DOCUMENTS OF THE FIRST CHAMBERS OF COMMERCE
IN BRITAIN AND IRELAND, 1767–1839

Records of Social and Economic History is a British Academy Research Project.

The British Academy, established by Royal Charter in 1902, is the national academy for the humanities and social sciences, promoting, sustaining and representing advanced research. As an academy composed of senior scholars throughout the UK, it gives recognition to academic excellence and achievement, and plays a leadership role in representing the humanities and social sciences nationally and internationally. As a learned society, the British Academy facilitates the research of individuals and groups of scholars.

More information can be found at www.britishacademy.ac.uk

RECORDS OF SOCIAL AND ECONOMIC HISTORY
NEW SERIES 55

DOCUMENTS OF THE FIRST CHAMBERS OF COMMERCE IN BRITAIN AND IRELAND 1767–1839

Edited by
ROBERT J. BENNETT

Published for THE BRITISH ACADEMY
by OXFORD UNIVERSITY PRESS

Oxford University Press, Great Clarendon Street, Oxford OX2 6DP

First published 2018

British Library Cataloguing in Publication Data
Data available

Library of Congress Cataloging in Publication Data
Data available

Typeset by
New Leaf Design, Scarborough, North Yorkshire
Printed in Great Britain
on acid free paper by
CPI Antony Rowe Limited
Chippenham, Wiltshire

ISBN 978–0–19–726624–3

Foreword

Professor Bennett has established himself as the leading interpreter of the earliest British chambers of commerce that began to secure their presence in the second half of the eighteenth century. He has done so through the relatively recent publication of two important monographs that assess the activities of these organisations nationally and locally (Liverpool). In this 55th volume in the Records of Social and Economic History series Professor Bennett makes available a large body of primary sources used in the preparation of those monographs and some more besides, that are located in repositories throughout the British Isles and North America. These records relate principally to the earliest years of the chambers that succeeded and some that failed, extending from the 1760s to c. 1839, the terminal date falling after the passing of the Municipal Reform Acts. Chambers were founded in part to lobby governments on matters of economic policy but they also came to offer services to the business community and also provided a context for wider social interactions among their members. Material is edited relating to all of the 27 places that are known to have established or re-established chambers in this early period. These sources reveal the means by which chambers evolved towards a standardized rule-based governance model and how in so doing they provided local economic groupings means of limiting rent-seeking behaviour at a critical stage in Britain's economic development. An interesting section concerns sources relevant to the short-lived phase between 1785 and 1787 of the General Chamber of Manufactures which show so clearly just how much more successful were the contrasting localised chambers with their broader concerns for commercial and trading matters. The roles that chambers played in periods of economic crises (such as the American war in the 1780s), as providers of local information to central government (to overcome information asymmetry), as generators of networks serving local economic and social needs as well as their links to London-based agents and the actual services they offered to their members are all themes revealed in the sources that have been so carefully selected. Professor Bennett concludes this very substantial edition with a particularly valuable appendix that lists, as far as possible, the membership of all the earliest chambers thereby offering a resource for a range of future researches on those individuals and their participation in broader business and social networks.

The Records of Social and Economic History committee thanks in particular Professor Julian Hoppit for his helpful comments on the introduction to this edition, the careful editorial assistance provided by Professor Vanessa Harding, the general editor of the series, in the effective and accurate presentation of a highly varied array of sources and the British Academy's Small Grants scheme and Ellen McArthur Fund of the University of Cambridge for their financial support towards the collection and keying of some of the sources used in the edition.

August 2017
R. M. Smith
Chairman, Records of Social and Economic History Committee

Contents

Illustrations

Figures

Plates
(following page xvi)

4. (a) Petition by 'the merchants of Liverpool' for the opening of Free Ports in Jamaica and Dominica in 1773, showing large scale activist involvement by chamber members, whose names are highlighted, immediately before the chamber was established (20 known or probable members of 33 signing; member number may be under-estimated since not all chamber members are known). Almost all those not highlighted were corporation Aldermen, past or current, who did not join the chamber one year later, illustrating the fracture of Liverpool's civic leadership (TNA: T 498 f. 182; Photograph: R. J. Bennett).

(b) Liverpool Stamp Act Committee request to Bristol for support, 31 December 1765: full text in Chapter 5, Section 5.2 (Bristol SMV in-letter; Bristol Record Office, BRO SMV/2/4/2/10 (7(a)); Photograph: R. J. Bennett)

Preface

This volume draws on the documents used in two previous studies of chambers of commerce by the editor of this volume: *Local Business Voice* and *Voice of Liverpool Business.* For these studies, original documents were consulted in all known archives that hold early chamber material in Britain, Ireland and North America: local record offices, national archives, the records of the national association (ACC, ABCC, BCC: at the London Metropolitan Archives), and in private hands of the chambers in Britain, Ireland and Chambers Ireland. To these records this volume adds significant new documentary material. First, further efforts have been to trace other early chambers, with some limited success; e.g. for Exeter, Guernsey in 1769, Nottingham, Portsmouth, and Wolverhampton. For other chambers significant new material is included from previously well-known chambers, and others that have been little covered: notably Kirkcaldy and North Staffordshire. Second, as a result of mounting the lists of members of the early chambers on a website and inviting comments and updates, significantly more information has been discovered from descendants and family historians on some important early chamber figures: notably John Dobson, the first chair, and Joseph Dalterra one of the founding members of the Liverpool chamber in 1774; and Thomas Peter Foxlow in the Manchester Committee of Trade. Third, the opportunity has been taken to update with new references and information. For example, the minutes of the West India Committee in London covering exchanges with Liverpool, Bristol, Liverpool and Jamaica are additional to previously quoted material in *Local Business Voice* and *Voice of Liverpool.* Also, after the author drew attention to the significance of Heywood's 'Curious Papers' held in the Liverpool Athenaeum Library, this very damaged and disjointed document was archivally restored and re-bound. This drew attention to doubt about its exact provenance. Whilst it is labelled 'Benjamin Heywood's Curious Papers' on the cover in pencil, as referred to in *Local Business Voice*, it is not clear when this was written, or by whom. Whilst there is no doubt it was one of the Heywoods and the library staff at the Athenaeum still believe this to be Benjamin's book, it is possible that it was Arthur Heywood's, brother of Benjamin and treasurer of the first chamber. Here it is referred to as 'Heywood's Curious Papers'.

The documents in several locations are still held by the modern chambers. I am grateful to the following chambers for allowing access to these private documents which has made possible their inclusion here: Cork, Hereford and Worcester, Hull and Humberside, Kirkcaldy. In the case of the modern Kirkcaldy chamber I am also very grateful to the current chief executive Bill Main for making available transcripts he prepared of some of the chamber's early papers. Additional acknowledgement is also gratefully given for the permission to access the Wedgwood papers at the Wedgwood Archive, Barlaston, and to all the other archives cited in the sources listed with the documents, including the Library Company of Philadelphia, and the Historical Associations of Massachusetts and Pennsylvania.

I am also grateful to the following individuals for comment, or for further information on individuals or chambers: to Professor Julian Hoppit for commenting on an earlier draft of the Introduction which has contributed greatly to its improvement; to Gregory Stevens-Cox, the leading local historian of Guernsey and St. Peter Port, for advice and information on the first Guernsey chamber, and for reading the sections on Guernsey and checking names; to David Senior, former executive of the London chamber for further information on London and for providing a copy of Payne's history of the chamber; to Matthew Dobson for much help on the early and later history of John Dobson the first Liverpool chamber chairman; to James Brennan for further information on Thomas Peter Foxlow, fustian manufacturer of Sharston, who was a member of the Manchester Committee of Trade in 1781 and its Cotton and Linen Committee; to the RSEH contact for this volume Professor Richard Smith for his support and help; and to RSEH series General Editor Vanessa Harding for improving many details of the text.

I am grateful for permission to reproduce photographs of archive records as follows: jacket illustration and Plate 2(a): Jersey Archives; Plates 2(b) and 4(b): Bristol Record Office; Plate 3(a): Watt Library, Greenock, Inverclyde; Plate 3(b): Manchester Libraries, Information and Archives, Manchester City Council; Plate 4(a): TNA. Figures 1 and 2 were drawn by Philip Stickler at the Cambridge University Department of Geography. Plate 1 is copyright of the author. I also owe a great debt of gratitude to Emily Noah who has painstakingly keyed many of the original documents, most of which were hand-written. This effort was supported by the British Academy Projects fund for the Records of Social and Economic History series and the Cambridge University, Faculty of History, Ellen McArthur Fund for Economic History.

The original process of accessing and collecting the documents for *Local Business Voice* from Archives and Record Offices around the British Isles and North America was supported by two British Academy Small Grants, SG39253 and SG44870. Some of the materials collected derived from the work of twenty-three Cambridge University students who visited some

Record Offices and Libraries over the summer of 2005; they are listed in the Preface of *Local Business Voice*. I am also very grateful for the advice received when preparing *Local Business Voice* and *Voice of Liverpool* from all the Archive Offices and chambers involved, and to a range of other sources of advice from local historians; particularly Todd Gray (Exeter), Rod Thorn (Macclesfield Silk Museum), and Joan Hanford (Liverpool Athenaeum library). I also wish to thank for help and advice the national associations of chambers in Britain and Ireland: Ron Taylor (Chief Executive of BCC, 1984–1998), Chris Humphries (Chief Executive, 1998–2001), David Frost (Chief Executive 2002–11), BCC staff Sue Deans, Alan Bartlett, Andrew Lansley, and Sally Low; and Ian Talbot, Chief Executive of Chambers Ireland. My wife Elizabeth also deserves special thanks for forbearance for enduring the mountains of material that accumulated during this book's preparation that impeded access to various parts of our house.

Editorial Principles

Most of the texts reproduced here are derived from hand-written minutes and correspondence; the remainder from printed reports, pamphlets and publications. Both offer challenges to presentation in a simple and readable form for modern use. In the documents the following conventions have been adopted.

As far as possible the original style and layout of material have been preserved to give as close as possible a flavour of the original. This includes preservation of capitalisation, italics and paragraphs. In handwritten material the use of italics and other emphasis is indicated by various conventions, most frequent of which is capitalisation. In only a few cases is the exact form of emphasis unclear, making it necessary to assume that either italics or capitals were intended. Where not used in the original, italics have been added to make clear the names of ships etc. Most spelling is preserved as the original, but for modern readers some contemporary conventions make reading cumbersome so that where a word is unambiguous the modern spelling is usually adopted; e.g. expense (for expence), public (for publick). All punctuation is as in the original, although in some handwritten material there are ambiguities resulting from trailing letter cursives, marks and blots. Original bracketing is indicated by ( ), editorial addition or interpretation by [ ]. Legible deletions are marked ~~thus~~. Text that is missing owing to damage to the manuscript, or illegible owing to deletion, is indicated by [ ] with an explanation or interpolation. Where a space is indicated in the original text, usually to indicate that a standard text or name is to be added, this is shown by underlining a space of equivalent size _____. All dates are as given in original sources. Only in rare cases was the old calendar (formally discontinued in Britain and its colonies in 1752) still used. Where this occurs the convention '1766/7' is used for the early months of a year to indicate the original old calendar date.

The spelling of personal names is problematic, both in handwriting and in some printed sources. The spelling is often inconsistent in the same document; it is frequently unclear or abbreviated; names of foreign origin, or in Jersey and Guernsey that are French-style, can be spelled in a variety of ways, sometimes anglicised and sometimes not; and in many locations there may be many people of the same or similar name, which makes precise identification uncertain. Whilst great care has been exercised to reproduce names as accurately as possible, and checks have been made with local sources, especially for Jersey and Guernsey, the reader still needs to be very cautious in using the personal names. The aim has been to accurately reproduce what was contained in the original documents. For this reason some of the spellings will not accord with published local histories, directories or other sources.

Where minutes contain long lists of those present and other conventional administrative comment, these have often been omitted (with an editorial note to this effect) in order to save space, though they are included where brief or of value to understanding. Similarly, in formal documents such as charters, the often extensive preamble and formalities are sometimes truncated, with an editorial note to that effect. Where lists of members are added to notices, these are sometimes the only available sources of a membership list. In this case, they are consolidated in the Appendix on membership, with the source indicated in both the original document reproduced here and in the Appendix.

Abbreviations

ABCC	Association of British Chambers of Commerce: title used 1919–96
ACC	Association of Chambers of Commerce (sometimes referred to as Associated Chambers of Commerce): title used 1860–1919
BCC	British Chambers of Commerce: association title used from 1996
BoT	Board of Trade (also used to refer to the Committee of Trade and Plantations in early years); became DTI in 1970, and BIS in 2009
BL	British Library
BSETC	Boston Society for Encouraging Trade and Commerce
CI	Chambers Ireland, the national association
City	'The City' refers to the City of London throughout
DAB	Dictionary of American Biography
ECCO	*Eighteenth Century Collections Online*
EIC	East India Company
LMA	London Metropolitan Archives
MP	Member of Parliament
MTMW	Making of the Modern World online resource
Newcastle	Refers to Newcastle-upon-Tyne throughout
ODNB	Oxford Dictionary of National Biography
PRONI	Public Record Office of Northern Ireland
RIA	Royal Irish Academy
RO	Record Office
SMV	Society of Merchant Venturers, Bristol
TNA	The National Archives of the UK (Kew)
TNAI	The National Archives of Ireland

PLATE 1

The Waterford Chamber of Commerce building, the oldest continuously occupied chamber building, since 1815 (Photograph: R. J. Bennett).

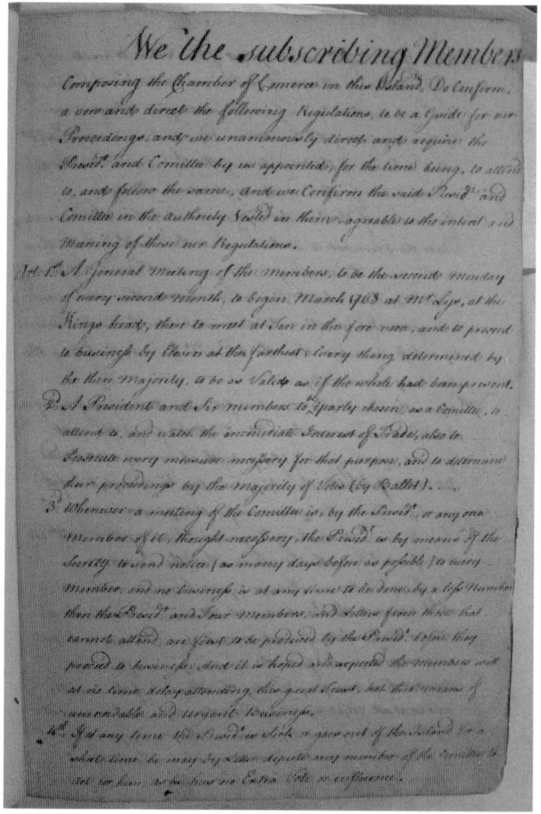

We the subscribing Members

Composing the Chamber of Comerce in this Island, Do Conform, a vow and direct the following Regulations, to be a Guide for our Proceedings, and we unanimously direct and require the Presid.t and Comittee by us appointed, for the time being, to attend to, and follow the same, and we Confirm the said Presid.t and Comittee in the authority Vested in them, agreable to the intent and Meaning of these our Regulations.

1st. A General Meeting of the Members, to be the second Monday of every second Month, to begin March 1768 at Mr Lys, at the Kings head, there to meet at Ten in the fore noon, and to proceed to business by Eleven at the farthest; every thing determined by the then Majority, to be as Valid as if the whole had been present.

2d. A President and Six Members to be yearly chosen, as a Comittee, to attend to, and watch the immediate Interest of Trade, also to Prosecute every measure necessary for that purpose, and to determine their proceedings by the Majority of Votes (by Ballot).

3d. Whenever a meeting of the Comittee is, by the Presid.t, or any one Member of it, thought necessary, the Presid.t or by means of the Secretary to send notice (as many days before as possible) to every Member, and no business is at any time to be done by a less Number than the Presid.t and Four Members, and Letters from those that cannot attend, are [illegible] to be produced by the Presid.t before they proceed to business, and it is hoped and expected the Members will at no time delay attending this good [illegible], but [illegible] unavoidable and urgent business.

4th. If at any time the Presid.t [illegible] out of the Island for a [illegible] time he may by Letter depute any member of the Comittee to act for him, as he has no Extra Vote or influence.

(a)

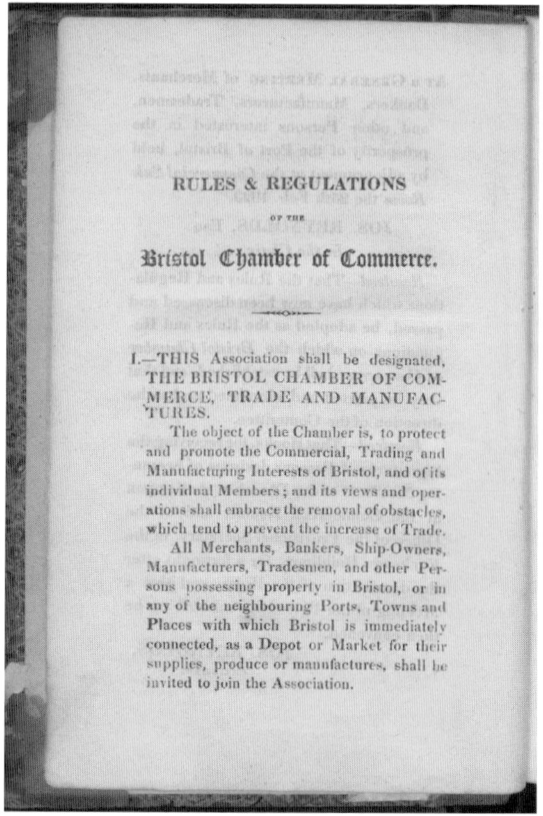

RULES & REGULATIONS

OF THE

Bristol Chamber of Commerce.

I.—THIS Association shall be designated, THE BRISTOL CHAMBER OF COMMERCE, TRADE AND MANUFACTURES.

The object of the Chamber is, to protect and promote the Commercial, Trading and Manufacturing Interests of Bristol, and of its individual Members; and its views and operations shall embrace the removal of obstacles, which tend to prevent the increase of Trade.

All Merchants, Bankers, Ship-Owners, Manufacturers, Tradesmen, and other Persons possessing property in Bristol, or in any of the neighbouring Ports, Towns and Places with which Bristol is immediately connected, as a Depot or Market for their supplies, produce or manufactures, shall be invited to join the Association.

(b)

(a) Regulations of the first early chamber, the Jersey Chamber of Commerce, as recorded in the first minutes in 1768, page one: full text in Chapter 1, Section 1.1 (Jersey Archives: L/A/38/A1/1; Photograph: R. J. Bennett).

(b) Regulations of the Bristol Chamber of Commerce 1823, arguably the foundation of a standardised set of rules for many subsequent foundations: full text in Chapter 1, Section 1.51 (Report and Rules; Photograph by Bristol Record Office, BRO 38605/A/1).

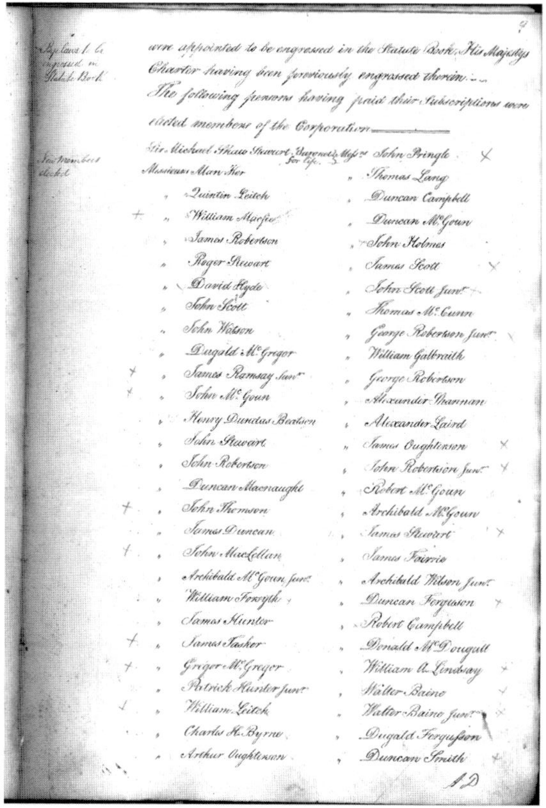

were appointed to be engrossed in the Statute Book, His Majesty's Charter having been previously engrossed therein.—
The following persons having paid their Subscriptions were elected members of the Corporation

Messieurs Alan Ker	John Pringle
Quintin Leitch	Thomas Lang
William Macfie	Duncan Campbell
James Robertson	Duncan McGoun
Roger Stewart	John Holmes
David Hyde	James Scott
John Scott	John Scott junr
John Watson	Thomas McCunn
Dugald McGregor	George Robertson junr
James Ramsay junr	William Galbraith
John McGoun	George Robertson
Henry Dundas Beatson	Alexander Shannan
John Stewart	Alexander Laird
John Robertson	James Oughterson
Duncan Macnaught	John Robertson junr
John Thomson	Robert McGoun
James Duncan	Archibald McGoun
John MacLellan	James Stewart
Archibald McGoun junr	James Fairrie
William Forsyth	Archibald Wilson junr
James Hunter	Duncan Ferguson
James Tasker	Robert Campbell
Gregor McGregor	Donald McDougall
Patrick Hunter junr	William A. Lindsay
William Leitch	Walter Baine
Charles H. Byrne	Walter Baine junr
Arthur Oughterson	Dugald Ferguson
	Duncan Smith

(a)

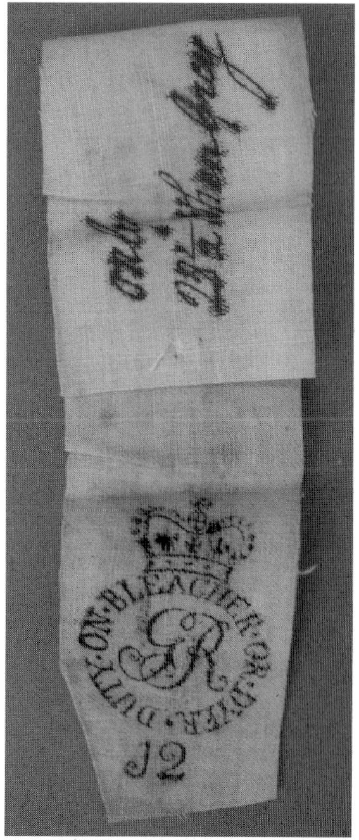

(b)

(a) The list of members who signed their commitment to the Charter of the Greenock Chamber of Commerce: full text in Chapter 1, Section 1.38, members listed in Membership Appendix (Minute book, founding articles; Photograph by Greenock Archives, from TD 508/1).

(b) The focus for anger over the fustian tax in 1785. The stamp of Excise Officers on a roll of fustian cloth. Stamped 'J2 DUTY ON BLEACHER OR DYER', with ink addition in hand 'only 28½ When Grey'. The cloth has been cut from across the end of a roll and is less than 28½ inches wide, evidencing the claim that the cloth shrinks with bleaching from grey to white and therefore should bear a lower Excise duty. It is folded in the photograph (Manchester Central Library: GB 127.M503 f.15; Photograph: R. J. Bennett).

PLATE 4

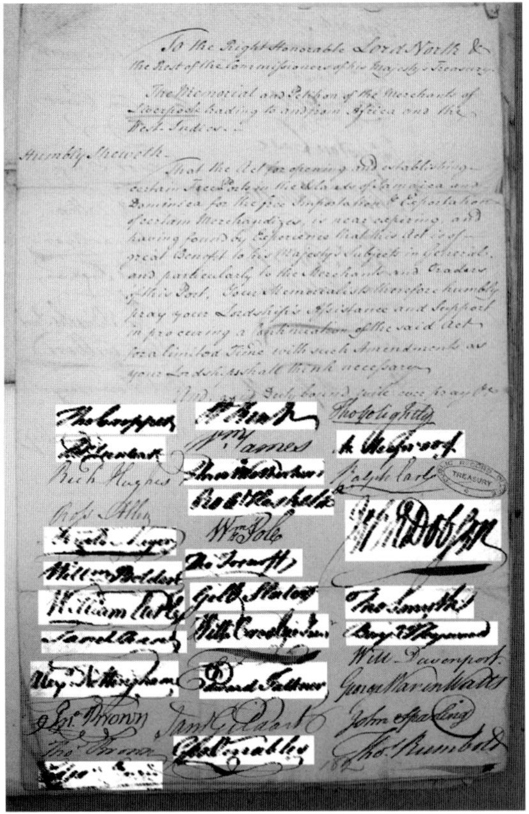

To the Right Honorable Lord North & the Rest of the Commissioners of his Majesty's Treasury

The Memorial and Petition of the Merchants of Liverpool trading to and from Africa and the West Indies

Humbly Sheweth

That the Act for opening and establishing certain Free Ports in the Islands of Jamaica and Dominica for the free Importation & Exportation of certain Merchandizes, is near expiring and having found by Experience that the Act is of great Benefit to his Majesty's Subjects in General and particularly to the Merchants and Traders of this Port. Your Memorialists therefore humbly pray your Lordship's Assistance and Support in procuring a [illegible] of the said Act for a limited Time with such Amendments as your Lordships shall think necessary

And your [illegible]

(a)

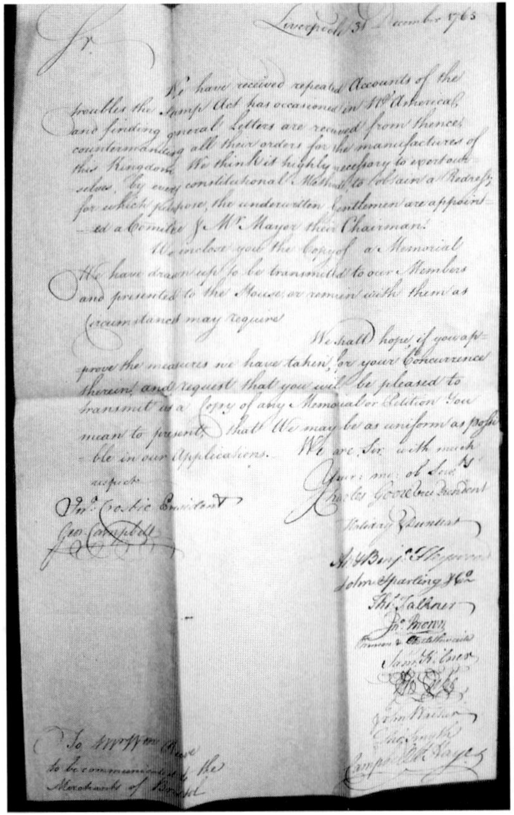

Sr.

Liverpool 31 December 1765

We have received repeated Accounts of the troubles the Stamp Act has occasioned in N. America, and finding general Letters are received from thence countermanding all their orders for the manufactures of this Kingdom, We think it highly necessary to exert ourselves, by every constitutional Method, to obtain a Redress; for which purpose, the underwritten Gentlemen are appointed a Comitee & Mr. Mayor their Chairman.

We inclose you the Copy of a Memorial We have drawn up to be transmitted to our Members and presented to the House, or remain with them as Circumstances may require.

We shall hope, if you approve the measures we have taken, or your Concurrence thereon, and request that you will be pleased to transmit us a Copy of any Memorial or Petition You mean to present, that We may be as uniform as possible in our Applications. We are Sir with much respect

Your most ob. Serts.

To Mr Wm. Reeve to be communicated to the Merchants of Bristol [illegible]

(b)

(a) Petition by 'the merchants of Liverpool' for the opening of Free Ports in Jamaica and Dominica in 1773, showing large scale activist involvement by chamber members, whose names are highlighted, immediately before the chamber was established (20 known or probable members of 33 signing; member number may be underestimated since not all chamber members are known). Almost all those not highlighted were corporation Aldermen, past or current, who did not join the chamber one year later, illustrating the fracture of Liverpool's civic leadership (TNA: T 498 f. 182; Photograph: R. J. Bennett).

(b) Liverpool Stamp Act Committee request to Bristol for support, 31 December 1765: full text in Chapter 5, Section 5.2 (Bristol SMV in-letter; Bristol Record Office, BRO SMV/2/4/2/10 (7(a)); Photograph: R. J. Bennett).

Introduction

1. Documents of the Early Chambers of Commerce

The earliest private-law bodies called ‘chambers of commerce’ in the British realm were initiated in 1767. They differed from earlier organisations by seeking to represent *general* business interests and by establishing a *permanent* presence. This volume takes as the five defining characteristics of the early private-law chambers that they sought to act permanently as a voice of the local business community, were voluntary, represented general interests (not individuals, firms or sectors), were locally rooted in a specified area, and their governance was formally open and transparent. Earlier examples of private-law chambers had been established in Bremen in 1451, Hamburg in the 1460s, and Marseilles in 1599. There were also other European ‘chamber’ bodies for insurance (as in Paris in 1750) and other specialised purposes. There were also examples of societies and associations with many of the attributes of chambers of commerce, both in the British Isles and elsewhere; of which the Boston (Mass.) Society for Encouraging Trade and Commerce (BSETC) of 1733 is one of the more important examples. However, the 1767 chamber foundation in the Channel Islands at Jersey for most purposes represents a turning point where a new concept was initiated. This concept differs from the state-backed public law chambers of much of Europe and is important as an example of a network of interrelated voluntary membership bodies. They were not founded as a ‘system’, since they were definitionally local, drawing from the community networks of the major cities and ports. However, they became a systematic network of local leadership developing local initiatives independently of each other, but also increasingly developed a cooperative structure through various experiments with London-based agents and collective national bodies. As the documents demonstrate, they were primarily founded to lobby government on economic policies, and this was their main field of growing cooperation, but they were also early providers of collective business services and other activities, and as leading milieus (well illustrated in Plate 1) for deliberation, economic engagement and mercantile social interactions.

There had been no systematic scholarly study of these early organisations until the author’s *Local Business Voice* (2011) and the case study of Liverpool in *The Voice of Liverpool Business* (2010).[1] These two books required the assembly of a substantial body of primary material from local and national archives around Britain, Ireland and the Channel Isles, and to a lesser extent from the USA, Canada and Jamaica. It is from this collection of documents that this volume is drawn. Other material for these two books led to the construction of an aligned database of statistics on chambers from 1790 up to 2005. This, together with an aligned database of urban populations used in those books, has been deposited at the UK Data Archive.[2] *Local Business Voice* also provides a systematic bibliography on chamber histories, including all local chamber histories, and a full listing of archive sources and their location. These are not repeated here. Any new sources are however fully listed here, and Chapter 1 of this volume gives a full chronological list of all chambers now discovered that includes several not known at the time of writing of *Local Business Voice*.

This introductory chapter seeks to put the documents in their historical context. It includes interpretations that have emerged since the publication of *Local Business Voice* that mainly draw on the wider connections and political networks of the members. Whilst *Local Business Voice* emphasised the chamber system as a whole, this chapter summarises the significance of the documents, the extent to which localities varied, and also assesses how far their foundations, purposes, activities and rules converged as the early chambers evolved.

2. The Area and Period of Documents Covered

The main coverage of this volume is from the 1760s until 1839: from origins until immediately after the Municipal Reform Acts. This was a period in which chamber initiatives can be interpreted as local responses to an interrelated set of political tensions and needs across the British Atlantic world. The chamber developments included the Channel Isles, North America and Jamaica, as well as Britain and Ireland. Hence bodies around the British

[1] R. J. Bennett, *Local Business Voice: The History of Chambers of Commerce in Britain, Ireland and Revolutionary America, 1760–2011* (Oxford, 2011); *The Voice of Liverpool Business: The First Chamber of Commerce and the Atlantic Economy, 1774–c.1796* (Liverpool, 2010). Also valuable are A. R. Ilersic and P. F. B. Liddle, *Parliament of Commerce: The Story of the Association of British Chambers of Commerce 1860–1960* (London, 1960), and a study by the retired chief executive of the national chamber association, R. Taylor, *A History of chambers of commerce in the United Kingdom: 1768–2007* (London, 2007), though both have only brief cover of, and contain some errors and omissions, for the early period.

[2] *Database of chamber of commerce financial and other benchmarking information 1790–2005*, UKDA deposit SN 6878; *Database of urban population C17th and 1801–1911* (Law-Robson-Langton database), UKDA deposit SN7154.

Atlantic are included in this volume where they are relevant and offer additional insights.[3] This was an important period of economic growth in the British realm, punctuated by wars; with the wars as important for the development of chambers as the times of peace. The period can be treated as one in which there was a general pattern of economic development which applied not only to the metropolitan state, but also to the whole colonial realm that remained with Britain after the American secession in 1776. Even in Ireland, Cullen shows that there was no long-term depression in trade over this period, and that the difficulties that the Irish economy was to experience followed not from the 1800 Act of Union, but mainly began in the 1840s when Irish domestic industries increasingly suffered competition from more technologically advanced British ones,[4] as well as the removal of protections when the transition to Union ceased after equalisation of British and Irish duties in 1823.

The end date of 1839 is used for four reasons. First, it draws to a close a period over which chambers evolved towards a governance model that became relatively standardised, and which formed the basis for most subsequent developments. This evolution provides a valuable addition to the information available on the development of bodies with rule-based governance for the period. Innes and Hoppit have suggested that the political system of this period became steadily more open to demands from organised local interests (such as through private parliamentary Bills), provided they did not arouse opposition from others and had demonstrably 'democratic' structures of involvement (such as demonstrating the 'general interest').[5] This was a 'reforming' period through local initiative. It was an 'associational age' which Langford and Pearson and Richardson have identified as encouraging the transition of business organisations from informal to formal structures with rules-based constitutions.[6] Within Britain, Hoppit has shown how increasing numbers of business-led direct lobbies for local economic improvements began to dominate much parliamentary attention.[7] Chambers vividly illustrate the argument by Mokyr and Nye that new economic groupings contributed

[3] There is no attempt to cover the early US chambers in depth. More discussion of their activities is given in Bennett, *Local Business Voice* (2011) 132–5, 174–8, 247, 750–1; see also recent history of US chambers in C. Mead, *The Magicians of Main Street: America and its Chambers of Commerce, 1768–1945* (Washington D.C., 2014).

[4] L. M. Cullen, *Economy, Trade and Irish Merchants at Home and Abroad* (2012) 11–17.

[5] J. Innes, 'The local Acts of a National Parliament', *Parliamentary History*, XVII (1998) 23–47; J. Hoppit, ed., *Parliaments, Nations and Identities in Britain and Ireland, 1660–1850* (Manchester, 2003).

[6] P. Langford, *Public life and the Propertied Englishman 1689–1798* (Oxford, 1991); R. Pearson and D. Richardson, 'Social capital, Institutional Innovation and Atlantic Trade before 1800', *Business History,* 50 (2008) 660.

[7] Hoppit, *Parliaments* (2003).

to institutional development that supported rapid industrialisation in Britain by reducing the scope for rent-seeking coalitions that sought to maintain obsolete economic arrangements and allowed potentially blocking interests to accept change (especially in parliament).[8] The chambers are such a group of bodies that became established in the 1760s and proved extremely durable; arguably they are the oldest continuing economic organisations in the British realm. Although some were short-lived, most early foundations managed to maintain themselves over periods of at least ten or twenty years, with most being re-founded again after short gaps, and some early foundations have been maintained continuously up to the present day. Clearly they had something about them that provided more than the typical incentives of the period to maintain collective action, which usually stopped when urgent issues of concern were resolved. Their early development well illustrates Wootton's comment that the period is one where modern forms of interest representation 'peep tentatively out'.[9] As discussed later, Olson's *Logic of Collective Action* suggests how this was achieved. Whilst the transaction costs and sheer time and effort of maintaining collective representational bodies may have been off-putting or sometimes preclusive, a mix of service activities with representation provided chambers with large enough portfolios of incentives to membership that the transaction costs and effort required were supported.[10] Mixed portfolios also prove to be the modern chambers' solution to collective action problems.

Second, the cut-off of 1839 falls immediately after the Municipal Reform Acts of 1835 in England and Ireland. As highlighted by Innes, the discourse in the period before this was dominated by reform debates that ranged across the spectrum, with 'reform' a generic concept that could build wide support, provided it did not become too radical.[11] The 'great' Reform Act of 1832 changed all this. It extended the election franchise and restructured parliamentary constituency seats in Britain, which was critical to the structure of national government. The Municipal Reform Acts of 1835 were equally or more important at local level, followed by the Scottish Reform Act of 1846.[12] These acts together form an important watershed for how lobbying by all

[8] J. Mokyr and J Nye, 'Distributional Coalitions, the Industrial Revolution, and the Origins of Economic Growth in Britain', *Southern Economic Journal*, 74, 1 (2007) 50–70; see also D. C. North, 'Transaction costs in history', *Journal of European Economic History,* 14 (1985) 557–76.

[9] G. Wootton, *Pressure Groups in Britain 1720–1970* (London, 1975) 11.

[10] M. Olson, *The Logic of Collective Action: Public Goods and the Theory of Groups,* 2nd ed. (Cambridge, Mass., 1971) 132–5.

[11] J. Innes, 'Reform' in English public life: the fortunes of a word, in A. Burns and J. Innes (eds.), *Rethinking the Age of Reform: Britain 1780–1850* (Cambridge, 2003) 71–97.

[12] Although the Scottish reforms had had little effect in the larger towns; it was not until 1888 that the Scottish guildery was finally abolished.

organisations had to be conducted; for local bodies they represented a sea-change in local processes, the allies that had to be used, and the potential routes and reception by government ministers and departments. Although arguments continue about the significance of the great Reform Acts, as Salmon has recently emphasised there is no doubt about the significant changes that occurred to the practice of representation and lobbying that had to be followed by interest groups seeking to influence government after 1832–5.[13] Annual voter registration lists, standardised election procedures, and registration processes that were largely independent of local and national government redefined the legal and constitutional framework. One of the most critical changes was the shift from 'corporate bodies' with freeman lists that could be managed and manipulated, to individuals who possessed their votes by local qualification, which restricted scope to interfere with the franchise. Municipal corporations had governed most of the large towns and were the cause of considerable friction that contributed to stimulating the foundations of several of the most prominent early chambers: notably in Liverpool in 1774, Dublin in 1783, Londonderry in 1790, Cork in 1814–19, and Bristol in 1823. Conversely, where major towns had not previously had direct local representation but had relied on the overlying county representatives, the Reform Acts enfranchised local voters on local issues for the first time and paved the way for a level of engagement impossible in the pre-Reform state at both national and local level. This was particularly important for cities like Birmingham, Manchester and the Staffordshire potteries. The Reform Acts began to bring these local peculiarities into a single system; or, as Salmon puts it, 'helped to impose a far more nationally-oriented political system upon local parochial, municipal and administrative life', that led to 'new types of party-based attachments and more permanent forms of party organisation across all levels of British politics'.[14] Hence the structure of lobbying before and after 1832/5 changed markedly.[15]

Third, the cut-off at 1839 means that the later debates on Corn Law abolition and free trade, with which many chambers were heavily involved, are largely omitted from this volume. Major Corn Law abolition campaigning began in 1838 and was eventually successful in 1846. Abolition represented a significant political watershed for how parties operated, re-orientated political alignments especially within the Tory interests, and stimulated organised, more persistent political engagement among a much wider range of interests than previously (including the landed interests and trades unions), which fundamentally changed how business interests operated. For chambers

[13] P. Salmon, *Electoral Reform at Work* (2002).
[14] Salmon, *Electoral Reform* (2002) 10–11.
[15] See also J. Brewer, *Sinews of Power: War and the English state, 1688–1783* (1989).

it was also an important watershed for the crystallisation of the free trade movement which came to dominate most chamber policy positions for the 70–90 years after 1846. Fore-shadows of the Corn Law campaigns can be seen in the earlier chamber documents in the volume, not least with 'Corn Law reform' as part of Glasgow's founding purposes in 1783, and Liverpool chamber's opposition to Pownall's Corn Law reforms proposed in 1774. Moreover Glasgow mounted a substantial opposition to attempts by the Scottish gentry to revise the Law in their favour in 1787, publishing a substantial 32-page report with additional technical appendices on prices.[16] However, in the earlier period the Corn Laws were only one of many issues concerning chambers, did not then carry as much of the freight of political meaning that they subsequently acquired, and in any case were not generally as onerous as followed the 1815 restructuring of the Corn Laws.

Fourth, the whole parliamentary process also experienced significant administrative changes by the 1840s, changing the representation process for chambers and others at Westminster. Over the period 1836–51 the process for presenting and receiving private Bills in parliament came under the first systematic Code, largely precipitated by the load of business resulting from the numerous Acts promulgated during the railway boom of the 1840s. Reforms to establish a Private Bill Office occurred in 1817, and to abolish the parliamentary agency by clerks in 1840, and other changes that made Bills easier and more secure in their processes.[17] Though Bills still had to follow the same processes for finding support, these changes made the procedures more open and accessible, opening the way for less expert promoters with more diverse objectives to come forward. The closed and rather special world that early chambers and a few others had inhabited now became more open and potentially conflictual with other interests. This was a strong contrast to the way in which elite lobbies, municipal local corporation elites, or colonial agents and chambers could operate during the eighteenth century.[18]

Despite the cut-off at 1839, however, the main documentary cover here is not made too water-tight. Some coverage is given to intellectual debates about representative bodies dating back to the 1680s which resonate with

[16] *Report of a Committee of Directors of the Chamber of Commerce and Manufacturers of Glasgow on the Corn–Laws* (Glasgow, 1787); Glasgow Mitchell Library and ECCO. For a detailed discussion of Scottish Corn debates in this period see K. J. Cameron, 'Anti-Corn-Law Agitations in Scotland' (Edinburgh, 1971) 18–34.

[17] O. C. Williams, *The Historical Development of Private Bill Procedure* (1948) 52–124; see also D. L. Rydz, *The Parliamentary Agents* (1979); Brewer, *Sinews of Power* (1989).

[18] Brewer, Sinews of Power (1989); M. G. Kammen, *A Rope of Sand: The colonial agents, British politics, and the American Revolution* (Ithaca, 1968); A. G. Olson, 'The London Mercantile Lobby and the coming of the American Revolution', *Journal of American History,* 69, 1 (1982) 21–41; *Making the Empire Work: London and American interest groups 1690–1790* (Harvard, 1992).

later developments, and some reference is made to the evolution after 1840 to illustrate the continuity or changes that occurred.

The volume includes, as far as possible, all chambers of the period. This will allow other researchers to investigate cross-linked questions in any subsequent study (such as cross-memberships, networks, campaigns and similarities of structures/governance). There were about 27 places where major chambers had been founded by 1839 in the British Isles, though the documents supporting the establishment often cover two or more phases after early foundations lapsed and had to be re-founded. They were entirely in major urban or maritime centres: see Table 1.

This group of chambers is covered as systematically as possible to include all surviving documents on rules and founding purposes, and a selection of major initiatives and activities of their early years. Because of the relevance of exchanges across the British Atlantic realm, some briefer coverage is also be given to the first US chambers (Boston 1764, 1785 and 1794; New York 1768; Charleston 1773; and Philadelphia, proposed in 1784), Quebec (proposal 1776), Halifax Nova Scotia (1803), Kingston Jamaica (1778), and 'delegate' chambers in Britain (those that were primarily led by a few individual spokespeople) in Norwich, Exeter, Halifax, Sheffield, Portsmouth, Rochdale, etc. The General Chamber of Manufacturers (1785–7) is also covered; this has had substantial academic attention but has rarely been seen against the wider context of local chambers, which changes its interpretation substantially. The locations mainly concerned are shown in Figure 1.

Table 1: The first local chambers of commerce in the Britain and Ireland 1760–1839, with dates of foundation

Date of foundation	Chamber	Date of foundation	Chamber
1767	Jersey	1801	Liverpool American
1769 / 1808 / 1832	Guernsey	1807	**Limerick**
1774 / 1781/ 1794 / 1820	Manchester	1813	Plymouth
1774	Liverpool	1813	**Greenock**
[1782] / 1817 / 1822	London	1815	Newcastle
1783	**Glasgow**	1819	Cork
1783 / 1788 / 1805 / 1820	Dublin	1819 / 1835	Forfar/Dundee
1783	Belfast	1819	Wolverhampton
1783 / 1813 / 1820	Birmingham	1823	Bristol
1784	N. Staffordshire	1825	Kirkcaldy/Fife
1785	Leeds	1835	Nottingham
1785	**Edinburgh**	1837	Hull
1787 / 1804	**Waterford**	1839	Worcester
1790	Londonderry		

Chartered bodies are shown in **bold**; secondary dates refer to re-founding; excludes bodies that did not start, and delegate bodies.

Figure 1. The early chambers of commerce in Britain and Ireland, 1767–1839

In addition to the chambers that were actually established, attention is also given in this volume to proposals for early chambers that did not succeed. These give insights into the difficulties and barriers experienced. Of course documents for establishments that did not happen are scarcer and less likely to survive. But this volume attempts to track down evidence of all these failed chambers as well as those that were successful. These are included in Chapter 1, Rules [as bracketed items], where documents on attempted start-up and statements of purpose survive. They are also covered in various other chapters where a valuable document has been discovered evidencing a local body's existence and activity. The main initiatives discovered are summarised in Table 2. Further research on these bodies, and on possible initiatives in other areas, is clearly desirable.

Table 2: Chamber of commerce known initiatives 1760–1839 in Britain and Ireland that failed to develop, had very restricted development, or where documentary evidence is too meagre to be certain of establishment; with approximate dates

Date	Chamber	Date of known initiative	Chamber
1779	Lancaster	1813	Nottingham
1779	Blackburn	1817	London
1782–1802	Weskett's London chamber	1823–4	London
1785–7	General Chamber	1820	Newry
1785–7	Nottingham	1820	Sligo
1785	Perth	1822	Enniskillen
1797–8	Portsmouth	1822	Galway
1801	Hull	1830	Tralee

3. Significance of the Documents

The importance of the documents reproduced here is to open a light on a world of collective action for political and service activity that has been previously largely unknown, or misunderstood. For the first time, in one place, it is possible to see, and for other researchers to use, the main primary materials from the early chambers. It is arguable how politically significant these bodies were, or how valuable their services were to their members. But they were certainly as significant as many other bodies of the period to which more scholarly attention has been given, they have continued to survive for over 250 years, and some of their activities throw entirely new light on wider and significant historical developments that have been previously misunderstood. The documents, like the two earlier studies by the author, open at least eight major new lines of evidence for scholarly study.

First, the documents evidence the status of many chamber bodies that have not been previously investigated. Although there were many early failures and false starts, in most major centres they were relatively stable and persistent. They formed a corpus of activity, and a corpus of discourse, which gathered momentum from the 1760s, reaching a level of considerable significance and geographical breadth by the early 1780s. To their political pressure can be attributed key changes in the trade policies of North's and Pitt's governments, and some of the shifts in the political attitude to America after loss of the colonies in 1783, such as resolving disputes by arbitration of war claims and elements of the Jay Treaty of 1795, pressure to repeal the Orders in Council in 1812 (although too late to avoid a new American war), and of course the victories in defeating the fustian tax and Irish Propositions in 1785.[19] The policy shifts they initiated also began to ground the dominant

[19] Bennett, *Local Business Voice* (2011) 374–423.

policy paradigm towards 'open trade' within the empire, and wider opening of bilateral trade policy elsewhere. This was not 'free trade' but represented significant shifts towards 'reciprocal trade' or 'equality of trade' that were important steps on the way to the free trade championed by later chambers, especially in Manchester.[20]

Second, the numerous local chambers, committees, or bands of 'delegates' that had developed by the early 1780s throw a very different light on the General Chamber of Manufactures which operated over 1785–7. There has been a dominant tendency for historians, if they mention early chambers at all, to focus overwhelmingly on the episode of the General Chamber; yet it was the exception. As shown in Chapter 8, the General Chamber was short-lived, centralised in London, used a confused committee or managing board which was highly unstable, had a dominating manufacturing focus, and collapsed in faction and recrimination. This focus has also thrown too much emphasis on personality, especially the figures of Josiah Wedgwood, Samuel Garbett, and Thomas Walker. Partly this is because the records exist and Wedgwood was, in almost every sense, a 'great man'. But there were other men with less prominent profiles who were just as important locally and who were often rather more effective than Wedgwood in terms of managing a chamber-like organisation. In contrast to the General Chamber, the emerging and successful model was not centralised in London, but localised; not confused or lacking in rules, but with a transparent and agreed architecture of rule-based decision-making that generally worked; not manufacturing or any single sector, but general commercial and manufacturing interests; and normally much longer-lived without the same extent of fracture and recrimination —though tensions, conflicts and collapses certainly occurred.

Third, the documents reproduced in Chapter 3 demonstrate that the General Chamber in many ways reflected an 'antique' view of how to organise and react to growing government intrusion. Advocacy of a *national* body based in London to represent and manage local trading interests through a few delegates had been running since being proposed by Whiston and Davenant in the 1690s. The ideas had originally sought to restrict the powers of the Crown after the accession of William III in 1689. Subsequently they became central to some radical and Dissenter discourse to limit the influence of both Crown and the aristocracy. These came into chamber discourse not so much to limit the king, but reduce control of offices and other routes to patronage and control of electorates. Local electoral franchises had come almost entirely under control of patrons and government by mid-century. In 1700 about 20 per cent of MP seats were influenced by patronage; by 1741 it

[20] Bennett, *Local Business Voice* (2011) 438–68.

was 45 per cent; 60 per cent by 1780, and 82 per cent in 1816.[21] In Ireland it was almost all seats, with almost all occupied by English aristocrats, with the boroughs almost entirely 'venal'.[22] Patronage assured enduring control by the landed elite whose interest in trade was often ephemeral or at best limited to crises. Concerns with landed elite control increased as the century progressed in line with parliament sitting for much longer and becoming more intrusive into commerce. This resulted in growth of government itself becoming a key business issue. As identified by Hoppit, there was significant new taxation and increased burdens specifically on industry and trade, especially after 1760. Similarly special Acts of parliament also became much more frequent: 5,354 Acts over 1760–1800 have been classified as 'economic' by Hoppit, which were 71 per cent of all acts over 1660–1800.[23] These developments brought chambers directly into the discourse about the wider 'reform' issues identified by Innes.[24] The criticisms of government intrusion were often led by Dissenters (and Catholics in Ireland), who formed a significant minority of many chambers. Dissenters were also very active in other societies, which provided access and opportunities for them as 'a neutral arena: territory where political and social contact between landed and elite families could be maintained … without risk of political acrimony'.[25] But the wider discourse also resonated with a large number of other interests, among which the major merchants and manufacturers were a significant and powerful group.

Chapter 3 shows how the early concepts persisted in many quarters for a nationally-based body to become a new Board or Committee of Trade, formed from a nested set of local committees and/or delegates that represented three constituencies: the localities, merchants and manufacturers, and major fields of overseas trade (e.g. West Indies, America, East India). Whiston and Davenant's proposals in the 1690s have an uncanny resemblance to the structure and rhetoric behind the General Chamber of the 1780s. The documents show how the discourse advocating an independent national Committee of Trade continued throughout the eighteenth century through writers such as Cary, Child, Bennett, Ashley, Mun, Smith, Temple, and Gee. From 1766 Samuel Garbett in Birmingham began pressing (unsuccessfully) for a national

[21] All figures quoted from F. O'Gorman, *The Emergence of the British Two-party System* (1982) 18–21; see also E. Porritt and A. G. Porritt, *The Unreformed House of Commons,* Vol.2, 8–63.
[22] Porritt and Porritt, *Unreformed House*, Vol. 2 (1903) 339–41; L. B. Namier and J. Brooke, *The House of Commons* (London, 1964).
[23] Hoppit, *Parliaments* (2003).
[24] Innes, '"Reform" in English public life', 71.
[25] P. Clark, *British Clubs and Societies 1580–1800* (Oxford, 2000) 80; also Black (1963); I. R. Christie, *Wilkes, Wyvill and Reform* (London, 1962), *War and Revolutions* (Cambridge Mass, 1982); J. E. Bradley, *Religion, Revolution, and English Radicalism* (Cambridge, 1990); P. Langford, *A Polite and Commercial People* (Oxford, 1989).

council or chamber using the MPs William and Edmund Burke.[26] In 1782–3 Garbett revived this plan, with the Birmingham Committee a first building block. This also influenced Wedgwood towards a General Chamber, drawing on the experience he had developed with the committee of Staffordshire Potters he had chaired since 1767, and which he turned into a chamber in 1784 (see Chapter 1).[27] However, the documents in Chapter 3 from Postlethwayt and Mortimer, and to a lesser extent from Weskett, demonstrate how a rival structure was emerging that was local; and it was this that came to underpin the successful chambers of the period. The concept of a national body, however, also continued, in part stimulated the General Chamber, and was given prominence by Edmund Burke in his 1780 speech on 'economical reform' which led to the abolition of the Board of Trade (BoT) over 1782–6. 'Economical Reform' had been a key aspect of the wider 'reform' discourse since Whiston and Davenant, and was to continue and become enmeshed with debates on Corn Law abolition.[28] Against the rival concept of locally-based chambers, therefore, the demise of the General Chamber had little long-term impact. Instead the local model succeeded, with only later a national cooperative structure emerging, in which many local chambers appointed their own London agents from the late 1780s, and for which a 'union' of chambers emerged in the 1790s, as shown in Chapters 7 and 9. However, the debate between local and national resurfaced again in the 1860s when the first national chamber association was developed (ACC).[29] Indeed the debate continues today.

These rival concepts often centred around the political position of the BoT, which was a central theme of 'reform' discourse for the period and hence for the early chambers. The BoT had been given executive powers over 1748–61 under Lord Halifax, but was stripped of cabinet status as soon as Halifax left office in 1761. By 1768 it had been reduced to an adjunct of the Secretary of State for the Colonies, becoming entirely 'subservient' to the Crown and government.[30] Political objectives in America took precedence over commerce following George III's objective to overcome 'the perplexed

[26] Garbett letter to Edmund Burke, 29 October 1766; quoted in J. M. Norris, 'Samuel Garbett and the early development of industrial lobbying in Britain', *Economic History Review,* 10, (1957) 452.

[27] Norris, 'Samuel Garbett'; J. Money, *Experience and Identity: Birmingham and the West Midlands, 1760–1800* (1977).

[28] P. Harling, *The Waning of 'Old Corruption': The Politics of Economical reform in Britain, 1779–1846* (Oxford, 1996) 16–25, 32–59; D. S. Klinge, 'Edmund Burke, Economical Reform, and the Board of Trade, 1777–1780', *Journal of Modern History*, 51 (1979) D1185–D1200.

[29] Bennett, *Local Business Voice* (2011) 303–63.

[30] A. H. Basye, *The Lords Commissioners of Trade and Plantations* (New Haven, Conn., 1925) 32–104; A. G. Olson, A. G. 'The Board of Trade and London-American interest groups in the eighteenth century', *Journal of Imperial and Commonwealth History,* 8 (1980) 33–50.

mode of joint interference' of the Southern Secretary and the BoT and avoid 'future jarrings of departments'.[31] These changes were fundamental drivers for business leaders, especially if they were already radical in outlook. With the demise of the BoT as a powerful body, and the rest of the State apparatus more closed and obdurate, it was inevitable that ideas for creating representative organisations for businesses along the lines suggested by Whiston, Davenant and others would gain traction. An *independent* Committee of Trade, or chamber of commerce, was an obvious solution. However, its design and rules could follow different routes: as a local equivalent of Westminster's BoT, with members appointed from local dignitaries having access routes to the oligarchic State such as a local corporation, as first attempted in Liverpool in 1773–4; or openly elected from a defined 'business membership', which was the final Liverpool model of June 1774. It could be a 'board' where officers were empowered to act as an executive committee (as appears to be the case in Manchester in 1774–85) or it could be operated under continuous exchange with members through general meetings (as defined in many chamber rules). Also open to tension was how it was to be paid for and free riders controlled (those who benefited from the representational activity, but who were not prepared to subscribe), which appears to have been an issue in Manchester in 1774–82,[32] and pervades private-law chambers up to the present.

Fourth, the documents evidence the key problems of information asymmetry for government, and power asymmetry for the business community, which were heightened by emasculation of the BoT from1760, and its abolition over 1782–6. Although the government had massive sources of information (especially through its Customs and revenue services),[33] there were, and are, major limitations to government making effective policy interventions in business and the economy without cooperation and engagement with commercial and business interests. This was the core of the conceptual challenge that chambers addressed from the outset. Thomas Mortimer's 1772 view, reproduced in Chapter 3, was that government undermined the economy through incompetent legislation on trade, taxes, treaties, and the colonies:

> the effect of ignorance in commercial affairs becomes more fatal, when it gets in possession of the administration of government. … The history of England furnishes too many instances of the imbecility of entire administrations in this respect; the very department peculiarly charged with the inspection and care of

[31] Basye, *Lords Commissioners* (1925) 179–89 and Appendix A.

[32] For details of the debates about the Liverpool and Manchester models, see Chapter 4 and Bennett, 'Searching for new models' (2014) 270–9; 'Alignments, interests and tensions' (2014) 65–75.

[33] J. Hoppit, 'Political arithmetic in eighteenth-century England', *Economic History Review*, 49, 3 (1996) 516–40.

> commercial affairs [the BoT], having often been filled with gentlemen, who could not claim to the least mercantile knowledge … and (unhappily) the superior offices of state … [are] likewise occupied by men equally deficient in this point'.[34]

The need to overcome such ignorance or mistakes was a common objective embodied in most chamber founding statements: see Chapter 1. The weaknesses of government information only began to be tackled by government itself in the 1830s with reorganisation of the BoT. This was arguably the first initiative towards what is now termed 'evidence based policy' as part of 'scientific administration', or the 'statistical movement'.[35] With sympathetic support from the president of the BoT Lord Auckland and chancellor Francis Baring, the Statistics Department of the BoT was established in 1832. However, as discussed in Chapter 6, this BoT initiative proved initially of limited value. Asymmetries were not really tackled until the establishment of reorganised government statistical services in the early 20th century.

Fifth, the documents evidence how crises and other periods of tension raised temperatures and caused a level of anger sufficient to precipitate busy business people to act together: for example during the Stamp Act crisis of 1765–6, the abolition of the BoT over 1782–6, the recriminations after the failed American war in the 1780s, and the tensions of the French Wars of 1793–1815. Crises acted as stimuli for several chambers to set up, with war convoying being a major catalyst. Crises demonstrated most evidently the extent of government information deficiencies in the views of chamber leaders. They raised the temperature and drew new attention and support for attacking the old problems of 'reform', and exposed the inadequacies of control by the aristocratic state. The documents evidence a chamber system that was evolved to deal with and seek influence through a pre-Reform structure that only occasionally gave trade and manufactures a priority. It shows how a group of voluntary private-law bodies adopted increasingly formalised approaches to lobbying to maintain and expand trade. Under pressures of war or conflict they asserted merchant influence on imperial managers to maintain trade by linking local and colonial interests with the political classes at the centre of metropolitan power.

The American war (1775–83) brought these contentions to a climax, subsequently transforming ideas about the Empire.[36] These changes profoundly influenced not only America, but also Jamaica (leading to a cham-

[34] T. Mortimer, *Elements of Commerce (1772)*, Introduction, vi; see Chapter 3.

[35] M. J. Cullen, *The Statistical Movement in Early Victorian Britain* (New York, 1975) 19–27.

[36] V. T. Harlow, *The Founding of the Second British Empire, 1763*–1793 (1964); P. J. Marshall, *The Making and Unmaking of Empires: Britain, India, and America c.1750–1783* (Oxford, 2005); A. J. O'Shaughnessy, *An Empire Divided: The American Revolution and the British Caribbean* (Philadelphia, 2000).

ber foundation in 1778) and other parts of the Caribbean, and were proximate catalysts to the mainland chambers in Liverpool and Manchester. These early foundations subsequently provided a blueprint for other chambers across the British Empire. Some of the impact of wars is evident in Figure 2, which shows how strongly the chronology of chamber establishment interrelates with periods of war. Key foundation periods were the beginning and end of the American War (the mid- and late-1770s, and 1783–8), and the end of the French Wars (1813–19). The exceptions are the establishments in the 1820s in Ireland that relate to growing crises of food supply and lobbying to reduce competition from the rest of the UK in the lead-up to equalisation of British and Irish duties in 1823 following the 1800 Act of Union. However, after crises abated, some of these chambers proved to be short-lived. As indicated in Figure 2, 13 of the early locations (38 per cent) did not sustain an

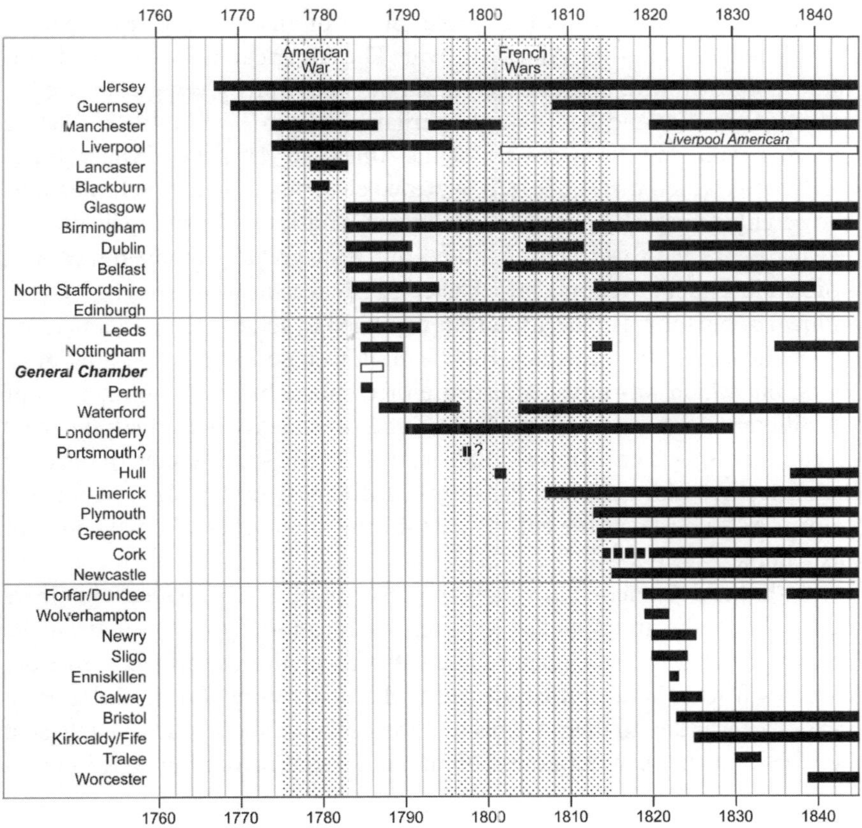

Figure 2. Chamber establishment and existence 1767–1839 compared to periods of war

early chamber for more than 2–4 years.[37] Yet the majority did have sustained, or at least renewing, activity with relatively short gaps; and the proportion sustained is much higher if the rather special cases in Ireland in the 1820s are excluded.

Until 1832–5 the chambers worked with the pre-Reform structure of influencers and patrons to provide information and press for their 'cases' for action. The documents show how MPs were frequently used, as well as members of the House of Lords, the Irish Lord Lieutenant, colonial governors, municipal corporate boroughs, counties, Courts Leet, parochial vestries and other pre-Reform local, colonial and national structures. In the Channel Islands the routes to influence were through the local States and then directly to the Crown through the Privy Council. Often the focus devolved on to the BoT. This in turn meant that many contrasts between chamber actions relate to the position of the BoT itself, with strong differences before and after the period 1760–82, with the restructuring of the Board in 1760 to be more directly controlled by the King being one of the prime influences on chamber foundation in the first place. Some of these structures began to change radically after the American War. The American colonies could now follow their own way, and other colonies were generally given greater leeway and attention. Ireland had its own parliament from 1783 until the Act of Union in 1800, and the aftermath of the American war presented a political opportunity which was supported by varied elements of patriotic Protestants who resented English control of commerce, politics and privileges, propertied Catholics who were marginalised and saw greater opportunities in a more independent Ireland, and Ulster Presbyterians who sought to gain political opportunities. These interests managed to achieve the parliamentary independence for Ireland 1783–1800 leading to a period of economic prosperity, but which was unstable because of conflicts between the interests of the different Irish groups,[38] evident in the documents here. Despite these developments, which showed the metropolitan state under increasing challenge, the state itself remained largely unchanged until the 1835 Municipal Reform Acts chosen as the cut-off date for the main series of documents for this volume.

Sixth, the documents show how the network of emerging local chambers drew on new dynamics which were mostly locationally different from the General Chamber. The General Chamber was predominantly formed from delegates from inland centres; the local chambers were almost all based in ports. This was key to their origins and their relative success. It also reflected their basis in the 'new economy' of the 'industrial revolution' and interna-

[37] Excluding the General Chamber from both numerator and denominator.

[38] P. Langford, *The Eighteenth Century: 1688–1815*, (2002) 23.

tional trade, rather than in traditional centres like Norwich, Exeter or York. Local chambers drew from extensive existing but rapidly growing mercantile trading networks, within which high-trust relationships were the primary mechanism of commercial agreements, underpinning the use of financial instruments such as bills of exchange and wider credit supports. These were intimately interlocked with the emergence of provincial banking, another major feature of the 'new economy', with which chamber leaders normally strongly overlapped: at least 39 per cent of bank partners that were chamber members held chamber offices, of which at least 14 per cent were presidents or vice presidents of early chambers.[39]

In the provincial port cities the merchants, merchant-manufacturers and merchant-bankers were the most significant businesses then in existence. Many were large and economically powerful. They formed a natural economic elite that already closely collaborated with each other for trade and credit. The emergence of collective action to form a chamber was thus a fairly natural step—it just needed a catalyst to make it worthwhile. The inland manufacturing centres certainly participated in similar and overlapping networks with the ports, but they were usually in secondary positions to the merchants and had a lesser expertise in the trade networks that were emerging to take increasing volumes of their manufactures. The balance was to change later, but in the period 1760–1800 most manufacturers were only beginning to participate directly in international trade networks on a significant scale. In this regard Wedgwood was again exceptional and far ahead of most of his manufacturing peers. Even a man of wide experience like Garbett was taken aback by the scale and breadth of activity on his first visit to Liverpool. And the Manchester manufacturer Thomas Walker emerges as a figure of broad intellectual-political links but with little economic grasp beyond his own medium-sized fustian business.

Seventh, the relatively high cohesion in the major ports that underpinned chambers leads to very different inferences about the dynamics of business associations from those drawn from the General Chamber and most later manufacturing groups. In his history of the Leeds chamber, Beresford states that 'dissolution and reformation occur regularly', due to 'sectional troubles ... [that] plagued the eighteenth century chambers'; and 'the union of chambers in the eighteenth century had floundered because of divergent interests'.[40] In Manchester, Bowden concluded that 'the city's industries early developed a diversity of interests as well as an excess of individualism' that

[39] R. J. Bennett, 'Network interlocks: The connected emergence of chambers of commerce and provincial banks', *Business History*, 55, 8, (2013) 1288–1317.
[40] M. W. Beresford, *The Leeds Chamber of Commerce* (Leeds, 1951) 13, 62, and 103.

led to 'difficulties of maintaining a general and harmonious organisation'.[41] Similarly for Manchester, Redford claimed that the decline of commercial societies (i.e. the chambers) at the end of the eighteenth century was due to fundamental divergence of opinion over tariff policy as well as general 'dissatisfaction with the financial results of collective action'.[42] Fragmentation has also been claimed to arise from tensions between 'old' and 'new' manufacturers.[43] The detailed evaluation of local chambers given here and in *Local Business Voice* provides little evidence for these assertions, which were based on a few specialised instances. Recent reassessment of the heavily used Manchester experience, for example, shows a different pattern, of progression between organisations and not the breakup claimed in the 1780s and 1790s.[44] Helm, Bowden, Ashton, Redford and Beresford have also argued that there was a split between protectionists and free traders in this period.[45] This is a misinterpretation, which is why the contemporary terms, 'reciprocal' and 'equal' trade, are employed here. Rather, there was strong favour for opening trade through bilateral treaties, or within the empire, but in a controlled way against external threats from protection, especially by France. The conclusion by Helm that the Manchester merchants were 'not yet emancipated from the thraldom of protection'[46] is misleading. Similarly, Redford's conclusion that there was growing 'apathy', so that 'the commercial societies of the 1790s met with little success, and there can be no doubt that their failure to secure substantial and tangible benefits for their members contributed largely to the general decline of the movement after 1798' is incorrect. Unfortunately these assertions have been frequently restated: from an early date by Bladen and Bowden, and in more recent chamber histories such as Ilersic and Liddle, and Taylor.[47] Similarly, modern historians such as Rose, using Redford, Bowden, and so on, makes claims not supported by the

[41] W. Bowden, *Industrial Society in England Towards the End of the Eighteenth Century* (1965) 167.

[42] A. Redford, *Manchester Merchants and Foreign Trade 1794–1858* (Manchester, 1934) 45; also 60.

[43] Redford, *Manchester Merchants,* 205–7; A.P. Wadsworth and J. de L. Mann, *The Cotton Trade and Industrial Lancashire, 1600–1780* (Manchester, 1931) 164–70, 224–30, 241–48.

[44] R. J. Bennett, 'Alignments, interests and tensions over 'Reform' in eighteenth Century Britain', *Northern History*, 51, 1 (2014) 61–90.

[45] W. Bowden, 'The English manufacturers and the commercial Treaty of 1786 with France', *American Historical Review,* 25 (1919–20) 18–35; J. H. Clapham, *An Economic History of Modern Britain, Vol. 1:* (Cambridge, 1926); T. S. Ashton, *Iron and Steel in the Industrial Revolution*, 3rd edition, (London, 1963).

[46] E. Helm, *Chapters in the History of the Manchester Chamber of Commerce* (London, 1897) 60.

[47] V. W. Bladen, 'The Association of the Manufacturers of Earthenware (1784–86)', *Economic History, Supplement to Economic Journal*, 1 (1928) 363–5; Ilersic and Liddle, *Parliament of Commerce* (1960); Taylor *A History of Chambers* (2007).

evidence of this volume: that 'the majority of early associations were a localised response to a specific set of circumstances, [hence] it is not surprising that they were generally short-lived and ineffective'.[48] They were localised responses but, as shown in Figure 2, many were not short-lived and, in the terms they sought, they were certainly often effective.

Eighth, the evidence of cohesion and stability also runs counter to many claims within business history and political science about the general instability of business associations. Generally the view has been that businesses have difficulty maintaining coherent interests, unless they have a high concentration of a few large firms that dominate their markets, or a strong sectoral or other sources of similarity, that makes management of collective action processes easier and increases the willingness of members to cover its costs. Normally it is claimed that competition and differences of economic needs between different businesses and sectors leads to endemic fragmentation and instability of business associations.[49] However, the studies that have found such fragmentation and instability are dominated by analysis of employer associations concerned with wage and productivity negotiations with their employees, or with sector associations that have tried to organise price and market cartels. These are all narrow-interest bodies, specialised and focused on market and wage controls. In contrast, this volume shows how instability and fragmentation was often more readily controlled and managed in general-interest business associations concerned with generic issues where some theoreticians argue it was supposed to be more difficult. The chambers show that, especially where the generic issues were *local*, there was the potential for strong internal cohesion drawing from historically high inter-firm trust on the issues that were of concern.

Hence, the evidence provided by this volume contradicts much earlier literature. Empirically local chambers did survive, becoming a broad-based local and national movement up to the present. Moreover the early foundations established a model that diffused across Britain and Ireland, spread through North America, and was adopted in most British colonies and the Commonwealth, and after 1990 was used instead of the public law model in most of central Europe and many former Soviet republics.

[48] M. B. Rose, *Firms, Networks and Business Values: The British and American Cotton Industries since 1750* (Cambridge, 2000) 135.

[49] e.g. S. E. Finer, 'The political power of private capital, Parts 1 and 2', *Sociological Review*, NS 3 (1955) 279–94; NS 4 (1955) 5–29; W. Grant, *Business and Politics in Britain,* second edition (1993), *Pressure Groups and British Politics* (2000); G. Jordan, G. and J. Richardson. J. *Government and Pressure Groups in Britain* (Oxford, 1987).

4. Services and Activities

Chambers differ from many other business associations by having a strong focus on services as a well as representation, as reflected in Chapter 6 of this volume, and in terms of their premises, as shown in Plate 1. Chambers in the British realm are, and always were, private law bodies that have to behave like businesses or other private associations. This means that they have to meet member demands, otherwise their members will not join or will leave, resulting in weak resources and reduced credibility—there is no law of compulsory membership as in Germany or France. They also have to make budgets balance—there is no underwriting by the state as de facto occurs in public law chambers—otherwise they become insolvent, as indeed many have done over the years. The British chambers thus have had continually to adapt their services and activity to new demands in order to maintain their membership and resources. Over time this has resulted in considerable changes punctuating long periods of relative stability. Also, since the core services were not laid down by law, as in public law systems, chambers varied considerably depending on local demands and priorities. Their essence was and is local variety. All chambers have a core activity of representing and lobbying in the interests of their members (covered in Chapter 5). This has not changed over time, although the methods and topics have changed markedly. For all chambers, representation continues to be regarded in modern times as their unique selling point: the core service to their members. However, as well as representation, almost all chambers now and in the past have also provided a range of service activities directly to individual businesses, ranging from 'tailored services' (such as advice and information provision to a specific business) to collective services (such as information provision, meetings and networking between member businesses).

It has been argued that, as private law chambers do not have compulsory membership, they face significant challenges because the core collective service of representing on behalf of their members is non-excludable. Representation is delivered on behalf of members but it is impossible to prevent consumption by others who are not members and who do not contribute to the costs ('free riders'): for example, all relevant firms benefit from a change in government regulations that a chamber encourages, such as a new Treaty or a tax reduction or tax reform; and all businesses benefit from new local infrastructure that an association provides or encourages others to provide, such as a road or harbour. It is claimed that normally business associations can only survive by combining the lobby and representation function, which is non-excludable and beset by free riding, with exclusive services (combining the 'logic of influence' and the 'logic of services'). In effect chambers do this. But the argument then runs that this distorts association management decisions so that representation becomes a 'by-product', resulting in ineffectiveness and tensions for member motivation which reduces commitment and leads to lapsing ('exit').[50] As a result it is often argued that it is necessary for government to 'organise' business interests, which introduces other types of distortions and tensions by requiring a 'logic of partnership' with government.[51]

However, the by-product problem is overstated. As shown by the documents here, chamber members and officers were well aware of the tensions and, in practice, they developed an *interlocked* dual service structure, or 'bundling'. Bundling does not just combine services, it encourages each to gain from the other: in modern management terminology it encourages 'cross-shopping'. A member joins or retains membership not just for one service, but also for other services including the representation function. This is a general solution to collective action problems used widely in trade association and other bodies as well as chambers.[52] Bundling generally strengthens retention in member organisations, because it offers economies of scale and scope for both association members and managers, by combining management, marketing and delivery costs for collective and individual services.[53] It mitigates free-rider behaviour by restricting access to some services to incentivise membership and also raises entry barriers for competitors, favouring incumbents.[54] This has been a particular advantage for chambers as the oldest established business associations in the UK. Although market entry is in theory easy, since in a private law system anyone can set up a chamber,

[50] M. Olson, *Logic of Collective Action* (Cambridge, Mass., 1971).

[51] See Bennett, *Local Business Voice* (2011) 64–5, 590–661; also W. Streeck and P. C. Schmitter, 'From national corporatism to transnational pluralism: organised interests in the single European market', *Politics and Society*, 19, 2 (1991) 133–64; D. Sadowski and O. Jacobi, *Employers' associations in Europe: Policy and organisation* (Baden-Baden1991).

[52] F. Van Waarden, F. (1991), 'Two logics of collective action?' in D. Sadowski and O. Jacobi (eds.), *Employers' Associations in Europe: Policy and organisation* (Baden-Baden,1991) 51–84; R. J. Bennett, 'The logic of local business associations: an analysis of voluntary chambers of commerce', *Journal of Public Policy*, 15 (1996) 251–79; R. J. Bennett and M. Ramsden, 'The contribution of business associations to SMEs: Strategy, bundling or reassurance?', *International Small Business Journal*, 25, 1 (2007) 49–76.

[53] C. B. Bhattacharya, 'When customers are members: Customer retention in paid membership contexts', *Journal of the Academy of Sciences*, 26, 1 (1998) 31–44; R. J. Bennett and P. J. A. Robson, 'Exploring the market potential and bundling of business association services', *Journal of Services Marketing*, 15, 3 (2001) 222–39; M. Dixon and R. Verma, R. 'Sequence Effects in Service Bundles: Implications for Service Design and Scheduling', *Journal of Operations Management*, 31 (2013) 138–52.

[54] Olson, *Logic* (1971); Bennett and Robson, 'Exploring market potential and bundling' (2001) 230; Bennett and Ramsden, 'Contribution of business associations to SMEs' (2007) 54.

successful large associations take time and costs to develop, with established brand a valuable asset that reduces search costs for members and raises status with those lobbied. Hence, over time, chambers have tried to develop a mix of excludable and non-excludable services which have tended to remain relatively stable over long periods, as long as the environmental conditions change slowly.[55]

Bundling allowed (and continues to allow) chambers to manage what Hirschman argues are the transaction cost benefits which non-excludable services gain from the loyalty and commitment of their members: through loyalty, voice and involvement with the chamber's management.[56] Bundling offers unique service benefits by using the commitment and solidarity of members as a strategic asset, e.g. using networking and marketing opportunities that businesses would find difficult to access without membership. In any case the actual process of self-selection by joining private law chambers indicates interests in common that, in effect, pre-screen contacts that will be made to be like-minded and hence relevant in terms of supply, markets or sector concerns: what the early chambers called the '*principal* merchants and manufacturers' of their locality. This made them a self-declared and self-identified local elite. Such 'pre-scrutiny' is an advantage over other networks since it encourages trust between firms. This would also be encouraged by the local sense of community, clustering, and group solidarity as a form of 'social capital'. No historical surveys of the motivations of members of the early chambers exist (though there is information on why they lapsed), but modern surveys show that members often join and remain members of chambers from such multiple causes: a sense of responsibility in relation to their community or commitment to a common cause, as well as for specific services.[57]

Bundling offers some significant transaction cost advantages for chambers. Trust and commonality of interest reduces costs where uncertainty and risks are higher, where transactions have high volumes and frequency, and where asset specificity is high introducing 'lock in' effects.[58] Survey evidence from

[55] Olson, Logic (1971); H. E. Aldrich, *Organizations and Environments*, (Englewood Cliffs, NJ, 1979); R. J. Bennett, 'Management adaptation of business association services: Long-term stability 1783–2012 and "change points" for Irish Chambers of Commerce', *Irish Journal of Management*, 35, 1 (2016) 58–73.

[56] A, O. Hirschman, *Exit, voice and loyalty* (Cambridge, Mass., 1970), *Shifting involvements* (Oxford, 1982); Bennett, 'The logic of local business associations' (1996) 260.

[57] Bennett, *Local Business Voice* (2011) 719–62.

[58] E. Ostrom, 'Collective Action and the Evolution of Social Norms', *Journal of Economic Perspectives*, 14 (2000) 137–58; see also R. J. Bennett, 'Can transaction cost economics explain voluntary Chambers of Commerce?', *Journal of Institutional and Theoretical Economics,* 152 (1996) 654–80; M. Schneiberg and J. R. Hollingsworth, 'Can Transaction Cost Economics Explain Trade Associations?' In *Political Choice: institutions, rules, and the limits of rationality*, in R. Czada, and A. Windhoff-Héritier (eds.), (Frankfurt, 1991) 199–256; M. Taylor, M. and

modern UK chamber managers shows how transaction cost advantages derive from combining specialist staff skills with member-member and chamber-member marketing opportunities.[59] Bundled outcomes give cost reductions because of service inter-connectedness, for high frequency, medium cost, and medium intensity services, where there is high personnel and transaction specificity. For this the provision of multi-function accommodation was often critical, as illustrated in Plate 1. In-house bundling allowed cost advantages from combining two type of trust: 'calculative' or 'self-interested' trust (to get something from membership), and social-personal and local trust to others which provided social rewards. Trust could also lead to improved service quality because 'soft' support of advice and information could yield 'hard' impacts (on profit and turnover), with chambers offering more benefit from this combination than most other associations. It gives advantages over the general market for consultancy and business advice, where quality control is notoriously difficult.[60] The effects are greatest where uncertainty and risks are higher, for services with high volumes and frequency, and where asset specificity and 'lock in' effects are strongest. This explains why many early chambers were founded, or grew stronger, in times of crisis.[61]

These rather theoretical distinctions were not fully in the minds of chamber founders, but they were well aware of the need to develop a body that did more than just represent. It had to establish a high status, and it also had to be meaningful as a focal point locally, as projected through its accommodation. This led to an emphasis in most of the early chambers on a set of services that continued in a fairly stable form throughout the period discussed in this volume: from the mid-eighteenth century until the 1830s. After the Municipal Reform Acts of 1835 the service mixes began to change as the local government structures offered both more and less potential for service involvement. Less potential because municipalities were no longer able to

S. Singleton S. (1993) 'The Communal Resource: Transaction Costs and the Solution of Collective Action Problems', *Politics and Society,* 21 (1993) 195–214; and R. F. Donner and B. R. Schneider, 'Business Associations and Economic Development: Why Some Associations Contribute More than Others', *Business and Politics*, 2 (2000) 261–88.

[59] Reviewed in Bennett, *Local Business Voice* (2011) Chapters 14–15.

[60] R. J. Bennett and P. J. A. Robson, 'The role of trust and contract in the supply of business advice', *Cambridge Journal of Economics*, 28 (2004) 471–88; M. Ramsden and R. J. Bennett, 'The benefits of external support to SMEs: 'Hard' versus 'soft' outcomes and satisfaction levels', *Journal of Small Business and Enterprise Development*, 12, 2 (2005) 227–43; D. D. Dawley, R. D. Stephens and D. B. Stephens, 'Dimensionality of Organizational Commitment in Volunteer Workers: Chamber of Commerce Board Members and Role Fulfilment', *Journal of Vocational Behavior*, 67 (2004) 511–25.

[61] Ostrom, 'Collective Action' (2000); Bennett, 'Management adaptation of business association services' (2016).

delegate market management (as had occurred in several Irish chambers before 1835, such as Limerick and Dublin), but more potential because reform allowed broader access and influence locally that was to evolve into major joint infrastructure and improvement initiatives, and subsequently into later nineteenth-century 'gas and water socialism' that was often led by chambers and their members.[62]

5. Membership

This volume also provides an Appendix with a complete listing, as far as possible, of the membership of the earliest chambers. It was these individuals who initiated the system and it is important to understand and record who they were. This opens a resource for a range of other research on individual involvements and networks of interrelationships. The member lists also contain some objective or 'exogenous' characteristics of chamber members: e.g. their business field, sector of activity, etc. Perhaps more significant were their 'endogenous' characteristics: the sense of commitment or feelings that led them to join with others. Unfortunately little information on endogenous characteristics survives, but where possible their religious affiliation is listed in the Appendix. One explanation for the emergence of chambers is that they were an outcome from a more general need for political expression by those leading business people who felt excluded and un-represented by the political system.[63] The chambers offered particular attractions as one of the few organisations where business people were the leading figures; they were often only minor participants in most other societies in the eighteenth century where they were usually greatly outnumbered by small traders or artisans,[64] which was particularly valuable to Dissenters. Chambers were also highly focused on the major economic concerns of the day and, despite some exclusiveness, had fewer barriers to entry than most other major organisations (such as the corporations).[65] The only significant rivals to the chambers as economic bodies were sector-based organisations (of which there were few, and most were short-lived), agricultural societies, and some of the societies for improvement, invention, or 'philosophical' discourse (scientific and technological discussions), which often had high status and sometimes attracted the patronage of the aristocracy and leading political figures, thus perhaps

[62] Bennett, *Local Business Voice* (2011) 596–9.

[63] S. G. Checkland, 'Economic attitudes in Liverpool 1793–1807', *Economic History Review,* 5 (1952) 58–75; Bradley, *Religion, Revolution* (1990); Clark, *Clubs* (2000) 96.

[64] Clark, *Clubs* (2000) 152.

[65] See N. Rogers, *Whigs and Cities; Popular politics in the age of Walpole and Pitt* (Oxford, 1989); O'Gorman, *Emergence* (1982); Langford, *Polite and Commercial* (1989).

offering stronger access to political elites: as in the case of the Society of Arts, Royal Society, some Agricultural Improvement Societies, and some of the literary societies that had broader remits. But leading chamber members were also members of most of these, including the major agricultural societies (as in Manchester and Liverpool), drawing some coordination between chamber and non-chamber business leadership.[66]

Religious dissent was a major endogenous feature. Dissenters were disproportionately frequent members of chambers. Dissenters were often the leaders of many of the protests and reform initiatives of the eighteenth and nineteenth centuries. They were leading figures in many more populist campaigns, such as Wilkes elections campaigns 1769–76, Wyvell's County Association 1780, and the anti-slavery movement of 1787–1807. Dissenters were also very active in many societies so it is natural that business leaders among them would engage with chambers. In the earliest chambers of Liverpool, Manchester, New York and Charleston Dissenters formed over 30 per cent of all members at a time when their proportion of the local population was no more than 10 per cent. In the Stamp Act committees of the 1760s the proportion was even higher: 35–50 per cent.[67]

Whilst we have insufficient surviving information to fully understand all 'endogenous' member characteristics and motivations, it is clear that the early chambers were certainly composed of a disproportionately high number of activists. Analysis of the participation by Liverpool's chamber members in other major petition and pressure activities over 1765–80 demonstrates that they were among the most active people locally: 10–53 per cent of those involved. Similarly activists made up a large proportion of chamber membership: 34–47 per cent of the members were involved in other major local petition activities.[68] Similarly in Manchester over 1765–80 chamber members made up 10–52 per cent of all petition activists, with almost all the chamber board particularly active.[69]

We can be more certain of the exogenous characteristics of chamber members. The analysis in *Local Business Voice* demonstrates that over 1767–1819, 52 per cent of members were partnership businesses, much higher than the average. Membership was also dominated by merchants in almost all chambers. 'Merchants' were the leading entrepreneurs and key figures in financing and trading products for other businesses, with many evolving into banking and becoming the leading intermediaries in credit and finance.[70]

[66] Bennett, *Local Business Voice* (2011) 103–6, 669–87, discusses some of the interactions and overlaps with other societies.

[67] Bennett, *Local Business Voice* (2011) 683–5.

[68] Bennett, *Voice of Liverpool* (2010) Tables A4–A7.

[69] Bennett, 'Alignments, Interests and Tensions' (2014) Table 1.

[70] Bennett, *Local Business Voice* (2011) 669–78.

They typically had the highest status among business people in the national and local economy.[71] Thus the chamber 'interest' was very much from the business elite who were the central figures of the global trading companies of the day, as well as in inland trade. Their involvement in chambers was natural since they relied on the ports, and the trade and treaty policies of the government. Merchants and shippers were particularly numerous in chambers such as Jersey, Liverpool, Glasgow, Greenock, Dublin, Cork, Limerick, and Guernsey. But there were also chambers such as Manchester, Birmingham and Dundee where manufacturers made up the majority of membership, or Belfast and Newcastle which had a more equal mix of merchants and manufacturers. The detail is available for each chamber in the Appendix.

6. Chamber Management and Governance

A major part of the documents presented here covers the governance structure, rules and processes used by chambers to manage themselves. As far as possible I have sought to reproduce the founding articles of each early chamber, and any significant amending statements during their early life. This is an important field since governance underpinned the status and legitimacy of chambers both internally (to their members) and externally (to those to whom they were representing interests). It was also part of the general shift to rule-based organisation of the period.

Chambers had a different portfolio of activity from most other organisations. As noted, they bridged service, social and political dimensions. However, it would be expected that their governance would draw from precedents elsewhere, and deal with similar problems of governance in similar ways. Three strands of literature provide relevant comparators: that on companies, that on societies, and that on protest movements. Each has been extensively studied, but none has included chambers in a meaningful way. For example, Freeman et al. provide an important benchmark study of how the rules of early corporate forms were evolving, but do not include the rules of any chambers of commerce.[72] A second strand is that of societies. Clark, in a major and wide-ranging study of societies for this period, touches on chambers but, although his sample of societies is never fully clear, it is apparent that chambers form no meaningful part. He refers to chambers on only four occasions: two are comparative comments that societies differ from merchant bodies, and two comments cover specific places (Dublin and New

[71] Bowden, *Industrial Society* (1965) 136, 140.

[72] M. Freeman, R. Pearson and J. Taylor, *Shareholder Democracies? Corporate Governance in Britain and Ireland before 1850* (Chicago, 2012).

York) where the chamber is seen as part of a panoply of societies with no attempt made to assess it or draw on the published studies of these two bodies.[73] The third strand of literature has assessed political movements, but almost all of this is on social and modern action groups. There has been little systematic inclusion of business bodies. Much of this literature is therefore only partially relevant: it shows that such movements seek to maximise the scale of membership or number of activists, develop methods of direct action, and maximise media or other publicity.[74] Chambers and other business bodies, in contrast, tend to emphasise select membership of business 'elites', subtle and often confidential exchanges, with publicity used only for occasional and limited objectives. However, the political movement literature is important as a counterpoint because most of the chambers were founded in a period where external social and economic pressures affected the population and businesses alike. Many business leaders shared the anger of social movement activists, and they were usually similarly excluded from the mechanisms of the state. But the business community had more to lose, had some privileged routes of access, and had more leverage as a result of their significance to government as providers of wealth, economic resources, and often also of logistical materials (such as ships and men required during wars). Hence, they generally trod a careful line between confidential and publicised engagement, activism and more subtle methods of influence.

The neglect of these previous literatures to include chambers in their analysis is also of some utility, since it means that the previous studies of the corporate form, societies and political movements are essentially exclusive of chambers and hence can be used as independent comparative samples. The following discussion highlights the patterns of governance from the three comparator bodies: corporations, societies, and protest movements, attempting as far as possible to systematise comparison with chambers.

6.1 Corporate bodies

Corporate bodies relevant to comparisons here took two main forms in the eighteenth century: municipal corporations for local government, and business corporations. The former were the realm of formal and state powers, the latter the world of business. Both offered precedents for chamber organisation. The emergence of chambers can be seen in the light of the general evolution of these corporate forms. The merchant and manufacturing interest, as a separate interest, had always existed, but had never been numerically

[73] Clark, *Clubs* (2000) 152.
[74] See e. g. G. Jordan and W. Maloney, *The Protest Business* (Manchester, 1997).

large. Across Europe until the 15th or 16th centuries the old order was dominated by church control or the King, prince or manor. As Cooke argues, the merchants and manufacturers did not fit into that hierarchy, generally having no significant land holding, located in urban centres (especially the main foci of trade), and deriving income from outside the traditional fields of control by ecclesiastical licence, state license, or manor privilege—all of which they saw as restraints on freedom to trade and inefficient monopolies that needed to be circumvented, if necessary by interloping.[75] They invented new corporate forms through trading partnerships, with a well-established structure of agents, factors, and correspondents, with its own legal process of the law merchant (*Lex Mercatoria*) that was essentially self-governing and became internationally understood and recognised by other local and state courts largely independently of state political decisions. It worked because a code of conduct underpinned the trust needed for reliable transactions, payment of debts, and provided a basis for credit and banking (or its precursors). At various stages this voluntary system recruited the state. The law merchant was based on contract notes and bills of exchange which was backed by an increasingly sophisticated case law that was enforced through the normal courts: in England through the higher courts of Chancery, and the lower courts of local magistrates or under local mayors and burgesses as Courts Merchant.[76] In all trading states the same processes developed, though the institutional supports would locally vary: developing early in Florence, Venice, Genoa and many Mediterranean trades, and later in the Dutch, German and French trades.

The response of the state apparatus varied, but was usually slow to adapt. Generally concessions were won when state rulers were in crisis, when short of funds, or in conflicts that needed support from the merchants and manufacturers as sources of additional funds and credit, and as controllers of significant parts of the infrastructure that could be pressed by the state to fill its needs: for example, logistical organisation to gather and distribute supplies to victual troops and navies; production of additional weaponry such as ships, cannons and ordnance; and means to transport it all through chartering shipping, carts, horses and other necessities.

The local boroughs and corporations were often allies in developing the new facilities needed: e.g. dock, harbour, canal and river improvements. The new merchant classes could exercise some control over these as freemen. However, as corporations became increasingly valuable as means to control parliamentary elections they became more corrupted by ruling elites. Hence, by the mid-eighteenth century corporations were less reliable as economic

[75] C. A. Cooke, *Corporation, Trust and Company* (Manchester, 1950) 183–6.
[76] C. Gross, *Gild Merchant: A contribution to Municipal History* (Oxford, 1890).

supports and other means were recruited: parliamentary Acts, statutory companies and charters, private joint stocks and partnerships.

6.1.1 Municipal corporations

Municipal corporations performed four important roles that influenced businesses: (1) Property owning, to supply facilities such as harbours; (2) Regulatory, to oversee industry and commerce, manage local markets, and supply urban services such as street cleansing, policing etc.; (3) Legal, to manage courts and tribunals; and (4) To guard a town's interests and promote it through lobbying and petitioning.[77] They were natural arenas for business to engage with in order to influence local conditions and to direct representations to the Westminster government. They were the target for one of the first chamber initiatives in Liverpool in 1774, when the initial proposal was to operate a joint committee of trade between the corporation and the wider merchant community. However, corporations attracted increasing criticism through the century, as identified by Innes.[78] First, they were exclusive to a limited and increasingly controlled electorate, often de facto operating through co-option to offices and hence easily controlled by a single party, family or factional interest, and increasingly focused on the influence of Westminster government politics. This was particularly strong in Scotland and Ireland, where almost all Burghs and corporations were venal,[79] with religious groups such as Catholics formally excluded and Dissenters often limited in access. This undermined their legitimacy and popular support, especially among an increasingly large group of prosperous merchants and manufacturers who were significant figures in their own worlds, who saw a petty and odious local elite controlling access to local facilities and resources, and controlled by government interests. Municipal exclusiveness indeed proved fatal to the 1774 Liverpool joint committee of trade proposal, as shown in the documents in Chapter 4.

Second, there was criticism of financial burdens. The corporations financed themselves from tolls, fees and levies. These bore chiefly on traders and manufacturers, which inevitably produced a conflict with the largely landed interest who paid little and who controlled corporations (either directly or through their freeman-elected dependents). Also, although some corporations were effective in using revenue for improvement and service functions, this often benefited the insiders who made gains through land speculation or new fees, whilst many corporations were perceived as dilatory,

[77] J. Innes, 'Governing Diverse Societies', in P. Langford ed. *The Eighteenth Century: 1688–1815* (Oxford, 2002) 111.

[78] Innes, 'Governing Diverse Societies' (2002) 111–4.

[79] Porritt and Porritt, *Unreformed House* 1903); Namier and Brooke, *House of Commons* (1964).

inefficient and neglectful of their locality, and more interested in dining, petty privileges, establishing local hierarchies, or pursuing political advancement with the national government or Crown. There were increasingly calls for transparency about elections and finances as the eighteenth century developed. Elections and dock fees were the centre of the disputes in Liverpool in 1774 leading up to the chamber's establishment, where a current of discord about control of formerly 'free quays' and land speculation by aldermen and had been going on for decades. Similarly in Manchester, the Lord of the Manor power over the court Leet became increasingly resented by the merchants and manufacturers in line with its increasing neglect or misuse.

Third, the municipal corporations were often increasingly irrelevant. The freeman status of municipalities had become of little or no significance in its original meaning of limiting and controlling traders, and many functions that were needed could not be easily developed by a municipal corporation alone. Instead private Acts and subscription initiatives had to be deployed which required evidence of, and the financial backing from, broader local support than a corporation's common council alone. The new Acts and subscription bodies also provided opportunities for a range of new leaders that demonstrated a converse, more active and effective way of doing business that a corporation. They appeared more 'modern' and reforming, open, transparent and creating 'improvements'. In comparison corporations appeared backward, inward looking, preoccupied with maintaining hierarchy and the status quo, supporting the external rather than the local state, or just indulging themselves. Also, in an increasing number of important 'rising towns' such as Birmingham or Manchester, corporations did not exist and other models of organisation had to be developed to achieve anything. Alternative institutional structures such as counties, manor courts Leet, and parishes might be effective in some minor fields, but were usually unable or uninterested in improvement and new ventures, especially the major economic and commercial undertakings sought by the business community. Hence the local institutions of the state in the eighteenth century were not well-tuned to improvement. This naturally led to others taking a lead where they could, for which chambers became one leading stream of initiatives. As Innes observes, the question of who held power in the towns became increasingly complex and confused.[80] However, the outcome of many of these initiatives for private Acts of Parliament predominantly lined the pockets of the landed classes or corporations because they owned most of the land on which canals, turnpikes and dock improvements were built. The promoters and shareholders of canals and other improvements were often merchants

[80] Innes, 'Governing Diverse Societies' (2002) 113.

and smaller business interests who took most risk but received small financial rewards because the bigger gains were to be made from land speculation rather than running the infrastructure: again this was a major issue in Liverpool.[81]

6.1.2 Business 'corporations'

For the counterpart of companies, there were the options of formal incorporation, or so-called 'un-incorporated companies' constituted as partnerships. Freeman et al. provide a valuable analysis for both types of governance structures covering 514 companies in Britain and Ireland founded between 1720 and the Companies Act 1844. This time period and geographical coverage is almost exactly coterminous with that which is of interest for early chambers. The Freeman et al. sample contains those companies with 13 or more partners and transferable shares for which governance papers could be found. It is estimated that their sample covers about one third of all companies established over the period.[82] Their analysis also seeks to compare companies with other bodies such as municipal corporations, voluntary societies and commissioners for bodies such harbours, streets and sewers, but no chambers were included.

Chambers were a hybrid of a business body and a political body and it can be expected that they would draw on precedents from company structures as well as other more diffuse and varied precedents. However, one of the major issues on which the analysis of companies focuses is less relevant to chambers. The extensive discussion of principal-agent problems, a major focus of company analysis, usually has little importance for chambers in this period, though it was to become a major concern in modern chambers when highly paid chief executives were appointed.[83] Agency issues arise from the different incentives influencing members and managers, to ensure that managers are aligned with member interests. Most early chambers had no staff other than a record-keeping clerk, a part-time secretary or a member-volunteer, so agency had very limited scope to arise. However, all chambers

[81] e.g. where dock improvement enclosed former free quays, or made it difficult for chamber members who were landing cargoes directly on to the shore or were using it for ship building, as occurred for Richard Kent and John Walker; and over the Sankey and Leeds-Liverpool canal routing, where chamber members concerned with the Sankey were left isolated when the route through Wigan was by-passed, which affected Nicholas Ashton, Thomas Staniforth and others, and perhaps the chamber's chair John Dobson: Wigan Archives, Liverpool-Wigan Canal letterbook D/D2 A13/38. Also see Bennett, *Voice of Liverpool* (2010) 79–81, 103, 119, 122–3; also Barker and Harris, *Merseyside Town* (1959) 38.

[82] Freeman et al., *Shareholder Democracies* (2012) 14–16; see also B. R. Cheffins, *Corporate Ownership and Control: British Business Transformed* (Oxford, 2008).

[83] Bennett, *Local Business Voice* (2011) 236–43.

had 'managerial' committees/boards that usually sought to act as an executive. How the authority of that executive operated was a major concern, and detailed governance structures were evolved to manage it. This was the counterpart to the managerial challenges of aligning the board and shareholders of a company. But there was no concept in this early period that there should be a separation of the interests of a chamber's executive and its shareholders (the members) to ensure good governance. Indeed the reverse was true. The governance structures sought to ensure that the executive closely followed the members' *collective* concerns.

A second strand of the literature on governance of companies focuses on how new initiatives sought innovative structures that met their needs, but within the constraints of the common law structure governing the status of legal bodies then available in England and Wales, Scotland, Ireland and the colonies. This was fundamental to chambers. They had no counterpart to the status granted to the public law chambers as in France or Germany, where their governance was defined by statute. Instead in the British realm various devices deriving from the law of partnership had to be used.

Partnership law was a fundamental influence on chamber governance. The only other formal ways to establish a 'body corporate' were by parliamentary Act (like a canal company or turnpike trust) or by Royal charter. Several chambers sought charters and six were successful, but there is no example of a chamber seeking an Act, presumably because the purpose was not a specific trading initiative to make a profit that might meet with parliamentary success. In any case both Acts and charters were difficult to obtain and expensive, and hence most chambers sought an alternative. In contrast, partnership law offered a general means to organise a collective enterprise that was cheap, readily available, familiar and unfussy.

Partnership offered the obvious precedent for chamber governance. It was the main means for business organisation throughout the eighteenth and nineteenth centuries. Under English law, partnership had the convenient feature that the firm was not a separate entity distinct from the partners (members) who composed it. For a chamber, the members were the body: the individuals and the collective were one. This sums up the explicitly defined purpose of many chambers: to act together for the benefit of the locality.

English partnership law differs from that in Scotland, European states and the later USA, which treat partners as 'an association' or separate entity, including co-ownership of partnership property. This allowed Scottish chambers some benefits of more formal laws of co-partnership, though in practice this mainly influenced only the size of the partnership and its wider acceptance as a model. In contrast, in England and Wales partners were (and are) both principals and agents for each other; the firm's name is a mere expression, not a legal entity; the firm is no more than the names of the individuals operating under the name.[84] Partnership law was based on common law and equity. This in turn was part of the law of agency where each partner constituted their co-partners as their agents for carrying on the business.[85] The courts since the 1690s had recognised this structure: common contract and agency law 'worked' and evolved to meet new needs 'developing slowly with the growth of trade and commerce and representing generally perceived views of justice' deriving from normal commercial practices.[86]

For chambers it allowed the constitution as an 'entity' or legal personality to be defined, and hence allowed it to act as a collective to undertake activities, and undertake legal agreements with others. However, partnership law imposed some important limitations that made the operation cumbersome, especially for large bodies like chambers. First, it was not an entity distinct from its members: it could not sue or be sued as an entity, or own or rent property as a body, but only in the names of all partners/members who all agreed to take on liabilities jointly and severally. Second, any change in the membership required any legal arrangements to be re-established with the new group of members. The strict consequence of these two legal constraints was that each member had to agree to take on liabilities, which could be off-putting, and each time the chamber membership changed all legal agreements had to be terminated with former members and contracted with the new members. This explains why some of the chambers sought to establish themselves for fixed periods (see Chapter 1 for Jersey in 1767 and Liverpool in 1774; both had fixed three-year terms) which bound all members to joint activity, with the chamber reconstituted with a new group of members after the fixed term.

As a result, partnership law was very cumbersome: although the law was very supportive, it 'permitted the spontaneous creation of partnerships, yet [it] denied them the privileges of limited liability or separate legal entity'.[87] Partnerships were de facto restricted by the high transaction costs of establishment, monitoring of the partners by each other and by others, and making changes such as dissolution and re-establishment.[88] None of these costs arose for municipal bodies or corporations with charters which were constituted from their outset as a single entity which had independence from their members and 'permanence'. Moreover the costs and complexity rise more than proportionately as the number of partners increases, because of

[84] N. L. Lindley, *A Treatise on the Law of Partnership* (London, 1878) 18, 236–7.
[85] Lindley, *Partnership* (London, 1878) 236–7.
[86] W. S. Holdsworth, *History of English Law,* vol. 8 (1925) 242–3.
[87] R. Harris, *Industrialising English Law* (Cambridge, 2000) 1.
[88] H. Hansmann, and R. Kraakman, 'The essential role of organizational law', *Yale Law Review*, 110, 3 (2000), 387–440.

the greater number of permutations of inter-partner and extra-partner interrelationships to manage changing risks.[89] Thus for a body like a chamber with numerous members, this becomes preclusive. In addition there will be increasing risks of moral hazard with large partner numbers increasing the potential for free-riding, opportunism or delinquency among partners, and potential for hold-ups and inefficiencies which all increase with larger partner (and member) numbers.[90]

As a result of these constraints, although chamber governance was usually *formally* constituted as an partnership entity for all members, for practical reasons the rules normally sought to limit *de facto control* to a small group of officers or a board operating 'in trust' for the membership as a whole. Thus monies were almost always held by the treasurer in his name, or held within a local bank 'in trust', or by a small group of the officers (usually the president and vice president)[91] on behalf of all. Similarly any actions requiring the chamber to make legal agreements with others were made through its board[92] or most commonly by one or a few officers in their own names acting in trust for the whole. The contortions to make these structures work in practice is evident in some of the convoluted text of the rules reproduced here, and in many of the deliberations in the minutes where there were legal issues to be resolved. Although agency issues might arise from these structures, the minutes and activities of the early chambers rarely show it. In the examples here the main case where the board created agency problems was Dublin in 1788.

Formal incorporation was possible from the 1844 Company Act for existing bodies, but for a new body became possible only under the Company Acts of 1856 and 1862. Once this legal structure was created, an alternative approach to legal status existed, and the chambers were among the earliest organisations to use it: 16 of the first 1,000 limited companies in England and Wales.[93] Formal incorporation also became a recommended route for chambers to follow in the twentieth century, usually as companies limited by

[89] Hansmann and Kraakman, 'Essential role' (2000) 406ff.

[90] N. R. Lamoreaux, 'Partnerships, Corporations, and the Theory of the Firm', *American Economic Review, Papers and Proceedings*, 88 (1998) 67–8.

[91] The term president is used uniformly here; many chambers also referred to the chief officer as chairman.

[92] Boards were so named in many cases, but also the title 'Committee' was widely used, and 'Council' occasionally used, for the governing body. Here the generic title 'board' is used throughout.

[93] See L. Richmond and B. Stockford, *Company Archives: The Survey of the records of 1000 of the first registered companies in England and Wales* (Aldershot, 1986); the first chambers incorporated in this way, all after 1860, were Oldham, Swansea, Newport, Ipswich, Bolton, Manchester, Lincoln, London, Leeds, Cardiff, Hull, Kendal, Spen Valley, Batley and Birstal, Liverpool, and Middlesbrough.

guarantee, more recently also including community interest companies (as for Liverpool chamber in 2011).[94] Incorporation was first advocated by Leone Levi, who drafted a Bill in 1857 for incorporating chambers of commerce as a special form of company registration under the 1856 Act. This was taken up by the national Association of Chambers (ACC) when it was established in 1860. Jacob Behrens (Bradford chamber) and the ACC in 1866 began to explore Levi's proposal with the BoT, using a private Bill to seek a separate incorporated status for chambers.[95] This was unsuccessful, but use of general incorporation laws, with approval via the BoT, did begin to take off in the 1870s. Incorporation assured an independent legal personality, and a form of governance through the company's memorandum and articles of association with perpetual succession, the ability to contract and take legal proceedings in its own name, especially to own property, with its officers and members freed of personal liability. For chambers it also became an important means to prevent others from assuming the title of 'chamber' and passing themselves off as a similar body for a specific locality.[96] Full protection was not, however, finally achieved until an Act formally protecting the title 'chamber' in 1999.[97]

6.2 Charters

Chartered status was desired by many of the early chambers, and achieved by six. It offered the advantages of a separate legal entity that could act without the constraints, costs and complexity of a partnership. Such an entity could act as a legal personality that could sue and be sued, own and convey assets such as meeting rooms and buildings. It made it easier to receive bequests and donations, and it offered more ready redress in the courts against officers where there were misdemeanours.[98] A Royal charter also provided permanence independent of the commitment or survival of its members. A charter could limit liability and had to provide a mechanism for transferability of shares. A charter also provided authority for the body to regulate itself, such as setting membership subscriptions, settling disputes between members, and acting collectively for the chamber with outsiders in any transactions or disputes. Such powers allowed a chamber to take on a contract for delivery of a

[94] Bennett, *Local Business Voice* (2011) 252–8.

[95] LMA: ACC, Standing Committee minutes, 24 February 1862, 20–22 February 1866, and following.

[96] LMA: ABCC, Home Affairs Committee, 1 July 1936.

[97] Company and Business Names (Chamber of Commerce etc.) Act, 1999; see Bennett, *Local Business Voice* (2011) 273–5.

[98] Without incorporation, the courts often failed to protect societies from mismanagement and fraudulent conduct by their officers: Clark, *Clubs* (2000) 180; also 98.

service or activity, e.g. by acting as a harbour commissioner, managing a hide or butter market, enforcing quality controls on products such as textiles or agricultural products, or acting as an agent in promoting a canal or other infrastructure schemes.[99] Most importantly, a charter allowed the corporate body to own property. These aspects were critical to the activities of the early chambers for which, as large membership bodies averaging 40–100 founding members, a charter simplified many day-to-day administrative processes of services and premises management.[100] For such bodies the partnership model under common law was extremely burdensome in terms of the transaction costs involved, both internally and externally. Where used, a charter defined the constitution and rules of operation of the body, and sought to protect it from external suits or abolition. These are features of the charters reproduced in Chapter 2 of this volume.

However, the chief advantage of a charter for most chambers that sought it went far beyond pure transaction costs, ability to own property and administrative convenience. These were certainly desirable. But the key benefit was to give *status*, especially an equality of status, with those other bodies with which a chamber co-operated, or against which it sought to lobby. Most specifically chambers sought charter status against the various elements of the administrative structures of the state most relevant to their issues, which of course explains why charters were difficult for chambers to obtain. The opposition was often especially vigorous locally. Most of the early chambers arose specifically to provide a voice as an alternative to municipal corporations, to manorial courts Leet, to colonial Governors or Assemblies, and to administrators operating local bodies corporate such as harbour commissioners, ballast offices, or Trinity House. The chambers also needed status with central metropolitan administrative arms of the state such as the Treasury, Admiralty, Post Office, and especially local Customs officers. But most of all they needed status with parliament. Early chambers were sometimes in positions akin to modern chambers where they were helping government, facilitating the flow of information to administrators or ministers which encouraged improved decision making. But most chambers were born in the most fraught periods of political tensions, many during or after wars, where advocacy of the views of outsiders and commercial interests ahead of the political class was at best seen as irrelevant, more generally as an incon-

99 Freeman et al., *Shareholder Democracies* (2012) 46–7; Bennett, *Local Business Voice* (2011) 540–3.

100 The only other formal alternatives available, as for companies, was letters patent, which was generally irrelevant to chambers as it was only granted in pursuit of specific adventures (such as infrastructure, or in earlier periods, foreign trade). It also became of little relevance to companies, and efforts to revive use of letters patent by an 1834 Act had limited impact; see e.g. Freeman et al., *Shareholder Democracies* (2012) 32–3.

venience that had to be managed and diverted, and at the most extreme as viewed as seditious. Chambers laboured on numerous occasions against the political position that their lack of status made them irrelevant: they had no 'right' for their voice to be heard.

During the eighteenth and early nineteenth centuries pressing for a charter was a lengthy and specialised process, which was usually costly and required engaging supporters in parliament and the Privy Council, which had become the main decision making bodies. However with the right entrée charters were more easily granted. For example, Patrick Colquhoun, the first president and founder of the Glasgow chamber in 1783, was able to use his position as Provost of Glasgow to seek support from individuals in high office who would have been difficult for the Privy Council to refuse (such as Henry Dundas; some of this correspondence is reproduced in Chapter 4). It also helped that the request came from Scotland which was less challenging to government. Colquhoun was advised by London agent John Seton that 'a Royal charter will add permanency and weight to the establishment of your chamber of commerce'.[101]

But in the pre-Reform state everything depended on patronage. The request for a charter from the Jersey chamber was refused in 1787, and repeatedly thereafter.[102] Efforts to establish a London chamber through a charter in 1817, 1823 and 1850–70 were all resisted by government.[103] Dublin purportedly considered seeking a charter in 1783, but abandoned it.[104] The other chambers able to obtain charters all reflected the different circumstances of Scotland and Ireland: Greenock in 1813; Leith in 1852; Limerick, founded in 1807, gained a charter in 1815 largely as a result of its de facto licence as an arm of the local corporation;[105] and Waterford, founded in 1787, sought a charter in 1807, eventually granted in 1815 largely on the basis of the debenture structure of shareholders that it had developed for purchase of its building.[106]

The difficulties arising from the lack of a charter were experienced frequently in the 1780s. When Thomas Stanley, MP for Lancashire, presented to parliament the petition of manufacturers of Manchester concerning the

[101] *The Scots Magazine*, vol. 48, February 1786, 99.

[102] Jersey Archives: chamber minutes, 23 April and 18 August 1787; 3, 9 and 24 January, 5 February, 3 December 1788; 12 January 1789; see Chapter 2. Jersey became a limited company in 1900.

[103] Bennett, *Local Business Voice* (2011) chapters 5 and 7; see also Chapter 4 below.

[104] TNAI: Dublin chamber, *Report of Council* (1823) 5.

[105] Quoted in Limerick entry in Bristol chamber, *Yearbook* (1908–9): Bristol RO 38605/Pu/35; for Ireland see D. P. O'Connor, *The history and functions of the Limerick chamber of commerce 1807–1902* (Dublin, 1938).

[106] Waterford Archives: chamber minutes, 17 July 1807; *Charter text* (1815).

fustian tax in 1785, the president of the BoT, Charles Jenkinson, was quick to note that 'undoubtedly the House could not recognise any meeting or aggregate body of men, who assembled without either the authority of the Crown or parliament'; i.e. they lacked a formal charter. This was all part of the political play, the 'twitting' as Wedgwood called it. However, Jenkinson was eventually prepared to accept the petition in the name of one signatory, Thomas Walker, not the Manchester chamber (committee of trade), or the claimed 50,000 signatories that had been involved.[107]

In the Irish parliament, when Travers Hartley, president of the Dublin chamber and an MP, presented a petition from the chamber for reform of the navigation laws in 1785 (see Chapter 5), Mr Fitzgibbon, the Attorney General, could not 'consent to receive a petition from a body of men styling themselves—a council of a chamber of commerce—a title utterly unknown to this House, either as a chartered or a corporate body, and therefore however respectable the petitioners, this House can take no cognisance'. He went on: 'what is a chamber of commerce. Merely a self-elected body, and the name a title usurped'. This theme was continued by Mr Beresford MP, who said the 'House cannot recognise a body unknown to law … [but] they may come as a guild of merchants of the City of Dublin, or as individual merchants'; and John Scott MP argued that the 'usurped titles of president and vice president of the chamber of commerce—titles that we in vain look for in the Statute Book … or in the charters of corporations'[108] should mean that their views could be set aside. There was no refusal to receive petitions from individuals, since everyone had the right to petition parliament and the Crown. Again the issue was resolved by accepting the petition from Hartley as MP and his co-signatories as individuals, not from the chamber.[109]

6.3 Societies

Chambers had some activities and objectives identical to those of societies, particularly to encourage meetings and discourse. For chambers this provided opportunities to obtain commercial intelligence, open market opportunities, and engage in purely social exchange. These exchanges were key 'services' in their own right, but were also part of the platform from which political and policy initiatives could be developed; meetings were the essential

[107] Namier and Brooke, *House of Commons*, 11 March 1785 (1964) 350.
[108] TNAI: *Parliamentary Register or History of the House of Commons of Ireland*, October 1783–May 1784, 205–7.
[109] The Dublin chamber decided not to attempt to acquire a charter in the early 1800s, as it was not going to have property, stock, or capital: P. L. Prendeville, *History of the Dublin Chamber of Commerce 1760–1860,* M.Comm Thesis (University College Dublin, 1930) 101.

way to deliberate, form and marshal 'opinions', gather evidence, and prepare convincing policy statements. Hence, socialising, discourse and deliberation interacted as part of the core bundle of early chamber activities, and as an important means to allow the development of the cases and memorials that were part of the lobbying process, both through formal meetings and informal exchanges. This explains their heavy emphasis on prestigious accommodation (as illustrated in Plate 1). Deliberation increased the strength of lobby arguments, moving beyond assertion or 'protest' to a reasoned 'case' and credible statement of a policy position. A 'case' was a key means to try to overcome government's information asymmetry. As stated by one London chamber member in 1823, fully quoted in Chapter 4 of this volume, 'Ministers would themselves derive a sort of security for the consideration that every subject had undergone the investigation of such a body before it was propounded to government'.[110] 'Conveying to the councils of the nation the *deliberate opinion* of the great mercantile body upon any public commercial question … [and] in many cases remove misconceptions'.[111] Studies of societies thus provide useful comparators for some of these processes.

There was an explosion in the numbers of voluntary societies in late eighteenth-century Britain and the British colonies. Langford and Clark refer to an 'associational age' of 'dynamic, open, and pluralistic world voluntary societies';[112] Morris refers to an 'associational culture' that allowed experimentation with various social and economic initiatives.[113] This was directly coincident with the rise of chambers.[114] Similarly in Ireland, Cullen has demonstrated how societies transformed the economic and political life of the main cities, especially Dublin.[115] This was part of a rapidly emerging 'public sphere' which opened government and political decisions to much greater scrutiny and discussions, through the press, pamphlets and other publications, but especially through public meetings and social engagement within the larger commercial communities. Societies facilitated political engagement, debate, and discourse about 'improvement', as well as offering purely social, drinking and dining functions (that of course acted as other incentives within the bundle). It was also about what Morris called 'the order-

[110] R. Shaw, report on establishing a London chamber of commerce, *Morning Chronicle*, 29 August 1823.

[111] Report of committee to form a London chamber, *Morning Chronicle*, 19 March 1824; emphasis added.

[112] P. Langford, *A Polite and Commercial People*; Clark, *Clubs* (2000) Chapters 6 and 7.

[113] R. J. Morris, 'Urban Associations in England and Scotland, 1750–1914', in G. Morton, B. de Vries and R. J. Morris eds., *Civil Society, Associations and Urban Places* (Aldershot, 2006) 139, 148–9.

[114] Compare Clark, *Clubs* (2000) Figs 4.1 and 4.2; 128, 132.

[115] Cullen, *Economy* (2012) 219–236.

ing of order in the growing commercial and industrial towns': implicit and explicit rules by which collective and voluntary decisions were made about urban development.[116] Studies of societies recognise the most active locations to be the major cities, just where chambers were also mainly to be found.[117]

As well as being vibrant and flexible, Clark identifies societies as becoming more formalised through the century, with increasing use of rules, and increasing numbers of rules: to manage the election of officers; admission of members; organisation of services and activities; and collection of subscriptions, financial management, control of arrears, and audit. Generally the extent of formality and number of rules increased with the number of members, especially for societies of over 20–40 members; most societies had 10–12 rules in the mid-1700s, but this increased to 20–30 by 1800.[118] Committees and sub-committees also tended to proliferate, again generally in larger numbers in larger societies, with audit committees and audit processes becoming more prominent in later societies.[119] Increasingly societies sought 'to ensure a controlled context for social interaction and co-operation'.[120] Clark argues that societies seldom sought charters, though a few did after 1760; rather, they found a legal form through registering with the high court, or through elaborate rules that sought to define themselves as a partnership entity to protect the interests of the society, and protect the officers.[121] Clark does not explicitly recognise the role of partnership and trust law in these rules, but many societies were essentially copying approaches used for corporate bodies, as used by chambers and outlined above.

The interpretation of a chamber as a society was part of the process of social acceptance and personal advancement which was a core element of societies.[122] This influenced the content of the reading rooms which many chambers catered for either directly, or in partnership with other local initiatives for subscription libraries or coffee houses and hotels.[123] The conventions of societies also included the rhetoric of 'politeness', which was very significant in eighteenth-century discourse and a strong influence on chambers. The

[116] R. J. Morris, 'A Year in the public life of the British Bourgeoisie', in R. Colls and R. Rodger eds., *Cities of Ideas: Civil Society and Urban Governance in Britain, 1800–2000* (Aldershot, 2004) 128.
[117] e.g. for Dublin, see Cullen, *Economy* (2012) 219–33.
[118] Clark, *Clubs* (2000) 245.
[119] Clark, *Clubs* (2000) 195–261.
[120] Clark, *Clubs* (2000) 196.
[121] Clark, *Clubs* (2000) 97–8.
[122] Clark, *Clubs* (2000) Chapters 6 and 7; Langford, *Polite and Commercial People*; P. Borsay, 'The Culture of Improvement', in P. Langford ed., *The Eighteenth Century: 1688–1815* (Oxford, 2002) 183–212; R. H. Sweet, 'Topographies of politeness', *Transactions Royal Historical Society*, 12 (2002) 355–74.
[123] Bennett, *Local Business Voice* (2011) 510–36.

chamber rules, and actual practice recorded in minutes, show care to ensure that conflicts were avoided, or if they arose were reconciled through discussion (and for commercial disputes were resolved through the chamber by arbitration).[124] This facilitated the development of unity, though it could encourage acquiescence and withholding from action.[125] Thus we find few examples in minutes or reports of chambers of disputes or disagreements, and if recorded this is usually discreet or opaque.

The rhetoric of 'politeness' was also increasingly sought for a locality. Members could access a 'wider social universe',[126] as part of the efforts to make places attractive to current residents and to visitors. This meant having specific and visible institutions or buildings: parks, walks, museums, theatres, libraries, and the development of leading buildings and institutions, Assembly Rooms, Exchanges, coffee rooms and respectable hotels.[127] These were social milieus and business milieus which both promoted and served the locality through encouragement of social networking and meetings. They supported the same mechanisms of discourse as those that underpinned chamber governance.

For many societies there were also issues of exclusiveness. As Clark notes, this was both a marketing tool so that people felt prized as members, and also a means to focus on including the major interests.[128] In some chambers exclusiveness was fostered by 'black balls' and restrictions on the number of members. The early New York chamber in 1768 geared the entrance fee so that it increased with membership size, which strongly limited numbers to the most significant merchants.[129] Five chambers had explicit blackballing provisions (Jersey 1767, New York, 1768, Dublin 1783, Waterford 1805, Belfast 1830), whilst in others this was more subtly operated through board recommendation. The existence of such rules was probably as important as their use as a symbol of exclusiveness. Other chambers sought to police the wider community of traders, not just members. Overall, 10 of 35 chambers (29 per cent) with surviving rules had some type of 'policing' function in their rules: such as 'keeping trade on a respectable footing' (Jersey 1767) or 'preventing smuggling' (Guernsey 1808). Manchester in 1794 had a 'black book' to

[124] Langford, *Eighteenth Century*, p. 315; on arbitration see Chapter 5 of this volume.

[125] F. G. Castles, 'Business and Government: a typology of pressure group activity', *Political Studies,* 17, 2 (1969) 160–76.

[126] Clark, *Clubs* (2000) 230.

[127] R. H. Sweet, 'Topographies of politeness', (2002) 372–3.

[128] Clark, *Clubs* (2000) Chapters 6 and 7.

[129] Bishop, *Chronicle* (1918) 6–7, 64–8, 230. Initially there was a flat rate entrance fee of $5 in 1768; in 1770 it became $10 rising in $2.5 stages above 80, 100, and 120 members.

identify 'chicanes' and 'swindlers, and exposing persons void of principle and honour'.[130]

Whether deliberate or not, chambers were also almost all exclusively male, and much of the language of their rules is gendered. Although Davidoff and Hall claim the 'age of societies' opened the way for participation by middle-class women, this did not really occur in the commercial world of principal traders on any scale until much later.[131] The only two women who can be definitively identified as early chamber members are Mrs Norton, in Manchester in 1782, who was probably a fustian manufacturer who became a member on the death of her husband; and the 'widow of Symons & Sons' who was one of the first proposers of the Plymouth chamber in 1813. The small presence of women, and only as widows, reflects their limited opportunities to enter into significant businesses on their own account in the eighteenth and early nineteenth centuries.[132]

6.4 Political and protest movements

Political and activist protest movements also had some similarities with chamber governance structures. They required a similar demonstration of a wider public interest if they were to have any chance of being successful. This involved public meetings, which might be preceded by private canvassing, and the establishment of committees, with the central objective of drafting a petition or memorial stating the objective of the protest and the remedy sought. There were, however, four critical differences from seeking a 'body corporate' for campaigning.

First, the objectives were usually one-off rather than permanent: to meet the needs of a particular and immediate grievance and campaign. There was thus, at least initially, not the same aim of establishing long term and 'permanent' rules of governance. Second, the significant drafting and approval of documents had to be maintained during all the crucial stages at a visibly public level (or at least had to appear to be transparent), whereas chambers could be more private: the alternative to incorporation was the 'body politic' —local collective opinion and 'community of interest'. The private promoters had to bury their personal interests as far as possible within wider arguments for common or local good; indeed direct personal profit from the

[130] Manchester Central Library: Proceedings of the Manchester Commercial Society, 2 October 1794 ff.; see also Helm, *Chapters* (1897) 2; Redford, *Manchester Merchants* (1934) 22–23.

[131] L. Davidoff and C. Hall, *Family Fortunes: Men and Women of the English Middle Class 1780–1850* (1997) 416, 436.

[132] For more on the gender of chamber members see Bennett, *Local Business Voice* (2011) 679–80, 712.

body was not the objective, unlike a company, but improvement in trade conditions which would indirectly increase business opportunities for all, including the state as an entity.

Third, protest inevitably ran counter to current political decisions or priorities, and thus had much more potential to meet local or national resistance. This required trying to recruit members of the administrative state to its support. The aim was to turn 'protest' into 'measured and reasonable opinion' represented by existing state elites and interests; most fundamentally it sought to transform protest into a 'case' that it was expected any reasonable minister or administrator should be able to accede to. The process could thus be very long: deliberation and interpersonal exchange was potentially far more intense than for a company promotion. It was also potentially much more risky: to protest against the government carried all sorts of risks to current positions. As the frequency of such petitions from similar local groups increased it also required increased care, greater effort, and potentially higher risk to align those seeking changes with 'reform' rather than to 'challenge authority' or appear to be seeking 'revolution'. The distinctions between reformers and the minority of ideologically committed, often the 'rational dissenters', represented by figures such as Manchester's Thomas Walker, became an increasing dividing line where care had to be exercised.[133] Walker himself recognised this, attacking the timidity of those who had 'constantly fallen short of their own principles ... [and] have been so strongly the advocates of overstrained moderation ... [with] an excess of caution, or a timid kind of prudence'.[134] For a memorial or petition it was thus particularly important to try and obtain signatories and supporters from the moderates, and from those in authority such as the local municipal corporation, local MPs, or other sympathetic state interests to demonstrate that it came from within the existing state structures. Supporters of local improvements, such as a canal or street commission initiative, would also try to recruit municipal and other supporters. But the stakes were far higher for the local elites with a political campaign than for a local improvement. This led to chambers having to rely to a greater extent on a few skilled promoters, who had the specialised balance of personality and skills required, and a level of recognition and authority enabling them to act as intermediaries between the established state and the often angry protesters. There were dangers of jeopardy from both sides: ostracism by state dignitaries at all levels, and alienation and local

[133] J. C. D. Clark, *The Language of Liberty, 1660–1832* (Cambridge, 1994) 29–36; J. Seed, 'A Set of Men Powerful Enough in Many Things': Rational Dissent and Political Opposition in England, 1770–1790, in K. Haakonssen (ed.) *Enlightenment and Religion: Rational Dissent in Eighteenth-Century Britain* (Cambridge, 1996) 141–2.

[134] Walker, quoted in A. Prentice, *Historical Sketches and Personal Recollections of Manchester* (London, 1851) 20; Seed, 'Rational Dissent, (1996) 167.

ostracism from other traders if nothing was achieved; and for both groups the potential to be lampooned in the press or pamphlets so that many people focused on their businesses and might avoid the campaign. Thus for chamber leaders there were higher stakes and risks, financial and non-financial, at all levels than for company promoters or most activist protesters.

Moreover, fourth, chambers could not usually buy off or intimidate opposition. A railway or canal company could reduce opposition by providing profitable opportunities or discounted shares to disgruntled landowners or political opponents. This was a form of what would be recognised as modern 'pork-barrel politics'. This was not generally open to those arguing for political rather than profit advantage. Although Freeman et al. are right to argue that 'the pervasiveness of political metaphors in the pamphlet literature and procedural records of … companies is evidence that … balances were viewed in political terms, reflecting the reshaping of the governmental landscape' of the period,[135] this affected everyone who wished to achieve something through the state. Chambers had similar but also some very different hills to climb to be successful.

Nevertheless, most chambers had one of their central objectives to campaign for new or amended laws: this was part of the founding purpose of 18 of the 35 (51 per cent) surviving rule documents reproduced here, but was higher in practice since all chambers campaigned for law changes when required even if this was not part of their founding purpose. The early chambers also focused on specific 'causes' within a broader attack on reform. Protests and campaigns usually responded to a specific problems or threat: 'bads' were usually the major stimulus for campaign development, particularly if potential threats were large. These generally became strongest when existing agents and networks were ineffective, and where shared ideas and agendas motivated a common cause.[136] Generally businesses are much more reluctant and risk-averse at low-level threats, making them less willing to engage, but they become more willing if threat levels are high and direct against their profit and trading interests. However, even then they are reluctant to align with unpredictable forces which challenge the existing state structure and which may be economically dangerous.[137] This balance was frequently apparent in the early chambers in response to major threats, as indicated in their periods of establishment shown in Figure 2. But they usually kept apart from potential and real 'revolutions': for example the

[135] Freeman et al., *Shareholder Democracies* (2012) 240.

[136] See J. M. Hansen, 'The political economy of group membership', *American Political Science Review,* 79 (1985) 80–1; D. McAdam, S. Tarrow and C. Tilly, *Dynamics of Contention* (Cambridge, 2001).

[137] A. Meister, *Participation, associations, development, and change* (New Brunswick, 1984) Chapter 4.

many public campaigns around Wilkes in the 1760–70s and especially the American revolt and the period of the French revolution. They tended to position themselves within established routes of influence, but often had to use methods and supporters outside the main centres of political power. Hence, whilst social and political movements are rife with examples of civil disobedience, riots and boycotts,[138] civil disobedience was not common by chambers. It had high cost and high risk. But activism akin to political movements was mobilised when government appeared otherwise deaf: e.g. during the Stamp Act crisis, the American War, over the fustian tax and Irish Propositions, or convoy needs. For the fustian tax campaign visible symbols were used to raise anger. The Excise Duty stamps on rolls of fustian cloth were shown at meetings to whip up support. It was claimed that the Excise was over-charging because the cloth shrank after bleaching. Plate 5 shows an example of the cloth passed around at a meeting, with its Excise stamp and hand-inked statement that it was 'only 28½ When Grey' [i.e. before bleaching]; other examples were quoted: 'No. 75 23¾ yards charged 25 yards', and 'No. 9 35¼ yards charged 37 yard'.[139]

Campaign success depends on the receptiveness of government or others being lobbied. It is most successful when supported by powerful established agents and existing mechanisms of consultation; i.e. when existing mechanisms and power brokers could be recruited. However, one of the challenges for early chambers was that many of the normal routes of influence became closed or less receptive because the crown and wider state apparatus turned to a set of political objectives, particularly in America, that ignored economic interests (or at least ranked them well behind political objectives), and the king after 1760 curtailed the role of the BoT. This was a period that has been termed one of 'transgressive contention': when the state agents were not interested in resolving challenges.[140] As shown in Figure 2, the proximate origin of chambers derives from the contentions of the 1760s to 1780s. For business associations Castles has classified business mobilisation into categories based on the extent of need or 'strain' and the degree of legitimacy of the government. In periods of severe strain and low government legitimacy, such as the 1760s–1780s, business are more likely to press their cause through protest activism, public campaigning and alliances with political parties (particularly the opposition); where government has higher legitimacy or is more accommodating there is a stronger tendency to use existing government

[138] See e.g. R. J. Morris, *Class, power and social structure of British nineteenth century towns* (Leicester, 1986); McAdam et al., *Dynamics of Contention* (2001); A. Goodwin, *The friends of liberty: The English democratic movement in the age of the French Revolution* (London, 1979).
[139] Plate 5; Manchester Central Library: GB 127.M503 f.15. Examples quoted: Ibid. f. 16.
[140] McAdam et al., *Dynamics of Contention* (2001); Bennett, *Local Business Voice* (2011) 68–72, 108ff.

machinery and to compromise.[141] Campaigning is also more likely in a common law system like Britain's, where there is no 'right' to be consulted, compared to public law systems of Europe where chambers and some other business bodies have a statutory public status. Campaigning was thus a significant similarity, but also a point of departure between chambers and protest movements.

Although the templates of companies, societies and protest provided guidelines, it is clear that the evolution of the chamber governance also had unique features and appears to have been highly empirical, reflecting different experiences and personal visions in each place. Although there was common ground, a single template did not begin to evolve until the 1820s.

7. Analysis of Chamber Rules

Chapter 1 in this volume, Rules, allows analysis of trends and patterns, which is briefly undertaken below. It is important to bear in mind that this analysis is restricted to explicit statements in the rules, which may not have been followed fully in practice, whilst other de facto rules may have been followed that were not written down or have not survived. Also for comparison over time, many rules carried forward from the earlier foundation of the same chamber; e.g. the audit provision of Manchester in 1782, which was early among chambers, was carried into all the subsequent foundations at Manchester; similarly the casting vote of the president tended to be carried forward in those chambers that used this. This to some extent leads to a pattern at any one time with a mix of former and newer rules across the chamber system. The analysis here is restricted to the rules at establishment and formal re-establishment; not all changes in continuing chamber rules are tracked.

The legal world into which chambers became established required extensive prior activity to frame the chamber's rules and carry sufficient support locally. The most widely used structure of partnership required enough people to be prepared to finance and commit themselves jointly and severally; the more specialised use of a charter required substantial funding and major political effort. As a result, the *process* of establishment and definition of purpose was often as important as the rules themselves in achieving a successful foundation. The support of the local community also had to be gained, or at least sources of criticism and resistance had to be overcome, managed or contained. The process of establishment is included with many of the chamber rules reproduced here. The purposes for which chambers were established were varied, but converged on the general promotion of

[141] Castles, 'Business and Government' (1969) 164.

trade. Thirty-seven of the first 39 surviving rules can be analysed. They specify, in date order, aims to promote: 'well-being of trade', 'promotion of trade', 'encourage industry', 'encourage trade and manufactures', 'attention to trade', 'help West India commerce', 'security and encouragement of trade', 'improve trade', 'represent the trading interest', 'promote interests of commerce', 'approach parliament', 'treaty negotiation', 'develop trade and manufactures', 'promote the interests of trade', 'improve trade and safety', 'promote trust', 'develop American trade', 'promote commerce & intercourse', 'promote 'commerce and manufactures', 'improve regulations', 'develop trade', 'expand trade', 'promote commerce and manufactures', 'prepare memorials', 'improve the trade of this port', 'develop trade', 'assist traders', 'commerce and manufactures', 'trading interest', 'commerce, trade & manufactures', 'public measures & reliefs', 'commercial interest', 'trade', 'protect trade', 'the commerce of this port', 'local improvements'. These brief statements demonstrate a dominant focus on trade, local supports, concern with commerce and increasingly with manufactures, and advocacy to parliament.

The law of partnership also influenced the language used in the rules, and the attempt to encourage a close correspondence between the interests of the individual members and the collective entity. As part of their stated purpose, an explicit statement of collective intent exists for 24 of the first 39 chambers. These statements established the chamber to act 'in trust' (three cases), promote 'mutual wants', seek the 'general benefit', pursue 'common or general interests' (twice), act for the 'the whole community' (twice) and for 'trade or community at large' (three cases), act for the 'public interest or advantage' (six times) or 'public and national interest', operate as a 'united liberal body', and promote 'harmony', 'union,' 'union and cooperation', and 'fellowship'. These statements demonstrate the close link of solidarity and trust, combining advocacy with service activities, as expected from 'bundling' strategies and partnership law.

There was also close similarity with many early company and society establishment processes. The establishment of chambers, societies and companies usually followed a process of private meetings between projectors, followed by private canvassing, recruitment of patrons with significant social status and recognition (usually aristocrats and the politically influential), appointment of a promotional committee, drafting a plan, circulation in local newspapers and pamphlets, a series of meetings, with a final launch of a published prospectus to attract subscribing investors. Both public *and* private interests had to be promoted; i.e. there had to be at least some level of potential profit from the investment. The object was to construct a 'body corporate' out of a private initiative.[142] Chambers used all these mechanisms,

[142] Freeman et al., *Shareholder Democracies* (2012) 32–5.

and seem to have used mechanisms of engagement based on circulars and newspapers to a greater extent than companies and trusts.[143] The chambers therefore followed a well-trodden path of business practice which had been used by promoters of companies since the early eighteenth century, and became progressively more frequent from mid-century.[144] They also benefited from the general political shift from crown to parliament after 1688 that provided growing scope to promote initiatives through local Acts of Parliament.[145] However, they also had another set of precedents originating from protest, reflecting their position of sitting on the cusp of commercial and political interests. This allowed them to call on a fount of anger and commitment to action in some cases, as evidenced by the widespread use of general meetings evident in their rules, and occasional extra-legal or direct action in what they viewed as extreme circumstances ('transcendental contention'). The Stamp Act resistance, which included enforcing trade embargoes, was one of the main direct predecessors of chamber organisation, from which many of the main local chamber-like bodies derived. Chambers and related bodies used the same embargo activities during the American War in both America and in Ireland, though supported to a lesser extent in England.[146] Some aspects of these actions are evident in the documents in Chapter 5, whilst an embargo on paying Customs duties was used by Waterford chamber, as reproduced in Chapter 6.

The legal model of partnership was used by the majority of chambers. Freeman et al. argue that the widely-recognised dormancy of the Bubble Act of 1720, the positive opportunities offered by the law of partnerships and trusts, and the diffusion of associational culture based on formal rules and an open process allowed a variety of un-incorporated forms to proliferate. A ruling of 1673 had determined that assets held on trust could not be claimed by trustees' creditors. This could be achieved through vesting assets through a deed of settlement, thus allowing establishment of a quasi-body corporate, with rules (Liverpool's 1774 deed is a good example). Rules specified procedures: such as current subscriptions to be fully paid, processes for election of officers (as trustees) to ensure a perpetuity and continuance, amendment of rules, accounting conventions, holding of assets in the name of trustees, and

[143] Compare Freeman et al., *Shareholder Democracies* (2012) Table 6.4.

[144] See Freeman et al., *Shareholder Democracies* (2012) Figure 1.1.

[145] See J. Hoppit, ed. *Parliaments, nations and identities in Britain and Ireland, 1660–1850* (Manchester, 2003); J. Innes, 'The local Acts of a national parliament: Parliament's role in sanctioning local action in Eighteenth-century Britain', *Parliamentary History*, XVII (1998) 23–47.

[146] Bennett, *Local Business Voice* (2011) 108–64; T. M. O'Connor, 'The Embargo on the Export of Irish Provisions, 1776–9', *Irish Historical Studies*, 2, 5 (1940) 3–11.

transfer of shares.[147] Though imperfect, trusts provided the legal basis for 93 per cent of the un-incorporated companies in the sample investigated by Freeman et al. Their sample showed 77 per cent to be established indefinitely, with those established for fixed terms varying between seven and 99 years, with a mode of 21 years. For chambers 85 per cent of establishments over 1767–1839 were in partnership 'trusts' and 15 per cent through charters. All chambers were established in perpetuity except the initial foundations of Jersey 1767 and Liverpool 1774. The three-year fixed term in these two cases was encouraged by worries that an un-incorporated body should not appear to claim perpetuity, and it also allowed the original investors to recover their capital at periodic re-establishments.

To manage the process of large numbers of 'partners' (i.e. members), chambers vested significant authority in their boards who became the executive named as those who were legally liable. In practice, this contraction of numbers to deal with partnership obligations was usually then further contracted to a few named officers who acted in trust for all other members. For the 38 early chambers with known rules the officers most commonly numbered four: a president, vice president, treasurer and secretary (45 per cent), with one chamber (2 per cent) having a president, two vice presidents and a secretary. Eight chambers had only three officers (21 per cent), in three cases by combining secretary and treasurer roles, and in five by having no treasurer. Six (16 per cent) had just two officers, a president and secretary, or president and vice president; and two (5 per cent) had only one specified officer, a secretary or a president. Four chambers (11 per cent) had more than four officers, all through additional vice presidents: two had two vice presidents, one had three, and one had four vice presidents.

In companies Freeman et al. show that the executive board had the power to appoint trustees (the officers) in 48 per cent of cases. In only 24 per cent did this fall on general meetings; the remainder had no specified process. There was some geographical variation with more Scottish and Irish companies having fixed terms for the trust but lower frequency of shareholder appointment/election of trustees than in England. This was not the case in chambers. General meetings appointed through elections the executive board in all chambers, in all locations, though the turnover through rotation of board members might be slow and often imperfect. Similarly proxy voting was seldom or never used by chambers, though in 14 of the early chamber rules (36 per cent) the president had a casting vote. This compares with 85 per cent of companies using proxy voting in the eighteenth century. The numbers

[147] Freeman et al., *Shareholder Democracies* (2012) 53–5; R. Harris, *Industrialising English Law* (Cambridge, 2000).

required to call for special meetings were usually very small for chambers compared to companies (where it was 2–4 per cent of shareholders).[148]

Similarly the members 'at large' frequently elected the officers (86 per cent of cases), though in five chambers (14 per cent) these were elected by the board not the members. The explicit specification that board members and officers should rotate, through requirements for re-election and limits on tenure, tended to increase over time. Of the chambers before 1800 only six of eighteen had known requirements for board members to stand for re-election, which generally varied from every three to five years, though Liverpool of 1774 specified two-thirds to stand down each year. After 1800, 13 of 19 with known rules specified a fixed term, with rotation now generally every three or four years. This reflected the shift towards more standardised rules, though of course those with constitutions continuing from earlier periods, especially the chartered chambers, retained earlier provisions. In comparison, the term of office of company directors, where specified, was generally restricted to one year. After the change in the East India Company constitution in 1773 introduced a rotation of one quarter of the board each year, Freeman et al. argue that there was some impact on other companies, with annual elections being reduced from 93 per cent before 1800, to 50 per cent 1800–9, 30 per cent 1830–4, and 20 per cent in the 1840s.[149] However, the majority of companies still did not specify terms at all and despite such provisions many companies were criticised as acting like 'close corporations'.[150] Such 'formal' permanence of boards did not occur in chambers, which all had rules for elections and most developed rotation rules. However, in practice, some members of boards continued uninterrupted for long periods, and rules providing for outgoing directors to be ineligible for re-election for a specified period were rare: only four cases (12 per cent), whereas this was about 20 per cent for un-incorporated companies. In both early and later chambers the de facto rotation of board members was often very low as the same individuals were frequently re-elected for a further term. This generally seems to have reflected the willingness of members to pass to others what they considered as a relatively tedious role, though occasionally there were outbursts of engagement and 'voice' when some of the old guard were turned out.

Constitutions of chambers were often long and complicated. Some implicitly tried to ensure protection from challenges of acting outside the Bubble Act. For companies, constitutions were generally drafted by a solicitor in private, with little shareholder scrutiny. This was not the case for chambers

[148] Freeman et al., *Shareholder Democracies* (2012) 163, 165–7.

[149] Freeman et al., *Shareholder Democracies* (2012) 87–8.

[150] Cheffins, *Corporate Ownership* (2008) 30–2; Freeman et al., *Shareholder Democracies* (2012) 90–2.

where drafts were brought back to general meetings for agreement, usually by a drafting committee of the leading potential members (and sometimes by a mayor); a lawyer does not seem to have been widely used except for charters. Chamber constitutions were agreed entirely internally, usually through consulting the entire membership, frequently through large and repeated public meetings, and not infrequently challenged and amended at large meetings that might be called specifically for the purpose of agreeing changes to a rule. Some proposals for chamber charters fell away during these stages, as shown for Jersey and Dublin in the following documents. Rules were also often subject to frequent and detailed amendment by the executive committee/board who then sought agreement from an annual meeting of all members, either to modify the rules, or establish bye-laws. Disputes over whether rules had been followed or not were regular occurrences in chambers, especially where this affected controversial decisions over politically-charged policy positions: some of the most divisive being over slave trade abolition in 1788, the positions of the General Chamber on the French Treaty of 1786–7, and repeatedly over Open Trade in Ireland from 1768 to the early 1800s (see Chapter 5).

In general the powers of open meetings and the annual general meeting were considerable in chambers compared to companies, and they were more generally decisive, or required the executive to come up with proposals for changes. This was also true of chambers compared with societies: chambers were generally more accountable to the mass of members, and in this they were more akin to political movements. General meetings were usually critical and definitive. The frequency of general meetings was initially very high in some chambers: monthly in Jersey 1767, New York 1768, Charleston 1773, Leeds 1785, and bi-monthly in Dublin 1783. In these cases the officers were restricted in the scope of their executive responsibility so that a general meeting had to be called to agree on any policy or initiative. This was characteristic of places with significant conflicts and/or lack of trust, as in Charleston and Dublin. In Jersey and Leeds it seems to have arisen because of the very small membership and tight location that encouraged frequent general gatherings. In other places the provision was that all major decisions were agreed in special general meetings, reflecting the high commitment to moving in unity and also using meetings as a means of mass engagement and collective deliberation akin to political mobilisation, especially during periods of high tension, as in New York, Jamaica, Birmingham, Boston or North Staffordshire. In one case the general meeting was explicitly as 'viva voce' (in order to expel undesirable members who had tried to subvert and close the chamber: Guernsey 1832). As time progressed, the specification for general meetings moved towards a norm of one or two per year, doubtless reflecting the practicalities of getting everyone to assemble in sufficient numbers, with special meetings (ad hoc, but often frequent) used when urgent discussion was needed. This was generally much lower than societies, where general meetings were the norm, usually fortnightly or monthly, but where social activity was the aim and business was seldom undertaken. Of course the majority of most chamber meetings was routine, and it was common for board meetings to be postponed or deferred because they were not quorate or there was 'no business to be done'. But if there was dissension this almost always had to be resolved by open meetings rather than the alternative of executive action. There was not usually the focus in chambers that commonly occurred in societies of using annual meetings for a feast,[151] though chamber board meetings were often associated with dining.

The requirements for calling special meetings adapted. From the outset these usually were called by the president, vice president, or board of the chamber, sometimes by the secretary with a requirement for a minimum number of the board to have approved. This latter process became the norm, with the board or officers calling special general meetings as required by the nature of the business and initiatives being taken. Conversely, the provision that special general meetings could be called by a number of the members (external to the board), tended to move towards a higher threshold. In the earliest chambers it was often explicit, or occurred de facto, that any single member could request a special meeting because of an urgent issue. These were tight bodies with a core group of highly involved and committed members; if one individual was concerned, it was understood that all should be once they were made aware. The minutes often show the concerned member leading the discussion and usually receiving the ready collective support of all after a discussion. Indeed, such meetings were often called by some of the most prominent chamber members outside of the formal officers. Individuals carried weight because of their prominence as 'principal merchants', with the board almost always also prominent people, but only as primus inter pares. Only from the 1783 foundations did a minimum threshold begin to be specified for special general meetings. Until about 1810 this was quite small, ranging from five to six members (only Edinburgh's charter in 1785 specifying a larger number at 15). From 1820 the norm generally moved upwards to ten, 20 or 25, with Bristol in 1823 specifying 40. However, the numbers required to call special meetings in chambers usually remained very small compared to companies (where it was normally 2–4 per cent of shareholders, which could number hundreds).[152]

The frequency of board meetings also interrelated with the scope and role of general and special meetings. Until the foundations of the 1790s the

[151] Clark, *Clubs* (2000) 238.
[152] Freeman et al., *Shareholder Democracies* (2012) 163, 165–7.

frequency of boards meeting ranged widely, from a minimum of four per year, to 12 or 52. But the predominant pattern was frequent: 36 per cent specified weekly, and 36 per cent monthly board meetings. After 1790 the majority specified monthly (79 per cent), with the remainder quarterly.

The shifts in the balance between special and general meetings and the role of the board also interrelated with the size of the board. A few chambers had very large boards in early years; e.g. Birmingham had a board of 60 in both its 1783 and 1813 rules, and the Glasgow and Edinburgh charters specified 30 and 33 respectively. Apart from these, half had 19–22, with the rest having 12 or 15, and Leeds and Boston having five. After 1800 no new board was larger than 26, with the mode becoming 24, usually composed of 21 plus three officers (with the secretary often not a voting member). Only Limerick 1807, and Kirkcaldy 1825, had small boards, each of nine, with the rest mostly ranging from 12 to 15. Later, there was some tendency for an increase in size: Belfast grew from 15 in the 1780s to 21 in the 1850s. Size remained similar throughout the century: for a sample of 55 chambers in 1892, the range of board size was from eight (Dundee) to 48 (North Staffordshire), with an average of about 24, the same as the early 1800s. However, the quorum for boards moved downwards, reaching a mode of five after 1800 with little variation (largest ten). The early chambers with quorums for boards of 12 or more were only retained in the chartered chambers of Glasgow and Edinburgh. There is some evidence throughout of smaller boards, and board quorums, in smaller places.

For societies Clark states that officers became more numerous over time. By the 1760s a common size for societies was an executive board of 12, but this had risen to 20 by 1800, although some of these might be honorary and chiefly there to add weight and status to the society.[153] This is similar to the shifts in board size of chambers. For companies in the sample of Freeman et al. only four did not specify a board size, but the specifications varied considerably from boards of one to 70, with a mode of 12, and a range strongly concentrated between five and 20 that contained 87 per cent of cases. This was similar to chambers, though slightly smaller. Insurance and canal companies had the largest ranges. There was some trend for large companies to have larger boards and more complex committee and sub-committee structures, sometimes with frequent changes and experimentation over time,[154] but in chambers no rules specified sub-committees until the 1820s (except for Manchester in 1782 which established three sub-committees from its outset in order to balance different sector interests).

[153] Clark, *Clubs* (2000) 251–6.
[154] Freeman et al., *Shareholder Democracies* (2012) 78–84.

Chamber subscription rules ranged from half a guinea (11s.) to two guineas (£2 2s.), with only Glasgow having the higher figure of five guineas. After 1804 no new rules required subscriptions over one guinea. Fifteen of eighteen (83 per cent) used one guinea or £1; the three others that are known had half a guinea or 7s. 6d. These levels were similar to many societies of the time.[155] It was common in chambers to have an admission fee as well as an annual subscription. Seventeen of 34 with known rules (50 per cent) had admission fees. This appears to have been mainly aimed at generating a capital sum at establishment, which new members were obliged to pay in order to maintain equality with founding members. Admission fees ranged from 10s. to five guineas, with the most common being either one guinea or £1 (one third), or two guineas (one third). The trend from 1822 was towards £1 or no fee at all for admission.

Most chambers had an annual subscription, often with the provision that it could be covered through a one-off life fee. A twenty-guinea life fee was used by Glasgow in 1783, reduced to ten guineas in 1786, five guineas in 1794, maintained until 1913. Bristol set it at twenty guineas from 1823, only reducing this to ten guineas in 1870. A sample of chambers in 1892 showed 44 per cent using life fees, of which 21 per cent used five guineas, and 75 per cent ten guineas.[156]

Only in five cases was there something more complex than an annual or life subscription. In the case of Jersey in 1767 and Liverpool in 1774 there was annual fee but for a committed period of years of annual fees. It was de facto a form of capital provision. In Limerick a complex fee structure was used based on levies on exports and imports per barrel, hide or other measure, or some proportion of customs duties levied. In Manchester in 1774 it appears that the initial subscription was explicitly perceived as endowing a capital sum, raised from an open subscription with variable levels depending on individual's donor choices. This was akin to many other subscription initiatives, such as for town improvements, for the poor, for militia volunteers, etc. The other example was the Waterford structure developed in 1812 and embedded in its 1815 charter reproduced in Chapter 2.[157] This called for an endowment of £50,000 made up of £25 shares in common stock, though only to be owned by chamber members, with a requirement for the stock to

[155] A guinea was a common subscription for industry bodies in the eighteenth and nineteenth centuries; e.g. Ashton, (1963) 178. Many non-commercial societies used of one or two guineas: Clark, *Clubs* (2000) 194–233; early trade unions and friendly societies most frequently used £1 6s. (6d. per week).

[156] Royal Commission on Labour, *House of Commons Papers*, 1892, XXXIV, Part V, p. xxxiv, and Appendix.

[157] Entirely different from Waterford's initial foundation in 1787, which had a standard annual subscription.

be sold to other members when a member deceased or resigned. This was specifically designed to raise the capital required for purchase of a building to house the chamber. In some other chambers capital was raised in a similar way, but this was done through specific calls for contributions and was not part of its rules. Waterford is the only known parallel to companies where formal shares were issued for membership. For companies the share subscription needed averaged £28–244; £1 shares became common only in the 1840s. Waterford's share subscription was thus at the bottom of the range used by companies and was easily raised.

Non-payment of subscriptions resulting in arrears was a common problem in all voluntary bodies, made complex because continuing membership decisions were often not explicit: lapsing and resignation could not be distinguished from failure to pay, and for life subscribers lapsing usually occurred only with death, which made it difficult to maintain membership lists.[158] The rules reproduced here show that only 31 per cent of chambers had explicit rules to ensure members continued only if they had paid, though this increased over time from 25 per cent before 1800 to 40 per cent after 1800.

As a result of a generally open process, most chambers did not have specific qualifications for membership, with few examples akin to the property ownership qualification of municipal corporations. The main qualification invoked was to be a 'principal' trader, merchant or manufacturer, which was assessed by the board. More specific qualifications were rare; e.g. Jersey 1767 and Limerick 1807, to own a specific tonnage of shipping (or equivalent). This contrasts with companies where qualifications were more frequently invoked by requiring directors to own a specific minimum number of shares, and these tended to become more onerous over time.[159]

As far as can be determined no chamber remunerated its directors or board, nor paid an attendance fee; indeed many chambers levied fines for non-attendance. The only payments by chambers to committees or members was reimbursement of delegates' or officers' expenses, such as travelling to London to facilitate a lobby. This is a strong contrast to directors of companies where, although the majority were not remunerated, a growing number of companies made payments, and attendance fees became common by the mid-1800s.[160] Remuneration of staff was a different matter. Whilst many chambers relied entirely on voluntary inputs, it was common for the clerk or secretary who kept records, wrote letters and called meetings to receive a small honorarium. Less commonly the treasurer might also receive an

[158] See Bennett, *Local Business Voice* (2011) 757–8, 788–90; also Clark, *Clubs* (2000) 242, 'arrears and mismanagement … was common'.
[159] Freeman et al., *Shareholder Democracies* (2012) 95–98.
[160] Freeman et al., *Shareholder Democracies* (2012) 102–5.

honorarium. Where these were basic clerks the figure was similar to that paid by companies, £20–30 per year. However, in some cases it was ambiguous whether these people were members or not. Some were clearly people of considerable status who were volunteers for whom the honorarium was a thank-you gesture; for others it was a payment towards the time that their clerks had devoted to the chamber's business.

The analysis of rules and comparison with corporations, societies and political movements shows that chambers borrowed concepts from each of these organisations. This drew on the experiences of their members with these other bodies. They were closest to companies. However, they also reflected the character of societies, with some elements also akin to political movements. Chambers also developed their own governance structures that were in several ways relatively unique in their emphasis on the whole membership being frequently engaged, their mix of general 'elite' or 'principal' trader status qualification with political activism, and their concern to press for radical reform objectives on specific issues largely through normal routes of influence in parliament or localities. As a result, although often radical in intent, they generally worked within the existing state apparatus.

8. Conclusion

A major insight that emerges from the analysis here and the documents reproduced, particularly the rules of governance, is that early chambers were a composite. They did not fit any single model of activism and association; nor did they conform to the expectations of any one theoretical perspective. Perhaps this is why they have received somewhat confused and sometimes misleading academic commentary. They were a composite of social, deliberated and elite discourse; they reflected and sought to assert an alternative, more independent and legitimate status than the pre-Reform structures of patronage and corporation control, but to work within it. They were an elite but their members suffered from the political asymmetry of the period, and were usually as excluded as the poor artisan; they attempted to tackle this by developing their own structures, to overcome both political and information asymmetries. They were pro-reform, generally ecumenical, though often led by Dissenters, often highly radical individuals, but normally cautious as collective bodies only moving where all members supported (or at least acquiesced in) a campaign. They sought to bend and influence the state, not change it. They operated generally within a corporate structure of partnership law, sometimes using charters, but even then with a collective partnership-like character of equality between members. They were not usually 'managerial' or 'top-down', but endemically subject to the general membership and 'bottom-up', so that agency rarely arose. Their composite character was also reflected in their bundling of services to offer a wide cover of what the major traders thought they 'needed'.

The whole concept of the early chamber was most readily projected through a physical presence. The Waterford chamber building shown in Plate 1 is an excellent example. Occupied by the chamber continuously since 1815, it was located at the head of the most prominent street intersection of the city, dominating the view down the short street linking the harbour quays to the commercial district, a similar strategic location to that of the Dublin chamber in the Commercial Exchange opened in 1779. Waterford's records and the surviving features of the building show that the rooms were deployed in a structure that was similar to all the other early chambers that had significant premises. Its ground floor, accessed directly off the street under the entrance staircase, was let to the Harbour Board (which chamber members dominated) and to the Ballast Office. There were post boxes and bags in the entrance foyer between these two offices where outgoing mail was assembled ready to go to the next ship leaving for a specified destination and where incoming mail would be sorted into the boxes for the main businesses and firms. The tallest, largest and most attractive rooms, on the first floor, were devoted to the library and newspaper room, and the coffee room; waiters were the main early chamber employees and attended the needs of the members and their guests, the main public face of the chamber other than its leading members, who would have been prominent in these rooms during the main social periods of the day. The rooms would have been quietly and discreetly abuzz. On the second floor the most prestigious room of all, with elaborate plasterwork, was the chamber's council room for the board's meetings and other formal occasions. On the upper floors and in the basement was domestic staff accommodation, some rooms let as an hotel, coal and wine cellars, lavatories, and other functional facilities. Many features survive today, even the post-boxes[161] and the early nineteenth-century labelling over the doors.

Unfortunately we do not have a significant surviving first-hand account of Waterford's chamber in these early years. However, for Glasgow's chamber we have accounts of the members' use of its rooms which were similar in their use to Waterford. For a member: 'here he learns whatever is new or interesting at home or abroad, in politics, commerce; and often in literature. His mind recovers, or acquires here tone and elasticity; and each returns to his family or his business with new vigor'.[162] 'At the daily arrival of the mail, a

[161] The heavy mahogany boxes may be of slightly later manufacture that the 1815 occupation of the building.

[162] I. Lettice, *Letters in a Tour through various parts of Scotland in the year 1792* (1794) 87–8.

more stirring, lively, and anxious scene can hardly be imagined. Indeed, no part of the day passes without some concourse of subscribers, or of strangers'.[163] 'The manufacturers and merchants … make a point … of appropriating the afternoon and evening to convivial enjoyment,—with the abstraction of a short interval, in which rising, in gay spirits, from the table, they rejoin to the tontine coffee house to talk over the news of the day, and the transactions of the week'.[164]

We are fortunate that Waterford's building survives in such an historically resonant condition. It personifies the chamber as composite of business self-governance, social focus, bundled business service facility, an elite projection of status onto the urban landscape, and marking its political objectives as a counterweight to the pre-reform local state structures: a place of rationality, expertise and considered judgement. In 1796 it was even a place from which to challenge local officials by agreeing to boycott the payment of Customs House fees.[165] It was at once a society, a business body and partnership of elite equals projecting their status, and a place from which to focus opposition to dilatory or corrupt local state officials and to government. The documents in this volume provide vivid access to this world and the way it was organised. This should open the way for further understanding of the historic role of chambers in local communities, national political debates, and the discourse on trade, treaties and imperial structure.

[163] J. Denholm, *An Historical Account of the City of Glasgow* (Glasgow, 1797) 109.

[164] R. Heron, *Observations made in a journal through the Western Counties of Scotland in 1792* (Glasgow, 1799) Vol.1, 382.

[165] With enough subsequent worry about status and political exposure for the names of the signatories to have been cut from the minute book: see Chapter 5, Waterford minutes on Customs House. In 1796 the chamber was based in the chamber's former building at the Old Assembly Rooms.

PART 1

Chapter 1

Founding Principles, Rules and Governance

This Chapter of documents covers the principles which were followed in establishing local chambers, and presents *all* the surviving rules of chambers up to 1839. These are in chronological order of foundation, with any substantially new set of early rules that were agreed (usually as part of a re-establishment after a period of lapse or occasional activity) placed at the later date when the new rules were adopted. The value of a complete listing is to record the totality of information currently available, to demonstrate the variety, and to show the increasing convergence of process and rules.

The chronological list covers all known chambers in Britain and Ireland, with the early chambers in America and other parts of the Atlantic realm, as far as they have been discovered, included up 1794. The chambers with no surviving rules, and any that possibly existed, are also noted in the chronological presentation. Some more specialist bodies related to local chambers (such as the Dublin Ouzel Galley Society, John Weskett's London 'chamber' of 1782, and the General Chamber of Manufacturers 1785–7) are noted where they arise, but their rules are given in other chapters of this volume. Other early suggestions for chamber-like bodies by Whiston, Davenant, Mortimer and others are reproduced in Chapter 3 of this volume.

The rules of the chambers frequently contain information about the principles they were to follow, the foundation process, the stated aims at foundation, and previous meetings leading up to the agreement of the rules. These are included in some the material reproduced here as they indicate the sort of issues that were being addressed by those seeking to define the most appropriate rules, and the motivations involved. Similarly, the rules were often modified in detail. The major modifications, where detected, have been included here in the immediate years after foundation

Six chambers obtained chartered status (New York, Glasgow, Edinburgh, Waterford, Limerick, and Greenock). They each have rules and byelaws in addition to their charters. In this chapter the rules and any statement of purpose are given. The charters are reproduced in Chapter 2 of this volume. The chartered chambers differed in how they used their charter to define their detailed rules: detailed for Glasgow, but for Greenock only sought to provide a framework to establish the chamber as an independent legal entity. Most charters were somewhere between these extremes.

The evolution of the rules, discussed in the Introduction, reached a point of stability and similarity largely as a result of the efforts made by Bristol in 1823 when it gathered other chamber rules and collated them in a single format. A similar collation was undertaken by Dundee with its new constitution in 1855 which claims to be based on having 'collected the Rules of twenty different bodies of a kindred character, from Great Britain Ireland, America, and France'.[1] Similarly Leone Levi claimed that rules he drafted for the re-foundation of the Liverpool chamber in 1849–50 were copied by many of the chambers established by the 1880s.[2] The extent of exact copying was limited, but by 1823, and certainly by the 1850s something of a 'settled' design for chamber rules had been reached.

1.1 Jersey Chamber of Commerce 1767

Jersey chamber was founded in May 1767. However, its foundation is often incorrectly stated as 1768 in most sources.[3] Its minutes show its first AGM to be on 9 May 1768, re-electing a committee that had 'served for a year'. Foundation in 1767 is thus definite, and further confirmed by the first three-year anniversary occurring on 14 May 1770 when it was agreed that the chamber should continue 'for three more years', as required by Articles 14 and 26 (q.v. below). Hence, the chamber was formally first established and had operated from about 14 May 1767, with its first surviving recorded minute being 8 March 1768. This minute shows the chamber to be already ongoing and taking action on 'routine' business; the first record was 'to take immediate steps for relieving the trade of the island from the persecutions carried out by Thos. Jas. Gruchy, receiver of sixpences for Greenwich Hospital'. Hence, as in *Local Business Voice*, Jersey's foundation is taken as May 1767 making it the first in the British realm. The founding articles were modified in 1785, though they remained substantially similar.

The 14th Article of the chamber stated that 'Each subscription is to be for three years certain, … the payment to be made only to the day of contin-

[1] Dundee Archives: Dundee Baltic Coffee House Chamber of Commerce, 1855 printed rules and report, 15 October, and 12 and 26 November 1855; the Coffee House was the de facto chamber.

[2] L. Levi, *The Story of my Life: The first ten years of my residence in England, 1845–1855* (London, 1888) 32; it is unlikely that Levi's claim is correct. However, Levi contributed many other things to chambers from c. 1848 onwards, especially regarding concepts about tribunals of commerce: L. Levi, *Chambers and Tribunals of Commerce and proposed General Chamber of Commerce in Liverpool* (London: 1849); see Bennett, *Local Business Voice* (2011) 262–5, 275–86.

[3] See e.g. A. G. Jamieson, ed., *A people of the sea: The maritime history of the Channel Islands* (1986) 249; *Bulletin Societé Jersiaise*, 'The Jersey chamber of commerce—the early years', 19 (1968) 300.

uance'; the 26th Article stated that the subscription was 'to be renew'd every third Year, at the last General meeting for the Year'. This indicated a quasi-debenture structure where subscribers were committed for fixed three-year terms and could then exit. The additional comment in Article 26 also stated that 'if there is but one Subscriber he is to have the disposal of the Stock & Interest, and manage it in the manner he shall think best'. This turned the debenture into a type of Tontine where the last survivor received all assets. This structure of periodic renewal and reaffirmation continued until 1837. In 1785 it was amended to a five-year renewal process. This continued in an orderly way for 1790, 1795, 1800, and 1805; it then slipped to 1811, and was not used explicitly again. The chamber was reconstructed with new articles in 1826, reverting to 3-year renewal, but the first subsequent explicit renewal was not until 1834. The periodic renewal structure was finally abandoned at a meeting on 2 March 1837, which voted for a 20s. annual subscription and £2 entrance fee.[4]

The periodic renewal process created problems of two types. First, the chamber was not always precise about remembering that the period had ended and that a reaffirmation was necessary. Second, it gave a fixed opportunity and an incentive to a group of members to vote to dissolve the chamber and disperse the assets, either for personal reasons or because they were dissatisfied with activities. In a more typical process of annual subscription disenchanted members would just lapse; they did not have the 'hold-up' power which was a source of weakness in Jersey and other partnership structures. The explicit reaffirmation process, however, did provide a powerful lien over a chamber, compared to chambers that 'continued' but actually just faded away.

An action by a group of members to dissolve the Jersey chamber occurred at its annual meeting on 25 May 1772 where the minute reproduced below sought to revoke the agreement to continue the chamber and instead to dissolve it and invest the assets (valued at 575 livres) in lottery tickets, the proceeds of which were then to be distributed to the subscribers. The minutes state that there were not enough 'willing to join in maintaining the commerce of the Island on a proper footing', but does not give enough detail to interpret this decision: we do not know if it was due to dissatisfaction with activities and leadership, or if there was a sudden flight of fancy to speculate and distribute the assets. The decision has led some commentators to conclude that the chamber indeed did dissolve in 1772.[5] However, the minutes show continuity until November 1775. It appears that, in fact, only some of the chamber's assets were used to buy lottery tickets, probably some of the

[4] Jersey Archives: Minute books L/A/38/A1/2–4.
[5] Jamieson, *A people of the sea* (1986) 251.

accumulated interest and part of the principal, as permitted under Rules 17 and 28. A minute of 12 May 1773 shows that £75 had been won in prizes, which it was agreed should be invested in further tickets. At first sight it appears that there is a gap in the minutes from November 1775 until 5 February 1784, when the Treasurer Philip Hamon was reported to have £577 in lottery receipts and prizes, and the Articles of the chamber were renewed for 'a third time' a month later on 2 March 1785. However, detailed examination of the minute books suggests that a considerable period of 1775–84 had chamber activity. The first minute book of the chamber is filled up by the last meeting of 5 February 1780, and it appears that a second minute book was then begun.[6] Close inspection of the second minute book, which begins with the meeting of 2 March 1785, however, shows that pages have been torn out of the front of this volume, with sufficient edge-paper remaining to show that a first record of 15 February 1780 had existed (i.e. continuous from the end of the previous minute book), and perhaps other meetings. It thus appears that there was indeed probably a gap in minute-keeping after 1775, but they were re-established at least by 1780 though not under the formality of the continuing Articles for renewal. The statement by *Bulletin Societé Jersiaise* seems most accurate, that 'during this period the chamber met irregularly'.[7] The renewal in 1785 marks formal reestablishment. But the torn sheets indicate that Hamon acted on various matters at least over 1780–84 using a new minute book.

Source
First minute book: Jersey Archives L/A/38/A1/1

Founding Articles May 1767

We the subscribing Members Composing the Chamber of Commerce in this Island, Do Confirm a vow and direct the following Regulations, to be a Guide for our Proceedings and we unanimously direct and require the President and Committee by us appointed, for the time being, to attend to, and follow the same, and we Confirm the said President and Committee in the authority Vested in them, agreeable to the intent and meaning of these our Regulations.

Art: 1st. A General Meeting of the Members, to be the second Monday of every second Month, to begin March 1768 at Mr. Lys, at the Kings Head, there to meet at Ten in the fore noon, and to proceed to business by Eleven at the farthest; Every thing determined by the then Majority, to be as Valid as if the whole had been present.

[6] Jersey Archives: Minute books L/A/38/A1/1–2.
[7] *Bulletin Societé Jersiaise*, 1968, 300.

2nd: A President and Six members to be yearly chosen, as a Committee, to attend to, and watch the immediate Interest of Trade, also to Prosecute every measure necessary for that purpose, and to determine their proceedings by the Majority of Votes (by Ballot).

3rd: Whenever a meeting of the Committee is, by the President, or any one Member of it, thought necessary, the President is by means of the Secretary to send notice (as many days before as possible) to every Member, and no business is at any time to be done, by a less Number than the President and Four Members, and Letters from those than cannot attend are first to be produced by the President before they proceed to business; And it is hoped and expected the Members will at no time delay attending this great Trust, but thro' means of unavoidable and Urgent Business.

4th: If at any time the President is Sick or goes out of the Island for a short time he may by Letter depute any member of the Committee to Act for him, as he has no Extra Vote or influence.

Art: 5th. But if the President should go out of the Island to reside or Depart or by a continued ill state of health cannot attend the Duty of his Trust, In this Case a General meeting is to be summoned by the members of the Committee in order to choose a new President who is to be one of the Members of the then Committee and a new Member for the Committee is also to be chosen.

6th: If members of the Committee by going out of the Island, or Sickness reduce the number to do business, to the President & three, then in this case, the Secretary may give his Vote; but if more of the members should be Sick, or absent, then other Members to be appointed, as above, because no business can be transacted by a less Number then the President & Four, including the Secretary occasionally.

7th: Upon the Death of a Member of the Committee or going out of the Island to reside, another is to be Balloted for, at the next General Meeting, but if by death, absence, or a continued Ill state of Health, there happens two Vacancies; to be filled up, by a General Summons for that purpose.

8th: Two Boxes with Locks & Keys to be kept by the President are to be provided, with the words: For the Question, Influenced by no Person upon honour, on the one; And against the Question, with the same words on the other. Also a Ball or Tally for each member. The Boxes to be put in a room separate from the Company, and after any Matter has been proposed by the President of the Committee, who is at all Meetings to preside, the members being called by the Secretary, are by turns as they are upon the List, to go in the room, the Door being shut, The Person if approving will put his Tally in the Box for the Question, but if he disapproves of the measure, he will put his Tally in the Box against the Question, by which means the Box with most Tallies carries it.

9th: And in order to give more Consequence to this method of proceeding, every Member must recollect that he pledges his honour, that he is not influenced by any person to put his Tally (or Vote) for or against the Question, but merely the Dictates of what he thinks best for the public Interest.

10th: The President and Members of the Committee are to Vote at the General Meeting as if they did not belong to the Committee.

11th: The Same Method is to be practised by the Committee, as in Art: 9 who in their proceedings are to say, That after having duly considered the matter before them, they upon honour have thought it for the Interest of their Trust to Etc. [the public Interest].

12th: The President as well at the General meeting, as at the Committee is to Vote last.

13th: And in order to forward this very essential purpose, to the well being of Trade, and to support and keep the Merchants upon a Respectable footing (in Unity) A fund of Three Pence Sterling per Ton per annum is hereby agreed upon to be raised upon the Tonnage belonging to each respective member & the Vessels to be measured by direction of the Committee. Condemned Vessels for break up not included. The Tonnage to be enter'd in the Book of the Chamber.

14th: Each subscription is to be for three years certain, unless alteration happen in Society's, by Augmenting, lessening, or Dissolving, the payment to be made only to the day of continuance.

15th: All subscriptions for Tonnage to be paid in, to the President and one of the members of the Committee, who shall attend with the Secretary in the usual place appointed for a General Meeting, there to receive the same Viz. The first Monday, Wednesday, & Friday in March between ten & one o'clock in the forenoon and the Person paying the same, to enter in the Book for that purpose Viz. March 1768 Paid in to the Committee of the Chamber of Commerce the Tonnage for 1767 on account of _____ to _____ & Signs the same, which note of payment is to be Countersigned by the Secretary. The Members of the Committee will take it by turns to attend the President in this Duty.

16th: Any [member of the] Society failing to pay as above, is to forfeit Fourteen Sols, Four Deniers ~~French currency~~ (the Exchange to receive state of the account) per Day until it is paid. No Money to be received after the hour of one is past; unless as above, forfeiting a day (those waiting in the room to be dispatched excepted) Which money so arising from such forfeiture is to be added to the General Stock or Capital.

17th: When the Money arising from the said Collection amounts to a Sum equal to the purchase of half a Stock, it shall be remitted to London to be placed in the 3 or 4 Per Cent Annuities or other Government securities in the name of the President for the time being, for which he is to enter a bond in the Book of Records belonging to the said Chamber of Commerce, obliging himself to transfer the same to the Person who shall succeed him as President of the Committee, the Interest to be applied to forward the above purpose, at the Direction of the Committee, but if at any time, any part of the Principal is requisite [required], then the body of Subscribers must be summoned & Consulted, and are to determine upon it by Ballot as above.

18th: And if any of the Principal is Voted to be used, to forward the public Interest of Trade in this Island, a Power of Attorney to be executed in favour of the person who may be appointed to manage the money matters in England, by the President & of the Committee, in presence of the full meeting, or majority of subscribing Members attending that day, limiting the Sum to be sold out of the Funds, whether a half or full Stock, because nothing less than a half can be sold: And if any overplus, it may be left in the hands of the person managing the money matters in England, or drawn for by the president & of the Committee and lodged in the hands of our Secretary, to answer Contingencies at the direction of the Committee.

19th: If at any time the President and members of the Committee think it necessary, to bring any one or more of the Members together, to consult them, & to have their opinion upon any point too material, or in their opinion too intricate for them to determine, they may do it by a particular or a General summons for that purpose, sent by a trusty person to every subscribing member at the public Expense, which Method is to be practiced, upon every Extra meeting, giving some days notice if Possible.

20th : The days for General Meetings, also the place, may at any time be changed, to be determined by Ballot, but always to be in Town, because Books of Records, proceedings, and Accounts, must be kept by the Secretary, under the Inspection of the Committee, and may at times be called for, but cannot be carry'd out of Town.

21st: As all the payments for Tonnage, are to be made the first week in March, the Committee are to remit the money and produce Vouchers for the same, and settle their accounts for the year, and lay them, together with the record of their proceedings, before the General Meeting in May, for their being inspected, by any one, or the whole Members, & the General State of the Accts is then to be signed by the President and members of the Committee (Present) and Countersigned by the Secretary.

Art 22: The Secretary to keep all Money paid in until remitted.

23rd: The Accounts of the Year being signed and settled as above, A Percent of members for a Fresh Committee, are to be Balloted for, & that being done, the Secretary is to insert their Names in the Book of Records, as being appointed to carry on the business for the ensuing Year, the old President and Members, or any of them, may again be chosen.

The manner of choosing a President and members of the Committee to be as follows—Viz.

24th: Every member going in the room, where one of the Boxes, only is to be put for the purpose, will write on one piece of paper the Name of the person he chooses for a President, as also the names of those he approves for [Committee] Members, and roll it up & put it in the Box, by which means they may be fixed upon, & no person know the Voters, as they may easily disguise their writing.

25th: The Members are to go in by turns as before directed, by which means no more papers can be in the Box, than there are Members present. If any two or more have equal Votes or Tallies, they are to be canvass'd for a Majority.

N.B: Pen, Ink & Paper to be on a Table in the room where the Box is put, for the purpose.

26th: This Subscription to be renew'd every third Year, at the last General meeting for the Year, but if there is but one Subscriber he is to have the disposal of the Stock & Interest, and manage it in the manner he shall think best, for the Interest & purpose above mentioned.

[2]7th: After the first Year none to be chose President or Members of the Committee, that have not been subscribing Members a Twelve Months.

28th: The Interest of the money in the Funds or other Government Security, if not wanted, to be added to the Capital, or at least when ever there is a sufficient Sum even to purchase a half Stock; And when the Capital comes to £500 Stock in the 3 or 4 Per Cent or other Government security, the Interest if not otherwise wanted, May Yearly be applied, together with such part of the Yearly amount of the subscription, not exceeding one half, as the Committee may think right (which then may be lessen'd) to relieve distress'd Families of Seamen, Dying or Meeting with accidents, so as to be disabled in the service of any subscribing Member, being recommended to the Committee by a Member, Certifying the same in writing, and producing Vouchers of the Nature of the Accident, signed by the Master; And of the man being a Sober, good & diligent Man, and that he was in every particular equal to his Trust.

Also the particulars of the distressed family sign'd by the Clergy Man & Church Wardens of the Parish they Live in: All which is to be enter'd as Vouchers, by which the Committee will determine how best to relieve them. By which the Seamen will more cheerfully exert themselves for the Int[erest] of their Owners.

Art 29th: The President of the Committee will in all his Summons request the Members intending to dine at the place, to send their names to the Landlord, or to who else it may be thought right, by the Friday, preceding the day for a General meeting, that provision may be made accordingly, and the

Members after sending, are to pay their Ordinary [dinner costs] tho' they should not Dine there. And no one to stay to Dine that do not send.

30th: The Meeting to adjourn at 1 o'Clock, unless business of Consequence requires the contrary, but no second meeting for business on the same day, neither at the General Meeting nor Committee.

The hour of Dinner at 2, unless prevented as above.

31st: The Expense for the Ordinary to be 24 sols French Currency per head, And after 4 o'clock, the Bill may be called for by any Member, at Dinner.

32nd: None but Members to be admitted in the room for business. At Dinner Merchants from abroad may be admitted as a Guest to those that bring them, but no body else on any account Whatever.

33rd. The Owners of the London, [South]Hampton & other Coasters, to pay Tonnage, otherwise, they & those sailing with them are to expect no relief in case of needs, nor shall they get any freight but when subscribers are not in the way, for which purpose necessary orders shall be given by us respectively.

34th: And as a greater Security to our Common Interest, Shipping, & Cargoes, Much depending upon the Condition of the Harbours & Quays, we think it right to recommend it to the particular attention of the Committee.

Art. 35th: Any Member disturbing the Harmony and Friendship, necessary to subsist, in prosecuting these essential regulations for the Interest of Trade & the public Good in this Island is to be expelled by Ballot.

36th: Members not concerned in Shipping may subscribe for what Tonnage they think proper—Not less than thirty Tons.

37th: Form of Summons _______ Island of Jersey 7th March.

> The members of the Chamber of Commerce in this Island are desired to Dine together on Monday next 14th March, being a day appointed for a General Meeting. The Members intending to come to Dinner are desired to send their names to ____ by Friday 11th Inst. that he may on Saturday provide accordingly. No business is expected. Dinner at 2 o'Clock ___ by Order of the President & Committee.
>
> If for business [Form of Summons]:
>
> The members of the [Committee] to meet at ____ at 10 o'Clock for the dispatch of business, Members intending to [be present ….]

38th: The Secretary to be chose by Ballot in the same manner as the President and Members of the Committee, & to continue in his office for three Years, being the time limited for the subscription.

39th: The Secretary to be allowed Thirty two Livres according to order per Annum.

[49 Signatures follow: see Appendix, no. 12].

Minutes 25 May 1772

At a general Meeting of the Chamber of Commerce held this day, Pursuant to the resolution passed the 11th May 1772 all the Members in the Island having been particularly Summoned Voted:

That it appearing there is due to Mr. James Hemery Sixty four Livres one Sol six Deniers for Balance of Account upon the former Transactions the said Sum shall be paid to the said Wm. Hemery from the Fund belonging to the Chamber, after being Balloted for has been unanimously resolved in the affirmative.

That the present Establishment of the Chamber with a proper fund and supported by the General Harmony of the Merchants might have been highly advantageous to the Trade of the Island as has been seen in the Confirmation of our Right to the Newfoundland Fishery, but as a Considerable part of the Merchants are Notwithstanding unwilling to join in maintaining the Commerce of the Island upon a proper footing, which consequently throws the whole Burden and expense of the Public affairs upon the present Subscribers of the Chamber, and as the fund belonging to the same is too limited to answer such expense as public Exigencies might require it has therefore been resolved that the Agreement entered into the 14th May 1770 to continue the Subscription to the Chamber for three years longer shall be and is hereby revoked and annulled & that the Subscribers shall be obliged to pay no longer than for the Year 1771 after which their Subscription shall be determined; And that the Chamber be and is hereby dissolved and that from this day all Agreements relating thereto remain of no Force. After having been Balloted for the above [deleted word indecipherable] has been unanimously resolved in the Affirmative.

After having examined the Accounts of the Chamber it appears there is in the hand of Ph. Hamon the late Secretary the Sum of Five hundred and Seventy Seven Livres one Sols Six Deniers French Currency which it has been resolved shall be laid out in the purchase of two Lottery Tickets or as far as the Money in hand may go toward Purchasing the said two Tickets or share.

That as soon as the Success of the said Tickets can be known the Produce shall be paid to the Present Subscribers upon account which shall be made according to the Several Subscriptions for the Year 1771 as they have been paid into the Chamber.

That Ph. Hamon be appointed to Purchase the said Tickets and to manage the Same as above directed.

The Books and Box to remain in the hands of the Secretary.

[Signed:]

Thos. Pipon & Co.

Thos. Durrell & Co.
Thos. Durrell for de Gruchy etc.
Will. Patriarch & Co.
Ph. Robin for self
John Flue

Thos. Hilgrove for Clement [Hilgrove of Southampton]
Edwd. Combes & Co.
Mattw. Gosset & Co.
Peter Mallet
James Hemery
Philip Laurens

Minutes 29 November 1775

Notice having been given to the Gentlemen who belong to the Chamber of Commerce that a general Meeting was to be held this day at Mr Phil Lys, at the King's Head for Particular Business, Mr George Rowcliffe having Proposed that the Money now remaining belonging to the Chamber should be applied toward Supporting his Appeal before King and Counsel against Mr Thos. James Gruchy Receiver for Greenwich Hospital relating to obtaining Damages, for his having Unlawfully detained the Brig George.—Messrs. John Robin, James Hilgrove, Mattw. Gosset, Thos. Hilgrove, John Hue, George Rowcliffe, Rchd. Combes, Peter Mallet, & James Hemerry being Present. It was carried in the Affirmative, and Mr James Amice Lempriere not being a Member of the Chamber of Commerce agree to contribute in the proportion of one Hundred Tons towards carrying on the Said Lawsuit. It is also further agreed that Mr George Rowcliffe will pay in whatever Damages he may receive toward defraying the Expenses of the said Lawsuit.

1.2 New York Chamber of Commerce 1768; also see charter 1770 in Chapter 2

A Register of Proceedings of the New York Chamber of Commerce survives and has been completely transcribed and published by John Austin Stevens in 1867. Here the objective is to abstract only those parts that give insight into the Rules and organisation of the chamber to allow it to be compared with those developed in the rest of the British Realm. There is no simple listing of the Rules in the early years. Instead the minutes give the specification of each aspect as a separate listing from April 1768, with small amendments later that year. A charter was sought in 1769, and granted in 1770. Numbering has been added to rules for clarity.

Source
John Austin Stevens, 1867, *Register of Proceedings of New York Chamber of Commerce*, New York, vol. 1.

Minutes *5 April 1768*

WHERE AS, mercantile societies have been found very useful in trading cities for promoting and encouraging commerce, supporting industry, adjusting disputes relative to trade and navigation, and procuring such laws and regulations as may be found necessary for the benefit of trade in general;

For which purpose, and to establish such a society in the city of New York, the following persons convened on the first Tuesday in, and being the 5th day of, April, 1768:

[List of 20 member names][8]

Who agreed that the said Society of Merchants should consist of

A President,
A Vice-President,
Treasurer,
Secretary,

And such a number of merchants as already, or hereafter may become members thereof, to be called and known by the name of THE NEW YORK CHAMBER OF COMMERCE.

The Members present unanimously chose the following Gentlemen their officers for this year, to commence the first Tuesday in May next:

John Cruger, President.
Hugh Wallace, Vice-President,
Elias Desbrosses, Treasurer,
Anthony Van Dam, Secretary.

Then the following resolutions, being read, were agreed to.

[1] That the members of the Chamber of Commerce shall meet the first Tuesday in every month, to transact such business as may come before them; and establish such rules for the order and good government of the Society as they may think proper and find necessary.

[2] That the first Tuesday in May, August, November, and February in every year are declared to be the Grand Quarterly Meetings, at which times the accounts of the Chamber are to be settled, and any new members who desire it and are chosen by ballot are to be admitted.

[3] The officers of said Chamber of Commerce to be chosen yearly by ballot on the first Tuesday in May, and to continue for one year.

[4] Every member of the Society who now is or hereafter may be admitted into the same, shall pay unto the Treasurer for the use of the said Chamber of Commerce five Spanish dollars on his admission, and shall also pay unto the said Treasurer for the aforesaid use the further sum of one Spanish dollar on each of the four quarterly days before mentioned, and such members shall

[8] Full membership lists at http://www.geog.cam.ac.uk/research/projects/chambersofcommerce/newyork.pdf.

faithfully and truly keep, obey, and conform to all rules and regulations made and entered into by said Chamber of Commerce, which are to be entered into the Books of the said Society to be kept for that purpose, on pain of being dismissed the said Chamber of Commerce, and having his or their names struck off the list.

[5] Any merchant choosing to become a member of this Chamber of Commerce must give in his name to the President for the time being on the first Tuesday in the month preceding the Quarterly meeting, and the person proposed is to be balloted for, and if three nays appear he cannot be admitted during the government of the President in whose year he was so refused, but may be proposed the succeeding or any year after, and if not again opposed by three nays then to be admitted, but if any person is three times refused, he is never to be admitted.

[6] A proper room for the meeting of the members of the Chamber of Commerce is to be provided at the expense of the members so that it doth not exceed one shilling per man, which each person is to pay to the Treasurer at their respective meetings.

[7] The members of the Chamber of Commerce doth agree that the Treasurer shall provide for their use a strong chest wherein shall be deposited their cash, books and papers which is to have three different good locks and keys — one key to be kept by the President, one by the Treasurer, and the third by the Secretary; the chest for the present to be kept at the Treasurer's.

[8] No business to be done by the said Chamber of Commerce unless there be twenty-one members present, of which the President or Vice-President to be always one (unless by committees to be appointed for particular purposes), the meeting on the first Tuesday in May next only excepted, when thirteen or more members may do business, and every thing proposed or transacted to be by vote of the members present, and the opinion of the majority of votes to be conclusive and binding on the members, except in admitting new members, which is to be done as is herein before directed.

[9] The President, with the advice of the members of the Chamber is to appoint the place of meeting, nothing to be done but by application to him, who is to examine and sign the Treasurer's accounts, and in general to superintend all the Society's affairs.

[10] The Vice-President in the absence of the President to have the same power and authority as if the President was personally present, who is to keep the President's key when absent.

[11] The Treasurer to provide a proper book at the expense of the said Chamber for keeping the receipt of all money paid to him, and all money laid out by him for the use of the said Society, which are to be fairly entered at the meetings held from time to time, and which are to be audited on the first Tuesday in May in every year, and signed by the auditors to be appointed for

that purpose, when he is to deliver over the cash remaining in hand, books and his key to the Treasurer elected, or in the absence of the Treasurer so elected, then to the President, or in his absence to the Vice-President.

[12] The Secretary is to keep a fair register of all proceedings, orders, rules, and regulations of the said Chamber of Commerce, which are to be entered in a proper book to be provided for that purpose at the expense of the said Society. In the absence of the Secretary, the President to appoint one of the members to officiate in his place for the time being, to whom, by a written order from the President, the Secretary is to deliver his key.

[13] Every member not attending the monthly meeting, to forfeit and pay to the Treasurer two shillings, and such who do not attend the quarterly meeting, to pay four shillings for non-attendance, unless some cause, judged reasonable by the Society, is admitted by them as sufficient. Sickness, and being absent at least six miles from the city, to be always allowed sufficient reason for non-attendance.

[14] The President is to appoint a proper person, to be approved of by the Society, as their Doorkeeper and Messenger, who is to be paid by the Treasurer such sums as may be hereafter directed by the President, for his services.

[15] It is agreed that no new rules, regulations, or orders for the government of this Society shall be made, unless proposed at a preceding meeting, that there may be time for the general sense of the Society to be known.

[16] The President, or, in his absence, the Vice-President, hath power on any emergency to call a meeting of the said Chamber, and all meetings to be at six o'clock in the evening of every day that their attendance may be required.

Minutes 6 September 1768

Having taken into consideration the proposal of admitting members monthly, instead of quarter days. Resolved unanimously, that any persons offering to become members of this Chamber, that they be balloted for the meeting after that their names be proposed.

Minutes 6 December 1768.

... The draught [RULES] proper to be inserted in the newspapers — the use and design of this Chamber — which, being read, was in the words following:

'As Mercantile Societies have been found very useful in trading cities for promoting and encouraging commerce, adjusting disputes relative to trade and navigation, supporting industry, recommending such laws and establishing such regulations as may be found necessary for the benefit of trade in general,

A considerable number of the Merchants of New York formed themselves into a Society in May last, and have since been joined by the greatest part of the other Merchants in the city, in order to advance so truly laudable an Institution.

They are called the New York Chamber of Commerce; who meet the first Tuesday of every month, and hear all proposals for the better regulating, encouraging and extending trade and navigation.

[17] A Monthly Committee is appointed, who adjust accounts and settle, gratis, all disputes between merchants and traders which the parties may think fit to submit to their decision.

[18] The Chamber, in general, do everything in their power for the interest of the Community.

A plan of the Institution, with the Rules and Regulations relating to the Chamber, and the method of admitting members,[9] may be seen by applying to

ANTHONY VAN DAM, Secretary.'

Ordered — That the Secretary deliver a fair copy of the Articles now read to the printer, and request him to print 300 copies thereof, and that each member be furnished with one.

Ordered — That a fair copy be made of the writing proper to be inserted in the newspapers, to acquaint the public the use and design of this Chamber, and desire the printers to publish it in the next papers, and to continue it in their papers for six weeks.

Minutes 3 January 1769

The consideration of Mr. Low's proposal, That in case of sudden emergency only, when it may be thought necessary (agreeable to the established Rule of this Chamber) that a Special Meeting of the members shall be called, each of them shall be notified in writing of such meeting.

[19] Resolved unanimously — That in case any regulation which may be agreed to by a majority of the members then present at such meeting shall be binding on all the other members, under the same penalties and forfeitures as are provided for the observance of the other Rules and Orders of this Chamber.

Minutes 7 November 1769

[20] Resolved — That no Persons hereafter be proposed to be Members of this Chamber can be admitted unless they are Merchants Residents of this City.

[9] This does not seem to have survived.

Resolved unanimously — That all the Rules and Regulations already entered into be Printed for the use of the Members, and also that every future Regulation that may be agreed to shall be Printed every half year, for the same purpose.

Minutes 3 April, 1770

Mr. Low's Proposal that the Members of this Chamber shall in future leave to Arbitration matters of Account disputed to a Reference,

Ordered — That the consideration thereof be referred a future meeting.

Mr. Low's Proposal for admitting Members by paying a greater entrance having been very maturely considered of by the whole Chamber,

Resolved — That from and after there be Eighty Members belonging to this Chamber, Each Person admitted afterwards shall pay to the Treasurer for the time being the sum of Ten Spanish Dollars, until there be Ninety Members; that from and after there be Ninety Members belonging to this Chamber, Each Person admitted afterwards shall pay to the Treasurer for the time being the sum of Twelve and a half Spanish Dollars until there be One Hundred Members; and so on, ad infinitum Two and a half Dollars for every Ten Members, for the use of the Chamber.

Mr. Low's Proposal, that no less than Thirty Members be sufficient hereafter to compose a Chamber, having been considered of.

It is thought right there should be no alteration from the first mode. But that part of the motion which respects the admitting of New Members by a greater number of Nays, it is Resolved unanimously, that instead of Three Nays to disqualify a Person from being hereafter elected, there shall be Three Nays when only Thirty Members are Present at an Election; whenever more than Thirty Members present, Four Nays; when more than Forty Members present, Five Nays; and so on. One Nay for every Ten Members after the Number present exceeds thirty Persons.

1.3 Guernsey Chamber of Commerce 1769

The modern Guernsey chamber was founded in 1808, for which full information survives. However, an earlier chamber existed which was founded in about 1769. No rules survive, but its existence is evident from its actions. Its foundation date is evidenced by the historic badge of office of the current chamber bearing that date, as quoted by Cox from material at the chamber.[10] The badge appears to derive from the 1808 re-establishment of the chamber and indicates that at that date the existence of the earlier chamber was known

[10] G. S. Cox, *The Guernsey Chamber of Commerce 1808–1983* (Guernsey, 1983) 9.

and acknowledged as a point of continuity. Cox in both his earlier and later history of the chamber quotes evidence 'that the Priaulx family acted in concert with other leading merchants of the 18th century, and this may have constituted a Chamber, *de facto* if not *de jure*'. Both also quote a presentation in 1801 by the Guernsey merchants to William Le Marchant 'as a testimony of the gratitude and respect for his uniform and unwearied zeal in support of the commerce and privileges of the Island'.[11] This indicates some possibility that the initial foundation continued from 1769 perhaps until 1801, with Le Marchant as its prime mover and probable chair/president. There are a few documentary records showing its activities. There is one reference to Guernsey chamber in the Jersey minutes in 1785,[12] and a record by Arthur Young in 1786, stating that 'a chamber of commerce has been lately established in Guernsey'.[13] The 'Canary Wine petition' of 1776 reproduced in Chapter 5 of this volume perhaps is attributable to the chamber. In addition, Cox has drawn my attention to a Sociétié de la Chambre at St. Peter Port for which an account book for the period 1737–67 survives. It was established in 1737, with formalised rules laid out in 1738. In 1767 its last minutes do not formally close and it is possible that had there been survival of further minutes, or another minute book, these would have shown its transition into the chamber from 1769 (as occurred with the evolution of some commercial societies elsewhere; e.g. Dublin in 1783, or for Dundee from a former coffee house in 1832). Cox states that the Sociétié 'membership was very small and select, focused on William Le Marchant and his coterie. They had a club room and dined and drank together. The rules laid down that no members could remove a newspaper from the premises'.[14] This was similar to the rules of other chambers of commerce that had coffee rooms or libraries.[15] It would appear that this Sociétié de la Chambre provided the infrastructure for the 1769 chamber foundation, which was probably based in its premises and may have been an evolution from it. As with other chambers it is probable that the 1769 foundation marked the need for a new title and formalisation when the activities of the previous society were extended. A more formal status was required for specific lobbies and to claim a generality of support for acting on behalf of the wider community than just to act as an elite meeting and dining group.

[11] Cox, *Guernsey Chamber* (1983) 9; Guernsey Chamber, *The Guernsey Chamber of Commerce, 1808–2008* (Guernsey, 2008) 4.
[12] Jersey Archives: Jersey chamber minutes 4 July 1785.
[13] Arthur Young, *Annals of Agriculture* (1786) 370.
[14] Gregory Stevens-Cox, personal communications November 2014; Guernsey Greffe: Account Book of Sociétié de la Chambre, Sausmarez Papers 15/20.
[15] For example, see the rules for Waterford and Cork at 1.23 and 1.42 below; also Bennett, *Local Business Voice* (2011) 508–22.

1.4 Charlestown [Charleston], South Carolina, Chamber of Commerce 1773

The foundation of the Charleston chamber cannot be separated from the need for local coordinated action as a result of the American rebellion, especially the emergence of tea parties in the different main trading ports. One of the chamber's first actions in December 1773 was an attempt to moderate. Local radicals were intent on preventing unloading tea from the East India ship, the *London*. Negotiations led to the town council and chamber offering protection to the collector of Customs, who seized and landed the tea, impounding and storing it in the Exchange. This was still seen as insulting by the British, but the Charleston radicals accused chamber members of lack of patriotism. A meeting of radicals on 16 March 1774 established a standing committee to act in future crises, and discussed calling it a 'chamber of counterpoise.'[16] Although tensions continued the chamber acted as a general body up to 1780 when the British evacuated; it chiefly responded to disruptions to credit and trade.[17] The chamber was revived in February 1784 with similar rules.

Source
RULES OF THE CHARLESTOWN CHAMBER OF COMMERCE, CHARLESTOWN: Printed by Robert Wells, 1774, 19pp. Library Company of Philadelphia 13194.

Printed pamphlet 16 December 1773

The Advantages arising from Commerce to every State are so universally acknowledged, that it has been an Object of their constant and utmost Attention. The Grandeur, Strength, and Opulence of Great-Britain, her Improvement in Knowledge and the Polite Arts, and the present flourishing Condition of her Colonies, are peculiarly indebted to it: Hence, any Attempt to extend Commerce, encourage Industry, and adjust Disputes relative to Trade and Navigation, must deserve the Approbation of every Well-wisher to his Country. With these Views, Mercantile Societies have been formed in trading Cities, and proved equally beneficial and useful: In order, therefore, to effect in this Town an Institution of the like Nature, a considerable Number of Merchants met on the 8th of December 1773, when they agreed to call a General Meeting of the Gentlemen in Trade. This Meeting was held on the

[16] C. Bridenbaugh, *Cities in Revolt: Urban Life in America 1743–1766* (New York, 1955) 87–8; G. C. Rogers, 'The Charleston tea party: the significance of December 3, 1773', *South Carolina Historical Magazine*, 75, (1974) 162–6; Bennett, *Local Business Voice* (2011) 137–40.
[17] L. Sellers, *Charleston Business on the eve of the American Revolution* (Chapel Hill, 1934) 72–3; *Wells Almanac and Register*, from Bridenbaugh, *Cities in Revolt* (1955), 287–8; see also modern chamber: www.charlestonchamber.net/about/history.

9th of the same Month, where the Design being proposed was unanimously approved of, and the following Persons elected from the whole Body, viz. John Savage, Miles Brewton, Edmund Head, George-Abbot Hall, James Laurens, John Edwards, John Dawson, Andrew Lord, James Jamieson, Roger Smith, Alexander Inglis, Peter Bacot, Thomas Shirley, John Hopton, John Simpson, Gabriel Manigault, William Ancrum, John Neufville, John Smyth, David Deas, and Alexander Gillon, were declared to be a CHAMBER OF COMMERCE, who might make such Rules as they, or a Majority of them, should think expedient for such an Institution: The Chamber, therefore, framed and ratified the following

RULES.

I. This Society shall be called the CHARLESTOWN CHAMBER OF COMMERCE, and shall meet on the First Thursday in every Month, to dispatch such Business as may be brought before them, and establish such farther Regulations, for the good Government thereof, as may be found necessary.

II. The First Thursday in February, May, August and November, in every Year, shall be the Quarterly Meetings; at which the Treasurer's Accounts shall be audited, and any other necessary Business done.

III. The PRESIDENT, VICE-PRESIDENT, TREASURER and SECRETARY, shall be chosen yearly, by Ballot, on the First Thursday in November; and any Person, so elected, refusing to serve, shall forfeit, if President, Twenty Pounds, if Vice-President, Fifteen Pounds, if Treasurer, Ten Pounds, and if Secretary, Ten Pounds current Money; unless the Excuse offered for such Refusal be approved of by a Majority of the Chamber: And no Person shall be obliged to serve, in any of the aforesaid Offices, oftener than Once in Five Years.

IV. The President shall preserve Decorum and Regularity, sum up all Debates and put Questions, appoint the Place of Meeting and all Committees; he shall sign all Orders on the Treasurer; and at every Meeting, after taking the Chair, he shall first order the Minutes of the last Meeting to be read, then the Reports of the Committees, and afterwards proceed to any other Business of the Chamber.

V. The Vice-President, in the Absence of the President, shall act in his Stead, and be vested with the same Powers.

In Case both are absent, then the Members met at any monthly, quarterly or extraordinary Meeting, shall, by a Majority of Votes, taken by Ballot, elect one of their own Number to preside for that Time.

VI. The Treasurer shall provide, for the Use of the Chamber, a Common Seal; on which shall be engraved such a Device as shall be agreed on by a Majority of the Members; also, a Strong Box, wherein shall be deposited the Cash, Books and Papers belonging to his Department.

He shall keep an Account of all Monies received and paid by him; and the Seal, Books, Papers, Cash and Box he shall, on the First Thursday in November, deliver to the Treasurer then chosen, or, in his Absence, to the President, Vice-President, or Person elected to preside at that Meeting.

He shall, on his Election, give Bond for the Trust reposed in him, with sufficient personal Security, to the President and Vice-President, to the Amount of the Monies paid into his Hands by the preceding Treasurer, together with the Amount of the Contributions during the preceding Year; which Bond shall not be cancelled but by the President or Vice President, with the Consent of a Majority of the Members at any monthly or quarterly Meeting.

VII. The Secretary shall keep a fair Register of all Proceedings, Orders, Rules and Regulations of the Chamber, in a Book provided for that Purpose. He shall, at the stated or extraordinary Meetings, read the Minutes of the last Meeting; also, all Applications to the President relating to the Chamber, and the Reports that may be given in by the Committees.

At every monthly Meeting, he or his Assistant shall report to the President the Names of such Members of the Committees as neglected to attend at their appointed Times of Meeting, during the preceding Month.

VIII. If either the President, Vice-President, Treasurer or Secretary should die, resign, or depart the Province, a Meeting of the Chamber shall be called, to choose, by Ballot, a new Officer or Officers, in the Room of such Officer or Officers, who may die, resign, or depart the Province.

IX. Any Person desirous of becoming a Member of this Chamber, must apply, by Letter, to the President, at any of the stated Meetings, when it shall be read; and after a second Reading, at the next monthly Meeting, the Person, so applying, shall be balloted for, and admitted a Member, provided he is voted in by not less than Two-thirds of the Members present.

X. Every Person who now is, or may hereafter be admitted, a Member, shall pay to the Treasurer, for the Use of the Chamber, the Sum of TWENTY POUNDS currency; and on each of the quarterly Meetings he shall also pay to the Treasurer, for the aforesaid Use, the Sum of TWO POUNDS currency.

If any Member delay the Payment of his Contribution Three Months after the Time it ought to have been paid, he shall not be entitled to vote at any Meeting, until his Arrears are paid up; and if he neglect the Payment thereof Nine Months, he shall then be struck off the List, and no longer be deemed a Member.

Every Member shall punctually observe, and conform to, all Rules and Regulations made and entered on the Books, on Pain of being dismissed from the Chamber.

XI. The Chamber shall have a Committee of Eight Members, the whole to be chosen at the first monthly Meeting. At every monthly Meeting thereafter,

Four new Members shall be appointed, and the Names of the first Four, on the List of the last Committee, shall then be struck out; and this Method shall be followed, in Rotation, through all the Members, except those elected to Offices, who, during their Continuance in them, shall not be obliged to serve on Committees.

The Committee shall meet on every Thursday, or oftener, if Business require it, and shall report on the Matters committed to their Charge, at every monthly Meeting, or whenever desired by the President; and three of them shall be a Quorum to do Business.

Every Member of the Committee, not attending their stated or extraordinary Meetings, shall forfeit Twenty Shillings currency, for each Default, at the next monthly Meeting, unless his or their Excuse be admitted by a Majority of the Members then present.

Any Person appointed a Member of the Committee and refusing to serve shall forfeit, for such Refusal, Ten Pounds currency.

XII. Any Member, not attending the Meetings of the Chamber, shall, for every Default, forfeit and pay to the Treasurer the following Fines; if a monthly or quarterly Meeting Fifteen Shillings, and if an extraordinary Meeting Twenty Shillings currency, unless the Excuse offered for such Default be approved of by the Chamber.

XIII. The President shall have Power, on any Emergency, to call a Meeting; and all Meetings shall be held at Six o'Clock in the Evening, except on the Anniversary, when the Chamber shall meet at Eleven o'Clock in the Forenoon; and after the Business is over, the Members shall dine together.

Every Member in the Province, whether present at, or absent from, the Anniversary Meeting, shall pay to the Treasurer Thirty Shillings currency as his Quota of the Expenses of the Day, unless the Excuse made by such Absentee by approved of at the next Meeting.

XIV. When any Member speaks, he shall address himself, standing, to the President; and if two or more Members offer to speak at once, the President shall determine who ought to speak first.

No Member shall speak more than twice to the same Question, or longer than ten Minutes each Time, unless called upon by the President, to explain any Thing he may have said.

XV. Whenever the Chamber shall be possessed of One thousand Pounds currency, by Contribution or otherwise, the Majority, at a monthly Meeting, shall determine whether it shall be applied to any public Benefit, or lent on Interest; and if the latter be resolved upon, the Treasurer shall not lend the same without the Advice of the Committee and Consent of the President; nor shall any Monies, so lent out, be for a longer Term than one Year to any Person borrowing the same, who shall give sufficient personal Security, for the Repayment thereof.

All Bonds, for Monies lent, shall be made payable to the President and Vice-President, in Trust and for the Use of the Chamber: And,

No Member shall be permitted to borrow any of the said Monies, or become Security for any Borrower thereof.

XVI. All Questions, at monthly, quarterly or extraordinary Meetings, shall be determined by Majority of Hands, or by Ballot if required by any two Members present: And, if Votes are equal, the President shall have the casting Vote.

XVII. During the first Year of the Chamber, not less than Eleven Members shall be a Quorum to do Business, at any monthly, quarterly or extraordinary Meeting; and after the Expiration of the first Year, not less than Twenty-one Members shall be a Quorum.

XVIII. All reasonable Expenses incurred in conducting the Business of the Chamber by the Officers and Committees thereof, and at their monthly, quarterly and extraordinary Meetings, the Anniversary excepted, together with the Salary of a Doorkeeper, hereafter to be appointed, shall be defrayed out of the General Fund.

XIX. No Motion, for altering or repealing any of these Rules, or for enacting any new Rule, shall be made otherwise than in Writing, and addressed to the President, who shall order the same to be read by the Secretary; then, if it is seconded, all the Members shall be specially summoned to attend at the next monthly Meeting, when, exactly an Hour after the stated Time of Meeting, the Motion shall be again taken up, and if Two-thirds of the Members present vote in Favour of it, it shall then be declared to be carried. If the Motion be for adding a new Rule, the President and Vice-President shall sign it in the Journal Book; if it be for repealing a former Rule the Rule, so repealed, shall be struck out, and the President and Vice-President shall sign their Names in the Margin. Nor shall any new Rule be of Force, or any former Rule be considered as repealed, unless all and every of these Particulars be complied with.

XX. Any Doubt that may hereafter arise concerning the Meaning of any of these Rules, shall be determined by a Majority, at any monthly or quarterly Meeting, provided not less than Two-thirds of the Members, then in the Province, are present.

1.5 Manchester Committee of Trade 1774 and 1781

The Manchester Committee of Trade established on 1 February 1774 is generally credited as the first chamber-like body in that city.[18] However, in some

[18] Redford, *Manchester Merchants* (1934); Bowden, *Industrial Society* (1965).

ways it was more limited than a full chamber concept. A detailed evaluation analyses the establishment period and compares it with the contemporaneous municipal corporation Committee of Trade in Liverpool for 1775, which shows similarities.[19] The conclusion is that the 1774 Manchester Committee of Trade was independent and chamber-like but was restricted in its engagement with members, acting more like a Board of Trade. Its re-foundation in 1781–2 may have improved its engagement.

For the original foundation in 1774 no compete set of Rules survives. The most complete items are newspaper notices which indicate its general character. These evidence a large subscription being raised of £2,000 which, it subsequently became clear in the 1781 reports, was mainly derived from a small number of people. If each had subscribed between 5 and 10 guineas (a frequent sum at the time for major subscribers), this would indicate a membership of 200–300. This is remarkably close to the list of members of 1781–2 (of 293) when the subscription was only one guinea. For the re-establishment in 1781 a set of Rules was published and these probably indicate many of the characteristics of the 1774 structure. Hence the two periods of 1774 and 1781–2 are presented together here. However, given some deficiencies in the period 1774–81, particularly getting subscriptions paid and continued support, some of the 1781 Rules were clearly different from those in 1774. The differences probably mainly focused on the level and payment of subscriptions, the development of sub-committees, and a structure of auditors, which seem to be the main issues that focused debates in 1781–2 and were aimed at increasing participation and trust.[20] The Committee of Trade seems to have lapsed in c.1786 as the Fustian Tax Committee locally, and the General Chamber nationally, attempted to take on the roles of the Committee. The 'quasi-minutes' of the Fustian Tax Committee show it had no intent to be a chamber, either in general objectives (being sector-based) or in having continuing formal Rules seeking permanency.[21] The General Chamber lapsed in 1787 (see Chapter 8). Successor bodies were founded in 1794 as a Manchester Commercial Society, and as a chamber in 1820 (q.v. later below).

Sources
[a] *Manchester Mercury*
[b] *The London Magazine of Gentleman's Monthly Intelligencer*, vol. 43, 1774.

[19] Bennett, 'Searching for new models' (2014), 'Alignments, interests' (2014).
[20] Bennett, 'Searching for new models (2014).
[21] Manchester Central Reference Library: J. Whitaker, 'quasi-minutes of the fustian tax committee'; missing from box at GB127.MS 336.27 M9: 1785, but fortunately preserved on microfilm (MF801). The only formal processes of the fustian committee were the calling of meetings, reporting of proceedings, and appointing of delegates. There appears to have never been a chair or other officers, though Whitaker was 'appointed Solicitor and conductor of this present course' (quasi-minutes 11 March 1785).

Notice of establishment 8 March 1774[a]

On Tuesday the first Day of February last, in Pursuance of a public Advertisement, "A general MEETING of the MERCHANTS and MANUFACTURERS, was held at Crompton's Coffee House, in Manchester, to consider of proper Measures for the Security and Encouragement of the Cotton, Linen, and other Manufactures of this Town and Neighbourhood." At this Meeting a Committee was appointed for these Purposes, consisting of the following Gentlemen.

THOMAS B. BAYLEY, of *Hope*, Esq; Chairman.
Mr. ROBERT HAMILTON, Deputy Chairman.
Mr. JOHN MARKLAND, Treasurer.
Mr. JOSEPH CHIPPINDALL, Secretary.

Mr. Josiah Birch	Mr. Tho. Chadwick, jun.	Mr. James Touchet
Mr. Edmund Radcliffe	Mr. Daniel Whitaker	Mr. James Potter
Mr. James Harrison	Mr. Thomas Starkie	Mr. Thomas Barrow
Mr. Joseph Ryder	Mr. Thomas Tipping	Mr. Tho. Withington
Mr. James Hodson	Mr. Thomas Stott	Mr. Robert Hibbert
Mr. William Walmsley	Mr. Peter Crompton	Mr. Robert Hyde
Mr. John Ridings		

This Committee has regularly met, and has adopted several Measures relative to the present State of Trade, which, it is hoped, may have the most beneficial Consequences, all their Proceedings are regularly minuted, and Copies taken of all Letters sent and received by the Committee.

The great extent and variety of the Manufactures and commercial Interests of *Manchester* and the Neighbourhood, render the Appointment of such a Committee, not only proper, but necessary; for there are scarcely any Regulations of Trade that can be proposed in Parliament by which they may not be affected.

The Committee have resolved to apply to the Gentlemen in Trade for their Subscriptions, to enable them to carry on the Business in which they are engaged, and some of them will take the Trouble of collecting these.

To leave the whole Expense and Trouble of promoting these public Interests, to a few generous Individuals in *Manchester*, has on former Occasions been matter of very just Complaint; it is now reasonable to expect the generous Aid of all Persons in Trade; not only in *Manchester*, but in the several Towns and Villages in the Circuit of its Manufactures. Such an universal Concurrence is as necessary, as it is just, and will raise a very considerable Sum, without laying too heavy a Burden on any Individual.

The Interests of our Manufactures are of the greatest Consequence, and too much Care and Attention cannot be paid in order to protect and extend them, and as the Cause is of general Concern, so ought to be the Support it meets with free and universal.

Whatever Sums are subscribed, will be applied under the Direction of the Committee, with the utmost Care and Frugality, and a just and regular Account kept, which will be open to the Inspection of the Public.

N.B. Half of the Money subscribed is to be immediately paid into the Hands of Mr. *Markland*, Treasurer to the Committee.

Printed report 22 April 1774[b]

At a general meeting of the merchants and principal manufacturers held at Manchester, to consider of proper measures for the security and encouragement of the trade of that town and neighbourhood, a committee was appointed for those important purposes. The usefulness and necessity of this association has instantly appeared, in the detection of some persons who were attempting to carry out of the kingdom most of the implements used in the cotton and linen manufactures, and engaging workmen in the different branches to accompany them; and the people are so fully satisfied of the great utility of this patriotic undertaking, that near 2000l, have been already subscribed for the support of the chamber of commerce in Manchester.

Reestablishment 26 June 1781[a]

A COMMITTEE for the Protection and Encouragement of Trade in this Town and Neighbourhood, having subsisted ever since the 1st of *February*, 1774, and the Members of it having a thorough Conviction, from Experience, of the great Benefits arising from such an Indication, and the great Extent of the Manufactories seeming to render a Measure of this Sort still more necessary; they thought it proper that the Sense of the Public should be taken on this Occasion: Therefore the said Committee have dissolved themselves, and by public Advertisements called this General Meeting.

AT WHICH SAID GENERAL MEETING, HELD THIS DAY, AT THE BULL'S-HEAD, IN MANCHESTER, IT IS RESOLVED.

1st. That we whose Names are hereunto subscribed, Merchants and Manufacturers within *Manchester* and the Neighbouring Towns, being fully convinced of the real Necessity of raising a Fund for the public Support and Protection of the Commercial Interests of this Country, and that the most effectual Method of establishing a Capital for that Purpose will be by an Annual Payment of such Sums as each Gentlemen may think proper to subscribe: THEREFORE we do hereby severally bind and oblige ourselves each to the other, that we will pay the several Sums of Money set opposite to our respective Names, Annually, to such Persons as are authorised to receive the same, for the Purposes above mentioned, (but for no other Use) the First Payment thereof to be made this Day, and every other Annual Payment progressively on every Tuesday next before the 24th of June.

2d. That the Boroughreeve and Constables of *Manchester*, for the Time being, are always requested to attend the Election of the General Committee, on every *Tuesday* next before the 24th of *June*, at Three o'Clock in the Afternoon, ________ in *Manchester*; at which Time and Place every Subscriber shall meet Annually, and shall proceed by Ballot, in like Manner as at the India-house, in the Choice of their Directors, to elect and choose nineteen Gentlemen Subscribers hereto, to be a General Committee, to continue for one Year next ensuing the Election, under the Title of the General Committee of Trade, for the Town of *Manchester* and the Neighbourhood, which Committee shall consist of viz.

THREE Auditors,
TEN Linen or Cotton Manufacturers, }
THREE Silk Ditto, } To be *Committee-men.*
THREE Small-ware Ditto, }

and each Trade (the Auditors excepted) shall select themselves into separate Committees, and act separately respecting their own Branch of Business; but shall have no Power to dispose of any Money in this Fund without the Approbation of all the three Auditors, or a Majority of a decitive [= decision-making, executive] Committee of Nine Persons chosen out of the General Committee, consisting of three Gentlemen from each different Branch of Business, (the Auditors excepted) and they shall be summoned by the Clerk at least Forty-eight Hours before the Meeting, and that no Meeting of either the Auditors, General, Selected or Decitive Committees, shall be had or held at any Place whatever, but in a public Room that shall be hired or appointed for the present, or hereafter to be erected, for the Purpose of carrying this Design into Execution.

3d. That every Auditor and Committee-man shall acknowledge the Acceptance of the Trust within three Days after his Appointment (if in Town) and Notice given him, by subscribing his Name in a Book to be kept for that Purpose; but any Person so elected in the General Committee, shall refuse to act, his or their Nomination shall be void; or if any Person or Persons elected in the said General Committee, shall happen to die, or be otherways rendered incapable of acting within the Year, in any of these Cases, his or their Places shall be supplied by the Subscribers who are next in Number upon the Ballot for the nineteen elected.

4th That any Member of the selected Committees shall be empowered to order the Clerk to call occasional Meetings of his selected Committee, at any Time; and after any of the selected Committees have formed their Resolutions, the Clerk shall summons the Auditors to attend them; and if the said three

Auditors approve of the said Resolutions, they shall be confirmed, but if otherways, then the Clerk shall call the decitive Committees together, and a Majority shall confirm or disannul the same.

5th. That the General Committee first chosen, and in course each succeeding General committee shall have a Power to elect and choose an intelligent and competent Clerk, to be employed under them, and to pay him out of this Fund such annual Salary as they shall think proper, PROVIDED always that the Clerk so appointed by any General Committee shall give sufficient Security in the Penalty of __________ for the faithful Discharge and Performance of the Trust committed to him; and that proper Books shall be kept by such Clerk in the General Committee Room, in which shall be entered all Orders and Resolutions of the several Committees, and the Receipts and Payments of all Monies.

6th. That in Order to advance the Fund, the AUDITORS for each Year shall have Power as soon as Subscriptions are paid in the Amount of One Hundred Pounds, or upwards, to place the same at Interest in the Hands of a Responsible Banker, upon such Security as they shall approve, and that the same shall be so placed out liable to an Immediate Call of the Principal, or any part thereof, whenever the Purposes for which the Fund has been raised shall require it; and the same Monies shall be so placed out in the Names of the Auditors, declaring in the Deed, Bond, Bill, or Note which shall be taken for securing the same, that the Money so placed out is the Property of the Subscribers to the Fund for the Protection of Trade in the Town of *Manchester* and the Neighbourhood, and that their Names are only made use of in Trust for the said Subscribers, and permitting their or any of their Names to be made use of in order to recover the same, in Case any succeeding Committee or the major Part of them, shall disapprove of such Security.

7th. That every Subscriber shall be permitted to vote for, or become a Committee-man.

8th. That all Bills shall be paid before the Annual Settlement, or the Accounts owing, entered and signed by the Auditors, and the Accounts shall be printed Annually, and ready for a public Inspection at every Yearly Meeting, that each Subscriber may be apprised of the State of the Fund, as well as see the Resolutions of the Committees, &c.

9th. That if any Person shall choose to become a Benefactor of Twenty Guineas or upwards, he shall have the Privilege of an Annual Subscriber of Two Guineas.

10th. No Rules shall be altered, nor new ones made, but at a Yearly Meeting, by the Subscribers at large; the Alteration being proposed first in the public Advertisements.

11th. That at every Annual Election of nineteen Gentlemen for a General Committee, if the last acting Committee be Re-chosen,

{ONE Auditor, }
{THREE Linen and Cotton Manufacturers, }
{ONE Silk Ditto }
{ONE Smallware Ditto }

shall be Balloted out, and others shall be appointed by Ballot (as per Article 2d) to fill up their Places, and to act in their stead.

The following Gentlemen were appointed a GENERAL COMMITTEE for the ensuing Year:

AUDITORS.
T.B. Bayley, Esq.,
Mr. Wm. Rigby,
Mr. John Philips.

Cotton & Linen COMMITTEE.
Mr. John Hilton, *London,*
Mr. John Pilkington, *Bolton,*
Mr. Daniel Whittaker,
Mr. Josiah Birch,
Mr. James Touchet,
Mr. Thomas Potter,
Mr. Nathan Hyde,
Mr. B.L. Winter,
Mr. James Entwistle,
Mr. Thomas P. Foxlow.

SILK COMMITTEE.
Mr. Holland Ackers,
Mr. John Harmer,
Mr. Thomas Johnson

SMALL-WARE COMMITTEE.
Mr. Tho. P. Philips,
Mr. John Orme,
Mr. Thomas Gorton

A CLERK IS WANTED,

Apply to Mr. *B.L. Winter*, who receives Subscriptions. A Subscription Book is left at *J. Harrop's*.

N.B. The Subscribers will be advertised in the next Weeks Paper.[22]

1.6 Liverpool Chamber of Commerce 1774

The Liverpool *Deed* is the earliest formal articles of association of a UK chamber that survives in a printed form circulated to potential members and subscribers. It was 'rediscovered' by the editor at the Liverpool Athenaeum and also exists in the Liverpool RO, but neither copy had been referred to until the editor's study.[23] One key aspect of the *Deed*, to introduce an annual fee in place of a three-year payment, was modified following the publication of the *Abstract* in 1777 (q.v. Chapter 5). Two further modifications of the Rules in 1779 and 1781 are reproduced here. Both indicate, in the absence of surviving minutes, that the articles of the draft deed were the operating rules for the chamber. The 1779 modification sought flexibility, which must have been agreed, to re-open membership changing the original concept of a

[22] The full list of subscribing members is given in Appendix, no. 20.2.
[23] Bennett, *Voice of Liverpool Business* (2010).

closed debenture financial structure. The second modification re-interpreted the election rules for the committee (article five) which had originally sought that only one third of the previous year's committee continued. There is no comment in the notice or report of the 1781 change, just the comment 'seven from the former committee and 14 subscribers not on last year's committee elected' (*Williamson's Liverpool Advertiser* 26 June 1781). The original drafting may have been a specific design to prevent control by corporation interests following the conflicts over the chamber's establishment and the corporation's move to appoint their own committee of trade (see Chapter 4). However, in fact, only one third had resigned each year over 1774–5 – 1780–1 (termed in newspaper reports as the 'annual custom'). For the election in 1781–2 the members re-asserted the original drafting so that two-thirds resigned each year, which then continued for as long as records survive up to 1786–7.[24] By 1778 the chamber had a committee room, which had been desired in the 1777 *Abstract*, reproduced in Chapter 5. In 1783–4 the chamber was probably involved in the construction of the Tontine Hotel and Coffee Room. Given the constraints on associations and their ownership of property, because they were not legal corporate entities, the accounts for the Tontine Hotel were held by an individual member (the chamber treasurer, Arthur Heywood) and the initiative was led by four individuals, three of whom were known chamber members, and the other probably was a member.[25] The chamber was not re-established as a general body until 1849, but a more specialist Liverpool American chamber was founded in 1801 (see 1.29 below), with some members overlapping with the 1774 foundation.[26]

Sources
[a] Printed notice: LRO Holt-Gregson Papers 942 HOL/10 pp. 355–6; also at Liverpool Athenaeum, Gladstone Ms. No. 52, within Heywood's *Calculations and Curious Papers*
[b] *Williamson's Liverpool Advertiser*

Printed broadsheet 21 April 1774[a]

DRAFT of an ARTICLE, for Settling a CHAMBER of COMMERCE, in *Liverpool.*

Common utility, mutual wants, and the necessity of mutual services, gave rise to an ancient association in Liverpool, for the levying a small Tax, under the denomination of a Trade duty.

[24] See committee lists in Bennett, *Voice of Liverpool Business* (2010) Table 2.
[25] See Bennett, *Voice of Liverpool Business* (2010) 10–12.
[26] See Appendix, no. 16, and membership comparison in Bennett, *Voice of Liverpool Business* (2010) 335, n. 339.

The amazing extension of commerce during that period, affords a most convincing proof of the wisdom of those who projected and executed this salutary measure.

To give stability to that Trade, in its now extended state, requires an increase of attention, and an increase of public expense.

Therefore we whose names are hereunto subscribed, Merchants and Tradesmen, within the port of Liverpool, in the county of Lancaster, being fully convinced of the real necessity, of raising a fund for the public support of the commercial Interests of this port; and that the most effectual method of establishing a capital for that purpose, will be by an annual payment of such sums, as the Merchant and Tradesman of this port may think proper to subscribe.

Do hereby severally bind and oblige ourselves each unto the other, that we will pay the several sums of money, set opposite to our respective names, to such persons upon such terms, and to be applied to such purposes, as are herein after particularly mentioned.

First. That in order to fix this subscription upon the most equitable foundation, we the several subscribers hereto, do promise and engage, in order that the scheme may have a fair trial, we will severally continue to pay our respective annual subscriptions, for the term of three years certain, the first payment whereof, to be made on the 1st day of May next, and so on the 1st day of May, for the two succeeding years, to Mr. ARTHUR HEYWOOD who is hereby appointed Treasurer, or to such person as he shall depute or appoint to receive the same.

Secondly. That each Merchant and Tradesman so subscribing, shall meet on every twenty fourth day of June, unless the same happen on a Sunday, and if so, the day afterwards, between the hours of ten and twelve o'clock in the forenoon, the first meeting whereof, to be between the hours of ten and twelve o'clock in the forenoon, on Friday the twenty fourth day of June next, and they or the major part of them then present, shall proceed by ballot, to elect and choose twenty one of the Merchants or Tradesmen subscribers hereto, to be a committee for one year, under the style of *The Committee of the Chamber of Commerce, for the Port of Liverpool.*

Third. That every committee-man shall acknowledge his acceptance of the trust, within three days after his appointment, and notice given him, by subscribing his name in a book to be kept for that purpose: but if any person or persons elected on the committee, shall refuse to act, his or their nomination shall be void, or if any person or persons elected on the committee shall happen to die within the year, in either of these cafes public notice shall be immediately given, and the subscribers summon'd to meet, to fill up such vacancies; and when the committee of twenty one, so to be chosen by ballot, shall be complete, they the same committee shall proceed in like manner, by ballot, to choose out of their own body, one person to act as chairman, and one other person to act as deputy chairman, and that it shall be lawful for such deputy chairman, to preside and act in fulfilling the intentions of this Society, at any time whenever it shall happen that the chairman shall be absent.

Fourth. That each member of this committee shall be summoned forty eight hours before every stated meeting, and that no less than eleven committee-men, shall have power to dispose of any part of the fund, hereby intended to be raised, and that upon all questions arising in the committee, if upon a division the numbers shall be equal, the chairman, or in his absence the deputy chairman, shall have the casting vote, and that no meeting of the committee shall be had or held in any place whatever, but in a public room, that shall be hired, or appointed for the present, or hereafter be erected for the purpose of carrying this design into execution.

Fifth. That at the expiration of one year, from the twenty fourth day of June next, there shall be annually chosen by the subscribers at large, by ballot, from out of the committee of twenty one, seven of that committee to be continued of the committee for the succeeding year, and as soon as the balloting for those is over, the subscribers shall proceed to ballot for the remaining fourteen, to complete the number of the committee out of the body of subscribers at large.

Sixth. That no person shall be admitted to vote, or become a committee-man, who is a subscriber to this fund, for a less sum than the annual payment of *one pound one shilling*, and that every subscriber for that sum or upwards shall be entitled to vote, (provided he attends within the hours appointed for that purpose) in choice of committee-men, and that none but subscribers to the amount of *one pound one shilling* annually, have any claim upon this fund.

Seventh. That in order to advance the fund, the committee for each year, shall have power, as soon as subscriptions are paid in, to the amount of *one hundred pounds* or upwards, to place the same out at a very low or moderate interest; but upon a security to be approved of by the committee so placing out the same; and, that the same shall be so placed out liable to an immediate call of the principal, or any part thereof, whenever the purposes for which the fund has been raised shall require it; and that the same monies so placed out, shall be placed in the names of the committee so placing out the same, declaring in the deed, bond, bill, or note, which shall be taken for securing the same; that the money so placed out, is the property of the *Chamber of Commerce, for the Port of Liverpool*, and that their names are only made use of in trust, for that *Chamber of Commerce*, and permitting their, or any of their names to be made use of, in order to recover the same, in case the committee or eleven of them so placing out the same, or any succeeding committee, or eleven of them, or the subscribers to this fund, or the major part of them at their annual meeting, shall not approve of such security.

Eighth. That no person who on the twenty fourth day of June next, shall be a resident within the Port of Liverpool; and that time be concerned and interested in trade, or business, as a merchant or tradesman, shall be admitted as a subscriber to this fund, after the twenty fourth day of January, one thousand seven hundred and seventy five.

Ninth. That if it shall unfortunately happen that any subscriber to this fund, shall, by unavoidable misfortunes in the course of trade become necessitous, and the exigencies of commerce will permit an extension of relief from this fund; and the committee of twenty one, or the major part of them, shall deem him a proper object; that then such committee, or the major part of them, shall order him such assistance and relief, as they in their discretion shall think proper.

Tenth. That the committee to be appointed as aforesaid, shall meet the first Thursday in every month, after their appointment, between the hours of eleven and one in the forenoon, for the dispatch of business. And that the Chairman, or Deputy Chairman, (in case of absence or sickness or the Chairman) be empowered to call occasional meetings, upon any extraordinary emergency; and if the circumstances of such meeting, will not admit of time to send proper notice of forty eight hours, such Chairman, or Deputy Chairman, with the assistance of four other persons, being of the committee, shall have power to proceed in any such emergent business, (the disposal of the fund, or any part thereof, always excepted, and subject and liable to the fourth article.)

Eleventh. That the committee first chosen, and in course each succeeding committee shall have a power to elect and choose an intelligent and competent clerk, to be employed under them and to pay him from out of this fund, such annual salary as they shall think proper, provided always that the clerk so appointed by any committee, shall give sufficient security in the penalty of five hundred pounds, for the faithful discharge and performance of the trust committed to him; and that proper books shall be kept by such clerk in the committee room, in which shall be entered all orders and resolutions of the committee, and the receipt and payment of all monies.

Twelfth. That the annual accounts of each committee, shall be printed, published, and one copy delivered to each subscriber, on the twenty-fourth of June annually, that each subscriber may be then apprised of the state of the fund.

Thirteenth. That if any person shall choose to become a benefactor of twenty guineas or upwards, he shall have the privileges of an annual subscriber.

Printed notice 19 June 1778[b]

THE SUBSCRIBERS to the CHAMBER of COMMERCE are requested to attend of the Office of that Society, No. 172 Dale Street, near the Exchange, on Wednesday next the 24th inst. exactly at Ten o'Clock, to elect a Committee for the next year ensuing.—The second meeting will be at One o'Clock. [for the committee to elect the officers]

N.B. Attendance is given at the said office every day during 'Change hours.

Printed notice 26 June 1779[b]

A GENERAL MEETING of the SUBSCRIBERS to this FUND will be held on Monday next, the 28th instant, at the SOCIETY'S OFFICE, between the hours of Ten and Twelve o'clock in the forenoon, to determine upon the expediency of rescinding the Eighth Article of Association, by which it is enacted, that 'No person, who, on the 24th June 1774, resided in Liverpool, and was at the time concerned in trade, be admitted as a subscriber to this fund, after 24th of January 1775.'
CHAMBER OF COMMERCE, Liverpool, 24th June 1779

1.7 [Quebec, Canada, Chamber of Commerce; proposal 1776–7][27]

1.8 Kingston, Jamaica, Chamber of Commerce 1778

No copy of the Jamaica chamber rules survives. However, reference to various rules was made in reports of its meetings and these allow the main rules to be established. They are summarised as in the listing below, together with examples of some of the chamber's notices which are typical of most chambers of the period. Further detail of the development of the chamber is given by Bennett.[28] Also included is a minute of the London West India Committee announcing the chamber's establishment, with the agreement of the Committee to cooperate with it. The chamber's foundation date is stated as 'founded 1778' in the *Jamaica Almanack and Register* for 1780–85. The date is indicated as late 1778 by the letter to London West India Merchants. The exact foundation date of 26 November 1778 is deduced from the *Jamaica Mercury* report of the General Meeting of the chamber on 25 November 1779 (a Thursday) to elect new officers and committee 'for the next year'. Since the General Meetings were held on the equivalent Thursday date each

[27] No further papers appear to survive than a foundation proposal, which was agreed in principle by the Quebec Governor and the Westminster-based Committee of Trade; no rules were developed or survive, though the chamber may have operated under a few individuals for a few years; see Bennett, *Local Business Voice* (2011) 141–4. The first successful chamber in Quebec was formed in 1808 (not included here).

[28] R. J. Bennett, 'Collective action when needed: The Kingston chamber of commerce in Jamaica, 1778–85', *The Journal of Imperial and Commonwealth History* 43 (2015) 165–188.

year later, this indicates that the chamber's inaugural meeting was Thursday 26th November 1778. Note the chamber's official history incorrectly states the foundation date as 1779.[29]

Sources
[a] *Jamaica Almanack and Register*: BL, Bodleian, and National Library of Jamaica.
[b] *Jamaica Mercury*, later *Jamaica Royal Gazette*: BL and National Library of Jamaica.
[c] Analysis of officers and committee from sources [a] and [b].[30]
[d] Committee of West India Merchants: London Senate House M915/1.

Summary of known Rules (only Rules 1 and 3 reflect known numbering of the actual Rules):

1. Quarterly general meetings, open to all members, called 'according to rule 1', at least a week previously by published call or personal communication, on about 25th of February, August, May and November.[b]
2. Annual general meeting to hold election of officers and committee, and report accounts and activities, each year in November.[b]
3. Election of officers and committee 'according to rule 3';[b] tenure of committee and officers 'for the next year',[b] but seems to be for three years for officers;[c] one third of the committee to retire each year from the committee.[c]
4. Officers: President, Vice President, Treasurer, Secretary (Listed in *Jamaica Almanac* for all years 1779–1786, and most also listed in local newspapers).[a]
5. Committee of 18 including the 4 officers.[a]
6. 'Nine members [of committee] make a quorum' (*Jamaica Almanac*, 1781–85)[a]
7. Special meetings called in urgent circumstances, publicised in local press.[b]
8. Minutes to be kept and held by secretary,[31] but can be consulted at his offices or at meetings.[b]
9. Secretary to give notice of meetings a few days in advance.[b]
10. Secretary to hire room(s) to hold meeting where chamber's papers and newspapers were kept (usually a coffee house, e.g. Howard's 1779, Bentley's 1779–80).[b]

[29] J. Morgan, 'The chamber history', 10–17 in *The Bicentennial Handbook, 1779–1979* (Kingston, 1979) 10.
[30] Bennett, 'Collective Action when Needed' (2015).
[31] e.g. *Jamaica Mercury*, 29 May and 6 November 1779.

Printed notice Kingston, 18 November 1779[b]

Chamber of Commerce,

A General Quarterly Meeting of the Society will be held, at their Room in *Bentley's* Tavern, on *Thursday* next the 25th inst. at 11 o'clock in the forenoon; at which the Subscribers are requested to attend, in order to choose Officers and a Committee for the ensuing year, agreeably to THIRD RULE. J Hardwar, Secr.

Printed notice Kingston, 20 May 1780[b]

Chamber of Commerce,

A GENERAL QUARTERLY MEETING of this SOCIETY will be held on Thursday next the 25th inst. at their Room in BENTLEY'S Tavern, agreeably to *first* rule.
J Hardwar, Secr.

Minute London West India Committee, 27 April 1779[d]

A letter from Thos. Hibbert jun. President of the Kingston Chamber of Commerce in Jamaica was read. Ordered that an answer be sent expressing the desire of this meeting to co-operate with that Society, for the general benefit of the West India Commerce, as far as is consistent with the Institution of the Society of West India Merchants.

1.9 [Lancaster Committee of Trade 1779–81][32]

1.10 [Blackburn Committee of Trade 1779][33]

1.10 [Weskett's London Chamber of Commerce, 1782: see Chapter 3]

1.11 Glasgow Chamber of Commerce 1783; also see charter 1783 in Chapter 2

Glasgow had a statement of objectives which it published, printed identically in various sources. Its main operating rules were, however, contained in the very detailed specification given in its 1783 charter (see Chapter 2).

Source
James Denholm, *The History of the City of Glasgow*, Stewart and Meikle, Glasgow, 1798, pp. 172–4.

[32] Referred to in chapters 5.4, 5.7 and 6.4; no further evidence of rules or continued activity.
[33] Referred to in chapter 5.11; no further evidence of rules or continued activity.

Published Objectives 1783

The great outlines of the business committed to the charge of the directors of the Chamber of Commerce, is,

1. To consider of such plans and systems as shall contribute to the protection and improvement of those branches of trade and manufactures which are peculiar to this country, and which may be interesting to the members of the Chamber at large.

2. To regulate all matters respecting any branch of trade or manufacture, which may be submitted to the directors, for the purpose of establishing rules for the convenience and assistance, either of foreign traders, or manufacturers.

3. To read and discuss all public and private memorials and representations of members of the Chamber, requesting the aid of the directors in any matter regarding trade or manufactures.

4. To afford aid to members, whether as individuals or otherwise, who may apply for assistance in negotiating any matter of business, whether local, or of a nature which requires the weight and influence of the directors, in making application to the Board of Trustees, to the King's Ministers, or to Parliament.

5. To procure relief or redress in any grievance, hardship, oppression, or inconvenience, affecting any particular branch of trade and manufacture, carried on by the members of this society, by interposing the weight and influence of the directors in any public negotiation that may be thought necessary to effect such relief.

6. To consider of all matters affecting the corn-laws of this part of the united kingdom in particular, as being of the utmost consequence to its trade and manufactures.

And, in general, to take cognisance of every matter and thing that shall be in the least degree connected with the interests of commerce—to assist in pointing out new sources for promoting whatever may be useful and beneficial—and to attend to every application made to parliament, which may be thought injurious to the trade and manufactures of this country—to support an intercourse and friendly correspondence with the Convention of Royal Boroughs, and Board of Trustees for Fisheries and Manufactures, for the purpose of communicating new and useful improvements to their attention.

1.12 Dublin Chamber of Commerce 1783 and 1788

The first Plan for a chamber and its rules are contained in the 'Rough Minute Book of the Dublin Committee of Merchants', in the minutes and also as a loose paper of three pages (all handwritten). This follows a report of a larger open meeting at the Royal Exchange on 7 February 1783, Travers Hartley chair, which produced and recommended the Plan to the Committee of Merchants. This sequence is reproduced below. At some point in the development process in 1783 the Glasgow chamber was requested to send details of its charter and rules, so that it is clear that Dublin was influenced by them, but did not initially seek a charter, and the details differ considerably from Glasgow. By 1788 there were various tensions resulting in a new, or amended, set of rules which are reproduced below. The 1788 new rules explicitly embody the old rules (Rule 13), as well as some of the decisions made in intervening minutes; e.g. 23 September 1783 it was resolved that it was 'not within the province of this Council to interfere in difference between individuals', but instead to refer them to external arbitration. On 24 April 1784 it was agreed to send subscription demands 'to members by penny post who have not paid, who will not be admitted to votes of Council'; repeated on 25 May 1785. The new rules followed a discussion of 16 December 1787 'supporting continuity of mercantile association'—the chamber of commerce. The new rules were agreed on 19 December 1787 against some dissent; on 22 December they were agreed again with one change that Council members had to pay two guineas for membership to constitute them members of the chamber of commerce; a meeting on 2 January 1788 heard a counter proposal for one guinea, but the final discussion on 9 February agreed two guineas. It appears that some or all of the council had not been paying their annual dues or entry fees. The reaffirmation of 'continuity' appears to have been deemed necessary against some opposition to the Council members. It was also five years since the original chamber foundation in February 1783. The original Plan did not contain a fixed period for the chamber's existence, but did provide that the original subscribers should number at least 100 and each paid one guinea to create a fund. It appears that annual subscriptions had been collected regularly, but payments were difficult to get in. Formal accounts seem to have ceased in 1787, and only partial annual accounts for 1783–4 (Minutes 24 April 1784), 1784–5 (Minutes 26 May 1785), and 1785–6 (Minutes 12 August 1786), where expenditure amounted to about £24, £60 and £52, respectively, plus the £30 honorarium/salary for the secretary (Shannon). Also on 4 December 1783 £20 was allowed to Mr. Hamilton 'for coals & candles & cleaning the room for one year'. There were also other payments not accounted for at year end, e.g. 1 September 1785, 10 guineas for plate to the secretary Shannon as thanks for his efforts over the Irish propositions. Probably the annual expenditure was about £80, which would have been just possible to meet from subscriptions of 100 members at one guinea with some in arrears. New rules were developed again several times (see later below). Numbering added to rules for clarity.[34]

[34] Also see L. M. Cullen, *Princes and Pirates: The Dublin Chamber of Commerce 1783–1983*

Sources
[a] Rough Minute Book of the Dublin Committee of Merchants: RIA MS. 3 C 25
[b] Dublin chamber of commerce, Minute Book: TNAI

Minute 10 February 1783[a]

Present
Mr. Colvill
Mr. Hartley Mr. O Brien
Alderman Sutton Mr. Carothers
Mr. Cosgrave

At a meeting of the Committee of Merchants regularly convened by Summons for the special purpose of taking into consideration of a Plan for Instituting a Chamber of Commerce in this City [derived from the 7 February meeting].

Mr. John Patrick & Mr. Jo[shua] Pim presented to the Committee the Plan hereunto annexed which being received read & considered the following resolutions were entered into-

THAT we highly approve of said Plan as forming a broad & firm foundation on which may be expected to arise a superstructure of Eminent usefulness in the Commercial Department.

THAT from this measure the Trading Interest is likely to derive Great additional Importance and respect and the Public in general the advantages consequent thereto.

THAT on the great change expected shortly to take place in the Commercial System of Great Britain & Ireland and probably in that of some other Countries it is highly necessary and peculiarly seasonable by a scheme of this nature to collect the Experience & Abilities of every Intelligent Trader in the various lines of Commerce and Manufactures that their united Knowledge may be happily directed to the General good.

THAT this Committee do therefore most heartily recommend to their Fellow Citizens the carrying said Plan into Effect as speedily as possible and they will think themselves happy in resigning their appointment as the Committee of Merchants when on the Liberal & Extensive Plan now proposed a Council of the Chamber of Commerce shall be Elected.

PLAN

CHAMBER OF COMMERCE

The present important Situation of this Country, its lately renewed Constitution, its fond Hopes of rising Commerce and consequently increasing Opulence the variety of Commercial Regulations necessarily incident to

(Dublin, 1983); E. MacMahon, *A Most Respectable Meeting of Merchants: Dublin Chamber of Commerce: A History* (Dublin, 2014).

this change of circumstances and particularly requisite from the late Revolution in the Political System: every Consideration appearing to demand a general Union among Traders and a constant unwearied attention to their Common Interests; from a view whereof to promote these laudable Objects in this particular District, and to hold forth an Example for Imitation and Co-operation, to the rest of the Kingdom, it is proposed to institute forthwith:

A CHAMBER OF COMMERCE FOR THE CITY OF DUBLIN

[1] THAT any Merchant or Trader resident within the said City or its Dependencies shall be eligible as a Member of the Chamber on his paying one Guinea to Mr. John Patrick or Mr. Joshua Pim who have kindly undertaken to act as Treasurers until a Person shall be elected to that office; such Subscribers to continue Members so long as they shall respectively comply with the Rules which shall be adopted by the said Chamber for its good Government and for the continuation of a Fund to answer the purposes of its Institution.

[2] THAT when the subscribers shall amount to One Hundred the said Temporary Treasurers shall call a meeting by public Advertisement at which said first Meeting of the Chamber or at an adjournment of said Meeting the Members present shall choose by Ballot a certain number of Members who shall be called THE COUNCIL of the CHAMBER OF COMMERCE to continue in office until the first Day of May 1784 and that an Annual Ballot for such Council shall be held on every first Day of May not being Sunday, and when Sunday on the second day of May.

[3] THAT it shall be the business of said Council to attend to the Interests of Commerce and for that purpose to hold frequent Meetings to confer when necessary with Persons in high stations or others to have a watchful Attention to the proceedings of Parliament respecting Trade in both Kingdoms to inspect into the Methods of transacting business in Dublin and to contrive and recommend Improvements therein when such shall be thought expedient.

[4] THAT the said Council for the time being shall choose by Ballot from among themselves a President two Vice Presidents and a Treasurer and shall appoint a Secretary with a fixed Salary suitable to his Services.

[5] THAT it be understood that the Members of the Chamber shall be peculiarly entitled to the protection of the Institution on every proper occasion.

Minute: new rules 9 January 1788[b]

CHAMBER OF COMMERCE

1st RESOLVED that each Member of this Council do on or before the 1st day of February next pay to the Treasurer the sum of two Guineas which shall constitute him a Member of a Society to be henceforth called "The Chamber of Commerce of the City of Dublin."

2d RESOLVED that each Member of the said Society do pay an Annual Subscription of two Guineas.

3rd RESOLVED that the present Fund in hand together with all accruing Funds be vested in the said Society to be disbursed only on an Order signed by five Members of whom the President or a Vice President to be one.

4th RESOLVED that the present Officers continue until the first meeting in May 1788 when new Officers viz. a President, two Vice Presidents, a Treasurer, and a Secretary, shall be appointed by ballot and in like manner Annually at the first meeting in each Month of May the Officers to be capable of re-election.

5th RESOLVED that there be a regular meeting held the first and third Wednesday in every Month at seven o'Clock in the Evening the Months of July, August, and September excepted, and such other Meetings as shall be appointed by Adjournment of the Chamber or by appointment of the President either vice President or any three Members on Summons of the Secretary.

6th RESOLVED that such Members of this Council as shall not have paid the required Subscription by the 1st March 1788 be considered as having withdrawn from the Chamber.

7th RESOLVED that such Members as shall be in Arrear of their Subscription be deemed incapable of acting as Members or having the Rights of Members whilst in Arrear.

8th RESOLVED that any two Members shall be entitled to propose a new Member, which proposal shall be made in Writing and delivered to the Secretary together with a Deposit of the Admission Money which shall be returned in case of rejection.

9th RESOLVED that the new Members be chosen by Ballot to be held exactly at eight o'Clock and closed in an Hour on the stated meetings no person to be Balloted for sooner than two weeks after being proposed and the names of the Candidates to be posted up at every meeting from the time of proposing to the time of Balloting and to be inserted in a Summons to be sent to each Member.

10th RESOLVED that each new Member on his Admission pay two Guineas and the Annual Subscription afterwards.

11th RESOLVED that on the Ballot for new Members five negatives or the Majority present shall reject.

12th RESOLVED that a person rejected may be proposed again and the rejection is not to be recorded.

13th RESOLVED that the rules and orders of the late Chamber and Council be binding on this Chamber until altered or repealed.

14th RESOLVED that any Member paying down Twenty Guineas shall be a Member for Life.

1.13 Belfast Chamber of Commerce 1783

The minutes and papers of the Belfast chamber do not contain a full set of the first rules at its establishment in 1783, although we know from statements in them that they drew on Glasgow and Dublin chambers founded earlier in the same year. The Dublin Plan was primarily used with amendments (Minutes, 25 May 1783), even though this was very sparse (see above). The best that exists is an outline of procedures for establishing the chamber, reproduced below, to which is added extracts from the minutes indicating the main rules that operated. The first printed rules were for 1856, which are not reproduced here.[35]

Sources
[a] Belfast *News Letter*.
[b] Chamber minutes: PRONI D1857/1/AB/1

Report 22 April 1783[a]

At a Meeting of the Merchants of Belfast held at the Donegall Arms the 22d April 1783 Mr JAMES PARK in the Chair.

Resolved, That the Chairman do insert an advertisement in the next Belfast paper, summoning a general meeting of the Merchants of this town to be held at the Market-house, on Saturday the 3d May next, at 12 o'Clock noon, for the purpose of considering the propriety of establishing a Chamber of Commerce in the town of Belfast.

Report 20 May 1783[a]

Belfast 19th May 1783

At a meeting of the Merchants of Belfast to take into consideration the propriety of establishing a Chamber of Commerce in this Town.
THOMAS GREG, Esq. in the Chair.

Resolved unanimously, That in our opinion the establishment of a Chamber of Commerce in this town would be highly proper, and that great advantages may be expected therefrom.

That similar establishments in all the principal Trading Towns in this Kingdom might be productive of great advantages to the Nation, as by that

[35] Held at PRONI D1558/5/6/3; see also G. Chambers, *Faces of Change: The Belfast and Northern Ireland Chambers of Commerce and Industry, 1783–1983* (Belfast, 1983).

means a general union would be formed, the knowledge and experience of every intelligent Trader in the various lines of commerce and manufacture collected, and the united endeavours of the whole happily directed to the general good. …

Resolved, That the following gentlemen be, and they thereby are, appointed a committee to digest a plan for the above purpose, and that they do report the same to a general meeting on Saturday the 24th inst. at noon, of which public notice to be given.

Mr. Greg	Mr. John Brown
Mr. Cunningham	Mr. Joy
Mr. Thomson	Mr. Bradshaw
Mr Ewing	Any five to be a quorum.

THOMAS GREG, Chairman

Printed pamphlet 30 May 1783[a]

Belfast 27 May 1783

TO THE MERCHANTS AND TRADERS OF THE TOWN OF BELFAST

The Report of your Committee appointed to digest a Plan for establishing a Chamber of Commerce in said Town.

Having taken the business to us committed under our most serious consideration, we are unanimously of opinion, that we cannot so well discharge the trust reposed in us, as by recommending to your adoption the same plan which hath been adopted by our worthy and highly respected brethren, the merchants of Dublin, with some few variations which become necessary on account of the comparative smallness of our numbers.—We therefore recommend,

That every merchant or trader resident in the town of Belfast or its vicinity, shall at anytime become and be deemed a member of said Chamber of Commerce, on paying to the treasurer for the time being one guinea; such subscribers to continue members so long as they shall respectively comply with such rules as may be established by said Chamber for its good government, and for the continuation of a fund to answer the purposes of its institution.

That a subscription be now opened for that purpose, and that such gentlemen as shall now subscribe and pay one guinea each, do appoint from among themselves a temporary treasurer to receive subscriptions; and that as soon as the subscribers shall amount to fifty, the said treasurer do call a general meeting of the subscribers by public advertisement, at which meeting the members present shall choose by ballot fifteen subscribers, who shall form, and be called The Council of the Chamber of Commerce, to continue in office until the first day of July, 1784; and that an annual election by ballot for such Council shall be held on every first day of July, not being Sunday, and when Sunday on the second day of July.

That it shall be the business of said Council to attend to the interests of commerce; to have a watchful attention to the proceedings of Parliament respecting trade in both kingdoms; to inspect into the method of transacting business in Belfast, and to contrive and recommend improvements therein when such shall be thought expedient; to correspond with the Council of the Chamber of Commerce in Dublin, and with any others that may be established in this kingdom, as well as, when necessary, with those that are or may be established in Great Britain.

That the said Council, for the time being, shall, by ballot, choose from among themselves a President, Vice-President, and Treasurer.

And that the Members of the Chamber shall on every proper occasion be peculiarly entitled to the protection of the institution.

THOS. GREG,
Chairman of the Committee

Minutes, with subsequent amendments[b]

The purpose [of the chamber] is to attend to the interests of commerce, to have a watchful attention to the proceedings of Parliament respecting trade in both Kingdoms, to inspect into the methods of transacting Business in Belfast and to continue and recommend improvements. [27 May 1783]

Any merchant or trader is eligible to become a member. [27 May 1783]

Subscription annually of £1; reduced to 10s. [1822]

A ballot from the whole members attending the annual meeting, for the whole council and officers held each year. [27 May 1783]

Council of 12; increased to 15 [1 March 1802].

Fines for late attendance of council after 15 minutes of 1s.; changed to late attendance after 5 minutes 1s., and after 20 minutes 2s. 6d. with no excuse admitted for non-payment of fines, except sickness and absence from town, with President's permission [25 January 1785]; reverted to 1s. after 15 minutes [7 February 1792].

Council to meet weekly

Officers: President, Vice-President, Secretary who was also Treasurer.

Secretary (and other officers) honorary. [Secretary voted a salary of £20 at each annual general meeting from 1802].

No standing subcommittees established, but special committees to report to Council used extensively.

1.14 Birmingham Commercial Society 1783

Birmingham was the second inland location to found a chamber (or commercial society) after Manchester. Good records of many of its early activities and developments are given by Wright and Langford.[36] The chamber was re-founded in 1835 but had several intervening quasi-reestablishments. Numbering added for clarity.

Source
Aris's Birmingham Gazette.

Printed report Birmingham Hotel, 12 August 1783

—At a Town's Meeting held here, this Day, pursuant to the public Request of the Committee appointed to prepare proposals for the Establishment and Regulation of a General Commercial Committee, SAM. GARBETT, ESQ. in the Chair.

The following Resolutions passed unanimously, viz.:—

Resolved, That the Sketch produced by the Committee appointed at a public Meeting on the 15th of July last to prepare proposals for the Establishment of a General Commercial Committee has the unanimous Approbation of this Meeting.

[1] Resolved, that it is the Sense of this Meeting that it is highly expedient to establish a standing General Commercial Committee for the purpose of watching over and conducting the public Interest of this Town and Neighbourhood.

[2] Resolved, That a number of Persons, not less than Sixty, nor more than One Hundred, be now chosen for the Purpose of forming this Committee, who, from their Election, shall be considered as a public Body established for the Purposes above-mentioned, and that all future Applications to Parliament, or to Administrations for public purposes, be entrusted to them.

[3] Resolved, That this Committee shall not decide upon any Proposals that may be made to them, but at a Meeting called by public Advertisement in the Birmingham Newspapers, to be signed at least by five of their Body, in which the Business intended for the consideration of such Meeting shall be expressly mentioned; except in cases of real Emergency, admitted to be such by seven Members of the Committee, who shall in that Case be empowered to sign an Order to the Secretary for immediately summoning the whole Committee to a special Meeting.

[36] G. H. Wright, *Chronicles of the Birmingham Chamber of Commerce 1813–1913* (Birmingham, 1913); J. A. Langford, *A Century of Birmingham Life: or, A Chronicle of Local Events, from 1741–1841* (Birmingham, 1868).

[4] Resolved, That at all Meetings, whether public or special, seven Members shall form a board, and be empowered to Act in the Name of the Whole; but no meeting shall be held for any Business whatever without the Whole of the Committee being regularly summoned to it.

[5] Resolved, That the Committee shall keep an exact Register of all their Proceedings in a Book set apart for that Purpose, to which every Member of the Committee shall have free Access, and which shall be produced at the Public Meeting whenever the Committee shall find it necessary to call the Town together.

[6] Resolved, That if any of the Gentlemen nominated shall decline to Act, the Committee shall have power to elect others in their stead; and whenever the Number of the Committee be reduced to Fifty, by Deaths or Removals, the surviving Members are hereby authorised to fill up the Vacancies to a Number not less than Sixty, nor more than One Hundred.

[7] Resolved, That it is understood the Committee are to make Bye Laws for their own Government and Regulation in future. And Resolved, That it be and hereby is expressly enjoined upon them to correspond with any Commercial Committees, that are or may be established in any other Commercial Cities or Towns in the Kingdom, —and in particular that they receive and encourage a Coincidence and Connexion with the Towns of Wolverhampton, Walsall, and Dudley and their neighbourhood,

[8] Resolved; That the list of Names now produced by the Committee and filled up by this Meeting, to the number of One Hundred Persons, be adopted; and that the Gentlemen therein nominated be, and hereby are, duly elected Members of the General Commercial Committee.

[9] Resolved, That the Proceedings of this public Meeting be inserted in both the Birmingham Newspapers.

[10] Resolved, That the Thanks of this Meeting be given to the Chairman for the very Able and Candid Manner in which he has conducted the important Business of the Day.

(Signed) SAM. GARBETT.

1.15 North Staffordshire Potters Committee of Commerce 1784

A 'Potters' Committee of Commerce' for Staffordshire was first established in 1767 with Josiah Wedgwood a leading figure. This was essentially a potters' group that assembled when an issue needed attention, chiefly lobbies on trade and protection, prices and supply of clay.[37] It was more a sector association

[37] Wedgwood Archives: referred to in Wedgwood correspondence transcripts as a collective body of potters; e.g. Wedgwood letters to Bentley: concerned with 'getting higher duty on foreign china', vol.2, 14 February 1767; 'Our potters had a sort of General assembly the last week to

and was mainly ad hoc, assembled when needed, and does not appear to have had rules or used the title 'chamber'. This group, or their successors, moved on to become a more formal chamber in 1784 with a set of rules that sought to represent the whole neighbourhood where earthenware was produced. It thus had most of the characteristics of a chamber, but was sector-based and not a general body. It is included here as it was an important experiment and brought Josiah Wedgwood and the potters into contact with the rest of the chamber movement by which they were influenced and to which they contributed. It has been discussed previously in terms of its formation and lobby activities with Thomas giving a partial summary of some of the rules.[38] The text here is complete from the first meeting in its minutes through to the approval and additions to its rules at its third meeting, and then incudes the text from the fourth meeting where it relates to the rules. These meetings established fourteen rules, which have been numbered here to highlight their structure. The sequence of discussion demonstrates the origins of the Committee in the discussions then ongoing on the Treaty with France, and the related activities of other committees and chambers around the country. Committees/chambers in Birmingham and Manchester were written to at an early point, and later minutes show exchanges with Dublin and Edinburgh, as well as the General Chamber of Manufacturers. From the burning issue of the French Treaty, the Committee then proceeded to establish and refine its rules, with some elements reminiscent of the rules in Birmingham of 1783 and Manchester of 1781–2 (see earlier). Much of the activity of the Committee focused on the General Chamber after 1785 with a two-year gap in the minutes from 6 November 1787 until February 1789 during which the General Chamber had failed. The continuation of the minutes in 1789 in a different hand from Wedgwood (who recorded the minutes himself for all the early meetings) indicates his disillusionment, and also a shift in character of the potters' activities mainly to specific and technical issues about earthenware. But, without the General Chamber, the potters' committee itself seems to have also withered, with its last meeting recorded on 27 July 1790. It was revived in a form more like a local trade association in the 1830s.

---

consider upon a reduction of their prices and came to a resolution neme. cone. to lower them 20 p. ct. & I find that our Society & the whole potters abide by this resolution' vol. 7, 14 April 1773; 'a letter wrote yesterday by Mr. Byerley, in his official capacity, as clerk to the Committee of Potters, with their thanks to Lord North for his kind attention to the interests of our Manufactory', vol.10, 7 February 1776. Byerley was one of Wedgwood's clerks deputed to undertake the correspondence.

[38] V. W. Bladen, 'The Association of the Manufacturers of Earthenware (1784–86)', *Economic History, Supplement to Economic Journal*, 1 (1928) 356–67; J. Thomas, 'The potters of Staffordshire and their relations with the Manchester Committee of Commerce, 1784 to 1790', *Manchester Statistical Society, Papers* (1934–5) 6–7 partial text.

Source
Wedgwood Archives, Wedgwood MS. E39–28404 catalogued as 'Josiah Wedgwood's commonplace book', but in fact 'Potters' Committee of Commerce', minutes for 1784–1790, in the hand of Josiah Wedgwood until 1786, and then partly by Alexander Chisholm.

The Potters' Committee of Commerce 1784

MANUFACTORY OF EARTHENWARE IN STAFFORDSHIRE.

GREAT Inconvenience having been felt in this Manufactory in several recent instances from the want of a standing Body invested with powers to act as occasion required in the Conduct and Protection of its Public Interests and Concerns; A General Meeting of the Manufacturers, was held at Etruria Inn, on Thursday the 11th day of November 1784.

Present

Josiah Wedgwood Esq.	Charles Bagnall
Messrs. Charles Chatterley	James Robison
John Hales	Walter Daniel
Jacob Warburton	Ambrose Smith
William Clowes	Joseph Smith
Hugh Booth	Thomas Shelley
George Twenlow	Richard Barker

When Mr. Wedgwood, having at the request of the Gentlemen present, taken the chair, The expediency of forming a Committee of Commerce to watch over and conduct the Public Interests and Concerns of this Manufactory, upon a Plan similar to those already adopted by many other Commercial Bodies in this Kingdom, was taken into Consideration and having been maturely weighed and discussed,

It was unanimously resolved, That it is the opinion of this Meeting that it is expedient and will be highly advantageous to this Manufactory to establish such a Committee.

It being judged necessary, that a Memorial should be drawn up and presented to the First Lord of the Treasury and the Secretary of State for Foreign Affairs, setting forth the nature and importance of this Manufactory, and praying that the interests of it may be attended to in the Treaty now negotiating between the Courts of London and Versailles, the following one [Memorial] was accordingly prepared, read, and unanimously approved, Viz.

The Manufactures of Earthen Ware in Staffordshire, being informed that a Treaty of Commerce is now Negotiating between the Courts of London and Versailles beg leave humbly to represent,

That the exportation of the Manufactures into France is at present Prohibited; although French Manufactures of a like kind are admitted into this Country upon a certain Duty,

They beg leave further to represent, That the value of their Manufacture consists altogether in the labour bestowed upon it in this Kingdom no foreign Materials being employed in it.—That it gives employment to many thousands of poor labouring people.—That it furnishes Tonnage for the Coasting Trade, all raw materials being carried several hundred miles along the Coast, from Gravesend, Tinmouth [Teignmouth, Devon], and Pool[e] in Dorsetshire, to Liverpool and Hull and from thence to the potteries by River and Canal Navigation.—That when the goods are Manufactured, they are again carried by the same Course of Navigation to every part of the Coast of this Island, as well as to every Foreign Market where we have any Commercial Intercourse, Inasmuch that scarcely a ship leave any of our Ports without more or less of this cheap and therefore important Article.

They therefore humbly hope that their Manufacture will be thought worthy of some Attention, as a national object, in the present, or any other Treaty of Commerce. For themselves they only wish, that whatever Duties the Earthen Ware of any Foreign Nations shall be admitted into this Country, theirs may be exported into the same states respectively, on the same Terms. And may they be permitted just to hint, that they apprehend high Duties upon so cheap an Article must either amount to a prohibition or encourage elicit modes of Importation, nor have they any fears from the Competition of Foreign Manufacturers upon such an arrangement taking place, being full persuaded that low duties will, in this instance, promote their Interest as well as that of the Revenue.

Ordered

That Copies of the above Memorial addressed to the Right Honourable William Pitt and the Marquis of Carmarthen be signed by the Chairman and sent to the Right Honourable Earl Gower, with a request from this Meeting that his Lordship will be pleased to present the same.

That notice of the next meeting be given to all the Principal Manufacturers, and that they be particularly desired to attend on special Affairs.

Adjourned to Thursday the 18th day of November Instant at the same place, at Ten O'Clock in the forenoon.

[signed] Jos. Wedgwood

AT A GENERAL MEETING of the Manufacturers held at Etruria Inn on Thursday the 18th day of November 1784 pursuant to adjournment, and to Notice given according to directions of the last Meeting.

Present In the Chair	Josiah Wedgwood Esq.
Messrs. Ralph Baddeley	Charles Chatterley
John Yates	Charles Bagnall
Thomas Twenlow	James Bourne
Ephraim Chatterley	Jacob Warburton
Willm. Adams, Burslem	James Robison
Joseph Warburton	John Daniel
Josiah Spode	John Hales
John Rogers	Thomas Wedgwood
Hugh Booth	

The Chairman reported That Copies of the Memorial prepared and approved at the last meeting addressed to the First Lord of the Treasury; and the Secretary of State for Foreign Affairs, had pursuant to the Order for that purpose, been signed by him, and transmitted to Lord Gower, with a request that his Lordship would be pleased to present the same.

The Resolution of the last meeting relative to the establishment of a Committee of Commerce having been read, and that measure again taken into Consideration,

The following Resolutions passed unanimously. Viz.

[1] That a general meeting of the Manufacturers be held annually at such time and place, and under such Regulations, as shall be agreed upon at the next Meeting.

[2] That the Committee of Commerce do consist of Twenty one Members; That Fourteen be now drawn by Lot out of all the Principal Manufacturers, who shall at their First Meeting elect seven others persons, or so many more as shall be necessary from Refusals to Act or otherwise, to make up the number Twenty one; and that after such Election the Committee shall be considered as a Public Body, established for the purposes before mentioned.

[3] That seven of the Committee to form a Board, and be invested with power to act in the name of the whole.

[4] That seven members of the Committee shall be changed annually, by ballot at the general Meeting.

[5] That the Committee shall keep an exact Register of all their Resolutions and Proceedings, in a book set apart for that purpose, to which every Member shall have free access, and which shall likewise be produced at all general annual Meetings.

[6] That the Resolutions and Proceedings of this and their former Meeting be entered in such a book.

The following Fourteen persons were drawn by Lot Members of the Committee, Viz.

Messrs. Thomas Twenlow
John Yates
Charles Bagnall
Benjamin Godwin
J. Wedgwood, Burslem
Elijah Mare
Taylor Brindley
Enoch Wood
James Bourne
John Prince
Richard Barker
Charles Whitehead
Daniel Mellor
John Graham

ORDERED

That Mr. James Bourne, Mr. Charles Bagnall, Mr. Ephraim Chatterley, Mr. John Hales, Mr. John Rogers and Mr. William Adams, be desired to wait upon the Principal Manufacturers in their respective Districts to communicate to them the Proceedings of this and the former Meetings to take their Sentiments thereupon, and request their Attendance at the next meeting and that they be likewise desired to acquaint the Members of the Committee with their having been drawn by Lot, and enquire whether it will be agreeable to them to attend and act in that Capacity.

[7] Messrs. Sparrow and Caldwell of Newcastle under Lyme were appointed Secretaries to the Committee.

ADJOURNED to Tuesday the 30th day of November instant, at the same place at 11 o'Clock in the Forenoon.

[signed] Jos. Wedgwood

AT A GENERAL MEETING of the Manufacturers held at Etruria Inn on Tuesday the 30th day of November 1784 Pursuant to adjournment

Present Josiah Wedgwood Esq.

In the Chair

[33 others present]

The following Letters from Right Honourable Mr. Pitt and the Marquis of Carmarthen in answer to the Memorial … were produced by the Chairman and read. …

Six of the Gentlemen who had been drawn by Lot Members of the Committee having declined acting Thirteen others were elected conformably to the directions of the last Meeting to make up the number to Twenty one and the Committee was afterwards formed of the following Members[39]

Messrs. Josiah Wedgwood
Walter Daniel
John Rogers
Hugh Booth
John Turner (Lane End)
Anthony Keeling
Ralph Baddeley
Thomas Twenlow
John Yates
Charles Bagnall

[39] Wedgwood Archives: These members evidently continued for at least a year as they are listed again in Wedgwood's commonplace book: MS E39–28408, 210.

William Clowes	Benjamin Goodwin
Jacob Warburton	Elijah Mayer
John Hayles	Richard Barker
Robert Wilson	Charles Whitehead
Charles Chatterley	John Graham
John Mare	

The Resolutions of the former Meetings were read and Unanimously approved.

Ordered

[8] That a general Quarterly Meeting of the Manufacturers be held instead of an Annual one on every last Tuesday in the Months of February, May, August, and November, and at such place as the Meeting shall from time to time appoint.

[9] That the first general quarterly Meeting be held on the last Tuesday in February at Etruria Inn.

[10] That the Secretary do at any time by Order of the Committee or at the request in writing of any seven or more of the Persons who have attended at this of the former Meetings call a Special general Meeting to be held at such time and place as they shall respectively appoint signifying at the same time the reason of such Meeting being called.

[11] That the Chairman be desired to communicate the Proceedings of this and the former Meetings to the Committee of Commerce established at Birmingham and Manchester and request their friendly Intercourse and Correspondence.

The Committee adjourned to the last Tuesday in January at Etruria Inn at 11 o'Clock in the forenoon.

[signed] Jos. Wedgwood

AT A GENERAL MEETING of the Committee held at Etruria Inn on Tuesday the 25th day of January1785 Pursuant to Adjournment

Present Josiah Wedgwood Esq.

In the Chair

Messrs. Ralph Baddeley	John Hales
John Yates	Charles Chatterley
Thomas Twenlow	Jacob Warburton
Joshua Heath	William Clowes
Hugh Booth	John Graham

...

Ordered

[12] That the persons who have expended any money in the public business or concerns of this Manufactory be applied to for their Accounts and that a general Account of such expenditure be made out and delivered to the next General Meeting

[13] That a subscription be now opened for the purpose of defraying all such Expenses and that the Overplus, if any, be applied towards the Establishment of a General Fund for the disbursement of all such expenses as shall be incurred in future on Account of the said Manufactory under the direction of the general Meetings of the Manufacturers and the Committee of Commerce. [Expenses incurred by the Manufactory, exclusive of the expenses of the Committee, were authorised to be paid at the next meeting 28 February, of £124 10s. 6d.]

[14] That such Subscription be handed through the different districts of the Manufactory by a select Body of the Committee.

The Subscription was accordingly opened by the Members of the Committee present and Messrs Chatterley. Yates. Baddeley, Warburton, Hales, Thos. Twemlow, and Heath, undertook to present the same through the Manufactory.

The Chairman produced a Letter which he had received from the Chairman of the Committee of Commerce at Manchester containing an Assurance that the proposal of a Friendly Intercourse and Correspondence which had been made pursuant to the directions of the last Meeting would be accepted with great pleasure by that Committee.

Great Loss and Inconvenience having been repeatedly sustained by the Manufactory by reason of Clays of a Quality injurious to the Manufacture being sent into the Country, It was Ordered that it be submitted to the Consideration of the next General Meeting whether it will not be expedient to appoint an Agent at the places where Clay is raised to superintend the same and to take care that none but such as is of a proper Quality for the purposes of the Manufactory be sent away. …[40]
[signed] Jos. Wedgwood

1.16 Philadelphia, Penn., Chamber of Commerce 1784

A first chamber of commerce in Philadelphia appears to have been planned in 1784, though it is not certain that this was actually implemented. The plan reproduced here is clearly a personal proposal by Tench Coxe, who was the prime mover; it is not a finalised and agreed set of rules. Coxe was a merchant who was also a leading Anglican and low-profile loyalist. The plan was to be promoted among an identified list of over 313 merchants. It sought to promote manufactures and stimulate trade. It was an attempt by the merchants after American independence explicitly to 'counter-balance' the 'country' interests in the state Congress, by supporting federalist Republicans, and

[40] The proposal was subsequently discussed many times but appears not to have been taken up.

counteracting plans to move to Confederation with greater state autonomy.[41] Additionally it was a major attempt to heal rifts between the more loyalist and radical parts of the community that had occurred during the war with Britain. It also reflects Coxe's long-standing interest in promoting manufactures in America. The documents reproduced here are the list of potential members Coxe identified, which are ff. 1–6 of his plan, ff. 9–12 which summarise the purpose of the chamber, and then on the last partially filled page (f. 12) a start on defining the powers to be invested in the chamber. Two pages (ff. 7 and 8) have not survived, which may have contained the rules or may have been blank. Most of the paragraphs stating the purpose have been contemporaneously bracketed in the left hand margin and ticked, as shown here by <> below, which have been numbered here but not in the original. The bracketing and ticking probably indicates the purposes that had been agreed in discussion with others. The two paragraphs that were not bracketed concerned arbitration and a mercantile school. It is notable that Coxe saw arbitration as a source of income to the chamber, evidencing his awareness of the free rider problem and difficulties of raising enough resources (as discussed in Chapter 6). A reconstituted chamber was formed in 1801 (not included in these documents).

Source
Tench Coxe Correspondence and General Papers, microfilm reel 46, fo. 1–6, 9–12: Historical Society of Philadelphia

A Plan for a Chamber of Commerce of Philadelphia 21 October 1784

Alphabetical list of the Merchants of the City of Philadelphia Oct. 21 1784
Made out for the purpose of forming a Chamber of Commerce.
Chamber of Commerce of Philadelphia

1st. The purpose for which it should be instituted—

<1> To unite the mercantile Body.

<2> To form a city interest, that may create some small counter-balance for the great weight of the Country interest in this state.

<3> To regulate the commissions of sales, insurance, agencies & negotiations which are extremely uncertain & various.

<4>To restore the ancient intercourse that subsisted between the different parties in the city, and by a mutual exchange of private kindness and public services to restore our old good humor, & promote the peace and interests of the state.

[41] Further discussion in Bennett, *Local Business Voice* (2011) 225; T. M. Doerflinger, *A vigorous spirit: merchants and economic development in revolutionary Philadelphia* (Chapel Hill, 1986) 275.

<5> To promote the perfection of such manufactures as are adapted to our Situation, and particularly of our principal raw staples, as wheat, Ind[ia]n corn, Hemp, Iron, lumber &c., all of which are carried on to a very beneficial degree, &c. are exported to our great advantage. In considering thus the saving of the dear articles of labor, provisions, & may be effected in a great measure by the use of water works. This Country, the middle States especially, abounds with mill seats, and appears to me that it would be very useful to have a return made of all the mill Seats <u>near</u> this city [location of mills], or upon navigable waters within 50 miles of it. What would be the effect of premiums for the best flour &c.

<6> To increase the facility of bringing our produce to market by the improvement of our fine waters the Delaware & Schuylkill, as well as our other rivers, & our roads; also by making Canals.

To form something which perhaps might be properly enough called their Merchants Court, to adjust disputes arising among Mercantile men. This is an important object in point of convenience. The duty falls heavy now upon a few, who can [act as arbitrators] through a good deal of it. It might be well to arrange this Matter so that the parties might pay something to the referees or to the public or both. In London, tis said, the sum of 5 guineas per Right has been often charged, and that for each referee.[42] This must be in capital Business; much larger than the Sums to which transactions usually run here. It might also form a source from which an annual income might be drawn to defray the contingent expenses of the Chamber.

<7> The fisheries of this country require our particular attention & I think would pay Us well for it. If the French & English can make that trade do so far from home as Newf[oun]dland Mosquito [? meaning the fishing banks off Mosquito, spelling unclear], & the New England States, at Cape Horn I cannot see an impediment in our Way.

<8> To ascertain the line that should be drawn between our own Vessels & those of Foreigners, and lay the same before the assembly of the states—This cannot be so well done as by the Merchants & a few cannot do it so well as the collected body. Besides as long as it continues only generally interesting to all individuals alike, no one will take the lead. This would not be the Case if it fell to the turn [of] 28 or 30 [as a chamber board] to exert themselves in convenience with their Engagements.

<9> A constant general correspondence between the Mercantile bodies of this & other of our Cities upon new discoveries in trade or the arts must be very useful. Every new regulation, measure or Scheme adopted in any

[42] This may refer to Weskett's London chamber, the plan for which was published two years earlier in 1782, and copies of which certainly reached America; it sought to charge such fees: see chapter 6.1.

place should be provided in its digested form from one to another: it would therefore be very useful to have such a Chamber in New York, Boston, Baltimore, Charleston &c.

<10> Attention should be paid to making use [of] some public property belonging to the Merchants—for the purpose of building Coffee houses, Exchanges &c. which never can be begun till they are collected into a body. But were they a body it would soon follow.

The Chamber of Commerce might in my opinion institute a very useful Mercantile School in which should be taught the modes of calculating the exchange, weights, & measures of foreign Countries, tonnage of Ships and the quantity of the various kinds of goods they would carry—the different kinds of manufactures or other modes of manufacture by samples.

2ndly. The powers which should be invested in the Society & the Board of Directors—also the duties of the Pres[iden]t, Directors & other Officers—and the qualifications, which they should be required to possess. [rest of page blank, hence details left undeveloped]

1.17 Leeds Chamber of Commerce 1785

The first Leeds chamber was founded in March 1785. Its first minuted meeting was held on 27 April, with its main business being the postal service and the 'shameful practices that prevail amongst the Mill Searchers of false stamping of cloth and coatings' which it sought to suppress. A minute of 26 October 1785 resolved to take offenders to JPs for prosecution. There were rules drafted by committee (reported to a general meeting on 23 March), but these do not survive. However, the surviving minutes for 1785–93 give indications of what the rules must have been.[43] There was a gap between 15 June 1787 and 27 October 1788; then meetings resumed approximately monthly until a gap from 5 January to 19 May 1789; then a large gap between 28 May 1790 and 17 April 1793. The chamber then appears to have lapsed until its modern foundation in 1851. Some newspaper reports give a small amount of other detail. From the surviving information the following rules are clear:

1. Officers elected: Chairman; no mention of vice chairman.
2. Secretary appointed.
3. Secretary acted as Treasurer

[43] Leeds University Library: Leeds chamber of commerce minute Book, MS Dep. 1951/1; see also M. Beresford, *The Leeds Chamber of Commerce* (Leeds, 1951) 12–22.

4. Committee elected, probably of five members. No further election reported after 1785 so election appears to have run for a period of years, perhaps like the Manchester Committee of Trade 1774–81.
5. Fixed general meetings of its committee, probably monthly
6. Committee meetings probably weekly (though becoming irregular), and as required.
7. Appointed delegates to act for it.
8. Major petitions or public positions had to be referred to a general meeting
9. No requirement to publicise meetings in local press, so secretary must have sent personal notices.
10. Invited delegates to attend its committee and general meetings from nearby towns: including Rochdale, Wakefield, and Saddleworth.
11. Cooperated with other chambers through General Chamber of Manufactures, and bilaterally.

Source
Leeds Mercury

Report 22 March 1785[a]

A General Meeting of the Merchants and Manufacturers of this Town and neighbourhood and towns adjacent is to be held this afternoon to take into consideration the present Commercial Treaty with Ireland and other matters of importance to the trade in general.

Tomorrow General Meeting is to be held at the Old King's Head to receive the report of the Committee appointed at a late General Meeting to prepare Heads and Regulations for the Establishment of a Chamber of Commerce.

Jer. Dixon, Mayor

1.18 Boston, Mass., Chamber of Commerce 1785 (and BSETC 1764)

The first body formally adopting the title 'chamber' in Boston was formed in 1785 after the American War, for which the rules are reproduced here. However, like many other places, this first chamber drew from an earlier body. This was the Boston Society for Encouraging Trade and Commerce (BSETC) established in 1733. This body undertook chamber-like functions to promote the trade of the area. But it also had political objectives, founded primarily to resist the Molasses Act. A reconstitution in 1764 was again primarily designed as a resistance body against renewal of the Act, as the Sugar Act of 1764. However, in both 1733 and 1764 it appears to have had a wider remit to encourage trade and commerce. By 1764 it definitely had formal governance procedures and broad lobby objectives, and in most respects acted as a de facto chamber.[44]

No copy of the first rules of BSETC for 1733 has been found, but its title was reaffirmed and the new 'Rules and Orders' agreed in April 1764 are reproduced here as an example of an early predecessor of a chamber. It is likely that the 1764 rules were similar to those of 1733, but adapted and extended to the new circumstances. The evidence of correspondence about the 1764 Society's activities in the papers of Ezekiel Price, one of its leading members, shows it was concerned among other things with promoting fisheries, hemp spinning of 'duck' textiles, extending the bleaching industry, and regulating the rates paid for spinning and weaving (reasserting and extending rates previously agreed in 1756). In 1768 it also was the leader of subscriptions to help the poor, drafting proposals for employing the poor in local manufacturing, and employing poor women and children.[45] This was partly linked to overcoming hardships as a result of promoting the non-importation ban against imports from Britain. As well as becoming a general promotional body for the leading merchants, it became the main Boston organisation to operate as a non-importation committee and develop other resistance to British legislation in the run-up to the American rebellion. This became an increasingly political and radical process.[46]

The 1764 rules reproduced here show that its governance and purpose was exclusively mercantile and non-political; hence the tensions as the pressure from radicals built up. A committee had been constituted on 14 April to draft the rules. The papers reproduced here constitute a note of 21 April, which appears to refer to the meeting where the committee's draft 'Rules and Orders' were agreed, with the election of officers deferred until 28 April, one week later. A few amendments or additions to the text shown here can be assumed to have been added at the 28 April General Meeting, and thus the

[44] C. McL. Andrews, 'The Boston merchants and the non-importation movement', *Transactions of the Colonial Society of Massachusetts*, XIX (1916) 159–259; J. W. Tyler, *Smugglers and patriots: Boston merchants and the advent of the American Revolution* (Boston, 1986) 161–5.
[45] Massachusetts Historical Society: Ezekiel Price papers.
[46] BSETC was initially a moderating voice but was overwhelmed by local radical leaders. Using Tyler's data, I have shown BSETC members moved from accommodation to breakdown with radicals at the point of the 'Solemn League and Covenant' in 1774. Only 15 per cent of BSETC members were willing to sign this. Where known, 22 per cent of BSETC members became 'loyalist', of which 16 per cent supported British occupation under General Gage, 13 per cent were declared to have been loyalists after British withdrawal, and 14 per cent were subsequently banished by the State of Massachusetts, compared to 42 per cent that became patriots, with the remainder neutral or unknown: Tyler, *Smugglers and patriots* (1986) appendix; Bennett, *Local Business Voice* (2011) Table 4.3.

document constitutes the final rules adopted. The sequence of the other Ezekiel Price papers makes it clear that the papers are almost certainly for 1764, but may be for 1763. The formality and structure of the process, and its emphasis on harmony and exclusion of political issues is identical to most early chambers.

The 1785 rules reproduced also derive from the Ezekiel Price papers, with gaps left to fill in subsequently agreed details. They indicate that the draft was intended as an interim document on which to base a charter to be sought from the State of Massachusetts. The initial text refers to 'the Office', which implies that an organisation already existed, which was presumably the continued BSTEC in some form. It also implies that an operation was underway that was probably already delivering most of the activity listed in the rules; e.g. commercial arbitration. The 1785 chamber was probably only limited in its activities and was reconstituted in 1794 (see later below).

Source
Ezekiel Price papers: Massachusetts Historical Society

Loose single sheet with handwritten note, f. 73 (item 22) 21 April 1764

Voted that we choose our Chairman & Officers at the Next Meeting.
Voted that this meeting be adjourned to 28 April at 7 o'clock afternoon.

Articles and Rules, handwritten copy, ff. 75–8 (items 23–24); 21 April, with subsequent amendments on 28 April 1764

The Committee appointed by the Company at their Meeting of the 14th Instant, to draw up some general Rules and Orders for their Government do report as follows.

That the Company form themselves into a Society, by the Name of The Boston Society for Encouraging Trade and Commerce within the Province of the Massachusetts Bay.

That this Society shall consist of Merchants and others concerned in Commerce, and of any other Persons of Ability and Knowledge in Trade, who may be desirous to encourage the same.

That there shall be a General Meeting of the Society some time in the Month of April or May Annually, to consider of the State of Trade and to determine upon any Matters relative thereto, that shall be laid before them, And that the particular Day of such General Meeting, shall be appointed by the Standing Committee for the time being.

That at the General Meeting a Chairman shall be chosen by written Votes (The greatest Number of Votes to determine the Choice) Whose Business shall be to moderate at the Meetings and put the Questions, to be determined by Vote: At such Meeting a Clerk also shall be chosen to minute down the Proceedings, & record the Votes of the Society.

That Business may be carried on with greater Decency & Order, any Member who may have anything to propose, shall address himself to the Chairman, and Care shall be taken to avoid as much as possible, all Party disputes, & every Thing that may tend in any Measure to dissolve the Union of the Society, or to interrupt the good Harmony which ought to subsist among the Members of it.

That at the General Meeting annually, there shall be a Standing Committee chosen consisting of fifteen (of whom 9 shall be a Quorum).[47] The Members of which Committee shall be chosen singly by written Vote the Majority of Voters to determine the Choice.

That this Committee shall meet together Monthly (or oftener if they see Cause) to consult upon the Affairs of Trade, to take Notice of any Thing which may be judged prejudicial to it, & to receive any Proposals that may be made for its Advantage, and shall make Report of the same to the general Meeting, to be acted upon there as shall be judged proper.

That the Standing Committee (if they think there is sufficient Reason therefor) may occasionally call a General Meeting of the Society, at which Meeting the Business shall be regulated and carried on, in the same manner as at the stated Annual Meetings.

That upon Request in writing subscribed by Twenty or more of the Members (without assigning any Special Reason) The Committee shall call a General Meeting.

That the Committee either in the public News Papers or some other Way, as they shall judge most proper shall cause Notice to be given of the Time and Place of the General Meetings two Days at least before the Same.

That any Persons of other Towns in the Province who are Friends to Trade & desiring to advance the Interest thereof, ~~and who may be in Town~~ at any Time when the Standing Committee meets, may be invited to be present with them.

That at every General Meeting any Member present shall before he departs leave with the Clerk a pistareen[48] or what the Company shall deem sufficient in order to defray the Expenses of the Meeting: And the Clerk shall account with the Society, for what he receives.

That the Tavern Expenses of Committees shall be born[e] by themselves; but all other Charges which ~~they~~ may [be *added*] incur[ed *added*] for the

[47] The numbers 15 and 9 added subsequent to the original draft in a space left for the purpose, presumably agreed on 28 April.

[48] Pistareen subsequently added in a space left for the purpose; this was a small Spanish silver coin.

Service of the Society, shall be defrayed by the whole. An Account of which shall be laid before the Society at their Annual Meeting.[49]

That any Person who shall Subscribe his Name to the foregoing Articles shall be deemed a Member of this Society.

[signed by 145 members; see partial list at http://www.geog.cam.ac.uk/research/projects/chambersofcommerce/boston–1763–76.pdf]

Articles: ff. 391A–401 (item 103); many pages blank for 'remarks' 7 July 1785

Articles for Conducting a Chamber of Commerce submitted to the Gentlemen of the Office for their Inspection and Remarks.

CHAMBER OF COMMERCE

Whereas advantages may be desir'd to the Merchants, Traders, & Manufacturers of this Commonwealth as well as to the Community at large from the Establishment of a Chamber of Commerce in the Metropolis in which the collected Wisdom & Experience of the Trade might be applied both to the Adjustment of matters of a commercial Nature in Controversy between any of the Members, & to the forming necessary general regulations; tending on the one hand to promote Trusting Fidelity, Oeconomy & Punctuality, & to prevent or expose every species of Fraud & Imposition in mercantile Transactions; and on the other [hand] to avoid all unnecessary Perplexity, Litigation & Expense: We the Subscribers do agree to become members of such a Chamber upon the following Plan, Viz.

Article 1st. That the Chamber shall consist of Merchants & others concerned in Trade, with such Gentlemen as have retried from Business.

The Chamber shall be organised in Conformity to an Act of Incorporation, to be obtained of the Legislature, for that Purpose.

2d. At the first Meeting the Officers of the Chamber shall be chosen, Viz. one President, one Vice President, twenty five Directors, one Treasurer & one Secretary—the choice to be renew'd on the first Wednesday in April next ensuing & to be made on the first Wednesday in April annually forever.

All Elections shall be by Ballot & determined by the Votes of two thirds of the Members present.

At the first Meeting of the Chamber each Member shall pay to the Treasurer ten Spanish milled Dollars to be appropriated as the Chamber shall direct.

3d. Four of the Directors with the President or one of the Vice Presidents shall meet once at least in every Week to receive Communications & Complaints & to arrange & prepare Business for the monthly meetings of the Directors & for the stated meetings of the Chamber. They shall also by

[49] This last sentence subsequently added, presumably on 28 April.

themselves or suitable Persons to be by them appointed, hear & determine as far as may be convenient to them all the Cases [for arbitration] of a Commercial Nature which shall be submitted to them by any of the Members—making report to the Directors each Month of such Cases as have been left undecided upon by them or by the Referees by them appointed; & the Directors shall take Cognizance thereof, & the same order thereon, as though the same had been Originally submitted to them by the Parties.

4. The President, Vice President & Directors shall meet once in every Month & may continue their Meeting by adjournment—Not less than fourteen shall constitute a Quorum for doing Business.

The President, or in his absence, the Vice President or the first Director shall always moderate at the Meetings of the Directors & of the Chamber & whoever may preside shall have a casting vote. The Directors shall at their Meetings make & pass such Rules & Orders relating to Commerce as they shall think proper & may be competent to; to be from Time to Time laid before the Chamber at their next stated Meetings, and not to continue in Force unless approved by at least two thirds of the Members present.—They shall also by themselves or suitable Persons to be by them appointed hear & determine all such controverted Matters in Commerce between any of the Members as they shall desire to have settled by Reference [referees], in Conformity to such Rules as shall be established by the Chamber—the Parties to lay the same before the sitting Directors of the Week, fourteen days at least before the monthly meeting of the Directors. The Vice President when not in the chair shall always sit & act as a Director.

5. The Sitting of the Directors for the purpose mentioned in the 3rd Article shall be in alphabetical Rotation & of four Gentlemen in & for each month: Excepting that at the expiration of the first Month the two first named shall go out & the two next in the Order aforesaid shall come in & so on from Month to Month through each Year.

6. Any Gentleman appointed an Arbitrator or Referee and having served within _____ Weeks, & refusing, unless for just & satisfactory Causes, shall be considered as withdrawing himself from the Chamber—and any Member refusing Compliance with the Rules & orders which shall be agreed upon by the Chamber, or to abide by the Decisions of the Directors, or the Referees by them appointed, shall be expelled [from] the Chamber, and be rendered ever after inadmissible.

7. The Chamber shall be convened twice in every year after the first meeting Viz. on the first Wednesday in April & on the first Wednesday in October, at which time the Proceedings of the President & Directors shall be communicated; the Rules & Orders made & passed by them either confirmed or refuted [possibly 'repealed']; new Members admitted; the Treasurer's Accounts adjusted; Provision made for paying the Debts of the Chamber if

any, or surplus stock, if any, appropriated; Vacancies in the several Chamber offices filled up & such other Business transacted relating to Commerce & to the Chamber as shall be thought expedient. The President or Vice President or in their absence the first Director may convene the Chamber oftener if necessary & may adjourn the several meetings if Business require it.

At the half yearly Meetings each Member shall pay to the Treasurer two Spanish milled Dollars to be appropriated as the Chamber shall direct.

Article 8. No Person after the first Meeting of the Chamber shall be admitted but at the general stated meetings, Nor then unless he shall have given in his Name and Desire of Admission to the Directors at the Monthly Meeting next immediately preceding the same.

Each new Member shall pay to the Treasurer ten Spanish milled Dollars on his Admission.

9. In Order to promote punctual Attendance at the several Meetings of the Chamber & of the Directors the President shall reasonably notify by Advertisement in the Public Newspapers the stated Meetings of the Chamber; & shall also send a written Notification to the Dwelling Houses of the Directors three Days before each such Meeting & one Day before each monthly meeting—And every Member not attending the Chamber at the calling the List which shall be done by the Secretary at ____ o'Clock at each meeting, shall forfeit & pay to the Treasurer the Sum of _____. If absent the whole of the Time of the Meeting the Sum of _____. The same at Adjournments.

10. In Cases of the Absence of one or more of the Directors the Vacancy or Vacancies shall on Notice given by the Gentleman who may preside at the Meeting be supplied by the next Director or Directors in the Alphabetical Course aforesaid—who shall not be unavoidably prevented from attending.

11. All Fines shall be collected by the Treasurer & not remitted but by the Vote of at least two thirds of the Directors present at the next monthly Meeting.

12. The Treasurer shall keep a fair set of Books containing regular Accounts of all Monies received by him, & all Appropriations & Payments & shall balance them once in six months & lay the same before the Chamber at every stated Meeting for Examination.

Fines to be entered in a Petty Ledger & not transferred to the Cash Account until decided upon by the Directors.

13. The Secretary of his Deputy shall always be present at the Meetings of the Directors & of the Chamber & shall keep a fair Record of the Acts of Incorporation & of all subsequent Statutes relating to the Chamber & of the Proceedings of the President & Directors & shall lay the same on the Table at every stated Meeting.

1.19 [General Chamber of Manufactures 1785: see Chapter 8]

1.20 Edinburgh Chamber of Commerce & Manufactures 1785; also see charter 1786 in Chapter 2

The chamber was first proposed by David Steuart, who called a meeting on 9 November 1785 to gain support for a plan. A committee was established to prepare the plan, chaired by William Creech. It reported in December with a set of purposes and rules, reproduced below. It had support from the leading figures of Edinburgh, including the Earl of Rosebery and almost all leading Edinburgh bankers. It was one of the chambers most interconnected with bank directors.[50] David Steuart was a leading private banker (Allan & Steuarts), described as the leading spirit of the chamber, whilst William Creech was a leading local bookseller. It initially had ambitions to be a chamber with the title *General Chamber of Commerce & Manufactures for Scotland*. This mirrored the proposals current at the time for the General Chamber in England. The existing Glasgow chamber objected to this title, which was modified in order to receive consent for Edinburgh's charter (see Chapter 2).[51]

Source
Reprinted papers in *A Brief Account of the Rise, Progress, & Present Position of the Chamber of Commerce & Manufactures in the City of Edinburgh*, printed by the chamber 1861: National Library of Scotland, pp. iv–vii.

Printed notice 21 December 1785

Report of the Committee.

SCOTLAND, which in times past could scarcely be considered in any other light than that of a warlike nation, has of late years made rapid advances in trade and manufactures. The great body of the people, while under a feudal system, were engaged either in national contests or in civil broils. Commerce and the arts of peace were little cultivated: and absence from the field was generally passed in indolence, and improvement lost in inactivity. Those days, however, are now happily over; and the present spirit of trade, and of rising manufactures, which actuates this country, must be highly pleasing to every patriotic mind. To support and regulate this growing spirit of industry becomes an object of national concern; and it will be felt as a duty by every good citizen.

[50] Bennett, 'Network interlocks' (2013).
[51] See Bennett, *Local Business Voice* (2011) 164–5.

If ever there was a time when attention to Trade and Manufactures was necessary, it is the present; at the end of an expensive war, with an enormous load of national debt, heavy taxes upon every article of life or convenience, and the treaties of commerce with *Ireland*, *France*, and *America*, unsettled.

It is only by united virtue, and united industry, that such a situation can be raised to prosperity and eminence; and Societies of men exerting their efforts to this noble purpose, deserve the applause of every well-wisher of his country.

It must be obvious that a Society of Merchants and Manufacturers, with united liberal views, may be highly useful to Commerce. They may, as a body, establish plans and systems that may greatly contribute to improvement, and check others that might be detrimental: but which, as individuals, they would neither have planned, nor had ability to execute.

The increase and improvement of Trade and Manufactures is also deeply connected with the landed Property; and every advancement in the first has an evident tendency to promote the interest of the latter.

The protection and encouragement of Commerce and Manufacturers, and the rules and practices of Merchants, have hitherto been little attended to in the code of our municipal laws. It was even lately found, that the sinking of ships wilfully could not be punished as felony; and this crime, so daring in itself, and detrimental to the interests of Commerce, only received a slight arbitrary punishment.

An united body of Merchants and Manufacturers, whose rules are understood among themselves, have it in their power to prevent tedious and expensive litigations, the bane of harmony and industry. They have it also in their power to bring forward important questions; to apply for laws for the good of the whole, which no divided or separated interest could do with effect. They have it in their power to suggest new improvements, and to give aid to such as are worthy of pursuit; to assist the views of Parliament, in so far as they may be beneficial to the country; or to point out mistaken or partial measures that might be hurtful.

In short, to give spirit and vigour to Commerce and Manufactures; assistance to genius and industry; to protect the just rights of individuals; to encourage the active, and discourage the idle; are objects which have a manifest tendency to render a people great, prosperous, and happy: And such are the avowed purposes of the present Institution.

The good effects of such Societies are conspicuous in the examples of those Chambers of Commerce that have been already established in different parts of *Great Britain*; and it is to be hoped that similar good effects will soon result from the establishment of one in *Edinburgh*.

But the success of every institution, however well intended, must depend, in a great measure, upon the laws that are formed for its regulation. The

following rules have been approved of, for present direction; and it is to be hoped that they will contribute to promote the interests of Trade and Manufactures in this part of the *United Kingdom*.
William Creech, Chairman.

Rules—also see Charter 1786 21 December 1785

I. That every Merchant, Manufacturer, or Trader, residing in *Scotland*, shall have a right to become a Member of this Chamber, on his paying into the hands of the Treasurer for the time being, the sum of Two Guineas at the time of his admission, and the further sum of One Guinea annually, on the first *Monday* of *January* of every year, so long as he chooses to continue a Member. And any person paying the Chamber the sum of Ten Guineas shall be deemed a Member of the same for life, without being subjected to any future payments.

II. That any Member who chooses to vacate his place may do so at pleasure, on giving such intimation to the Secretary. Every member who fails to pay his annual subscription on or before *Candlemas* shall *ipso facto* be considered to have withdrawn.

III. That no person so withdrawing shall ever have it in his power again to become a Member of the Chamber, or be entitled to any of the benefits of the institution; nor shall any practitioner in law, although a Merchant or Manufacturer, have it in his power to become a Member of this Chamber on any account whatever.

IV. That the business of the Chamber shall be conducted by a Chairman, two Deputy Chairman, and thirty Directors. The Chairman, or one of the Deputies, and twelve Directors to be a quorum.

V. That the six senior Directors shall go out of office annually, and six others be elected in their room:—Also, the Chairman and the two Deputy Chairman to go out of office alternately, one of them each year; the vacancies to be filled up by the Members at large, and the seniority to be determined at the first election.

VI. That a Secretary shall be appointed, who must be a Member of the Chamber, and whose business shall be to keep the books and papers belonging to the Chamber, to write the minutes, and to carry on correspondence.

VII. That there shall be a Treasurer, who must likewise be a Member of the Chamber, who shall keep an account of all the moneys received and paid out by the Chamber; and he shall pay whatever money he may receive from time to time into the *Royal* Bank of *Scotland*, or such Bank or Banker as the Members shall from time to time direct, whenever the same shall amount to Fifty Pounds Sterling.

VIII. That there shall be five Members, not in the direction, named to audit the Treasurer's accompts, three to be a quorum.

IX. That there shall be a General Meeting of the Members held at *Edinburgh*, annually, on the *Monday* preceding the Convention of the *Royal Boroughs*, for the purpose of choosing a Chairman, or Deputy Chairman, as the vacancy may happen; six Directors in room of those going out; five Auditors; a Secretary, and a Treasurer, which two last offices are to be filled up every year, and the persons holding them may either be continued or removed, as the Members shall think fit.

X. That all elections shall be made by ballot.

XI. That there shall be another General Meeting held on the third *Wednesday of January* every year, for the special purpose of reading the Minutes of the Chamber, and giving such other general directions as shall to the meeting, or to the majority, appear proper.

XII. That any fifteen Members, not in the direction, may call a General Meeting whenever they think proper, on their giving ten day's previous notice by advertisement in the *Edinburgh* newspapers.

XIII. That every order for money must be signed by the Chairman, or a Deputy Chairman, and three Directors, in presence of a quorum, and the same minuted by the Secretary.

XIV. That every Member shall have a right to inspect the Minutes, by applying to the Secretary on the *Wednesday* of every week, between the hours of noon and three o'clock in the afternoon, but at no other time, unless by order of three Directors.

XV. That all questions which come before the Chamber, shall be decided by a majority of votes; and in case of an equality, the Chairman shall have a casting vote, besides his own.

XVI. That the Directors shall not have it in their power to contract any debt in name of the Chamber, on any pretence whatever; but shall have it in their power to engage the funds of the Society for the purposes of its institution.

XVII. That the Chairman or Deputy may call a Meeting of Directors whenever the same is thought to be necessary.—All Meetings are to be held in *Edinburgh*, in such room or hall as the Directors may appoint.

XVIII. That an account of the proceedings of the Directors shall be printed annually, and a copy sent to every Member.

XIX. That any additions or alterations to the present rules may be made by a General Meeting.

1.21 [Nottingham Chamber of Commerce 1785–7: see Chapter 4.3]

1.22 ['Chamber of Manufacturers at Perth'][52]

1.23 Waterford Chamber of Commerce 1787; see also charter 1815 in Chapter 2

Outline rules for the chamber are recorded in the minute book for 30 March 1787 as the first surviving minute, which appears to be the first recorded meeting. However, two pages are missing at the start of the book and these may have contained the first rules or earlier minutes. In the document below the outline rules are summarised, together with subsequent amendments. The chamber was reconstituted in 1804 after a period of little (recorded) activity. A charter was sought and granted in 1815 (see Chapter 2).

Source
Waterford chamber minutes: Waterford Archives, WCOC 1/01

Minutes 30 March 1787

1. Minutes to be kept in a proper book.
2. Committee (probably of 12) to be elected every year at annual meeting.
3. Chair elected at general meeting.
4. Chamber Committee to meet in the Coffee Room at the Exchange every week.
5. A fine of 1s. to be levied for non-attendance unless excuse accepted by majority of Committee.
6. Regularly consult members and representatives [MPs] to know if Bills are pending in House of Commons.
7. Collect subscriptions, which were initially set at voluntary level.

Minutes 6 April 1787

8. Special subscription to be raised to establish a fund to suppress smuggling

Minutes 20 April 1787

9. More subscriptions needed; to be set at a minimum of half a guinea.

[52] Glasgow Mitchell Library: referred to in Glasgow chamber minutes, 20 February 1785 in relation to a memorial on the Irish proposals: no other information available.

10. A Committee member in person or a clerk to attend chamber's room every Tuesday and Friday 1.30 to 2.30 'to transact bill business', with a fine of 1s. for non-attendance.

Minutes 27 April 1787

11. 'Finding that a few individuals [members] have been called on as arbitrators which interferes with their business, to refer requests to the Committee' which will meet every week on Fridays to act as arbitrators.

Minutes 11 December 1795

12. Committee number increased to 18 plus chairman.

1.24 Londonderry (Derry) Chamber of Commerce 1790

There are no surviving Rules for the first Londonderry chamber, but a few surviving documents give insights into its aims and organisation. Its foundation is given as July 1790 in a 1793 publication by the chamber. A petition of November 1790 (see Chapter 5) demonstrates a concern with Customs duties. Londonderry had a locally special case of a corporation appointed by the City Corporation of London, the so-called 'Irish Society' of London deriving from a charter of 1662 that constituted 26 citizens of London into a 'plantation society'.[53] Most were absentee and never visited. This author argues that the foundation of the chamber in 1790 reflected efforts by the Irish Society to exert stronger control, annoyance about local abuses of tolls and fishing, as well as more general ferment and attacks on landlords in Donegal.[54] However the chief concern of the chamber was the parliamentary electoral franchise and its control by two major families, the Hills and Alexanders.[55] In July 1830 the chamber repeated its efforts to improve local administration by putting pressure on the Irish Society by obtaining a legal opinion on the charter, following a dispute over a mayoral election.[56]

[53] See J. S. Curl, *The Honourable The Irish Society and the plantation of Ulster, 1608–2000* (Chichester, 2000).

[54] Bennett, *Local Business Voice* (2011) 209–10.

[55] D Murphy, *Derry, Donegal and Modern Ulster, 1790–1921* (Londonderry, 1981), Chapter 1; Municipal Commission, Ireland (1837) *Parliamentary Papers*, XXVI, 16 and 191–3.

[56] Londonderry chamber (1830) *Case relative to the elective franchise in Londonderry, with the opinion of Mr. Harrison, taken on behalf of the chamber of commerce*, BL: 8139.df.35/1(1.).

Source
Translation of the Charter Granted by King Charles II To the Mayor and Community and Citizens of the City of London-Derry, Carefully Compared with the Original in the Roll's Office, Dublin, and Published by the Direction of the Chamber of Commerce, London-Derry, W. Haseltine, 1793: BL general collection 1384.f.10; also ESTC.

Printed pamphlet Londonderry Chamber, May 1793

To the Citizens of London-Derry.

In the month of July 1790, a respectable number of the Merchants and Traders of this City associated as a Chamber of Commerce—They were actuated by a sincere desire to promote the interest of Trade; they hoped, by the union of men of commercial knowledge, to render the institution useful to their Fellow Citizens; and, they feel satisfaction in reflecting, that their exertions have not been altogether fruitless.

Sensible that it was the right of the Citizens of Derry to enquire into their privileges, the Chamber of Commerce deemed it their duty to procure an authentic copy of the Charter granted by King Charles the Second "to the Mayor and Community and Citizens of London-Derry," which having been accordingly obtained, directions were given to publish a Translation of it, in order that every Freeman might have an opportunity of knowing his just Rights and Franchises.

The Chamber of Commerce have now the pleasure of offering to their Fellow Citizens a correct translation of their Charter; and they flatter themselves, that the whole Incorporation will be well pleased to see, in a plain English dress, the important instrument by which they are entitled to so many valuable privileges.

The Chamber of Commerce have only to add, that in publishing this translation of the Charter, it is their earnest wish to promote that union, and strengthen that harmony, which have so long prevailed in this City; and they trust, that the strong interest which they are known to have in its happiness and prosperity, will be deemed a convincing proof of the purity of their motives, and the rectitude of their conduct.

1.25 Manchester Commercial Society 1794

The Manchester Commercial Society of 1794 succeeded the Manchester Committee of Trade of 1774–c.1786 after a lapsed period. There was probably little direct link to the earlier body as it was primarily occupied with different tasks, operated in a more democratic and chamber-like way, and was primarily made up of members trading in Europe who were stressed during the French wars. A formal minute book survives with a formal set of rules minuted. This was succeeded by the first body formally titled a chamber in 1820 between which there is clear evidence of continuity (see later).

Source
Commercial Society of Merchants, minute: Manchester Central Library GB127 M8/1/1–2

Minute 27 February 1794

Proceedings of an adjourned Meeting of the Commercial Society of Merchants trading On the Continent of Europe held this day at Spencer's Tavern to discuss the Rules for the Society agreeable to the Resolutions of the last meeting. Mr. James Entwisle Chairman [and twenty other members present].

The following Propositions and Rules were made and agreed unanimously.

The Commercial Society of Merchants Trading on the Continent of Europe for the following Purposes. viz.

1st. To resist and prevent as much as possible the Depredation Committed on Mercantile Property in Foreign Parts, detect Swindlers, expose Chicaners, and Persons void of Principle and Honour in their Dealings.

2nd. To adopt such Regulations as may tend to the Benefit of their Trade, add to its Safety and promote more regular Payments.

3rd. To watch over the Interest of their Trade at Large and co-operate jointly in all Applications to Government or in any Measure, which may from time to time be thought necessary for the Good of the Whole.

And in order to support and conduct this Society with Respectability and promote Confidence with every one of its Members the following Rules are adopted as the Fundamental Principle of its Establishment.

1st. This Society shall elect Annually one of its Members to be President who shall be chosen by a written Majority of Members present, and that one Gentleman only of any Firm shall be allowed to vote for the Election of the President, such first Election to take place at the next Meeting of this Society.

2nd. In the Absence of the President at any of the meetings of this Society, a Chairman shall be appointed for the Day out of the Members then present, who shall cause the Proceedings of such Meeting to be reported to the President.

3rd. At the next Meeting a Person shall be appointed Secretary for one Year, to transact the Business of this Society under the Direction of the President with an Allowance of Twenty Pounds.

4th. Any Candidate who may hereafter wish to become a Member of this Society shall be proposed at one of its ordinary Meetings, be balloted for at the next, and that three fourths of white Balls be necessary for his Admission.

5th. This Society shall regularly meet every first Thursday in the Month at Ten O'clock in the Forenoon.

6th. The President shall have the Power to call extraordinary Meetings, whenever he is requested by Five or more of the Members.

The above Rules having passed unanimously, it was Resolved

That: This meeting be adjourned to the Sixth Day of March at Ten O'clock in the Forenoon, to be held at Spencer's Tavern for the further Discussion of Business, and that a printed Notice of the Adjournment be sent to each Member, acquainting him, that a President and Secretary will be appointed on that Day at which time his Attendance is requested.
Jas. Entwisle

Minute 6 March 1794

Proceedings of an adjourned Meeting of the Commercial Society of Merchants trading on the Continent of Europe held this day at Spencer's Tavern to discuss the Rules for the further discussion of business. Mr. James Entwisle Chairman [and 19 other members present].

The following Rules in Addition to those proposed at the last Meeting were formed and unanimously agreed upon.

Rule 7th. Every Firm or House admitted into this Society shall pay Annually the Sum of Two Guineas to form a Fund to defray the necessary Expenses which may be incurred, and if on account of any extra and unavoidable Expenses the Disbursements should exceed the Fund raised by this Yearly Subscription, every such Firm or House shall pay its quota to make up the Deficiency at the end of the Year.

8th. The frequent Depredations committed upon Trade, the Chicanery, and want of Regularity we have experienced, render it highly expedient that every Member of this Society be recommended to give up such Correspondents as are found guilty of unjustifiable Abatements, Chicanery, Prolongation of Payments beyond the time actually agreed by the Parties, or any other unmercantile Proceedings whatever.

Rule 9th. After the Society have found the Complaints alleged against such a House on the best Information they can obtain to be well founded, the same shall be entered in the Book of this Society with the Ground of Complaint.

10th. The Pretensions of the Merchants abroad in making the Exporters suffer a Loss by the Exchange on their Remittances being against all Mercantile Laws ought to be and must be uniformly resisted.

11th. This Society ought to consider it as a firm and fundamental Principle of Trade, that they sell their Goods here (in England) in English Measure, Weight, and Money, and are no ways responsible for the Fluctuation in the Exchange, and that their Goods once shipped become the absolute Property of those who ordered them.

[President, Charles Frederick Brandt, then elected by majority of votes for current year]
Jas Entwisle Chairman.

Minute 13 March 1794

Proceedings of a Meeting of the Commercial Society of Merchants trading on the Continent of Europe held this day at Spencer's Tavern. Mr. Charles Fred. Brandt President [and 29 other members present].

John Orme was elected Secretary for one Year.

Resolved that President be Treasurer for the current year, and that the Subscriptions for the present year be immediately paid.

That the absentees from this meeting be waited upon by the Secretary for their Subscriptions.

Resolved unanimously:

That the Secretary shall not suffer any Books or Papers belonging to this Society to be taken out of his hands by any Person whatever except the President nor inspected but by such as are Members of the Society.

The Rule which was denominated the 10th and proposed at the Meeting of the Society on the 6th instant with the Amendment as transcribed below, the Discussion of which was postponed to the Day having been read, the previous Question on both was moved, seconded and carried unanimously.

Rule 10. That after a Member of this Society has made a Charge against any one of his Correspondents, and the Matter he has brought against him has been found deserving of his being entered in the Book of the Society; no Member of this Society who was not in actual Correspondence with the Person or House so charged prior to the Complaints being made,[57] shall execute any Orders he may receive from such House, until the Matter in Dispute be settled or given up by the Party injured, under the Penalty of being excluded from this Society.

That this Article may not admit of a wrong Construction, or be evaded, in explanation of the Clause being in actual Correspondence is meant, where Orders have been received or executed within two Years prior to the Complaint being made.

Amendment proposed

Instead of the Words in the Rule printed in Italics, shall execute any Orders he may receive from such House,[58] shall be inserted, after the Date of

[57] Dashed underlining in handwritten text

[58] Dashed underlining in handwritten text.

its being entered in the Book, nor any Orders which may have been taken by its Agents or Traveller, after two Months from the above Date.

Resolved

That such Rules as are proper to be selected and printed in several Languages, be selected against the next Meeting of this Society.

[signed] Charles Fred Brandt, President.

Minute 20 March 1794

Proceedings of a Meeting of the Commercial Society of Merchants trading on the Continent of Europe held this day at Spencer's Tavern. Mr. Charles Fred. Brandt President [and 14 other members present].

The 1st. 2nd. 8th. 9th. 10th and 11th Rules having been selected and proposed for Publication in Foreign Languages in Consequence of the Resolution passed for that purpose at the last Meeting, they were read and a Letter produced by the President on that Business being also read, containing as follows.

> Sir,
>
> The Merchants and Manufacturers of Manchester trading to the Continent of Europe, united into a Society for the Support and Improvement of Trade and Commerce, having taken into their Consideration the many Injuries they have individually sustained from some of their Correspondents by Chicaneries, Irregularity in Payments, and other unmercantile Practices, proceeding from a want of Principle and of that Honour so necessary in mercantile Transactions, are desirous to adopt such Measures as may tend to correct these Abuses, and add to the Safety of Trade in general.
>
> They do it in Justice to themselves, as well as for the Benefit of such of their Correspondents, as are by their honourable Dealings, entitled to their full Confidence, and to every Advantage their Trade can afford; but who of late Years have been equally injured by these Depredations, as they have enabled those who committed them to undersell and Rival the fair Dealers in the different Markets where they came in Competition
>
> To effect this Salutary Purpose, every Member of this Society who finds himself injured by any of his Correspondents, is to lay the Matter open to this Society, with the grounds of Complaint, and every Document necessary, arising from the Correspondence or otherwise, and on its being clearly proved that he has been ill-treated, either by his Correspondent not fulfilling his Engagements, or by his making groundless Complaints and futile Chicanery. The Name of such Correspondent is to be entered upon the Register of this Society, with the ground of Complaint, to prevent others from experiencing similar Treatment, and in particular Cases,

the Society will support and assist such of its Members so injured, in order that he may obtain Redress and Justice.

This Society will likewise correspond with other principal Manufacturing Towns of England, to communicate on all matters of common Interest, and to promote the above salutary Purposes.

This Society also thinks it necessary thus publicly to declare that it considers it as a fundamental Principle of Trade, that Orders being transmitted and agreed upon to be executed in English Measure, and the Invoices being made out in Sterling Money, the Manufacturer is no ways answerable for the fluctuation in Exchanges, but ought to be remitted in Sterling Money; and the Members of this Society will uniformly resist any attempt to the contrary.

This Society will moreover watch over the general Interest of its Trade and adopt every Method which may lend to give a decided Advantage to the fair Trader, both at home and abroad, by which Means Hopes may be entertained that Trade will return to its usual fair Channel, and increase in Prosperity by the uprightness and fairness of dealing of those concerned in it.

I am Sir Your Most obedient humble Servant
by order of the Society
John Orme Secretary

Resolved: That this Letter which contains Extracts of the Subscribers, be adopted in lieu thereof shall be printed in such languages as are hereafter enumerated be signed by the Secretary, and delivered in such quantities to the Members of the Society as they may apply for. That there be printed on Post Paper:

1000 copies in English
3000 Copies in French
3000 Copies in German
3000 Copies in Italian.

Minute 8 March 1798

At the Annual Meeting of the Commercial Society held this Day at Spencers Tavern

Present

Mr Joseph Hardman in the Chair

Mr Brandt	Mr Worthington
Mr Norman	Mr Thexford
Mr Harris	Mr William Pilling
Mr Krauss	Mr Dawson
Mr Crompton	Mr Lawre. Peel

Mr Norman desired to withdraw his Motion of which he gave Notice the last Monthly Meeting

The Rules of this Society having been read, the following Alterations were proposed

In Rule 2nd In the absence of the President for the time being, the President of the preceding Year shall Act for him and take the Chair at any of the Meetings of this Society, and in Case of absences of both, a Chairman shall be appointed for the Day out of the Members then present, who shall cause the proceedings of such Meetings to be reported to the President.

Rule 5th being Rescinded—the following substituted

Rule 5th The Society shall have four Quarterly Meetings for the Transactions of the Ordinary Business at this Society, to be held every first Thursday after Quarter Day precisely at 11. o'Clock in the Forenoon

In Rule 6th The President shall have power to call extraordinary Meetings whenever he shall deem it necessary, or is requested so to do by five or more Members of this Society

Resolved That the Alterations in the Rules proposed this Day, be Printed and circulated amongst the Members of this Society in order to be confirmed or rescinded at the next Monthly Meeting

1.26 Boston, Mass., Chamber of Commerce 1794 (re-establishment of 1785 body)

Source

RULES AND REGULATIONS of the Boston Chamber of Commerce, Established March 17, 1794; Printed by Ezra W. Weld and William Greenough, at the Magazine Office, No. 49, State Street, 1794. 10 pages, plus 6 pages of member list. Library Company of Philadelphia, 26686.

Member list at: http://www.geog.cam.ac.uk/research/projects/chambersofcommerce/philadelphia.pdf

Printed report 1794

RULES AND REGULATIONS.

I. The Members shall have Quarterly and Monthly Meetings, at such Place as the President shall appoint, until some permanent Provision be made for that Purpose by the Chamber.

II. The Quarterly Meetings shall be on the first Monday of *January, April, July,* and *October*; the Monthly Meetings on the first Monday of each Month, at six o'Clock, afternoon.

III. Annually, at the Meetings in *April*, shall be elected, by Ballot, a President, two Vice presidents, and a Secretary, to continue in Office one Year; a Majority of the Members present making a Choice.

IV. The President shall appoint a Doorkeeper and Messenger, who shall receive quarterly such Pay for their Services as the Chamber shall direct.

V. It shall be the Business of the President, and in the Absence, of one of the Vice presidents, to preside at all Meetings; to call special Meetings when he shall think necessary, or when he shall be requested so to do by the Committee; to receive all Communications or Information, written or verbal, that can in any Way interest the Society, and lay the same before the Chamber. And in Case of the Absence of the President and Vice presidents, a Member shall be elected to preside *pro tempore.*

VI. It shall be the Duty of the Secretary to attend all Meetings; to record the Names of Members who attend, and every Transaction of the Chamber, in proper Books, procured for that Purpose; to receive all Monies; to pay all Bills, approved by the Committee; and to deliver to his Successor in Office, all the Books, Records, Papers, Monies, and other Effects of the Chamber.

VII. On the first Monday in *March*, annually, shall be appointed, a Committee of Three, to examine the Accounts of the Secretary, and report the State of them to the Chamber, on the first Monday in *April*, and what Compensation they may think will be adequate to his Services.

VIII. Five Members shall be chosen monthly, by Ballot, who shall be called the Committee of the Chamber, whose Duty it shall be to hear and determine all Causes, Controversies, and Disputes, referred to the Chamber for Decision; to give an Opinion on all Questions submitted to their Judgment, respecting Commerce, Insurance, or Maritime Affairs, any three of whom shall make a Quorum. The Secretary shall publish monthly the Names of the Committee, in one of the Boston Newspapers, and shall attend their Meetings. No Member shall be chosen two Months successively; nor shall any one be obliged to serve more than two Months in the Year; each Committee to finish its own Business, and report upon all Cases referred to them respectively. The Members of the Committee shall be balloted for separately, and a Majority of the Votes present be necessary to constitute a Choice.

IX. Any of the Members, or other Merchants not of the Chamber, having disputed Accounts, or doubtful Questions respecting Commerce, Insurance, or Maritime Affairs, which they mutually agree to submit to the Determination of the Chamber, shall make known their Desire to the Secretary, who shall communicate it to the Chairman of the Committee.

X. Previous to hearing any controverted Cause, the Parties shall exhibit in writing to the Committee, the Points they intend to submit, and shall legally obligate themselves to abide the Award.

XI. The Committee shall always give their Award in Writing, accompanied with such Observations and Reasons as they may think proper to assign, which shall be delivered to the Parties, after it is recorded by the Secretary; and the Secretary shall at all Times, when required, give either of the Parties an attested Copy of any Award.

XII. Any Person desirous of becoming a Member of the Chamber, shall make known his Wish, by a Billet to the President; and at the Expiration of one Month from such Application, he shall be admitted by Ballot, provided three fourths of the Members present are in his Favour.

XIII. Merchants and Insurance Brokers only can be admitted Members.

XIV. Every Member, on his Admission to the Chamber, shall pay to the Secretary two Dollars; and shall also pay fifty Cents, at every Quarterly Meeting, till further Order of the Chamber.

XV. Every Member, for non Attendance at Quarterly Meetings, shall pay a Fine of fifty Cents; and for non Attendance at Monthly Meetings, twenty five Cents; and the Secretary is directed annually, at the Meeting on the first Monday in *March*, to call upon the Members and collect the Fines.

XVI. Twenty one Members shall be necessary to constitute a Chamber for the Transaction of Business.

XVII. Any Rules or Regulations proposed to be established, shall be made in Writing, and remain on File with the Secretary, at least one Month previous to their final Adoption.

XVIII. All Letters and Communications intended to be made to the Chamber, shall be directed to the President of the Boston Chamber of Commerce.

XIX. The Members at every Meeting are requested to lay before the Chamber such Information upon the Subject of Commerce as they may think will be useful.

XX. Such Additions and Alterations shall from Time to Time be made to the foregoing Rules and Regulations as may appear expedient.

1.27 Portsmouth Chamber of Commerce ? c. 1797–8

It has been suggested that there was an early chamber in Portsmouth, 'according to local newspaper reports'.[59] Taylor relied on various secondary histories but unfortunately gives no further information for the claim for this Portsmouth chamber. Searches of the local histories, the local Record Office and library, TNA, BL, ECCO and other on-line sources yield no confirmatory information. A search of all issues of the *Portsmouth Gazette and Weekly Advertiser* for 1795–99 yields only slender confirmatory information. This was the main local newspaper and the only one with a surviving continuous series. It is briefer (only four pages) and less discursive than some local newspapers, but it is unlikely that it would not report foundation meetings of a chamber. Hence, because of the absence of substantial newspaper comment,

[59] Taylor, *History of chambers of commerce* (London, 2007) 13.

it seems safest to assume that if a chamber existed it was of a more informal kind, a form of delegates' committee.

The *Portsmouth Gazette and Weekly Advertiser* reports a range of initiatives that were taken by local merchants and business leaders in the period 1795–99. Many of these were similar to those in other major centres: e.g. subscriptions to help man the navy (2 February 1795), petitions of disapprobation of the Convention Bills (23 and 30 November 1795), Subscriptions to found a Portsea Company for Fisheries (6 January 1796; first annual meeting 19 December 1796), A Loyal Volunteers Association to exercise small arms (28 November, 12 December 1796), a subscription for the relief of seamen's widows and wounded seamen (23 October 1797; 15 October 1798), a further long list of subscribers to help the government resist invasion (listed 19 February–30 April 1798), and several subscriptions to help the poor (e.g. 24 January 1795 and 30 December 1799). There was also an ongoing Commission for Paving the Town, with trustees and subscribers, that mirrors improvement initiatives in other urban centres of the period; and also a Portsmouth and Portsea Society for Prosecution of Thieves and Felons. These subscriber initiatives would have helped to stimulate wider civic involvement and bring business leader together; they were closely linked with chamber members in most other places that developed chambers. Hence it may be that they had a similar effect in Portsmouth to stimulate chamber-like activities. The two activities that are closest to a chamber relate to financial issues. The first of these was initiated 2 March 1797 (reported 6 March) at a meeting of the principal inhabitants of Portsmouth, Portsea and Gosport, chaired by the Portsmouth mayor John Carter, responding to the Order of the Privy Council to the Bank of England to forbear issuing cash in payments. This led to a local declaration from a list containing 99 prominent merchants, bankers and other business leaders from Portsmouth and Portsea, and 20 from Gosport: to agree to receive as cash the notes of the banks. The second was a meeting of December 1798 which, whilst they supported the government raising new revenue, warned that further support for burdens on businesses was difficult and they requested a 'more equal and effective' method for laying the burden. Unfortunately only the single name of the chair of this meeting, D. Garrett, is reported (senior bank partner of D. Garrett & Son; who, with the other main local bank W. Pike & Co., was the first to sign the 2 March declaration). Since these initiatives are the closest to a chamber activity, both documents are reproduced here.

Source
Portsmouth Gazette and Weekly Advertiser

Printed Report 6 March 1797

GUILDHALL, PORTSMOUTH,
March 2, 1797.

At a Meeting of the principal Inhabitants of Portsmouth, Portsea, Gosport, and their Environs, held here this day to consider the necessary means to remove the present inconvenience occasioned by the scarcity of Cash,

Sir JOHN CARTER, Mayor, in the Chair,

Resolved,

That the late Order of his Majesty's Privy Co. to the Bank of England, dated the 16th of February, 1797, to forbear issuing any Cash in payment, &c. may possibly occasion a temporary scarcity of Specie, for, the necessary circulating medium of this Country, We, whose Names are hereunto subscribed, do agree to receive as Cash the Notes of both the Banks of Portsmouth, as well as those of the Bank of England, as heretofore.

Sir JOHN CARTER; Mayor.

W. Pike & Co.	W. Turner,	T. Sharp
D. Garrett & Son	J. Keet	B. Woolfe,
J. Bettesworth,	P. Adams	H. Hill
W. Baker & Son.	J. Binstead,	H. Starkey,
J. Consens,	J. Chillingsworth	J. Gibbs,
T. & J. White	T. Boys,	W. Gibbens,
A. Atcheson,	C. & E. Creswell,	J. Judson,
J. Bradley,	W. Churcher,	A. Clarke
W. Hammond,	J. P. Yeomans,	E. Fowles,
J. Lear,	J. Brent,	J. Gain,
W. J. Porter,	R. Stroud,	R. Rood,
A. Moody,	J. Jacob,	M. Harty,
J. & A. Atkins	J. Hancock	E. Tollervey,
M. Greetham,	J. Goodeve,	T. Passard,
J. Diaper,	T. Eastman,	S. Wise,
S. Scarlett,	J. Mottley,	T. Croxton,
J. Bradley, jun.	W. Clark,	T. B. Costollo,
W. Harward,	T. Naters,	E. Taswell,
T. Walcott,	T. Buckley,	J. Brent,
T. Pratt,	H. Allen,	J. Cross,
Morris & Shenstone,	W. Dawes,	W. Andrews,
J. Googeve, jun.	W. Goldson,	J. White,
R. Callaway,	W. Veale,	W. Howell,
R. White,	J. Cousens,	W. Damerum,
W. Burridge,	J. Budd,	J. Morey,

J. Marder,	E. Kirkman,	T. Perrin,
J. Pinhorn.	C. Lingren, for A. Lingren,	T. Slight,
R. Daw,	T. Walker,	A. G. Emdin,
W. Lang,	S. Hawkins,	J. Warren,
J. Knight,	J. Knapp,	F. Matthews,
J. Whitlow,	A. Mant,	T. Allen,
S. Spicer,	J. Richards,	J. Snook,
J. Bastard,	W. Grossmith,	
J. Bailey,		

Residents at Gosport

R. Forbes,	W. Gobson & Sons,	T. Hoskins,
J. Goodeve,	J. B. Timmins,	R. White,
Carter & Marshall,	E. Jukes & Sons,	S. Jellicoe,
M. March,	T. Morgan,	J. Paul,
M. March, jun.	T. Whitcomb,	E. Fiott,
Minchin & Wilkinson,	C. Hayter,	J. Battershell, sen.
	J. Westmore,	T. Curry.

Printed Report 10 December 1798

PORTSMOUTH, Nov. 30, 1798.
AT a MEETING, of MERCHANTS, BANKERS; TRADERS, and other Inhabitants of the Towns of Portsmouth, Portsea, and their Neighbourhood, holden this day at the Crown Inn, Portsmouth,

DANIEL GARRETT, Esq. in the Chair,

The following Resolutions of the Merchants, Bankers, Traders, and other Inhabitants of the City of London being read,

'1. That the Principle of Finance resorted to in the Session of Parliament, namely, that of raising, within the Year, a considerable portion of the sum necessary for the Public Service, has contributed, in an eminent degree, to the improvement of Public Credit, and the advantage of the Community.

2. That this Meeting are nevertheless of opinion that the Criterion then assumed, as the basis of that extraordinary Supply, has been found unequal in its operation, inasmuch as it had failed to call forth a due Ratio of Contribution from many descriptions of Persons.

3. That, impressed with full confidence that the Resources of these Kingdoms are adequate to the maintenance of our National Honor and Independence, this Meeting think it proper to declare their readiness to give their utmost support to such measures as the Legislature may deem best calculated to call forth those Resources in a more equal and effectual manner — trusting that its wisdom will devise such expedients for that purpose, as, combined with our late glorious Victories, may afford the means of further spirited resistance to the power and pretentions of the Enemy; and secure,

not only the blessings we now enjoy, but also that ultimate, object of all our exertions —a safe and honorable Peace.'

It was unanimously Resolved —That this Meeting do agree with, and heartily approve of, the Principle of the above Resolutions, as they tend at once to call forth the real Resources of the Country, and to prevent as much as possible any further Burdens being laid upon that class of the Community which is the least able to bear Taxation.

Resolved unanimously — That this Meeting, while they deeply lament the necessity thereof, cannot but be sensible, that powerful and National Exertions are at this period most particularly required, in order to follow up and secure to us, the good effects of our late glorious and splendid Victories, and that they do therefore most earnestly recommend to all loyal and well disposed Persons a cheerful acquiescence in those measures, which appear to be best calculated to produce an honourable, advantageous, and permanent Peace.

Resolved unanimously — That the Chairman be required to sign the above Resolutions, and to publish them in the following Papers, viz. the Sun, Star, Times, Oracle, Portsmouth, Winchester, and Salisbury.

D. GARRETT

Resolved unanimously — That the Thanks of the Meeting be given to the Chairman for his conduct on the occasion.

1.28 [Ouzel Galley Society, Rules 1799: see Chapter 6]

1.29 Liverpool American Chamber of Commerce 1801

The Liverpool American chamber was developed as a specialised body in terms of the field of trade covered, but in other ways was a typical chamber. Founded in 1801, it had a strong overlap of membership, aims and activities with the earlier chamber in Liverpool that operated over 1774–c. 1796; it also financed itself by a 'trade duty' like the initial concept of the first Liverpool chamber.[60] There was not to be a renewal of a general multi-sector chamber body for Liverpool until initiatives in 1849. As a result the American chamber to some extent filled this gap, acting not only on American but also some wider issues for the whole Liverpool commercial community. It merged with the Liverpool chamber in 1908. Its purpose is succinctly stated in its 15th rule. There have been previous discussions of the chamber's activities.[61]

[60] See Bennett, *Local Business Voice* (2011) 17, 135.

[61] Notably W. O. Henderson, 'The American Chamber of Commerce for the Port of Liverpool, 1801–1908', *Transactions of the Historic Society of Lancashire and Cheshire,* 85 (1933) 1–61; idem, 'The Liverpool Office in London', *Economica,* 18 (1933) 473–79.

The chamber often operated in an alliance with the municipal corporation and sector bodies in the town. It is notable as one of the first chambers to establish a major office in London to act on parliamentary and other representations, the activities of which have been summarised by Henderson.[62] The first chair, and purportedly one of the leading spirits behind the foundation, was James Maury, the American Consul in Liverpool. Maury had become established in Liverpool in 1790 and was 'frequently applied to by the masters of vessels & crews to settle and determine their disputes; in such instances I invariably endeavour to accommodate, but have not considered myself warranted in doing more'.[63] He clearly felt that, after the American War, he could develop a stronger base to encourage a greater activity to improve the American trade by re-kindling the earlier chamber concept in Liverpool but in a more focused way. With a strong background in New York he may also have used his experience of the chamber there. He subsequently was empowered to issue certificates against impressment to US citizens in Liverpool in 1803, and appears to have attended the Board of Trade in 1807 together with Philip Sanderson, the then chair of the Liverpool American Chamber.[64] It is an important example demonstrating the rapprochement with America after the rift in the 1770s, but this was to be severely tested by the UK embargoes resulting from the Orders in Council of 1808, and the war with America of 1812.

Source
Minute book: Liverpool RO 380 AME/4.

Minutes *7 July 1801*

Liverpool American Chamber of Commerce for the port of Liverpool.
RULES &c.

The Inconveniences that have been sustained in the American Trade by the Merchants in this Port having suggested the Expediency of a public Association for their mutual assistance and advantage, the following Rules and Regulations are this day agreed upon for the carrying their intentions into effect.

1st. This Association shall be known by the Name of the "American Chamber of Commerce for the port of Liverpool."

2nd. The Objects of this Association are hereby declared to be, the redress of existing and the prevention of future Grievances which may affect this

[62] Henderson, 'Liverpool Office' (1933).
[63] Maury to Thomas Jefferson, letter 2 March 1791; Transcripts from US Consular Reports from Liverpool, 1790–1830; Liverpool University Library S227/2(a).
[64] Ibid. Maury consular reports 19 November 1803 and 21 November 1807.

Branch of Trade generally: the Establishment of regular and settled rules amongst the American Merchants, in respect to the payments of freights, and the rate of fees in the Customs &c., and at the public boards and offices in London: and in general the attainment of such objects as involve the general interests of the Trade, and which it might be difficult or impracticable for the separate and isolated exertions of Individuals to effect.

3rd. This Association shall in the first instance, consist of such persons in the American trade now present, or who within one month from this date, shall subscribe the rules which may be now agreed to, and pay down their annual subscriptions, which shall in no case be less than two Guineas for each House: And in future any person desirous of becoming a Member may be proposed at any half yearly meeting of the Association by any existing Member: and if no Ballot be demanded by any other member, he shall be admitted on subscribing the Rules, and payment of his Subscription. If a ballot be demanded by any member, the majority in number shall elect or reject.

4th. That each Mercantile House, altho' composed of more than one persons shall be considered but as an individual Subscriber, except in the appointment of the Committee, to which each Individual (subject to the exception contained in the sixth rule) shall be eligible.

5th. There shall be two half yearly meetings of the Association, held in each Year, viz. on the last Tuesday in January at 11 o'clock in the forenoon, and on the last Tuesday in July, at the same hour: and it is proposed, that on the day of the general meeting in January, such of the Members as may be so inclined, shall dine together at such house, as the Committee may appoint, each Member being at liberty to bring with him any friend, whose Company he may believe will be agreeable to the meeting: and written notices of the time and place of these meetings shall be sent by the Secretary to each Member of the Association.

6th. At the half yearly meeting in January, a President, Vice-President, Treasurer, Committee, and Secretary shall be annually elected. The Committee shall consist of 15 Members, including the President, Vice-President, and Treasurers; all of whom shall be elected by Ballot, but the President, or in his absence, the Vice-President, may nominate, for the approbation of the Society, such Members as he may deem most eligible to succeed to the offices of President, Vice-President, & Treasurer. But it is understood and determined, that not more than one person in the same Mercantile House shall be competent to be of the same Committee; and if at the election of the Committee any more than one such Partner shall be elected, the partner who shall have the greater number of votes shall be considered as duly elected, and the election, as it respects the other, or others, of the said Partners, shall be null and void. And in case of an equality of votes between such Partners, a Ballot shall take place for the election of one of such partners.

7th. At the half yearly meeting in January the account of the Treasurer, together with all vouchers, and the particulars of expenditure shall be produced and read (having been previously examined by the Committee), and if approved of, a minute to that effect, shall be made at such meeting: and directions shall also be given to the Treasurer into which of the Banks the funds of this Association shall be paid.

8th. At each of the half yearly meetings, the minutes of the Committee shall be produced, and, if required, read for the general information of the Subscribers. And it shall be the further business of such meeting, to take into consideration, and decide upon any measures that may be suggested by the Committee, or any other Subscriber; to elect new Members; direct the appropriation of the Funds; to censure, fine, or expel any Member, offending against the rules of the Association; and to discuss and decide upon any business or question connected with the objects for which this Association is formed, Provided always, that no alterations shall be made in any of the rules now agreed upon, or to be agreed upon, at any half yearly or other general meeting of the Subscribers, unless information of the intention to make a motion for such alteration shall be expressed in the notice of such meeting, sent to each Subscriber, at least three days previously to the time of holding such meeting.

9th. The business of the meeting in July, and the powers of the members of this Society then assembled, shall be the same as those of the meeting in January, except in respect of the annual Election of Officers, the appointment of Bankers, and the examination of the vouchers, and reading over the particulars of the Treasurer's expenditure; which latter, the half yearly meeting in July may proceed upon, or omit, at their discretion; it being however to be regarded as a standing order of this Association, that the Treasurer's Books and accounts shall be produced, not only at the half yearly meeting in January, but at the half yearly meeting of the Subscribers in July, and at every stated periodical meeting of the Committee.

10th. The Secretary, at the request of the President, or in his absence, of the Vice-President, or in the absence of both, of any three of the Committee, or any five of the Subscribers, shall at any time convene a general meeting of the Subscribers, to take into consideration any particular business which may seem to require early attention: but it is required that such business shall be particularly stated in the notice to each Subscriber, of such intended meeting, to be sent at least three days previously to the time of holding such meeting.

11th. In case of the death or resignation of any of the officers of this Association, the vacancy so occasioned shall be filled up at the succeeding half yearly meeting, unless it shall appear expedient to the Committee to proceed to a new Election sooner, in which case a general meeting shall be called, as directed in the 10th Article.

12th. The President, or in his absence the Vice-President, or in case of the absence of both, a Chairman to be appointed for the time being, shall preside at all meetings on the business of this Association, and whenever the votes shall be equal, such president, vice-president, or Chairman, shall have a casting voice, and the minutes of the meeting shall afterwards be fairly copied by the Secretary in the Book kept for that purpose, and authenticated by the signature of the Chairman.

13th. The Treasurer shall collect and receive all Subscriptions, donations, fines, or bequests, due or belonging to this Association, and shall regularly pay the same in the name of this Association, whenever the amount may be £5 or upwards, into such Bank as may be directed at the general meeting in January, or at any other meeting convened for the purpose; and if any loss should arise in consequence of the funds being so placed, the Treasurer shall not be accountable for the same. The Treasurer's accounts shall be clearly kept and duly stated, and shall be regularly produced for the inspection of any Member of this Association at the general meetings, and at every stated periodical meeting of the Committee, and also at all other times to the Committee when required by them. And at a meeting of the Committee to be held preceding the annual meeting in January, the accounts of the Treasurer for the past year shall be examined, and the several vouchers produced and compared, and a report thereon be made to the succeeding half yearly meeting; when, if no objection be made to the report of the Committee, the balance of the account shall be understood to be finally settled, as stated in such Report.

14th. The Committee shall meet during the remainder of this year, on the last Tuesday in each Month, at 7 o'clock in the evening, at the house of the Star and Garter: and they shall afterwards assemble at such time and place as they by any written order or minute for that purpose made by themselves, and entered with the minutes of this Association shall direct, it being understood and determined that the Secretary shall send a note to each Member of the Committee, reminding him of each monthly meeting; and when regularly convened, any five of them shall be competent to act. The President, or Vice-President, or in the absence any two or more of the Committee, may at any time convene an extra meeting of the Committee, upon due notice, if they deem it expedient so to do. And if any Members of the Committee shall neglect to attend any meeting of the Committee punctually at the hour appointed for that purpose, he shall pay a fine of 5s. for such Neglect; and in case there shall not be five Members present at such Committee, so as to enable it to proceed to business, the fine on each absent member of the Committee shall be increased to 10s. 6d. No excuse for absence shall be admitted, except sickness or absence from Liverpool: and all fines for non-attendance, shall be immediately collected by the Treasurer, who is to keep a distinct account thereof, and the amount at the expiration of each year shall be appropriated as a majority of the Committee for such year, may direct.

15th. The Business of the Committee shall be, and they shall have accordingly full power and authority to adopt such measures, and establish such regulations for limiting the fees of officers in the Excise and Customs, for the adjustment of freight, and the mode in which it shall be paid, and for the attainment of any of the objects of this Association in general, (not repealing or infringing upon the resolutions of any general meeting) as they may deem necessary and expedient, conformably to the objects stated in the second law of this Association, which measures and regulations shall be binding, and obligatory upon the Members of the Society, until repealed by a general meeting of the Association; and that it shall be also part of the business of the Committee to prepare and digest such measures or applications for the more easy consideration and final determination of half yearly or other general meetings of the Subscribers: but it is understood, that no part of the funds of this Association shall, at any one meeting, be voted or appropriated, to any one particular purpose to an amount exceeding £10 10s, unless by a half yearly or other general meeting of the Subscribers, duly convened.

16th. The meetings of the Committee shall, at all times, be open to any of the subscribers who may be inclined to attend the same, but it shall be competent only to the Members of the Committee to vote upon any question which may come before it.

17th. The Secretary shall attend all half yearly or general meetings of this Association, likewise all the meetings of the Committee, to minute their proceedings; which he shall afterwards copy into the book kept for that purpose, and to lay the same regularly before the Chairman for his Signature: to take care that such book, and all other necessary books and papers be regularly produced at every meeting of the Subscribers or Committee, and to issue notices of all intended meetings according to the provisions herein before contained, or in such other manner as may be directed by the parties competent thereto; and for his attention to this business he shall receive such Salary as the Subscribers at their annual meeting may determine upon.

18th. The annual Subscription of every Member of this association shall become due and payable immediately upon such Member's admission; and all subsequent Subscriptions shall become due and payable on the 1st February in each year: and it is understood, that every Member of this Association is bound by his subscription to the rules and regulations, to pay his future Subscription for every current year provided he shall not have resigned, or ceased to become a Member on or before the 1st of February in such Year.

We whose Names are hereunder signed, or signed on the Page next, after the Page on which this our Engagement is written, do respectively agree to become, and be Members of the American Chamber of Commerce for the port of Liverpool: and do respectively accordingly engage to abide by perform, & fulfil the Rules & Regulations for the good Government of the said Association, its Committee & Members.

[signed list of names of members follows, heavily amended]

Rules adopted at a meeting of the Merchants & Gentlemen interested in the American Trade at Lillyman's Hotel in Castle Street, 7th July 1801

Resolved. That a Committee of 15 Gentlemen (of whom the Chairman be one) be appointed for conducting the business of the Association; five of whom (the chairman being one) shall be competent to act.

Resolved. That the following Gentlemen be accordingly appointed of the Committee:

The Chairman,	Mr. Sherlock,
Mr. Duncan,	Mr. Cropper,
Mr. Holland,	Mr. McCorquedale
Mr. Strickland,	Mr. Barber,
Mr. Ewart,	Mr. Long,
Mr. Rundle,	Mr. Gray,
Mr. Lodge,	Mr. Hamilton
Mr. Logan	

Resolved. That Mr. Brandreth be requested to accept the office of Secretary.

Resolved. That the Proceedings of the Meeting of the American Merchants of the 29th day of June last, & of the Meeting of the 6th of July Inst., be transcribed into the Book of the Proceedings of this Committee, & that they be adopted as the Resolutions of this Meeting.

Resolved. That the thanks of this meeting be given to the worthy Chairman, for his attention to the business of the Association.

Resolved. That this meeting be adjourned to the 29th Instant, to be held at this place at 12 o'Clock in the forenoon.

James Maury, Chairman [American Consul in Liverpool]

1.30 Hull Chamber of Commerce 1801

Hull had an active convoy committee 1757–60, revived in 1780–82 in renewed war conditions, and a committee of trade in 1784. It was one of the delegate committees of the General Chamber of Manufactures 1785–7, and a member of the Union of chambers and coordination of convoys in the 1790s (see Chapters 6, 8 and 9). However, a first attempt to establish an explicit chamber at Hull was not made until 1801. But even then, although a committee was established to develop a plan for the chamber, this appears to have been abandoned, and no rules seem to survive. According to Hope, the abandonment was due to the 'baneful influence of party politics'.[65] However, Hope's source for this comment, which he derives from the minutes of the Hull chamber founded in 1837, gives no further information, and attempts to find any contemporary comment in local newspapers have failed. The 1801 attempt appears to have derived from the committee that was liaising nationally with other places for convoying (see Chapter 9). There was a meeting in Hull in December 1800 of owners of vessels detained by the Emperor of Russia to support the continuation of payments to the families of the sailors detained; under the chairmanship of William Osbourne.[66] A petition to the Admiralty from the Hull merchants and shipowners requested a convoy in February 1801. In March it was noted that a convoy from Hull to Spithead would set off on the third and fourth of April, and a request was made to the Admiralty for the Hamburg convoy. Further information on the Hamburg convoy was received on 9 May.[67] All of these were under the Mayor's chairmanship. However, by 2 June there was a separate notice of convoy arrangement from the merchants themselves, which announced that a convoy would sail on 2 June next. By 3 November a further notice announced coordination with the London convoy arrangements, and in the following week the proposal for a chamber of commerce was announced (both documents reproduced below). Both meetings were chaired by William Osbourne, the chair of the committee to aid detained sailors in December 1800. He was not a corporation burgess, though a relative, Thomas Osbourne, was a Burgess and became an Alderman in 1801.[68]

It appears from this sequence of events that the Hull chamber proposal evolved from the committee already liaising with the other committees and chambers around the country over convoys. Previously this had been a more ad hoc body, or a continuation of the earlier committee on convoys originally established in 1757 and nominally under the authority of the mayor (see Chapter 6), but in 1801 an evolution into a chamber may have seemed more useful. The lack of subsequent development may have been stimulated by the preparations for the short-lived Peace of Amiens, which were reported in the Hull Newspapers on 3 November, when the corporation noted that this was

[65] W. J. Hope, *In the beginning was an orchard: A commentary on the origins of the Hull Incorporated Chamber of Commerce and Shipping* (Hull, c.1987) 1.
[66] *Hull Packet*, 16 December 1800.
[67] *Hull Advertiser*, 21 February, 28 March, 9 May 1801; celebrated in Hull in April, 9 April 1802; proclaimed May 1802.
[68] Hull Archives: Hull Bench Books, C.BRB/8.

now a good time to extend the wet dock.[69] For whatever reason, there was no further notice of the chamber's Plan. The abandonment of the chamber proposals therefore can be inferred to have probably arisen from both a perceived lesser need for formal convoy arrangements or resistance to the shift of authority to an independent body away from the mayor and corporation. The timing also coincided with a new private Bill for a wet dock at Hull, which proved controversial. Indeed it was the corporation that subsequently dealt with presentations to the local naval commanders and the Admiralty, as the following reports make clear:

January 1802. 'The corporation presented the freedom of the town and a silver cup of value 30 guineas to Captain Wm. Jones R. N. for his humane and exemplary conduct when for his time as regulatory officer in the Impress service at Hull' (Hull Bench Books, 4 December 1801; *Hull Advertiser,* 9 January 1802).

February 1802. 'The corporation presented the freedom of the town to Captain Cannon of the HM *Nonsuch* for his attention during the service on this station, and to Lieutenants Loter and Dane regarding the impress service' (Hull Bench Books, 2 January 1802; *Hull Advertiser,* 6 February 1802).

Source
Hull Advertiser.

Printed report 7 November 1801

Exchange Hull, Nov. 3, 1801
At a Meeting of the Merchants respecting the Convoy Duty, held this day at the Exchange,
WM. OSBOURNE Esq. in the chair;

It was Resolved

(In order to obtain information of the proceedings of the Committee in London on the same business) to adjourn this Meeting to one o'clock on Wednesday next, the 11th inst. when these interested are requested to attend at the Exchange, on this and other SPECIAL BUSINESS intended then to be discussed.

[69] *Hull Advertiser*, 3 November 1801.

Printed report 14 November 1801

At a Meeting of the Merchants of the town of Kingston-upon-Hull, holden at the Exchange, on Wednesday, the 11th day of November 1801, agreeable to public advertisement;
WM. OSBOURNE, Esq. in the Chair

Resolved unanimously,

That it appears to this Meeting, a Chamber of Commerce would be a very useful Institution, and that such should be immediately formed.

That the following Gentlemen be named a Committee for forming a Plan of such an Institution, to be laid before the Merchants, Traders, and Ship owners, so soon as convenient.

[list of 27 names follows: see Appendix, no. 11.2]

1.31 Waterford Chamber of Commerce 1804; see also charter 1815 in Chapter 2

The reconstituted chamber of 1804, originally established in 1787, defined a new set of rules after its first year in 1805. These are somewhat incomplete, but probably closely resembled the first chamber's rules (see earlier) for which a complete list does not survive; a charter was granted in 1815.

Source
Waterford Archives: Chamber of Commerce: minute book WCOC 1/02

Minutes 7 June 1805

1. No person eligible to be a Member who is not a Merchant, Trader or Banker.
2. All new members to be balloted on, with one black bean in four of members present considered a rejection.
3. A General Meeting requires 20 or more to attend to allow business to be transacted.
4. A ballot to be held every year to elect a Committee and Chair.
5. The Committee to consist of 12 members who make their decisions by ballot
6. The Committee to meet Monthly.
7. Any breach of confidential information will lead to a member being discontinued as a member if majority of a general meeting particularly summoned decide by ballot.
8. Summonses to meeting to be left at the Merchants counting houses.
9. Subscriptions one guinea per year
10. Fine for non-attendance by members at general meetings or committee at committee meetings of 1s.

Minutes 17 January 1806

11. Members to pay 2 guineas admission and one guinea per year.

1.32 Halifax, Nova Scotia, Committee of Trade 1803

The merchants in Nova Scotia had discontents with local governors and the metropolitan state akin to those in America. These was primarily focused on campaigns against governors and corrupt local officials. For example, in 1763 they achieved recall of the governor and in 1774–6 a purge on corrupt public accounts. Some of this mirrors the issues that led to the Jamaica chamber foundation (see above). Across Canada merchant committees were formed during the 1750s, certainly in Montreal, Quebec, and Halifax.[70] The first Halifax committee was formed in 1748–50 and seems to have been the strongest of these early bodies, and the proposal for a chamber in Quebec in 1776–7 may have been stimulated by its early committee. The 1748–50 Halifax committee has been claimed to be the 'first business group' in North America 'where the merchants of the town … formed themselves into an association to benefit trade'.[71] This is incorrect since the first Boston body (BSETC) was at least as active from 1733. However, Halifax was important: securing a local Assembly for Nova Scotia in 1758, and was part of the organisation that pushed for a loyal petition from the Nova Scotia Assembly in 1775. There is evidence of continued petitioning in the 1780s and 1790s, helping to form a Marine Insurance Association in 1794, attempts to initiate a Shubenacadie canal in 1798, and a bank in 1801. These initiatives certainly required an organisation, but there does not seem to have been a formal committee with rules like a chamber. It was more of an ad hoc and on-off structure, largely in response to specific issues, more a small committee or group of leading merchants than a formal body.[72] The first formal body was formed in 1803 as the Halifax Committee of Trade. This was broad-based and formalised, covering trade, agriculture and fisheries. It went through various re-establishments before an explicit chamber of commerce was founded in 1822,[73] though it also helped to stimulate the foundation of a Quebec chamber in 1808. The rules of the 1803 foundation have not been found and the later developments are not included here.

[70] D. Creighton, *The Empire of the St. Lawrence* (Toronto, 1937) 32–55; G. F. Butler, 'The early organisation and influence of Halifax merchants', *Collections of the Nova Scotia Historical Society*, 25 (1942) 1.

[71] B. Akins, *History of Halifax City* (Halifax, 1895) 27; 'The Halifax Board of Trade; An historical sketch 1748–1908', *49th Report of Halifax Board of Trade* (1908); B. Cuthbertson, *Voices of business: A history of commerce in Halifax, 1750–2000* (Halifax, Nova Scotia, 2000) 3 n.1.

[72] Bennett, *Local Business Voice* (2011) 140–1.

[73] Butler, 'Early organisation' (1942) 1–4; Cuthbertson, *Voices of business* (2000) 6–16.

1.33 Dublin Chamber of Commerce 1805

The second attempt to establish the Dublin chamber in 1805 followed lapse of the 1783 chamber in 1791 after disputes over 1788–91, probably resulting from its memorial on slave trade abolition, as well as other inter-member disputes (see Chapter 5). On re-establishment it continued to work with the Ouzel Galley Society (see Chapter 6).

Source
Dublin Chamber of Commerce, printed Articles of Association 1805: RIA HP 878/5

Articles of Association 16 April 1805

THE ARTICLES OF ASSOCIATION of the CHAMBER OF COMMERCE of the CITY OF DUBLIN.
ROYAL EXCHANGE, DUBLIN, the 16th Day of April, 1805.

AT a Meeting of Merchants, Manufacturers and Traders of the city of Dublin, convened by public notice from a voluntary association of Gentlemen, who with laudable and disinterested zeal have for some time been attentive to the commercial Interests of this City, the following Address was presented and read by Bartholomew Maziere, Esq.

To the Merchants, Manufacturers and Traders of the City of Dublin.

WE, the undersigned members of your body, have the honour to represent to you, that, with the acquiescence of a considerable number of our brethren, we have been induced, by motives of regard and solicitude for the public advantage, voluntarily to associate, and apply ourselves diligently, for a considerable time, in maintaining respectful communications with some of his Majesty's ministers, and in corresponding with the representatives in Parliament for the City of Dublin, and with commercial institutions and individuals at the outports of Ireland, respecting the regulation of several affairs interesting to that commercial prosperity, which is our common concernment.

That, during the correspondence incidental to the charge which we have thus assumed, we are become convinced of the necessity of forming, and giving permanent existence to, a local association in the City of Dublin, for superintending the general commercial, and manufacturing interests of the city, and also for suggesting improvements and alterations in the modes and rates of transacting commercial business in the city, and its vicinity; all which affairs were in the contemplation of the Chamber of Commerce which formerly existed in this city, when the trade and industry of Ireland acquired vigour and extent, by their liberation from partial restraints and injurious disabilities.

That the remoteness of the present seat of the Legislature has rendered the combined exertion of the experience and abilities of every intelligent trader of this city, of great importance, and peculiarly seasonable, for the purpose of reviving an institution fitted to offer respectful suggestions to his Majesty's ministers, and to the Legislature, on all proper occasions, with more weight and effect than our unauthorized, though well meant endeavours could accomplish, relative to the commercial and manufacturing interests of Ireland, and especially those of the metropolis.

That several of the principal cities of Ireland, by well regulated establishments of the nature that we recommend, have excited our emulation to have our body known by a permanent institution, qualified to communicate and co-operate with those provincial establishments, upon the commercial and manufacturing interests, which from the continual changes in the Fiscal laws of these countries, and other causes, are frequently the subjects of discussion in the Legislature, and as frequently require the merchants and manufacturers of Ireland to convey matured opinions upon those subjects.

In thus looking to present convenience, by giving existence to an institution so necessary, we are not unmindful of those considerations which happier times will suggest, for the extension of our manufactures, and the opening of all the sources of national industry and wealth, which local circumstances may place within our reach.

That we humbly conceive the revival of a Chamber of Commerce in the City of Dublin, is essentially necessary to the attainment of these important ends:— that it should comprehend the manufacturing as well as the commercial interests:— that the general body of the Chamber should be composed of Members, admitted upon well defined principles, and such as will ensure a perpetual [subsequently amended by hand to 'permanent'] existence to the institution, with the same efficacy as a charter of incorporation, for which we do not see any necessity, as the institution need not acquire any real property, or possess any transferable joint stock or capital; and above all, we recommend that the institution shall be invested with a permanent [subsequently amended by hand to 'fixed'] and constantly productive revenue, adequate to its probable expenses, and independent of periodical contributions; which revenue we conceive may be created, and with certainty obtained, by a declared concurrence of the commercial body, on a liberal view of the beneficial purposes to which that revenue would be applied.

To such an institution we shall with pleasure commit the documents, which the necessity that called for our interference hath placed in our hands; and we shall retire from the charge we have assumed, trusting that our brethren will acquit us of any arrogant pretensions, but proud of having originated, on lasting principles, an institution, which we fondly hope will manifest the consideration that is justly due to the City of Dublin.

Dublin, dated this 9th day of April, 1805.
[Signed, but printed; 13 names: see Appendix, no. 5.2]

No. I RESOLVED—On the motion of Richard Darling, Esq., seconded by Arthur Guinness, Esq., that Geo. F. Carleton, Esq., be requested to take the chair for this meeting.

GEORGE FREDERICK CARLETON, ESQ. IN THE CHAIR.

The following Resolutions were separately moved by Bartholomew Maziere, Esq., and seconded by Richard Darling, Esq.,

No. II RESOLVED—That the said Address be again read, and it having been read accordingly;

No. III. RESOLVED — That, duly weighing the reasons conveyed in the above Address, this meeting does therefore cordially, and with perfect conviction, concur in the opinion thereby conveyed of the indispensable and increased necessity of reviving, on permanent and comprehensive principles, a Chamber of Commerce in the City of Dublin; an institution at all times essential to the well being of every trading community, which acknowledges and acts upon the broad and liberal principle that public prosperity is the best source of individual advantage.[74]

No. IV. RESOLVED — That there shall be forthwith, and hereafter, a Chamber of Commerce in the City of Dublin, to superintend the commercial and manufacturing interests of the city and its vicinity, and to investigate and recommend improvements and alterations in the customary modes and rates of transacting commercial business, and also in the customary methods and forms of preparing and making up manufactures and others goods in the city and its vicinity; consisting of merchants, manufacturers and traders, as general members of the Chamber, who, at the time of admission, shall be established in the City of Dublin and its vicinity, and shall use and resort to the port and market of Dublin, and also consisting of such distinguished and eminent persons, whether foreigners or natives, as shall be admitted honorary members of the Chamber, with a Council consisting of twenty-one general members of the Chamber; which Council shall be invested with the executive powers of the Chamber, for the good order and conduct of its affairs and revenues; such Chamber and Council to be constituted and elected in the manner herein after mentioned.

No. V. RESOLVED — That the first Assembly of the Chamber shall be held on Thursday the 2d day of May next, at the Royal Exchange, Dublin, for the purpose of electing the Council; and that all merchants and traders of the City of Dublin, without regard to firms or assumed names of associated houses, who, previously to the 2d day of May next, shall sign a roll, containing

[74] Each subsequent Resolution III to XX is followed by the chair's initials G.F.C., indicating authentication by the meeting, as under Resolution IX, confirmed by Resolution XX.

a transcript of these resolutions, and thereby engage to observe and perform the regulations of the Chamber, during the time each subscriber shall continue a general member of the Chamber, and who shall at the same time pay the sum of two guineas as an admission fine for each subscriber, shall be, and be deemed general members of the Chamber, and competent to vote at the said election for general members so qualified to be of the Council; and that, until the said 2d day of May next, rolls, containing transcripts of these resolutions, shall be open for such signatures and subscriptions, at the respective offices of the Royal Exchange and Commercial Insurance Company's, in the Commercial Buildings, Dublin, preparatory to the said election of the Council by such subscribers on the said day.

No. VI. RESOLVED — That, from and after the election of the Council on the 2d day of May next, each general member of the Chamber, without regard to firms, or assumed names of associated houses, shall be admitted by a resolution for that purpose, ascertained by a ballot or close vote of the Council, or by a ballot or close vote of a special Assembly of the Chamber, on appeal from the decision of the Council, and not otherwise; upon which resolution for a general member, either by the Council or the Chamber, the negative of one-fifth part of the members voting shall exclude — and that each such general member do at the time of his admission, sign a roll, containing a transcript of the then existing regulations of the Chamber, and thereby engage to observe and perform the regulations of the Chamber during the time such person shall continue a general member; and also, that each such person do, at the same time, pay to the Treasurer of the Chamber the sum of two guineas, or such other sum in lieu thereof, as the Council shall appoint to be the admission fine of each general member. And it is further resolved, that each general member shall be at liberty to withdraw from being a member of the Chamber, on giving notice thereof in writing, signed by such member, to the Secretary, at the office of the Chamber.

No. VII. RESOLVED—That both the Chamber and the Council are hereby respectively invested with full power and authority, independently of each other, and without any appeal as before mentioned, but by ballot, or close vote, and not otherwise, to elect and admit as honorary members of the Chamber, by grace especial, and without payment of any admission fine, or signing the roll before mentioned, such distinguished and eminent persons, who, being foreigners, shall be deemed entitled to marks of hospitality and respect, or shall be deemed competent to promote the purposes of the institution, or who, being our fellow subjects, and not merchants, manufacturers or traders of the City of Dublin or its vicinity, shall, by their public services, merit to be adopted honorary members of the Chamber. And it is further resolved, that the Council shall cause a list of the Members of the Chamber to be accurately kept, distinguishing each member, according as he shall be a general or an honorary member.

No. VIII. RESOLVED — That, in order to constitute a permanent revenue for the Chamber, in addition to the fund which shall be formed by the admission fines of the general members, each merchant, manufacturer, and trader of the City of Dublin or its vicinity, whether a member or not of the Chamber, is hereby requested, from and after the thirty-first day of May next, voluntarily and uniformly to pay to a receiver, to be appointed by the Council, a contribution or toll of one shilling British sterling, on each and every such original and general entry of goods and merchandize, either inwards or outwards, not being a *post entry* or *entry advisum*, as shall be made by or in trust for him or her, or any firm or house of trade of which he or she shall be a partner, in addition and without prejudice to the duties now payable on such entries to the Trustees of the Royal Exchange, and to the Commercial Buildings Company, at the Custom-House of Dublin; and that each such merchant, manufacturer or trader, whether a member or not of the Chamber, who shall pay such voluntary contribution or toll, shall be entitled to the benefit of the consideration, influence, and advice of the Chamber and its Council, in all cases of a commercial nature, in which the personal and private interest of each such merchant, manufacturer, or trader shall involve any subject of public concernment, which shall fall within the province of the Chamber and its Council; and, that when the refusal of any general member to pay such voluntary contribution or toll, in any one instance, shall have been ascertained by the Council, the member so refusing shall forthwith cease to be a member of the Chamber. Provided always, and it is hereby resolved, that nothing herein contained shall justify or bind the Chamber or its Council to interfere in any differences between individuals, as the discussion of such private differences is foreign from the purposes of this institution, and is the peculiar object of our respected brethren of the *Ouzel Galley* Association.

No. IX. RESOLVED — That the Chamber shall hold its assemblies under the four distinct names of *Annual, Elective, Special, and Adjourned Assemblies*, and for the purposes herein after declared, and under no other names, and for no other purposes whatsoever, and that each such *Annual, Elective, Special, and Adjourned Assembly* shall nominate a President to regulate its proceedings; and that all questions and motions in every assembly, except the election of members, shall be decided by open vote, and, when necessary, by the casting vote of the President, who shall authenticate all the proceedings and decisions of each such assembly by his signature.

No. X. RESOLVED — That the annual assembly of the Chamber shall be held on the first Thursday in every month of May, and at such hours of such day, and at such place in the City of Dublin, as shall be appointed by the notice or summons to be issued and published by the Council five clear days previous to the day of meeting; and such annual assembly, after the first assembly herein before appointed, to be held on the said day, shall not transact any other business than that of receiving and determining upon the annual report of the then existing Council; and that the elective assembly of the Chamber shall be held on the first Thursday in the month of June, in the year 1806, and on the first Thursday of every succeeding month of June, at such hours of the said day, and at such place in the City of Dublin, as shall be appointed by a like notice or summons, to be in like manner issued and published by the Council. And such elective assembly of the Chamber shall not transact any other business than that of electing members to fill the annual vacancies in the Council, as herein after mentioned. And that every special assembly of the Chamber shall also be held at such other time and place in the city of Dublin, and for such purposes, as shall be specified by notice or summons to be issued and published by the Council five clear days previous to the day of meeting, either at the option of the Council, or upon the requisition of any other nine general members of the Chamber, signed by them, and lodged with the Secretary; and such special assembly shall not transact any other business than that which shall have been specified in such notice or requisition. And that such annual, elective, and special assembly, may adjourn for the purpose of further considering the business for which it shall have been convened, but for no other purpose whatsoever.

No. XI. RESOLVED — That, previously to the first Thursday in the month of June, in the year 1806, and previously to the first Thursday in every succeeding month of June, the members of the then existing Council shall re-elect from their own body sixteen members, to compose part of the Council for the succeeding year; and that the elective assembly of the Chamber, herein before appointed to be held on every such first Thursday in the month of June, shall elect five members to complete the Council to the before mentioned number of twenty-one, out of those general members of the Chamber who had not been members of the Council for the last preceding year.

No. XII. RESOLVED — That the members of Council, on meeting pursuant to summons or adjournment, and on appointing one of their number present to be the chairman of the meeting, shall have full power and authority, according to the tenor and effect of these resolutions, and of any other permanent bye-laws, or temporary orders and instructions that shall be made and given by the Chamber, on behalf and in the name the Chamber, to act for the whole body of the Chamber, and, upon all proper and requisite occasions, to hold respectful communications with his Majesty's ministers, the members of either House of Parliament, and other persons of high station and authority, and to correspond and confer with similar institutions and individuals, respecting the commercial and manufacturing interests of the Chamber, and also to investigate and recommend improvements and alterations in the customary modes and rates of transacting commercial business, and also in the customary methods and forms of preparing and making up manufactures and other goods in the City of Dublin and its vicinity, and generally to manage and regulate all the other concerns and affairs incidental to the objects and purposes of this institution; and for these objects and purposes to collect and appropriate the revenue of the Chamber, and to regulate and adapt the proceedings of the Council; and that, in all cases where these resolutions are silent, and where no such permanent bye-laws or temporary orders or instructions shall have been made and given by the Chamber, the Council shall have full and absolute power and authority at its own discretion, on behalf and in the name of the Chamber, to act for the whole body of the Chamber, and to communicate, correspond, and confer with, all and every of the authorities, institutions and persons abovementioned, of and concerning all and every of the interests, affairs, and objects of this institution, and also to collect and appropriate the revenues of the Chamber, and to regulate and adapt the proceedings of the Council as fully and effectually, to all intents and purposes, as any assembly of the Chamber might have done; and the existing Council is hereby authorized, upon all special occasions, and questions of difficulty and importance, to call in the assistance and advice of any general or honorary member of the Chamber.

No. XIII. RESOLVED — That the Council is hereby invested with full power and authority, at its discretion, and without the control or interference of the Chamber, to appoint a Treasurer and Assistant Receivers, and also a Secretary, and such other officers and servants as the Council shall deem requisite for the Chamber; and from time to time, at the discretion of the Council, to remove them, or any of them, and to appoint other persons to the same offices, and to pay such officers and servants such salaries and emoluments as the Council shall deem suitable and requisite.

No. XIV. RESOLVED — That the Council shall appoint and provide an office for the accommodation of the business of the Chamber, and shall also cause books of the proceedings of the Council and Chamber to be provided and kept; which books of the proceedings shall be on the table at every Assembly of the Chamber, and shall at all other convenient times be open for the inspection of the members individually.

No. XV. RESOLVED — That it shall be the undoubted right of every member of the Chamber to propose any subject relevant to the objects and purposes of the institution, for the consideration of the Council, by memorial or other writing to be lodged with the Secretary, to be by him laid before the Council; and every such member shall, at all convenient times, be at liberty to confer with the Council upon the subject of such written proposal.

No. XVI. RESOLVED — That every notice, summons, or requisition, addressed to the members of this Chamber, shall be posted in a conspicuous part of the Coffee-room of the Commercial Buildings, and published in one of the daily newspapers of the City of Dublin, for five clear days successively, and next before the day of meeting, for the purpose therein specified, and that such posting and publication shall be deemed equivalent to personal service of such notice of requisition on each member.

No. XVII. RESOLVED — That the Chamber shall at all times be competent to alter or revoke the regulations herein contained, or that shall be hereafter substituted for them, provided that such alteration or revocation, as shall have been resolved upon, by one assembly, shall be confirmed at a subsequent assembly, to be held within fifteen days next after such former assembly.

No. XVIII. RESOLVED — That the foregoing resolutions shall be the articles of association and regulations of the Chamber of Commerce of the City of Dublin.

No. IX. RESOLVED — That the forgoing address and resolutions be printed for the use of the members, and that a copy be delivered to each member, on signing the roll, and paying his admission fine.

No. XX. RESOLVED — That Geo. F. Carleton Esq., our Chairman, be requested to authenticate these resolutions by his signature, and that the thanks of the meeting be presented to him for his conduct in the chair.

1.34 Limerick Chamber of Commerce 1807; also see charter 1815 in Chapter 2

Initially the chamber was founded in 1807 with a set of rules listed in the first document below. It subsequently sought and received a charter in 1815, but its main rules were given in the second document below through bye-laws agreed at a general meeting three weeks after receipt of the charter. It is an important example of a complex fee structure to support the chamber related to the type and volume of trade. Limerick also had very active involvement in regulating and providing local markets which interrelated with the fee structure.[75]

[75] Bennett, *Local Business Voice* (2011) 540–1; see also D. P. O'Connor, *The history and functions of the Limerick chamber of commerce 1807–1902*, MSc. Thesis (University College Dublin, 1938).

Sources
Chamber of Commerce, Minute Book, p. 1ff.: Limerick Archives P1/1.

Minutes 1807

LIMERICK CHAMBER OF COMMERCE

The Committee appointed at a Meeting of the Merchants of Limerick to digest a plan for the establishment of a Chamber of Commerce propose.

1. That an institution for the promotion, regulation, & protection of Trade in all its branches be immediately formed under the Title of the Limerick Chamber of Commerce.

2. That those Merchants & Traders of Limerick, who are willing to become members thereof, shall sign an agreement to abide by its regulations. Resolved

3. That a Committee consisting of nine Members of the Institution shall be chosen by ballot. That an Election for a new Committee shall be had on the first day of May in every Year.

4. That no Merchant shall be eligible for the Committee who shall not have paid within the Year preceding the day of Election, either by himself or commercial Firm: the Sum of £1500 duties on Goods imported, or shall not have exported articles to the Value of £3000. And that only one partner of any commercial firm shall be eligible.

5. That after the first Committee shall be chosen, the name of any person desirous to become a Member of the Institution must be submitted to the Committee, who shall decide whether such person is a Merchant or Trader of Limerick within the meaning of the Institution & that the said Committee shall ascertain what shall be the future qualification of the Electors.

6. That the Committee shall annually choose a President, Vice President, & Secretary by ballot, that five Members shall constitute a Quorum, & be considered competent to act on all occasions.

7. That the Committee shall, from time to time, form such plans & regulations for the Trade in general as they shall deem advantageous and likely to extend it.

8. That all complaints of abuses or impositions shall be made to the Committee, who may either decide & publish their opinions thereon or submit the matter to a general Meeting.

9. That no general Meeting shall be called except by the Committee, and they shall summon such Meeting when required by the signatures of twelve Members of the Institution. That eight days previous notice of the proposed Meeting must be given, in which notice the precise matter to be discussed shall be inserted, & that no other subject shall be introduced at such Meeting. [*Subsequent annotation in pencil:* That extra general Meetings shall be called

by the Committee, and that the president shall summon a general Meeting when required]

10. That the Committee shall have the sole direction of the Butter Crane, & the management of the concerns of that Branch of Trade, and of the funds arising from it, whereby the necessity of a particular Butter Committee will be superseded.

[11] That in order to give Respectability & Effect [to] this Institution, & to enable the Committee to defray such expenses as must be necessarily incurred in forwarding the objects of it, but more especially to enable them to protect the Members from all illegal & unjust charges, innovations or abuses of what nature or kind soever. It is deemed proper that a fund should be placed at the disposal of the Committee, who shall account for the same to the General Meeting which shall annually assemble to elect a new Committee.

[12] That a voluntary contribution of the following rates by the Members of the Institution appears to be a proper mode of forming such fund, which rates may be continued, increased or diminished by the Committee which shall be elected at the next Annual general Meeting, viz.

EXPORT RATES

¼d. per Barrel on Oats Barley & Malt, & per Cask [?] on Oatmeal
½d. per Barrel on Wheat, Rapeseed, Peas & Beans & per Bag on Flour
1d. per Firkin & ¾d. per Barrel on Salted Provisions
½d. per Tub and ¼d. per Firkin on Butter Lard & Tallow
¼d. per Bale [? per back] on Bacon
½d. per Dozen of Calf Skins
½d. per Hide
1d. per Bag of Quills & Feathers
3d. per Hhd [Hogshead] of Tallow & Lard.

IMPORT RATES

12d. per £100 on the Amount of Duties on Goods imported, when the Duties in one entry exceeds £100, when under that amount one shilling per Entry—

And one shilling each upon all Inward & Outward Entries of Goods not rated as above.

[13] That as Millers, Brewers & Distillers do not export much of their Corn or the produce thereof, & yet may be interested in the promotion, regulation & protection of the Corn Trade, they may be admitted Members of this Institution & entitled to the Benefits thereof, on signing an engagement to contribute such Rates on the Corn they purchase as may be mutually agreed upon between them & the first Committee which shall be appointed.

[14] That the Rates on Articles exported shall be paid previous to the clearing out of the Vessel, to one of the Clerks of the Custom House

appointed to receive the same. That the Rates on Goods imported be paid at the time of passing the Entry to the said clerk, whom the Committee shall be empowered to recompense for his trouble.

[15] That should any Member refuse or discontinue the Payment of the above Rates, he shall be no longer continued a Member, & shall not be again admitted without the consent of the Committee.

[16] That each Member shall be at liberty to withdraw from being a Member of the Chamber on giving notice thereof in writing to the Secretary.

[17] That in case any Merchant or Trader shall refuse to subscribe to the engagement this year & shall hereafter be desirous of becoming a Member of the Institution, he shall not be admissible until he shall have paid all arrears which shall appear due by him, as if he had been an original Member.

Minutes of Bye-laws enacted at First General Meeting 25 June 1815[b]

Bye Laws of The Limerick Chamber of Commerce; Incorporated the 2nd day of June 1815

First. —That the following be the Rates of Contribution to be paid by the Members of this Corporation viz.

Rates

On the quantity of corn &c. purchased—

One halfpenny per Barrel, on Wheat, Rapeseed, Pease & Beans & per Bag on Flour

One farthing per Barrel on oats, Barley & Malt, & per Cwt. on Oatmeal

—On the following articles exported—

One halfpenny per Tierce & 1/4d per Barrel on Salted Provisions

One penny per Firkin on Butter Lard & Tallow

One Farthing per Bale on Bacon

One halfpenny per Hide & per Dozen of Calf Skins

One penny per Bag of Quills & Feathers

Three pence per Hhd of Lard & Tallow

—Import Rates—

Six pence per Pipe of Wine, Hhd of Sugar

Hhd of Tobacco, per Puncheon of Spirits

Three Pence per Hhd of wine & per Tierce of Sugar under 10 Cwt.

Two Pence per quarter Cask of Wine

Three Pence per chest of Tea

One Penny per Ton of Rock Salt

Two pence per Ton of white or Bay Salt

One penny per Bag of East India Sugar

Two pence per Ton of Iron or Steel

Two pence per Bag & one penny per Docket of Hops

One penny per Ton of Timber
Three pence per 120 Deals of 12 feet & over
Two pence per 120 Deals under 12 feet
Three pence per Ton of oak Bark
One Shilling & one penny per Ton of Hemp or Flax
One halfpenny per Barrel of Pitch or Tar
Three Pence per [hundred?] of Pipe & 2d. per [hundred?] of Hhd or Barrel Staves
Two Shillings two pence per One Hundred Barrels Herrings
Two pence per Ton of Newfoundland Cod Fish
Four pence per Ton of Oil
Two pence per Hhd of Flaxseed

—And on all Entries Inward & Outward not enumerated as above one Shilling per Entry

Second. The Qualification for a Member to Vote at General meetings & for the election of the chamber of Directors shall be, a payment by the regulated contributions of forty Shillings, or upwards within the preceding year. When the annual payment by a commercial Firm amounts to forty shillings and not to four Pounds, one only of the Partners shall Vote. Should the said payment of such firm, amount to Four Pounds, two shall be qualified, and so in gradation according to the number of Partners and amount of payments.

Third. No Member shall be qualified, to be a Director, who shall not have paid within the year preceding the day of election, either by himself or commercial firm, the Sum of Fifteen Hundred Pounds duties on goods imported or who shall not have exported articles to the Value of Three Thousand Pounds.—Only one Partner of any Commercial Firm shall be eligible.

Fourth. The name of any person desirous to become a member of this corporation shall remain on the record Book for one week, at least, after being duly proposed & seconded before the Directors decide on his admissibility nor shall he be a member unless he shall have paid up within a Week after being elected the full amount of all contributions to which he would have been liable, had he been a Member since the original formation of the Society in 1807.

Fifth. No person who was not a Member of the Society previous to the 13th April 1813, or who shall be hereafter admitted a Member of this Corporation, shall have the privilege of Voting on any matter at a General Meeting, or of being elected on the Committee of Directors, until he shall have paid by the regulated Contributions a Sum not less than Fifty Pounds. Except the person approved of should be the Son of a Member, or should have served a regular apprenticeship to one, he shall in such case be entitled to the privileges of Voting or of being elected a Director, when he Shall in like manner have Contributed a Sum not less than Twenty Pounds or if the Son of a Member whose Commercial firm has Contributed One Hundred Pounds to this institution, shall be approved of by the Directors, he shall at once be admitted to all the rights & privileges of the Corporation.

Sixth. Each member shall be at liberty to withdraw himself from the Corporation upon giving notice thereof in writing to the Secretary & paying all arrears of contribution &c. which may appear due of him to that period.

Seventh. When any member shall refuse or neglect to pay, any arrears due, for one month after a written notice (signed by the Secretary) has been left at his house, the Directors shall be empowered to deprive him of the privileges of this Corporation.

Eighth. As the Rooms of the Corporation are not to be considered as Public News Rooms, Residents of the City or Neighbourhood cannot be admitted except for purposes of Business with the Body. Strangers may be introduced by members, who are to enter the names of such Strangers, with their own in the Strangers Book, and which introduction shall entitle such stranger to frequent the Rooms for one week.

Ninth. Bankruptcy shall not disqualify any Member provided he shall have procured a certificate, & shall have paid all debts or arrears which may appear due of him to the Corporation.

Tenth. Any member who retires from Trade and who, either by himself or Commercial firm, shall have contributed Fifty Pounds, at least, to the Funds of the Society, shall be considered as an honorary Member.

Eleventh. Any person who shall not have contributed, either by himself or Commercial firm, Forty shillings, in any of the three years preceding the annual day of Election, shall cease to be a Member, except qualified to be honorary.

Twelfth. All Complaints of abuses or impositions are to be made to the Directors, who may either decide thereon or Submit the matter to a General Meeting.

Thirteenth. The President shall summon a General Meeting of the corporation when required by the signatures of twelve members, notice in writing of the proposed meeting to be left at the dwelling house, or Countinghouse of each member, five days previous to the appointed day, in which notice the precise matter to be discussed shall be inserted and no other subject shall be introduced at said meeting.

Fourteenth. No person shall be entitled to the privileges of this corporation until he shall give assent by his signature to become a Member of the Body, & Submit to its regulations.

1.35 Guernsey Chamber of Commerce 1808

The first chamber founded in 1769 lapsed sometime after Arthur Young's reference to it in 1786. For the 1808 re-establishment of the Guernsey chamber the full minutes are quoted showing the form of deliberations that led up to defining new Rules. The chamber continued actively until 4 August 1819, but there is then a gap in the minutes until 9 January 1832 when it was re-founded, probably following a period of limbo.

Source
Guernsey Chamber of Commerce Minutes: Guernsey Archives AQ/040/01

Minute, and notice printed and pasted into minutes 15 November 1808

CHAMBER OF COMMERCE.
We the undersigned Merchants of Guernsey, taking into consideration the critical state of the Island, and the necessity there is for taking steps to preserve the few channels of trade left open to us, have resolved to unite and form a CHAMBER OF COMMERCE, for the purpose of concerting together on the means best adapted for that purpose; and think it indispensable in the first instance to declare our resolution not to carry on from this said Island, directly or directly, any illicit trade with the mother country, but on the contrary, to assist with all our power in the execution of the laws and ordinances passed for its suppression; and farther, that no person shall be admitted as a member, but will previously agree to sign a declaration and give his word to the same effect.
GUERNSEY, the 15th. Nov. 1808.

The above Declaration having been signed with the utmost alacrity by the Merchants and Traders of the Island. A general meeting was held at the Rooms in the Market-Place, on the 16th. December, 1808, when Daniel de Lisle Brock, Esq. having been called to the Chair, it was

RESOLVED,

I.—That a Chamber of Commerce be formed on the grounds of the above declaration, which this meeting is unanimously of opinion to confirm, and render more explicit by disclaiming all idea or intention of carrying on any illicit trade with the mother country, not only directly from the Island, but indirectly through any other port or place whatsoever.

II.—That in addition to the chairman, the following members be appointed a committee to frame the rules of the Chamber of Commerce, which shall be printed and distributed to all the members, previous to the general meeting to be held on Friday, December, 23d. 1808, for the purpose of taking the said rules into consideration

Bonamy Dobree,	John Arnold,
Thomas Priaulx,	John Mellish,
William Collings,	John Tupper, Junr.
Charles Bishop,	David Macculloch,
Daniel de Lisle,	Matthew Brock.

(Signed) Daniel de Lisle Brock, Chairman.

Minutes 17 December 1808

REPORT OF THE SAID COMMITTEE

It appears to this committee, that the objects of the CHAMBER OF COMMERCE should be solely of a public nature, to watch over and preserve the commercial advantages and privileges now enjoyed by this Island; collect all the laws, orders in council and ordinances that immediately affect its trade, and generally procure all the information that can be anywise useful to the merchant; to suggest & submit to the Royal Court, all such regulations & ordinances as may concern the harbours, roads and pilotage, and such as may be requisite to give aid and protection to the regular inhabitants and traders, and prevent those abuses arising from strangers who come here with stolen goods, or to defraud their creditors, and which not only tend to injure the regular trader, but give, undeservedly, a bad name to the Island.

It appears also to this committee, that by adhering strictly to the principles of this institution, all attempts to revive an illegal trade will be prevented, and new channels of fair commerce opened to the industry and enterprise of the inhabitants. Representations or petitions coming from all the respectable merchants and traders of this Island, united in one body, for a fair and honorable purpose, cannot fail of being attended to, and this Island may look for an extension of its trade where the same can be granted without injury to the interest of the Mother Country; particularly at a moment, like the present, when the Island has the inestimable good fortune of having a Commander in Chief who has given so many proofs of kind attention to the interest of this community, and whose countenance and support this Chamber can rely upon in the attainment of the object here proposed, and with the views and intentions here professed.

And your committee recommends, not only with the view to such co-operation, but as a just tribute of respect; that the General Meeting do authorize your said Committee to wait on our said Commander in Chief, SIR JOHN DOYLE with an account of the establishment of this Chamber of Commerce, and its proceedings.

And for the interior management and carrying on of the affairs of the Chamber of Commerce, this Committee recommends the following rules to the General Meeting

I.—That for the running expenses naturally incident on such an undertaking, every member shall pay on admission, 20s. and yearly 7s. 6d. on the second Tuesday in January.

II.—That should any extraordinary occasion occur, in which a larger sum should be wanted to oppose any illegal pretension, or assert our just rights, a General Meeting be called and consulted on the propriety of such opposition or assertion, and on the means of raising the money wanted.

III.—That a permanent Committee be elected by ballot, to consist of thirteen members, which shall choose a president, vice-president and secretary out of its own number; that the Committee first elected, shall act, until the second Tuesday in January, 1810, when four members shall go out by lot, and the same number be elected on that day by ballot; on the second Tuesday in January of the succeeding year, four of the original nine shall go out by lot, and the year after, the five old members shall go out, and so on ever after in rotation.

IV.—That the president, vice-president and secretary serve for one year, and be chosen by the Committee after the ballot for new members—the same to be re-eligible, but not obliged to serve more than two years running. The members that have served already in the Committee to be re-eligible by the General Meeting.

V.—That the members elected by the General Meeting to serve in the Committee, be obliged to serve for the first time, under the penalty of 40s. but not liable to be again fined for two years.

VI.—That independently of those who have already signed the original declaration, no one be admitted a member of this institution, except he be recommended by the committee; when admitted, that no one be at liberty to withdraw himself without giving previous notice to the Committee, and then be obliged to pay the ensuing year's subscription.

VII.—That seven of the Committee form a quorum, the Committee to regulate its own meetings and manner of proceeding, and have power to call a General Meeting when it shall judge proper.

VIII.—That on the requisition of any ten members of the Chamber of Commerce, the Committee be bound to call a General Meeting.

IX.—That a fine of 2s. 6d. be paid to the General Fund by each member who does not attend the general yearly meeting, on the second Tuesday in January.

X.—That no law be passed at a General Meeting until it has been referred to the Committee, and reported upon at a future General Meeting, when the majority shall decide upon it.

Minutes of General Meeting 23 December 1808

RESOLVED. I.—That the Rules proposed by the Committee be approved of, as the standing Rules of the Chamber of Commerce.

II.—That where a larger sum shall be wanted as expressed in the second article, such money be raised in proportion to the quantity of Goods imported by each member, as nearly as can be ascertained for a year before.

III.—That the Committee be desired to wait on Sir John Doyle, Bart. our present Lt. Governor and Commander in Chief, with an account of the resolutions and proceedings of the Chamber of Commerce, the assurance of its sincere respect and esteem, and the request of his kind support.

IV.—That the present Committee be desired to act until the second Tuesday in January, 1809, when the general and yearly meeting will take place, and the permanent Committee[e] be elected, on which day, all the members are to attend without further notice.
DANIEL DE LISLE BROCK, Chairman.

1.36 Plymouth Chamber of Commerce 1813

Printed versions of the notices and various reports of the early chamber were brought together and published by William Burt in 1816. These provide the main surviving material on the early chamber.[76] The first public meeting on 7 December clearly followed a Plan that had been produced by George Soltau, a prominent Plymouth merchant and banker who was also involved in the London chamber proposals in 1823, where his opinions would have drawn on Plymouth's experience (see Chapter 4).

Sources
[a] Printed notice: Monkes of Saltram MS, Plymouth and West Devon RO
[b] Report reprinted in W. Burt, *Review of the Mercantile, Trading, and Manufacturing State, Interests, and Capabilities of the Port of Plymouth* (Plymouth, 1816): Plymouth Central Library P371.1, Accession No. L3730

Printed Notice 7 December 1813[a]

Borough of Plymouth.

At a very numerous and respectable Meeting of the Merchants, Ship-Owners, and other Persons interested in the Prosperity of the Port of Plymouth and the Neighbourhood, held this Day at the Guildhall of and within the said Borough, and convened by the Worshipful the MAYOR, by

[76] Burt was the first secretary of the chamber; brief discussion in R. N. Worth, *History of Plymouth from the Earliest Period to the Present Time* (Plymouth, 1871) 235–6.

Public Advertisement, in Pursuance of a Requisition for the Purpose to consider of the best Means to be adopted for converting the Facilities afforded by the recent Improvements in different Parts of the Port, to the permanent Extension of the Trade and Commerce thereof.

The Worshipful HENRY WOOLLCOMBE, *Esq. Mayor, in the Chair*.

Resolved—That it is the Opinion of this Meeting, that owing to the *increased*, and *increasing* Population of these Towns and Neighbourhood, it is a Matter of *essential* Importance, that every *Inquiry* should be made, and every Information obtained, as to the Possibility of *forming* and *establishing such a Trade*, as the peculiar Advantages possessed by the Port of Plymouth, may render practicable, and as may be commensurate with the Demands of the Public.

Resolved—That it is the Opinion of this Meeting, that the *great National Work* now carrying on in PLYMOUTH SOUND [the construction of the breakwater], as well as other *Public Improvements*, recently completed, should operate as an additional Inducement to all Persons interested, to give Effect to any Measure which promises such *general Advantages* to the Port and Neighbourhood.

Resolved—That it is the Opinion of this Meeting, that no Measure of any *permanent* and *substantial Efficacy* can be effected, without the *cordial Union* and *Co-operation* of the different Persons concerned.

Resolved—That a Committee be appointed to consider of the Means best calculated to give Effect to the above Resolutions, and to report their Opinion to a subsequent General Meeting, to be held on the 28th Instant, at the GUILDHALL, at Twelve o'Clock at Noon.

Resolved—That the Committee do consist of the following Persons, (viz.)

The Mayor	Messrs. James Slade	Messrs. J. Harris, Junr.
Lord Boringdon	W. Langmead	J. Elford
Messrs. J. Collier	W. Lockyer	J. Cleverton
E. Lockyer	P. Welsford	R. Fuge, Junr.
W.H. Hawker	A. Nicholls	D. Forrest
Rd. Bayly	J. Arthur	I. Blackburne
R. Fuge	H. Canning	and
G. Soltau	Geo. Forysth	Joseph Moore
W. Hodge	W. Prance	

And that any Seven of them be competent to act.

Resolved—That it be a special Instruction to the Committee, to consider and report how far it may be right to establish in the Port, SOME PERMANENT SOCIETY, with a View to the *Encouragement of Trade*, and that Mr. SOLTAU'S Plan for forming such Society, and any other of a similar Nature, which may be presented, do come under their particular Notice.

Resolved—That these Resolutions be signed by the Chairman, and published in Hand-Bills, and in the Plymouth Chronicle, and Dock Telegraph. HEN. WOOLLCOMBE, Mayor.

Printed Report 28 December 1813[b]

BOROUGH OF PLYMOUTH.

At a most numerous and respectable meeting of the Merchants, Ship-Owners, and other persons interested in the prosperity of the Port of Plymouth and the neighbourhood, held this day at the Guildhall of and within the said Borough, in virtue of a resolution of adjournment passed at the General Meeting, convened on the 7th instant.

The Worshipful HENRY WOOLLCOMBE, *Esq. Mayor, in the Chair.*

Resolved,—That the Report of the Committee, to whom was referred the consideration of the means best calculated to give effect to the Resolutions of the 7th inst. be read.

Your Committee further beg leave to express their opinion that when this Port shall become a considerable Depot for Colonial and Foreign produce—when the Fisheries shall have been duly extended—and the Manufactories increased,—the Coasting and Inland Trade will both be necessarily augmented, by furnishing at a lower rate the different articles heretofore supplied to them by Bristol, London, and other Ports.

And altogether the opportunities for Trade and Commerce appear to your Committee multifarious and prodigiously extensive, presenting to the Merchant a full scope for enterprise and perseverance, and to the various classes of Inhabitants full employment, and a vend for their Manufactures and produce. *To the Proprietors of Mines*, by the export of Tin to Canada, Newfoundland, East Indies; and by supplying the Arsenal. *To the Proprietors of Quarries*, by the export of Lime to the West Indies, Slates to Canada, Halifax, and Newfoundland—by the supply of Lime for manure and various purposes in the interior, also of Slates and Marble Slabs coastways.—*To the Woollen Manufacturers*, by the exports to Canada, Halifax, Newfoundland, and the Baltic.—*To the Proprietors of Salt Works*, by the increase of the Pilchard, Herring, Ling, and Hake Fisheries, and of the Newfoundland Fishery, by export to the Baltic, by supplying Salt for salting Provisions for the West Indies, and to the Victualling Office. *To the Proprietors of Fisheries*, by the export of Pilchards to the West Indies and Mediterranean, Salted Herrings and Ling to the West Indies and the Continent, and Red Herrings and Salted Hake coastways and into the interior. *To the Farmers, Graziers, and Landholders*, by the demand for Cattle for the Victualling Office and increase of Shipping, Salted Provisions for the West Indies, Hay and Oats for Transports, Vegetables and Poultry for Shipping, Cheese, Bacon, and Butter for the West Indies and Victualling Office, Barley (for Malt) and Hops for Private Breweries and the King's Brew-House, Grain for the Distilleries, Flax and Wool for the Manufactories, Potatoes to Gibraltar, Mules for the West Indies. *To the Proprietors of Breweries*, by the export of Porter to the West Indies, East Indies, Canada, Newfoundland, Halifax, Gibraltar, the Mediterranean, and different parts of the Continent; by the supplies to the Arsenal, and the increased Shipping in the Port.—*To the Rope-makers and Twine Spinners*, by export of Cordage to the West Indies, Newfoundland, Canada, and for the Southern Fisheries, for increase of Shipping to the Port; and Twine for the Fisheries, Sail Cloth Manufactories, and the Arsenal.—*To Paper Makers*, by the supplies of Stationery to the Government departments at the Port, and the export to the West Indies, Canada, Halifax, and Newfoundland.—*To the Taylors, Hatters, Shoemakers*, &c. by exports to the West Indies, Canada, Newfoundland, and Gibraltar.

Under the fourth head of this Report, your Committee would flatter itself with the hope that it might suggest some new arrangements and facilities beneficial to the public interest.

[extensive *Report* is then printed, which lists various initiatives needed for Plymouth to develop greater participation in various commodity trades and navigational improvements, including extension of the Breakwater. It also notes (p. 27) 'there having hitherto been at this Port no place of general rendezvous for those engaged in commerce, [and] there had not been upon all occasions, an entire co-operation among the Merchants'. Published document then continues:]

Your Committee agreeably to the order and arrangement which they prescribed to themselves in the outset of this Report, have thus, in the FIRST instance, detailed the information they have collected relative to the important subject confided to their investigation.

They have, in the SECOND place, set forth some of the impediments which in their view have hitherto contributed to oppose the establishment of an extensive Trade to this Port.

THIRDLY, they have specified different lines and objects of Trade which they conceive may be worthy of the more minute enquiry, and the attention, diligence, and enterprise of the Merchants.

FOURTHLY, they have humbly submitted their sentiments as to the creation of new arrangements and facilities for the establishment of an advantageous Commerce.

Having done this, they beg at the same time, to be permitted to express their decided opinion.

That the information which they have collected will best be improved.

That the existing impediments against Trade, will be effectually removed.–

That the different lines and objects of Trade which they have enumerated will be most advantageously opened.

That the new arrangements which they have suggested will be most judiciously effected, by the permanent establishment of

A CHAMBER OF COMMERCE,

Under the Rules and Regulations hereinafter mentioned.

1.—That the following Noblemen and Gentlemen having signified their intention of becoming Members of the Chamber, be Directors of the same.

His Grace the Duke of BEDFORD
The Right Honourable the Earl of MOUNT EDGCUMBE
The Right Honourable Lord ELIOT
The Right Honourable Lord BORINGDON
The Right Honourable R.P. CAREW, M.P.
Sir WILLIAM ELFORD, Bart.
Sir CHARLES POLE, Bart. M.P.
Sir MASSEH LOPES, Bart. M.P.
Sir JOHN PERING, Bart. M.P.
J.P. BASTARD, Esq. M.P.
BENJAMIN BLOOMFIELD, Esq. M.P.
FRANCIS GLANVILLE, Esq.
JOHN HARRIS, Esq.

2.—That a Managing Committee consisting of twenty Members be elected by ballot, at the Guildhall, between the hours of twelve and two, on Tuesday the fourth day of January next, by the then existing Members of the Chamber, (the Chairman of this Committee taking the ballot) and in future years, such election, by ballot, shall take place at the Annual Meeting, hereinafter appointed to be held.

3.—All those Persons shall be considered existing members of the Chamber on the fourth day of January next, who shall before that day inscribe their names in one of the Books to be opened for that purpose at the Banks in the Town.

4.—That the Committee when elected do immediately proceed, by ballot, to the appointment of their Chairman, Deputy Chairman, and Treasurer, and do also appoint a Secretary, with a proper Salary.

5.—That all Persons who shall subscribe one guinea per annum, and otherwise conform to these Rules and Orders shall become Members of the Chamber.

6.—That in aid of the above Subscription, and for the better establishing and continuing a Fund to defray the expenses of the Chamber, all Members shall pay upon the entry inwards and outwards of each Ship or Vessel, at the Custom House, and for the Goods and Merchandize on board such Ship or Vessel, which is consigned, or belongs to them, or for which they act as

Agents, the several sums set opposite the respective articles enumerated in the annexed Schedule [this does not survive].

7.—The Committee shall meet monthly, and oftener if necessary, and at such Meetings, the Chairman, Deputy, Chairman, or Treasurer, and four Members shall be competent to transact Business, and shall be empowered to convene Special Assemblies of the Chamber whenever they may deem it requisite.

8.—An Annual Meeting of the Chamber shall be held on the second Tuesday in December, to appoint Officers for the ensuing year, to audit the accounts of the past, to revise the Rules and Orders, if necessary, and transact all other business that may be requisite for the welfare of the establishment.

9.—That at such Annual Meeting a Report shall be made by the Committee upon all the various matters which have engaged their attention in the preceding year,[77] and which they may deem necessary or useful to be communicated.

10.—That those members who shall refuse or neglect to pay up their subscription for two years following, shall cease to be considered as belonging to the Chamber.

1.37 Birmingham Commercial Society 1813

The first Birmingham Commercial Society had fairly continuous existence from 1783 into the early 1800s, and appears to have operated under essentially the same rules throughout (see earlier). However, after a period of inactivity is was revived in 1813 with new rules and for the first time explicitly took the title of chamber. This was short-lived, needing further efforts in 1820. The modern chamber was founded in 1842.[78]

Source
Aris's Birmingham Gazette

Printed Leaflet 19 July 1813

The following Prospectus of the BIRMINGHAM COMMERCIAL SOCIETY

Having been circulated amongst the merchants and manufacturers of this town, we are desired to lay it before the public.

[77] Presumably this meant by ballot by the committee who appointed officers under rules 2 and 4.
[78] See Wright, *Chronicles* (1913) 49–58.

The vast importance of the commerce and manufactures of this country to its welfare—the necessary dependence of its public revenue upon the resources of its merchants and manufacturers—and the reliance of a large proportion of its population for subsistence upon a foreign demand for the produce of its well-directed industry—all demonstrates the propriety of adopting some place by which these very general interests may be fairly appreciated, and efficiently supported.

The strong and immediate interest which the middle classes feel in the commercial prosperity of the country, leads them to investigate and discriminate the bearings of public measures upon its commerce and manufactures: but the members of that class of society of which the legislature is composed have seldom a personal acquaintance with trade, cannot be expected to possess that intimate knowledge of its relations which is so essentially requisite in all cases where it becomes the object of legislative control.

Hence it has frequently happened that the interests of the manufacturing districts have been unintentionally sacrificed to erroneous commercial and political regulations, whilst the landed, the shipping, the Colonial, and other great and powerful interests have been protected by their advocates in Parliament, by concentrating their information and influence, and directing their attention to such proceedings of administration and the legislature as they conceived likely in any degree to affect their interests.

Since a watchful superintendence has been found thus beneficial to obtain interests, surely the manufacturers of the United Kingdom (consisting of nearly a fourth part of its population, and, according to the calculation of Mr. Pitt, as far back as the year 1798, employing a capital of £120,000,000) ought to exercise a similar vigilance, to investigate the causes which have a tendency to retard or promote their prosperity, and endeavour to establish a bond of union which would render the influence of their joint exertions co-extensive with their national importance.

The preceding observations, though general in their nature, are particularly applicable to Birmingham and its neighbourhood, unquestionably one of the most important manufacturing districts in the kingdom, the value of its manufactures being principally made up of the labour bestowed upon them by a very numerous population, employed, not only in raising a native and abundant raw produce, but in converting the metals so raised into all those useful and ornamental forms which contribute so largely to the necessities, conveniences, and elegance of life: whilst they augment the national prosperity by the collective industry and ingenuity required by their production.

Happily for the commercial and manufacturing part of the community, members of both Houses of Parliament have recently evinced a greater desire than at any former period, justly to appreciate the relations of commerce to the general interests of the Empire, and have found that they involve some of the most important principles of political economy that they are totally inconsistent with a narrow system of municipal arrangements for the benefit of a few, and that the diffusion of the commercial spirit has been most instrumental in advancing the national welfare.

These considerations, especially when viewed with reference to the unparalleled efforts which have been made to exclude our manufactures from the Continent of Europe, and the increasing competition consequent on the suspension of intercourse with America, forcibly indicate the necessity of establishing a Commercial Society in Birmingham, composed of its most respectable and intelligent merchants and manufacturers, for the purpose of collecting and comparing their opinions—of acting as a medium of communication with ministers and the legislature on the subject of trade, and of co-operating with other parts of the kingdom on all questions affecting the general prosperity of manufactures and commerce of the British Empire.

Such an institution, it is conceived, would be no less advantageous to the Government than beneficial to the trading part of the community; since it would enable the former to avail itself of a greater mass of intelligence than could be collected by any other means, and ensure to the interests of the latter that protection to which they are so amply entitled, and which, there can be no doubt, it is the wish of ministers at all times to afford.

Printed report 14 July 1813

To Richard Spooner, Esq., High Bailiff of Birmingham.

We, the undersigned, considering that it is expedient to establish a COMMERCIAL SOCIETY in the town of Birmingham, for the purpose of collecting and comparing the opinions of its principal merchants and manufacturers—of acting as a medium of communication with ministers and the legislature on the subject of trade and of co-operating as occasion may require with other parts of the United Kingdom on all questions affecting the general prosperity of the manufactures and commerce of the British Empire, do request you to call a Town's Meeting, to take the same into consideration.

...

In consequence of the above highly respectable requisition, I do appoint a Meeting of Merchants, Manufacturers, and other INHABITANTS of this town, to be holden in the ROYAL HOTEL, on WEDNESDAY NEXT, the 21st instant, at ELEVEN O'clock in the forenoon.

Printed report Birmingham, July 21st 1813

At a General Meeting of the Merchants, Manufacturers, and other Inhabitants of this town, held this day at the Royal Hotel, convened by the

High Bailiff, in compliance with a requisition addressed to him for the purpose of taking into consideration the propriety of establishing a Commercial Society in the Town of Birmingham.
Richard Spooner, Esq., High Bailiff, in the chair.
Resolved unanimously —

(1) That it is expedient to establish a Commercial Society in the Town of Birmingham, for the purpose of collecting and comparing the opinions of its merchants and manufacturers, of acting as a medium of communication with ministers and the legislature on the subject of trade, and of co-operating, as occasion may require, with other parts of the United Kingdom, on questions affecting the general prosperity of the manufactures and commerce of the British Empire.

(2) That the proposed Society be called 'The Chamber of Manufacturers and Commerce of Birmingham.'

(3) That all persons interested in the manufactures and commerce of this town and neighbourhood, subscribing a sum of not less than one guinea per annum, be considered members of the Society. Subscriptions to be received by the treasurer or secretary, and paid in advance for the first year. Subsequent subscriptions to be paid when called for by the Committee, providing that not more than one call be made in each year. Every member intending to leave the Society shall give six months' notice of his intention to the secretary, in writing, or be liable to pay the subscription for the ensuing year.

(4) That sixty members be chosen as a Committee to manage the affairs of the Society, and that ten be competent to act.

(5) That fifteen members of the Committee shall annually go out, for the first three years, by ballot, of the original Committee, and afterwards by rotation, and that such fifteen shall not be re-eligible for that year.

(6) That the Committee shall annually elect a Chairman, Deputy Chairman, Secretary, and Treasurer, and supply any vacancies that may occur in their number during the year. Any person chosen to supply a vacancy shall go out in the same rotation as his predecessor would have done.

(7) That the Annual General Meeting of the Society shall be held on the first Tuesday in June, at which Meeting of the Committee shall report their proceedings. Auditors shall be appointed, and fifteen members be elected upon the Committee to supply the places of those who go out, by each member then present, personally delivering a list of fifteen names eligible to serve on the Committee.

(8) That printed lists of the Members of the Society eligible to serve on the Committee, shall be sent to each subscriber at least seven days previous to the Annual General Meeting.

(9) That the Committee shall be empowered to make Bye Laws for their own Government; such Bye Laws to be approved by two-thirds of the Committee specially summoned for that purpose.

(10) That the Committee shall keep an accurate register of all their proceedings in a book to be prepared for that purpose, which book shall be open for the inspection of any member of the Society at any meeting of the Committee.

(11) That any twenty of the Committee shall be empowered to call a Special General Meeting of the Members of the Society on giving seven days' notice by a circular letter to each member, or by advertisement in the Birmingham papers.

(12) That it shall be imperative on the Chairman, or, in his absence, on the Deputy Chairman of the Committee, to call a Special General Meeting of the Subscribers, on receiving a written requisition from one hundred members of the Society, or any smaller number, constituting not less than one-fourth of the whole; such requisition to state the object of the Meeting.

(13) That the conduct of the Committee on all questions shall be subject to the control and be regulated by the decisions of the Annual and Special General Meetings.

(14) That the gentlemen who signed the requisition for the Town's Meeting, together with the High Bailiff, be elected a Provisional Committee, and that they be directed to call a General Meeting of the Subscribers at the expiration of three months, when a Committee shall be elected for the current year, by the members then present marking lists previously laid on the table for that purpose. Any appointment made by the Provisional Committee to cease at the formation of the permanent Committee.

(15) That the Secretary shall keep a correct list of all subscribers to this Society, which list shall at all times be open to the examination of any subscriber.

(16) That Paul Moon James, Esq., be appointed Treasurer, and that he be requested to obtain signatures and to receive subscriptions.

(17) That these resolutions be printed in such papers as the High Bailiff shall think proper.

— Richard Spooner.

1.38 Greenock Chamber of Commerce and Manufactures 1813; also see charter 1813 in Chapter 2

The chamber at Greenock was founded in 1813. However, before this a very active body acted like a chamber: the Merchants House of Greenock. It is cited in the Glasgow chamber's records as lobbying on various issues; e.g. on 10 September 1790 Glasgow reports Greenock's grievances about the Customs House fees on certain goods. In this case the Glasgow chamber formed a committee of four merchants from Greenock to cooperate with the Greenock Merchants House in order to procure redress and send a memorial if necessary. The Glasgow chamber also made strong efforts to recruit members from Greenock. However, the 1813 initiative demonstrates a desire for greater independent voice for Greenock. The following document is a listing of bye-laws to its charter.

Source
Chamber minute book: founding articles: Greenock Archives TD 508/1

Minute 5 January 1814

At a General meeting (being the first) of the Chamber of Commerce and Manufactures of Greenock; incorporated by Royal Charter; held in the Tontine Inn on Wednesday the fifth day of January Eighteen Hundred and fourteen.

Mr Alexander Dunlop was called to the Chair. The meeting proceeded to Consider the transactions of the Committee which had been appointed for the purpose of drawing up a System of Rules and regulations for the Society; An abstract of these proceedings was laid before them by the Chairman of the Committee in the following Report.

"On the third of March last, the following Gentlemen Messers. George Robertson, James Hunter, Robert Ewing, James Tasker, David Hyde, Rodger Stewart, James Leitch, John Denniston Junior, James Ritchie, John Buchanan Junior and Gersham Stewart were appointed a Committee for the purpose of drawing up regulations; which having been framed, were approved of at a general meeting of Subscribers held in the Underwriting room on the twenty eighth April: and at the same meeting the above named Gentlemen were appointed a Committee to take the requisite steps for incorporating the Society into a body Politic; and a Subscription was raised for defraying the necessary experience.

As the Lord Advocate is the official person through whom all charters of the kind in question passes, it was thought advisable prior to any application to Government, to explain to his Lordship the views of the Merchants of Greenock on the subject; and at same time, to lay before him a copy of the proposed regulations. He expressed himself favourable to the resolution, and approved of the regulations that had then adopted, with the exception of one clause of little consequence, which the committee expunged. After a course of correspondence, between the Committee or their Secretary, and the Lord Advocate, Mr Richardson of London and other professional Gentlemen, the Royal warrant for the Charter was transmitted in the month of November, and the Charter was received from Edinburgh in this town in the middle of December.

In laying the Charter before the Corporation the Committee by way of explanation beg to Remark, that in matters of this kind, it being essential either that the whole system of Regulations of the Society should be engrossed into the body of the Charter; or that the Charter should bestow powers, whereby such regulations might be afterwards introduced in the form of Bye Laws: The committee resolved to adopt the latter method; chiefly, because in that way a considerable sum was to be saved to the institution; since the expense in the London offices is in a great measure determined by the number of words which the Charter contains. And therefore by keeping out that part of the regulations which related chiefly to Internal management, the object of oeconomy was in some degree gained. On this Account the Corporation at their first General meeting will require to enact those parts of the Regulations, that have been left out of the Charter, into bye Laws. And upon looking at their charter they will find that they have ample powers of doing so. The committee on the same principle of avoiding expense resolved that the Charter should nominatim incorporate [those specifically named above] only those persons who had been elected to the office of Directors and Secretary; because a considerable fee is charged at the London Offices in the name of each individual in the Charter. By these means the persons who form the Corporation at present are the Directors and Secretary alone; and the General subscription fall to be formally admitted by them at the next general meeting, as members of the Corporation.—The Committee farther state, that the Subscriptions Collected by them amount to Four hundred and four Pounds five Shillings Sterling. That the sum laid out as expenses of framing the regulations and procuring the incorporation of the society Amounts to Two hundred and Thirty four Pounds one Shilling and eight pence halfpenny Sterling; leaving a balance of One hundred and Seventy Pounds three Shillings and three pence halfpenny Sterling in their hands; which with the consent of this meeting they will hand over to the Directors for the general purposes of the institution. With this statement the Committee beg leave to close their Report."

[Signed] T. Leitch, Chairman

The meeting having taken the previous into Consideration resolved unanimously that the thanks of the corporation be presented to the members of the Committee, for their exertions in behalf of the society. And direct the above balance of One hundred and Seventy Pounds three Shillings and three pence half penny Sterling be paid over to the Directors. The Secretary then produced to the meeting their Royal Charter of Incorporation, which having read aloud by appointment of the meeting, he was afterwards ordered to express in the Statute Book of the Chamber, and lay it up with the Society's papers. THE MEETING then proceeded to consider that WHEREAS by that charter, the corporation by a Majority of voices of the members present at any General meeting, periodical or Extraordinary, are empowered to make and Establish bye laws, Constitutions, ordinances and regulations for the conduct of the said Corporation in the transaction and management of all its affairs, and for the election and admission of members; And fixing as to the fees of admission, and annual Subscriptions or compositions therefore to be paid them; And the penalties and forfeiture of privileges in case of not regular payment of annual Subscriptions; for fixing as to the Meetings ordinary or extraordinary of the directors, the time and place of meeting; the mode of Convention and Generally all matters in any manner of way connected therewith; for ascertaining the mode of the acceptance of the Office of Directors when elected and declaration thereof; for Supplying vacancies in the Direction, in case of none acceptance death or otherways; for the determination and regulation of the whole business and duty of the Directors, and of their Chairman, Deputy Chairman, Secretary or other officers, that may be appointed and the responsibility of any of them; and generally for the Regulations and Conducting of the affairs of the said corporation, as fully freely and effectually as the members of any other like Corporation may or can do, and as is not inconsistent with the Laws and practice of Scotland;—provided always that no byelaw which should fix, alter, or affect the fees of entrance or annual contributions to be paid by the members shall be binding, or of force unless it should be agreed to by two thirds of the members of the Corporation present at any General meeting. AND WHEREAS for the reasons mentioned in the Report of the Committee it is expressed that certain byelaws and constitutions should be enacted for the better regulating and conducting the affairs of the Corporation. The meeting therefore unanimously resolved upon the following; which had been recommended by the said committee for adoption, conform[able] to their minute dated the fifteenth December Eighteen hundred and thirteen years

PRIMO It shall be understood that the Society is established upon the most liberal and equitable foundation, and all Merchants traders or Manufacturers who shall reside in Greenock and its vicinity shall have the privilege of being Committee members of the Corporation. The sum of Five guineas shall be paid by each Member on his admission and one Guinea per annum thereafter. Those who shall subscribe Twenty Guineas in the first instance shall be considered as members for life and entitled to all the privileges of the Society without any annual payment. Those who enter at Five Guineas and fail afterwards to pay one guinea per Annum, shall forfeit all right and Title as the privileges of the Corporation so long as the arrears shall remain unpaid.

SECUNDO The great outlines of the business committed to the charge of the Directors (exclusive of that pointed out in His Majesty's charter) shall be to read and discuss all public and private Memorials and representations of members of the Chamber requesting the aid of the directors in any matter regarding Trade and Manufacturers.—To afford aid by their advice and influence to members whether as individuals or otherways, who may apply for assistance in regulating any matter of business, whether local or of a nature which requires the weight and influence of the directors in making application to the public Boards, to the King's ministers, to Parliament, or otherways.—To procure relief or redress in any grievance, hardship, oppression or inconvenience affecting any particular branch of Trade or Manufactures carried on by the members of this Society, by interposing the weight and influences of the Directors in any public negotiation that may be thought necessary to effect such relief; and in general to take Cognisance of every matter and thing that shall be in the least degree connected with the interest of commerce.—To assist in pointing out new Sources for promoting whatever may be useful and beneficial, and to attend every application made to Parliament which may be thought injurious to the Trade and Manufactures of this Country.—To support an intercourse and friendly correspondence with the Members of Parliament for the Boroughs and County, as also the Board of Trustees for Fisheries and Manufactures and the Boards of Custom and Excise; the other Chambers of Commerce and Manufactures established throughout the Kingdom, and others for the purpose of Communicating new and useful improvements to their attention.—In addition to the above mentioned duty of the twelve Directors it shall be incumbent on them to accept of arbitrations in disputes upon Mercantile Cases among those who are privileged by being members of the Chamber in order to save them the heavy expense attending Law suits. And for this purpose the directors or their quorum shall choose two of their number best qualified according to the nature of the dispute; who in case of difficulties shall state the Case to the Chamber of Directors at Large; in order to obtain every advantage which may be supposed to arise from the Combined ideas of the most intelligent Members who preside for the time.—After which the arbiters chosen shall again reconsider the matter in dispute, and in case of ultimate disagreement the Chairman or in his absence the deputy Chairman shall act as umpire or oversman and shall pronounce a final Decree within a period not exceeding four months from the time the matters at issue came under his Cognisance.

TERTIO It shall be the peculiar province of the Chairman and in his absence the Deputy Chairman to convene all extraordinary meetings of the Directors; to prepare all business to be brought under discussion, to superintend the Correspondence of the Chamber; and in general to do and perform all matters and things which are understood to belong to the office of Chairman or President of any similar Society.

QUARTO It shall be the province of the Secretary besides what is pointed out in His Majesty's Charter, to receive Memorials, letters and applications on the Subject of the Public business; to assist in the arrangement of the same for the Consideration of the directors, to frame and engross the Minutes and resolutions of the directors or of the Corporation at large; to have the charges of Convening all ordinary periodical meetings as well of the Directors as of the Members at large; to keep the accounts of the Society, and in general to take the whole executive charge of the matters Connected with the affairs of the Society; for all which he is to be allowed an annual Salary, and in his capacity of Treasurer he shall lodge the money belonging to the Corporation in such place as the Directors for the time may appoint; and the Directors shall further have the power of specifying an amount, any sum beyond which it shall not be lawful for the Secretary to retain in his hands at any period, It shall be also part of the Secretary's Office to act and clerk in all arbitrations which may fall under the cognisance of the Chamber of directors; To bring the same regularly before the Arbiters, and in general to do and perform all those duties, which are understood to belong to the Clerk of an arbitration for which he shall be allowed the usual fee paid for such business, to be recovered according to the award of the arbiters; But he shall always record the cases and decisions in a Book for the purpose

QUINTO Each Director shall accept the Trust committed to him when within three days after his election if in town; and if absent within three days after his return; and that by subscribing his name in a Book to be kept for that purpose by the Secretary. And in case of failure so to do, the nomination to be void and a new election to take place; And in case at any time there shall be casual or occasional vacancies not exceeding three, among the Directors, by declensions to act, death or otherways, then and in that case the remainant Directors themselves without the necessity of a general meeting of the Corporation shall have power to nominate and appoint new directors who shall accept of the office in manners above specified.

SEXTO Besides the procedure directed by His Majesty's Charter at the two general meetings of the Corporation in January and July—The Chairman or Deputy Chairman shall state to the meeting all matters of business under the consideration of the Chamber of Directors for the time being, together with full information regarding what may be the subject of discussion for the ensuing half year, at these meetings;—also a state of the funds of the Society shall be exhibited by the Secretary;—and it shall be competent for any member to recommend to the consideration of the directors any matter whatsoever connected with Trade and Manufactures where the assistance or interference of the Chamber of directors may be thought necessary.—In case it may be found necessary the general meetings may be adjourned by the chairman or deputy chairman.

SEPTIMO The Directors shall hold four general periodical meetings to be called by the Secretary by notices in writing on the last Wednesdays of January, April, July and October each year. At these meetings the transactions of the last periodical Convention shall be read over by the Secretary as well as proceedings and resolutions of any extraordinary meetings which may have been held during the interval; and such further resolutions shall be formed for the benefit of the Society and the trade of the Country as shall occur to be proper at the time.—In cases of urgent necessity it shall be lawful for the Chairman or Deputy Chairman in his absence to call an extraordinary meeting of Directors on the shortest notice and proceed to business provided there are a proper quorum.

OCTAVO And further to save trouble and confusion it was enacted that all business to be brought before the directors should be done by Memorial or letter alone.—The Directors were appointed a Committee to consider and make choice of the device and form of a Seal to be used as the common seal of the Corporation And thereafter to cause such Seal to be made and given to the Secretary for the purpose of being appended where required.—The aforesaid bye laws were appointed to be engrossed in the Statute Book, His Majesty's Charter having been previously engrossed therein.

1.39 [Nottingham Chamber of Commerce proposal 1813: see Chapter 4]

1.40 Newcastle-upon-Tyne Chamber of Commerce 1815

Source
Newcastle first chamber minute book: Tyne and Wear Archives 2401/1/1

Printed leaflet glued into minute book 5 January 1815

AT a MEETING OF MERCHANTS, MANUFACTURERS, and SHIP-OWNERS of the port of Newcastle, held at the Merchants' Court, on the 5th January 1815;
BENJ. SORSBIE, Esq. in the Chair;
The following Rules and Resolutions were adopted for regulating the Proceedings of "The Newcastle upon Tyne Chamber of Commerce".

1st,—That all merchants, manufacturers, and ship-owners, and others interested in the Commerce of the Tyne, be eligible as Members of the Chamber of Commerce.

2d,—That a list be formed of the names of such gentlemen as are present, and desirous of becoming Members, and that such gentlemen immediately proceed to the election of a Committee, which shall consist of a President, three vice Presidents, and twelve other Members; the Committee having power to appoint its own Secretary and Treasurer.

3rd,—That the purposes of the present institution are, the addressing of all Grievances in any wise affecting the Trade of the Port—the facilitating of any Measures calculated to promote the Interest and Prosperity of our local Commerce—and generally the Attainment of such Objects, connected with the Commerce of the Port, as the exertions of individuals may be less adequate to accomplish.

4th,—That the Committee shall meet at the Merchants' Court, at 12 o'clock, on the first Thursday in every month, for the consideration and regular dispatch of business; that five members shall be a quorum; and that in any case of an equal division of the Committee, or of the body at large, the Chairman shall, as usual, be entitled to a casting vote.

5th,—That there shall be a general meeting of the Members once a year, on the first Thursday in January, and that at such meetings the whole of the Committee shall annually be elected by ballot.

6th,—That each house or individual on becoming a member, shall pay an admission fee of 3 guineas, and be liable to an annual subscription (to be paid in advance) of 1 guinea; this annual subscription being however to be commuted by a subscription at any one time of 10 guineas. The Committee for the time being to be vested with the entire distribution of the funds.

7th,—That persons wishing to become Members shall procure the recommendation of some gentleman already a Member, and shall be admitted with the appropriation of three of the Committee, such application being signified at a regular meeting of the Committee.

8th,—That any subject to which it may be thought proper to draw the attention of the Committee, shall be submitted to them in writing; and that for such purpose a minute book shall be provided, and remain with the Secretary, such book being at all times freely accessible to the Members of the Chamber at large.

9th,—That the Committee shall have power to call, at any time, a general Meeting of the Members for any particular object; but a written notice shall be given to each Member at least three days previous to such meeting, and the notice shall state the purpose for which the meeting is convened.

10th,—That only one person, in any single mercantile concern, shall be competent to be upon the Committee at one and the same time; and that no single establishment shall, at any general meeting of the Members, be entitled to more than one vote, which, in case of dispute, shall be given by the senior partner present.

11th,—That the Treasurer shall regularly make up, and lay before the Members at their annual general meeting, an account of the receipts and disbursements of the institution for the year preceding, and shall state the balance remaining in hand.

12th,—That the Secretary shall attend all the meetings of the Members, and of the Committee, and shall keep a regular journal of their proceedings; such journal being at all convenient times accessible to the different Members of the institution.

13th,—That these rules and resolutions be entered in a book, and signed by each Member of the Chamber of Commerce.

14th,—That no rule shall be altered, nor any new rule adopted, excepting at the annual general meeting, and after notice, of at least one month, having been given in "the Minute Book", of the proposition to be moved.

The thanks of the meeting were afterwards moved to the Provisional Committee, for their trouble in drawing up the rules, &c.
(signed) BENJ. SORSBIE, Chairman

1.41 [London Chamber of Commerce 1817 and 1823–4, proposals: see Chapter 4]

1.42 Cork Chamber of Commerce: Reading Room Rules 1819

Detailed rules for the chamber established in 1819 do not survive, though various of its procedures can be deduced from its minute books. However, a formal set of rules for its reading room, which was one its main activities, indicate its approach to governance. The room was described in a minute of 31 December 1819 as 'useful to the merchant, instructive to the politician, and amusing to the stranger and light reader with which the subscribers themselves are not already acquainted'.[79] An earlier attempt to establish a chamber occurred in 1814 (see Chapter 4). There was no established chairman in 1819, the committee elected a chair at each meeting.

Source
Chamber minute book: held by modern Cork chamber.

Minute 13 November 1819

1. The room is the property of the subscribers who refuse or consent to grant the use of it.
2. Election of the committee on January 1st by ballot.
3. Petitions may be freely introduced into their room for signature.
4. Annual subscription of one guinea for all resident in the City and liberties and the room free to country Gentlemen and strangers being introduced by a Subscriber.
5. No introduction is necessary for any Gentleman of the Army or Navy.

[79] Bennett, *Local Business Voice* (2011) 214–6, 516–8.

6. Half yearly subscriptions for Gentlemen of the Revenue or other Public Departments who are liable to be removed [i.e. may be transferred to another location by the Revenue Service].
7. Subscriptions payable by 1 November, any person in arrears by 1 December will no longer be considered a member.
8. The Committee will expel anyone who takes away, tears or defaces any newspaper of the room.
9. Any complaint against waiters [who manage the room] will be acted on by the Committee.
10. No newspaper to be held longer than 15 minutes after being applied for [by another member].
11. Twelve subscribers may call a General Meeting.
12. The Room will be open at 7.00 from 25 March until 29 September, and 8.00 in other months, until 10.00 in the evening.

1.43 Forfarshire 1819, and Dundee Chamber of Commerce 1835

The Forfarshire chamber of commerce was the first to cover the Dundee area, and despite its name it was essentially based on Dundee City. Its rules of 1819 were largely maintained continuously until a major review took place in 1855. But in 1835 the chamber was re-established after something of a lapse and the name was changed to the Dundee chamber; it was closely linked with the Baltic Coffee House in Dundee.[80] The new formal rules were agreed at its first general meeting on 25 May 1836. The rules stayed very similar to 1819 but were supplemented. The 1819 rules are reproduced below with their original Roman numerals. New rules agreed in 1835/6 were similar in many respects. These are shown by the new numbering of clauses and additional clauses in brackets, thus: <>. The additions mainly related to (i) the removal of the Treasurer, whose role was taken on by the Secretary; (ii) the imposition of a geographical quota to balance the interests of the members, with one quarter of the Directors to come from Arbroath and outside Dundee, as well as giving three days' notice of meetings so they could attend; and (iii) the establishment of an arbitration service, with rules for appointment of arbiters, umpire, and use of the whole committee to resolve 'difficulties'. The 1855 rules, not reproduced, were printed and are contained within the chamber's minute book; they took over most of the 1835–6 terminology and detail but were far more extensive on procedures.

[80] Bennett, *Local Business Voice* (2011) 519–20.

Source
Dundee Plan and Regulations, 1819; Constitution and Regulations, 1835; both hand-written in Chamber of Commerce minute book: Dundee Archives GB251/GD/CC

Plan and Regulations 3 March 1819

<1> I. That the Chamber of Commerce and Manufacture be established on the most liberal Basis by admitting as Members all Merchants, Bankers, Traders, Manufacturers Flaxspinners and Shipowners residing in the County of Forfar.

<2> II. That all persons subscribing the Rules of the association and contributing as afterwards specified shall be admitted Members thereof.

<3> III. That the objects of this Association shall be

1. To afford assistance to individuals Members in the redress of any grievance affecting trade or Manufacturing or in the negotiation of any particular Business <interesting to the association and> which may require the influence of the Chamber in making application to <the Convention of the Royal City Burghs, The Board of Trustees, the King's Ministers or> Government, to Parliament or to any public Body.
2. To procure relief from any general grievance, opposition or <any apprehension of> inconvenience affecting any particular branch of Trade or Manufacture carried on by the Members of this Society by interposing the Weight and activity of the Association in any public measures that may be thought necessary to effect such relief.
3. To afford advice and assistance in <foregoing replaced by 'To regulate'> all matters respecting any Branch of Trade or Manufactures which may be submitted to the Directors in regard to the establishing of Rules for the convenience and assistance either of Foreign Traders or Manufacturers, or otherwise.
4. To form a regular Channel for the procuring and speedily conveying of information on Subjects of general interest to trade and Commerce.
5. To assist in pointing out new Sources of Trade and to consider and encourage such plans and Systems as shall contribute to the protection and improvement of those branches of Trade & Manufacture which are peculiar to this Country and interesting to the Chamber at large.
6. To attend to every application made to parliament which may be thought injurious to the trade and Manufactures of this Country.

7. The attainment of all other objects which may involve the general or particular Interests of these branches of Trade and Manufactures where the same can be conducted with more effect by an associated Body than by individual exertion.

<4> IV. That a fund be raised to defray the Expenses and be applicable to the objects of the Institution and for that purpose that each Member shall pay One Guinea of Entry Money, [and] thereafter ____ <one guinea> Shillings per annum, and failing to do so he shall be deprived of the benefits and privileges of the Association. <Those who shall have paid ____ Guineas shall be relieved of all further payment> [precise annual and life subscriptions left blank in 1819 draft and not subsequently reported, but was probably one guinea annually and 20 guineas for life]

<5> V. That the executive power be lodged with twenty four Members as Directors of the Chamber of which five shall be a quorum. <That at least a fourth of these twenty members be elected from members residing in Arbroath and the other parts of the Country at a Distance from Dundee.>

These Directors shall be chosen by a majority of the Members present at the annual General Meeting to be held on the first Thursday of April and from among these Directors and at said General Meeting a Chairman and Deputy Chairman shall be chosen. The Chairman or Deputy Chairman for the time being at any General Meeting of the association or of the Committee of Directors having a Casting vote in case of an equality of Votes, besides his own as a Member of such Meeting.

<6> VI That the Committee of Directors shall have the General management of the concerns of the Association and the application of the Funds as they may judge expedient for the purposes and benefit of the Association and that they be empowered to appoint annually a Secretary and Treasurer. <'Treasurer' deleted, replaced by 'Clerk for Arbitrations with power to vest both Offices in one person, if they shall at any time find it expedient'; plus additional amendment added at meeting 'that Secretary and Clerk for Arbitrations be elected by a Majority at a General Meeting'>

<7> VII The Chairman or in his absence the Deputy Chairman shall preside at all meetings of the Chamber & Directors: his particular province shall be to convene all extraordinary Meetings, to prepare all business to be brought under discussion and to superintend the correspondence of the Chamber.

<8> VIII The Secretary shall receive all Memorials, Letters and applications to be presented to the Chamber on the subject of

Public business & shall assist in the arrangement of the same, Shall frame Petitions or Memorials to Public Bodies and shall have the charge of convening all ordinary Meetings. The Treasurer <deleted and left with Secretary> shall collect the Subscriptions, Keep the accounts of the Society and at each annual Meeting produce his Account of receipts and payments clearly posted up and Balanced. <and in short shall execute the detail of the Affairs of the Chamber—He shall be allowed an annual Salary to be fixed by the Directors.>

<9> <In addition to the Duty of the twenty Directors as Guardians of the Trade and Manufactures of this part of Scotland it shall be incumbent upon them to accept of Arbitrations in disputes upon Mercantile cases, among those who are privileged by being Members of the Chamber in order to save them from the heavy expense and vexatious delay attending on Law Suits and for this purpose that two out of the Committee of Directors shall be chosen, one by each of the disputing Parties, who before proceeding with Arbitration shall appoint the Chairman or the Deputy Chairman of the Directors as an Umpire.—In case of difficulty they may state the same to the Committee of Directors, in order to obtain every advantage which may be supposed to arise from the combined ideas of the most intelligent Members who preside for the time being—After which the Arbiters chosen shall again consider the Matter in dispute.>

<10> <An intelligent and fit person educated to the Law shall also be chosen by the Directors at their first Meeting each Year whose province it shall be to act as Clerk to all Arbitrations which may fall under the cognizance of the Committee of Directors to bring the same regularly before the Arbiters, and in general to do all those duties which are understood to belong to the Clerk of an Arbitration, for which he shall be allowed the usual fee paid for such Business, to be recovered according to the award of the Arbiters the said Clerk always recording the cases and decisions in a Book for the purpose.>

<11> IX. That at the annual General Meeting the records of the Association for the preceding Year <'preceding' replaced by 'last'> be read over and a Statement of the Funds exhibited by the Treasurer <replaced by 'Secretary'> and that a Statement of all Business at present engaging or likely to engage the attention of the Committee of Directors during the ensuing Year be afforded by the Chairman or Deputy Chairman. At this as well as all extraordinary Meetings of the Chamber it shall be competent for any

Member to recommend to the consideration of the Directors any matter whatever connected with Trade or Manufactures where the Aid, Assistance or interference of the Directors may be thought necessary.

<12> <That for the convenience of those Members residing at a distance from Dundee where the Meetings will be held, three days' notice be given of all ordinary and extraordinary Meetings whether convened by the Chairman or Secretary.>

<13> X. Meetings may at any time be called upon a requisition signed by not less than Ten Members and addressed to the Chairman.

<14> In cases of urgent necessity it shall be lawful for the Chairman to call an extraordinary Meeting on the shortest notice and proceed to Business provided there be a quorum of Eight Members present.

<15> XI. That it shall be competent for a General Meeting upon a Month's previous notice stating the object of the Meeting to alter or annul all or any of these Rules & Regulations and also to enact new Regulations better adapted to the interests of the Association.

1.44 Wolverhampton Chamber of Commerce 1819

The first body with the title Wolverhampton chamber of commerce is noted in a report dated 12 November 1819 signed by 27 'subscribers to the Wolverhampton chamber of commerce', a document which is listed by Beaumont.[81] The names are given in Appendix, no. 27. No rules or other surviving papers have been found for this chamber, which may not have proceeded beyond an initial meeting. However, one report in the local newspapers gives some further insight into it, indicating that it had some basic rules and an elected committee. The document referred to by Beaumont thus appears to be the first list of subscribers who had attended an open meeting on 12 November 1819. The only other possible document related to the chamber that has been found is a petition on the condition of workers in February 1820, reproduced below. Though this was a general action of all 'merchants, manufacturers and other traders' it closely followed the chamber's foundation and was chaired by Joseph Pearson who had been appointed the chamber's treasurer and secretary. The chamber may have been precipitated by calls for a normalisation of commerce with France after the end of the wars in 1815. There was also a revival of civic spirit following efforts in September–October 1819 to expand the *Act of 50th Geo III* for repairing

[81] V. B. Beaumont, *The Wolverhampton Chamber of Commerce 1856–1956* (Wolverhampton, 1956) 3.

roads (*Wolverhampton Chronicle*, 8 September 1819) and the preparations for the *Act of 1 Geo IV cap viii for lighting with Gas the Town of Wolverhampton*. These civic activities, though, were fraught with conflicts among the elite;[82] and this fracture of local leadership may have made development of the chamber difficult. This was also a time of great ferment with the recent Peterloo Massacre at Manchester resulting in local meetings censuring the Manchester magistrates; e.g. at Hanley 10–25,000 had attended (*Wolverhampton Chronicle*, 10 November 1819). Continued local unrest led to the foundation of a local loyalist association: 'The radicals seem determined to keep the public mind in a state of ferment' (*Wolverhampton Chronicle*, 15 December 1819). The modern chamber was founded in 1859.

Source
Wolverhampton Chronicle

Printed Report 17 November 1819

WOLVERHAMPTON

At a MEETING *of the Merchants and Manufacturers, held this* 12th November 1819;

MR. JOSEPH PEARSON IN THE CHAIR;

It was unanimously resolved,

That a Memorial should be presented to the Lords Commissioners of the Treasury, on the Subject of a Commercial Intercourse with France.

On a Motion of Mr. Jos. Walker, seconded by Mr. Ryton,

It was unanimously resolved.

That the Memorial now produced be adopted by the present meeting.

Resolved unanimously.

That the Memorial be signed by the Gentlemen present, and others interested in its Success, and that it be transmitted to the Lords Commissioners of the Treasury.

Resolved

That these Resolutions be advertised in *The Wolverhampton Chronicle* and *Aris's Birmingham Gazette*.

JOS. PEARSON, Chairman.

[82] See e.g. G. P. Mander, *A History of Wolverhampton to the Early Nineteenth Century* (Wolverhampton, 1960) 159–175; Wolverhampton Public Library, *Wolverhampton: The Town Commissioners 1777–1848: Their Story in their Minutes and the files of 'The Wolverhampton Chronicle* (Wolverhampton, 1976); C. J. L. Elwell, 'Black Country Essays and Reviews, Black Country Society' (Wolverhampton, 1988) 32–57.

At a MEETING of the Merchants and Manufacturers held this 12th November 1819;

MR. JOSEPH PEARSON IN THE CHAIR;

On a Motion of Mr. Tarratt, seconded by Mr. Ready,

It was unanimously resolved,

That it is highly expedient that a Chamber of Manufactures and Commerce should be established in this Town.

Resolved,

That it shall be entitled, 'The Chamber of Manufactures and Commerce of Wolverhampton and its Vicinity.'

Resolved,

That each Individual subscribing One Guinea per Annum, be admitted a Member.

Resolved,

That a Committee of twelve Members be appointed to manage the Affairs of the Establishment, for the Space of two Years.

Resolved,

That Mr. PEARSON be appointed Treasurer and Secretary, and that he be empowered to call a General Meeting of the Subscribers, for the Purpose of choosing a Committee, and other Business.

Resolved,

That these Resolutions be advertised in *The Wolverhampton Chronicle* and *Aris's Birmingham Gazette*.

JOSEPH PEARSON.

Resolved,

That the Thanks of the Meeting be given to the Chairman.

Printed Report Wolverhampton, 8 February 1820

At a MEETING of the Merchants, Manufacturers, and other Traders of this Town, held at the PUBLIC OFFICE, convened by the Constables, in Compliance with a Requisition addressed to them, for the Purpose of "considering the Propriety of Petitioning Parliament to inquire into the Causes of the present distressed State of Trade, and Manufactures, and the best Means of relieving them"

MR. JOS. PEARSON IN THE CHAIR;

It was unanimously resolved,

That it has been with Feelings of deep Anxiety, we have observed the lamentable State of Manufactures and Commerce of the Kingdom, and the unexampled Distress which the harbouring Mechanics have so long endured.—In this Town and its Vicinity their Condition is so deplorable, that numberless Instances of Individuals are known, who, after working 14 or 16

Hours daily, can acquire only the small Pittance of 7*s.* or 8*s.* per Week, while a full third of the Population are nearly dependent on parochial Allowance, and the gratuitous Distribution of Soup for Existence and Support.

That notwithstanding the official Statement in the last Session of Parliament of the Export of British manufactured Goods for the Year ending 31st December, 1818, being nearly to the Amount of 49 Millions of Pounds sterling, a Sum far exceeding any former Period, it is well known that the manufacturing and mercantile Classes never experienced so great and general Distress, as during the Whole of the Year 1819.

That it appears to this Meeting, there is not a sufficient Demand for manufactured Goods in the Markets hitherto usually frequented, and that it is highly desirable commercial Advancements should be made with other Countries not at present accessible to the British Merchant.

That the long continued Stagnation of Trade, the wretched Condition of the Labourers and Mechanics, and the dreadfully alarming Increase of Pauperism, are subjects requiring the serious and deliberate Consideration of Parliament.

That Petitions to both Houses of Parliament be presented, praying they would institute an inquiry into the Causes of such Distress, and adopt such Measures as may appear necessary to remove them.

That the Petition now read be approved, and that the Most Noble the Marquis of STAFFORD be requested to present it to the House of Lords, and the Right Hon. Earl GOWER and E.J. LITTLETON, Esq. to the House of Commons, and that they be solicited to bring forward or sanction a Motion in its Behalf.

That Copies of these Resolutions be printed, and transmitted to those Members of Parliament who are connected with the manufacturing and mercantile Districts, and that they be respectfully requested to aid and assist the Object of the Petition.

That these Resolutions be advertised in *The Wolverhampton Chronicle, Staffordshire Advertiser, Aris's Birmingham Gazette,* and the *Times London Newspaper.*

JOS. PEARSON, Chairman.

Resolved.

That the Thanks of the Meeting be given to the Chairman for his Conduct in the Chair, and for the Attention he has bestowed on the Subject.

1.45 Dublin Chamber of Commerce 1820

The foundation in 1820 of the Dublin chamber was the third attempt, after 1783 and 1805. This proved durable as the foundation of the modern chamber.

Source
Dublin Chamber of Commerce, Published laws and regulations 1820: RIA HP 1220/5

LAWS AND REGULATIONS 1820

I. THE name of the Association shall be, "The Chamber of Commerce of the City of Dublin."

II. The object of the Association shall be, to promote the commercial and manufacturing interests of the city of Dublin; as well as to take cognizance of, and investigate such matters, as, affecting the commerce and manufactures of Ireland generally, must necessarily influence those of the metropolis. — For the attainment of this object, the Council of the Chamber, to be constituted as here-aftermentioned, shall hold respectful communication with the ministers of the crown, and other officers of the government, the members of either House of Parliament, and other persons of high station and authority; and shall correspond and confer with similar associations, and with individuals, respecting the objects of this association. The Council shall also support and assist, in the manner it may deem advisable, any member who shall be exposed to expense or inconvenience, by asserting the legal rights of a merchant or trader.

III. All persons paying one guinea annually, and one guinea admission fee, previous to the 1st. January, 1821 shall be members; after which period, no person shall be admitted a member of the Association, except by a ballot of the Chamber.

IV. An assembly of the Chamber shall be held on the first Tuesday of December in each year, which shall be called, The Annual General Assembly of the Chamber, for the purpose of electing by ballot, a President, four Vice-Presidents, and twenty-one other members, who shall form a Council for the ensuing year, and who shall act for and on behalf of the Chamber in promoting the objects of the Association: At the election of the Council for the second and every following year, not more than fourteen of the twenty-one members of the preceding Council shall be eligible.

Assemblies of the Chamber shall also be held on the first Tuesdays of March, June, and September in each year, for the purpose of admitting members, and transacting such other business as shall be brought before them.

Special assemblies of the Chamber shall be called by the Council, giving ten days notice, upon the requisition of twenty-one members; stating the object.

The Council may also at any time, convene special assemblies of the Chamber, giving ten days notice thereof, and stating the object.

V. The Council shall meet on the first Thursday in each month with liberty of adjournment; and at its first meeting it shall elect from amongst its members, a Secretary and Sub-treasurer, who shall fill those offices for the ensuing year, without any pecuniary remuneration whatever.

The Bank of Ireland shall be requested to act as Treasurer to the Chamber: and any monies lodged, shall not be drawn thereout, otherwise than by drafts signed by the President or a Vice-President and two other members of the Council.

VI. The Council shall have the appointment of a Clerk, and such servants as shall be found necessary to conduct the business of the association; allotting the salaries and other remuneration for their services.

VII. In the event of any member of the Council not attending its meetings at least twice in three months, without assigning a satisfactory reason to the Council; such member shall be considered to have vacated his seat.

VIII. The Council shall provide a room or rooms for the accommodation of the members of the Association, shall cause registries of the proceedings of the Chamber and the Council to be properly kept, and the monies received and paid on account of the Chamber, to be duly entered in books provided for such purpose; said registries and books shall be on the table at every assembly of the Chamber.

IX. The Council shall fix upon and procure such commercial lists and publications, and such revenue, parliamentary, and other papers, as they shall from time to time judge proper, to be deposited in the rooms of the Association, to which the members shall have access at such hours as shall be fixed on.

X. Every member of the Chamber shall have an undoubted right to propose in writing any subject, relevant to the objects and interests of the Association, for the consideration of the Council; and every such member shall at all convenient times, be at liberty to confer with the Council upon the subject of such written proposal.

XI. Every member of the Chamber shall have the privilege of introducing any person, not residing within fourteen miles of Dublin, to the rooms of the Association for a period not exceeding one week; the name and place of residence of such stranger, together with the name of the member introducing him, shall be entered in a book provided for that purpose.

XII. The Council shall make a report to each annual assembly of the Chamber, of such transactions of the year as it shall judge needful, together with a statement of receipts and disbursements.

XIII. The Chamber shall at all times be competent to alter, revoke, or create laws for regulating the Chamber and its Council, provided that all such alterations, revocations, or creations, as shall have been resolved upon by one assembly, shall be confirmed at a subsequent assembly, to be held not earlier than fifteen, nor later than thirty days, after such former assembly; and provided that not one of the said assemblies be a quarterly one.

[followed by 'OFFICERS of the ASSOCIATION': see Appendix, no. 5.3]
Register,
Thomas Jameson, Esq.
Office, Commercial Buildings.

1.46 Manchester Society of Merchants (Chamber of Commerce and Manufactures) 1820

This was the first Manchester body formally titled a chamber, initially called the Society of Merchants and immediately re-labelled as Chamber of Commerce and Manufactures. It directly derived from the former Society of the Protection of Trade at Manchester of 1794, although there had been a lapse of about 20 years. The *Proceedings* begin with letters as if continuing the earlier Society, and Mr. Peel 'communicates the willingness of Richard Yates Esq. [former Treasurer of the Society of 1794] to pay over for use of this chamber, on receiving an indemnity, a balance (about £172) which remains in his hands, and which belonged to Society of the Protection of Trade, long since dissolved' [minutes 14 November 1821]. Hence funds were held by the treasurer as an individual, on behalf of and on trust for the Society, as common in the non-chartered chambers. The Society was revived by a public meeting in June 1820 with a constitution drafted and board of directors appointed by November, reported in the *Manchester Mercury* 19 December 1820. The minute book (*Proceedings*) began one year later in November 1821. There is confusion about the formal date of establishment. Redford considered the chamber to have been initiated in November 1820, formalised in February 1821, and he termed the 'first annual report' to be in 'January 1822'.[83] Actually the Proceedings show this was February 1822, and it was not explicitly called 'first'. Redford's chronology is contradicted by the numbering of subsequent annual reports, indicating that the founders considered the chamber to have begun in 1820. Hence the annual meeting of 11 February 1822 received the Second Annual Report, though numbering did not begin until 1825.

Source
Proceedings of the Chamber of Commerce: printed and glued into inside back cover, Manchester Central Library GB127 M8/2/1. The details of the rules show that this was printed soon after the annual meeting of February 1823, i.e. after the initial two years referred to in Rule 25. The minutes show most rules were agreed at the outset, with the text below recording the additional changes over the first two years.

[83] Redford, *Manchester Merchants* (1934) 69–70.

Printed sheet 1820–23

1. The objective of the Chamber to be the promotion of measures calculated to benefit and protect the Trading Interests of its Members, and the general Trade of the Town and neighbourhood of Manchester.

2. The Chamber to consist of Merchants, Manufacturers, and others, British subjects, interested in the Trade of the Town of Manchester and the neighbourhood, on payment of an annual sum of £1. 1s. to be paid in advance, or of £10. 10s. at any one time, in commutation of the annual subscription. [Initially subscriptions had an admission fee of 3 guineas and an annual subscription of 1 guinea. This was amended at a Special General Meeting to have only an annual subscription; minutes, 28 November 1822].

3. The business of the Chamber to be arranged by a Board of Directors, to consist of twenty-four Members, to be elected annually, by the Chamber at large ['by lots'; minutes, 10 February 1823];—Five Directors to be competent to transact business.

4. Six Directors to retire annually from the Board, and to be ineligible for one year, or till a vacancy occurs;—the exclusion to fall on those who, having been Directors during the whole year, have attended fewest Meetings;—equal cases to be decided by lot of the Directors.

5. Vacancies in the Direction, by death or resignation, to be supplied by the Board: all vacancies to be declared at the next Meeting: the Directors to be specially summoned, three days prior to each of the following Meetings, to nominate Successors at the former, and to elect (by ballot, if required) at the latter Meeting. The Boroughreeve of Manchester for the time being, to be a Member of the Board ex officio. [Board was de facto increased to 25 with Borough Reeve ex officio: Annual Meeting, 10 February 1823].

6. A President, Vice-President, and Treasurer to be annually chosen by the Directors, out of their body, at their first Meeting: the Vice-President to enjoy the powers of the President in his absence.

7. A Secretary to be appointed annually by the Directors, and to be allowed a competent salary.

8. Partners may be Members collectively or individually; but one Subscription to confer only one vote, to be given by any one Partner of the House.

9. Any Member intending to withdraw from the Chamber to give notice in writing to the Secretary, three months prior to the 31st of December, or to be liable to the payment of his subscription for the year ensuing.

10. A General Meeting of the Members to be held the Second Monday in February, at eleven o'clock in the forenoon, at which the Board shall be elected:—and four Quarterly Meetings of the Directors the Second Monday in the months of February, May, August and November, at twelve o'clock.

—Notice for the Annual Meeting to be given in writing to each Member, and to be inserted in not fewer than two of the Manchester papers. The places for meeting to be appointed from time to time by the Directors.

11. Special Meetings of the Directors to be called by the President, or, in his absence by the Vice-President, at any time, on his own authority, or on the requisition in writing of five Directors.—In the case of the absence or refusal of the President, or Vice-President, the Secretary, on requisition, in writing of eight Directors, to call such Meeting; giving not less than three days notice in writing of the Meeting and its object.

12. On requisition in writing of not fewer than half of the Directors, or one-fourth of the Members at large, the President, or Vice-President, or in the case of their absence or refusal, the Secretary to call Special General Meetings, giving notice in writing to each Member. The object of such General Meeting to be stated in the requisition and notice.

13. In the absence the President and Vice-President at any Meeting, the Members present to elect a Chairman for the day.

14. No person to be entitled to vote on any question, whose subscription is in arrears.

15. The Chairman, on all occasions, to have a casting vote, as Chairman, in addition to his vote as Member.

16. The Board of Directors to make Bye-Laws for their own Government; —such laws to be proposed at one Meeting, and decided at the ensuing Meeting; the Directors to be specially summoned for that purpose, and a Copy of the intended Laws to be inserted in the Notice.

17. Personal communications from Members of the Chamber to the Board of Directors, or in writing, addressed to the President, relating to the General Interests of Trade of the District, to be always entitled to the early consideration of the Board.

18. The Funds of the Chamber to be under the control of the Directors for the time being;—but no sum exceeding £20 to be paid without being proposed at one Meeting of Directors, and confirmed at the next Meeting.

19. No money to be paid by the Treasurer without an order by the President, (or, in his absence, the Vice-President) and the Secretary; such order to be first sanctioned by a vote of the Directors.

20. The Treasurer to make up his Accounts to the 31st of December, to be laid before the Annual Meeting. Auditors then to be appointed, and, as soon as the accounts are examined, the same to be printed, and a Copy to be transmitted to each Member. [Annual Meeting elects two auditors; Annual Meeting minutes, 11 February 1822].

21. The proceedings of the Chamber to be recorded in a book appropriated for that purpose; such book to be open to the inspection of Members at the Meetings of Directors, or at General Meetings.

22. The Secretary to keep a correct list of Members, to be at all times open to their inspection.

23. On any change to a Firm, the Interest in the Chamber to cease, unless the same to be notified in writing to the Secretary; in which case the Directors to be empowered to decide on their discretion whether the change in the Partners in the House is of a nature to warrant a continuation of the Interest.

24. General Meetings to be empowered to exclude any Member whose conduct may have been such as, in the opinion of the majority present, to render him unfit to continue as a Member of the Chamber.

25. During the first two years the Rules may be altered at any General Meeting, especially convened in due form for the purpose, after which period no alteration to be made but at an Annual Meeting. Notice of any New Rule, or of alteration in a Rule, to be inserted in the minute book, signed by six or more Directors, at least one month previous to the Meeting at which the proposition to be entertained.—The Secretary to send a copy of the entry to each Member at least seven days before the Meeting.

26. No one to be considered as a Member until he has signed his name to the Rules of the Society in a book provided for the purpose.

1.47 [Newry Chamber of Commerce 1820][84]

1.48 [Chamber or Committee of Merchants of Sligo, 1820][85]

1.49 [Galway Chamber of Commerce, 1822][86]

[84] Two catalogue records at TNAI refer to an early Newry chamber. First, two letters of 15 April 1820 from Isaac Glenny, president, Chamber of Commerce, Newry, County Down: 'for government assistance in improving navigation on Newry canal and river', and to Lord Viscount Castlereagh, 'making application for government assistance in improving navigation on Newry canal and river, outlining the benefits to be derived from completion of project including faster, less troublesome access by sailing vessels, advancement of trade' and the 'great public advantage to be derived from the employment and consequent relief this undertaking would afford to a distressed peasantry'. Second, an undated draft letter (for c. 1850 or earlier) to the president of Newry chamber of commerce concerning the tolls on the Newry canal. Unfortunately neither of these records can be found by TNAI as they appear to be mis-catalogued. However, there is no doubt about the existence of the documents themselves which indicate a Newry chamber active in the 1820s and later. The chamber is referred to in 1832 when it was contacted by the Board of Trade Statistics Department, 3 September 1832: Copy letters in minutes: TNA BT 24/1. No further records have been found.

[85] Referred to in Belfast chamber minutes, 4 February 1822, in relation to proposal for an agent for Irish chambers in London. Belfast also refers to it as established in 1820 or 1821: Belfast minutes 13 February 1822; PRONI.

[86] Evidenced by advocacy efforts; included in Chapter 5.

1.50 [Enniskillen branch of the Belfast Chamber][87]

1. 51 Bristol Chamber of Commerce 1823

Bristol was surprisingly late to develop a chamber, given its size and status as a major port. This was largely due to the presence of the Bristol Society of Merchant Venturers that acted like a chamber throughout the eighteenth century and earlier. It collaborated with other chambers: as shown by correspondence with the Liverpool chamber reproduced in Chapter 5. The city corporation had also generally been supportive of commercial lobbies. However, cooperation and mutual support broke down in Bristol in the early 1800s after the development of the 'floating harbour' and the creation of the Bristol Dock Company which charged heavy fees on shipping. The committee that prepared a draft set of chamber rules (see below) was at pains to claim that the chamber would not conflict with any existing organisations, but in practice it was aimed at pressuring the Docks and being more effective in lobbying than the Venturers and Corporation had now become.[88] The report can therefore be read as trying to tread around these local sensitivities. This was not successful, and attacks on the chamber followed from the corporation, who attempted to take it over and suppress it. This was similar to attempts by Liverpool corporation in that city; both these actions are reproduced in Chapter 4. Its foundation in 1823 coincided with an attempt to found a London chamber, with which it was clearly in contact (see Chapter 4). London's attempt failed because of conflicts with existing local institutions from the outset, especially lack of support or antipathy from the government.[89] Bristol was successful and its rules had some influence on the London proposals, or vice versa, and can also be seen directly in the Worcester founding purposes of 1839, as well as in aspects of the rules in Nottingham 1835, Dundee 1832, and Hull 1837 (see later below). Indeed the chamber's committee proposing Bristol's rules claimed to have looked at the rules of other chambers. As a result, by 1823 a level of stability towards a shared set of rules and objects had occurred for British chambers, initiated by Bristol, that began to diffuse, albeit with significant local adaptations.

[87] Agreed to be established, though not clear that it was: Belfast chamber minutes, 4 February 1822: PRONI.

[88] Bennett, *Local Business Voice* (2011) 201–4.

[89] Bennett, *Local Business Voice* (2011) 193–9.

Source
Report and Rules; Bristol Record Office 38605/A/1

Printed 13 February 1823

REPORT OF THE PROVISIONAL COMMITTEE

THE Committee appointed to frame Rules and Regulations for the formation of a CHAMBER of Commerce in BRISTOL, are now prepared to lay before their Fellow-citizens, the result of their proceedings. To assist them it the execution of the task confided to their care, they have had recourse to the Rules and experience of similar Associations at this time flourishing in different parts of the United Kingdom; and the Committee have much satisfaction in stating, that their enquiries on this subject have uniformly been answered, by the strongest assurances of the high character in which these various Institutions are publicly recognized; the attention paid by official authorities to their representations and interposition; as well as, of the activity, vigour, and general success by which their proceedings have been marked. And from the practical benefits, thus experienced by other places, the Committee are induced to form a sanguine expectation of similar advantages to accrue to Bristol from the establishment of an efficient Chamber of Commerce within its walls. …

The BRISTOL CHAMBER OF COMMERCE is intended to embody and represent the *Commercial*, *Trading*, and *Manufacturing* Community of the City and its vicinity; and on *this* community at large, and on *every individual* who shares in the advantages of the general prosperity, it relies for the countenance and support, which are necessary to invigorate and give efficiency to its operations. It looks with confidence for this general support, because the *Merchant, Manufacturer*, and *Tradesman*, will alike find their interest secured and advanced by its exertions. Land,— and every investment of Capital, the value of which is dependent on the fluctuations of Commerce, must participate in its success; and in short, the only interest to which it will not afford protection or prospect of advantage, is that interest, whatsoever it may be, which is opposed to the *general good*. The views and designs of the Association are strictly and exclusively Commercial; and upon the rigid exclusion from the Chamber of every topic and feeling opposed or irrelevant to its proper objects, its very existence will depend. To every class and individual, therefore, of the Community, without distinction, its doors are alike Open. The subjects which will engage its attention belong properly to the *Public*; they are of great and general concern, but from the natural backwardness of individuals to undertake such matters, they are commonly lost sight of and neglected; in *these* it is the object of the Chamber to interpose and exert the *Public Voice*, as well as in various cases of general interest, in which, through the difficulty of obtaining redress, the exertions of individuals may be stifled, discouraged, or be raised in vain.

It is needless for the Committee to debate, on the *peculiar* want under which BRISTOL labours, of such a representative Association. The effects of it are apparent on every side; it is seen in the *decay of trade* and *enterprise*; the *local impediments* which weigh down and paralyse commercial activity, and in the apathy with which advantages and opportunities are suffered to escape; but more accurately it may be judged of, by the Commercial improvement which during the same period has attended other places, where Associations for similar purposes have been in operation; and by the necessity at this moment felt in the Metropolis itself, for the establishment of a similar Institution. It way suffice to remark, that *every branch* of this subject and the *utmost practicable alleviation* of the evils referred to, come within the scope and view of the Association, and are the field of its public labours. The Committee do not give a pledge, that these accumulated inconveniences will be removed by the influence of the Chamber; although even that event might he looked with confidence, if the active concurrence of the Citizens should support its exertions, and call forth the natural advantages which Bristol possesses. The disease is making alarming advances, the remedy is innocent, and has elsewhere been found efficacious; what then but *despair* or *indifference* can discourage the application of it here?

But in addition to the advantages, which each private member derives, through the prosperity of the Community; in addition to the increased value, which the interests of property will receive from measures of public service rendered by the Chamber, it offers assistance to the man engaged *in Trade*, which he alone can duly appreciate. If to obtain concessions or relief from inconveniences, he has bad occasion to approach the Customs, Excise, or other Public Departments of Government, he must be acquainted with the distrust which necessarily attaches to applications, in which personal interest is involved, and must have learnt the too general insufficiency of his own single efforts. He, therefore, can value the assistance and weight of a respectable Association of his Fellow-citizens, who, after examining the circumstances of his case, would attest and support his representations, and use its influence in forwarding their object.

The Committee would close this part of the subject, by distinctly avowing their conviction, that in the origin and design of the present Institution, neither the slightest glance of disrespect has been intended to the Corporate Societies of this City, nor a wish to interfere with their functions or authority; nor does there, as they conceive, exist a reason, which should prevent the estimable individuals who compose them, from enrolling their names among its Members; they cordially hope, therefore, that their cooperation and support will not be withheld from an Institution, which the Committee believe to be fraught with the highest advantage to the Public good, and for the success of which *Union* is so necessary. The *objects* of the Chamber, it may be observed, are widely distinct from those which employ the attention of any other Body; and are such, as a Constitution similar to its own, is alone qualified to effect. Its sole aim is the furtherance of the *Public good*, and in that of the welfare of each, and of all; and only where the conflicting rights of others are proved unnecessarily burdensome and oppressive to this common interest, may the Chamber interpose its efforts to reduce them more just and more moderate limits! ...

[Text continues to review parts of the Rules proposed, some of which are amended in the final document]

STEPHEN PRUST
CHAIRMAN

Printed pamphlet 25 February 1823

RULES REGULATIONS

Settled and Adopted at a General Meeting, Held at the Commercial Sale Room, the 25th of Feb. 1823.

I.—THIS Association shall be designated, THE BRISTOL CHAMBER OF COMMERCE, TRADE AND MANUFACTURES.

The object of the Chamber is, to protect and promote the Commercial, Trading and Manufacturing Interests of Bristol, and of its individual members; and its views and operations shall embrace the removal of obstacles, which tend to prevent the increase of Trade.

All Merchants, Bankers, Ship-Owners, Manufacturers, Tradesmen, and other Persons possessing property in Bristol, or in any of the neighbouring Ports, Towns and Places with which Bristol is immediately connected, as a Depot or Market for their supplies, produce or manufactures, shall be invited to join the Association.

II.—Individuals shall be received as Life Members of the Chamber, on payment of Twenty Guineas, and signing the Regulations. All other persons admitted Members shall sign the Regulations, and pay on entrance the sum of Two Guineas and an annual sum of One Guinea, to be due and payable on the 1st of January for the current year. But the Chamber shall have power from time to time to increase the entrance-money subscriptions.

Any Member, intending to leave the Association, shall give written notice to the Secretary, at least one month before the 31st December, or shall be held liable for his Subscription for the ensuing year. Where such Subscription shall by notice be withdrawn, or shall be discontinued for more than one year without notice, the party shall forfeit the entrance-money and cease to be a Member; and no Member shall be entitled to any privilege of the Chamber whose annual subscription is unpaid.

Firms becoming Members of the Chamber shall be represented by one partner only, whose name shall be given in at the time of paying the subscription, and may be changed once at the commencement of each year, and not oftener; unless in case of the death or incapacity of the partner so nominated. The other partners may be present at meetings of the Chamber, but shall not be allowed to take part in the discussion, or to vote on any question, except on their becoming Members individually.

III. — A Meeting of the Chamber shall be held on the last Monday in January in every year, at a place and hour to be fixed by the Board of Directors; of which ten days' notice shall be given in each of the Bristol Papers. The regular business of the Annual Meeting shall be — first, to receive and pass the audited Accounts of the Chamber, to supply the vacancies in the Board of Directors, and to elect from the Board a President and two Vice-Presidents; to appoint a Banking Firm in Bristol to be Treasurers, and also to elect three auditors of Accounts (not being Directors), for the correct year. The Board of Directors shall also make a full report to this meeting of their proceedings during the past year; with such further communications as they shall deem requisite. And it shall then be competent to the meeting to recommend to the consideration of the Directors any subject of a general nature within the design of the Chamber, in which the interference of the Board way be thought expedient. No previous notice shall be required of any business to be transacted at the annual meeting; but every motion proposed at meetings of the Chamber shall be in writing, nor shall a verbal motion be put from the Chair.

IV. — The President, the Vice-Presidents, or any ten Directors may convene a special meeting of the Chamber; and the President or one Vice-President, or in their absence, the Secretary shall forthwith call such a meeting, on receiving a written requisition from one-fourth part, or forty in number of the members of the Chamber.

Seven days notice, by Post, of every such meeting, and of the business to be then brought forward, shall be sent to each member; nor shall any business, of which due notice has not been so given, be transacted or discussed thereat.

At all meetings of the Chamber and Board of Directors, the Chair shall be taken by the President, or in his absence by one of the Vice-Presidents, or in their absence by some other Director; who shall have a casting vote only.

No addition to, or alteration in, the fundamental Regulations of the Chamber shall be adopted, until the same shall have been discussed and decided on at one special meeting, and confirmed at the next.

The election of Officers, and all matters relating to personal character, shall be decided on a by ballot; but all other questions before the Chamber by open vote.

If the business regularly brought forward at any meeting of the Chamber cannot conveniently be concluded thereat, the same may be adjourned; and such unfinished business only be proceeded with at the adjourned meeting, without a new notice.

V.— All business and negotiations of the Chamber shall be managed and transacted by a Board of forty-two Directors, elected by ballot from the Chamber at large (with the exception of members who may be of the legal profession). Of these Directors when regularly convened, five shall be competent to act; except for making or altering Rules for the government of the Board, for which purpose the concurrence of twenty-two Directors shalt be necessary, and unless where it is otherwise provided for.

Of the first Board of Directors, fourteen members shall at the first, and also at the second annual meeting, retire by ballot amongst themselves; and afterwards the fourteen members entered first on the list shall retire annually, and shall not for one year be re-eligible; their places shall be supplied at the yearly meeting in addition to vacancies caused death or otherwise; which, when they occur, may be filled either at the yearly or (with notice) at a special meeting of the Chamber; the Directors chosen to supply casual vacancies going out as their predecessors would have done. To every newly-elected President, Vice-President, Director, and Auditor, a written notice of his appointment shall be sent, requesting him to signify his acceptance in writing; which, if he neglect to do for one week, if in Bristol, or if absent for one week after his return, his election will be void, and the member next in succession upon the ballot shall be considered elected in his place.

VI.— The Board of Directors shall annually, after their election, appoint a Secretary, being a practicing Attorney or Solicitor, who shall be the acting and ostensible Officer of the Chamber, and shall receive communications, notices, and applications addressed thereto.

The Secretary shall give all notices, and attend all meetings of the Chamber and Board, the standing Committee, and such other Committees as the Board shall direct, and shall keep a Journal or Minute Book of their proceedings. All Apartments, Books, Papers, and Effects of the Chamber, shall be under his charge, but shall be delivered up by him to the Board on demand: He shall act under the directions and control of the Board, who shall have power to remove him, and to direct such salary to he paid him as they shall think fit.

VII.—A monthly meeting of the Board of Directors, for dispatch of business, shall be held on the first Monday in the month, at any place and hour to be fixed by them, and notified in their Minute Book. And the President, or either of the Vice-Presidents, or any three Directors, may at any time order a special meeting of the Board to be convened.

A standing Committee of six shall be appointed in rotation from the Directors, of whom, the first two on the list shall retire and be replaced at each monthly meeting of the Board. This Committee shall meet weekly, and three members of it shall be a quorum. Its duty shall be, to carry into effect the resolutions of the Board; to receive and attend to applications and other business, and to prepare the same for the Board. Any meetings of the Board, or Weekly Committee, may, for proceeding with business, adjourn at their convenience.

The Board may also, at its discretion, depute Committees of its members to effect or attend to any definite object or special matters; and should the purpose of any such appointment be still in progress and incomplete at the time of the Annual Meeting, and it shall be so reported by the Directors, then such Committee may be continued by the Meeting for any time not exceeding the current year, notwithstanding the retirement of any of its members from the Board of Directors.

VIII. — It shall be competent to a meeting of the Board of Directors, at which at least twenty-two Members shall be present, to refuse admission to, or to expel from, the Chamber, any Individual whose conduct has in the opinion of three-fourths of the members present, been disgraceful, either by offending against the law of the land, or by his mercantile or trading transactions having been grossly and notoriously dishonorable. Reserving to such individual the right of appeal to the Chamber, if he shall consider himself aggrieved.

IX.—The Board of Directors shall, after the first year, undertake the arbitration of differences upon matters of Trade and Accounts, where both or either of the parties shall by Members of the Chamber; and the Board shall, at the meeting of the Chamber in January, 1824, propose, a Plan for that purpose.

X. — The Funds of the Chamber shall be managed by the Board, and shall be invested in Exchequer Bills, or in other Government Securities in the names of the Treasurers.

Every payment shall be ordered at a meeting of the Board, and by a majority in which five at least of the Directors present shall concur, and all cheques on the Bankers shall be signed at such meetings by the Chairman and two other Directors; but no gratuity shall be voted except by the Chamber at large. The Accounts shall be kept by the Secretary, and shall be examined at every Monthly Meeting of the Board, and be signed by the Chairman.

The Directors may employ a person, giving security to their satisfaction, to collect the Entrance and Subscription Monies, allowing a compensation for his trouble, and they shall not be liable for his default.

XI.— Every member of the Chamber shall have access at all reasonable times to the Journals, Minute and Account Books of the Chamber and Board of Directors; but shall not take extracts therefrom without consent of the Board. Every application made by Members for the interference of the Board, with the statement of facts on which such application is grounded, shall invariably be made in writing.

Additional Rule of the Chamber,

Passed at the Annual Meeting, on the 26th January, 1824,—[See Rules and Regulations of the Chamber, and Report of Provisional Committee, p. 18, and First Annual Report of Board, pp. 5, 23].

ARBITRATIONS.

XII. — That in cases where a difference shall arise upon any matter relating to Trade or Accounts, between persons one or both of whom shall he Members of the Chamber, and the parties are desirous of submitting the matter to the decision of an Arbitration, under the direction of the Board, the same shall be received; subject nevertheless in each ease to the discretion of the Board.

In order to such a proceeding, the parties shall state in writing the subject matter of the dispute to the Standing Committee or the Secretary, who shall submit the same to the Board of Directors at the next Monthly Meeting, or at a Special Meeting.

At such Meeting the Board shall proceed to Elect by ballot five of its Members, as a Deputation for the Arbitration; which number shall be reduced by each party in difference striking out one name, and the remaining three Directors shall then undertake the arbitration.

Instruments of reference, to be approved by the Arbitrators, shall then be executed by the respective parties; such instruments reserving a power of compensating the Arbitrators for their time, and also a power of moderate extension of the time for the determination of such difference; but, previously to the availing themselves of such power of extension, the Arbitrators shall report in writing their reasons to the Board, and obtain its sanction to such delay, — and for this purpose the Arbitrators shall have power in every case to extend the time for their decision until the next Monthly Meeting of the Board.

GRESLEY HELLICAR, SECRETARY

1.52 Kirkcaldy Chamber of Commerce 1825

Kirkcaldy chamber was founded in 1825 for which there is a set of rules within the chamber's minutes. These were clearly used as they are reported in some secondary sources; for example, Leighton in 1840 stated that 'The increase of trade and manufactures of this town led, in 1825, to the formation of the Kirkcaldy chamber of commerce, of which the principal merchants and manufacturers are members; and the object of which, as elsewhere, is to attend to the varied interests of the mercantile and manufacturing community. It is managed by a committee of directors, and a chairman'.[90] A contemporary report states 'the third clause of its rules and regulation' was 'to watch over every public measure, whereby the trade and manufactures, in which its members are engaged, may be affected, …'.[91] Some account of its early foundation is recorded in David Landale's 1826 autobiography, and a modern biography, which notes that Landale called the initial meeting at the George Inn which 'agreed unanimously that a Chamber of Commerce and Manufacturing be established on the most liberal basis by admitting as members all manufacturers, flax spinners, bleachers and shipowners, residing in Kirkcaldy and its districts.' David Landale was elected the first chairman of the chamber. He is also notable for taking part in the last duel in Scotland, with a local bank manager, George Morgan in 1826. Morgan, in an argument in the High Street about whether Landale could pay his creditors, hit Landale with a cane; Landale felt forced to defend his honour and in the following duel shot and killed Morgan. He was tried for murder, but was acquitted, probably owing to support from chamber members (among others), some of whom swore affidavits in his support.[92] The incident is illustrative of the strength of local networks where honour and trust were foundations of business practice. The early activities of the chamber led to several petitions, e.g. in March and May 1830 the chamber together with the magistrates and councils of Dysart, Kinghorn and Kirkcaldy petitioned Parliament for an end to the East India Company's trade monopoly.[93] On 2 June 1841 a petition was presented by Mr. Colquhoun from the chamber against any reform of the banking system.[94] The chamber also lobbied against the Corn Laws.

[90] J. M. Leighton *History of Fife from the earliest period to the present time*, vol. 3 (Glasgow, 1840) 145

[91] *The Edinburgh Magazine and Literary Miscellany*, 96, July (1826) 365.

[92] D. Landale, *Report of the trial of David Landale Esq* (Perth, 1826); J. Landale, *Duel: A True Story of Death and Honour* (Edinburgh 2005).

[93] *Fife Herald*, 18 Mar. 1830; also *CJ*, lxxxv. 193, 382; *LJ*, lxii. 93, 114, 115, 158, 305.

[94] J. H. Barrow ed. *The Mirror of Parliament*, Vol III (London, 1838) 2013.

Source
Kirkcaldy chamber of commerce minute book: held at modern Kirkcaldy Chamber, transcribed by its chief executive Bill Main.

Minutes 18 July 1825

RULES AND REGULATIONS OF THE CHAMBER OF COMMERCE AND MANUFACTURES OF KIRKCALDY

1. That the Chamber of Commerce and Manufactures be established on the most liberal basis by admitting as members all manufacturers of linen cloth, traders in those articles made use of in that manufacture, flax spinners, bleachers, and ship owners, residing in Kirkcaldy and in its district, and also any person or persons engaged in these branches of trade and manufactures within the County of Fife, desirous of becoming members.

2. That the district of Kirkcaldy shall be understood to comprehend the bounds of the presbytery.

3. That the principal object of the association shall be to watch over every public measure whereby the trade or manufactures in which its members are engaged may be affected, and to lend its weight and influence for procuring relief from any general grievance; as well as for the attainment of any other object which may involve the general or particular interests of those branches of trade and manufactures, where the same can be conducted with more effect by the association than by individual exertion.

4. That there shall be procured for the benefit of the member of this association, in so far as their funds will admit, any public documents that may be considered useful to the Chamber; such as acts of Parliament, Custom House and Excise regulations, rules and lists of dues leviable at all the principal sea ports in Great Britain, and also the law and regulations established in the principal shipping ports of foreign nations; these to be under the charge of the secretary, and open at all times to the inspection of the members.

5. That to accomplish these objects a fund shall be raised to defray the necessary expenses for carrying the measure of the Institution into effect; and for that purpose each members shall pay at entry one guinea, and such a sum annually as shall be fixed by the directors for time being, not exceeding 10 shillings and sixpence, declaring that no members shall be liable for more than these sums respectively; and those failing to pay shall be deprived of the benefits and privileges of the association. In the event of the death of any member during the existence of the association his interest in its funds shall cease, and in no way be considered the property of his heirs or executors but applicable to uses and purposes of the Chamber.

6. That a general meeting shall be held on the first Wednesday of October annually, at which there shall be elected by a majority of the members present nine members, who shall be denominated a committee of directors, five of

whom to be a quorum; and these shall choose from their own number annually a chairman and deputy chairman to preside at all committee meetings, these and likewise the chairman who may be appointed to preside at general meetings to have a casting vote in case of an equality of votes occurring at any such meetings.

7. That the committee of directors for the time being, shall have the general management of the affairs of the association and of the application of the funds in the way they may judge most proper for the purposes and benefit of the institution; and it shall be their peculiar duty to watch over every public measure likely to affect the interest of their constituents, adopt such measures as they may deem necessary under the circumstances, and report to the annual general meetings the proceedings of the Chamber for the bygone year.

8. That the directors shall annually appoint a treasurer who shall have in charge the funds of the association which must be lodged in a bank, as directed by the committee of directors. He shall be responsible for his own intromissions only; and at every annual general meeting he shall produce account of his receipts and disbursements with a clear state of the funds of the association.

9. That the directors shall annually appoint a secretary whose duty shall be to attend all general and committee meetings, to take charge of the documents of the Chamber, to receive all memorials or letters, and applications, to be presented to it on the subject of public business, to frame petitions or memorials to public bodies, to collect the subscriptions for the purpose of paying them over to the treasurer, and generally to execute the detail of the affairs of the Chamber, but always subject to the control of the directors. He shall be paid annually such a compensation for his services as may be fixed by the directors for the time being.

10. That it shall be in the power of the committee of directors to appoint one person to do the duties of treasurer and secretary, and in either ease the treasurer shall give security to the satisfaction of the directors for his intromissions.

11. That the chairman or in his absence the deputy chairman may, with consent with the majority of the committee of directors, call general meetings and at all times shall do so upon the requisition being addressed to him stating the object of meeting and subscribed by at least ten members.

12. That notices shall be sent by the secretary in name of the chairman of the committee of directors to each member at least three days previous to any ordinary general meeting being held stating at same time the object and purpose of the meeting, but in case of urgent necessity, it shall be lawful for the directors to call extraordinary general meetings on the shortest notice, and proceed to business provided there be twelve of members present; and in the

event of any alteration to be proposed in the law of the association, then and in that case fourteen days' notice at least must be given to each member.

13. That, in the event of any person wishing to become a member of the Chamber of Commerce and Manufactures, application must be made to the committee, who shall have power to admit him.

14. That it shall be in the power of the general meeting, specially called for that purpose by at least one month's previous notice being given, to dissolve the association, upon there appearing to be two thirds of the members voting for that purpose at said meeting; and in that case the property of the Chamber shall be converted into cash; the whole of which with the balance in the treasurer's hands to be delivered over to the committee of directors acting at the time, and by them apply such charitable purposes, and in such proportions, as they may deem proper.

1.53 [Chamber of Commerce at Tralee (Kerry) 1830][95]

1.54 Guernsey Chamber of Commerce 1832

After the re-establishment of the Guernsey chamber in 1808, it went into some form of limbo after 4 August 1819, when there is a gap in the minutes until 9 January 1832. It must have continued some form of life since in 1832 the chamber went through internal discords when a group of members sought to disband it and use its assets, whilst another group sought to re-establish it, remove old officers and recover its assets. This led to a statement of the 'fundamental principles of a chamber of commerce' with a new set of rules. These were not all-embracing principles but Guernsey-specific, a response to the local discords.

Source
Guernsey Chamber of Commerce Minutes, Guernsey Archives AQ/040/01

Minutes, also printed as pamphlet 25 January 1832

FUNDAMENTAL PRINCIPLES OF THE CHAMBER OF COMMERCE

We, the undersigned Merchants, Traders and other Inhabitants of the Island of Guernsey, fully concurring in the Resolutions passed at a General Meeting, held at Cole's Hotel on the 20th December, 1831, hereby agree to unite and renew the Chamber of Commerce first established on the 16th of

[95] Referred to as one of several 'petitions of the freeholders against an additional duty of one shilling a gallon on Home made spirits', *Hansard*, N. S. xxxiv, 29 (1830); *General Index Hansard*, John Philippart ed., Baldwin & Craddock, London, 1834, 392.

December, 1808: the general object of which shall be as heretofore, to watch over the commercial interest of the Island, and to deliberate on and adopt all such means and measures as shall appear best calculated to promote and protect the same, and to preserve inviolable our remaining privileges, and faithfully determined to adhere to the pledge given in 1808. We again solemnly proclaim our unalterable Resolution not to countenance either directly or indirectly, any illicit trade with the United Kingdom; but, on the contrary, to assist with all our power in the execution of the Laws and Ordinances enacted for its suppression; and we further declare that we shall not admit to Membership any person who will not previously bind himself to the same effect.

[List of 59 names follows]

At a General Meeting, held at Cole's Hotel, on Tuesday Feb. 14, 1832, pursuant to public notice, Joseph Collings, Esq., in the chair, resolved:

1.—That the Chamber of Commerce be founded on the principles of the foregoing declaration, which this Meeting unanimously adheres unto.

2.—That the following rules proposed by the Committee for the management and support of the Chamber of Commerce be, and they are hereby approved of.

RULES OF THE CHAMBER OF COMMERCE.

1.—That for defraying the current expenses of the Establishment every Member shall pay on admission Ten Shillings, and yearly Seven Shillings and Sixpence on the second Tuesday in February.

2.—Should any extraordinary occasion occur requiring a larger sum to oppose any illegal pretensions, or to assert our just rights, a General Meeting shall be called and consulted on the propriety of such opposition or assertion of our rights, and on the means of raising the money that may be wanted.

3.—That a permanent Committee of Management be elected VIVA VOCE, to consist of thirteen Members, who shall choose a President, Vice President, and Secretary, out of their own number. That the Committee first elected shall serve until the Second Tuesday in February, 1833, when four members shall go out by lot, and the same number be elected on that day to replace them. On the Second February of the succeeding year four more of the original thirteen Members shall go out by lot, and the year after the five remaining old Members shall quit the Committee, and so on ever after in rotation.

4.—That the President, Vice President, and Secretary be chosen by the Committee after the election of its Members, and be obliged to serve for one year; that they be re-eligible, but not compelled to serve more than two successive years, and that the Members who have served already in the Committee be re-eligible by the General Meeting.

5.—That the Members elected by the General Meeting be obliged to serve for the first time under the penalty of Forty Shillings; but they shall not be liable to be again fined for two years, if being re-elected they refuse to serve; in which case others will be elected in their place.

6.—That independent of those who have already signed the original declaration, no one be admitted a Member of this Institution except he be recommended by the Committee; and that no one once admitted be at liberty to withdraw without having first signified his intention to the Committee and paid the ensuing years' subscription.

7.—That seven Members of the Committee form a Quorum. That the Committee be bound to meet on the first Tuesday in every month, at Ten o'clock in the forenoon, and that every absentee pay a fine of One Half-crown to the general fund.

8.—That the Committee shall have the power of convening a General Meeting whenever it shall deem it expedient, and that on a requisition to that effect, signed by at least ten Members of the Chamber of Commerce, and setting forth the matter to be taken into consideration, it be bound to call a General Meeting.

9.—That every Member be bound to attend the General Yearly Meeting except for reasons satisfactory to the Committee; and every absentee pay a fine of One Half-crown to the general fund.

10.—That every Member of the Chamber of Commerce shall have the right of submitting his commercial disputes and differences to the arbitration of a quorum of at least five Members of the Committee, whether the adverse party of parties be or be not a Member or Members of the Chamber, providing that each disputing party pay beforehand One Guinea to the general fund for each case so submitted, whether it compromise one or more articles in dispute, and every award given shall be final.

11.—That no individual who is not a Member of the Chamber of Commerce shall be entitled to claim the services or assistance of the Managing Committee in any case of private concern.

12.—That no Member shall remove, or cause to be removed out of the Committee Room any books, documents, papers, or any other article belonging to the Chamber under the penalty, for each article removed, of One Guinea for the benefit of the general fund.

13.—That no law or rule shall be passed at a General Meeting which shall not have been previously submitted to the Committee for its consideration and reported upon.

14.—That the vote of the majority shall in all cases be binding under the minority.

[Subsequently, at a General Meeting of the Chamber held 29 March 1849, it was resolved that the new 1832 Rules of the Chamber be printed and sent round to every Member. These are pasted in the minute book: AQ/040/02]

1.55 Nottingham Chamber of Commerce 1835

There were previous initiatives to form a chamber in Nottingham as part of the response to the General Chamber in 1785 (see Chapter 8) and in 1795 and 1813, which each collapsed as a result of tensions with local hosiery workers (see Chapter 4). The only initiative that actually resulted in rules and seems to have had some form of operation before the modern chamber was founded in 1860 was that in 1835, as reproduced here. This foundation has been usefully covered by Walton, who provides a valuable source.[96] Walton was unable to discover much activity, but found some actions continuing into 1837. Most notable was a petition almost immediately after foundation for the chamber to take immediate steps 'to memorialise the Board of Trade upon the occasion of the great distress amongst English lace embroiderers which arose from the facility with which foreign embroidered goods were imported by smuggling into England. The charge by smugglers into England was 5% to 7% only; while, by the superior vigilance of the French Officers of Customs, the charge on their frontier was 50%'.[97] This memorial may indicate the primary motivation for the 1835 foundation as occasioned by unrest among local workers resulting from poor economic conditions. The 1835 initiative seems to have collapsed by 1838. An initiative in 1838 to set up a parallel chamber of workers, with the two collaborating also collapsed and perhaps led to the demise of the more general 1835 foundation (see Chapter 4). Nottingham was perhaps the chamber most concerned to act partly as an employer association, setting wages and prices, in its initiatives in 1795 and 1813, and some of this continued after the successful foundation in 1860.

Source
Walton, R., *The History of the Nottingham Chamber of Commerce 1860–1960*, Nottingham, 1960) 17–18.

Resolution 19 May 1835

1. That a Chamber of Commerce now be established having for its object the promotion of all measures calculated to benefit and protect the interests

[96] Walton, *History of the Nottingham Chamber* (1960) 16–21.
[97] Walton, *History of the Nottingham Chamber* (1960) 17.

of the members and of the manufactures, trade and commerce of the country, and more especially the town of Nottingham and its neighbourhood.

2. That this Chamber consist of Merchants, Bankers, Manufacturers, Tradesmen and others interested in the trade of Nottingham and its vicinity. A subscription of one guinea annually be paid in advance on the 1st May to constitute a member; Persons paying ten guineas to be members for life.

3. That the business of the Chamber should be managed by 15 directors, the first 15 to be appointed at this meeting. Five of those who have attended the least frequently to retire annually, and to be ineligible for one year and five others to be chosen at the Annual General Meeting by written lists containing five names and signed by the subscriber, the Mayor of Nottingham to be ex officio. Five directors to be competent to transact business.

4. A Secretary to be appointed annually by the directors and to be paid a suitable salary. He should keep a record of the proceedings which will be open for inspection of the Members at the meetings; and also a list of all the members to be open for their inspection at all times.

5. A President, Vice President and Treasurer to be chosen annually by the directors out of their body at their first meeting. The Vice President to exercise the powers of the President in his absence.

6. An Annual General Meeting of the Members shall be held in May for the transaction of business at which five directors shall be chosen in place of those who retire. Notice of such meeting to be given to the members.

7. Quarterly Meetings of the directors shall be called by the Secretary by circular for the transaction of general business. Communications from members shall receive prior consideration to any others.

8. Special Meetings of the directors may be called by the President on his own authority or on the written requisition of three directors or in the case of absence or refusal of the President shall be called by the Secretary on the written requisition of five directors, giving not less than three days' notice in writing of the meeting and its object.

9. Special General Meetings of the Members at large shall be called by the President, or in the case of his absence or refusal by the Secretary on requisition in writing of not less than half the directors or one fourth of the members, the requisition and notice to state the object of such a general meeting.

10. The Chairman of any meeting to have a casting vote only.

11. The funds to be under the control of the directors for the time being. The Treasurer shall sanction all payments by previous vote and always signed by the Chairman and the Secretary, and any sum above £20 shall not be paid without being proposed at one meeting of directors and sanctioned at the next.

12. General Meetings shall be empowered to exclude any members whose conduct may have been such in the opinion of two-thirds of the members present to render him unfit to continue to be a member of the Chamber.

These resolutions having been passed, a ballot took place for the appointment of Committee members for the first year. Those successful were Samuel Adams, Thomas Adams, William Boden, Samuel Carledge, D. S. Churchill, William Felkin, John Hall, John Heard, Thomas Hind, Samuel Hollins, Charles Leavers, Henry Leaver, T. B. Milns, John Rodgers and Thomas Wakefield.

On the following day, Wednesday, 20th May 1835, a meeting of those directors took place. Thomas Wakefield was appointed the first President, John Heard the first Vice President, Samuel Adams the Treasurer and John Hutchinson the Secretary.

1.56 Hull Chamber of Commerce 1837

An earlier attempt to found a chamber in Hull in 1801 seems to have failed to get underway (see section 1.30), though it may have been involved in convoy organisation (see Chapter 6). Hope claims that it failed because of the influence of party. No evidence of this has been found, but it is echoed in 1837 in the chamber's first annual report of 1838: 'Chambers of Commerce, imperfectly as they are at present constituted, possess advantages for combined and immediate operations which are not attained by any other institutions, and so long as they keep aloof from the baneful interference of party politics (with which they neither can or ought to have any connection) they may fairly be looked forward to as the precursors of great and substantial benefits.'

Source
Minute books of chamber: held at the modern Hull and Humberside Chamber of Commerce and Industry.

Minutes 1 March 1837

Laws of the Hull Chamber of Commerce

1st That a Chamber of Commerce be established, to consist of Merchants, Bankers, Manufacturers, Ship Owners, Underwriters, Ship & Insurance & Mercantile Brokers and Agents, parties conducting the Export, Coasting, and River Trades, and proprietors or Occupiers of Warehouses, resident in Hull and its vicinity.

Consuls and Vice Consuls to be Members, ex officio; and Non-Residents may be elected Honorary Members.

2. That the objects of the Chamber are to take into consideration questions affecting the Commerce of the Port of Hull, communications from other Chambers of Commerce, to endeavour to obtain redress of any grievance or inconvenience affecting the commerce of the Port, and to arbitrate disputes

3. That the Subscription be One Guinea per annum, to be paid in advance

4. That the executive power shall be vested in twenty one subscribing Members, to be chosen by ballot (the Voting papers to be signed by the Member, and if delivered by another Member to be countersigned by him) who shall be denominated *The Directors of the Hull Chamber of Commerce*, seven of whom shall be a quorum, and they shall continue to act until the first Meeting of their Successors. The first election to take place on the ______ and afterwards at the Annual Meeting. Seven Members to retire annually, the first Seven being those who have the fewest votes, the second seven those having the next lowest number of votes, and afterwards by rotation of the retiring members to be eligible for re-election; Vacancies to be filled up by those having the next highest number of votes, in case of equality of votes, then by lot. Only one member of a firm to be in the Directory at the same time

5. That a Chairman and Deputy Chairman shall be elected annually by the Directors, from their own body, at their first meeting, the Chairman, or in his absence, the Deputy Chairman shall preside at all Meetings of the Directors or Members, but in case neither of them are present, the Meeting shall appoint a Chairman for the occasion.

6. A Secretary, with an annual Salary, to be fixed by the Directors, shall be elected at the first Meeting of the Directors in each year, who shall have the custody of all Books and Documents belonging to the Chamber, shall summon the Members to all Meetings, arrange the business intended to be taken into consideration, draw up the awards in cases arbitrated, record all proceedings, collect the Subscriptions, and Keep a particular account of receipts and disbursements; he shall give up all books, papers, and documents belonging to the Chamber, when required by the Directors, and, if they think requisite give security for the faithful discharge of his duties.

7. The Directors shall meet the first Monday after their election, and once a month afterwards for the dispatch of business, by summons from the Secretary, stating the nature thereof, at least two clear days before the Meeting. Special Meetings of Directors may be called by the Chairman or Deputy Chairman or any five Directors.

8. Members wishing to refer disputes to the Chamber, shall apply to the Directors, through the Secretary, in writing, who at their first Meeting shall appoint a Committee of three of the Members, to whom the reference will be certified by the Secretary, but if preferred by the parties in dispute, each may

appoint one Arbitrator from the list of Members, these having power to appoint a third, and in case of their not agreeing, such nomination of a third shall be vested in the Board of Directors. The decision of any two of the Arbitrators to be binding, but before the investigation takes place, both parties shall sign a declaration in the Arbitration Book, agreeing to abide by the decision of the Arbitrators.

9. The Arbitrators shall send their decision to the Secretary to be countersigned by the Chairman, or in his absence by the Deputy Chairman, and a copy thereof shall then be delivered to each of the parties in disputes, on payment of the following fees—two thirds to the Arbitrators, and one third to the funds of the Chamber exclusive of expenses actually incurred—where both parties are Members not less than Two nor more than Five Guineas, when one or both of the parties are not Members not less than Two nor more than Ten Guineas, the Arbitrators to decide by whom it is the Fees and expenses shall be paid. The names of the parties in dispute, the point at issue, the names of the referees, and the Award shall be registered in the Arbitration Book, a reference to it being also made in the Minute Book of the Directors

10. The Annual General Meeting shall be held on the first Monday in February. Special General Meetings may be called by the Directors, or Twenty five of the Members, on their giving each Member three days' notice thereof, the object of the Meeting being stated therein

11. The Secretary's accounts shall be made up to the 31st December in each year, and having been audited by two of the Directors, shall, with a list of the Members, and Copies of any motions intended to be made at the Annual Meeting (which must not be received by the Secretary after the 15 January) be printed and sent by post to every member on or before the 22nd January

12. The funds shall be under the control of the Directors, and placed at interest in a Bank in the Town. No payment to be made unless authorized in writing by the Chairman of the Meeting; and no payment exceeding Ten Pounds shall be voted unless Twelve Directors are present

13. All decisions of General Meetings, or of the Directors, shall be by Ballot, if required, and the Chairman, shall have a casting vote, in addition to his vote as a member

14. That the name and occupation of every person desirous of becoming a Member shall be given to the Secretary, in writing, signed by two Members recommending him, and shall be balloted for at the next Meeting of the Directors or Members, but shall not take any part in the proceedings until he has been three months a Member.

15. That any Member becoming Bankrupt or Signing over his property to his Creditors, shall in consequence, cease to be a Member, but he may be again proposed and elected, as stated in Law 14

16. That General Meetings be empowered to exclude any Member, whose conduct may have been such as, in the opinion of two thirds of the Members present, renders him unfit to continue a Member of the Chamber

17. That no Law shall be expunged, altered, or added, except at the General Annual Meeting, or at a special General Meeting.

18. That the minute & account Books of the Chamber shall be open for the inspection of the Members from 12 to 3 o'clock every Wednesday

19. That where each partner in a firm does not subscribe, he only who signs the Laws shall be the member of the Chamber

20. That these Laws be entered in a Book and signed by each Member

We the undersigned hereby agree to be members of the Hull Chamber of Commerce, subject to the preceding Laws, and such alterations and additions thereto, as may from time to time, be duly made.

1.57 Worcester Chamber of Commerce 1839

The Worcester foundation papers were printed and contain the purpose and rules of the early chamber. They bear a strong resemblance to the committee report and rules of Bristol for 1823, indicating that by this date the format of chamber rules was being widely shared and had become relatively standardised.

Source
Printed *Report with Rules and Regulations agreed upon for the Formation of the Worcester Chamber of Commerce together with Bye-Laws*: held at the modern Hereford and Worcester Chamber of Commerce

REPORT OF A PROVISIONAL COMMITTEE APPOINTED TO PROMOTE THE FORMATION OF THE CHAMBER 7th May 1839

THERE is now scarcely a seaport or manufacturing town in the kingdom of any importance that has not seen the advantage of forming a Society from amongst its inhabitants for the protection of its local interests, and the redress of its local grievances in trade, whether they arise from public or private causes.

There are few inland cities in the kingdom more advantageously situated than Worcester for carrying on an extensive trade. Placed in the centre of a populous and fertile county, prolific in every article which gives a stimulus to agriculture as well as employment to capital in manufactures and commerce, together with a noble river and canals intersecting the very heart of the county, its citizens must at all times be sensible of the many advantages inherent in the natural position of their city.

That they are so is evidenced by the attempts they have recently made (though they have hitherto been unsuccessful) to keep pace with the general improvements of the nation, by promoting the formation of the Railways projected within their neighbourhood, and more particularly by their endeavours, at many thousand pounds expense, to render the navigation of the Severn available for far more extended usefulness than it is at present.

It is not meant to be asserted that the inhabitants of this city have hitherto failed in their attempts to attain those objects through want of such an Association as that which is now proposed; but it is capable of proof that there are many minor benefits which might be derived therefrom, and that occasions may arise when it might, by its interference and influence, assist in the attainment of highly important and extended schemes of improvement.

In short, it must be evident to every reflecting mind that a body of individuals, associated for one common object, is far more likely to succeed than one individual by his single exertions; and that in petitioning Parliament, addressing the executive Government, or treating with another public body, the weight and authority of the one will bear no comparison with the other.

The peculiar advantages, if not the necessity, of such an Association are apparent at the present time, when there is a prospect, by timely interference and vigorous exertion, of showing that this city has perhaps far greater, if not more rightful claims, to participate in the privileges and benefits of the Bonding System than many other places that are applying; and an application for a reduction in the rate of postage would at this crisis be more likely to succeed by the combined efforts of such an Association than by those of single individuals

The objects contemplated by the Chamber may be stated to be fourfold:

First: To effect the redress and removal of any *local* impediments or burdens which may obstruct or impede the trade and manufactures of the city.

Second: To keep a watchful eye upon and to guard against the injury which may arise from the imposition of any *public* burdens, which by their *partial* operation sometimes become serious local injuries.

Third: To endeavour, as a Body, to promote those interests of their fellow-citizens which as private individuals they frequently find it difficult, if not impossible, to attain.

And Fourth: To correspond with other Institutions of a similar nature. And thereby promote a general co-operation and commercial intercourse with each other.

It should be borne in mind that the views and designs of the promoters of this Association are strictly and exclusively *commercial*; and upon the rigid exclusion of every topic and feeling opposed or irrelevant to this its avowed object, its very existence will depend.

RULES AND REGULATIONS OF THE WORCESTER CHAMBER OF COMMERCE.

I. The Association shall be called the WORCESTER CHAMBER OF COMMERCE.

Its object shall be to protect and promote the commercial, trading, and manufacturing interests of Worcester; and its Inhabitants generally are invited to join the Association.

II. Individuals may be received as Life Members of the Chamber, on payment of Ten Pounds, and signing the Regulations.

All other Members shall sign the Regulations, and pay an annual sum of 10s, to be due and payable in advance on the 24th of June, for the current year.

Any Member intending to leave the Association shall give written notice to the Secretary at least one month before the 22nd of June, or shall be held liable for his subscription for the ensuing year. Where such subscription shall by notice be withdrawn or shall be discontinued without notice, the party shall cease to be a Member; and no Member shall be entitled to any privilege of the Chamber whose annual subscription is unpaid.

Firms becoming Members shall be represented by one partner only, whose name shall be given in at the time of paying the subscription. The other partners may be present at meetings of the Chamber, but shall not be allowed to take part in the discussion, or to vote on any question, except on their becoming Members individually.

III. A general meeting of the Chamber shall be held on the third Tuesday in July in every year, and at a place and hour to be by the Board, of which seven days' notice shall be given by the Secretary, through the Post-office. The regular business of this annual meeting shall be, first, to receive and pass the audited accounts of the Chamber; to supply the vacancies in the Board of Directors, and to elect from the Board a President and Vice-President; to appoint a Treasurer, and to elect two Auditors of Accounts (not being Directors) for the current year.

The Board of Directors shall at this meeting make a full report of their proceedings during the past year, with such further communications and suggestions as they may consider will promote the objects of the Chamber; and it shall also be competent to the meeting to recommend to the consideration of the Directors any subject of a general nature within the design of the Chamber, in which the interference of the Board may be thought expedient. No previous notice be required of any business to be transacted at that meeting; but every motion proposed at meetings of the Chamber shall be in writing, nor shall a verbal motion be put from the chair.

IV. The President, Vice-President, or any five Directors, may convene a special meeting of the Chamber; and the President, Vice President, or, in their absence, the Secretary, shall forthwith call such a meeting on receiving a written requisition from one-fourth part, or twenty in number of the Members of the Chamber; seven days' notice, by post, of every such meeting, and of the business to be brought forward, shall be sent to each Member; nor shall any business, of which due notice has not been so given, be discussed or transacted thereat.

At all meetings of the Chamber and Board of Directors the chair shall be taken by the President, or, in his absence, by the Vice-President, or, in their absence, by some Director, who shall have a casting vote only.

No addition to or alteration in the fundamental regulations of the Chamber shall be adopted, until the same shall have been discussed and decided on at one special meeting, and confirmed at the next.

The election of Officers, and all matters relating to personal character; shall be decided on by ballot (if required by any Member); but all other questions before the Chamber by open vote.

V. All business and negotiations of the Chamber shall be managed and transacted by a Board of fifteen Directors, elected by ballot (if required by any Member) from the chamber at large. Of these Directors, when regularly convened, five shall be competent to act, except for making Bye-laws, or altering Rules for the government of the Board, for which purpose the concurrence of eight Directors shall be necessary, unless where it is otherwise provided for.

Of the first Board of Directors, five shall at the end of the first year retire by ballot among themselves, and in each succeeding year the five senior Members shall retire by rotation, but they may be re-eligible at the discretion of the general Members. Vacancies by death or otherwise to be filled up at the yearly, or (with notice) at a special meeting of the Chamber. Notices to be sent by the Secretary to every newly-elected President, Vice-President, Director, Treasurer, and Auditor, requesting him to signify his assent in writing; if he neglect to do so for the space of one week, his election to be void, and the Board shall elect another Member in his place.

VI. The Board of Directors shall annually after their election appoint a Secretary, being a practicing attorney or solicitor, who shall be the acting and ostensible Officer of the Chamber, and shall receive communications, notices, and applications addressed thereto.

The Secretary shall give all notices, and attend all meetings of the Chamber and Board, the Standing Committee, and such other Committees as the Board shall direct, and shall keep a journal or minute-book of their proceedings. All apartments, books, papers, and effects of the Chamber, shall be under his charge, but shall be delivered up by him to the Board on demand; he shall act under the directions and control of the Board, who shall have power to remove him, and to direct such salary to be paid him as they shall think fit.

VII. A monthly meeting of the Board of Directors for dispatch of business shall be held on the first Tuesday in the month, at any place or hour to be fixed by them and notified in their minute-hook; and the President, Vice-President, or any three Directors, may at any time order a special meeting of the Board to be convened.

It shall be competent to the Board of Directors to appoint Committees out of their own body for any special purpose

VIII. It shall be competent to the Board of Directors, at which at least two-thirds shall be present, to refuse admission to, or to expel from the Chamber, any individual whose conduct has, in the opinion of three-fourths of the Members present, been disgraceful, either by offending against the law of the land, or by his mercantile or trading transactions having been dishonourable; reserving to such individual the right of appeal to the Chamber at large, if he shall consider himself aggrieved.

IX. That in cases where a difference shall arise upon any matter relating to trade or accounts between persons, one or both of whom shall be Members of the Chamber, and the parties are desirous of submitting the matter to the decision of an arbitration under the direction of the Board, the same shall be received; subject, nevertheless, in each case to the discretion of the Board.

In order to facilitate such a proceeding, the parties shall state in writing the subject matter of the dispute to the Standing Committee or the Secretary, who shall submit the same to the Board of Directors at the next monthly meeting, or at a special meeting.

At such meeting the Board shall proceed to elect by ballot five of its Members as a deputation for the arbitration, which number shall be reduced by each party in difference striking out one name, and the remaining three Directors shall then undertake the arbitration.

Instruments of reference, to be approved by the arbitrators, shall then be executed by the respective parties, such instruments reserving a power of compensating the arbitrators for their time, and also a power of moderate extension of the time for the determination of such difference; but previously to the availing themselves of such power of extension, the arbitrators shall report in writing their reasons to the Board, and obtain its sanction to such delay; and for this purpose, the arbitrator shall have power in every case to extend the time for their decision until the next monthly meeting of the Board,

X. The funds of the Chamber shall be managed by the Board; but no gratuity shall be voted except by the Chamber at large, to be decided by a majority of Members present. The accounts to be kept by the Secretary.

XI. Every Member of the Chamber shall have Access, at all reasonable times, to the journals, minutes, and account books of the Chamber and Board of Directors, but shall not take extracts therefrom without consent of the Board. Every application made by Members for the interference of the. Board, with the statement of facts on which such application is grounded, shall invariably be made in writing.

BYE-LAWS for the GOVERNMENT OF THE BOARD OF DIRECTORS.

1.—All meetings of the Board shall be held on the first Tuesday in every month, at ten o'clock in the morning, unless in cases of manifest inconvenience.

2.—Notice of all meetings of the Board (except adjournments for not more time than eighteen hours) shall be sent by the Secretary to the Members, directed to them at their residences or usual places of business; and the summons shall be issued two days at least prior to the day of meeting, by post or otherwise.

3.—That the President, Vice-President, or three Members of the Board, shall have power, in cases of emergency, to call the Board together without two days' notice, when no fine shall be exacted for non-attendance.

4.—In every summons the Secretary shall specify the business to be transacted, unless, in the special case above alluded to, the party calling the meeting shall think in unadvisable; but eh Board shall not be precluded from considering and deciding upon any business not mentioned in the notice, unless at meetings specially convened for a particular object, provided that such business be not the rescinding of any former resolution of the Board.

5.—Members shall be fined one shilling for non-attendance five minutes after the time specified in the summons, according to Saint Nicholas's clock, unless excused by illness or absence from the city.

6.—At every meeting of the Board, previously to entering upon any business, the Secretary shall call over the names of the Directors, marking the absentees, detailing the fines incurred at the previous Board; which fines, if not then remitted, shall be considered as confirmed. Fines to be paid to the Secretary, and be subject to the disposal of the Board.

7.—The minutes of the last Board Meeting shall then be read by the Secretary, or in his absence by the Chairman, and afterwards the Reports from the existing Committees, and the business arising therefrom shall be first disposed of.

8.—No Member of the Board shall be required to act on more than two existing Committees, unless he acquiesced in the appointment; and an appointment to an arbitration shall be considered an exemption from serving on more than one Committee.

9.—No resolution of one meeting of the Board shall be altered or revoked at a subsequent one, unless a special notice of the intended alteration be given in the summons, in which revocation two-thirds of the Board shall concur.

10.—Every Member of the Board proposing a subject, or desirous of expressing his sentiments on any measure under consideration, shall rise and address the Chairman, and shall on no account interrupt another speaker, except on a point of order. No member shall leave any meeting of the Board previously to the Chairman having quitted the chair without his permission; and if he do so, he shall be subject to the foregoing fine of one shilling.

11.— That all payments ordered by the Board shall be made by cheque, signed by the Chairman and any Member of the Board who is present.

THE COMMITTEES

12.—On the appointment of a Committee, the hour and place of its meeting shall be fixed by the Members proposing it, and, if practicable, at the Board when the same is appointed, and one clear day's notice, specifying the business, shall be sent to each Member of it; but when all the Members composing a Committee, being present, shall concur in fixing the meeting for business, such agreement shall supersede the necessity for notice.

13.—If a Committee adjourn the business under their consideration beyond eighteen hours, then notice of the adjourned meeting shall be sent to each Member.

14.— At the first meeting of a Committee (the President and Vice-President being Members, *ex officio*) they shall elect a Chairman, by whom, in the absence of the Secretary, the minutes of the business transacted at each meeting shall be taken.

15.— At each monthly meeting of the Board every existing Committee shall present a written Report of its progress, signed by the Chairman, and, if necessary, may call a special meeting of the Board to receive a Report.

16.— Notice of the existing Committees, their objects, and times of meeting, to be kept by the Secretary, and to be shown by him to any Member of the Chamber making enquiry relative to the object on which the Board is engaged.

Chapter 2

Charters

Chartered status was desired by many of the early chambers, and achieved by six: New York in 1770, Glasgow 1783, Edinburgh 1786, Greenock 1813, Limerick 1815, and Waterford 1815. These six charters are reproduced here. It is notable that none of these was in England. Attempts to gain a charter by the General Chamber in 1786–7, Jersey in 1788, and Dublin in 1823 (and perhaps in 1783) were all unsuccessful. Efforts to establish a London chamber through a charter in 1817, 1823 and 1850–70 were all resisted by the Westminster government.[1] The issues are clear in the unsuccessful attempts by Jersey and Dublin reproduced here. Gaining a charter was a lengthy and specialised process, which was usually costly and required engaging supporters in parliament and the Privy Council, which had become the main decision-making bodies. It was fatal for there to be opposition from another body or major interest, as shown for Jersey and Dublin. To be successful the application had to be essentially unopposed, and supported by major figures.

All the charters reproduced here have standardised marginal notation to indicate the main powers. These are omitted for clarity and to save space, but some additional paragraphing has been added. Most of the charters have extensive preambles and repetitive text which has been omitted, though its location noted.

2.1 New York 1770

The chamber began the process of applying for a charter on 5 December 1769 and received it from the Lieutenant Governor in April 1770.

Source
John Austin Stevens, 1867, *Register of Proceedings of New York Chamber of Commerce*; this is a complete transcript of the chamber's minute books.

Minutes of Special Meeting 15 February 1770

The Committee appointed to draw up a draft of a Petition to His Honor the Lieut. Governor praying him to Incorporate this Society, and to draw up

[1] Bennett, *Local Business Voice* (2011) 193–9, chapters 5 and 7.

a draft of the Charter, Report that they had drawn a draft of the Petition, which being read was in the words following:

To the Honourable Cadwallader Colden, Esquire, Lieutenant Governor and Commander-in-Chief of the Colony of New York, and the Territories depending thereon in America, In Council.

The Petition of John Cruger, Esquire, President of a Society of Merchants of the City of New York, associated for promoting Trade and Commerce in behalf of the said Society,

Most Humbly Showeth

That the said Society, sensible that Numberless inestimable benefits have accrued to Mankind from Commerce, that they are in proportion to their greater or lesser application to it, more or less opulent and potent in all Countries; and that the Enlargement of Trade will vastly increase the value of real Estates as well as the general opulence of this Country; have associated together for some time past in order to carry into execution, amongst themselves, and by their Example, to promote in others such measures as were beneficial to these Salutary Purposes. And the said Society having, with great pleasure and Satisfaction, experienced the good Effects which the few Regulations already adopted have produced, are very desirous of rendering them more extensively useful and permanent, and more adequate to the purposes of so benevolent an Institution.

Your Petitioner, therefore, in behalf of the said Society, most humbly prays your Honor to Incorporate them as a Body Politic, and to invest them with such Powers and Authorities as may be thought most conducive to answer and promote the Commercial, and consequently the Landed Interests of this growing Colony.

And your Petitioner, as in duty bound, shall ever pray.

Resolved—That the Petition be engrossed and signed by the President, and that he does wait on His Honor the Lieut. Governor with the same when perfected, and that the Committee before mentioned do attend the President, and such other Gentlemen of the Chamber as please to go.

Minute 6 March, 1770

The President reported to the Chamber that he had with the Committee waited on His Honor the Lieut. Governor, and had presented the Petition praying him to Incorporate this Society, who was pleased to say:

I think it a good Institution, and will always be glad to promote the Commercial Interests of this City, and shall deem it a peculiar happiness that a Society so beneficial to the General good of the Province is incorporated during my administration.

It is proposed, that for the good Offices the Attorney-General has shown in his readiness to forward the Charter to Incorporate this Chamber, that he be paid Twenty Guineas for his trouble, by the Treasurer.

Minute 3 April 1770

On Saturday, the 24th March 1770, a Committee of THIS Chamber waited on His Honor the Lieutenant Governor with the following Address:

To the Honourable Cadwallader Colden, Esq., &c., Lieutenant Governor and Commander-in-chief of the Colony of New York and the Territories depending thereon in America.

The Address of the President and Members of the Corporation of the Chamber of Commerce of the City of New York.

May it please Your Honour,

We, the President and Members of the Chamber of Commerce of the

City of New York, sensible of Your Honour's desire to encourage every Measure that may tend to promote the Interest of the Colony; take the earliest opportunity of returning you our sincere thanks for the Royal Charter with which you have been pleased to invest us. And we entertain the most grateful sense of the confidence thereby reposed in us by Government.

The important Light in which Your Honour views this Institution has been abundantly evinced by that Readiness so conspicuously manifest in every part of your conduct, from our first Application to its last happy Conclusion.

The Merchants are now, by Your Honour's favour, enabled to execute many Plans of Trade, which, as Individuals, they could not before accomplish, and we flatter ourselves many and great advantages will result to this Colony from their Incorporation—

We beg leave to assure your Honour that our utmost Ambition is to approve ourselves useful Members of the Community, submissive to the Laws, zealous for the Support of Government, and our happy Constitution, and firmly attached to our most Gracious Sovereign ; and that we will exert ourselves on all occasions to promote the General Interest of the Colony, and the Commerce of this City in particular ; that the Utility of the Institution and the Wisdom of its Founder may be equally applauded by the latest Posterity.

Signed by Order of the Chamber,

John Cruger, President.

To which his Honour was pleased to return the following Answer:

I return you sincere thanks for this very obliging Address:

The extensive Property of so considerable a Body of the Merchants of this City, united with Principles of Loyalty, afford the strongest assurance of your Zeal in the Support of the Government and our happy Constitution; while your good Example will, at all times, have the most favorable Influence by promoting that due Obedience to the Laws which is essential to the Security of the Subject. I ardently wish success to this Institution so well adopted to increase the Trade and Opulence, and advance the Prosperity of the Colony.

Fort George, New York, March 24th, 1770.

CHARTER [as copied in the minutes]

GEORGE THE THIRD, by the Grace of God, of Great Britain and Ireland, King, Defender of the Faith, and so forth—To all to whom these presents shall come. Greeting:

… [preamble repeats chamber's petition: minute 15 February 1770]

Know ye. That … [73 names listed], all of our City of New York, in our said Province of New York, Merchants, and their Successors to be Elected by Virtue of this our present Charter, shall for ever hereafter be one Body Corporate and Politick in Deed, Fact, and Name, by the Name, Style, and Title of "The Corporation of THE Chamber of Commerce in the City of New York, in America," and them and their Successors by the same Name, We do by these Presents really and fully Make, Erect, Create, Constitute and Declare One Body Politick and Corporate in Deed, Fact, and Name for ever; And Will, Give, Grant, and Ordain, that they and their Successors, The Corporation of the Chamber of Commerce in the City of New York, in America, by the same Name, shall and may have perpetual Succession, and shall and may by the same Name, be Persons capable in the Law to Sue and be Sued, Implead and be Impleaded, Answer and be Answered, Defend and be Defended, in all Courts and elsewhere, in all Manner of Actions, Suits, Complaints, Pleas, Causes, Matters, and Demands whatsoever, as fully and amply as any other our Liege Subjects of our said Province of New York may or can sue or be sued, implead or be impleaded, defend or be defended, by any lawful Ways or Means whatsoever; And that they and their Successors by the same Name, shall be for ever hereafter Persons Capable and Able in the Law to purchase, take, receive, hold, and enjoy, to them and their Successors, any Messuages, Tenements, Houses, and Real Estates whatsoever, and all other Hereditaments of whatsoever Nature, Kind and Quality they be, in Fee simple, for Term of Life or Lives, or in any other manner howsoever, and also any Goods, Chattels, or Personal Estate whatsoever, as well for enabling them the better to carry into Execution, encourage and promote by just and lawful Ways and Means, such Measures as will tend to promote and extend just and lawful Commerce, as to provide for, aid, and Assist, at their Discretion, such Members of our said Corporation as may be hereafter reduced to Poverty, and their Widows and Children: Provided always, the clear Yearly Value of the said Real Estate doth not at any Time exceed the Sum of Three Thousand Pounds Sterling, lawful Money of our Kingdom of Great Britain. And that our said Corporation of the Chamber of Commerce in the City of New York, in America, and their Successors for ever, by the same Name, shall and may have full Power and Authority to Give, Grant, Sell, Lease, Demise and Dispose of the same Real Estate and Hereditaments whatsoever, for Life or Lives, or Year, or for ever; and all Goods, Chattels, and personal Estates whatsoever, at their Will and Pleasure, according as they shall judge to be most beneficial and advantageous to the Good Ends and Purposes above-mentioned. And that it shall and may be Lawful for them and their Successors forever hereafter, to have a Common Seal, to serve for the Causes and Business of them and their Successors, and the Same Seal to Change, Alter, Break, and Make new from time to time at their Pleasure. And also that they and their Successors by the same Name, shall and may have full Power and Authority to Erect and Build out of their Common Funds or by any other Ways or Means, for the use of the said Corporation hereby Erected, any House, Houses, or other Buildings, as they shall think necessary and Convenient. And for the better carrying into Execution the Purposes aforesaid, our Royal Will and Pleasure is, and We do hereby Give and Grant to the Corporation of the Chamber of Commerce in the City of New York, in America, and their Successors for ever, that there shall be for ever hereafter belonging to the said Corporation, one President, One or more Vice President or Vice Presidents, One or more Treasurer or Treasurers, And One Secretary; And for the more immediate carrying into Execution our Royal Will and Pleasure herein. We do hereby Assign, Constitute, and Appoint the above named John Cruger, Esq., to be the present President; the above named Hugh Wallace to be the present Vice President; the above named Elias Desbrosses to be the present Treasurer, and the above named Anthony Van Dam to be the present Secretary of our said Corporation hereby Erected, who shall hold, possess, and enjoy their said respective Offices until the first Tuesday in May now next ensuing:—

And for the keeping up the Succession in the said Offices, Our Royal Will and Pleasure is, and we do hereby for us, our Heirs and Successors, establish, direct, and require, and give and Grant to the said Corporation of the Chamber of Commerce in the City of New York, in America, and their Successors for ever, that on the said first Tuesday in May now next ensuing, and Yearly, and every Year forever thereafter, on the first Tuesday in May in every Year, they and their Successors shall meet at some convenient place in our said City of New York, to be fixed and ascertained by some of the Bye-Laws or Regulations of our said Corporation, and there, by the Majority of such of them as shall so meet, shall by Ballot, or in such other manner and Form as shall be regulated by the Bye-Laws or Regulations of our said

Corporation, Elect or choose One President, One or more Vice President or Vice Presidents, One or more Treasurer or Treasurers, and One Secretary, to serve in the said Offices for the ensuing Year, who shall immediately enter upon their respective Offices, and hold, exercise, and enjoy the same respectively from the time of such Elections, for and during the Space of one Year, and until other fit Persons shall be Elected and chosen in their respective Places, according to the Laws and Regulations aforesaid. And in case any of the said Persons by these Presents Nominated and Appointed to the respective Offices aforesaid, or who shall hereafter be Elected and Chosen thereto respectively, shall die, or on any Account be removed from such Offices respectively before the time of their respective appointed Services shall be expired, or refuse or neglect to Act in and execute the Office for which he or they shall be so elected and chosen, or is or are herein nominated or appointed, that then, and in any and every such Case, it shall and may be Lawful for the Members of our said Body Corporate hereby erected, to meet at such Time and Times, and at such Place and Places within our said City of New York, and upon such Notices or Summons as shall for that Purpose be established and directed by the Bye-Laws or Regulations of our said Body Corporate, and there, by the Majority of such of them as shall so meet Elect and choose other or others to the said Offices respectively, in the Place of him or them so dying, removing, neglecting or refusing to Act in manner and Form, and after the same method to be observed in the Annual Elections of the like Officers respectively, by Virtue of these our Letters Patent, and the said Bye-Laws or Regulations of our said Corporation, Hereby giving and granting, that such Person or Persons as shall be so Elected and Chosen by the majority of such of the said Members as shall meet in manner aforesaid, shall have, hold, exercise and enjoy such the Office or Offices to which he or they shall be so Elected and Chosen, from the time of such Election until the first Tuesday in May then next ensuing, and until other or others be legally Chosen in his or their Place and Stead, as fully and amply to all Intents and Purposes whatsoever, as the Person or Persons in whose place he or they shall be chosen might or could have done by Virtue of these Presents. And our Will and Pleasure is, and We do hereby for us, our Heirs and Successors, ordain, direct and require, that every President, Vice President, Treasurer and Secretary to be Elected by Virtue of these Presents, shall, before they Act in their respective Offices, take an Oath or Affirmation to be to them administered by the President, or in his Absence by One of the Vice Presidents of the preceding year, (who are hereby Authorized to Administer the same,) for the faithful and due Execution of their Respective Offices during their Continuance in the same respectively. —

And We do further, for Us, our Heirs and Successors, Give and Grant to the Corporation of the Chamber of Commerce in the City of New York, in

America, and their Successors forever, that besides the Annual Meeting of our said Corporation herein before Directed and Appointed to be held on the first Tuesday in May in every Year, it shall and may be Lawful for them, their Heirs and Successors, forever hereafter, for promoting and carrying into Execution the laudable Intents and Designs aforesaid, and for the Transacting the Business and Concerns of our said Corporation, to meet together on the first Tuesday in every Month, for ever, at such Place or Places in our said City of New York as shall for that Purpose be established, fixed, ascertained and Appointed by the Bye-Laws and Regulations of our said Corporation:—

And that the Members of our said Corporation being so met, or so many of them in Number at the least as shall by the Bye-Laws or Ordinances of our said Corporation be for that Purpose from time to time established, directed, Ordained or Appointed, shall, together with the President, or any one of the Vice Presidents of our said Corporation for the Time being, be a legal Meeting of our said Corporation; and they, or the Major part of them so met, shall have Power and Authority to adjourn from Day to Day, or for any other Time, as the business of our said Corporation may require, and to do, Execute, and perform all and every Act and Acts, Thing and Things whatsoever which the said Corporation of the Chamber of Commerce in the City of New York, in America, are or shall by these our Letters Patent be Authorized to do, Act or Transact, in as full and ample manner as if all and every of the Members of the said Corporation were present:—

And that at any such legal Meeting of the said Corporation, they shall and may in Writing, under the common Seal, make, frame, constitute, establish, and ordain from Time to Time, and at all Times hereafter, such Laws, Constitutions, Ordinances, Regulations, and Statutes, for the better Government of the Officers and Members of the said Corporation, for fixing and ascertaining the Places of Meeting of our said Corporation as aforesaid, and for regulating all other their Affairs and Business as they, or the Major Part of them so legally met, shall Judge best for the general Good of the said Corporation, and profitable for the more effectually promoting the beneficial Designs of their Institution; All which Laws, Constitutions, Regulations, Ordinances, and Statutes so to be made, framed, constituted, established, and Ordained as aforesaid. We Will, Command, and Ordain by these Presents for Us, our Heirs and Successors, to be from Time to Time and at all Times hereafter, kept, obeyed, and performed in all things as the same ought to be, on the Penalties and Amercements in the same to be imposed and limited, so as the same Laws, Constitutions, Regulations, and Statutes be reasonable in themselves, and not repugnant or contrary to the Laws and Statutes of that Part of our Kingdom of Great Britain called England, nor of our said Province of New York.—

And, for the keeping up and preserving for ever hereafter a Succession of Members for the said Corporation, our Will and Pleasure is, and We do hereby for us, our Heirs and Successors, Ordain, and Give and Grant to the said Corporation of the Chamber of Commerce in the City of New York, in America, and their Successors for ever, that at any of the Stated legal Meetings of the said Corporation, to be held on the first Tuesday in every Month for ever hereafter, but at no other Meeting of our said Corporation, it shall and may be Lawful for them and their Successors for ever, to Elect and choose in such manner and Form, and upon such Terms and Conditions, as shall be directed, ordained, and established for that Purpose by any of the said Bye-Laws, Statutes, Constitutions, or Ordinances of the said Corporation, such and so many Persons to be Members of the said Corporation as they shall think beneficial to the laudable Designs of the said Corporation; Which Persons, and every of them so from Time to Time Elected and Chosen, shall by Virtue of these Presents and of such Election, be Vested with all the Powers, Authorities, and Privileges which any Member of the said Corporation is hereby Invested with. And in case any other extraordinary Meeting or Meetings of the said Corporation shall at any Time or Times be judged necessary for the promoting the Interest and Business of the said Corporation, We do hereby for us, our Heirs and Successors, Will, Declare, and Ordain, that it shall and may be Lawful for our said Corporation to meet from Time to Time, at such Days and Times, and at such Places in our said City of New York, and upon such Notices or Summons as shall for that Purpose from Time to Time be Settled, Established, and Ordained by the Laws, Ordinances, or Statutes of the said Corporation; And that the Members of our said Corporation being so met, or so many of them in Number at the least as by the said Laws, Ordinances, and Statutes aforesaid shall from Time to Time be Established, Directed, Ordained, and Appointed for that Purpose, shall together with the President, or One of the Vice Presidents of the said Corporation for the Time being, be a legal Meeting of the said Corporation; And they, or the Major part of them so met, shall have full Power and Authority to Act, Transact, do, and Perform all and Singular whatsoever may be Transacted, done, and Performed at any the hereby Stated Meetings aforesaid of the said Corporation, saving and Except the Electing Members, Making laws, Ordinances and Statutes, and Disposing of the real Estate of the said Corporation.

And our Will and Pleasure is, that until the same shall be otherwise Regulated as aforesaid, that the Meetings of the said Corporation shall be held in the great Room of the Building commonly called the Exchange, situate at the lower End of the Street called Broad Street, in the said City of New York: and that until the same shall be also otherwise regulated as aforesaid, that no Act done in any Meeting of the said Corporation shall be Legal,

Good, or Valid, unless the President, or one of the Vice Presidents, and Twenty others of the Members of the said Corporation at the least, be Present, and the Major Part of them consenting thereto. And We do further Give and Grant to the said Corporation of the Chamber of Commerce in the City of New York, in America, that it shall and may be lawful for the President of the said Corporation, at all times hereafter for ever, to Appoint a Door-Keeper, One or more Messenger or Messengers, And all such other Inferior Officers as shall by him be thought necessary for the said Corporation, and to displace them and any or every of them at his Will and Pleasure. Provided nevertheless That no such Door-Keeper, Messenger, or other Officer shall hold his or their Office or Offices by Virtue of any such appointment, longer than until the then next lawful Meeting of our said Corporation, unless such Person or Persons so appointed shall be then approved of by the Majority of such of the Members of the said Corporation as shall then be met.—

And We do further, of our especial Grace, certain Knowledge, and mere Motion, for us, our Heirs and Successors, Grant and Ordain, that when and as often as the President, or any Vice President, Treasurer or Secretary of the said Corporation, shall misdemean himself in his or their said Offices respectively, and thereupon a Complaint or Charge in Writing shall be exhibited against him or them, by any Member of the said Corporation, at any legal Meeting or Meetings of the said Corporation, that it shall and may be lawful for the Members of the said Corporation then Met, or the Major Part of them, from Time to Time, upon Examination and due Proof, to suspend or discharge such President, Vice President, Treasurer or Secretary, from their Offices respectively, although the Yearly or other Time for their respective Services shall not be expired, anything before in these Presents contained to the Contrary thereof in any wise notwithstanding.—

And further, We do by these Presents, for us, our Heirs and Successors, Give and Grant unto the said Corporation of the Chamber of Commerce in the City of New York, in America, and their Successors forever, that this our present Charter shall be deemed, adjudged, and construed in all Cases most favourably, and for the best benefit and advantage of our said Corporation, and for promoting the good Intentions and Designs herein before expressed, inducing us graciously to grant the same; And that this our present Grant, being entered on Record as herein after is expressed, or the Enrolment thereof, shall be for ever hereafter good and effectual in the Law, according to our true Intent and meaning hereinbefore declared, without any other License, Grant, or Confirmation from us, our Heirs and Successors, hereafter by the said Corporation to be had or obtained, notwithstanding the not reciting or misrecital, or not naming or misnaming of the aforesaid Offices, Franchises, Privileges, Immunities, or other the Premises, or any of them. And although no Writ of ad quo damnum or other Writs, Inquisitions, or

Precepts hath been upon this Occasion had, made, issued, or Prosecuted, Any Statute, Act, Ordinance, or Provision, or other Matter or thing to the contrary thereof in any wise notwithstanding. In testimony whereof We have caused these our Letters to be made Patent, And the Great Seal of our said Province to be hereunto Affixed, And the same to be Entered on Record in our Secretary's Office, for our said Province, in one of the Books of Patents there remaining.

Witness our trusty and well-beloved Cadwallader Colden, Esquire, our Lieutenant Governor and Commander-in-Chief of our said Province of New York, and the Territories depending thereon in America, by and with the Advice and Consent of our Council for our said Province, at Fort George, in our City of New York, this thirteenth Day of March, in the Year of our Lord One thousand seven hundred and Seventy, and of our Reign the Tenth.

2.2 Glasgow 1783

The Glasgow charter was the first to a chamber in the British Isles and aspects of it were used by several other chambers for their own rules. The process is discussed more fully in the Introduction, whilst John Seton's role as Glasgow's parliamentary agent in London is covered in Chapters 4 and 7; and some of his financial accounts are reproduced in Chapter 5. The rigidity of most charters is demonstrated by the Glasgow experience. By 1860 its first charter 'had been found not to be well adapted to the altered circumstances of the present period'.[2] It made successful applications for a new charter in 1860, granted 28 July 1860, and supplemental charters in 1907 and 1967. The requested changes had to pass through detailed assessment by civil service officers in the Privy Council offices, who in turn requested legal advice from the Attorney General's staff, and the Scottish Lord Advocate. Various queries were raised on each requested change and this could have led to difficulties that resulted in a necessity to rely on the old charter. In 1967 the civil servant commented that the request for free authority to make bye-laws 'would not be allowed in a modern case'.[3] Requests for change also brought potential for opposition from others. For example, in 1967 the Ayr chamber objected to any attempt to expand the membership of Glasgow chamber to cover West Scotland, and this led to a formal exchange of correspondence resulting in Glasgow having to withdraw its expansion of geographical coverage.[4] In fact one of the changes in the 1860 charter had already stated its aim that 'every

[2] TNA PC 15/120: 1860 charter, published text, 2.

[3] TNA PC 15/199: File memo.

[4] TNA PC 15/199: Letter from Forsyth Brash, Secretary of the Ayr chamber of commerce, 3 April 1967.

Banker, Merchant, trade, or Manufacturer in Glasgow, or the West of Scotland, shall be eligible as a member',[5] though the title of the chamber had not been changed, so that formally Glasgow's 1907 and 1967 supplemental charters still contained this aspiration.[6] The other major changes in Glasgow's 1860 charter were to increase its powers to dispose of property (where the original charter had bound it to a particular building), to introduce a distinction between Ordinary and Honorary members, and to change the entrance fee to five guineas and allow annual subscriptions to be modified as required. There was a continuing debate about the advantages and disadvantages of entrance fees within chambers, and their interaction with life subscriptions. Glasgow and Edinburgh were both particularly affected by the perverse dynamics that could be created.[7] Although Glasgow's bye-laws allowed modification of the level of entrance fee, which it did several times, its 1907 decision finally to remove the fee required a charter change.

Source
TNA PC/15/20

Glasgow charter 31 July 1783

TRANSLATION OF THE ROYAL CHARTER GRANTED TO THE Chamber of Commerce and Manufactures of Glasgow.

[Preamble] GEORGE, by the Grace of God, King of Great Britain, France, and Ireland, Defender of the Faith: To all good men to whom these our present letters may come, greeting. Whereas, Patrick Colquhoun, Esquire, Lord Provost of the City of Glasgow, [29 other names listed], all Members of the Society known by the name of "The Chamber of Commerce and Manufactures in the City of Glasgow" by their humble petition, have represented to us, that the City of Glasgow is a town of the greatest importance in Great Britain as regards Commerce and Manufactures; and that, in order to give stability and encouragement to the commerce and manufactures of the said city, and of the towns and villages in its vicinity, the petitioners had formed themselves into an association by the name of "The Chamber of Commerce and Manufactures in the City of Glasgow," and had collected, by voluntary subscription among themselves, a sum of money to be applied to the purposes above-mentioned, under certain laws and regulations; which Institution they verily believed would be of great benefit, not only to the

[5] TNA PC 15/120: 1860 charter, published text p. 4.
[6] The competition between chambers for territory became a sensitive issue in the twentieth century as the scope for new chambers became limited by existing bodies, with various conflicts and rules developed: see Bennett, *Local Business Voice* (2011) 692–5.
[7] Bennett, *Local Business Voice* (2011) 757–60.

individual Members of the said Society, but to the community at large: That the petitioners were advised, and firmly believed, that if they and their successors in the administration of the affairs of the said Society were invested with corporate privileges, the said Society would be rendered more extensive and useful to the community, and its funds would be managed more judiciously, and with greater security: And, therefore, the petitioners humbly prayed that we would be graciously pleased to grant them a Royal Charter, incorporating them and their successors in the administration of the affairs of the said Society into a body corporate and politic, by the name of "The Chamber of Commerce and Manufactures in the City of Glasgow," with perpetual succession, and with power to use a seal, to sue and to be sued, to purchase lands, to make bye-laws, and with other necessary and usual powers.

[Grant of Charter] We, according to the said petition, and being willing to grant to the said society all proper encouragement; therefore, we in furtherance of the said humble petition, and by virtue of our royal prerogative and special favour ... have granted that the above mentioned [names listed] and other such persons as shall be duly admitted Members, and shall contribute to the funds of the said Society, in manner after-mentioned, shall be one Corporation and body corporate and politic, and shall be called "The Chamber of Commerce and Manufactures in the City of Glasgow;" and that they, and their successors in all time coming, shall have perpetual succession, for the purposes of better and more efficiently administering, directing, ordaining, and constituting, in all matters and things relative to the said Society, and pertaining to its funds: And we, for the aforesaid purposes, do present [names listed] and other such persons as shall be duly admitted Members, and shall contribute to the funds of the said Society, into a Corporation, or body corporate and politic [names listed]; and that the said Corporation, by its said name and title, may and shall be empowered, and legally capable of purchasing, holding, and enjoying perpetually, a house or tenement, to be used by them as a place of holding meetings of the Directors and general meetings of the Members of the said Society, (as by this Charter is permitted) of lending money on heritable and personal security, of holding goods and chattels, and of receiving and holding donations and bequests for the foresaid purposes; and it shall also be lawful for the said Corporation, by the name and title aforesaid, to sue and be sued, to carry on suits, and to prosecute and defend in all courts and places, and before all constituted judges, and other tribunals, in all actions, suits, defenses, causes, matters, and claims whatever, and in such manner and form as any of our subjects, or any other body politic and corporate, may legally and competently do: And, also, that the said Corporation shall have a common seal for using in all manner of business and causes belonging to them and their successors; and that it shall be lawful to them and their successors to break, change, or renew the said seal from time to time, as to them, or a majority of them, shall seem proper; which seal shall remain in the possession of the President, Vice-President, or Secretary of the said Society, one of whom shall attend with the said seal at all meetings at which it shall be required:

And we, for ourselves, and our heirs and successors, direct, ordain, and appoint, that two general meetings of the said Corporation shall be held annually, on the first Tuesday of January, and on the first Tuesday of July; to which meetings the Secretary, to be elected in manner hereinafter-mentioned, shall cite each Member by a written notice, directed to his dwelling-house, at three days before the day on which such meeting respectively shall be held; and that the first general meeting of the said Society shall be held on the first Tuesday of July, in this present year 1783, betwixt the hours of eleven forenoon and one afternoon, in the hall or chamber of meeting provided in the buildings called the Tontine, in the said city of Glasgow, or in any other convenient place within the said city; in which building, so provided, all subsequent meetings of the said Corporation and its Directors shall be held; the records, books, and documents belonging to the said Corporation shall be preserved; and all business whatsoever relative to the same shall be transacted. Moreover, we grant and declare that the said Patrick Colquhoun shall be the first President, and James M'Grigor shall be the first Vice-President, and [all the other listed names], shall be the first Directors of the said Corporation, and that Gilbert Hamilton shall be the first Secretary; and that the persons above-named shall remain in their respective offices until the first Tuesday of January, in the year 1784; and that the Members of the said Corporation shall have full power and authority at the said general meeting, on the first Tuesday of January 1784, to elect, for the succeeding year, thirty of their Members to be Directors (of whom twelve shall constitute a quorum) for transacting business, and administering the funds of the said Corporation in all respects, except those hereinafter excepted, and with power of adjourning as to them shall seem proper: Declaring always, as it is by these presents expressly provided and declared, that six of the said Directors shall be annually disqualified by Ballot for the first four years following the said first Tuesday of January 1784; after which period the six senior Directors shall go out each year in rotation. And at the annual meeting of the said Corporation, on the first Tuesday of January, in each year, six new Directors shall be elected, by the voices of the major number of the Members then present, in the room and place of the six Directors disqualified or retiring in manner above-mentioned; and each Director shall accept his appointment, within three days after his election, by subscribing his name in a book, to be kept for that purpose, otherwise his election shall be void; and in case of such voidance, or of the death of any Director or Directors for the time being, it may, and shall be lawful for the survivors, or the majority of those remaining in the

Direction, specially to convene the Members of the said Corporation, in order that they may elect another Director, or other Directors, in the room of the Director or Directors then dead, or demitting, notice in writing of such meeting being always given by the Secretary to each Member of the said Corporation, directed to him at his dwelling-house, at least three days before the day on which the said meeting is to be held.

And we direct and ordain, that the said Directors shall meet within eight days, or earlier, after the annual general meeting on the first Tuesday of January, for the purpose of electing, by the votes of the majority of the Directors then present, from their own number, a President and Vice-President, and also a Secretary, from the Members of the Corporation: Providing always, and declaring, as it is by these presents provided and declared, that no person shall be continued in either of the offices of President or Vice-President for a longer period than two years at one and the same time; and that the President, when elected, or, in his absence, the Vice-President, shall have the right of presiding at all Meetings of the Corporation, and of the Directors, and of having therein a deliberative as well as a casting vote in every question where the votes of the Members then present shall be equal; and, further, of convoking all extraordinary Meetings, of preparing all business for discussion, of conducting the correspondence of the Corporation and Directors, and, generally, of transacting and managing all business and affairs which are usually transacted and managed by the President, or, in his absence, by the Vice-President, of other Corporations.

And it is by these presents declared, that at each of the said two general Meetings, to be held on the days above-mentioned, the transactions and minutes of the Directors for the preceding six months shall be laid before the Meeting; and the President, or, in his absence, the Vice-President, shall submit to the Meeting all matters under the consideration of the Directors for the time being, together with full information touching matters to be discussed during the six months following; and at these Meetings, also, a statement of the funds shall be presented by the Secretary, to which statement it shall be competent to any Member to object. And we ordain and appoint, that, at the first Meeting of Directors held after their election, they shall elect fit persons to be Clerks and other officers; and that it shall be lawful for the Directors, at their Meetings, to deliberate upon and suggest any useful improvement in those branches of commerce and manufactures with which they are conversant, and which they shall judge to be useful to the community, by premiums or otherwise, to afford every kind of encouragement thereto, and to prosecute such counsels and plans for promoting the commerce and manufactures of the city of Glasgow, and the places in its vicinity, as may accord with the nature and intention of this Institution.

And we direct and appoint that there shall be four general Meetings of the said Directors annually, that is, one every three months, on the second Tuesdays of January, of April, of July, and of October, to which Meetings respectively the Secretary shall cite each of the Directors, by a written notice, directed to his dwelling-house, at least three days preceding that in which such Meetings respectively may be held, at which Meetings all the transactions of the Directors during the preceding three months shall be laid before the Meeting, and the said Meetings shall have the power of adjourning from time to time, in order that they may be able, more efficiently, to prosecute the business of the Corporation. And it is by these presents declared, that twelve Directors shall constitute a Quorum for transacting ordinary business; but that no money shall be voted unless twenty Directors be present. And we empower and authorise the President, or, in his absence, the Vice-President, in cases of urgent necessity, to call Meetings of the Directors, even upon the shortest notice, for the discussion or any particular business which cannot lie over, provided that no money be voted at such Meeting.

And we direct and ordain that the Secretary, to be elected as above-mentioned, shall keep the records of the Corporation; that he shall act as Treasurer of its funds, keep the accounts, receive all memorials, letters, and applications, arrange them for the consideration of the Directors, insert the resolutions and minutes of all the Meetings in a book to be kept for that purpose, transact and perform all business in conformity to the lawful orders which he may, from time to time, receive from the Directors of the Corporation, for which services an annual salary shall be paid to him, and (if required) he shall give security for the faithful performance of his duty; Provided always, as it is by these presents expressly provided, that the Secretary shall deposit the money belonging to the said Corporation in one of the Glasgow banks, at the highest interest which can be obtained for it; and that he shall never keep in his hands at any one time a sum exceeding fifty pounds sterling. And we direct and appoint that the funds of the said Corporation shall be under the sole administration and inspection of the Directors, with power to them, at any of their Meetings which twenty Directors shall be present, to disburse and apply any sums of money which may be necessary for discharging expense, incurred, or to be incurred, in conducting the affairs of the Society.

And we will and declare, that no person shall be admitted a Member of the said Corporation until he shall have paid to the Secretary, for the use of the said Corporation, five pounds five shillings, as the fees of his admission; and that, when any Member shall be admitted into the said Corporation, his name shall be inserted by the Secretary in a book to be kept for that purpose; and he shall remain and continue a Member so long as he shall continue to pay the sum of one pound one shilling, on the first Tuesday of January yearly;

or such other annual sum as hereafter may be fixed and ordered to be received from each Member of the said Corporation, by a regulation or bye-law made for that purpose, the said regulation or bye-law not being valid without the consent of two-thirds of the Members of the Society; and any Member in arrear of the said annual payment shall be expelled from, and shall lose his place in, the Corporation, until he shall have paid his arrears, and been re-elected by a majority of the Members assembled at one of their general Meetings: Provided always, that any Member who shall pay twenty-one pounds as the fees of his admission shall be freed and relieved from making any annual payment whatever, and shall have right during his life to all the privileges of the Society.

And we, for ourselves, our heirs and successors, give and grant to the Members of the said Corporation and their successors, full power and authority, in general meetings from time to time convened, to appoint, ordain, and make such and many bye-laws, constitutions, rules, and ordinances, as to them, or a majority of their number, then and there present, shall appear proper and necessary for the government and direction of the said Corporation, and to alter and abrogate the said bye-laws, constitutions, rules and ordinances, or any of them, as to the said Corporation so convened, or a majority of them present, may appear necessary. And we will that all such bye-laws, constitutions, rules, and ordinances, as are made as aforesaid, shall be rightly observed and kept: Provided that, the same shall not be in any wise contrary or repugnant to the laws of this kingdom, or the tenor of this Charter; and provided that the said bye-laws, constitutions, rules, and ordinances, from time to time so enacted, and every abrogation or alteration of them, or of any of them, be, in like manner, agreed on, established, and confirmed by the next general meeting of the said Corporation, held after the enactment thereof. And we, for ourselves, our heirs and successors, declare that these our letters patent shall be valid and effectual in law to all intents and purposes, according to their true meaning and intent; and that they shall be received, interpreted, and construed in the sense most favourable and beneficial for the said Corporation, wrong reading, defect, uncertainty, or imperfection in these our letters patent notwithstanding. And we, for ourselves, our heirs and successors, covenant, grant, and agree, that we, and our heirs and successors, from time to time, and at all times, will give and grant to the humble request and petition of the said Corporation or body politic, and to their successors, all such further and other privileges, authorities, things, and matters, for rendering this our grant, according to its true intent and signification, more efficacious, as we or they may lawfully grant, and which may be reasonably proposed or devised by the advisers of the said Corporation or body politic for the time being, and which may be approved by our Advocate or Solicitor-General in Scotland, or the Advocate or Solicitor-General of our heirs and successors, on our part or on theirs. In testimony whereof, we have ordered that our seal, appointed by the Treaty of Union to be kept and used in Scotland, in place of the great seal thereof, be appended to these presents. Given at our Court of St. James's, in the ninth day of the month of June, in the year of our Lord 1783, and in the 23d year of our reign.

Indorsed by the sign-manual of our Sovereign Lord the King.

Written to the seal, and registered the 31st of July, 1783.

(Signed) ALEX. WATSON, Depute.

(Signed) JOHN WAITCHOPE, Depute.

Sealed at Edinburgh, the 31st day of July, 1783.

2.3 Edinburgh 1786

The original request for a charter was initiated by David Steuart on 15 February 1786 shortly after the chamber was established in late 1785.[8] A minute from Glasgow chamber (reproduced below) sent to the Lord Advocate objected to use of the founding title of Edinburgh's chamber as the 'General Chamber of Commerce and Manufactures for Scotland' as originally proposed.[9] Under advice from their solicitor-agent, Edinburgh modified the title to 'The Chamber of Commerce and Manufactures in the City of Edinburgh' and advanced £200 to their agent to carry forward the proposal, which was granted 10 July. However, its rules (or bye-laws: see Chapter 1) still contained 'Scotland' as its constituency; indeed Glasgow also referred to covering 'this country' many times in its documents (see Chapter 1). The Edinburgh Charter allowed Bye-Laws, which were printed in each Annual Report of the Chamber, and were used among other things to modify subscription levels. The charter closely resembles Glasgow's, and like that it embedded the principle of entrance fees and life subscriptions. Like Glasgow this caused considerable problems when the two rates were modified. For discussion of the development of entrance fees and life subscriptions see above section 2.2.[10]

Source

[a] Glasgow Chamber of Commerce minutes; Glasgow Mitchell Library TD 76/1

[b] Printed charter; translation contained in *Edinburgh Chamber of Commerce and Manufacturers 160th Anniversary 1785–1945* (1945), Chamber of Commerce, Edinburgh; BL 8231.f.88. The original charter was in Latin.

[8] Edinburgh Archives: Edinburgh chamber minutes 15 February 1786

[9] Edinburgh minutes 8 May 1786

[10] An evaluation of these subscription structures is given in Bennett, *Local Business Voice* (2011) 757–60.

Minutes Glasgow, 7 June 1786[a]

The Chamber of Commerce at Edinburgh had applied for incorporation under the name of General Chamber of Commerce and Manufacturers of Scotland. … Objected to and would support the title Chamber of Commerce and Manufacturers of Edinburgh as not conveying the appearance of assuming upon the antecedent rights of others.

Edinburgh Charter 10 July 1786[b]

George, by the grace of God, of Great Britain, France, and Ireland King, Defender of the Faith; to all true men to whom these present letters shall come, greeting.

WHEREAS [32 names listed] All members of a Society known at present by the name of the General Chamber of Commerce and Manufactures for Scotland, by their humble petition have represented to us that the petitioners, to promote the interests of trade and manufactures in that part of the United Kingdom in which they reside, have formed themselves into a Society, and have collected a sum of money by a voluntary subscription among themselves, to be applied to the purposes set forth above, under definite laws and regulations; which institution, they truly believe, will be of great profit not only to the individual members of the same Society but to the whole State: that the petitioners have been advised and firmly believe that if they and their successors in the administration of the affairs of the said Society should have been invested with corporate powers, the same Society would be rendered more extensive and useful to the State, and the funds of the same would be spent more suitably and with greater security: the petitioners therefore have most humbly prayed that we should be graciously pleased to grant them our royal charter incorporating the petitioners and their successors in office in the administration of the affairs of the said Society, with such other persons as shall have been elected members of the same into a body corporate and politic by the name to be set forth hereafter, with perpetual succession, and with the power of using a seal, of suing and being sued, of buying land, of passing private laws, and with all other necessary and usual powers.

We granting the said petition and wishing to give all proper encouragement to the said Society, therefore in accordance with the said humble petition and by virtue of our royal prerogative and of our special grace, with definite knowledge and mere motion, have granted, determined, declared and ordained, as by the tenor of these presents we grant, determine, declare and ordain, that the aforesaid [names repeated], and such other persons as shall duly be admitted as members and shall contribute to the funds of the said Society in the fashion to be set forth hereafter, shall be and shall be called one corporation and a body corporate and politic by the name and style of The

Chamber of Commerce and Manufactures in the City of Edinburgh, which name of the said Society shall be in future in the place of the name which they now use; and that they and their successors for ever in the future shall have a perpetual succession for the purposes of better and more efficiently administering, directing, ordering and determining all the business and affairs concerning the said Society and the funds of the same.

And *We* for the purposes aforesaid by these presents make, create, determine and establish the said [names repeated], and such other persons as at first shall duly have been admitted as members and shall have contributed to the funds of the Society in the manner to be set forth hereafter, into a corporation or a body politic and corporate for ever by the name and title of **The Chamber of Commerce and Manufactures in the City of Edinburgh**, and that the said Corporation by the name and title aforesaid may be able and capable in law to buy, hold and enjoy for ever a house or tenement to be used by it as a place for holding the meetings of the Directors or the general meetings of the members of the said Society (as is permitted by this charter), to lend money upon heritable or personal securities, to hold goods and chattels, to receive and hold gifts and legacies for the purposes aforesaid. Also in the name and title aforesaid it shall be right for the said Corporation to sue and be sued, plead and be impleaded, defend and be defended in whatsoever courts and places, and before whatsoever judges, justices and other officers in all actions, lawsuits, accusations, accounts, matters and demands whatsoever, and in such manner and form as may be right and lawful for any of our subjects able and capable in law or any other politic and corporate body.[11] And also that the said Corporation shall have a common seal for the carrying on of every kind of business and causes of them and their successors; and that it may be and shall be lawful for them and their successors to break, change or make anew the said seal from time to time as shall seem good to them or to the majority; which seal shall be in the possession of the President, Vice-President, or Secretary of the said Society, one of whom shall be present with the said seal at all meetings if there shall be need.

And *We* for ourselves and our heirs and successors direct, ordain and determine that any merchant, manufacturer or trader residing in Scotland can be co-opted as a member of the said Chamber if he has paid into the hands of the Treasurer for the time being the sum of two pounds and two shillings sterling at the time of admission and in addition a sum of one pound and one shilling of the said money yearly on the first Monday of January of every year as long as he wishes to remain a member; and any person who pays to the Chamber a sum of ten pounds and ten shillings sterling shall be deemed a member of the same throughout his life, being not subject to any further

[11] Translation corrects original Latin grammar.

payment; that it shall be lawful for any member to vacate his place at his wish after making intimation to the Secretary; and any member who fails to pay his annual subscription either before or on the feast of the Purification of the Blessed Virgin shall *ipso facto* be deemed to have withdrawn and shall thereafter be entitled to none of the benefits of the institution: And it shall not be lawful for any practitioner in law, even though doing business as a merchant or a manufacturer, to be a member of the said Chamber: That the business of the Chamber be administered by a President, two Vice-Presidents and thirty Directors; the President or one of the Vice-Presidents and twelve Directors being a sufficient number, in the common tongue 'a quorum'.

Further *We* grant and declare that those who now act as President, Vice-President and Directors and other officers of the said Society shall continue and have power of administering in the said offices up to the Monday immediately preceding the first meeting of the Convention of the Royal Burghs in Scotland in this present year 1786, when a general meeting of the members of the said Chamber shall be held at Edinburgh for the purpose of electing a President, two Vice-Presidents, thirty Directors and other necessary officers for the following year: that thereafter the six senior Directors shall leave office annually, and other six be elected in their place: also the President and the two Vice-Presidents shall leave office alternately, one of them every year; the vacancies should be filled from the members in general and seniority should be fixed at the first election: that a Secretary shall be appointed who ought to be a member of the Chamber and who shall keep the books and papers of the said Chamber, shall write the minutes, and carry on the correspondence: that the said Society shall have a Treasurer who ought also to be a member of the said Chamber, who shall keep account of all sums of money received or spent by the Chamber, and shall pay all money which he shall receive from time to time into the Royal Bank of Scotland, or to such bank or banker as the members from time to time shall direct whenever the same amounts to fifty pounds: that five members not of the number of the Directors shall be named to audit the Treasurer's accounts, three being 'a quorum' in the common tongue: that after this year has passed a general meeting of the members shall be held yearly at Edinburgh on the Monday preceding the Convention of the Royal Burghs for the purpose of electing a President or Vice-President as a vacancy may occur, six Directors in place of those leaving office, five Auditors of the Accounts, a Secretary and a Treasurer, which last two officers are to be filled annually and a member who holds the same may be continued or removed as shall seem suitable to the members: that all elections are to be made by ballot: and another general meeting shall be held on the third Wednesday of January every year for the special purpose of reading the minutes of the Chamber and of giving such other general directions as shall seem good to the meeting or the majority: that it shall be lawful for any fifteen members not of the number of the Directors to call a general meeting, previous intimation being given by a notice in the Edinburgh press ten days beforehand: that every order for money must be signed by the President or a Vice-President and three Directors in the presence of those who are called 'a quorum' in the common tongue, and the same is to be noted by the Secretary: that each member shall have access to inspect the minutes after making application to the Secretary on Wednesday of each week between the hours of noon and three in the afternoon, but at no other time except by the instruction of three Directors: that all questions which are put before the Chamber shall be settled by a majority of votes, and if it happens that the number of votes is equal the President shall have a casting vote besides his own: that it shall in no wise be lawful for the Directors to borrow any money in the name of the Chamber on any pretext whatsoever; but it shall be lawful for them to pledge the funds of the Society for the purposes of its institution: that it shall be right for the President or Vice-President to call a meeting of Directors whensoever the same shall be judged necessary, all meetings to be held in Edinburgh in such a room or hall as the Directors shall determine: that an account book of the proceedings of the Directors shall be printed annually, and a copy of it shall be sent to each member. And *We* direct and ordain that it shall be lawful for the President, Vice-President and Directors at their meetings to discuss and suggest any useful improvements in those branches of trade and manufactures with which they have a connection or which they shall judge to be useful to the State; and by rewards or otherwise to give encouragement of that kind; and to pursue such plans and methods for promoting the trade and manufactures of the city of Edinburgh and its neighbourhood as shall agree with the nature and intention of the institution.

And *We* direct and determine that there shall be four general meetings of the said Directors in every three-monthly period yearly, on the second Tuesday of January, the second Tuesday of April, the second Tuesday of July, and the second Tuesday of October, to which respective meetings the Secretary shall summon each Director by a written notice addressed to him at his dwelling place at least three days preceding that on which such meetings respectively are to be held,[12] at which meetings the whole of the proceedings of the Directors during the previous three months shall be put before the meeting; and that at the same said meetings there shall be the power of adjourning from time to time so that they can more effectively pursue the business of the Corporation.

And *We* for ourselves, our heirs and successors give and grant to the members of the said Corporation and their successors full power and authority in general meetings called from time to time to determine, ordain, and

[12] Translation corrects original Latin grammar.

make such and so many private laws, constitutions, rules, and ordinances as shall seem suitable and necessary to them or a majority of them then present in the same place, for the better governing and direction of the said Corporation, and to alter and annul as shall seem necessary to the said Corporation or a majority of them then present the said private laws, constitutions, rules, and ordinances, or any of them; which private laws, constitutions, rules, and ordinances, to be made as is aforesaid, we wish all and several to be duly kept and fulfilled, provided that the same shall be in no way contrary or repugnant to the laws of this realm and the tenor of the said charter, and so long as the same private laws, constitutions, rules and ordinances, to be so imposed from time to time, and each annulment or alteration of the same or any of them, shall likewise be agreed, established and confirmed by a general meeting of the said Corporation to be next kept and held after the same have respectively been made. And *We* for ourselves, our heirs and successors declare that these our letters patent shall be in all things and by all things valid and effective in law according to the true intent and understanding of the same, and to be accepted, interpreted, and adjudged in the sense most favourable and advantageous for the greatest benefit of the said Corporation notwithstanding any misrecital, defect, uncertainty or imperfection in these our letters patent. And *We* for ourselves, our heirs and successors covenant, grant and agree with the said Corporation or body politic and their successors, that *We*, our heirs and successors from time to time and at all future times at the humble request and petition of the said Corporation or body politic and their successors, will give and grant to them all further and other privileges, authorities, things and matters to make more effective this our grant according to the true intention and understanding of the same, which *We* or they can rightly grant, and which shall be reasonably proposed or devised by the counsel learned in law of the said Corporation or body politic for the time being, and which shall be approved by the Lord Advocate and Solicitor General in Scotland of ourselves, and our heirs and successors on behalf of us or them. *In witness of which matter*, to the presents we have ordered to be affixed our seal by the treaty of the Union to be kept and used in Scotland instead of and in place of the Great Seal of the same. At our Court at St. James', on the fifth day of June in the year of our Lord 1786, and in the twenty-sixth year of our reign.

By the signature in the hand of our Sovereign Lord the King aforementioned.

Sealed at Edinburgh the tenth day of July, one thousand seven hundred and eighty six years,
JOHN WAUCHOPE,
Dept. Lord Seal.

Written to the Seal and registered the tenth day of July 1786.
ALEX. WATSON,
Dept.

2.4 Greenock 1813

Source
CHARTER with RELATIVE BYE-LAWS of The Chamber of Commerce and Manufactures of Greenock, Incorporated 6th November 1813, printed 1900, W. Hutchinson, Greenock: Watt Library, Greenock; BG1/3/1. R34593, 647.9625.

Greenock Charter 6 November 1813

WARRANT FOR CHARTER.
In the Name and on the behalf of His Majesty (Superscribed) George, P.R.,

Our Sovereign Lord, Considering that a Humble Petition has been presented by [13 names listed], Merchants, Shipowners, and Manufacturers in Greenock and vicinity, setting forth, That the establishment of Chambers of Commerce and Manufactures in the Commercial and Manufacturing Cities and Towns of Scotland will prove highly conducive to the prosperity of such Cities and Towns, and beneficial To the Commercial and Manufacturing interests of the country at large,—

That the Town of Greenock is the principal seaport in the West of Scotland, and it would tend much to the encouragement and promotion of the Trade and Manufactures already extensively Established and carried on there, and in the vicinity of that Town, If the petitioners were incorporated as a Chamber of Commerce with the powers and privileges usually conferred on such bodies; and therefore humbly praying that His Majesty would be graciously pleased to grant them a Royal Charter for incorporating them, and such persons as might thereafter be duly admitted Member of the said Corporation, into one body corporate and politic, by the name, style, and title of the Chamber of Commerce and Manufactures of Greenock, with a perpetual succession and power to acquire and hold property heritable and moveable; to use a Common Seal; to sue and be sued; to make bye-laws, and with such other powers and privileges as are usually granted to other bodies corporate and politic of the like nature, in such manner and form as to His Majesty in his Royal wisdom should seem fit; and His Majesty being certified that the prayer of said Petition is just and reasonable Ordains a Charter to be made and passed under the Seal Appointed by the Treaty of Union, to be kept in Scotland in place of the Great Seal thereof, constituting, erecting and incorporating as His Majesty by His Royal prerogative and special favour for him and His Royal successors by these presents, constitutes, erects and incorporates the said [names repeated], and such persons as shall be duly admitted Members, shall contribute or shall have contributed to the Funds, and in other respects conform to the regulations of the said Corporation in manner after-mentioned, into an incorporation and body, corporate and politic, or legal incorporation by the name, style and title of 'The CHAMBER OF

COMMERCE AND MANUFACTURES OF GREENOCK'; and under this name and title to have perpetual Succession and Endurance, with power to the said Corporation of Acquiring, holding and enjoying, and also of disposing, alienating and selling all kinds of property, real and personal, heritable and moveable; and also power of suing, prosecuting and defending, and of being sued, prosecuted and defended in any of His Majesty's Courts of Justice, and before all and whatsoever His Majesty's Judges, Justices, and other Officers of the Law in such manner and form as any of His Majesty's Subjects, or any other body, Politic and Corporate, may or can sue and be sued.

With Power also to the said Corporation to have and use a Common Seal which May be changed or renewed from time to time as the said Corporation or a majority thereof assembled at any General Meeting shall deem expedient, and His Majesty directs and appoints that the first meeting of the said Corporation shall be holden on the first Wednesday in the month of January, Eighteen hundred and fourteen, between the hours of Eleven before and One afternoon, in a place to be provided therefor, and that there shall thereafter be holden in the same place Two General Half Yearly Meetings of the said Corporation, viz. upon the first Wednesday of July and upon the first Wednesday of January in each year, with power of adjournment, as they shall see cause, to which meetings the Secretary of the Corporation shall summon every Member by notice in writing, directed to him at his dwelling place at least three days previous to the day on which such meetings are respectively to be holden, at which two General Meetings the records and a state of the transactions of the Corporation and also the accounts of the Secretary or Treasurer for the preceding six months shall be exhibited, and any question arising at such meetings shall be decided by a majority of the voices of the members present, and His Majesty hereby directs and appoints that the management of the funds, the acquisition and disposal of property, and the ordinary concerns of the said Corporation shall be committed solely so twelve Directors to be called the Chamber of Directors, five of whom shall constitute a quorum, capable of acting in all the ordinary matters of the Corporation, but no money belonging to the Corporation shall be paid or disbursed, or ordered to be paid or disbursed, by any number less than seven Directors, and the said Directors shall have power to consider of, and suggest such plans and systems as may contribute to the protection and improvement of those branches of Commerce and Manufactures with which they may be connected, or which they may think conducive to the interests of the Country, and by premiums or otherwise to give such encouragement to and follow out such plans and measures for promoting the Commerce and Manufactures of the Town of Greenock and its neighbourhood as may be consistent with the nature and design of the Institution.

And His Majesty further directs and appoints that [names repeated] shall be the first Directors, and John Dunlop aforesaid first Secretary, and they continue in office from and after the said first meeting of the Corporation till the meeting to be holden upon the first Wednesday of January, Eighteen hundred and fifteen, at which last mentioned meeting three of the Members of the said Chamber of Directors shall be disqualified by Ballot and three new Directors shall be elected in their place by a majority of the voices of the whole of the Members of the Corporation present at such meeting, and so on in like manner; three from among the eldest Directors shall at the General Meetings to be holden in January, Eighteen hundred and sixteen, and January, Eighteen hundred and seventeen, be disqualified by Ballot and three new Directors be chosen at each of said meetings, and thereafter and in all future years the three senior Members of the Chamber of Directors shall go out annually at the General Meeting on the first Wednesday in January, and three new Directors be elected in their stead by a majority of the Members present, the former or ex-Directors being again eligible after they shall have been respectively a year out of office:

And His Majesty further directs and appoints that the said Chamber of Directors at their first meeting each year after the General Meeting in January (such meeting of Directors to be appointed and holden at such time as shall be fixed by the Regulations and Bye-Laws which the Corporation are hereinafter empowered to make) shall out of their own number choose a Chairman who shall do and perform all the matters and things which the Corporation may, by the Charters to follow hereupon, or by the Bye-laws hereby after authorised to be made, direct to be done, or which to the Office of Chairman or Preses [presiding officer] of such Corporate bodies is known to belong, and who shall, in cases of necessity have the power of summoning General Meetings of the Corporation; and at any meeting of the Corporation or Chamber of Directors, voting upon any question, the Chairman, Deputy-Chairman, or other Preses of the meeting shall have an original vote or deliberative vote, and in case of equality of voices at such meetings, the Chairman, Deputy-Chairman or Preses shall have moreover and besides his deliberative vote, a casting vote; and in any suit or action to be raised or pursued or to be defended on the part of the Corporation; the same shall be so raised or pursued or defended in name of the Chairman alone or Deputy-Chairman, for and in behalf of himself and the said Corporation, and the investiture of any property, heritable or moveable, had or acquired or to be had and acquired by the Corporation may be taken in the name of the Directors for the time; and any Deeds or Writings for the conveying and disposing of the property, heritable or moveable, of the Corporation, or otherwise with regard to the transactions thereof, may run and be granted in name of the Directors for the time alone; And the said Chamber of Directors is hereby also appointed to choose a Deputy-Chairman, who, in absence of the Chairman, shall have full power to act in all respects in the same manner as the Chairman might have acted if present; and the Chamber of Directors shall also at such meeting appoint a Secretary, to whom the care of the records of the Corporation and other duties to be prescribed in the Bye-laws shall be committed, and who shall act also as Treasurer to the Corporation, and shall, if required, give security for his faithful management; and the Records, Books, Vouchers and Papers of the Corporation shall remain and be deposited in a Room, apartment or house to be provided or appointed for their meetings by the Corporation, which Chairman and Deputy-Chairman shall remain in their respective offices for two years only at a time:

And His Majesty further directs and appoints that the said Corporation shall, by a majority of voices of the members present at any General Meeting, periodical or extraordinary, have the power of making and establishing bye-laws, constitutions, ordinances and regulations for the conduct of the said Corporation in the transaction and management of all the affairs; for the election and admission of Members, and fixing as to the fees of admission and annual subscriptions, or composition therefor to be paid by them, and the penalties and forfeitures of privileges in case of not regular payment of annual subscriptions, for fixing as to the Meetings ordinary or extraordinary of the Directors, the time and place of Meeting, mode of convention, and generally all matters in any manner of way connected therewith, ascertaining the mode of the acceptance of the office of Directors when elected, and declension thereof; for supplying vacancies in the direction, in cases of non-acceptance, or death, or otherways; for the determination and regulation of the whole business and duties of the Directors, and of their Chairman, Deputy-Chairman, Secretary, and other Officers that may be appointed, and the responsibility of any of them, and generally for the regulation and conducting of the affairs of the said Corporation, as fully, freely, and effectually as the Members of any other like Corporation may, or can do, or as is not inconsistent with the laws and practice of that part of the United Kingdom called Scotland: Provided always that no bye-law which fixes, alters, or affects the fees of entrance or annual contribution to be paid by the Members shall be binding, or of force, unless it shall be agreed to by two-thirds of the Members present at any General Meeting; and that the Corporation shall also have power by a majority of the voices of the Members present, as aforesaid, to repeal, alter, or add to their bye-laws and rules; such repeal, alterations, or additions being proposed at a Meeting held at least thirty lawful days previous to the Meeting at which they are to be so made and enacted, repealed and altered; and We do farther will and command that this our Charter do pass the Seal appointed by the Treaty of Union, to be kept and used in Scotland, in place of the Great Seal thereof without passing any other Seal or Register. For the doing whereof this shall be as well to the Directors of our Chancery for writing the same, as to the Keeper of the said Seal for causing it to be appended thereto a sufficient warrant. Given at His Majesty's Court, at Carlton House, the sixth day of November, 1813, in the fifty-fourth year of His Majesty's reign.

By the command of His Royal Highness the Prince Regent, in the name and on behalf of His Majesty,
(Signed) SIDMOUTH.

2.5 Limerick 1815

Source
Limerick Chamber of Commerce, Minute Book 1: Limerick Archives P1/1.

Minute: Copy of the Charter 2 June 1815

[Preamble omitted] [9 names listed], and all such other persons as shall be duly admitted members and shall contribute of shall have contributed to the funds, and in other respects conform to the regulations of the said corporation, in manner herein after mentioned; into one body politic, and corporate, or legal incorporation by the name stile and title of 'The Chamber of Commerce of Limerick', and under this name and title to have perpetual succession, and endurance, with power to the said corporation, or acquiring, holding, and enjoying real estate, to the value of one thousand pounds per annum, but not more, and also of alienating, disposing and selling All kinds of the same, and of acquiring, holding, and enjoying, all kinds of personal estate, and also power of suing, prosecuting, and defending, and of being sued, prosecuted and defended, in any of the courts of justice and before all and whatsoever judges, justices, and other officers of the law, in such manner and forms as any of our subjects, or any other body politic and corporate, may or can sue and be sued, with power also to the said corporation, to have and use a common seal, which may be changed and renewed, from time to time, as the said corporation, or a majority of them assembled as a general meeting, shall deem expedient; and our further will and pleasure is, and we do hereby declare and grant, that the first meeting of the said corporation, shall be holden within one month after the date of this charter, between the hours of eleven before noon, and two after noon, in a place provided therefore, and that there shall thereafter be holden, one general yearly meeting of the said corporation, viz., upon the first Monday after the twenty ninth day of September in each year, with power of adjournment as they shall see cause, to which meeting the secretary of the corporation shall summon every member, by notice in writing directed to him at his dwelling place, at least three days previous to the day on which such meeting shall be holden, at which general meeting the records and state of transactions of the corporation, and also the accounts of the secretary or treasurer, for the preceding twelve months shall be exhibited, and examined, and any question arising at such meeting, shall be decided by a majority of the voices of the members present.

And our further will and pleasure is, and we do hereby declare and grant, that the management of the finds, the acquisition and disposal of property, and the ordinary concerns of the said corporation, shall be committed to nine directors to be called the chamber directors, five of whom shall constitute a quorum, capable of acting in all affairs of the corporation; and the said directors shall have power to consider of and suggest, such plans and systems, as may contribute to the protection and improvement of those branches of commerce with which they may be connected or which they may think conducive to the interest of the country and by premiums or otherwise to give such encouragement to, an follow up such plans and measures, for promoting the commerce of the City of Limerick, and its neighbourhood, as may be consistent with the nature and design of the institution.

And our further will and pleasure is and we do hereby declare and grant, that [names repeated]; shall be the first directors, and John Carroll first secretary, and that they shall continue in office from and after the said first meeting of the Corporation, till the meeting to be holden upon the first Monday after the twenty ninth day of September one thousand eight hundred and fifteen; at which last mentioned meeting, and at any future annual meeting, a new chamber of Directors shall be elected by ballot, in which there shall be at least three members who had not served the preceding year.

And our further will and pleasure is, and we do hereby declare and grant, that the said chamber of directors at their first meeting in each year, after their general meeting on the Monday after the twenty ninth day of September, (such meeting of directors to be appointed and holden at such time as shall be fixed by the regulations and bye laws, which the corporation are herein after empowered to make) shall out of their own number choose a president, or Chairman who shall do and perform all the matters and things, which the corporation may by this charter, or the bye laws hereby after authorized to be made, direct to be done; or which to the office of president or chairman of such corporate bodies is known to belong; and who shall in case of necessity, have the power of summoning general meetings of the corporation, and at any meeting of the corporation, or chamber of directors, voting upon any question; and that the president or chairman, the vice president or deputy chairman, or other president of the meeting, shall at such meeting, and upon every question there arising, have an original or deliberate vote, and in case of equality of votes at such meeting, the president, vice president; or chairman, shall have moreover and besides the deliberate vote, a casting vote; and in any suit or action to be raised or pursued, or to be defended on the part of the corporation; the same shall be so raised or pursued, or defended, in their said corporate name of 'The Chamber of Commerce of Limerick'; and the investure of any property real or personal, had or acquired, or to be had or acquired, by the Corporation, be taken in their said Corporate name of 'The Chamber of Commerce of Limerick'; and any deeds or writings, for the conveying or disposing of the property, real or personal, of the corporation, or otherwise with regard to the transactions thereof may run, and be granted, in the name of 'The Chamber of Commerce of Limerick'; and the said chamber of directors, is hereby appointed to choose a deputy chairman, who shall have full power in the absence of the president or chairman, to act in all respects as the president or chairman might have acted if present; and the Chamber of directors shall also at such meeting, choose a Secretary, to whom the case of the records of the corporation and other duties to be prescribed, in the bye laws, shall be committed; and who shall, if required give, Security for his faithful Management, and the record books, vouchers, and papers of the corporation shall remain and be deposited in the room, apartment, or house, to be provided or appointed for their meetings, by the corporation; which president or chairman, and the vice president or deputy chairman, shall remain in their respective offices for one year only at a time.

And our further will and pleasure is, and we do hereby declare and grant, that the said corporation shall by a majority of voices of the members present at any general meeting, periodical, or extraordinary; have the power of making or establishing bye laws, constitutions, ordinances, and regulations, for the conduct of the said corporation, in the transactions and management of all its affairs, and the repealing or altering the same; for the election, admission, or removal of members, and fixing as to the rates of contribution to be paid by them, and the penalties and forfeitures of the privileges, in case of not regular payment of such contribution; for fixing also the meetings ordinary or extraordinary of the directors, the time and place of meeting, made of convention, and generally all matters in any manner or way connected therewith; ascertaining the made of acceptance of the office of directors when elected and declining thereof; for supplying vacancies by death or other ways, for the determination and regulation of the whole business and duties of the directors, and of their chairman, deputy chairman, secretary, and other officers; that may be appointed, and the responsibility of any of them, and generally for the regulation and conducting of the affairs of the corporation, as fully, freely, and effectually, as the members of any other like corporation may or can do; or as shall not be inconsistent with the laws and practices of that part of our united kingdom called Ireland;

Provided always, that no bye laws, which fixes alters, or affects, the rates of contribution to be paid by the members, shall be binding or of force, unless it shall be agreed to by two thirds of the members of the corporation present at any general meeting; and that the said corporation shall also have power, by a majority of the voices of the members present, as aforesaid, to repeal, alter, or add, to the bye laws and rules, such repeal, alterations or additions being proposed at a meeting, held at least eight lawful days previous to the meeting, at which they are to be so made and enacted, repealed and altered.

And our further will and pleasure is, and we do hereby strictly change, and command, all justices, mayors, aldermen, sheriffs, bailiffs, constables, and all officers, ministers, and subjects, whatsoever of us, our heirs, and successors, to be from time to time, aiding and assisting, unto the said corporation, in and about all things, according to the true intent and meaning of these our letters patent.

And our further will and pleasure is, and we do hereby grant to the said corporation, and their successors that these our letters patent, or the enrolment or exemplification thereof, and all and singular, matters and things, in the same contained, shall and may be good, valid, sufficient, and effectual, in the law; according to the true intent and meaning of the same, and shall be taken, construed, and adjudged, in the most favourable and beneficial sense, for the best advantage of the said corporation and their successors; as well in all our courts of records, as elsewhere, by all and singular judges, justices, officers, ministers, and other subjects whatsoever; of us our heirs and successors; any omission, imperfection, defect, cause or thing, whatsoever to the contrary thereof, in any wise notwithstanding; provided always, that these our letters patent be enrolled, in the rolls of our high court of chancery, in that part of our said united kingdom called Ireland, within the space of six months from the date hereof; otherwise these our letters patent to be null and void; and of no effect, anything herein contained to the contrary in any wise notwithstanding

In witness whereof we have caused these our letters to be made patent

Witness our aforesaid Lieutenant General and General Governor of Ireland at Dublin the second day of June in the fifty fifth year of our reign

[Signed] Granard

Examined Thos. Bourchier, Deputy Clerk of the Crown

Enrolled in the office of the Rolls of His Majesty's high Court, of Chancery in Ireland the third day of June in the fifty fifth Year of the Reign of King George the third, and Examined by R. Wogan Deputy Keeper of the Rolls

2.6 Waterford 1815

The Waterford chamber was first founded in 1787, and after some lapse in activity was re-founded in 1804, soon after which it sought a charter. The chamber was continuous from 1804, with the 1815 charter a development of its 1804 rules plus the need for a new financial structure to own property. Its charter is distinctive in being motivated by and largely concerned with establishing the legal personality of the chamber to hold property. This was stimulated by the desire to purchase a large building as the premises for the chamber's coffee house, library and hotel in the former 'House of Concerns'. The charter underpinned the debenture structure for the members to hold shares in the assets of the chamber (the building).[13] The shares for this had already been issued in £50 units in 1812 for the purchase (cost £3,000), with three trustees and seven to form a committee of management, who were to be remain as officers for seven years; no trustee or committee member could transfer shares except to a member of the chamber (minutes 10 and 21 February 1812). There were 46 initial shareholders, one of whom held four shares, two held three, nine held two and the rest held one share (List of purchasers of House of Concerns: WCOC 2/01 10 February 1812). The charter was amended in 1908, with Bye-laws produced as published booklets from 1851.[14]

Source
Printed booklet, John Bull Bookseller: Waterford Archives WCOC 18/01

Printed booklet 16 September 1815

CHARTER OF INCORPATION OF THE CHAMBER OF COMMERCE OF THE CITY OF WATERFORD, Granted in the Year 1815.

[Preamble omitted] On behalf of themselves and other Persons, Merchants, Bankers, and Traders of the said City of Waterford, have by their Petition to our trusty and well-beloved Counsellor CHARLES VISCOUNT WHITWORTH, our said Lieutenant General and General Governor of that part of our said United Kingdom called Ireland, SET FORTH that the convenience of Commercial Dealing AND Intercourse within the said City of Waterford, would be essentially promoted by the funding of Buildings to be appropriated to that purpose, situate in the central part of the said City, and properly constructed and regulated; and that the Petitioners and the said

[13] For further detail of the structure of shares and the history of the coffee house, library and hotel, see Bennett, *Local Business Voice* (2011) 514–6. Further background in D. Cowman, *Perceptions and Promotions: The Role of the Waterford Chamber of Commerce, 1787–1987* (Waterford, 1987).
[14] Waterford Archives: WCOC 18/02–19.

persons had entered into a voluntary Society, and had subscribed certain sums of money in shares, to the amount of £25 sterling each share, towards constituting a Capital Stock for the formation and support of such an Establishment, and had appointed a Committee of Management, consisting of nine members of the said Society, with certain powers, by virtue whereof the said Committee of Management, on behalf of the said Society, had been paid, and had received from the Members of the said Society respectively, deposits in money payment of the said Subscriptions, in order to enable them to carry into execution the above-mentioned plan of improvement; and had, out of the Fund so subscribed, purchased the fee and inheritance of an House, with the Appurtenances, situate in the said City of Waterford, and had caused the same to be fitted up in a manner suited to the convenience of Commercial Dealings AND Intercourse, within the said City of Waterford.

[Further preamble omitted] ... KNOW ye, therefore, that we, taking the premises into our royal consideration, have, agreeably to our uniform desire of encouraging Institutions, fitted to promote the convenience of the Commercial Dealings and Intercourse of our trusty and well beloved subjects, exercising trade within the said City of Waterford, in that part of our said United Kingdom called Ireland, thought fit to grant the said Charter. We, of our special grace, certain knowledge, and mere motion, by and with the advice and consent of our right trusty and right well beloved Counsellor CHARLES VISCOUNT WHITWORTH, our said Lieutenant General and General Governor of that part of our said United Kingdom called Ireland; and according to the tenor and effect of his Royal Highness the Prince Regent's Letter, in our name, and on our behalf, and under our Privy Signet, bearing date at our Court at Carleton House, the tenth day of July, one thousand eight hundred and fifteen, in the Fifty-fifth Year or our Reign, now enrolled in the Rolls of our High Court of Chancery, in that part of our United Kingdom called Ireland, have made, ordained, established, authorized, constituted, and appointed, and by these presents, for us, our Heirs and Successors, Do make, ordain, establish, authorize, constitute and appoint our trusty and well beloved [9 names listed], and all such other persons, whether natives or aliens, as now have and are possessed, or hereafter shall have and be possessed of any share or shares to the amount of £25 sterling each share as aforesaid, of and in the Capital Stock of the said Subscribers, or in any augmentation of the said Capital Stock hereafter to be made, either as original Subscribers or otherwise, according to the provisions herein contained, being thereunto first duly elected and chosen in manner herein-after provided, for and during such time as they shall respectively have and be possessed of such share and shares and no longer, to be and be called for ever hereafter one Body, politic and corporate in deed and in name, by the name of the CHAMBER OF COMMERCE OF THE CITY OF WATERFORD, and by the same name to have perpetual succession and continuance, conformably to the provisions herein after contained in that respect, for the purposes of founding, constructing, regulating, and maintaining the aforesaid Buildings, and all such other Buildings or Improvements as they or their successors, in their said corporate capacity, shall deem necessary for the convenience of their said Society, and the purposes of Commercial Dealings and Intercourse, and to enable them at any time or times hereafter, as they or their successors may think fit, to contribute to the accommodation of persons exercising trade within the said City of Waterford or the Liberties thereof; and our further will and pleasure is, and we do hereby grant and ordain, that in all times coming, they and their successors, in their said corporate capacity, shall be able and capable by the same name to sue and be sued, plead and be impleaded, answer and be answered, act and defend before all Judges and Ministers, and in all Courts of Law and Equity, in all actions, pleas, suits and complaints of what nature and kind soever, as fully to all intents and purposes as any body politic or corporate within that part of our said United Kingdom called Ireland, and by the same name, to purchase, have, hold, and enjoy, lands, tenements, or other hereditaments, of whatsoever nature or kind, not exceeding however in the whole the clear yearly value of One Thousand Pounds, sterling, at the time of purchasing or acquiring such estates, together with, and over and above, and in addition to the House and Appurtenances aforesaid; and our further will and pleasure is, and we do hereby empower the said Company to take and receive full and absolute conveyances, such purchases and conveyances to be good and valid, notwithstanding any statute or statues of Mortmain; and our further will and pleasure is, and we do hereby enable the said Society, by the same name, to grant, alien, mortgage, demise, sell, assign, or otherwise dispose of all their estates, revenues, and effects, or any party thereof at their will and pleasure; and that in all times coming, they and their successors, in their said corporate capacity, shall and may have and use one common Seal, such as they shall think proper for the use of the said Company, and shall and may from time to time, at their discretion, change, alter, or make anew the said Common Seal.

AND our will and pleasure is, and we do hereby, for us, our heirs and successors, ordain and appoint, that the said Joint and Capital Stock of the said Company shall consist of and be divided into shares of Twenty-five Pounds each; and that Twenty-five Pounds of said Capital Stock and no more shall be and be deemed to all intents and purposes a share thereof; and that the said Capital Stock shall not in the whole exceed the sum of Fifty Thousand Pounds, unless increased in the manner hereinafter mentioned; and that it shall and may be lawful for any General Assembly of the said Company, duly summoned for the purpose at any time or times hereafter, and either at once, or twice, or from time or time, to augment their said

Capital Stock to any sum or sums not exceeding in the whole amount the sum of One Hundred Thousand Pounds, sterling, by increasing the number of Members and Shares, or by increasing the number of shares only, and by empowering the Committee of Directors for the time being, to receive subscriptions for such purpose, provided the act, order, or proceeding of every such General Assembly for that purpose, shall have been ratified and confirmed by an order, or proceeding of a subsequent General Assembly, to be duly convened and held within not less than seven nor more than fourteen clear days after such former Assembly, excluding the days of holding both Assemblies; and in case such augmentation shall be at any time take place, then, and as often as the same shall happen, the said Company shall have the same powers over every such augmentation of the Capital Stock as over the original Capital Stock; and the person or persons entitled to such augmentation of the Capital Stock being Members of the said Society, shall be entitled to all the privileges, and subject to all the regulations granted by and contained in these presents, or in any bye law or bye laws duly made, whether previous to or after such augmentation.

AND our will and pleasure is, and we do hereby, for us, our heirs and successors, ordain and appoint, that the aforesaid subscription, entered into by the said voluntary Society, shall constitute (as far as the same shall extend) a part of the Capital Stock of the said Company, being first paid over to the proper officer of the said Company for that purpose; and that all deposits already paid by the Members of the said Society respectively, on account of their respective shares of the said subscription, shall be allowed by the said Company to the said Members or their Representatives, in part payment of similar shares in the said Capital Stock.

AND our will and pleasure is, and we do hereby, for us, our heirs and successors, grant, ordain and appoint, that such Company from time to time, for ever hereafter, shall be under the direction and management of nine or such greater number of Directors, not exceeding at any time the number of fifteen, as shall from time to time be ordained by any bye law or bye laws of the said Company; all such Directors to be elected and chosen from the Members of the said Company, according to the bye laws and regulations thereof. And we do hereby nominate and appoint the said [repeats names] … , the present and first Directors, and to continue in their said offices respectively, until other persons shall be chosen in their respective rooms, according to the bye laws and regulations hereafter to be prescribed by the said Company in that respect, unless the said persons or any of them shall previously die, be removed from, resign, or otherwise vacate, or be deprived of their said office respectively; and that such Committee of Directors, and also all subsequent Committees of Directors, to be elected and chosen as aforesaid, shall, on their election, become and constitute a Committee for ordering, managing, and disposing of all the Capital Stock, estates, revenues, effects, affairs, and concerns of the said Company, conformably to the provisions of such bye laws, as the said Company shall so as aforesaid enact and constitute; and that the aforesaid House and Appurtenances, and all other the Capital Stock, estate, effects, and revenue of the Company, shall be for ever hereafter vested in the said Corporation and their Successors, and shall be from time to time under the control and direction of such Committee of Directors, and all subsequent Committees of Directors, as soon as they shall be elected and chosen respectively, TO THE USE NEVERTHELESS of the said Company; and said Company shall and may at all times hereafter, whenever they may think proper, meet together for the purposes of the said Company, at such times, and at such convenient places within the said City of Waterford, as they may from time to time appoint.

AND that said Directors, immediately after the passing of this Charter, and all subsequent Directors, immediately after their election, shall from time to time elect one of their number to be Chairman of said Committee of Directors, which election shall be made by the majority of the votes of the Directors then present; and the Chairman so elected, shall preside at all their Meetings, and shall regulate the proceedings thereof, but shall have no vote at said Meetings, except in case of an equality of votes, in which case he shall have a casting vote, and that he shall authenticate all acts, orders, and proceedings of such Meetings by his signature, and without such signature, such acts, orders, and proceedings, shall not be valid or effectual; and through and by him all questions or subjects that it shall be necessary to communicate to the Company at large, shall be so communicated.

AND our further will and pleasure is, and we do hereby, for us, our heirs and successors, ordain and appoint, that said Committee of Directors shall, upon such their election, nominate, and appoint two of the said Committee to be Keepers of the common Seal of the said Company, to whom, upon their entering on the duty of their office, said common Seal shall be delivered, and who shall from thenceforth have the actual custody thereof, until the next election of officers, or until such Keepers respectively shall die, resign, or be removed from the said office; and such Seal Keepers shall from time to time, affix the said Seal to all such writings or instruments as shall be vouched and authenticated by the said Committee of Directors, as proper writings or instruments for that purpose; and further, that the Keepers of said Seal or any of them, shall not affix or permit the said Seal to be affixed to any other writings or instruments whatsoever than as aforesaid; and in case such Keepers of the Seal or either of them shall die, resign, or be removed from being Keepers thereof, or shall be necessitated to absent himself or themselves from two successive Meetings of the said Seal Keepers, which absence shall be considered as a resignation of that office, then and in each of the said cases, the said Committee of Directors shall thereupon elect one other Keeper or Keepers of said Seal, who shall, together with the other person theretofore elected to that situation, and then continuing therein, from thenceforth act as the Seal Keepers of the said Company for the time being, until their offices of Seal Keepers respectively shall expire, such Seal Keepers to be however from time to time subject to the bye laws of the Company, enacted for their government.

AND our will and pleasure is, and we do hereby ordain and direct, that said Committee of Directors shall, during the continuance of their office, be subject to the control and direction of the bye laws of the Company, to be prescribed for their government, and shall annually on the expiration of their office, or at any other time when thereunto required by a General Assembly of the Company, cause to be laid before them just and fair accounts in writing, to be duly kept, of all receipts and payments, and doings of them, their officers, and agents, for the approbation and inspection of said Company; and that all such sum or sums of money as shall be paid by said Committee, or which they or any other person at their instance, are or may be liable by any contract or contracts to pay, for or on account of the said Company, shall be considered as paid or agreed to be paid on account of the Company, and shall be allowed in account with them to the said Committee, or to such other person or persons to whom such sums of money shall be payable; and said Directors and Seal Keepers are hereby required, on the expiration of their offices, to deliver up to the President of the Company for the time being, or such other person or persons as the said Company shall appoint for that purpose, the said Common Seal, and all and every the books, papers, securities, or other documents, the property of said Company then in their custody, power, or possession respectively.

AND our further will and pleasure is, and we do hereby, for us, our heirs and successors, ordain and appoint, that the first General Assembly of the said Company shall be convened and held within twenty days next after the passing of this Charter, excluding the day of passing thereof; on such day, within that time, and between such hours of such day, and at such convenient place within the County of the City of Waterford aforesaid, as shall be appointed by summons in writing, signed by three or more of said Directors hereby nominated, to be inserted in one or more of the public Newspapers, published in the said City of Waterford, and to be served upon each Member, either personally, or at the usual place of his residence within the said City, but such insertion in the public Newspapers to be considered as a sufficient summons to all persons not having a known residence within the said City of Waterford, and said Committee of Directors shall thereupon summon said Company accordingly; and the Members who shall be present at the Assembly so convened, and who shall respectively be qualified to act and vote therein, according to the provisions herein contained, shall constitute such first General Assembly.

AND that from thenceforth said Company shall have four general stated Meetings in each year, viz.—On the first Monday in the month of January, first Monday in the month of May, first Monday in the month of September, and first Monday in the month of December, at which last mentioned general stated Meeting, the Members who shall be present thereat, shall, before any other business be transacted, proceed to be the election of a Committee of Directors for the ensuing year, from the Members of the Company qualified as aforesaid, and appoint the other officers of the Company for the said ensuing year, who shall, immediately after the general stated Meeting of the Company on the first Monday in the ensuing month of January, or as soon after as may be, enter upon the duty of their respective offices, under the control of the bye laws of the Company, and shall hold and continue the same until the first Monday in the next ensuing month of January, and until there shall be a new Committee of Directors chosen, or officers appointed: AND that at such Meeting, shall be also elected from among the Members of the Company, two persons to fill the situation of President and Vice-President of the Company for such ensuing year; which President, or in his absence, the Vice-President, or Chairman of the Company for the time being, shall preside at all Meetings of the Company, to be held during such ensuing year; and until there shall be a new President and Vice-President chosen respectively, and shall authenticate all acts done at any such Meeting in manner and form to be prescribed by the bye laws of said Company; and shall likewise, together with the Keeper of the Seal aforesaid, be the person alone competent to sign and authenticate all acts of the said Company. But if there shall be no Meeting of said Society on said day, or that it shall be deemed advisable to postpone the same, then each and every such election as aforesaid, to be made at such subsequent Meeting of said Society as shall be appointed for the purpose.

AND our will and pleasure is, and we do, for us, our heirs and successors, ordain and appoint, that the said President or Vice-President, or the person or persons officiating as such, and the Chairman of said Committee of Directors respectively while they shall officiate as President, Vice-President, and Chairman respectively, but no longer, shall have power and authority to administer oaths or affirmations as the case shall require, to all Members, Officers or Servants of the said Company, and to the several Witnesses, which shall be produced before any such Assembly or Meeting, as to all matters touching or concerning the qualifications of the Members of the said Company, or the support and good government thereof, or to the investigation of truth, relative to such property, affairs, and concerns of the said Company, as may be inquired of and decided upon at such General Assembly or Meeting, pursuant to the powers granted to them respectively, and pursuant to the bye laws of the said Company.

AND our will and pleasure is, and we do hereby, for us, our heirs and successors, ordain and appoint, that nothing herein contained shall in any manner prevent the said Company from meeting together at any time or times, besides said general stated Meetings, provided the same shall be an adjournment of such stated Meeting, or be a regularly summoned Meeting, according to the bye laws of the Company: And further, that each General Assembly of the Company or adjournment thereof, shall represent the whole body of the Company; and that all the acts, orders, and proceedings, which shall be done, made, or agreed to in manner aforesaid, by the majority of the Members who shall constitute any such General Assembly, or an adjournment thereof, shall be deemed and considered as the acts, orders, and proceedings of the whole Company, and shall have the same force and effect to bind and charge the whole Company, and the Committee of Directors, Members, Officers, Servants, Capital Stock, Estates, Revenue, Effects, Affairs and Concerns of the Company, as fully and effectually to all intents and purposes, as if every individual Member of the Company had been present, and personally assented to such acts, orders, or proceedings; provided that such acts, orders, or proceedings shall be conformable to the bye laws of the Company; and provided that no act, order, or proceeding of any General Assembly or any adjournment thereof, for the conveying, alienating, demising, mortgaging, or otherwise encumbering the grounds, buildings, or revenue of the Company or any part thereof, shall be valid or effectual, unless such act, order, or proceeding shall have been ratified and confirmed by an act, order, or proceeding of a subsequent General Assembly convened for that special purpose.

AND our further will and pleasure is, and we do hereby ordain and appoint, that at such first Assembly, or any subsequent Assembly of the said Company, it shall and may be lawful for them, and they are hereby fully authorized and empowered from time to time hereafter, to make, ordain and constitute, and also to alter and repeal all and every such bye laws or bye law, for and concerning the good government of the Company, the Committee of Directors, and the Members, Officers and Servants of the Company, and the regulation, management, and disposal of all the Capital Stock, estate, revenue, effects, affairs, and concerns of the Company, and the imposing reasonable mulcts, fines, and penalties, upon offenders against such bye law or bye laws, as such Assembly shall judge proper and requisite; PROVIDED always, that the ordaining, altering, or repealing of any such bye law shall not be or be deemed, or considered valid or effectual, unless each act, order, and proceeding of a General Assembly for any of the said purposes, shall have been ratified and confirmed by an act, order, or proceeding of a subsequent General Assembly, to be duly convened for that purpose, under the rules and regulations of the Company; and unless every such act, order, or proceeding of such two General Assemblies, at which such bye laws shall be so made, altered, or repealed, shall be authenticated under the Seal of the Company, AND PROVIDED also, that such bye laws be not repugnant to the laws and statutes of that part of our said United Kingdom called Ireland.

AND our further will and pleasure is, and we do hereby for us, our heirs and successors, ordain and appoint, that every such bye law, when duly ordained, confirmed, and authenticated as foresaid, shall be and be deemed, and considered, until altered or repealed as aforesaid, and no longer, as valid and effectual, for the purposes aforesaid, as if the contents and matter thereof were specifically set forth, and contained in our said Letters Patent; and that all forfeitures, mulcts, fines and penalties, shall be to the use and benefit of the Company, as part of their annual revenue, without any account or payment thereof to be rendered to us, our heirs or successors, and shall and may be so received and recovered by sale of such share, or by deduction out of such interest, dividend, salary, or other allowance, as shall belong, or be payable by the Company, to the person or persons who shall have incurred any such forfeiture, mulct, fine, or penalty; and shall accordingly, when adjudged by virtue of the authority granted by these our Letters Patent, attach and be levied on said dividends, salary, or other allowance, and shall and may be recovered as aforesaid, or in such other manner, consistent with the laws and statutes of that part of the United Kingdom called Ireland; and by such person or persons as the said Company or Committee of Directors for the time being, shall from time to time order and appoint.

AND our will and pleasure is, and we do hereby, for us, our heirs and successors, ordain and appoint, that each General Assembly of the said Company shall have power from time to time, upon complaint being made of the improper conduct of any Member or Members, Director or Directors, Officer or Officers, Servant or Servants, of nonconformity to the several bye laws of the Company, or any of them, to summon the parties so offending to appear at the next General Assembly of the Company; and by examination into the truth of the complaint, determine whether the person be guilty thereof, and shall thereupon award such punishment, as shall be prescribed by the aforesaid bye laws.

AND our will and pleasure is, and we do hereby, for us, our heirs and successors, ordain and declare, that no person shall continue to be a Director or Member of the said Company after he shall have so forfeited or ceased to possess a share or shares in the Capital Stock of the Company; nor shall any person or persons, becoming possessed of any share or shares, be entitled to act or vote in any general, or other assembly of the Company, by virtue of such share or shares, unless he or they shall have been previously elected a Member of the Company, according to the laws and regulations thereof.

AND our further will and pleasure is, and we do hereby for ourselves, our heirs and successors, ordain and direct, that all shares of the Capital Stock of the Company, shall be deemed and considered to be personal and not real Estate; and if any Member of the Company shall die possessed of a share or shares in said Capital Stock, such share or shares shall not accrue to the surviving Members, nor go or descend to the heir of such deceased Member, but shall vest in the executors or administrators of such deceased Member, and be disposable for his, her, or their benefit, in the manner, and according to the bye laws of said Society; nor shall any share or shares in said Capital Stock, or in any augmentation thereof, or any dividend arising therefrom, be liable to any foreign or other attachment, save and except such attachments as shall affect such share or shares, by virtue of the provisions contained in those our said Letters Patent: and that no act, order, or proceeding of the Company, or of the Committee of Directors shall operate so as to subject the private or personal Estate of any Member of the Company, not being part of such Capital Stock or property of the said Company, to any forfeiture or loss in any case.

AND our will and pleasure is, and we do hereby for us, our heirs and successors, ordain and appoint, that all securities and instruments, duly authenticated according to the aforesaid bye laws, shall be at all times assignable and transferrable in the manner, and according to the manner to be prescribed by such bye laws; and that same, authenticated as aforesaid, shall be evidence of the facts therein respectively contained and recited, as against the Members of the Company respectively.

AND our will is, and we do hereby, for us, our heirs and successors, grant and declare, that these our Letters Patent, and the enrolment thereof in our High Court of Chancery, in that part of our said United Kingdom called Ireland, shall be valid and effectual to the said Company, according to the true intent and meaning thereof, without further Licence or Grant from us, our heirs and successors, and shall in all things be construed and adjudged in the sense most favourable to the said Company.

PROVIDED always, that these our Letters Patent be enrolled in the Rolls of our High Court of Chancery of that part of our said United Kingdom called Ireland, within the space of six months, next ensuing the date of these presents; in witness whereof, we have caused these our Letters to be made Patent. Witness our aforesaid Lieutenant General and General Governor of that part of our said United Kingdom called Ireland, at Dublin, the sixteenth day of September, in the fifty-fifth year of our Reign.
[signed] GRANARD.

Enrolled in the Offices of the Rolls of His Majesty's High Court of Chancery in Ireland, the twenty-third day of September, in the Fifty-fifth

Year of the Reign of King George the Third, and examined by R. WOGAN, *Deputy Keeper of the Rolls.*
[followed by list of 87 'Original Members': see Appendix, no. 25.2]

2.7 Unsuccessful charter bids: Dublin 1783 and 1823

The Dublin chamber had ambitions to become chartered but appears to have been put off by early exchanges and does not seem to have made a formal approach. It is claimed by MacMahon[15] that failure to obtain a charter left the chamber in a weakened position in the later 1780s; but there is no evidence that a charter was actively sought then. The first record of Dublin seeking a charter occurs in 1823, but this was abandoned.[16] Prendeville (1930, p. 101) suggests that the chamber decided not to attempt to acquire a charter because it was not going to have property, stock, or capital. However, there was appreciation of the difficulties of acting without the formal status of a legal body corporate. The document reproduced here records the response of having a petition being rejected by the Irish parliament because of the chamber's status—not being a body corporate. The petition was 'to permit the import of tobacco to Great Britain from Ireland'.[17] This seems politically innocent enough, but it challenged English control of Irish trade and suggested an attempt to use Ireland as a base for smuggling. It was also very divisive between the chamber council members. The discussion of the petition had begun in August as a more general 'memorial on measures for the improvement of trade'. Various committees had considered this, with over 20 meetings postponing final drafts through September and October. The final petition agreed on 30 October was much weaker and more general. The tobacco import petition was a more specific aspect carved out of this. Travers Hartley, president of the Dublin chamber and an MP, had presented the petition,[18] but as noted in the Introduction, it had been rejected as coming from 'a self-elected body, and the name a title usurped'. The issue was resolved by accepting the petition from Hartley as MP and his cosignatories as individuals, not from the chamber. Thus the device used in the quoted document did not serve the purpose.

[15] MacMahon, *Most Respectable Meeting* (2014) 72.
[16] TNAI: Dublin chamber, *Report of Council* (1823) 5.
[17] TNAI: minutes 22 November 1783.
[18] See *ONDB*; biography related to chamber in Cullen, *Princes and Pirates* (1983) 35–57; Prendeville, *History of the Dublin Chamber* (1930).

Source
Dublin chamber of commerce, Minutes: TNAI.

Minute 25 November 1783

It having being mentioned to the Council that there Petition to Parliament would not be received by the House of Commons from an objection to the Title.

Resolved that the following do stand the Title of the Petition of this Council to Parliament.

The Humble Petition of Merchants who have been nominated a Council by a numerous body of Traders associated under the Title of the Chamber of Commerce of the City of Dublin.

Resolved that the following be the Subscription [in whose names it was given] to the Petition—

Signed at the Desire and in behalf of the said Merchants

by the President and Vice President

Resolved that our own worthy President be requested to present said Petition to Parliament

2.8 Unsuccessful charter bid: Jersey 1787–8

The chamber sought a charter in 1788, but was unsuccessful. The records in the minutes indicate the difficulties encountered and the critical importance of ensuring that there was no local opposition to the formal process. The chamber had anticipated some local opposition and to prevent this 'it was unanimously agreed and resolved to keep secret among the members of the committee' the charter proposal until the final papers were ready to be laid before the whole membership of the chamber. This was 'particularly recommended' by John Dumaresq, their London agent and a Jersey merchant and member. The papers were agreed at a chamber meeting in August 1787, and a petition with letters sent to solicit support from the Governor, Bailiff and jurats.[19] However, by January 1788 a caveat had been lodged 'with the Attorney General by William Heythuyson one of 60 clerks in Chancery against the petition'.[20] The chamber resolved to fight this, raising new funds if necessary. The first document shows that papers were prepared by the secretary evidencing the contribution of the chamber to the 'commercial advantage to this country' (i.e. to the whole of Britain), and Dumaresq was sent to England to assist the lobby. Dumaresq pressed matters, and a hearing

[19] Jersey Archives: chamber minutes, 23 April and 18 August 1787; L/A/38/A1/2.
[20] Reported by Paul Le Mesurier; Ibid. minutes, 3 January 1788.

before the Attorney General was held at which the caveat was lodged by various 'gentlemen of this Island' supported by legal 'counsel for these gentlemen'. The second document shows that, as a result, the Attorney General suspended his report on the charter until he was further informed.[21] Dumaresq briefed the chamber on the objections, prepared a reply, which the chamber approved. He was then instructed to pursue the matter,[22] but no further developments are recorded. The Jersey experience shows how critical it was to ensure that there were no local objections.

Source
Jersey chamber minute book: Jersey Archives L/A/38/A1/2

Minutes 24 January 1788

The Committee has approved of the Steps taken by Mr. Dumaresq in communicating to Paul Le Mesurier Esq. the Resolutions of the Chamber respecting the Caveat laid against the Prayer made for a Charter of Incorporation & in desiring Mr. Le Mesurier to pursue that matter with the utmost vigour & Soliciting a continuance of his Zeal & Assistance in the Prosecution of this business.

Resolved that it is best to wait the further information of Mr. Paul Le Mesurier upon the Caveat before the Committee agrees upon any instructions to be sent, in support of the Prayer of the Chamber in as much as the reasons of opposition whatever they may be are unknown to the Committee. In the mean time however the Secretary is desired to make extracts of all Resolutions of the Chamber or Committee by which any relief has been given to individuals or any Steps taken or any Money Spent or advanced toward the promotion of the Trade and Navigation of this Island also extracts of any contributions made by the old Chamber of Commerce to obtain commercial advantage to this Country, with the date of the first establishment of the said former Chamber of Commerce such extracts being likely to prove proper documents for instruction and to be in readiness to transmit over when occasion shall offer.

Mr. Dumaresq is further authorized by the Committee to correspond with Mr. Le Mesurier on the subject of the Caveat above mentioned and to communicate to him such information & instructions from time to time as Mr. Dumaresq shall think conducive to remove this obstacle to the Unanimous wishes of the Chamber.
Ph. Hamon Sec.

[21] Ibid. reported by John Dumaresq; minutes, 24 January 1788; the names of the objectors are not recorded.
[22] Ibid. minutes, 12 January 1789; Dumaresq's observations are not recorded.

Minutes 3 December 1788

Resolved that for the future such Members as cannot attend the General Meetings on important business are to send to the President their excuse for non-attendance in time that they may be produced to the Chamber previous to their Name being called

Mr. Dumaresq has informed the Chamber that there has been a hearing before the Attorney General upon the application of the Chamber for a Charter of Incorporation in which Mr. Thos. Leckeswrier appeared as Counsel for the Society & Mr. Hardings Counsel for the Gentlemen of this Island who have laid a Caveat against the said Application: that the Counsel for these Gentlemen was instructed to deny various facts and Services alleged to have been done by the Chamber for the Good of Trade & of the Public in General; that on the other hand the said Counsel delivered in writing before the Attorney. Genl. sundry Objections and pretentions advanced against the Chamber a Copy of which Mr. Dumaresq has delivered to the Committee of the Chamber at his return from England, that upon the different allegations & pretentions of the parties the Attorney General has suspended his report until the matter should again appear before him, or that he should be further informed on the Subject. The Chamber upon the whole considering that the Copy of the Objections above mentioned have been put by the Committee in the Hands of Mr. Dumaresq to make his observations thereupon & to prepare a reply to them he judged proper to defer any further resolutions on the Subject until the Chamber is Acquainted with the Nature of the said Objections and Observations upon them. And to this effect Mr. Dumaresq is desired by the Chamber to prepare matters as soon as he conveniently can do it & when done to acquaint the Committee with it that the whole may regularly come before the Chamber.
Ph. Hamon Secretary

Chapter 3

Wider Discourse

The documents presented in this chapter are key elements of the wider published, memorial and pamphlet literature that informed founders and developers of chambers of commerce. This thinking has not been previously brought together, which has inhibited understanding of the evolution of representational bodies from the 1688 Revolution through the eighteenth century into the early nineteenth century. This material provided an interlinked stream of discourse in which each writer tended to draw on earlier sources and reshape them to the current circumstances. From Davenant, Whiston, Cary and Child, through Bennet, Ashley, Mun, Smith, Temple, Gee, to Postlethwayt, Mortimer and others, these writers built a prolific range of book-sized publications, pamphlets and hand-written advice to ministers, advisors and anyone else who would listen. This percolated into the commercial community by private circulation and from the 1750s through subscription libraries. These writings confirmed what the merchants and traders already knew, but provided an intellectual case, wider dissemination, and some concepts for practical plans for improvement by modifying institutions which can be seen in some of the chamber rules.

Key themes of the discourse were: the need to reduce high taxation, especially on excise or exports; the need to prevent unnecessary wars, or fight wars only with greater emphasis on commercial gain; the inefficiency of government decision making; inefficient Treaty negotiation that neglected commercial interests; lack of commercial skills and knowledge on the part of ministers and administrators; a parliament that contained too few members with commercial knowledge; corruption of parliamentary elections, public offices and appointments; resistance to existing monopolies and vested interests such as the East India Company (EIC), Royal African Company, and plans for Fishery Companies; lack of attention to the colonies, and bad government in the colonies by weak and corrupt Governors; and the need for improved management of convoys and naval protection. The control of sale of offices was also bound up with the need to improve elections by open ballots, and to limit the time over which parliament would sit. Commercial discourse was thus entangled with wider debates about 'reform', parliamentary representation, and the political writings of Bolingbroke and Burgh. Much of this was to be wrapped up in later discourse, led by Burke in 1780, under the catch-all of 'economical reform'. It was also interlinked with the conflicts over the Stamp Act in 1765, the American Rebellion and War 1774–83, the Wilkes election affairs, and reform of the East India Company, among many other specific issues of 'reform'. The writings evidence the tension of ideas between viewing the crown as an absolute source of enlightened decisions, parliament as a more democratic source of decisions, and the (often coded) view of the potential incompetence of both.

A running theme, deriving from Whiston and Davenant, was the claim that a committee of trade could be a 'commercial parliament', removing from government—or better informing ministers on—key aspects of trade, treaties and the Navy. This forms the platform for arguing that merchants and manufacturers can give a more informed view than those of 'ignorance' in government, what would be termed today information asymmetry. This led to a collision of ideas between the concept of independent voluntary chambers and a government-appointed Committee, or Board of Trade, which is evident in the sometimes contradictory claims in the documents reproduced here. At local level the same collision of ideas and power could occur between the chambers and committees appointed by municipalities of county bodies (as evident in Liverpool: see Chapter 4). Various elements of the commercial parliament idea are developed in the documents in greater detail, and were pursued by the early chambers, notably: (i) settlement of commercial disputes through arbitration in a court merchant, or commercially appointed body (avoiding lawyers and their costs); (ii) development of insurance and other supports for markets; (iii) control of naval convoys; (iv) advocacy of freedom to trade within broad regulations rather than through statute companies (especially the EIC); (v) encouragement of marine societies for care of widows and orphans of seamen; (vi) improvement of fisheries and training of seamen; (vii) improvement of the skills of consuls abroad; (viii) advocacy of ending imprisonment for bankruptcy. All the themes, in different ways, point to a rule-based system of representation and making decisions (as shown taken up in Chapter 1). The idea of a national-level council or 'parliament' appears to have had a particularly strong influence on the General Chamber of 1785–7. The interlinkage between chambers and courts merchant, or courts of arbitration, formed a strong element of the 'services' provided by most early chambers (see Chapter 6). It also developed as part of an argument that chambers deserved public recognition as 'tribunals of commerce' and deserved some form of public law status, that continued into the twentieth century.[1]

The most direct influence of the early discourse on actual chambers appears to be through Postlethwayt, Mortimer and Weskett, who acknowledged the various early writers, and whose work, appearing in the 1750s–1770s,

[1] Bennett, *Local Business Voice* (2011) 275–89.

forms the main bridge between earlier writers and practical chamber foundations. Postlethwayt in many writings, but most fully in *Great-Britain's True System*, drew attention to the benefits of the French Council of Commerce, its twelve elected members representing the principal trading centres in France, complemented by local chambers of commerce in each centre. Postlethwayt's most widely circulated and reprinted book, his *Dictionary of Commerce*, first published in 1751–5 in instalments, and reissued in 1766 and 1774, widely disseminated the ideas in a brief 'popular' format. Postlethwayt was a populariser whose writings were almost universally known in the intellectual and merchant communities. He had been an advisor to Walpole and Henry Pelham. He was an advisor to the African Company 1744–6; and one advisor to Rockingham during the Stamp Act crisis 1765–6.[2] He was a professional 'writer', well trained and experienced in writing to influence.

Mortimer also popularised information on French chambers, but additionally offered a specific blueprint for UK chambers in *The Elements of Commerce* of 1772.[3] This was very widely disseminated, being reissued in 1774, 1780 and 1802 editions, translated into German in 1783, and enlarged as a *General Commercial Dictionary* in 1810, which went through three further editions by 1823. Mortimer explicitly acknowledged Child, Cary, Mun, Davenant, Postlethwayt and others, and it is likely that this book was the source for Burke's reference to Whiston-Davenant in his 1780 speech on 'Economical Reform'. Mortimer was subsequently denounced by the landed interest for proposing independent chambers.[4]

Weskett's 1782 book, *Plan of the Chamber of Commerce*, had lesser conceptual impact, but did lead to a practical specialised chamber being set up in London as an advice and arbitration body 'open all days … Saturday afternoons and Sunday's excepted'. Although it was not a broad representa-

[2] Malachy Postlethwayt, 1707–1767, was a prodigious author on commerce and economics, including the African and slave trades. The *ODNB* has various gaps for his genealogy and makes no comment on his advocacy of French institutional models or chambers. His brother, James Postlethwayt, 1711–61, was also a major commentator: see R. J. Bennett, 'Malachy Postlethwayt: Genealogy and influence of an early economist and spin doctor', *Genealogists' Magazine*, 31, June (2011) 1–7, for new coverage of genealogy and influence.

[3] Thomas Mortimer, 1730–1810, was a well-placed son of the Master of the Rolls. He was an extensive author, and continued to advocate chambers into the 1800s, e.g. lecture 10 of *Lectures on the Elements of Commerce, Politics and Finance* (1801). His *Universal Director* (1763, p. 19) lists him as a compiler and author, private teacher of languages and 'the art of acquiring a correct style fit for the press'. He began as junior clerk to Court of Chancery, then merchant and consul, later clerk to the Chief Baron of Exchequer (1792) and to the Lord Chief Jurie of Common Pleas (1793–8).

[4] See Bennett, *Local Business Voice* (2011) 98–100.

tional chamber, it lasted for 18 years, 1782–1800.[5] Weskett's chamber, like the suggestions of the early writers, was also intended to have a 'council of *merchants* and *traders* … to confer on, communicate to government the properest measures',[6] though this aspect never seems to have been implemented.[7] Apart from his *Plan* the only other direct record that has been found is his letter to the Glasgow chamber reproduced here (Section 3.2) which makes clear that his chamber was chiefly or solely for dispute resolution.

The documents reproduced show a continuous line of discussion of the need for a council of commerce in order to better inform government, from the 1690s through to the 1780s. By 1770 the concept and title of 'chamber' was becoming as frequent as that of council or committee, and once chambers were actually established over 1767–74 then it was natural that they were used as examples of what was needed. The texts were mostly published or semi-published as pamphlets, but are also contained in records of senior government ministers. Those reproduced here focus on the elements covering the specifics of chambers, which interleave with a mixed collection of wider issues of reform. In the documents the main title is underlined for each source, as referred to in this volume. Footnotes within texts are as in the original documents, but re-numbered; any additional footnotes are restricted to the document title.

Sources throughout this chapter
[a] Davenant's Memorial; BL Harley MS. 1223 f. 184–8.
[b] Correspondence of John Cary of Bristol; BL Add. MS. 5540, f. 84
[c] Pamphlet by James Whiston; BL MS. 816.m.12 (.5)
[d] Printed works in ECCO
[e] Goldsmith's Kress Papers, London Senate House Library; also in MTMW.
[f] *Morning Chronicle* 7 February 1783; also *London Chronicle* 8 February and *Whitehall Evening Post* 13 March 1783; repeated *General Evening Post* 12 June 1784.
[g] *The British Magazine and Review or Universal Miscellany*, Vol. 2, 1783, p. 47.
[h] Glasgow chamber papers, Glasgow Mitchell Library: TD 1670/4/15

[5] Listed in *Browne's General Law List* for all years 1787–1800, and local directories, e.g. *The London Companion;* Wakefield, *General Directory;* Bowles, *New London Guide*.
[6] Weskett, *Plan of the Chamber of Commerce* (1786) 6–7, emphasis in original.
[7] Little is known of John Weskett beyond his insurance and chamber publications. He lived c.1730–1800, and was an underwriter; see L. S. Sutherland, *A London Merchant 1695–1774* (Oxford, 1933) 56–7. He wrote a major treatise on insurance, and is listed in directories as a merchant. He was assistant secretary of the African Company from about 1751 until at least 1767, which suggests he was probably a participating African merchant; TNA: T 70/144–5; *The Court and City Kalender or Gentlemens Register* (London, 1767) 239.

3.1 Charles Davenant, James Whiston, and their legacy

Davenant (1656–1714), an MP in 1685–8 and 1698–1701, was a strong political influence, wrote memorials, and assisted Bills often as an agent for commercial interests. He mainly worked through Robert Harley, 'the most important parliamentarian of his day', and was an important pamphleteer.[8] In the parliamentary debates in 1695–6 over a council of commerce Davenant became a prominent source of information, with his *Memorial* reprinted below forming an important contribution to the debates. Lees refers to the debates as regarded by contemporaries as 'a political and constitutional crisis of the greatest importance', which also influenced later historians and politics.[9] Langford notes that Burke's 1780s references to the Council of Trade referred to attempts by the Tories in 1695–6 to enable the House of Commons to encroach on the Crown's right to the patronage of offices.[10] Despatches by L'Hermitage, the Dutch emissary in London at the time, are an important record of the discussion of the actual events which are used as a central source by Lees, but would not have been widely available to outsiders, nor to subsequent external observers. In contrast, Davenant's memorial was later extended and adapted in his published writings, particularly the *Discourses* of 1698. They also influenced Whiston, whose own writings and thinking were significant influences on Davenant, as recognised by L'Hermitage in Lees's interpretation.[11] Reproduction of Davenant's memorial and Whiston's text (in Section 3.1) shows how they sought to influence the debate, and demonstrates how ideas about a council of commerce were current among those in the highest levels of government. Similarly, correspondence from John Cary, merchant of Bristol who was author of one of the other celebrated books on trade of the time, was also influential in the debates. One letter reproduced here is part of a larger correspondence reproduced by Lees;[12] see also Cary's books, part reproduced here (see Section 3.1).

James Whiston was perhaps a greater conceptual influence than Davenant. In writings in 1681, 1693 and 1695–6 he conceived the concept of a 'commercial parliament' elected from leading merchants. The parliamentary Bill of 1695–6 backed this plan. It was subsequently a key part of Whiston's *Discourse on the decay of trade*, which went through many editions into the 1770s. One version, reproduced in Section 3.1, demonstrates the availability

[8] See: *History of Parliament*; *ODNB*; *Biographical Dictionary of British Economists*.

[9] R. M. Lees, 'Parliament and the proposal for a Council of Trade, 1695–6', *English Historical Review*, 54 (1939) 38.

[10] P. Langford, ed., *Writings and Speeches of Edmund Burke*, Vol.3 (1996) 536–7, n.2.

[11] Lees, 'Parliament' (1939) 44.

[12] Lees, 'Parliament' (1939) 57–61.

and currency of these ideas at the time of chamber foundations. Whiston (c. 1641–1706) was a broker to merchants at the Royal Exchange, and developed a range of publications to promulgate his views.[13] *The Merchant's Weekly Remembrancer*, which he issued 1681–1707, was an important four-page journal that included price and trade information with political commentary. He first produced his *Discourse on the decay of trade* in 1693, reproduced here, as a lobby pamphlet. It was re-published in amended form in *The Causes of our present calamities* (1695), repeated with modification in many later versions, and also in *A short account of the grievances of the nation* and other pamphlets. Whiston took up many causes and probably served as a professional 'writer' to frame cases and lobby, in the same way as Postlethwayt. Whiston's later memorials ranged widely: e.g. for exemption of apothecaries from duty; in favour of a duty on foreign books; and for a duty on imported paper. However, his early and most personal lobbies concerned trade and commerce, as reproduced here. Davenant's and Whiston's writings were almost continuously in print in one form or another throughout the eighteenth century, with a 1771 collection of Whiston's works abstracted, demonstrating the currency of proposals for a 'council of commerce' during the critical years in which chambers were being established.

Davenant and Whiston provided sources for Burke's 1780 speech on Economical Reform, in Lees's view probably transmitted through Burnet's *Complete History of England*,[14] though it is perhaps more likely that Mortimer's *Elements* was used.

James Whiston, A Discourse of the Decay of Trade, *The Necessity of Recovering: The Danger of Neglecting: The Advantage of Effecting: With the proper Means to Accomplish the same. Whereby the War itself will become as certainly Advantageous as a Peace will be Destructive.* Printed for Samuel Crouch, Cornhill, London.[15] 1693[c]

… How absolutely necessary is it then that all possible endeavours be made (as the Examples of our Neighbours Successful Industry, and our own Sloth and Neglect sufficiently warn us) to study the ablest Means and Methods for the improvement of Trade, to be considered and discussed by proper Judges of the Case, (Viz. A Select *Society* or *Committee of Traders*

[13] See *ODNB*; *Biography of British Economists*.

[14] Burnet's *Complete History of England*, vol. III (1706) 707 ff.: Lees, 'Parliament' (1939).

[15] See also *J. Whiston*: The Causes of our Present Calamities *in reference to the Trade of the Nation, fully discovered with the most proper expedient to remedy the same … Humbly presented by James Whiston.* Pamphlet printed several times by the author, now corrected and enlarged [Jan–March old calendar] 1695–6[c]. This is similar to *Decay of Trade*, with the Committee identical to the 1693 document.

accordingly Skill'd and Experienced) by which we shall soon feel the warm Beams thereof extending their bountiful influence over the whole Nation.

Upon the fitness of Persons Chosen, depends the Good or Ill Success of this great Design, for the Arts-Man is ever the best Counsellor in his own Profession, and every honest able Man is safest to be Credited in his Opinion about means for the better improvement of the Mystery he Professes; if an enquiry be about Salvation, we apply ourselves to some professing the *Ministry*: if the Dispute be concerning the *Title* to an Estate, we desire the Judgment of a *Lawyer*; if Sick, we Consult a *Physician*: So when the *Trade* of a Nation is to be Secured or Advanced, the *Merchants* and *Tradesman's* Advice is questionless best able to accomplish the same: For let any Vers'd in *Trade* but reflect, how many Interesting Accidents belong to that Mystery, and how many various Shapes every Branch of it hath taken before it arriv'd at perfection; and they will conclude it impossible for Noblemen and Gentlemen not Educated in *Trade*, ever to arrive at a perfect Understanding of the Matters in Question; for want of which their Judgments are Abus'd by Clamour, Importunity, Prejudice, Partiality, or some other prevailing Bias; and seldom or never if the Matter be of Importance enough to require Debating, come to a right Decision; to the manifest Abuse of the People, Damage the Nation, and Disparagement of that *Council* or *Committee*.

Therefore that the Predominancy of that *many headed-Monster*, Private *Interest*, that hath Spun so fine a Thread, and twisted itself into so many Disguises, may not any longer insinuate Prejudice against this Proposal; This Establishment [of a Committee of Trade] will no ways be an infringement of *Royal* Prerogative, nor any Entrenchment upon the Privileges, or Invasion of the Province of our *High Court of Parliament*. On the contrary, it will be an useful Assistance and Ease to both, more especially to that great Council, necessarily Sub-ministering to them, in the due Inspection and Enquiry into Matters, and Things, which cannot so fully fall under their Cognizance and Examination, and accordingly be more Reputably and Commodiously handed up to them for their Approbation; Their Doors and Ears being always open to the Poorest Person, that shall offer any thing of Public Advantage.

This Committee must be more capable of opening a yet fairer Light, and insight into Trade, (with submission) even to the Wisdom of *Parliaments* themselves; who may be thereby be the better enabled to redress all these Mal-Administrations and Non-Improvements of *Trade*, which through the difficulty of Access, and the Multiplicity of their other Affairs and Fatigues, cannot so easily fall under a sufficient *Parliamentary* Inquiry.

It is an infallible Truth that we cannot long continue as we are; and that we can never Meliorate but by this, or such like Method as here proposed; Without some such Helps and Succours as may be drawn from hence, we must go from one Distraction to another, till we come to be utterly destroyed.

So that if the Earnest Expectations of the People be disappointed, by making use of Unsuitable Expedients, the *Ship* of this *Common-Wealth* (which by embracing the proposed Methods may be in a fair way of entering into a Safe *Harbour*) on the contrary will be driven to Sea in a Storm, and must expect another favourable Wind to save it, and God knows whether ever that may come. For the Poise and Balance of Affairs is not now as in former Ages. The Bulk of *France* is grown too unwieldy for the rest of the World; And we have (morally speaking) no hopes of Redemption, from being Crushed by her, if any yet greater Weight be added to her Scale.

It's humbly proposed that an Order be Issued forth to the Sheriffs of each County, Commanding them to give Notice to the several Merchandizers and Traders (as hereafter mentioned) to meet at a certain time to choose Annually Representatives, By a *Balloting* Box, according as the aforesaid Order shall Direct, To sit at *Guild-Hall*, or some Convenient Place in *London*, as a Committee fully Authorized to Inquire and Examine into all Matters Relating to Trade.

In *London*

2 East-India-Company.	2 Nevis, Antigua, Montserrat and St. Christopher.
2 African- Company.	2 Jamaica.
2 Turkey- Company.	2 Virginia and Mary-Land.
2 Italy.	2 New-York and New-England.
2 Spain	2 East-Country.
2 Portugal.	2 Hambrough and Holland.
2 Barbados	2 Canaries and Madeiras.
2 Silk Manufacturers.	2 Shipwrights
12 Masters of Ships chosen by Trinity-House	
[outside London]	
2 Northumberland for Coals	2 Norfolk for Stuffs
2 Derbyshire for Lead	2 Birmingham and Sheffield for Iron-Ware
2 Cornwall for Tin	2 Devonshire for Fishery
2 Devonshire for Clothing	2 for Colchester, with some other Places as shall be thought fit may be added, &c.
2 Somersetshire for Clothing	
2 Wiltshire for Clothing	
2 Yorkshire for Clothing	
2 Norfolk for Fishing	
1 Gloucester and Worcester for Clothing	

Suppose the Number be a Hundred (or more) Persons in all, there will never meet one time with another above Forty, who may divide into Sub-Committees for the quicker despatch of Business, as they do in the *East-India* and *African* Companies; which at Ten Shillings a piece for each Time, and Meeting twice *per* Week is Forty Pound per Week, which for Fifty Weeks is — 3,000

The Chief Clerk and his Servants *per Annum* —	500
And for Coach Hire, Letters, Fire, Candle, and other necessary Expenses,	500
	£4,000

That they have power to Receive all Overtures relating to *Trade*, and to Grant Rewards suitable to those Discoveries or services that shall be rendered by any Person, out of the profit of such Discoveries, or otherwise, according as the Nature of such Discovery shall be. To which Effect there are Thousands who would offer considerable Matters of vast Improvements did they know once whom to apply to.

That there be a Register of their Votes for, and against every Matter.

That whatever Proposals are offered to the Committee, shall be read three times before they are Rejected, and their Reasons for such Rejection shall be Annexed.

That the Committee shall have Power to choose their Officers, and to allow *Salaries* (as before mentioned) which shall be Authorized and Obliged to pay same, together with the Ten Shillings apiece for the Commissioners, and such Rewards as cannot be taken out of some Proposals.

That the said Commissioners shall be obliged to give their Majesties (and Parliament, when sitting), an Account from time to time of the growing Emoluments of Trade, and of the Obstructions of the general Improvement; That so from such Reports Their Majesties and Parliament may be better Advised how to make Laws suitable for the Encouragement of the public Benefit.

Innumerable and almost Infinite are the Benefits which both King and People will reap from such a Committee; And this Proposer is ready to Impart to the said Committee several Proposals of considerable Importance whereby he doubts not but they will be Enabled to Accomplish all the great Designs here mentioned too Voluminous for him particularly to insert, or indeed to make Intelligible without mature Debates before Persons experienced in such matters.

Charles Davenant: *A Memorial concerning a Council of Trade;* [Hand-written: main arguments subsequently developed and published many times; e.g. in 1771 in collected and revised works of Davenant, by Sir Charles Whitworth, MP, printed for R. Horsfield, Ludgate St., and others].[16] 1697[a]

f. 184. … The ill-posture of our affairs seems to have disposed the Nation to desire that the Legislative Power Could interpose in the Care of Trade; And an Act of Parliament to that purpose will probably be obtained, if one side were agreed upon what they may reasonably ask, and if the other knew what may be safely granted.

f. 184a … in all likelihood every part of the constitution has a great interest that a Council of Trade should be settled in this Kingdom. …

f. 185… Negligence in the protection of trade is the worst part of ill-Administration, because it is depriving ourselves of Strength and Adding it to the Enemy

… If Trade cannot be protected in time of War, a trading Nation must avoid being long engaged in such a business. …

f. 185a. … The care of Trade does properly belong to those with whom the Government of a Nation is in Trust, which in England is the King, and such to whom his Executive Power is commissioned.

The original of Executive Power Springs from this, That the whole Legislative power cannot be always assembled and the Nature requires of many authorities that they should be acted by a single person.

All Executive power originally is in the King who not being able to perform every function of State in his own person commits part of his Authority to other People who represent him in his Courts of Justice, in his Armies, his Fleets, and Revenues. And when the Executive power is thus divided, if the Public Service require yet more help, it can be no breach into the Constitution for the Legislative authority to make yet a further Division and to commit new powers to new persons for the better Government of the Common business.

The erecting New Magistracy in times of Calamity and Danger has proved Fortunate to many Nations especially where the People have a share and interest in the Laws and where the Constitution has a mixture in of it of Popular Government. For next to a prosperous Administration men like that Matters should be administered according to their own Fancy and Direction. And many wise Lawgivers and [f. 186] Rulers and Directors of Kingdoms and Commonwealths have herein followed the Bent and Humour of the People by which Means, of the two points they gained one, either to have the Affairs of State better Managed, or to let the People see they could not be better Administered by Officers of their own Choice and appointment.

[16] Lees, 'Parliament' (1939) gives a shortened version which leads to some unfortunate differences in emphasis.

Perhaps the Circumstances of Time and Nature of the War could not permit that the trade of England should be better Looked after and protected than it has been hitherto. However in this declining Condition of the Nation it may peradventure be prudent to make an experiment whither the former Wealth and Prosperity of this Country may not be recovered by some after Game of Wisdom

If a Council of Trade to be Appointed by Parliament can find ways of better Governing and protecting Foreign Traffic 'twill much restore Our Affairs and Enable us to carry on the War. But if upon trial it be found that such a Council cannot remedy this Disorder nor prevent the Losses at Sea 'twill be a great justification to the past Conduct of the Ministers.

For the well-Governing and protecting of Trade many things must perhaps be done that may Thwart the Interest of other Nations, and this unpleasant Office may be performed more gracefully by Authority of Parliament than by any Single part of the Constitution. For those complements which are often expected from Princes are not looked for from Assemblies met to enact Laws for their Common safety and benefit.

Our Commerce abroad is not to be recover'd but by men of Skill and Courage who will make a severe Inquisition into the Advantages other Countries daily gain upon us, For which reason hardly any persons will have weight enough for so important a matter, but a Committee chosen out of both Houses of Parliament to whom may be added some wealthy Merchants not Engaged in Trade, and who are known to be of a Public Spirit.

The common notion is that no Effectual Service can be Expected from this Establishment, unless the Committee [f. 186a] have in their Direction, and at their disposal Such a number of the Fleet as may be needful from time to time for the due Guarding of the Seas.

'Tis true that Protection being founded in Strength and power, they to whom the care of Trade is committed should have at their Command and in their Disposal such a proposition of Frigates as may Convoy all the Merchants' Fleets.

Part of the Navy was ever Designed by the Parliament for the Uses of the War and part for the Service of our Commerce; nor is it at all Absurd that those different Allotments should be under the Direction of different persons. For all the Rights of the Admiralty that seem inherent to their Office, as appointing Commanders, punishing Offenders, etc., would be still preserv'd; though, for example Forty frigates should be Ordered by Act of Parliament to follow the direction of a Council of Trade in cruising and for convoys. …

Persons appointed by Parliament, can boldly represent, from time to time, what Infractions are made in the Treaties of Commerce, now subsisting or which we shall make hereafter.

Such a council can watch that matters relating to our Traffic be not neglected or betrayed by our Ministers Abroad; and that important points be not lost for Want of Courage to assert the Interest of England in Foreign Courts. …

f. 187 To avoid this Mischief and to take in that Party who seem so jealous that the Executive Power should run into any New Channel the following scheme of a Council of Trade is proposed by which the prerogative will not be entrenched upon nor the Rights and Jurisdictions of the Admiralty interfered with . . . and whereby the old course of business in the main will not be much altered and peradventure their ends fully answered who design nothing in this matter but the good of Traffic and Welfare of the Nation.

THE SCHEME

1. The Council of Trade to be established by Act of Parliament and to Continue two years.

2. The House of Commons to name Twelve persons, the House of Peers Six, and the King under the Great Seal to add thereunto four of his Chief Ministers of State (22 in all), and the quorum to be Ten.

3. That the Merchants of provincial Trading Companies [EIC etc.] to be Directed by this Act to lay before the said Council what number of Seamen will be necessary to man their respective Fleets which are their people, and proper Reasons for sailing,

4. That they [the trading companies] be likewise directed to lay before the said Council what convoys are needful to guard their respective Trades, in what stations the Cruising Ships, may from time to time, be posted to the best Advantage and for their greater Service.

5. That the said Council be directed from time to time to Examine & Consider what Complement of Men will be wanting for the Several Ships, and Principal Fleets, What Convoys will be needful, and by what Times these Convoys ought to be ready, and in what Station the Cruising Ships may be posted.

6. That they be Directed by the Act upon all those Matters to deliver Memorials in writing (Signed by Five at least of the Said Council) to the Board of Admiralty with their opinions what is fit thereupon to be done.

7. That the Board of Admiralty be directed to given an Answer within Seven Days to each memorial, SIGNED by Four at least of the said Board.

By this method the Delays will be prevented which happen to the Merchants between the Privy Council and the Admiralty. And that uncertainty and those false Excuses will be avoided which are ever frequent in verbal Transactions.

If by these Memorials the Council of Trade shall offer things out of reason, impracticable, or against the Public Interest, the lords of the admiralty will be justified in not complying with them. But on the Contrary, if what they propose is just, necessary, and for the Common Good, the Admiralty will be Accountable to the King, in Parliament for taking other Measures.

8. This Council of Trade should be directed to look into the General State and Condition of our Foreign Commerce, First how the balance of Trade Stands, whereto got, and whereto Loss in Our Traffic with other Nations, Then where to make Returns by our own Product, or only in Money or Bullion.

For if this were known, Stated and well understood this might show unto fit and Adept Sumptuary Laws such as might prohibit at home the use of Commodities from other Countries where we lose in the Balance, and where Trade is hurtful to us.

9. The King's Ministers abroad may be directed by the Act to correspond with this Council and to give them from [f. 188] time to time an Account how the Posture of our Trade Stands, and upon what Foot we deal with the respective Nations where they reside; What Improvements may be therein made; What Manufactures they have among them; What Commodities they take from other Countries, which may as well be furnished from England.

10. This Council of Trade may be directed to Inspect the Plantation Trade; For it is affirmed by Men of Knowledge in these Matters, That by the corruption of Governors, and through the general negligence here at home, Our Colonies abroad begin to set up Manufactures of their own, and so deal and Traffic with other nations contrary to Law; and much to the Mother Country: By which means, if not prevented, in process of time they may become independent of this Kingdom.

11. As this Council should have power to propose to the Admiralty Regular Convoys for the most important Fleets, so they must have Authority to Fix ultimate Days, in proper Seasons for sailing, and to lay an Embargo on such Merchant Ships, as are not ready by the Limited Time, And they must also have power to punish, and Fine such as lose their vessels by running without Convoys to [secure] Early Markets, and by this Method Trade will be hindered from hurting itself.

12. They may be directed to Enquire what Foreign Trades are near losing, or now lost to this Kingdom and by what Methods they are to be recovered.

13. They may be directed to Look into the Several Manufactures of England, and to see what Improvements may be therein made, and what Foreign Manufacturers may be Invited hither by good Encouragement.

14. They should have a general Power to Look into and Correct the Frauds committed in the goodness, weight, measures and fineness of our several Manufactures and Commodities sent to other Countries; in which a Nation that is defective does Lose its Credit and Reputation, and consequently its Trade abroad. [f. 188a]

15. They should, (in order to know the Balance of Trade) have Authority to inspect the Customs House Books; Nor can this business be well Managed without a power to administer an Oath, and to Send for Persons, Papers and Records.

16. Severe punishments must be Inflicted by the Act in case of bribery, or corruption in any Member of the Council, or in any of their Officers. …

Letter from ***John Cary*** *and others of Bristol* 16 December 1695[b]

To: Sr. Thomas Day and Major Yate [MPs for Bristol]

Having notice from different hands that the house of commons had voted a council or committee of trade, we think it a constitution which will tend very much to the interest of England if well settled in the beginning, and we cannot think this can be, except the trading cities are represented therein by able men such as they shall think fit to recommend, who are acquainted with their several interests; if it be made up of courtiers inexperienced in trade, 'twill become only a matter of charge to the nation; if of Londoners, they will endeavour to overrule things so as they shall best conduce to the bringing all trade to that great city, without respect to the other ports; now we recommend it to you as our judgment, that such a committee cannot be formed to the advantage of the trade of England in general so well, as when made up of persons sent up from all the parts thereof, as well the counties, as some particular trading cities and ports; we desire that you give us a true light of this affair, that when we better understand the meaning of it we may be more able to make you such proposals as we shall think best agreeable to the interest of this city; but if the members thereof are to be named out of hand by the king (as some this day advise) we desire you will please to take care that we may have the favour of recommending one or more to represent this city therein. …

Honoured Sirs, Your Honours' Most humble Servants (merchants of Bristol),

William Swimmer
Michael Pope
John Cary
William Andrews
George Mason, &c.

John Cary: *An Essay on the State of England, In Relation to its Trade, Its Poor, and its Taxes, For carrying on the present War against France*. Merchant in Bristol privately published. November, 1695[d]

… On the whole it appears to be the great Interest of *England* to advance its Manufactures, and this I humbly conceive may be done these several ways.

1. By providing Work-houses for the Poor, and making good Laws both to force and encourage them to work; but designing to speak larger to this before I close this Tract shall refer the Reader to it.

2. By discharging all Customs payable on them at their Exportation, and also on the Materials used in making them at their Importation; for as the one would encourage the Merchant to send more abroad, so the other would enable the Manufacturers to afford them cheaper at home, and 'tis strange that a Nation whose Wealth depends on Manufactures, and whose Interest it is to outdo all others (especially in the Woollen by underselling them in Foreign Markets), should load either with Taxes. …

3. By discouraging the Importation of Commodities already manufactured either from our own Plantations or other Places, such as clay'd and refined Sugars, wrought *Silks, Calicoes, Brandy, Glass, Earthen Ware, Irish Frizes, Tann'd Leather, Gloves, Lace*, &c. and instead thereof we should encourage bringing in the Materials whereof they are made, to be wrought up here; this may be done by Laws, and also by being in love with our Home Manufactures, and bringing their Wearing into Fashion.

4. By freeing the Manufactures from burthensome Excises, which do much discourage small Stocks, who are not able to carry on their Trades and make Provision for such great Payments. …

Taxes when laid on our Manufactures ought to be raised by such easy Methods as shall give least trouble to the Makers; Trade ought to be handled gently, and he that considers the Expenses of this Nation at Five Pounds *per Head* comes to Forty Millions, and the Lands of *England* but to Twelve, will imagine easier Methods may be found out to raise a greater Tax annually then we pay, without loading either Land or Trade as now we do, a Scheme whereof may be easily drawn up.

5. By prohibiting as much as may be the Exportation of things to the Plantations fit to be manufactured there till they are first done here. …

6. By defending the Merchants in their Trades who export the Manufactures, and making it as easy to them as may be; To this end good Convoys should be allowed, and good Cruisers maintain'd to preserve their ships, it being certain that what-ever is diminished out of the Merchants Stock doth so far disable him in Trade, and then consequently lessen his Exports and Imports; *Courts of Merchants* should be also erected for the speedy deciding all differences relating to Sea Affairs, which are better ended by those who understand them, than they are in *Westminster-Hall*, where all things are tried by the Nice Rules of Law, to whom after much Attendance and Expense they are often referred by the Judges, by this means they would see shore [sure] ends to their differences, and not be detained at home to attend long Issues; but there can be no general Rules given for these *Courts*,

which must be settled according as they best suit the convenience of every Trading City. …

The [Dutch] East-India Company is not settled on such a narrow Foundation as ours, which being limited to one City exclusive of all others sells their Commodities for greater Advance than any other Traders, whither we consider their Risk, or the time they are out of their Money, which should be the standing Rules in Trade; Nor can it be otherwise whilst they remain a Company, the Charges both abroad and at home being much more than when manag'd by private Stocks, besides the affected Grandeur in all, which must be paid by the Nation, whereon I take that Monopoly to be a Tax so far as it might be supply'd with them on cheaper Terms if the Trade were laid more open by a Regulation. …

I think it would be a consideration becoming the wisdom of the Nation if a standing Committee of Trade were appointed at the charge thereof, made up of Men both honest and discreet, and I doubt not such may be found, whose only business should be to consider the State thereof as to its Trade; to find out ways how it may be improved both in its Husbandry, Manufactures, and Navigation; to see how the Trade with Foreign Kingdoms grows more or less profitable to us; how and by what Methods we are outdone by others in the Trades we drive, or hindered from enlarging them; what is necessary to be prohibited both in Imports and Exports, and for how long time; to hear Complaints from our Factories settled in Foreign Kingdoms; to correspond with our Ministers abroad about Trade, and to represent all things rightly to the Government, with their advice what Courses are proper to be taken for its Encouragement; and generally to study by what Means and Methods the Trade of this Nation may be improved both abroad and at home; if this was well settled, the good Effects thereof would soon be seen; but then great care must be taken that these Places be not fill'd up with Courtiers, who know nothing of the Business, and so this excellent Constitution become only a Matter of Form and Expense; and herein I would propose for Pattern the Members of the Bank of *England*, who wisely foresaw if that project should fall into such Hands, 'twoud soon come to decay; therefore the first thing they did was by fundamental Rules to shut out all from having a share in the management, who had not a good Interest in its Profits or Losses, and next to choose out of that number such for their Officers, who being bred up in Business knew how to improve it to the best advantage: The *French* King found this Method very useful in the Management of his War, and his Opponents soon saw that Monsieur *Colbert's* Head did them more Mischief than an Army in the Field, because the latter only put in Execution abroad what he advised at home; and I think there is not more need of Policy in War than in Trade, the curious Fibres by which it moves are so fine and thin that if strained by injudicious Hands they are soon broken, and yet our Parliaments generally handle it very coarsely, and usually do more Hurt than Good when they meddle with it, not foreseeing the ill consequences of what they do will overbalance the Good they intend, and that the Methods they use will not answer their ends, the reason whereof is because the Conceptions they have of it are too gross for a thing so full of Spirit as Trade is; He that will but consider the *Irish* Prohibition Act, the Clogg put on *Distilling* by the Barley Act, and on Navigation by the Tunnage Act, will soon see they are in Truth Hindrances to what that Honourable Assembly intended by them, the Advancement of Land.

Charles D'avenant: *Select Dissertations on Colonies and Plantations. Dissertation II. On The Plantation Trade* [Originally Published 1698] Reprinted 1775 in *Select Dissertations on Colonies and Plantations. By Those Celebrated Authors, Sir Josiah Child, Charles D'Avenant, LL.D. and Mr. William Wood* [see later document]. 1698/1775[d]

… To preserve these Assemblies which are here proposed for the Northern Colonies, it will not only be necessary to take Care of the Manners of the People, but likewise to provide that the Assembly itself be not corrupted.

The ancient Custom in the mixed Governments formed in these Northern Countries (which will be the best Model for them to follow) was, that National Assemblies should be frequently called and sent Home, as soon as the Nation's Business was dispatched. The Wisdom of elder Times did never think it convenient, that one and the same Assembly should sit many Years brooding of Faction. …

What has been here said of great Empires, will, in some Proportion, hold in the Direction of less Matters, and in the Rule of our Northern Colonies; but, if the Governors now there, or to be sent thither, find the chief Magistrates and Officers in the Government, and the whole Mass of the People already corrupted, they will be but ill received and listened to, in their Endeavours to reform the general Vices and Immoralities of the Country; for Men, when they labour under any Disease, are fond of consulting Remedies; but it is not so with Governments sickly and distempered, it being then the Interest of a great many, that the Malady should be rather nourished, than any Cure hearkened after, and, at such a Season, they who would promote Ethics, in all Likelihood will meet but with a cold Reception: For, if in the respective Colonies wicked and ambitious Persons are got into Power, they will find their Account better in having Flattery promoted than in hearing Truth, since they would be undone, if the People should be wakened out of their present Lethargy; they will not desire to have Abuses corrected, as being their best Foundation; they will be afraid of wholesome Precepts and Examples, as being so many Reproaches to their Conduct; they will not dare to be brought to the Bar of right Sense and Reason, by which their Actings are never squared; they will not desire to have Morality advanced, as prejudicial so their Designs; they will dread Reformation of any Sort, as knowing they must be laid aside with Scorn, and return to their first Obscurity whenever things are capable of being mended. …

In forming that National Assembly which is here proposed for the better Government of the Northern Colonies, the Principal Matter to be recommended to the Common People is to elect Men of Fortune, Integrity, Public Spirit, and Virtue; and above all Things, to avoid those Pests of Human Kind, fine Talkers and busy intriguing Speakers, whom they anciently called Orators.

James Whiston: England's *State-Distempers, Trac'd from their Originals: With Proper Remedies and Means to make her Virtuous and Prosperous*.
1704[d]

Notwithstanding History has handed down many sad Examples of Flourishing Commonwealths, by their Corruptions brought to Destruction; and we even in our Memory have had sore Judgments inflicted upon us for our Crimes, yet 'tis deplorable to see how stupid we are grown, that we do not take warning, either at the Scourging of others, or our home Corrections, as if we were exempted from the Punishment due to the Vicious, and still obstinately refuse to put in Practice, Means that will effect our Deliverance, through Infinite Goodness still tendered to us; when we may yet by treading in Virtues Paths, not only become Happy our selves, but leave a Blessing to our Posterity, and give Examples to the rest of Mankind, how to be free from the Slavery that Vice produces; so no time (if we value our Wellbeings) ought to be neglected, for fear we afterwards should be denied like the Israelites access to Canaan, and Happiness at such time as we shall desire it.

Since Trade, the Converse with the World, is the Honest way to strengthen and enrich a Nation, and the great discourager of Idleness and Debauchery, &c. we being Situated by Nature, and of Geniuses proper for it, ought to make it our Study to manage it to its highest Capacity of Improvement, which if we would in earnest pursue, War its self would be such Advantage and Security to us, that we should not only be out of Danger from our Enemies, but command the Trade of the World; and on the contrary, if that be neglected, all the Miseries, attendants on Slavery and Poverty, that shall happen to the Nation, may be ascrib'd to our Improvidence and Inactivity. …

And whilst some Men in Authority are so Upright themselves that they scorn taking Bribes and the Selling of Places, yet tho' they do but tacitly permit these Crimes, they in effect are in conjunction with the Actors; for Connivance at Evil, is encouraging it, and they are like unjust Chyrurgions [doctors] that by powerful Medicaments force a surface Skin over the putrid

Sore, which masks the Corruption, till by its innate Corrosiveness it breaks out with violence, to the Destruction of the whole Body; so State Mischiefs let alone, unreproved and uncorrected, will gather Strength and Power to overturn, and unhinge the best constituted Government in the World. …

The Evils Springing from Sale of Places, Evil Disposals, and increase of needless Offices being so numerous, it shall suffice only to mention some of them, not questioning but every Reader will call to Remembrance some inconveniency and prejudice, that in his Transactions hath happened to him, by reason of this pernicious practice; without dispute, Places and Employs with Salaries, or Fees, were Originally given to Men as Rewards for their Labours, Fidelity, and ingenious Acquirements; but now they being disposed of, like vendible Commodities, to the highest Bidder, 'tis not reasonable to believe that Men will be satisfied with Labour and Salary only, for then, like Prodigal Fools, they part with their Money without Receiving an Equivalent, so as to reimburse them their purchase Money, they must exact beyond what is Legal, and thus by their evil Practices they make themselves great Gainers. …

In Order therefore to regulate all Abuses, it is humbly proposed, that every session of Parliament, by Lords and Commons, *A Council of State of Twenty One, Honest and Experienced Men be Chosen* by Balloting, not every of them to be Members of either House, or in any public Employ, or of Affinity one to the other, for there may likely be too great a parity, to be a grievance to the People.

That such a Council may be fully empower'd to Examine into the Actions practiced in every Office, or public Affair; and likewise to propose to Parliament, what Matters relating to the State, they shall think may conduce to the Nations Benefit, and to punish by suspension, or otherwise every Officer that shall act contrary to the exact Justice of their said Offices, wherein they shall be employ'd, and that no Officer may plead as an Excuse for his fault, that he was ignorant of the Duty required in his Office, every Officer upon his Admittance, *shall have given him full Instructions of the Duty of his Office*, which he shall be oblig'd to Read every Month, and no Man ought to be debarr'd access to this Council of State, who are to examine into all just Complaints, for if so, they must be Ignorant of Abuses, which ought to be corrected and amended. …

In order that the means of a complete Regulation may be made effectual, we propose to Consideration.

That the names of those that shall desire Public Places or Employs, by *Balloting*, shall be visibly fixed up (with the place of their Abode) in some convenient place, where the said Council shall meet, and in such other proper Public places as shall be appointed, and timely notice shall be given of the Election; so that whatsoever hath anything Material to Allege, either for, or against the Candidates, may be heard before the Election; that every person that recommends to this Council any one to be chosen into place of Service, be made responsible for his truth and good performance of his Duty, for 'twould be unjust in any Man to recommend one to be trusted by another, that he himself would not Credit.

That the said Council return three (amongst the Candidates to any Place or Office) that shall have the Majority by *Balloting* either to the Lord High Admiral, Lord Treasurer, or first Officer in managing such Office whereinto he would be Admitted; and such Officer, to choose one out of the three return'd by the said Council; by these Subministring Assistant's, examining and preparing matters fit for the Inspection and Discussion of Superiors, under whom such pretender is to Act, it will ease them of a great deal of trouble in Inquiries, being before hand accepted as fitting, and capable of such or such an Employment, and of good Reputation. …

By choosing all Officers in Trust by *Balloting* these, and many more Benefits will accrue, both to the public and to every private Man, the Advantages to the public are, *That the public Treasure will be managed according to direction of Parliament without Embezzlements, that Justice will be secured from being Bias'd, that the* Army *and* Navy *will be better Treated, and better paid, that the Trade of the Nation will be better managed and improved, &c.* And the Advantages to every private Man are, *That he shall have Justice done him without Partiality, or Dilatoriness, that he shall not be oppressed or exacted upon by those in Offices, either Civil or Military; that what he pays to Taxes, shall to the intent given, be laid out for the good of his Country, &c.* And the Reasons why such a Method will bring Benefits to the public as well as private, are plain, for if everyone in Office be Chose by *Balloting*, they may be concluded to be fitly Qualified for their Employments, because the Electors can have no private Interest to Choose any Man; no Reward being to be given to any by those Recommending, or those Chosen; the Honour and Satisfaction of serving their Country, being sufficient; but as to Pocket Expense, each Counsellor of State, may have Ten Shillings *per* Day to be Paid by the Treasury, for every Day he shall give attendance; and 'tis humbly supposed, that Her Majesty will out of Her Bounty (as She shall see what Benefits accrue to the Nation by their prudent and judicious Management) give them Encouragement, either by Advancing them to Honour with a particular distinction, or to higher Posts, or otherwise, as She in Her Wisdom shall think fit. But they should be oblig'd Three Days a Week to give Attendance, at least one third of the Council; and in case such a number shall not at such Times fit to dispatch Business, those absenting shall lye liable to be Fined by those attending, and the Fine forthwith to be paid to the Treasurer of *Greenwich Hospital*, for the Benefit of poor Seamen's Widows. …

And it may not be Foreign to the Antecedent Discourse to Remark, That the Author of these Papers did in the Year 1696, set forth in Print the

Grievances of Selling Offices; upon which, a Bill was brought into the *House of Commons*, in order to prevent their Sale for the future, which past that *House*; but because that Discourse was then more particularly levell'd at the Corruptions of the City of *London*, in Selling Offices to the highest Bidder; some of Her Magistrates, in conjunction with other favourers of a bad Cause, did in defence of their Mercenary disposal of Offices, use their utmost endeavours before the *House of Lords*, to quash the Bill with an useless Rider, and it being Introduced at the latter end of the Sessions of Parliament, the Bill did not pass, but was carried in the *Negative* by a very few Votes. But upon its Remembrance ought to be observed, that tho' the Author without any motive of Malice, or hopes of Reward, or Self-interest whatsoever, but purely for the good of his Country, did appear at the Bar of both *Houses*, and took the Field Armed, only with the Pebble from the Brook called *Truth*, to Combat the *Goliath* that insulted over his Native Country, yet the Opponents made use of all their strongest private Interest, and were very liberal of their Purses to Learned Mercenary Lawyers, who by florid Arguments, fine Rhetoric, shameful Falsities, and Sophistry endeavoured to set a Gloss upon their Briberies, Exactions and Injustice.

***James Whiston**: The Mismanagements In Trade Discovered: and Adapt[ed] Methods to Preserve, and Exceedingly Improve it. With an Appendix shewing the Decrease of Protestants in Europe.* 1704[d]

[develops further the committee idea, and defends the design]

The Proposal of a Committee for Trade.

[continues largely as in 1693 text] …

The Reason for choosing these Representatives by a *Balloting Box*, appears, first, in that it is humbly conceived, that neither Her Majesty nor the Parliament are, nor can be so proper Judges of the Ability of Persons fit to serve in this Committee, as Traders, most of the Members of that Honourable Body, being such whose Occasions never led them into any Deep and Intimate acquaintance with Affairs of this Nature.

Besides should they be otherways chosen, it might Create a Jealousy that they were not a free Committee; but under the Influence of that Power that chose them, which would discourage many Persons from making those discoveries which otherwise they would do, as well as obstruct the Committee (so wrong Chosen) from Acting and Reporting Impartially.

And it would be of unspeakable satisfaction to all sorts of Traders, to have the chief direction of their concerns, nay the very means of their Livelihood Committed to the prudent Manage and Assistance of such Persons, whom they themselves have approv'd of, and of whose Integrity and sufficiency they are fully convinced.

[Listing of committee in London, and its costs, as in 1693 and 1695 texts] …

That this Committee have Power to receive all Overtures, relating to Trade, and it shall be lawful and allowable for any Man to offer to such a Committee any thing in order to the preserving or advancing the Nations Welfare, and without delay Proposers or Opponents to Propositions shall be heard, and when their Discourses are ended, the Committee having by experience attained to a right understanding of Trade, and Mysteries that feed the Veins of the Nation, and being capable judiciously to make a true distinction of them, from those that will mock or exhaust the same, shall be the Moderators, and report their Opinions either to Her Majesty, Lord High Admiral, Treasurer, House of Parliament when sitting, or those, before whomsoever the matter in its Nature lies and they also to have full Liberty to grant Rewards suitable to Discoveries, or Services that shall be rendered by any Person out of the profit of such Discoveries, or otherwise, according as the Nature of such Services shall be; but as things are now managed, Thousands of Ingenious proposals have Died in the Embryo, for want of Encouragement of such a Committee, the Poor Trader, Navigator or Artist, that hath by experience found a good Consequence of an Experiment, has too few that he can have access to now, to encourage them to complete their well laid Schemes, but private Men, whose Avarice will defraud them, and make them that were the first Masters but very underlings in the Profit; but if such a Committee was Authorized, every Man would have opportunity to offer his well considered thoughts, and as they were found likely to be advantageous to the public, or not, would meet with due assistance, or Reasons, why not to be put in practice; for such a Committee set apart to consider of Trade, must from their constant converse about Trade, be the most able Judges; besides it would be their chief Study, encouraged by hopes of Advancement and suitable Rewards….

That every Proposal shall be Read three several Days before it be agreed unto, or rejected, that matters may be discussed with Mature Consideration; and that every Determination be by *Balloting*.

That the Committee shall have Power to choose their Officers by *Ballot* and to allow *Salaries* (as before mentioned) which they shall signify by Certificate to the Treasury, who shall be Authorized to pay the same, together with the Ten Shillings *per* Day to each Committee Man fitting, and such Rewards as cannot be taken out of some Proposals.

That the said Committee shall give Her Majesty, or Parliament, when sitting, or before any Board, before whom the Matter in its proper Nature shall lye, an Account from time to time of the growing Emoluments of Trade, and of the Obstructions of the general Improvement; that so from such Reports, those before whom the Matter shall lye, may be better Advised, how to make Orders or Laws, for the Advancement of the public Benefit.

That no Person be Chosen as a Member of this Committee, that holds any other Employment under, or receives any Rewards or Pensions from the Crown that herein mentioned.

Innumerable, and almost Infinite, are the Benefits which both Crown and Nation will Reap from such a Committee, and this Proposer is ready to impart to the said Committee several Proposals of considerable Importance (the Heads of which are hereafter annexed) [See proposals below] whereby he doubts not but they will be enabled to accomplish all the great designs here mentioned, too Voluminous for him particularly to Insert, or indeed to make intelligible without Mature debates before Persons experienced in such matters. …

The public Benefits and great End of this Committee of Trade will be this, That besides the Impoverishing of *France* by their care of securing our Navigation from the *French* Rapine, &c. they will likewise be able so far to improve our present Trade with the additional Advantages thereby gain'd to the Nation, that it shall more than pay the Charge of Her Majesties Navy to the easing of the Subject, and thereby cheering our Cause and edging our Swords. …

So the Committee of Trade ought to Command all Corporations, Societies and Persons experienced in every Merchandize, Mystery, and Mechanic Employs, on Penalty of being punish'd according to the several Laws for Neglect, to inspect into the due and regular making and ordering of all Commodities; and then by the Town's Mark, to signify to what degree and quality 'tis Manufactured and Ordered, and the Master Artist and Worker likewise to place his Mark, that unexperienced Chapmen may not be defrauded, and that by their imperfect making, packing, irregular Management, or making Commodities of less Value; the Value and Demand of our Manufactures, may not be slighted by our selves or other Nations, but to the discouragement of Art and Honest Manufacturing; the several Companies and Societies of Men, that either by Public or By-Laws, are to inspect the fraudulent practices in Trade of every Member, now, as if consenting to their exposing to Sale, Commodities not rightly made, undiscovered by any Mark distinguishing Degree of Quality; they neglect almost all manner of Inspection. …

There will also arise to the Nation by such a Council of State, and Committee of Trade; conjoined a further mighty Benefit and Prospect of Happiness, because such Men when Chosen into either Society, were Men of Abilities and Experience; and being by such Conjunction conversant with all the Public Affairs, will be the most proper Persons for Her Majesty to prefer to weighty Employs at home, and also to send Abroad about any Public Affair, because they will be capable as Ambassadors or Envoys to treat with Foreign Princes for the certain advantage of the Nation, which they must understand being well acquainted with our State Policy and Trade; *A Complete Statesman and Merchant is a Magazine of knowledge every way qualified to serve his Country*.

THE PROPOSALS

[various proposals follow; that using the council of trade for marine insurance is:] …

Proposals *of a* National Insurance *during the Present War, with the many and great Advantages thereof.* …

But we would here submit to Consideration, how a National Joint Insurance may be Established as well to the Security and great improvement of the Nation in general, as to the impoverishment of the Enemy, and to the Advantage of each Private Trader in particular.

It is proposed that by Act of Parliament, the Committee of Trade afore-mentioned, shall be empowered to set up a common Insurance under a National Security for Ships and Goods; The Act obliging every Merchants Ship to Insure Nine Tenths, but not the whole.

And towards the Encouragement of Merchants to Build great Ships and to fit them out with sufficient force of Guns and Men, that it be specified in the Act according to the number of Guns and Men, what *Premium per Cent.* shall be Paid to each part of the World; but providing an Obligation to Insure to any particular Parts, as *East-India* and *Guinea*, (where often, Ships lye till their Hulls are destroy'd) be found to the impediment of Trade by hindering Merchants to engage in that Branch of it, then that a convenient Toleration be given to such Traders.

That every Master of a Merchants Ship, under the Restriction of *Insuring*, shall be obliged to observe the times when the said *Committee* shall appoint them to depart from any *Port*, and not without absolute necessity by stress of Weather separate from his Convoy, and the proof to lie on the Masters side that so separated; but if upon the account of running for a Market, he shall leave his Convoy and comes to Damage, the Loss shall not be charged upon the Insurance, but the Proprietors must bear it, by reason, their Master of the Ship by such Separation, broke the Contract of the Policy; and if any Merchant Ship Arrive at his Port before his Convoy, he shall not break Bulk before the Arrival of his Convoy; but if the Convoy runs from the Merchants Ship, He to be brought to a speedy Trial, and the proof of the necessity of his Separation to be on his part.

This Public Insurance though under a National Security, to be paid out of the *Premiums* of the Insurance, cannot in reason be thought to be any hazard to the Nation's Public Treasure, by reason of Losses after such Insurances, as if there would be a Newer (not a more effectual) Contract and Obligation than is at present to defend and secure the Ships and Merchandizes; for now, when a private Loss happens, the Public is so insensible, as to think it self unconcerned; but if a Loss be entered in Capital Letters in the Nations Journal, *That* with due Punishment for default, will excite our Officers to their Duty and future Care, and by this Means, our Traffic and Navigation will increase, and those of the Enemy dwindle away, so that there can rarely happen any considerable loss from Enemies, whose Naval Power we still o're top, and shall then far more.

And the Merchant will be so far from having cause to complain of being compell'd to Insure that he will be hereby a Gainer; the *Premium* may be made very small, and the Government may afford to ease the Merchant, by taking off, or lessening the Customs on several Goods where it shall be found too heavy; and yet still, the Income of this Insurance after the Deductions made to Pay the Merchants Losses, will in all probability, together with the moderate Customs augmented by the increase of Trade, defray the whole Charge of the Royal Navy, &c. the Nation carry on the Universal Trade better than in time of Peace, because we shall keep our Enemies from it by daily disabling and reducing them. …

And this Proposal will be a farther Advantage and Strength to the Nation, because every Ship will pay for Insurance according to its Force; so Merchants will be prompted to Build their Ships larger, and consequently, will carry greater force to save paying Insurance, by which means, our Merchants Ships will be of such force, that from their own Strength they may defend themselves against Privateers; so the Nation by degrees will be so strong, that by our Civil Force at Sea, It will be able to cope with, if not o're power the Ships of War of other Nations.

3.2 Continuing discourse and developments

The ideas of Whiston and Davenant were attuned to the politics of their time. But the general concept of a council of trade became relevant in most of the major economic controversies of the next hundred years. The items reproduced here show the continuation and developments of the ideas in the works of Gee, Bennet, Cary, Ashley, Child, and Postlethwayt. Several were new editions of earlier works reprinted with additions and commentary by later writers, which appeared alongside new editions of Whiston and Davenant. This work culminated in the more practical blueprints by Mortimer and Weskett.

Joshua Gee: The Trade and Navigation of Great-Britain Considered, printed by Sam. Buckley, Amen-Corner. Gee's book was first published in 1729, then 1730, 1731 with new editions through to the seventh in 1767; Third edition of 1731 printed with a supplement after Gee's death, part of which is abstracted below. 3rd ed.1731[d]

THE PREFACE

… We are indeed very happy in the Constitution of our Legislature, who have made many excellent Laws for securing our Liberties and Properties, but we fear our Parliaments have sometimes have been missed when Matters relating to Trade have been brought under their Consideration; for as the two Houses consist of so great a Number of Noblemen and Gentlemen, whose Education has been quite different from the Study of such Improvements as might be made by Manufactures and Commerce, it is not to be expected that they should form a right Judgment therein without having Matters relating to Trade explained unto them. I was therefore willing to contribute my best Endeavours to set those Things in as clear a Light as I was capable, that the Members of both Houses might plainly see, the improving and encouraging our Manufactures, Commerce and Plantations, is improving and enlarging their own Estates; and as Commerce flourishes, Lands rise in Value; and as the Inhabitants of Towns and Cities increase, consequently the Consumption of Provisions, which is the Support of the Landed Interest; and doubtless as Gentlemen come to see, that in the turning the Wheel of Commerce they must have their Share of the Profits, they will soon find how necessary it will be for promoting their own Interest to put their Hands to so good a Work. …
[Main text goes through various improvements to trade that are needed, including Free Ports]

SUPPLEMENT

[added by printer to 1731 Third and subsequent editions]

The foregoing Treatise having met with so favourable a Reception, as that a *Third Edition* is desired; it hath been thought fit to add, by way of Supplement, some further Arguments and Observations made by the late Mr. *Gee* … ; and these Memoirs coming to hand since his decease are here communicated. …

Several ingenious Treatises have been written upon Trade by *Mun, Smith*, Sir *William Temple*, Sir *Josiah Child*, that which is entitled, *Britannia Languens*, &c. all which are well worth the Perusal of all Gentlemen who desire to inform themselves groundedly in that Subject. …

To conclude, if what has been said in the foregoing Papers shall convince Gentlemen that the Trade, and consequently the Wealth and Power of the Nation hath been for several Years past, and yet is in a declining State; but that if we will exert ourselves, we have still Resources in our Power to retrieve it; ‘tis to be hoped that all such who are in Stations which render them capable of performing so beneficial a Service to their Country, will apply their Thoughts, their Care, and their Interest to procure the speedy Execution of some at least of those valuable Improvements which have been humbly offered to their Consideration; always remembering that the Losing of Time often proves to be the Loss of Opportunities that can never be retrieved. And as I have observed, that at the Opening of every Parliament, four Grand Committees are always appointed, *viz.* for Religion, for Courts of Judicature, for Grievances, and for Trade, of which I have never known either to sit; if that Honourable House would be pleased to take these Matters into their Consideration, nothing seems to me to be a more efficacious Way to induce them to take the most proper Measures to repair our former Neglects, than the ordering the Committee for Trade to sit constantly to receive and examine such Proposals and Informations as might be offered to them, and to hear and judge of such Matters as might come to be debated before them; by which Means Gentlemen might come gradually to be so well instructed in Commercial Affairs, that they would not be so subject to be misled by the plausible Arguments of partial Men; and might grow up to be as it were a genuine Representative of Trade in the House of Commons: 'Tis true indeed, that a considerable Number of Merchants are always chosen into that House; but then it has been observed, that by the mutual Opposition of those who are engaged in different Interests, they rather puzzle than give light to the Argument in Debate; and I must confess, that I have usually found Gentlemen more ready to entertain right Notions of Commerce, as it respects the Advantage or Disadvantage of the Public, than most Men in Trade; few of whom, though otherwise knowing and well skill'd in their own Way, give themselves the Trouble to look further than what concerns their own particular Interest.

John Bennet: *The National Merchant: or, Discourses on Commerce and Colonies; being an Essay for Regulating and Improving the Trade and Plantations of Great Britain, by Uniting the National and Mercatorial Interests. To which are added, Some Considerations on providing for, and employing our useless and burdensome People. In several Letters to a Friend.* Printed for J. Walthoe, over-against the Royal Exchange, in Cornhill, and T. Osborn, in Gray's Inn. 1736[d]

To the Right Honourable Sir *Robert Walpole, &c.* and To the Honourable Sir *John Barnard, &c.*

Honoured Gentlemen,

These Letters having been published in separate Papers for every one's Consideration, are now collected together, and humbly submitted to Your joint Protection: For the Author is sensible, that the Public will receive little Benefit from them, unless approved and countenanced by *Those* who are able to carry their Design into Execution. …

THE NATIONAL MERCHANT.
Letter I. *Of the* Knowledge *of Trade, and its* Usefulness.
Sir,

Trade, with respect to the general Good of *Great Britain*, is a Science very extensive, and not to be rightly understood without a competent Share of Knowledge and Experience; for a Man should be able to comprehend all its Advantages and Disadvantages, to discover all its various Sources, and nicely to discern and distinguish those Branches which are more profitable, and tending to the public Benefit of the Nation, from those that are, or may be so, in a less eminent Degree. At present, most of the civilized Nations in the World, especially the *European*, seem to think their Safety, as well as Prosperity, greatly concerned in the Preservation and Enlargement of their Trade. Undoubtedly it is a Subject of the highest Importance; the Merchant, the Factor, the Tradesman, are not the only interested in it. Trade demands the Attention of the Ministry, the Parliament, and every Member of the Nation. …

ANOTHER Writer on Trade [probably refers to Davenant] has remarked, 'That we are indeed very happy in the Constitution of our Legislature, who have made many excellent Laws for securing our Liberties and Properties; but we fear our Parliaments have sometimes been misled, when Matters relating to Trade have been brought under their Consideration; for as the two Houses consist of so great a Number of Noblemen and Gentlemen, whose Educations have been quite different from the Study of such Improvements as might be made by Manufactures and Commerce, it is not to be expected, that they should form a right Judgment therein, without having Matters relating to Trade explained to them.'

MOST certainly it would be of singular Use and Benefit to the Public, if the Science of Trade were brought to some Certainty, by an established Set of Principles and Maxims, which might assist and direct our Conclusions. All other Arts and Sciences almost, by the Care and Industry of Men, have their Postulates, and fixed Principles methodized; why then should not the Science of Trade be cultivated and improved, and be brought to some Kind of Perfection? Is it not for want of some certain Rule to guide us, that private Interest has so often got the better of public Good in Deliberation of so much Concern and Importance, as are Matters of Trade and Commerce, upon which the Happiness and Glory of *Great Britain*, in the highest Degree, are known to depend?

I am SIR, *Your humble Servant*, The National Merchant. …

Letter XVIII. A Scheme *for* Regulating *the* Colonies, Trade, *and* Navigation *of* Great Britain, &c.

SCHEME

FIRST, That a *Court* be erected by Letters Patent of his most Sacred Majesty, revocable and subject to Modification or Alteration at Pleasure.

SECONDLY, that the said *Court* be named, *The Britannic Royal Court of Merchants*.

THIRDLY, that the said *Court* meet, at least, once every Week throughout the Year, on some certain Day and Hour, with a Power to adjourn, appoint Committees, &c.

FOURTHLY, that the *Place of Meeting* be in the **Royal Exchange**; and that the most commodious and most handsome Apartments there be fitted up for that Purpose.

FIFTHLY, That the said Court be composed of,

1. A President or Governor, to be nominated by his Majesty annually.
2. A Sub-Governor, to be elected by the Members themselves.
3. A Deputy-Governor, to be elected in the same Manner.
4. One or two Members to be appointed annually by the most noted *Towns in England for Trade and Manufactures*; and four by the City of *London*.
5. Four Members to be appointed by Scotland, and to be annually nominated by its Representatives in the *British* Parliament.
6. Four Members to be appointed by *Ireland*, to be nominated by the Representatives of that Nation.
7. Two Members to be appointed by every of our Plantations, to be nominated in like Manner.
8. One or two Members to be appointed by the Bank, and every great *Trading Company* in *London*, to be nominated annually by their General Courts.
9. His Majesty's *Lords Commissioners for Trade and Plantations* for the Time being, to be all Honorary Members, and have Right to be present at all Proceedings.

N.B. Every Member chosen to continue for one Year certain, and till superseded by the Nomination or Election of another to succeed him, which will prevent Interruptions and Disorders.

SIXTHLY, Any Twenty-one or more Members to make a Court, but the President (or Governor) or Sub or Deputy-Governor, to be one of the Number.

SEVENTHLY, the *Design* and *End* of the *Commission* to be, to inspect, hear and examine all Matters whatsoever relating to Manufactures, Trade, Navigation and Plantation, and to make Report thereof, and deliver their Judgments thereon in Writing, to his Majesty's *Board of Trade and Plantations*;

and to drawn up and offer for their Lordships Consideration, such Regulations and Improvements, as, from time to time, they shall conceive proper to be made; all to be submitted for their Lordships Approbation or Control; and by them to be laid before his Majesty in Council; or be recommended to *Parliamen*t; or otherwise, for them to do therein, as they shall find most expedient.

This is a very rough and short Sketch of the Scheme; but I suppose clear enough for every one to conceive a general Idea of it: Let us therefore examine its *Propriety* and *Usefulness*.

1. As to its Propriety.

[1] This *Court* is not proposed with a View to infringe or lessen, in the least, the Power of his Majesty's Board of Trade; it is rather to dignify and assist it; in a Word, to serve as a Grand Jury or Inquest, truly to represent Matters to it. And no doubt from such public and well digested Informations their Lordships will receive truer and clearer Lights, than they have yet been able to obtain from the partial Complaints or *disguised* Accounts, which often come from particular Persons. And from this Court their Lordships will have the best and freshest Advices of all Things touching their Commission, and thereby be the better and more certainly qualified to answer all its Ends.

2. As his Majesty will appoint the Governor or President, who, to be sure, will be always a Person of great Eminence, Worth, and Skill, and the Commission is only for *Probation*, and during Pleasure; it does not seem possible that any Disorders or Factious Designs should arise from it: On the contrary, it would tend to create a right and firm Good-Understanding between his Majesty and his Subjects, and engage them in all his Interests, as inseparable from their own. …

3. As to the several *Bodies* enumerated to appoint the Members of this Court, the Number to be sent by each, and the Manner of their Election or Appointment, they may be altered for the better, tho' I have not suggested these things without some Consideration.

4. As to the *Place for its Meeting*, I believe every one would rejoice to see the *Royal Exchange* once more inhabited; and such an Assembly, it may reasonably be presum'd, would give it a Splendor not yet thought of; which brings to my Mind Mr. *Addison's* Description of this no less useful than noble Edifice, and which I cannot omit, after pleasing myself, that Posterity in Crowds will make a full Stand at *George II, the Restorer of this Place, and the Mercantile Glory of the Nation.*—'There is no Place in the Town (says Mr. *Addison*) which I so much love to frequent, as the *Royal Exchange*. It gives me a secret Satisfaction, and in some measure gratifies my Vanity, as I am an *Englishman*, to see so rich an Assembly of Countrymen and Foreigners consulting together upon the private Business of Mankind, and making this Metropolis a kind of *Emporium* for the whole Earth. I must confess I look upon High Change to be a great Council, in which all considerable Nations

have their Representatives. Factors in the Trading World, are what Ambassadors are in the Politic[al] World; they negotiate Affairs, conclude Treaties, and maintain a good Correspondence between those wealthy Societies of Men that are divided from one another by Seas and Oceans, or live on the different Extremities of the Continent. I have often been pleased to hear Disputes adjusted between an Inhabitant of *Japan* and an Alderman of *London*, or to see a Subject of the *Great Mogul* entering into a League with one of the *Czar of Muscovy*. I am infinitely delighted in mixing with these several Ministers of Commerce, as they are distinguished by their different Walks and different Languages'. …

2. *As to the Usefulness of such a Court.*

… I shall therefore ask a few Questions … Whether *much* might not be done by it? And, whether there needs not *much* to be done?—For

ARE there no Stops and Hinderances to Industry and Honesty?

ARE there not many Livelyhoods, and great Estates obtained by what we may call *legal Dishonesty*, destructive of the *common Good*, and contrary to the true Nature and Reason of Things?

MIGHT not our Laws be reformed, digested, and regulated, in innumerable Instances, for the Ease and Benefit of our Colonies, Trade, and Navigation?

Is there nothing to be done for the Benefit of our Manufactures and Fisheries?

ARE no greater Rewards and Encouragements needful to revive the Loss of *Public Spirit*, and promote the National Welfare?

Is it not the prevailing Fashion at present for most Men to endeavour to *make their Fortunes*, as they call it, out of Trade and Traders, rather than by fairly trading themselves?

MIGHT not more Encouragement and Protection be given to honest Informers against public Abuses? And ought not such Information to be rendered honourable?

Are there not Abuses crept in, prejudicial to Trade, dishonourable to the Government, and of general ill Example?

HAVE we not lost many Branches of our Trade, and are we not losing others?

Is there nothing to be done to prevent Poverty, and relieve insolvent Debtors?

HAVE we not too many People depending on Divinity, Law and Physick? And might not many of these be provided for, and their too great Increase for the future be prevented?—I reverence the Professions, but speak against the Numbers of Professors, many of them fitter for other Employments.

ARE there not many unwarrantable, as well as useless Occupations?—And, if we take away the Labourer, honest Farmer, Manufacturer and Trader, what a happy People shall we be! *Many Mouths and no Bread*!

HAVE not *France* and *Muscovy*, of late, shewn us, by their prodigious Successes, the Benefits to be made by wise Regulations and new Institutions? …

I am, SIR, *Yours, &c.* The National Merchant.

John Cary: *A Discourse on Trade and Other Matters Relative to it*, Merchant of Bristol, 1745. First and brief edition 1712 [expands on Cary's 1695 *An Essay on the State of England*, reproduced above]. Second ed. 1745[d]

DEDICATION

THIS Second Edition, whereto I have added some sure and practicable Methods, for Discharging the Public Debts of the Nation, with most Ease to the People, I humbly Present to this Honourable House; If it may be Useful in your Debates, I shall think myself very Happy.

'TIS the Balance of our Trade, that supplies us with Bullion; if That be in our Favour, it brings it to us, if otherwise, it must be carried away.

THIS Balance is supported by our Manufactures, which keep our People at Work, and enable them to Maintain themselves by their own Labour, who must else stand still, and become a Charge on our Lands; and therefore I humbly conceive it to be our Interest, *First,* to encourage their being worn at Home, and then to give a Preference to such Things, as are Purchased for them Abroad, rather than to those, which are bought for Bullion; and if our Trade was well regulated, we shou'd soon become the Richest, and consequently the Greatest, People in *Europe.*

I have made some Essay at such Methods, as I doubt not, being Improved by your Wisdoms, and strengthened by your Authority, may Tend very much to the Effecting this great Work; And I humbly Offer the six Propositions following, as so many Fundamentals, necessary, for the better Ordering of our Trade, the Discharging of our public Debts, and Supporting the Credit of the Kingdom, whereby His Majesty will be rendered more Glorious, both at Home and Abroad.

THE First is, a Committee of Trade, made up of such Men as are well versed in the true Principles whereon it is Founded, and thereby enabled to make right Representations of such things, as shall be referred to them by the Parliament; who, Holding their Places, according as they are thought capable of performing them, will be careful to execute those Trusts with Judgment, Honour and Honesty.

THE Second is, a due Inspection into the Affairs of the Poor, and putting an End to that Pernicious Trade of Begging, …

THE Third is, the Keeping of our own Wool at home, and preventing the Wool of Ireland from being Transported any where else except to this Kingdom; …

THE Fourth is, the Encouraging the Linen-Manufacture of Ireland; …

THE Fifth is, the carrying on the Fishery, …

And for the better Encouraging the Trade of this Kingdom, I think it well worthy the Thoughts of a Parliament, whether a standing Committee, made up of Men well versed therein, should not be appointed; whose sole Business it should be to consider the State thereof, and to find out Ways to improve it; to see how the Trades we drive with Foreign Kingdoms, grow more or less profitable to us; how, and by what Means we are out-done by others in the Trades we drive, or hindered from enlarging them; what is necessary to be prohibited, both in our Exports and Imports, and for how long Time; to hear Complaints from our Factories Abroad, and to correspond with our Ministers there, in Affairs relating to our Trade, and to represent all Things rightly to the Government, with their Advice, what Courses are proper to be taken for its Encouragement; and generally to study by what means and Methods the Trade of this Kingdom may be improved, both abroad and at home.

If this was well settled, the good Effects thereof would soon be seen; but then, great Care must be taken, that these Places be not fill'd up with such who know nothing of the Business, and thereby this excellent Constitution become only a Matter of Form and Expense.

In the Management of Things of much less moment, we employ such who are supposed to understand what they undertake, and believe they cannot be carried on without them; whilst the general Trade of the Nation (which is the support of all) lies neglected, as if the Cogs that direct its Wheels did not need skill to keep them true: Trade requires as much Policy as Matters of State, and can never be kept in a regular Motion by Accident; when the Frame of our Trade is out of Order, we know not where to begin to mend it, for want of a set of experienced Builders, ready to receive Applications, and able to judge where the Defect lies.

Such a Committee as this, will soon appear to be of great Use and Service, both to the Parliament in framing Laws relating to Trade, and also to the Government in the Treaties they make with Foreign Nations.

As to the first, it hath sometimes been thought, that when that great and glorious Assembly hath meddled with Trade, they have left it worse than they found it; and the Reason is, because the Laws relating to Trade, require more time to look into their distant Consequences, than a Session will admit; whereof we have had many Instances. …

I mention these Things with great Submission to the Judgment of that glorious Assembly, the Wisdom and Strength of the Nation; to whom I only presume with all Humility to offer my Thoughts, that it would very much tend to the putting Matters of Trade into a true Light before them, if they were first referred to a Body of Men, well versed in the true Principles thereof, and able to see through the Sophistical Arguments of contending Parties, to be by them considered, and well digested, before they received the Sanction of a Law.

And as to foreign Treaties; I do not think our Trade hath been so much bettered by them as it might have been, for want of such a Committee; the

Representations made by private Merchants, (who generally differ according as their Interests clash with each other) tending rather to distract, than to inform the Government; which would not be, if their first Applications were made to an experienced Committee, who had Judgment enough to subtract out of them what was proper to be offer'd; by which means, our Demands might be rendered short and comprehensive.

John Ashley: *The Present State of the British and French Trade to Africa and America Consider'd and Compar'd; With some Propositions in Favour of the Trade of Great Britain.* BL: perhaps by Ashley Sabin. Printed for E. Comyns at the Royal Exchange. 1745[d]

The *English* Nation are very apt to have too mean an Opinion of the Trade and Navigation of other Nations, particularly the *French*, notwithstanding the Superiority they have *insensibly* gain'd over us in several Branches of Commerce since the Peace of Utrecht.

The Number of Prizes that have been taken from the *French*, and the frequent Arrivals of their numerous Fleets, have rouz'd and open'd the Eyes of many that would not be convinc'd before: And since our Indolence is at length awaken'd, our Security alarm'd, and every Breast seems to be fill'd with those Passions, which are enkindled by the Love of our Country, not only from this Instance, but also from many other Proofs, that the *French* have of late Years gain'd very great Advantages over us in Trade, surely no Opportunity ought to be lost to excite every *Briton* to the Exertion of all his Faculties to discover the Cause of such a surprizing Change, and to find out such Expedients as may enable us to bear up against the flourishing State and ambitious Views of the Common Disturbers of *Europe*.

In Order to answer so desirable an End, it will be necessary to search narrowly into the present State, Laws, Establishments, and Rules of Commerce, as well Foreign as Domestic, and to retrench what is superfluous and inconvenient, and to supply what is insufficient by prudent Regulations.

I shall therefore shew the wise Operations of the *French* in Support of their Commerce and Colonies, and the Consequences thereof; and shall then set forth what has been done by the *English* in Behalf of theirs; and, after touching upon the *French* Superiority and the Danger we are in from any further Delay in altering our Measures, I shall point out such Expedients as I humbly apprehend will put a Stop to the late rapid Increase of *French Trade, Wealth and Power*.

Lewis XIV, King of *France*,[17] 'having at all Times been sensible of what Importance it was to the Welfare of the State to favour and protect the

[17] Vide, The Arret for establishing a Council of Commerce, Done in the King's Council of State, his Majesty present, at *Versailles*, the 29th Day of June 1700. Sign'd *Phelypeaux* and seal'd.

Commerce of his People, as well within the Kingdom as out of it: And being, in the Year 1700, more dispos'd than ever to grant a particular Protection to Commerce to shew his Esteem for the good Merchants and Traders of his Kingdom; and to facilitate to them the Means of making Trade flourish *and extending* it: And judging that nothing could be more capable of producing this Effect than the forming a Council of Commerce, to be wholly attentive to the examining and promoting whatever may be most advantageous to Commerce, and, to the Manufactures of *France* in general', establish'd a Council accordingly, which consists of some of the principal[18] Officers of State, and twelve of the principal Merchants of the Kingdom, or such *who have been a long Time engag'd in Trade*; and of this Number two are of the Town of Paris, and each of the other ten of the Towns of *Rouen, Bordeaux, Lyons, Marseilles, Rochelle, Nantes, St. Malo, Lille, Bayonne,* and *Dunkirk*; and they are elected annually by the Corporation, Magistrates of the Town, and the trading Merchants in each of the said Towns, and every one of these Towns has a Chamber of Commerce within itself, which hear Representations concerning Abuses and Difficulties in Trade, and also Complaints concerning Impositions in Trade by Governors and other public Officers in their Plantations, which are represented by them to their respective Deputies elected as aforesaid.

In this Council of Commerce, which sits at least once in every Week at *Paris*, or where the Court resides, are discussed and examin'd all Propositions and Memorials which are sent to it, together with the Affairs and Difficulties which may arise concerning Commerce, as well by Land as by Sea, within the Kingdom and out of it, and concerning Fabrics and Manufactures.

Immediately upon the Establishment of this Council of Commerce, the Deputies[19] of the said Council apply'd diligently to the Duty of their Office, and the ensuing Year presented to the Royal Council no less than twenty Memorials concerning the Commerce of that Nation to their American Islands, Guinea, the Levant, Spain, England, Holland and the North; the raising nominally the Value of Coin, and the Effects that has upon Commerce; the granting Monopolies; the erecting of exclusive Companies; and other chief Points in Trade.

In these Memorials are contain'd several Propositions for Regulations and Remedies in Trade, many of which have since been thoroughly executed, *to the Honour of those Deputies, and to the great Advantage and Reputation of*

[18] Comptroller-General of the Finances, Secretary of State, and other particular Counsellors of State, who communicate what passes at this Council to the Royal Council, as Occasion may require.

[19] These Deputies have 10,000 Livres *per Annum* Salary, (which is near 500 l. Sterling) allow'd them by the respective Towns that elect them.

that Nation, as they have, since the Representations of the said Memorials to the Royal Council,[20] extended their Trade to the *Levant*, the *North, Africa, North America*, the *South-Seas*, and to the *East* and *West Indies*, even so far as to make more than double the Value in Sugar, Indigo, Ginger and Cotton in their *West-India* Island than what is now made by the *English*, who before that Time exceeded the *French* in this Branch of Trade abundantly. …

This Council of Trade is so wisely establish'd, that the Royal Council form their Resolutions, chiefly, upon the Informations they receive from it; and this Establishment seems more agreeable to the Intention of improving Commerce, as this Council is chiefly elected by Merchants, and other Persons experienced in Trade; and, besides, the Elected must be Men that have been a long Time engag'd in Commerce.

Josiah Child: *A New Discourse of Trade: Wherein are Recommended Several Weighty Points; Relating to Companies of merchants. The act of navigation, naturalization of strangers, and our woollen manufactures. The balance of trade, and nature of plantations; with their consequences, in relation to the kingdom, are seriously discussed. Methods for the employment and maintenance of the poor are proposed. The reduction of interest of money to 4 l. per cent. is recommended. And some proposals for erecting a court of merchants, for determining controversies relating to maritime affairs, and for a law for transferring of bills of debts, are humbly offered.* Printed by Robert and Andrew Foulis, Glasgow. Fifth ed.1751[d]

CHAP. III.

CONCERNING THE COMPANIES OF MERCHANTS.

It has for many years been a moot-case, whether any incorporating of merchants be for public good or not.

For my own part I am of opinion,

1. That for countries, with which his Majesty has no alliance, nor can have any by reason of their difference, or barbarity, or non-communication with the princes of Christendom, &c. where there is a necessity of maintaining forces and forts, (such as East-India and Guinea) companies of merchants are absolutely necessary.

2. It seems evident to me, that the greatest part of those two trades ought, for public good, to be managed by joint stock.

3. It is questionable to me, whether any other company of merchants are for public good or hurt.

[20] It is computed that before the Year 1720, there was no more than 30 Sail of Ships annually employ'd in the *American* Trade from *Bordeaux*, and that there are now 300 Sail employ'd *annually* in that Trade from that City only.

4. I conclude, however, that all restrictions of trade are nought, and consequently that no company whatsoever, whether they trade in a joint stock, or under regulation, can be for public good, except it may be easy for all, or any of his Majesty's subjects to be admitted into all or any of the said companies, at any time, for a very inconsiderable fine; and that if the fine exceed £20 including all charges of admission, it is too much, and that for these reasons. …

From whence may be inferred,

1. That restrained limited companies are not alone sufficient to preserve and increase a trade.

2. That limited companies, tho' established by act of parliament, may lose a trade.

3. That trade may be carried on to any part of Christendom, and increased without companies.

4. That we have declined more, at least have increased less, in those trades limited to companies, than in others, where all his Majesty's subjects have had equal freedom to trade.

The common objections against this easy admission of all his Majesty's subjects into companies or merchants, are;

Object. 1. If all persons may come into any company of merchants on such easy terms, then young gentlemen, shop-keepers, and divers others, will turn merchants, who thro' their own unskilfulness will pay dear for our native commodities here, and sell them cheap abroad; and also buy foreign commodities dear abroad, and sell them here for less than their cost, to the ruin of themselves, and destruction of trade.

I answer, first, Caveat Emptor, let particular men look to themselves, and so doubtless they will in those trades for which there are now companies, as well as they do in others for which there are no companies.

It is the care of law-makers first and principally to provide for the people in gross, not particulars; and if the consequence of so easy an admission should be to make our manufactures cheap abroad, and foreign commodities cheap here, as is alleged, our nation in general would have the advantage both ways.

Object. 2. If all should be admitted, &c. shop-keepers, being the retailers of the same commodities the company imports, would have so much the advantage of the merchant, that they would beat the merchant wholly out of the trade.

I answer, First, we see no such thing in Holland, nor in the open trades, viz. France, Spain, Portugal, Italy, and all our own plantations; neither can that well be; for to drive a retail trade to any purpose, requires a man's full stock, as well as his full attendance, and so does it to drive the trade of a merchant, and therefore few can find stock and time to attend both; from whence it follows, that of the many hundreds which in memory have turned merchants, very few continued long to follow both, but commonly after two or three years experience, betook themselves wholly to merchandizing, or returned to the sole exercise of their retail way; but whether they do, or do not, concerns not the nation in general, whose common interest is to buy cheap, whatever appellation the seller has, whether that of a mere merchant, gentleman, or a shop-keeper.

Object. 3. If shop-keepers and other unexperienced persons may turn merchants, &c. they will through ignorance neglect buying and sending out our native manufactures, and will send out our money, or bills of exchange, to buy foreign commodities, which is an apparent national loss.

I answer, That shop-keepers are, like all other men, led by their profit, and if it be for their advantage to send out manufactures, they will do it without forcing; and if it be for their profit to send over money or bills of exchange, they will do that, and so will merchants as soon and as much as they.

[three other objections follow, all also countered] ...

CHAP. VI.

CONCERNING A COURT MERCHANT.

I have conceived great hopes from the late most prudent and charitable institution of that judicature, for determination of differences touching houses burning by the late fire in London, that this kingdom will at length be blessed with a happy method, for the speedy, easy, and cheap deciding of differences between merchants, masters of ships, and seamen, &c. by some court or courts of merchants, like those which are established in most of the great cities and towns in France, Holland, and other places; the want of which in England, is, and has ever been, a great bar to the progress and grandeur of the trade of this kingdom; as for instance, if merchants happen to have differences with masters and owners of ships, upon charter-parties, or account beyond sea, &c. the suit is commonly first commenced in the admiralty court, where, after tedious attendance and vast expenses, probably just before the cause should come to determination, it is either removed into the delegates, where it may hang in suspense till the plaintiff and defendant have empty purses and grey heads, or else, because most contracts for maritime affairs, are made upon the land, (and most accidents happen in some rivers or harbours here, or beyond sea, and are not in Alto mari) the defendant brings his writ of prohibition, and removes the cause into his Majesty's court of king's bench, where after great expenses of time and money, it is well if we can make our own council, being common lawyers, understand on half of our case, we being amongst them as in a foreign country, our language strange to them, and theirs as strange to us. After all, no attestations of foreign notaries, nor even public instruments from beyond sea, being evidences at law, and the accounts depending, consisting perhaps of an hundred or more several articles, which are as so many issues at law, the cause must come into Chancery, where after many years tedious travels to Westminster, with black boxes and green bags, when the plaintiff and defendant have tired their bodies, distracted their minds and consumed their estates, the cause, if ever it be ended, is commonly by order of that court referred to merchants, ending miserably, where it might have had at first a happy issue if it had begun right.

From whence follows these national inconveniences.

1. It is a vast expense to the persons concerned.

2. It takes off men from following their callings to the public loss, as well as the particular damages of the party concerned, that time being lost to the nation which is spent in law-suits.

3. It makes men, after they have once attained indifferent estates, to leave trading, and for ease to turn country gentlemen, whereas great and experienced men are the only persons that must mate the Dutch in trade, if ever we do it.

4. It is in my opinion a great cause of the prodigality, idleness, and injustice of many of our masters of ships in England, and consequently a wonderful bar to the growth of our English navigation, who knowing that their owners cannot legally eject them, especially if the master have a part of the ship himself: but that remedy to the owners will be worse than the disease, which occasions masters to presume to do those things, and be guilty of such neglects as naturally they would not, if they stood more upon their good behaviour.

I could say much more of the damage this nation sustains by the want of a law-merchant, but that is so evident to all men's experience, that I shall not longer insist upon it, but proceed humbly to propose some particulars, which being duly considered, may peradventure by wiser heads be improved towards the cure of this evil, viz.

1. That it be enacted, that there shall be erected within the city of London, a standing court-merchant, to consist of twelve able merchants, such as shall be chosen by the livery men of the said city in their common hall, at the time and in the manner herein after limited and appointed.

2. That the said twelve persons so to be elected, or any three or more of them, fitting at the same time and place, and not otherwise, shall be accounted judiciary merchants, and authorized to hear and determine all differences and demands whatsoever, which have arisen, and are not otherwise determined, or may any ways arise between merchants, tradesmen, artificers, masters, and owners of ships, seamen, boatmen, and freighters of ships, or any other persons having relation to merchandizing, trade, or shipping, for or concerning any account or accounts of merchants, freight of ship, or goods, bill or bills of exchange, or bills of bottomry, or bumery, or for work done

upon, or materials delivered to the use of any ship, or money due for sale of goods, or any other thing relating to trade or shipping.

3. That any three or more of them, as the judges did lately at Clifford's-inn,[21] may proceed summarily to the hearing and determining of any such differences, and that their sentence shall be final, from which there shall be no appeal or review, otherwise than as is herein after-mentioned, nor any writ of error lie for the removal or reversal of the same.

4. That they, or any three of them may so issue out summons for convening all persons before them, as the judges did, &c.

5. That they be a court of record, as the judges were, &c.

6. That they take nothing for their own pains, directly or indirectly, but six-pence each for signing every final order in every cause, whereof the value of money to be paid does not exceed £10 and twelve pence for all causes not exceeding the value of £100 and only 2 s. each for all causes exceeding the value of £100.

The said fees to be due and payable only to such and so many of the said judiciary merchants as heard the said cause and causes, and signed the judgments or final decrees in them.

7. That for rewards to officers, the judiciary merchants do constitute a table of reasonable fees, to be confirmed by the two lord chief justices, and lord chief baron of the exchequer.

8. That in any case determined by a less number than seven of the said judiciary merchants, there may be an appeal to seven or more, as was lately practised in the afore-mentioned judicature.

9. That they may have power to levy executions upon estates real or personal, with such restrictions as the parliament shall please to appoint.

10. That the extent of the jurisdiction of the said court, shall be to all places within ten miles of London, or only to the late lines of communication, as the parliament shall think fit.

11. That the said judiciary merchants and their officers, before they exercise their authority, do take such oaths as the parliament shall please to appoint.

12. That if any of the judiciary merchants be prosecuted for exercising any of the powers that shall be committed to them, they may plead the general issue, and give the act in evidence for their defence.

13. That no writ or writs of supersedeas, certiorari, or injunction out of any of his majesty's courts, shall supersede, or stay execution, &c.

[21] This may refer to the Fire Court, set up to adjudicate disputes between ground landlords and leaseholders after the 1666 Fire. cf. P. Jones, *The Fire Court* (1966, 1970): I am grateful to Vanessa Harding for this suggestion.

14. The act to continue probationarily so long as the parliament shall think fit.

15. That the twelve judiciary merchants shall be chosen yearly by all the freemen, that are liverymen of London, in the Guild-hall of the said city, or by so many of them as shall be present at such election, upon every Monday yearly, next before the feast day of St. Michael, or as the parliament shall appoint, in manner following: every liveryman then present, to deliver unto any two such aldermen and four commissioners, as the lord mayor and court of aldermen for the time being, shall appoint to take the view or scrutiny of election, a paper containing the names of such twelve persons as he thinks best to be elected for the purposes aforesaid, setting his, the said elector's own name on the backside of the said paper; and the next Monday after in the said Guildhall, the said two aldermen, and four commoners, or so many of them as shall have taken the scrutiny, shall publicly declare unto the lord mayor, aldermen, and commoners then present, who are the twelve persons chosen by the majority of votes, and how many votes each of them had.

16. If it happen that any of the judiciary merchants die before the end of the year, or refuse to undertake the trust, it be lawful for the liverymen to choose another or others, toties quoties; and the lord mayor be enjoined to summon common halls to that purpose.

17. That every year six of the old judiciary merchants go off in course, and be incapable of being re-elected, and six new ones chosen in their stead, viz. all the twelve to be re-chosen, but only six of the old ones that had the most voices to hold the next year, although more of them should happen to be elected for the next year. …

Malachy Postlethwayt: *Great-Britain's True System: Wherein is clearly shewn, I. That an Increase of the PUBLIC DEBTS and TAXES must, in a few years, prove the Ruin of the Monied, the Trading, and the Landed interests. II. The Necessity of raising the SUPPLIES to carry on War, within the Year. III. That such a Design, however seemingly difficult, is very practicable: With a Sketch of various Schemes for that Purpose. IV. An EXPEDIENT which will support the public Credit, in all Times of public Distress and Danger. To which is prefixed An Introduction, relative to forming a NEW PLAN of BRITISH POLITICS, with Respect to our FOREIGN AFFAIRS, and our Connections on the Continent. Humbly Submitted to the Consideration of all GREAT MEN, IN and OUT of Power*, printed for A. Miller in the Strand; J. Whiston and B. White and W. Sandy in Fleet Street. 1757[d]

LETTER X.

Of Rivalship in Trade; *and more particularly with Relation to that which subsists between* Great Britain *and* France; *with its Application to the subject Matter of this Work.* …

The Council of Commerce was an admirable Establishment for the Benefit of Trade, and has been productive of unspeakable Advantages to *France*. This Council consisted of some of the principal Officers of State and others (as the Comptroller-General of the Finances, the Secretary of State, and other particular Counsellors of State) who communicate what passes at this Council, to the Royal Council, as Occasion may require. The Council of Commerce, consists also of twelve of the principal Merchants of the Kingdom, of such who have been long experienced in Trade: of this Number, two are of the Town of *Paris*, and each of the other ten, are of the Towns of *Rouen, Bordeaux, Lyons, Marseilles, Rochelle, Nantes, St. Malo, Lisle, Bayonne*, and *Dunkirk*; and they are elected annually by the Corporation and Magistrates of the several Towns, and the Trading-Merchants, in each of the said Towns, and every one of these Towns has a distinct CHAMBER OF COMMERCE,[22] within itself; which hears Representations concerning Abuses and Difficulties in Trade, and also Complaints relating to Impositions in Trade, made by the Governors, and other public Officers in the *French* Plantations, which are represented by them to their respective Deputies aforesaid, in Order to be laid properly before the Royal Council.

These Chambers meet twice a Week in one of the Rooms of the Town-House, in Order to confer together on the most proper Measures requisite to be taken, to make not only the Trade of their own Town flourish, but to increase both the inland and foreign Trade of the whole Kingdom; to which End, they receive all Informations and Proposals useful to any Branch of Traffic whatsoever; of all which they keep a Register, and of their Resolutions thereupon: of which they send Extracts every three Months, to their Deputies of the Royal Council, or in his Absence, directly to the Royal Council itself, on any Emergency.

These are most excellent Institutions, and have been productive of very great Prosperity to the whole Trade and Navigation of *France*: and such like Establishments, properly conducted, would certainly prove of inestimable Advantage to the Commerce of these Kingdoms, and contribute with other Measures, to enable us the better to support such a Rivalship against *France*, as will save our whole Trade from that Destruction, wherewith it is threatened. …

[22] The Establishment of a Royal Council at Paris, in the Year 1700, occasioned the setting up of *Chambers of Commerce* in the other chief Towns of the Kingdom, in the Year 1701. These Chambers of Commerce were instituted with an Intent to communicate to the respective Persons who attend the Royal Council, whatever they judged essential to the Interest of Trade and Navigation.

1. That these Regulations are grounded on the Representations of the Deputies of Commerce before taken Notice of, made from Time to Time, to the *Royal Council of State*; That those Deputies are Persons well skilled and experienced in Commerce, take due Pains to inform themselves in those Branches of Trade, concerning which they lay their Sentiments before the *Royal Council*.

2. That those Laws and Regulations, in general, are extremely minute, and appear to be derived from a very exact and circumstantial State of the Commerce, as carried on by the Merchants and Traders; which indicates that the Legislators in all Countries cannot be too fully and particularly informed of the various Methods and Arts, made Use of by Traders in the Prosecution of their respective Branches, the better to enable them so to adapt and conform their Laws to the Nature of peculiar Branches, that the national Prosperity cannot fail of being thereby promoted.

3. That the Fines and Penalties inflicted on Traders for violating those Laws, are very rigorous and severe; and that the *French* Nation are no less strict in the Execution of those Laws, than they are circumstantial and deliberate in the enacting them.

4. That the Laws of Trade in *France* should seem, suitable to the Nature of the Constitution of their Government, to be wisely accommodated to preserve the whole Trade of

their Island and other Colonies solely to themselves: in Order to render them absolutely subservient to the Prosperity of their Mother- Kingdom — And that, to this End, we find them, by their Laws, extremely vigilant to prevent all contraband Trade from being carried on with foreign Nations in their Colonies, they judging such Trade highly detrimental to the Interest of their Colonies, as well as of the Kingdom of *France* in general. …

Since the Establishment of the Chambers of Commerce in *France*, their Deputies thereby commissioned, and that also of the Royal Council of Trade, the *French* have increased in their Traffic to a Degree almost beyond our Belief. They have extended their Trade to the *Levant*, to *Africa*, to the *North*, to *North-America*, and the *South-Seas*, as well as to the *East* and *West-Indies*. In their *West-India* Islands they at present produce more than double the Value in Sugar, Indigo, Ginger, and Cotton, which is now made by the *English*, who, before that Time abundantly exceeded the *French* in this important Branch. …

LETTER XI.

Further Observations on Rivalship in Trade; with Regard to France *and other Nations.*

In the former Letter, we have taken a short View of some of the masterly Strokes of the *French* Policy, to raise their Trade and Navigation upon the Ruin of ours; and every impartial Man must discern the wide Difference there is between the *French* and the *British* System of commercial Policy; that the one is calculated, by the utmost Stretch of Wisdom and Sagacity, to raise the Commerce of our principal Competitor to its utmost Pitch of Splendor, and that the other is calculated to sink and depress the *British* Trade to its primitive Nothingness. …

That their Traders may labour under the less Difficulty and Discouragement in their private Affairs, and be the more at Ease and Tranquillity, to promote their own, as well as the public Prosperity, they have instituted *Court-Merchants*, for the short and inexpensive Decision, in a summary Way, of any Disputes which may arise in the Course of their trafficable Negotiations.

To give the *English* Reader the proper Idea of this Establishment, a Sketch of a genuine Edict for the Purpose may not be improper. That established by *Henry* II, King of *France*, concerning the *Court-Merchant* of the City of *Rouen*, runs as follows, viz.

> 'And, for the greater Ease and Advantage of the Merchants of our City of *Rouen*, and being desirous to gratify them in every Thing, as far as possible, that they may not be distracted, and drawn off from their Business and Affairs, by being obliged to give their Attendance at sundry Courts of Judicature, by Reason of Suits and Pleas occasioned by Litigations and Differences arising amongst them in their Traffic: Our Will and Pleasure is, that the Merchants of the said Town of *Rouen*, as well Natives as Foreigners, frequenting the said Place, shall every Year cause a Society of Merchants to meet in the Lodge of the Exchange, at what Time they think fit; out of which Society of Merchants they shall choose three Officers, *viz*. One *Prior* and two *Consuls*, who shall remain in Authority one Year; at the End of which new ones shall be chosen by the Plurality of Voices: which Election and Nomination being fully ended, the said *Prior* and *Consuls* shall have present Power in them to take Knowledge of, and to give Judgment between all Men, of what Estate, Quality, or Condition soever they be, of all Suits, Controversies, and Differences touching Matters Of Merchandizing, or buying and selling, in Manner as the Conservator of the Fair at *Lyons*, and the *Prior* and *Consuls* at *Toulouse* do, as well for Obligations, Bills of Debt, Receipts, Blanks, signed Bills of Exchange, Securities, Associations, and Partnerships of Merchants, either general or particular; Also of Assurances, Accompts, Transports and Contracts for Matters aforesaid, or any Thing belonging thereunto; with all full Power, and according to the Manner, Judgments, and Condemnations of the said Conservator of *Lyons*, and *Prior* and *Consuls* of *Toulouse,* &c. &c. Prohibiting all our judges to take Cognizance of any Matter or Plea thereunto belonging; which Command shall be noticed unto them, and unto all Persons to whom it shall appertain, by the first of our Officers or Sergeants that shall be required so to do, whom we enjoin to perform the fame accordingly, to the Intent that the EXTRAVAGANT CHARGE and EXPENSE that Merchants might otherwise be put to in prosecuting their Affairs before other Judges may be, by that Means, entirely avoided, &c. And in Regard to the Process in Writing, there shall another Record be

made, to the End that appeals may be ended in the SAME DAY, to avoid the PROLONGING OF SUITS, to the RUINING and CONSUMING OF THE MERCHANTS.'

The Domestic Consular Institutions in *France* are of the same Nature, and answer good Purposes to the Trading Interest: (1) As they also prevent tedious Litigations at Law between Traders; and (2) as they bring the *Consular-Courts* familiarly acquainted with the practical Affairs of *Commerce*, which renders their Decision easy to the Court, and no way Vexatious or expensive to the Subject. For, as their Determinations are all recorded in their Courts, from Time to Time; when any Point occurs that may not have been determined by their Predecessors, or which may be a new Case, they have, from an Index of References, immediate Recourse to Cases, as similar as they can find, and form a Judgment therefrom, in the Manner that our Courts of Law make their Decisions, from consulting a Similitude of Cases of their learned Predecessors, and weighing them consistently with the fundamental Principles of Law.

But these Consular-Courts, and *Courts-Merchants*, being restrained merely to Matters of Trade, they become more skilful, judicious, and expert, in this one Species of Cases, than any Court could possibly be, wherein they undertake the Decision of Cases of every Kind. Nor is this the only good national End that this domestic Institution answers to *France*; For this Court is a Kind of practical Seminary for the bringing up Persons for the Exercise of the Consular Jurisdictions in foreign Nations, with which *France* carries on their Commerce: And from amongst this Body, or from the Deputies of Commerce, (as taken Notice of in a former Letter) who make their Reports and present their Memorials to the Royal Council, their foreign Consuls are generally chosen. And as the Affairs of their Trade in foreign States and Empires are left to the Care of those Consuls, they think they cannot be too well qualified previously in Matters of Trade, before they are chosen for an Office of such Consequence: And indeed Persons cannot be presumed to acquit themselves with Honour and Credit in that Capacity abroad, unless they have been some how trained to it at home; for the Exercise of the foreign Consular Authority, is frequently in the Nature of a Judicial Power, when any Contests happen between the Subjects of one State and those of another in Relation to Affairs of Commerce: And by the prudent and wise Interposition of a judicious Consul, great Broils, and Heartburnings, have been happily reconciled; which might otherwise have terminated in Wars.

Thomas Mortimer: *The Elements of Commerce, Politics and Finances, in Three Treatises on those Important Subjects*, printed for S. Hooper, No. 25 Ludgate Hill, and others.[23] 1772[d]

INTRODUCTION.

The present and future grandeur, fame, riches, and happiness of Great Britain, depend so entirely on the ingenuity, industry, and commercial spirit of its inhabitants, and on the wisdom of its legislature, that no study seems more important than that which tends to convey proper ideas of those most essential subjects, COMMERCE, POLITICS, AND FINANCES …

On this foundation, and animated by this encouragement, the Editor of THE ELEMENTS OF COMMERCE, POLITICS, AND FINANCES [Mortimer], ventured to pursue the same plan; and having diligently collated, and accurately selected, from the best writers of every nation, the fundamental principles of the three subjects just recited, he had the honour to attend several of the young nobility and gentry of this kingdom, in the capacity of private tutor; inculcating, in the form of private lectures, a theoretical and practical knowledge of commerce, politics, and finances. A few years attention to this pleasing task naturally brought with it new improvements, drawn from observations on the practicable part of commerce; on the political state of Europe in general; and on the extension of public credit, and of the funded system in England and France during the late war; at the close of which, the Editor being appointed to an honourable station abroad,[24] had a favourable opportunity, in the course of five years residence, to collect and add to his plan, some modern improvements in the commercial and political departments, and also respecting the administration of the public revenues of different states on the continent.

On his return to England he again resumed the office of private preceptor on the same subjects, which profession he still continues; but observing, that the interesting state of public affairs, and the multitude of fashionable amusements, engrossed so much time in the polite world, that the requisite hours could very rarely be allotted for a regular course of study, he determined to revise and correct his manuscript, and to throw it into such a form, that from the press, it might find its way to the library, and prove an useful guide, to be consulted at leisure, by all those persons, who are, or may be hereafter, directly or indirectly, concerned in commercial, political, or revenue affairs. …

[23] Reference in this text to Mortimer's time as Vice Consul at Ostend (1764–6) are discussed at greater length in Bennett, *Local Business Voice* (2011) 98–100, which demonstrates how machinations between those who held offices and ministers resulted in excluding Mortimer, even though he had acted correctly in Ostend; this was doubtless an influence on his sense of grievance reflected in this text.

[24] British Vice-consul for the Austrian Netherlands.

The best writers on the maritime power and commerce of this country, concur with me in maintaining, that there is a manifest defect in the education of British youth of high rank and fortune, and of the sons of our opulent citizens, by neglecting to instruct them in this very important branch of knowledge, the commercial art. One, in particular, of great repute,[25] has gone so far as to assert, 'That though we are very happy in the constitution of our legislature, yet it is to be feared our parliaments have sometimes been misled, when matters relative to trade have been brought under their consideration'. He might have added, grossly imposed on by interested merchants and traders; which has been the occasion of such frequent amendments and repeals of acts of parliament respecting commerce.

Nor is this to be wondered at, when we consider the number of nobles, gentlemen, officers of the army and navy, lawyers, and spiritual lords, in parliament, whose education has been totally foreign from all enquiry into the means of improving arts, manufactures, and commerce; yet the education of a British senator ought to be so general as to include a competent knowledge of every subject that can possibly be brought into parliament. But above all, young gentlemen should not be permitted to make the tour of Europe, till they have acquired clear ideas of the firm principles of COMMERCE, POLITICS, and FINANCES. …

The errors of parliament may be rectified by amendments, or repeals of acts detrimental to commerce; but the effect of ignorance in commercial affairs becomes more fatal, when it gets possession of the administration of government in maritime and commercial states. The history of England furnishes too many instances of the imbecility of entire administrations in this respect; the very department peculiarly charged with the inspection and care of commercial affairs, having often been filled by gentlemen, who could not lay claim to the least mercantile knowledge. When this has been the case, and that (unhappily) the superior offices of state were likewise occupied by men equally deficient in this point, foreign powers have seldom failed to avail themselves of such junctures, to seduce our artificers, artists, and manufacturers; to violate treaties of commerce, by laying heavy duties and prohibitions on our merchandize entering their respective countries, contrary to express stipulations; and, by various other means, to annoy and disturb out merchants. But, when our Board of Trade and Plantations, which should be styled *the Council of Commerce*, has been composed of men versed in the commercial art, and capable of communicating all due information to the superior officers of state, Great Britain has ever rose superior to all other maritime powers, and has extended her commerce and national credit to the remotest parts of the globe. …

[25] Vid. Preface to Gee on *Trade and Navigation*, p. 13.

ON THE ADMINISTRATION OF COMMERCIAL AFFAIRS.

NOTWITHSTANDING the apparent prosperous state of the commerce of Great Britain, necessity obliges me to point out sundry defects in the conduct of our rulers, which strike at the root of some of its first principles, and make it nearly amount to a miracle, that we still hold the rank of the first commercial nation in Europe.

By stating generally, the regulations which are wanting to perfect the internal direction of an extensive commerce, we shall be enabled to deduce our capital errors, and to convey useful hints to government, not unaccompanied with some necessary reprehensions.

The celebrated French ministers, the DUKE OF SULLY, and Monsieur COLBERT: that most excellent French writer, MONTESQUIEU, and the latest British author we have on the subject, Sir JAMES STEUART, all agree in establishing this invariable maxim. …

BUT it will be asked, what minister will be so bold to introduce such innovations, however sensible he may be that they are for the public good? I readily answer, None, unless he's supported by the Crown, and has, at the same time, from his general good character, the confidence of the people. Such a statesman may bring about any beneficial revolution whatever; but he must first be made sensible of the truth of this maxim: 'That the present model of administration is by no means suited to the extensive commerce and vast territorial jurisdiction of Great Britain'. Such a plan might have done tolerably well in the days of ELIZABETH, when the sun of commerce was just risen; but in its present meridian splendour, we want a good board of trade, or more properly speaking, an intelligent COUNCIL OF COMMERCE in almost every county in England, and in every province of our American colonies. …

The wisest commercial states, both monarchical and republican, set him the example. France, Holland, Germany, Denmark, and some others of less note, have their chambers of commerce.[26]

SIR JOSIAH CHILD observes concerning the Dutch, 'That they have, in their greatest councils of state and war, trading merchants that have lived abroad in most parts of the world, who have not only the critical knowledge, but the practical experience of commerce, by whom laws and orders are

[26] It is true, we have a board of trade, but it takes no immediate cognizance of the commerce of the kingdom; so that it may properly be considered, as indeed it is commonly called, a Plantation Office; and that almost merely too for political use. In France there is an active and well informed council of commerce. In Holland the principal merchants have a great share in the government of the country. Here we appear to be all adrift in commercial matters, without pilot or compass, driving before the wind of accident, amidst quick-sands and rocks; so that if we long escape shipwreck, we shall have wonderful good fortune.

contrived, and peace with foreign princes projected, to the great advantage of their trade.'

And CARY, a more modern writer, recommends it to the consideration of parliament to appoint standing committees of trade, composed of men well versed therein, whose sole business it should be to consider the state thereof, and to find out ways to improve it. He adds, 'Great care must be taken, that these committees be not filled up with such who know nothing of the business, and thereby this excellent institution become only a matter of form and expense. In the management of things of much less moment, we employ such who are supposed to understand what they undertake. Trade requires as much policy as matters of state, and can never be kept in a regular motion by accident; when the frame of it is out of order, we know not where to begin to mend it, for want of a set of experienced builders, ready to receive applications, and able to judge where the defect lies.'
Considerations on the Commerce, Policy, and Circumstances of this Kingdom.

If only one council of commerce in this kingdom, and another in each of the American colonies, had subsisted on this plan, we should never have heard of the stamp act, nor of some other acts of parliament still unrepealed, which injured commerce to a very high degree, the instant they were made. Such, amongst others, was the act of the ninth and tenth of William III for the more effectual preventing the importation of bone lace, which caused a prohibition of British woollen cloths (our staple manufacture) in Flanders, and obliged the same parliament, in the next session, to repeal the act conditionally, viz. three months after the prohibition on our cloths should be taken off. This was accordingly done; but, by a subsequent act, the duties on those laces, as I have before remarked, were made so high, that, by way of reprisal, duties were laid on our woollen cloths and stuffs, by the Flemish government, which destroyed above two thirds of this valuable branch of commerce.

In short, as Cary says, 'Parliaments have very often made commercial matters worse than they found them'; one reason of which is, that the regulations of trade require more time to look into the distant consequences, than one or two sessions: another is, that the study of the theory of commerce is not made a part of the education of youth, who are likely to become British senators. The late worthy Sir JOHN BERNARD used frequently to complain of this in the House of Commons, and to tell our fine gentlemen, that they did not know so much of the matter before them (when the subject was commercial) as school-boys and young apprentices. Without any reflection on the members of the present Board of Trade in particular, I must add, that the same might be said of the lists of the members of it for twenty years back, or more; they ever were, and they now are, gentlemen promoted to those places by court interest, but whose education has been as foreign from all ideas of commerce, as from the Mahometan religion.

The expediency of instituting councils of commerce, needs no further proof; it rests on the best authorities, ancient and modern.

The good effects of such an establishment may be deduced from the various duties of their office, which I shall briefly point out; and from hence likewise shall discover the defectiveness of the present system of government, with respect to commerce.

1. It would be the business of the chambers of commerce, in the counties of this kingdom, to make reports, every three months at least, of the state of agriculture, population and manufactures, to the grand council of commerce at London. The members of these provincial chambers being elected annually, by the freemen of corporate towns, from the principal traders refilling in the respective counties, it would be their interest, as well as their duty, to mark any decline in agriculture, any symptoms of depopulation, any discouragement of manufactures, or any impediment to the general circulation of inland trade. No engrossing of farms; no razing of cottages; no monopolizing of provisions; no oppressions of the poor, working manufacturer, by low wages; in a country where high wages are the proof of riches and commercial prosperity; no combinations of workmen to prescribe illegal conditions to their masters; no frauds in the quantity or quality of manufactures could remain long unconcealed or un-redressed, if such institutions were general; the elections impartial; and the helm of government steered by an honest, discerning statesman.

2. In sea-port towns, these commercial juries would report any visible diminution in the number and tonnage of shipping usually trading to or from each respective port; they would watch over the increase or decrease of those useful subjects, British seamen; they would remonstrate on exorbitant port duties, which frequently occasion a diminution of foreign navigation to our ports; they would petition for redress of the tedious, perplexing mode of paying the Custom-House duties; they would notice when any merchandize usually exported to the benefit of the commerce of realm ceased, and point out the method of restoring it; they would present, as great grievances, all impolitic importations of articles of costly, effeminate luxury, from countries which do not consume any of our native products, or manufactures; they would effectually destroy smuggling, by their vigilance and activity in discovering the clandestine importers, the venders, and the fraudulent purchasers (a most easy talk, if the Treasury would part with only trifling sums, in comparison of what is idly lavished on worse accounts; to encourage the suppression of all contraband trade); in fine, they would make a proper representation to government of the oppressive excises on materials used in the mechanic arts and manufactures, which necessarily enhance their value at foreign markets.

3. They would frame a concise, complete mercantile code, or body of commercial laws, reforming those statutes which were well adapted to the

infant state of our trade, but which are by no means suited to the present extensive commerce of Great Britain. This code once digested, approved by the majority of the chambers of commerce in the kingdom, ratified by the grand council at London, and legalised by act of parliament, would enable the different chambers to exercise a judicial authority, and to terminate mercantile disputes in a summary way, as is practised in France, and other countries.[27]

4. They would most assuredly devise some means of employing the poor; of obliging the robust to follow a life of honest industry; and of punishing the idle and dissolute, in the first instance, to prevent their becoming criminals, which should be the first object of the police.[28]

5. They would alter the mode of satisfaction to be given by insolvent debtors to their creditors; they would not be so absurd as to shut up in prisons, at the will of the latter, a number of useful, laborious seamen, mechanics, manufacturers and tradesmen; most of whom, if not at all, might be employed in their several branches, partly for the benefit of their creditors, and partly for the support of their families, if a law were enacted to punish the wilful idleness of insolvent debtors; and to execute them as felons, if they ran away from their usual place of residence and employment, before they had paid a reasonable composition for their debts, in proper portions, from the fruits of their industry, or ingenuity.

The confinement of vast numbers of useful hands in prisons for debt, is one of the most inhuman, unmanly and impolitic steps, that ever disgraced a people asserting a spirit of liberty. …

6. They would most strenuously recommend an alteration in our criminal laws, more favourable to humanity and to the interests of a trading nation than those now subsisting, which are a disgrace to the British constitution and government. …

7. They would advise a law to be enacted, without loss of time, for the establishment of marine societies, in every capital town and sea-port in England, not only for the reception of boys, who after having been idle, profligate, abandoned wretches, take to the sea-faring life as their last resource; but for maintaining and educating a certain number from early youth for the sea-service; as well knowing that the strength of the British empire depends on having a sufficient quantity of able seamen always ready to man our fleets, and to navigate merchant-ships, without having recourse to

[27] In this opinion of a commercial or court merchant in every county, for deciding the ordinary contests in trade, without carrying them into the common law-courts, I am supported by the authorities of Child, Cary, Mun, Postlethwayt, and others, who all declare it to be an establishment much wanted in England.

[28] On this subject see Mr. Young's account of the industry-houses at Ipswich; and Cary's account of the management of the poor at Bristol.

that savage custom of pressing seamen; a custom which renders us unworthy of the character of a civilized nation.

And in order that the boys might join practice to theory, they would recommend the encouragement of fisheries on our coasts to the utmost extent.

8. To these chambers of commerce should be referred all memorials of our ministers and consuls abroad, concerning the decline of any branches of commerce carried on from the respective ports in the district of each chamber, to any foreign countries where such officers reside.

I will illustrate this proposition by an example. In 1764, while I had the honour to serve the King in the character of Vice-consul for Flanders, the Flemish government suddenly laid a very high additional duty on rock salt, which greatly affected the navigation and commerce of the people of Liverpool to the port of Ostend. If a chamber of commerce had at this time subsisted at Liverpool, the memorial I sent home upon that subject should have been transmitted directly to such chamber of commerce, instead of going to the Secretary of State's office, where its fate was to be neglected, in the multiplicity of more important business, or to be sent to our present flimsy board of trade, to be laid on the shelf.[29]

John Weskett: PLAN OF THE CHAMBER OF COMMERCE, (In the Building late the King's Arms Tavern, Cornhill) or OFFICE FOR CONSULTATION, OPINION AND ADVICE, INFORMATION AND ASSISTANCE, IN ALL COMMERCIAL, INSURANCE, AND MARITIME AFFAIRS, AND MATTERS OF TRADE in general. Sold by Richardson and Urquhart, Royal Exchange etc., London.[30] 1782[e]

PLAN OF THE CHAMBER OF COMMERCE.

It is every man's duty to be as useful as his talents and applications will admit of.—Every step that is made in the progress of knowledge, whether it proceed from reading, observation, or experience, ought to be applied to the affairs and transactions of life; for this, in truth, is the only proper use of all kinds of study.

Amongst those multifarious transactions, there are none which give rise to questions more difficult in themselves, more entangled with numerous and complex relations, or more perplexed with an endless diversity of circumstances, than those which relate to commercial affairs.—There are no ques-

[29] The Danish consul at Ostend is ordered, by his instructions, to correspond with the grand chamber of commerce at Copenhagen upon such occasions.

[30] Weskett's Plan seems to have been copied in London in 1817 by Bignold and Clarke's 'Equitable Trade Society and Chamber of Commerce' which probably did not become established. See Chapter 6.1.

tions which require so much personal knowledge of the subject to which they relate; nor any in which the opposition of particular interests so much incites to misunderstandings and disputes.

Whoever reflects upon the confused and precarious situation of the affairs of this country (whose very existence depends upon the preservation and prosperity of its commerce) and contemplates the manifold calamities of the times, both public and private, as reciprocally affecting each other, will be little inclined to discountenance such propositions, even of the meanest individual, as have honest foundations, to fair purposes, and a tendency to promote the public advantage, by *enlarging the means of private utility*.

Every aid to facilitate the transactions,—to obviate or diminish the perplexities,—to alleviate the vexations,—and to settle, compose, or moderate the differences, which, in various instances, and an infinity of shapes, are hourly occurring in the course of mercantile concerns (especially during such a complicated war as this nation is unhappily engaged in) is unquestionably entitled to some degree of attention from men of prudence; and can hardly be liable to the disapprobation of men of discernment and candour.

Several judicious and well-informed British merchants have, at different times, made public remonstrances against abuses; and ventured to raise their voice from amidst the multitude, to combat prejudice, and propose eligible remedies to remove, or lessen inconveniencies.—It is, nevertheless, surprising, and much to be lamented, that we remain, hitherto, entirely destitute of those *commercial establishments*, which have been found by long experience, in every other trading country, to be of the greatest national and private benefit; and which are usually sanctioned by legislative authority.

To the wisdom and policy of those establishments, particularly in *France* (in most of her trading places, as well as in all her chief cities and ports) and the special care that is taken by them, to remove all manner of impediments that might obstruct the progress and improvement of commerce, and embarrass the transactions, or affect the rights of individuals, is undeniably owing, in a very great degree, the present extent of the trade, and increase of the naval power of that nation:—and, to the *total neglect* of them in this, where they are so peculiarly applicable, may be justly ascribed no little share of the decline of our national grandeur and prosperity, and many public as well as innumerable private disasters.

The advantages are unspeakable which continually flow in France, Spain, Holland, Sweden, Denmark, &c. from their *councils* of *commerce*; their several and respective *chambers* of *commerce*; *chambers, courts*, and *commissioners* of *assurance*; *chambers* for *maritime affairs*, and *maritime law*; *judges-consuls*; and *merchant-courts*;—all of which, under these different appellations, have very similar objects.

They in general consist of *merchants* and *traders* of the first confederation, judgment, and experience, chosen annually; who meet weekly, or frequently, not only to confer on, and communicate to government, the properest measures of promoting and regulating both the foreign and inland trade of their own towns, and of the whole kingdom; and to receive all informations and proposals useful to every branch of traffic; but also, a *select number* of them, to take *speedy* cognizance of, to *hear, compose, determine*, and register *all causes* and *controversies*, arising *in matters of trade, commerce, navigation*, and *insurance*, in the most easy, summary, and inexpensive manner:—and being always on the spot, and daily conversant with the *practice* of trade; and, in their judicial capacity, restrained wholly to these matters; they necessarily become well acquainted with all *commercial doctrines, laws,* and *usages*, and more skilful and expert in *deciding* thereupon, than any court could possibly be, wherein they undertake cases of every kind.—Moreover, the parties are expressly prohibited from carrying their disputes to the ordinary courts of justice. Thus their differences are amicably and speedily settled; and a multitude of broils and inconveniencies avoided. —Nevertheless, in cases of great importance and necessity, an *appeal* lies, in some countries, to the superior courts of judicature; but, in most others, to a court of delegates, composed of a mixture of persons from some of the different orders following, *viz.* Merchants, well versed in foreign commerce and navigation; provost of merchants; magistrates, who are or have been merchants; sea-captains; college of burgomasters, who have been traders; sheriffs; college of trade; lieutenant general of police; counsellors of state; civilians; and sometimes common lawyers.

Similar establishments might, and certainty would prove highly beneficial in this kingdom; not only according to the opinion of some of the most judicious merchants[31] this country ever had; but according to the sentiments of our ablest statesmen, who have well understood the nature of trade, and have been desirous to remove all clogs and obstructions to it's prosperity;—and particularly that most baneful of all obstructions, the too frequent necessity of resorting to courts of law; *no other authoritative mode or means of justice whatever existing*.

In default of all such wise regulations here, it has been conceived that an institution, adapted to the circumstances of private commercial affairs, might be formed, established and conducted, in London, by, and under the direction of a man of competent abilities and experience, so as to answer several of the beneficial purposes of the chambers abroad; and be calculated to render many other needful services, to a variety of persons, according to their respective situations, concerns, and occurrences.

[31] Sir Josiah Child, Mr. Carey, &c.

In this view, it is deemed expedient to comprehend some particular objects of the foreign chambers, with sundry other matters concerning trade, in the following.

DELINEATION of the PLAN.

I. All persons who are engaged, or have any interest, concern, or connection, in COMMERCIAL, INSURANCE, or MARITIME AFFAIRS, or any other matter of TRADE, or in any transaction relating thereto,—may have a constant, or an occasional recourse to this office, personally or otherwise, for the several and respective purposes herein denoted;—in like manner as they might have to a confidential friend, agent, or correspondent.

II. Immediate, and continual opportunities are given for *verbal* CONSULTATION,

or conference.—The advantages of cool and deliberate discussion, with a judicious and impartial person, versed in the subject matter of it, and *professedly attentive* to it, are undeniably great to all persons; and to the inexperienced, or injudicious, they often prove inestimable.—No man, however large his experience or sagacity, particularly in what regards his own affairs, can be at all times competent, singly and alone, to direct all circumstances to the best effect; or sufficiently guarded, in the hour of perplexity, contrariety, or doubt, to foresee or obviate the ill consequences which are liable to ensue, sometimes from very sudden, and very small causes. *Nemo omnibus horis sapit*, is a maxim of just and universal application; but especially in matters of *trade*.—Besides the untoward nature and circumstances of many affairs in themselves, the *passions, humours, prejudices, ignorance,* or *sordidness* of the persons they must be transacted with, often puzzle the clearest head, and confound the most solid understanding: not to say, in what respects every man needs, occasionally at least, to be aware of some of those frailties in himself.—How many crude ideas, misconceptions, errors, dilemmas, might be instantly removed or elucidated,—how many disputes, litigations, embarrassments, enmities, might be early prevented, or more speedily stifled and ended,—by the opportunity of immediate and frequent consultation, with a proper person, seriously interesting himself to this effect. A single hint, or suggestion of a *right* measure, on the spot, or spur of the occasion, is sometimes of the utmost importance; and may be instrumental to avert a series of calamity and distress, at least of trouble and vexation, consequent of a *wrong* one.—*America* has been lost, through the error of a moment, in September 1775![32]—When men consult their acquaintance (whose attention is, perhaps, sufficiently engrossed by their own affairs) or those who are connected in the like concerns with themselves, the sentiments are often

[32] When the agents of the Congress were told, *'No answer would be given'* to their petition [Olive Branch petition].

superficial, partial, or too precipitate, if not dictated by interested or personal motives; and therefore fallacious, dangerous, or little to be relied on.—The life of the merchant, or trader, is a *conversable* one; and, from the variety, and quick progression of circumstances that daily occur to him, he stands continually in need of *convenient, liberal*, and *reiterated* communications.

III. From consultation, OPINION, ADVICE, and INFORMATION naturally result.—They may be obtained at this Office, either verbally (as intimated by the preceding article)—or *in Writing*, on *Cases stated* for that purpose; particularly respecting the *doctrines, laws, usages and practice, in commercial, insurance, and maritime affairs*, and all transactions of *trade* in general.—An assiduous study of these laws and usages has always accompanied the actual practice and experience of the conductor of this chamber; for he deemed it his duty to be acquainted with those with which he was immediately concerned; seeing it is to *them* that every one pretends, in argument at least, to appeal.—Without derogating, therefore, in the smallest degree, from the consequence and utility of the gentlemen of the law, as to the very extensive scale of their own professional knowledge and practice; or their indispensably necessary *agency* in the *courts*, on many occasions; it is certain that, in matters of *commerce* and *navigation*, their information must always be derived from traders themselves; whose affairs are, in general, regulated and *decided* by a law peculiar to them, called the LEX MERCATORIA, or *custom of merchants*; which often obtains even in occurrences of domestic trade.—In no other matters of law is it here meant to interfere: but, with respect to *commercial* laws and usages, several of the aforementioned gentlemen, themselves, may undoubtedly acquire very material information and assistance from this office, in many complicated mercantile and insurance cases that may fall under their care and management.

IV. The ASSISTANCE proposed to be given, is such *personal* and *actual negotiation, mediation, solicitation*,—such *management, superintendence, promotion*, or *execution* of any particular affair or matter, as falls within the scope of this institution, and may be performed by, or under the conduct of the director of it.—It being impossible to specify all the occasions on which such auxiliary services may, *at different times*, be required and rendered (for it would be an affront to common understanding to suppose them *all* to occur at the *same* time) it may suffice to give a general idea of them, in the following instances, *viz*.

1. In the applying to, attending on, or transacting with, any *private persons*;—any *public boards, companies, committees*, or *meetings*;—*arbitrators* (see Art. V.)—*commissioners, creditors, executors, &c.* on bankruptcies, insolvencies, and deaths (see Art. VII.)—*courts of judicature* (whether admiralty, equity, or common-law; in cases when no amicable accommodation, or medi-

ation, can have effect) ;— the *Ministers*;—either house *of parliament*, at committees or at the bar thereof (having often acted in like manner, particularly in behalf of one of our incorporated commercial companies).

2. In the forming and drawing,—or in the inspecting, perusing, correcting and approving,—or preparing minutes or instructions for, *memorials, petitions, remonstrances, appeals, proposals, plans*, and the like, to public boards, companies, or private persons,—to the several departments of administration, the crown, or parliament:—as also *agreements, contracts, securities*; occasional *letters*, or correspondence, and *translations*, in English, French, Italian, or Latin;—particular *accounts*, disputed or depending;—*cases*, with reasons and instructions, to be communicated to attorneys or solicitors, or laid before counsel, or arbitrators;—the regulation of losses, averages, returns, &c. on *policies of insurance* (see Art. VI.)—and all other papers or documents of a *mercantile* or *maritime* nature; with *abstracts* and *abbreviations* of, or *extracts* from them, suitable to the intent.

It is thought proper to point out, more distinctly, the matters contained in the subsequent articles, V. VI. and VII.

If an agent, mediator, &c. *professedly* acting in such capacity, be a man of discernment and experience, withdrawn from all engagements in trade, he can find better opportunities to discover in what any grievance, difficulty, or inconvenience consists; and to effect, or shew the means of redress, remedy, or moderation of them, than those who are immersed in actual business, biased or deterred by interest, passions, or connections; and whose attention to their own affairs does not even admit of their suitably exerting themselves, however able or willing; and by whose means, therefore, embarrassments are often increased, instead of removed or lessened.—With what facility, and mutual satisfaction, are many misunderstandings conciliated or prevented —and many disputes settled and terminated, by proper intervention, sometimes in a few minutes; which *could not otherwise be effected*, especially by the parties themselves, even in a number of years?

V. Parties in difference, who may choose to refer the matters of their dispute to the decision, or *sole* ARBITRATION of the director of this chamber;—or to join him with other persons; may firmly rely on the most deliberate, impartial, and conscientious discharge of that important and inviolable duty, in so far as depends on him, or his abilities.—Such parties disposed to choose other arbitrators, without joining him, may be usefully advised and assisted in making such choice; in properly preparing their papers and proofs, stating the case, and adducing the reasons.—And arbitrators *themselves*, at their own request, or at the request of either party, may be *attended* by him, for the purpose of aiding their inquiries and deliberations, or elucidating any matter within the scope of his intelligence.

VI. Matters of INSURANCE constitute one of the principal objects of this institution.— Every thing relating to policies of insurance, and the stating and adjusting of losses, averages, returns, &c. thereon, will be particularly attended to; and every aid given that is possible, to all those who shall have recourse to this chamber; whether merchants, insurers, brokers, or others; who either through multiplicity of business, want of time, or of sufficient skill or experience, or other cause, may find occasion for consultation, advice, or assistance; or confirmation of their own opinion and judgment.—The very extraordinary and peculiar attention that has, for many years, been given by the conductor of this office, both in the *study* and actual *experience* of the laws and usages of this branch of commercial knowledge; and investigating minutely the matters which relate thereto; he has reason to believe is generally and sufficiently allowed.—In truth the many public, as well as private *testimonies* that have been given, both at home and from abroad, of the very favourable reception, which his extensive work, lately published on that subject,[33] has already met with; while they afford him the satisfaction of having done the mercantile world some essential service, make it incumbent on him to seize the present opportunity of publicly expressing his respectful and grateful acknowledgments.

VII. In cases of BANKRUPTCY, INSOLVENCY, or the DECEASE of persons in trade; or of any whose depending affairs may relate thereto; it is proposed to their *assignees, trustees, executors*, or *administrators*, to act as their vice-assignee, trustee, &c. in the matters which concern these situations, as being well acquainted with the laws and customs in those respects.—There often arise very great delay, much inconvenience, and considerable prejudice to every person concerned and interested on those occasions; chiefly through the indispensably necessary engagements of assignees, &c. in their own affairs, and their want of time, and of such *proper assistance* as is hereby offered, in the management and liquidation of the said matters.—Bankruptcies and insolvencies are, unhappily, too frequent in the present times: some are the consequences of great misconduct, others of folly or inadvertency, many utterly unavoidable; for the supremest merit cannot always defend from distress.—Persons unfortunately under, or in danger of falling under the latter predicament, may also find advantage by application to this chamber.

VIII. It is requested that all PAPERS, DOCUMENTS, LETTERS, ACCOUNTS, POLICIES, and the like, left at this office, for any of the purposes herein-described, may be *previously* indorsed, arranged, and tied in the order of their *dates*; or in such other suitable method (together with a *list*

[33] Entitled *A Complete Digest* of the *Theory, Laws,* and *Practice* of *Insurance*— See after the conclusion of this Plan.

thereof) as may tend to the more convenient perusal of them, and the better *expediting* the business they relate to.

IX. For the purpose of discussing and transacting any such matters as have been herein specified, MEETINGS may be held, by any set of gentlemen, in the *large, commodious* room of this institution (where paper, pens, &c. will be provided); whether the conductor of it should be in any respect personally employed or concerned, or required to be present at such meetings, or not.

X. Proper ASSISTANTS or *clerks* will be employed as occasions shall require.—And convenient modes will be adopted, to obtain every useful *intelligence*, for the due prosecution and improvement of this undertaking.—To which end, every *communication, proposition*, or *hint,* will be respectfully and thankfully received.

XI. The EMOLUMENTS to be derived from the conduct of this institution, are intended to be, in all respects, regulated on the equitable principle of *reciprocation*; combining in this idea the *utility* of the services, the *number* of persons to whom, and of occasions on which they may be rendered, and (for this reason) the *moderation* of the charges.—In many instances, such as of consultation, opinion and advice, it would not be easy here, to make any determinate estimation; *mental* communications, arising from knowledge and experience, being indeed inestimable by any certain rule or measure:—and with regard to *personal* services and assistance, they depend as well upon the nature and circumstances of the respective affairs, as the time and exertions they require.

It is, however, thought proper to adopt the following methods; *viz.*

1. Every person paying not less than *three guineas*, is entitled to such a constant and familiar resort to the office as is described in Art. II. during *one year*; or *five guineas*, during *two years*;—for the purpose of *verbal* consultation, &c. as his occasions may require :— it being always left to the consideration of every such person himself, to *enlarge* the sum of his payment, either in the first instance or afterwards, (according to his rank, situation, or liberality) in such degree as *he* shall foresee, or find, may be more proportionate to the nature and *importance* of his occurrences, and the *frequency*, or *utility* of his conferences.

2. All other persons to pay, upon each application for such *verbal* consultation as aforesaid, a *fee*, not less than *half a guinea*;—but a *second* consultation may be had on the *same* identical matter as the first, without any further fee:—it being left to such person himself (in like manner as mentioned in the preceding item) to *enlarge*, or *repeat* such fee, as he shall judge to be expedient, according to circumstances.

3. For every *opinion* given *in writing*, on *cases stated* for such purpose (according to Art. III.) a *like fee* as mentioned in the preceding item, to be

paid (exclusive of all other considerations) on the delivery of such case;—or such *larger*, or *further* fee, as the party applying shall *himself* think proper, according to the importance, or length of the case, or opinion.

4. For all personal and actual *assistance*, negotiation, mediation, employment, &c. (as indicated by the IVth and subsequent Articles of this plan) such *compensation* only will be expected (regard being always had to any payment, or fee, previously received in consultation, &c. on the particular business in question) as may be justly deemed *reasonable*, in contemplation (as has been already said) of the nature and circumstances of the business; and the abilities, time, and exertions that may be requisite.

XII. This Office is open *every day* (Saturday afternoons and Sundays excepted) at all convenient hours of business.

The ADDRESS: *To the Director of the Chamber of Commerce*, near the *Royal- Exchange*, London.

The foregoing Plan has been approved by several very respectable merchants and other judicious persons, to whom the author has been long and best known, in terms too polite and flattering for him to repeat; both as to the expediency of it in itself, and his competency to execute and conduct it to the effect proposed. Far, however, from being actuated by any improper conceit of his abilities, or any unworthy motive, it is, and ever has been, the only wish of his heart, to give them, such as they are, a right direction. The best designs, and the most meritorious conduct, are liable to the shafts of prejudice and misrepresentation. But, if a man has devoted a whole life of application and industry to the study and practice of professional knowledge, and to indefatigable researches into the matters which relate to it;—if (being now abstracted from, and uninterested in all concerns of trade and employments, except such as constitute the duties of this undertaking) his chief ambition be, to render himself useful, in the exercise of those duties with zeal and integrity;—if the institution be *convenient*, and even *necessary*, as well as new;—the author (with that deference which is due to every candid reader) may reasonably expect, it will not only meet with protection and encouragement; but may also prove an incitement to more capable men, to unite in forming, and completing with public authority, a *commercial establishment* of greater consequence; and, at least, of equal utility with those abroad.—Of the plan, which has been here described, it is not necessary to say more; and he hopes it will not be found that truth requires him to say less.

Advertisement February—June 1783[f]

In the building late the King's Arms Tavern, Cornhill.
This day is published, price 6d.

PLAN of the CHAMBER OF COMMERCE,
or Office (which is open every day) for Consultation, Opinion and Advice, Information and Assistance, in all Commercial, Insurance, and Maritime Affairs, and Matters of Trade in general, and Laws, Usages, and Practice relating thereto—The address is, 'To the Director of the Chamber of Commerce, near the Royal-Exchange, London.'

To be had of Richardson and Urquhart, Royal Exchange; T. Whieldon, Fleet Street; W. Flexney, Holborn; and at the Office above-mentioned.

At which places may also be had, Mr. Weskett's Complete Digest of Theory, Laws, and Practice of Insurance.

Review of Weskett April 1783[g]

Plan of the Chamber of Commerce. 8vo. 6d. Richardson and Urquhart.

This little pamphlet, we think, might have been circulated *gratis* among the mercantile world, with more advantage to the ingenious author, than can possibly result from its publication by a bookseller. It contains a proposal for the establishment of an office for consultation, opinion, and advice, in all commercial transactions.

Great benefit is held to have been derived from interactions of a similar nature, in foreign countries; but though we apprehend something of this kind, on a larger scale, established by authority, might be attended with considerable advantages to the trading part of mankind, we cannot help entertaining doubts as to it's very extensive utility, under the auspices of an individual, invested with no particular legal power, however great his abilities.

Original letter 1 March 1783[h]

To Gilbert Hamilton, Secretary of the Glasgow chamber of commerce
Sir,

My Friends Messrs. James & Robt. Dunlop of this City having been so obliging as to recommend it to me to communicate to you the nature & purposes of the Office I have lately instituted, under the Title of the Chamber of Commerce, with the approbation of several respectable Merchts., Insurers & Brokers,—for enlarging the Means of private Utility (in Default of all public Commercial Establishments, in this Country, for judicial Purposes)—I take the Liberty of sending you the enclosed Plan, which fully explains the Design of the undertaking, I am flattered that, in the Course of your Occurrency, I may be able to render you some acceptable, & perhaps material Services; of which you & your Friends may freely & confidentially avail yourselves. I am respectfully, Sir
Your mo. Obedt. Servt.
John Weskett
Chamber of Commerce, London

P.S. At the end of the Plan you will receive an account of my Extensive Works on Insurance (which I was many years in Compiling)—many Copies of it have been ordered [by] agents to Scotland. The Price of a single Book is £2 5s—; but to Gentlemen who order six Books, or more, I make an allowance, or Deduction (the Work being my sole property) viz. %, on each Book —Some Captains of Vessels, and other Persons who sail from the Clyde, to the West Indies, North America &c might be inclined to take a few copies with them for sale.

3.3 Political admixture with national associations and 'economical reform'.

Two examples of the resonance of the chamber representational discourse with wider proposals for 'reform', by Burgh and Burke, are reproduced below. Burgh's concept of a national association had some interrelation with the concepts behind the General Chamber of Manufactures (at least as conceived by Thomas Walker in Manchester: see Chapter 8), had influence on Wilkes' organisation of local support committees, subsequently influenced the Society for Abolition of Slavery, and was contemporary with early chamber foundations. Burke's later intervention is crucial because it demonstrates the resonances from Davenant and Whiston, and provides a view of the ineffectiveness of the government in dealing with commerce over the critical period in which chambers were established, especially resulting in the recriminations over the disastrous events during the American War. Burke's proposal led to the abolition of the Committee of Trade over 1782–6 and also stimulated Bills and petitioning for the abolition of offices, which were part of a long-running campaign for 'economical reforms' in which many chamber members participated.[34]

James Burgh: <u>Political disquisitions</u>*: or, an enquiry into public errors, defects, and abuses. Illustrated by, and established upon Facts and Remarks extracted from a Variety of Authors, ancient and modern. Calculated To draw the timely Attention of Government and People to a due Consideration of the Necessity, and the Means, of Reforming those Errors, Defects, and Abuses; of Restoring the Constitution, and Saving the State*; printed for E. and C. Dilly, in the Poultry, London, Volumes 2 and 3. 1774[d]

Volume 2, CHAP. V.
Of Taxation without Representation

It appears … that our colonists have at all times had sufficient ground of complaint against the mother-country; and that if they had been of that

[34] See Bennett, *Local Business Voice* (2011) 121–9, 680–5.

turbulent disposition, and as desirous of shaking off the connexion with us, as the *Grenvillians* falsely pretend, they must have given repeated proofs of those bad dispositions. …

Gee, in his excellent piece on trade, remonstrates against all measures, which tend to hamper our colonies. What would he have said, if he had been told, that the time would so soon come, when we should, with horror, see our administration eager to send an armed force to dragoon them into submission to unjust laws, by which their property was to be seized contrary to their own consent, and those brave people by authority declared traitors, seditious, rebels, &c. for defending their property?

It has been said on the subject of taxing the colonists in parliament; Why may not the colonists. …

Suppose the *British* parliament should imagine a tax to be paid exclusively by those who have *no vote* for members of parliament, as the people of *Manchester, Ely, &c.* Would not this be universally decried as the most flagrant partiality? Yet this would be more plausible than a *British* parliament's taxing *America*; because the members cannot be supposed competent judges of the abilities of the colonists to bear taxes; whereas they are undoubtedly judges of the ability of their own countrymen, whether voters or not. Again: Suppose the parishes in the county of *Middlesex* to send two representatives each to a parliament, or legislative assembly, excluding only that of *Islington* from representation. Suppose this legislative assembly to lay taxes on the unrepresented parish of *Islington*; Could it with any reason be expected, that the parishioners of *Islington* should quietly submit to such gross abuse? Yet this would be less inconsistent with equity than a *British* parliament's taxing *America*, because the representatives of other parishes of *Middlesex* must be supposed competent judges of the ability of the Islingtonians; whereas the members of the *British* parliament can be no judges of the ability of the colonists. …

I do not pretend to justify all the steps that have been taken by the colonists. It is not easy for the most stoical individual to keep up his philosophy when provocation runs high, much less for a mixed multitude of all sorts of people. The first aggressors in all such cases, are chiefly to blame; though those who resist in an unjustifiable manner, are not innocent. …

A.D. 1765, Jan. 17, a petition was presented to the house of commons from the merchants of London trading to *America*, setting forth, that the colony trade, of infinitive advantage to *Britain*, suffered grievously by the colonists being reduced to a state of inability to discharge the debts owning by them to *Britain*, by means of taxes and restrictions laid on them by government, particularly by the Stamp-Act. There came afterwards petitions to the same purpose from *Bristol, Liverpool, Halifax, Leeds, Lancaster, Manchester, Leicester*, and other great trading and manufacturing towns. …

Volume 3, CONCLUSION: Addressed to the independent Part of the People of GREAT-BRITAIN, IRELAND, and the COLONIES.

My dear Countrymen and Fellow-subjects,

I have in these volumes laid before you a faithful and a dreadful account of what is, or is likely soon to be, the condition of public affairs in this great empire. I have exposed to your view some of the capital abuses and grievances, which are sinking you into slavery and destruction. I have shewn you, that as things go on, there will soon be very little left of the *British* constitution, besides the name and the outward form. I have shewn you, that the house of representatives, upon which all depends, has lost its efficiency, and, instead of being (as it ought) a check upon regal and ministerial tyranny, is in the way to be soon a mere outwork of the court, a *French* parliament to register the royal edicts, a *Roman* senate in the imperial times, to give the appearance of regular and free government; but in truth, to accomplish the villainous schemes of a profligate junto, the natural consequences and unavoidable effects of inadequate representation, septennial parliaments, and placemen in the house. All which shews the absolute necessity of regulating representation, of restoring our parliaments to their primitive annual period, and of disqualifying dependents on the court from voting in the house of commons. …

Nor have I, my good countrymen, advised you to repose your confidence in one set of men rather than another. I have not told you, that the *Rockingham* party can save you any more than the *Bedford* party. I have not advised you to put your trust in Lord *Bute* rather than Lord *Chatham*. The truth is, that any set of ministers must misconduct the affairs of the nation, so long as the nation itself is upon a bad footing. And it is equally true, that an incorrupt parliament will make any ministry upright. …

And now—in the name of all that is holy—let us consider whether a scheme may not be laid down for obtaining the necessary reformation of parliament.

Before all other things, there must be established a GRAND NATIONAL ASSOCIATION FOR RESTORING THE CONSTITUTION. Into this must be invited all men of property, all friends to liberty, all able commanders, &c. There must be a copy of the ASSOCIATION for every parish, and a parochial committee to procure subscriptions from all persons whose names are in any tax-book, and who are willing to join the Association. And there must be a grand committee for every county in the three kingdoms, and in the colonies of *America*.

'The people at large, when they lose their constitutional guard, are like a rope of sand, easily divided asunder; and therefore when the acting parts of the constitution shall abuse their trust, and counteract the end for which they were established, there is no way of obtaining redress but by associating together, in order to form a new chain of union and strength in defence of their constitutional rights. But instead of uniting for their common interest, the people have suffered themselves to be divided and split into factions and parties to such a degree, that every man hath rose up in enmity against his neighbour; by which they have brought themselves under the fatal curse of a kingdom divided against itself, which cannot stand.'[35]

By the readiness of the people to enter into the associations, it may be effectually determined, whether the majority are desirous of the proposed reformations. This, as has been observed before, is a matter of supreme consequence, for resistance to government, unless it be by a clear majority of the people, is rebellion. Therefore, with all due submission to the judgement of Bishop *Burnet* upon that point, the true criterion between rebellion and reformation consists not in the atrociousness of the abuses to be reformed, but in the concurrence of the people in desiring reformation. For whatever the majority desire, it is certainly lawful for them to have, unless they desire what is contrary to the laws of God.

Confederacies and associations have been usual in all countries, especially in *England* [continues by referring to Magna Carta, and earlier grassroots associations] …

The next question is, Who shall set himself at the head of this grand association? …

'The corporation of *London* has, since the Restoration, usually taken the lead in petitions to parliament for the alteration of any established law'.[36]

[continues by referring to 1688 Glorious Revolution] …

The objects of such a general association as I propose are, 1. The securing of public credit. 2. Obtaining the undoubted sense of the people, on the state of public affairs. 3. Presenting petitions, signed by a clear majority of the people of property, for the necessary acts of parliament. 4. To raise, and have in readiness, the strength of the nation, in order to influence government, and prevent mischief. …

Let the first business of the *London* association be, as I said, securing public credit; the next, for *petitioning*, exclusive of all views to any thing *farther*, and as taking for granted, that the petitions will be effectual. Let this example be followed by all the great cities, towns, counties, corporate bodies, and faculties, throughout the island, and the same in Ireland and the colonies. …

Members of parliament would hardly dare to reject the proposed reformation-bill, as knowing themselves not to be invulnerable, and remembering that they could not command a guard of 500 soldiers each at their country houses at all times.

[35] Hist. Ess. Engl. Const. 151

[36] Blackst. Comment. IV. 147.

Let the petitions be drawn up and presented in the most respectful and most unexceptionable way that is possible, so that the fault may all come upon government (if they reject the petitions) and none upon the people.

'Petitioning, in better English, is no more than requesting or requiring, and men require not favours but their due'.[37]

If the government shew themselves so wise and so friendly to the people as to grant the petitions, all is safe and secure. For an honest parliament will make every body else honest, and all will go well.

A government which opposes and refuses the undoubted demands of the people, in such manner that the people come to be defeated of their desire, be the subject matter what it will, is no government, but a proper tyranny. Supposing the government to be really and *bonâ fide* persuaded that the demand of the people is unreasonable, in this or any other case, and would prove hurtful to them if granted, they are only to remonstrate against it; and if the people still insist upon it, the government ought to a man to resign, not to resist the supreme power, the majesty of the people. Whoever undertakes to manage any person's or any people's affairs in spite of the proprietors, is answerable for all consequences. …

A grand national association for obtaining an independent parliament would make them tremble. For they know, that the nation, if in earnest, would have it, and that with the cessation of their influence in parliament, their power must end.

Edmund Burke: *Speech of Edmund Burke Esq., Member of Parliament for the City of Bristol, on Presenting to the House of Commons a Plan for the better Security of the Independence of Parliament and the Oeconomical Reformation of the Civil and Other Establishments*, 4th edition, printed J. Dodsley, London, 1780. Also reprinted in full in Langford.[38] 11 February 1780[r]

… Sir, … I will lay these principles fairly before you, that afterwards you may be in a condition to judge whether every object of regulation, as I propose it, comes fairly under its rule. … I conceive then,

First, That all jurisdictions which furnish more matter of expense, more temptation to oppression, or more means and instruments of corrupt influence, than do advantage to justice or political administration.

Secondly, That all public estates which are more subservient to the purposes of vexing, overawing, and influencing those who hold under them, and to the expense of perception and management, than of benefit to the revenue,

[37] Milt. Eikon, 109.
[38] Langford, *Writings and Speeches of Edmund Burke*, 3 (1996) 481–541.

ought, upon every principle, both of revenue and of freedom, to be disposed of.

Thirdly, That all offices which bring more charge than proportional advantage to the state; that all offices which may be engrafted on others, uniting and simplifying their duties, ought, in the first case, to be taken away; and in the second, to be consolidated.

Fourthly, That all such offices ought to be abolished as obstruct the prospect of the general superintendent of finance; which destroy his superintendancy; which disable him from foreseeing and providing for charges as they may occur; from preventing expense in its origin, checking it in its progress, or securing its application to its proper purposes. A minister under whom expenses can be made without his knowledge, can never say what it is that he can spend or what it is that he can save.

Fifthly, That it is proper to establish an invariable order in all payments; which will prevent partiality; which will give preference to services, not according to the importunity of the demandant, but the rank and order of their utility or their justice.

Sixthly, That it is right to reduce every establishment, and every part of an establishment (as nearly as possible) to certainty, the life of all order and good management.

Seventhly, That all subordinate treasuries, as the nurseries of mismanagement, and as naturally drawing to themselves as much money as they can, keeping it as long as they can, and accounting for it as late as they can, ought to be dissolved. They have a tendency to perplex and distract the public accounts, and to excite a suspicion of government, even beyond the extent of their abuse. … An œconomical constitution is a necessary basis for an œconomical administration. …

There is, Sir, another office, which was not long since, closely connected with … the American secretary; but has been lately separated from it for the very same purpose for which it had been conjoined; I mean the sole purpose of all the separations and all conjunctions that have been lately made—a job. —I speak, Sir, of the *Board of trade and plantations*. This board is a sort of temperate bed of influence; a sort of gently ripening hot-house, where eight members of Parliament receive salaries of a [£] thousand a year, for a certain given time, for doing little, order to mature at a proper season, a claim to [£] two thousand, to be granted for doing less, and on the credit of having toiled so long in that inferior laborious department.

I have known that board, off and on, for a great number of years. Both of its pretended objects have been much the objects of my study, if I have a right to call any pursuits of mine by so respectable a name. I can assure the house, and I hope they will not think that I risk my little credit lightly, that, without meaning to convey the least reflection upon any one of its members past or present,—it is a board which, if not mischievous, is of no use at all. …

I must say, that having till lately attended them a good deal, I have observed that no description of members give so little attendance, either to communicate, or to obtain instruction upon matters of commerce, as the honourable members of the grave board of trade. I really do not recollect, that I have ever seen one of them in that sort of business. Possibly, some members may have better memories; and may call to mind some job that may have accidentally brought one or other of them, at one time or other, to attend a matter of commerce.

This board, Sir, has had both its original formation, and its regeneration, in a job. … It was projected in the year 1668, and it continued in a tottering and rickety childhood for about three or four years, for it died in the year 1673, a babe of as little hopes as ever swelled the bills of mortality in the article of convulsed or overlaid children, who have hardly stepped over the threshold of life.

It was buried with little ceremony; and never more thought of, until the reign of *King William*, when in the strange vicissitude of neglect and vigour, of good and ill success that attended his wars, in the year 1695, the trade was distressed beyond all example of former sufferings, by the piracies of the French cruisers. This suffering incensed, and, as it should seem, very justly incensed, the house of commons. In this ferment they struck, not only at the administration, but at the very constitution of the executive government. They attempted to form in parliament a board for the protection of trade; which, as they planned it, was to draw to itself a great part, if not the whole, of the functions and powers, both of the admiralty, and of the treasury; and thus, by a parliamentary delegation of office and officers, they threatened absolutely to separate these departments from the whole system of the executive government, and of course to vest the most leading and essential of its attributes in this board [the Davenant-Whiston proposals]. As the executive government was in a manner convicted of a dereliction of its functions, it was with infinite difficulty, that this blow was warded off in that session. There was a threat to renew the same attempt in the next. To prevent the effect of this manœuvre, the court opposed another manœuvre to it; and in the year 1696, called into life this board of trade, which had slept since 1673.

This, in a few words, is the history of the regeneration of the board of trade. It has perfectly answered its purposes. It was intended to quiet the minds of the people, and to compose the ferment that then was strongly working in a parliament. The courtiers were too happy to be able to substitute a board, which they knew would be useless, in the place of one that they feared would be dangerous. Thus the board of trade was reproduced in a job; and perhaps it is the only instance of a public body, which has never degenerated; but to this hour preserves all the health and vigour of its primitive institution. …

But if all of these things were not more than sufficient to prove to you the inutility of that expensive establishment, I would desire you to recollect, Sir, that those who may be very ready to defend it, are very cautious how they employ it; cautious how they employ it even in appearance and pretence. They are afraid they should lose the benefit of its influence in parliament, if they seemed to keep it up for any other purpose. If ever there were commercial points of great weight, and most closely connected with our dependences, they are those which have been agitated and decided in parliament since I came into it. Which of the innumerable regulations since made had their origin or their improvement in the board of trade? Did any of the several East India bills which have been successively produced since 1767, originate there? Did any one dream of referring them, or any part of them thither? Was any body so ridiculous as even to think of it? If ever there was occasion on which the board was fit to be consulted, it was with regard to the acts, that were preludes to the American war, or attendant on its commencement: those acts were full of commercial regulations, such as they were;—the intercourse bill; the prohibitory bill; the fishery bill? If the board was not concerned in such things, in what particular was it thought fit that it should be concerned? In the course of all these bills through the house, I observed the members of that board to be remarkably cautious of intermeddling. They understood decorum better; they know the matters of trade and plantations are no business of theirs. …

It was but the other day, that the noble lord [Lord North] in the blue ribbon carried up to the house of peers, two acts, altering, I think much for the better, but altering, in a great degree, our whole commercial system. These acts, I mean, for giving a free trade to Ireland in woollens and in all things else, with independent nations, and giving them an equal trade to our own colonies. Here too the novelty of this great, but arduous and critical improvement of system, would make you conceive that the anxious solicitude of the noble lord in the blue ribbon, would have wholly destroyed the plan of summer recreation of the board, by references to examine, compare, and digest matters for parliament—You would imagine, that Irish commissioners of customs and English commissioners of customs, and commissioners of excise, that merchants and manufacturers of every denomination, had daily crowded their outer rooms. *Nil horum*. The perpetual virtual adjournment, and the unbroken sitting vacation of that board, was no more disturbed by the Irish than by the plantation commerce, or any other commerce. … neither the qualified propositions which were received, nor those other qualified propositions which were rejected by ministers, were the least concern of the board of trade, or were they ever thought of in the business.

It is therefore, Sir, on the opinion of parliament, on the opinion of the ministers, and even on their own opinion of their inutility, that I shall propose to you to suppress the board of trade and plantations; and to recommit all its business to the council from whence it was very improvidently taken; and which business (whatever it might be) was much better done and without any expense; and indeed where in effect it may all come at last.

Chapter 4

Opinion, Tensions and Disputes

The records that survive for chambers of commerce are often disappointing in the extent to which correspondence or exchanges exist that give insights into the personal motives and feelings of those involved. However, some more formal records and a few letters are valuable. The most important and insightful cases are gathered here, illustrating the sort of issues involved, their generality across the chambers, but also the specifics and tensions in each local situation. The first group of documents (4.1) are letters to Patrick Colquhoun during his efforts to establish the Glasgow chamber in 1782–3. He approached all the influential individuals in Scotland who he felt had to be aligned with and support the chamber. Many of the responses to his letters survive and provide some of the most vivid first-hand accounts of the motives for a chamber and how different individuals in varied positions of authority viewed the plans. Very clear in the general support for Colquhoun is the importance of the status of those involved, and the value of alignment with other interests to avoid tensions with established authority in the state. Also noteworthy is various advice about avoiding faction between interests within the chamber, always taking a general and public interest rather than taking up specific factional interests. Glasgow's successful foundation in many ways defined the British chamber model for the next 30–40 years.[1]

The second group of documents (4.2) relate to the foundation of the Liverpool chamber in 1774. This experienced quite the opposite of Glasgow, leading to highly public and severe tensions with the local Corporation, and with national government interests. This interlocked with more general demands for 'reform', and specific tensions over the American War where most chamber members were seeking conciliation with the Americans, whilst the Corporation supported the government policy of suppression. The documents show the confused chronological evolution of this period: first, in early 1774, a joint committee of trade was proposed between the merchants and the Corporation; this broke down and the merchants decided to establish their own chamber as an independent body in April 1774; a year later in April 1775 the Corporation set up a rival Committee of Trade of its own, made up of appointed members from the Corporation.[2]

[1] See Bennett, *Local Business Voice* (2011) 167–70.

[2] For more detail on Liverpool's rival initiatives see Bennett, *Liverpool Business Voice* (2010); 'Searching for new models'.

The third group of documents (4.3) show a different set of tensions in the various attempts to establish a Nottingham chamber of commerce in 1795, 1813, and 1835–8. Here the tensions appear to have been between, on the one hand, those seeking a body to liaise with workers and negotiate wages, prices and various other production agreements, and on the other hand, those seeking a chamber focused on more general commerce that did not get directly involved in negotiations with workers. The episode is an important early indicator of the bifurcation that occurred in the UK between 'employer associations' that were set up to negotiate with workers, leading up to the foundation of the EEF, FBI and CBI and other sector employer groups, and the mainstream chambers of commerce that generally did not get involved directly with employee negotiations.[3]

Documents 4.4 and 4.5 show tensions between the proposers of a chamber and the existing Company of Merchants in Cork in 1814, and between the founders of the chamber and the local Corporation in Bristol in 1822. The sixth set of documents (4.6) relate to the tensions in the attempts to establish a chamber in London in 1817 and 1823–4. The London discussions show how a campaign on a particular issue could evolve into a move towards founding a chamber, but also illustrate tensions with the national government over a chamber located on its doorstep, as well as divergence between the founders about its purpose; a successful London chamber was not to be founded until 1882.

4.1 Glasgow 1782–3

Patrick Colquhoun, who became to chamber's first president and who was already a major figure in Glasgow as the city's Lord Provost, well-understood how politics operated locally in Glasgow, in Scotland, and to a lesser extent at Westminster. Because of their length the letters are excerpted below. Colquhoun's efforts to secure support from powerful interests and individuals illustrates how these interests had to be aligned so that the chamber could progress to an establishment with all major individuals signed up, and no potential opposition to a planned charter.

Source
Glasgow chamber papers, Letters to Patrick Colquhoun: Glasgow Mitchell Library TD 1670/4/11–15

[3] For more discussion of Nottingham's difficult early attempts see Chapter 1.

Henry Dundas, Lord Advocate, 11 November, 1782: TD 1670/4/12.

Dundas 'assures of his support'. In a later letter he notes:

Henry Dundas, Lord Advocate, 8 January, 1783: TD 1670/4/14.

From the persons concerned I make no doubt of its being concluded upon the most beneficial principles in which case it will produce the effects the framers of it have in view. It sometimes happens that heats and jealousies get into institutions of that type; these I [hope] will be your forceful case to prevent and if you do I flatter myself you will have much credit by the institution.

John Seton, London lawyer and parliamentary agent, 11 February, 1783: TD 1670/4/14.

A Royal charter will add permanency and weight to the establishment of your chamber of commerce and there can be no objection to your obtaining it as I presume you will neither ask for powers to purchase lands nor to borrow money in your corporate capacity which are the great objections to His Majesty granting powers of incorporation. ... The only materials needed are a petition which will be referred to the Attorney General and Lord Advocate. ... I should conceive a conversation with yourself explaining the plain meaning of the institution.[4]

Thomas Miller, Justice Clerk in Edinburgh, 11 February, 1783: TD 1670/4/14.

At a former period such an institution would have been a public benefit. But at present, when the general system of commerce has undergone such a revolution, and our trade often suffering so much by the restraints of a complicated war, must now break out into new channels, under regulations, foreign and domestic, formerly unknown, it must be of great importance, to have the first effects ... directed and assisted by the ablest advice: and the many respectable names which I read in the list of members and directors of the chamber of commerce offered me, from the personal knowledge I have of them, the most flattering hopes. ... You judge wisely in prosecution of your plan, to establish a friendly and confidential intercourse with the Board of Trustees [of the Merchants' House].

William Wilson of Glasgow, 28 October, 1782: TD 1670/4/11.

Learnt with pleasure of chamber of commerce proposals ... with a view to stop, or at least lessen that confusion, uncertainty and expenditure which has hitherto attended the discussion of mercantile questions before the courts of law. ... Would save the community many thousands [of pounds] yearly in expenses, waste of labour and time ... and anxiety.

[4] See also discussion in Chapter 2 about the process of gaining charters and Seton's role for Glasgow; some of his accounts of fees as reproduced in Chapter 5.

James Dennistoun, leading member of Glasgow Merchants' House, November, 1782: TD 1670/4/12.

Unless there is more zeal among us than has shown on other occasions, the voluntary subscriptions may not yield what is expected, and may not be continued by the successors of the present generation; besides it appears not just that the great and small traders or manufactures should contribute alike. ... In choosing arbiters might not the choice be in the parties in place of the Directors. ... It will require some address to convince the smaller towns that the weight of Glasgow, where the meetings are to be held, does not too preponderate.

William Risk, 1 November, 1782: TD 1670/4/12.

[Colquhoun] a natural leader because of his ease of public speaking.

William Cunningham, 2 November, 1782: TD 1670/4/12.

Accounts hastily read over and audited in this public manner are very liable to be objected to, and justly. ... Records and Accounts should be printed ... and sent to each member. ... This method will prevent any misapplication of money and give satisfaction.

John Keppen of Greenock, 7 November, 1782: TD 1670/4/12.

Task undertaken by a chief magistrate of Glasgow whose abilities are equal to it; and whose zeal and exertions for the public welfare, do him such honour. ... It has been observed that though such institutions are active and useful at their commencement, they usually degenerate either into faction, or listless indolence in the end—there can be no danger of the latter while you continue in the direction.

Differences of opinion will naturally arise even among those who have the same ends in view, and partial and selfish motives will sometimes influence the members; as a palliative it might perhaps be not improper to communicate an oath to every director on his appointment 'that he should to the best of his judgment act for no other motives but such as tended to promote in the most effective manner, the general interest of commerce and manufactures, or the particular interest of such bodies as he may patronize without prejudice to the general interest' ... it may have the effect at least that it would keep the gentlemen awfully in mind of the original intent of the institution.

Sir John Dalrymple of Edinburgh, 18 November, 1782: TD 1670/4/12.

[Supports the chamber of commerce plan but suggests that] the Court Merchant [Merchant's House] should choose a few out of the 30 [directors] who have a turn and feeling for the business [of arbitration].

Ingenious men discover many in private but from their own situations often cannot take advantage of them. But when they are known to the public, others will.

Advantage will be to give weight of truth in applications to ministers. There are few mercantile favours that will be refused to the united voice of such a body of men. The Scotch members [MPs] are the worst channel in the world to get favours of trade, almost none of them are merchants. If they be men of straw they concentrate on getting places for themselves. [Also quotes differences in excise between England and Scotland].

William Wilson of Glasgow, 28 November, 1782: TD 1670/4/12.

[He suggested a regulation] like that for doctors and lawyers, with an examination for young merchants as a 'mark of worth' [recalls the ideas of Postlethwayt and Mortimer], giving proficiency … in the knowledge of trade …writing, figures and in keeping books. … Sends with this letter some extracts from a most elegant and sensible writer on the maritime affairs of England. He mentions the marine Ordinances of France. [These extracts focus on arbitration, and the sharing of costs between members and using the directors of the chamber as arbiters. The source of the extracts is unclear, but looks heavily based on Mortimer].

Hugh Moody of Greenock, 12 November, 1782: TD 1670/4/12.

Subscriptions here are at a standstill. The reason is they think five guineas paid immediately and one guinea annually is too much and would raise a very great fund, therefore a great number here do not choose to subject themselves to so much and all that have got to subscribe is myself, James Keppen, George Wood, John Hamilton and James Glammel expected.

Robert Douglas and William Howall, magistrates of Port Glasgow, 13 November, 1782: TD 1670/4/12.

We have done everything in our power to get subscriptions and are sorry to add the little progress we have made, as yet there are only seven that have signed. Mr. Hercules Ross[5] has sent 20 guineas. … They will keep open the subscription paper … a few days longer in hopes ... Objections are these—that nothing is allowed for a member should he fall back in the world nor to his children after his death, if they should want; another objection is that it does not appear a man can sign for himself and his company.

4.2 Liverpool 1774–5

The foundation of the Liverpool chamber was one of the most tension-laden of the earliest chambers. It well illustrates the difficulties of gaining support from traditional interests in a rapidly changing and tense political situation. Liverpool was now Britain's second largest port, surpassing Bristol about ten

[5] Formerly a member of the Jamaica chamber.

years earlier, and second only to London (and Dublin in Ireland). Like the new manufacturing centres which were finding it sometimes difficult to get their voice heard,[6] Liverpool also had to confront powerful existing interests. For Liverpool the issue was how to get a more effective voice than the Corporation; or alternatively, how to make the Corporation more effective and attuned to wider merchant interests rather than to a small group of long-standing merchant families and other interests dominated by personal interest and patronage from the national government.

The chronology of events is confusing and tight-packed in early 1774. The precipitation of discussions to form a committee to promote the trade of Liverpool seems to have developed partly as a result of disputes about the fees for landing at free quays, and partly deriving from proposals by John Phillips (supported by the Corporation) to build a lighthouse at the Smalls on which a fee on shipping would be levied. The Smalls light seems to have been the catalyst for developing a local 'committee' to manage the fees, chaired by leading member of the Corporation's Common Council, John Sparling. Sparling's management of this initiative later led to him being denounced as inappropriate. These tensions interlocked with long-running disputes about existing port fees, especially the very lucrative 'trade duty' levied by the Corporation,[7] as well as concerns about how local Aldermen profited from their positions through land speculation (again involving Sparling). Various public meetings in January and February 1774 led to some sort of accord to form a joint committee of trade between merchants of the port and the Corporation, which would have received a dedicated contribution from the Corporation's 'trade duty' of £250 per year. However, this possible accord broke down: either because key personalities on the Corporation's Common Council backed away (notably led by the Mayor John Parr, and the leading Councillor John Sparling), or because the merchants had been over-optimistic about what this sort of joint committee could ever deliver. The breakdown was public and acrimonious, as evident in press reports reproduced here. This led the merchant community to develop in April 1774 its own *Deed* for a chamber (see Chapter 1), and set up the chamber in June. This became immediately very active, including opposing the Smalls lighthouse and other Corporation pet projects (see *Abstract* in Chapter 5). Perhaps because of this success, the Corporation retaliated by setting up its own Committee of Trade in April 1775, the rules of which are presented here to demonstrate its differences with the rules of chambers. The

[6] See discussion by Redford, *Manchester Merchants* (1934); Norris, 'Samuel Garbett' (1957); Bowden, *Industrial Society in England* (1965).
[7] See Bennett, *Voice of Liverpool Business* (2010) 67–90.

detested Sparling was initially a member of this committee, though he rarely attended.

The detail of the Liverpool chamber and the committee of trade have been discussed before, but this is the first time the documents have been published.[8] They have important value because of the need to overcome the confusion created by Redford's statement that 'no general chamber of commerce was formed at Liverpool until 1849',[9] whilst several accounts have confused the chamber's activities with the Corporation's committee of trade.[10] Since these sources have been drawn on by many others without being aware of or scrutinising the original documents this has misled or confused subsequent scholars.[11] The documents illustrate two colliding visions: one for an independent chamber, and another for a body intermeshed with established interests and oligarchies of the local state. The collision is evident in the different views available on the meetings on 26 February recorded in the Corporation's minutes which give three pages of objections under seven headings from the merchants. The mayor himself took a party line when he 'dispersed in handbills through this town your address to the inhabitants dated 16 February, charging a considerable body of merchants with duplicity, and a public *breach of faith*'. This handbill was subsequently published in the London newspapers in order to influence the parliamentary decision on the merchants' petition to parliament. "A merchant of Liverpool" retaliated in the press on 11 March, by anonymous letter directed at the Mayor. This is believed to be from John Dobson, the first president of the chamber

As well as the specific local tensions, this was also a time of great national tensions. Some of this continued from earlier local disputes, and initiatives by the merchants. For example in 1765–6 a 'Liverpool American Committee' had been formed to manage opposition to the Stamp Act which brought the Corporation and merchants together, but had started with conflict.[12] In 1768 a more harmonious cooperation with the Corporation resulted in proposals for a set of local 'chambers' (in Liverpool, Bristol and Hull) to participate in a restructured EIC. These two initiatives are covered in Chapter 5. The tensions were however, revived. The EIC was still under pressure after a new Act

[8] For the chamber: Bennett, *Voice of Liverpool Business* (2010); for the committee of trade: Bennett, 'Searching for new models' (2014).
[9] Redford, *Manchester Merchants* (1934) 19.
[10] e.g. Major sources widely used that contain this confusion are: J. Touzeau, *The Rise and Progress of Liverpool from 1551 to 1835* (Liverpool, 1910) 553–7; J. A. Picton, *City of Liverpool: Municipal Archives and Records* (Liverpool, 1886) 236–8.
[11] e.g. Checkland, 'Economic Attitudes in Liverpool (1952), 58–9; T. C. Barker and J. R. Harris, *A Merseyside Town in the Industrial Revolution: St. Helens 1750–1900* (London, 1959) 37.
[12] See Bennett, *Local Business Voice* (2011) 117–26

passed in 1773 'for establishing better regulations for the better Management'.[13] There were also disputes over the governance of the Royal African Company in parliament; over Wilkes, whom the majority of chamber members supported; the Feathers Tavern petition of June 1773 was being re-initiated in January-March 1774 to give greater freedoms for Dissenters (many of whom were Liverpool chamber members); and the developing American rebellion produced even deeper divisions which interlocked with Wilkes, the EIC, and dissent.

Concurrent locally the promotion of local MP William Meredith as Controller of the Household, who was generally opposed to the Corporation interest, was a leading Rockinghamite during the Stamp Act crisis and was strongly interlinked with chamber members, led to hope by Corporation interests that a new writ would be issued for an election at Liverpool to replace him.[14] Meredith's appointment led him to being seen as a turncoat by those opposed to the growing danger of a war with America, which seemed to open electoral opportunities locally. Meredith also became embroiled in a complex exchange which allowed him to be portrayed as an enemy of the press. A letter (unsigned) of 11 February 1774 in the *Public Advertiser* to Sir Fletcher Norton, Speaker of the House of Commons, attributed to Meredith, criticised Norton's refusal to allow two petitions to be laid before the House (for enclosing lands in Tottington parish, Norfolk). A long letter from 'Brutus' attacked Meredith for his attack on the press (*London Evening Post*, 15 March 1774). An even more forthright letter from 'A Bold Britain' to 'Sir W____ M______' noted 'The astonishment which possessed every individual of your acquaintance, upon their receiving information of your ungenerous attack on the liberty of the press. ... One day animated and nervous in the service of freedom; next day enrolled under the banners of despotism, and sullying your sublime patriotism in subverting liberty of the press. ... Did a new election persuade you to a defection from the glorious band of patriots? ... What, the little hero afraid to appear before his constituents? What, will the *great maritime corporation* shun their champion, and espouse an interest repugnant to *his*? ... What carnal motive could then operate so unhappily? Surely not his finances! Omnes: obstipuere animi, gelidusque perima cucurrit ossa tremor [loosely: the senses are bent, an icy dread runs through the bones] (*London Evening Post*, 5 March 1774). Liverpool over the January-March 1774 period was thus a key fulcrum of attention for national politics through Meredith. The continuing support by leading chamber members for Meredith (as well as for the other local MP Richard Pennant, who was also usually

[13] See e.g. *London Chronicle*, 1 March 1774.
[14] *London Chronicle*, 10 March 1774.

with the 'opposition') was a key part of the local transmission of the national political tensions over elections and America.

Sources
[a] *Williamson's Liverpool Advertiser.*
[b] Liverpool Common Council Minutes; Liverpool RO.
[c] *London Chronicle.*
[d] *London Public Advertiser.*
[e] Minute book of Committee of Trade; Liverpool RO 353 MIN/COM I 2/1

Printed report 14 January 1774[a]

We hear that there was a very respectable meeting at the Council Chamber on Monday last, both as to weight and number, to deliberate on Mr. Phillips's plan [for the Smalls light]; but as the Model of his *distinguishable* Light-house was not ready, a discussion of the subject was deferred till this is produced, which the Workmen assured would be on Monday the 24th. instant, and the meeting was adjourned to that day.

In this model we are promised great matters: design and execution are united to convey an idea of general utility; no less than the means of discriminating every Lighthouse in the world from each other.

We have authority to say, that if Mr. Phillips is supported on his own bottom, *unconnected with the Skerries and Milford* [for which he had other initiatives], he intends to accomplish all he has already proposed; that is, build and support two Light-houses, and appropriate £12,000 to improvements, *under the direction of a committee at Liverpool*, at a duty of *an half-penny per ton.*

Printed notice [first public proposal for a committee of trade]
28 January 1774[a]

The Merchants and Masters of Vessels, both in the Foreign and Coasting Trade, are earnestly desired to meet at Pontack's Coffee House, in Water Street, Tomorrow, being Saturday the 29th instant, at Twelve o'Clock, upon Business of Importance to the Trade of this Place.
JOHN SPARLING Esq., Chairman

Printed notice 11 February 1774[a]

[meeting to agree petition to parliament for a committee of trade—details in council minute of 15 February]

The Merchants who have paid the TRADE DUTY, are desired to meet at the Town Hall on Saturday the 25th of February at Twelve o'Clock.

Council Minute 15 February 1774[b]

Whereas a Petition Copy of a Draft of a Petition hath been brought and read to this Council purporting to be a Petition to Parliament from the Merchants and Traders of Liverpool praying Liberty to bring in a Bill this Sessions for laying or imposing a Tax on the Importation of all Goods into the Port of Liverpool according to a printed Table of Rates thereof also delivered into the Council alleged to be for the Support and Benefit of Trade and any other public Occasion or to that Purport. And Whereas the said Merchants at a late public Meeting of them held in the Town Hall of this Town did openly declare that no such Application was intended or should be made at this Session for such Bill. This is followed by the Statement that no such Bill or draft of such Bill. And Whereas no such Bill or Draft of such Bill hath been prepared or laid before the public or this Council who conceive from the General Purposes of their Petition that such Bill may affect the Rights Interests good Order and Government of the Town. It is therefore now ordered that in Case any such Application be made of Bill brought into Parliament that an Opposition thereto on the behalf and at the Expense of the Corporation be made this Session of Parliament against the same passing into Law. And that Mr. Mayor, Aldermen Gildart, Blackburn, Sparling, Goore, Spencer, Hughes. And Gregson, and Mr. Peters, Mr. Birch, Mr. Bridge, Mr. Brown, Mr. Clemens, Mr. Treasurer and the Town Clerk be appointed a Committee to manage such Opposition in Parliament. And that a Petition be prepared and passed under the Common Seal of this Corporation and presented to the Honorable House of Commons for such Purpose, any five of such Committee to act and make a Committee and that the Treasurer of the Corporation do pay the necessary Costs and other Charges attending such Opposition.

Also Ordered that Mr. Treasurer do pay Mr. Alderman Spencer the Sum of Three hundred and fifty Pounds in Part of Seven hundred Pounds which the Corporation have at Interest of the Moneys belonging to a fund formerly called the Trade Duty.

Printed broadsheet 16 February 1774

[distributed by John Parr, Mayor, urging delay in signing the petition; no surviving copy found; subsequently re-printed in London newspapers, 28 February; q.v. below]

Council Minute 22 February 1774[a]

On a Representation made to the Committee appointed at the last Common Council, by several very respectable Merchants and Burgesses, and by that Committee to this Council now reported, that it is frequently necessary to send up Deputies, and that Resources are wanted to defray the Expenses of Deputies attending Parliament on their Deliberations and concerning that and other Purposes relating to, and to the Promotion and Support of such Trade, as it is the real Interest of this Town and Corporation to have promoted by reason that a late voluntary Contribution of the Merchants of this Town called the Trade Duty has ceased to be duly paid, tho' there are some remains thereof yet unapplied, the Mayor Bailiffs and Burgesses in this Council assembled now taking such Representation into their Consideration, and in as much as the Estate and Revenue of this Corporation have been improved and augmented; and are likely so to be, by the Increase, and much depend on the Promotion and Support of Trade, and this Council having the Welfare of this Town and its Trade at Heart do hereby declare they are convinced it is for the Interest of this Town and Corporation that a competent fund out of its Corporate Revenue be dedicated to the Service of that Commerce from whence the far greater Part of such Revenue immediately Springs.

It is therefore ordered enacted and ordained by the Mayor Bailiffs and Burgesses of this Town in this Common Council assembled (and who for their better Information touching the Premises have now enquired into the Accounts of the Sums which have been called for from the Trade Duty for the Support of Trade for many Years last Past) and by the Authority of the same, that from and immediately after such Part of the said fund called the Trade Duty as now remains shall be applied and expended to the Purposes to which and under the Directions of Persons by whom it is now applicable, and from and immediately after such expenditure shall by the Committee of Commerce to be established as hereafter mentioned or the major Part of them for the Time being under their Hands be certified so to be, to the Mayor of this Town for the Time being, any such Sum or Sums of money not exceeding Two hundred and fifty Pounds a year of this Corporation Revenue of which a Deposit of Two hundred and fifty Pounds, the first Year's Income shall immediately after such Expenditure be paid in Hand, and the aggregate fund of which Sum or Sums not exceeding and being hereby ordered not to exceed five hundred Pounds at any time, shall be annually set apart and paid by the Treasurer of this Corporation for the Time being from time to time to such Committee of Commerce and their Successors for the Time being, to consist of such number of Merchants Burgesses of this Corporation, provided an equal Part of them respectively be Persons chosen by the Mayor Bailiffs and Burgesses of this Town in Common Council to be assembled, and an equal Part of them by the Merchants and Traders Burgesses of this Town, at such Time and Times and from time to time is such manner and under and subject to such Rules Orders and Regulations for appointing a Chairman to be the casting Vote and other Purposes for their better Regulation and for the Common good of this Town as the Corporation Committee appointed at the last Council, of whom the Mayor and one Bailiff shall be two.

Printed notice 25 February 1774[a]

LIVERPOOL. FRIDAY, FEBRUARY 25.
THE MERCHANTS AND TRADERS WHO SUBSCRIBED THE PETITION TO PARLIAMENT TO RAISE A FUND TO BE APPLIED FOR THE ENCOURAGEMENT AND SUPPORT OF COMMERCE, ARE DESIRED TO MEET ON SATURDAY MORNING AT NINE O'CLOCK PRECISELY, IN WRIGLEY'S GREAT ROOM.

Council Minute [Morning] 26 February 1774[b]

It is hereby ordained that the Petition [based on the minute of 22 February for a Bill to formally constitute the Committee of Trade] of the Mayor Aldermen Bailiffs and Common Council of this Town, to the Honourable the Commons of Great Britain in Parliament assembled, now read in and approved of by this assembly and by Mr. Mayor and Bailiffs forthwith passed under the Corporation Seal.

Ordered at the same time, that Mr. Recorder and such other Council as choose to go with him, to meet the Merchants and read over the foregoing Act to them but not to leave the said Act with them, and that the Committee do require their positive Answer to be given the Corporation Committee in the Council Room at Six o'clock this Evening, whether they will desist to proceed in this Parliamentary Business or not and they have a Power after such Answer to give them a Copy thereof or not accordingly.

Council Minute [reconvened at 6 o'clock p.m.] 26 February 1774[b]

It is resolved and declared that several of the Proposals now offered by the Committee and Proposers of the intended Bill for a <u>Tax</u> on <u>Trade</u> now read to and considered by the Mayor Bailiffs and Burgesses in their Council assembled, being in their Opinion not proper to be complied with by them, they declare they cannot comply with the said Proposals and that if the Petition to Parliament for bringing in the said intended Bill is or shall be presented contrary to the Intent of the Order of the last Council the fund thereby established is or will be thereby void. Nevertheless the Mayor Bailiffs and Burgesses in this Council assembled still retaining and meaning in all things to shew a due Regard to the Commonwealth of this town, will always on all proper Occasions administer such Aids to the commercial Interests of this town as in the discretion of the Mayor Bailiffs and Burgesses from time to time in Common Council to be assembled, and in Experience shall be found Expedient for the Advancement of the Common Good of Liverpool.

[minutes continue uninterrupted, but with a clear break in business while the merchants' committee was consulted]

Same Day the following Paper was again brought into this Council from the Committee of Merchants in order to have their further Answer thereto being entitled—

Objections to, or Remarks on, the proposed Grant by the Council

[generally an objection is stated first, then a counter proposal]:

1st 'Tis thought an improper mention is made of the Residue of the Trade Duty as it retards an essential Condition of the Grant, if it does not defer its very existence besides that this Residue is not the Property of the Contracting Parties.

2d. The mode of electing Committee Men tends to keep up that unhappy Distinction of Party in the Town which it was the avowed Intention of the negotiations to prevent and the excluding of Merchants, who are not freemen Burgesses, from voting for the Choice of Committee Men appear a high injustice to many of the most respectable Contributors to that very fund that supplies our Exigencies and whose extensive Traffic enriches the Community. —We think the Right of voting for Committee Men should belong to every Person paying Twenty Shillings annually to the Town's Duty either for himself or upon consigned Merchandise, or who pays Duties to the amount of fifty Pounds annually or who is an Owner of Part Owner of some Ship belonging to this Port.

3d. Mr. Sparling being one of the Council it is suggested can't with propriety be named a Trustee in the Deed—The Gentlemen who are named with him, wish a few more Gentlemen may be nominated in the Trust, from motives of Delicacy.

4th. A small Committee was found injurious in the application of the former Trade Duty. This Evil can be guarded against by increasing the Number to Sixteen, Eight of whom shall be empowered to act and constitute a sufficient Committee, every member thereof to have a Summons in writing sent to him to attend, one Day before each meeting be appointed which shall be advertised in the public Papers, if publication of such Papers admit Time for such Notice—and any Committee Man not attending upon such Summons without giving such sufficient Reason for his absence as shall be approved of by the Majority of the members of the Committee, shall be expelled and another Person chosen regularly in his Room. But as a Committee of Correspondence is necessary and the Chairman may receive Letters of such immediate Urgency as not to permit a regular Summons according to the forms presented, The Chairman shall be empowered to send the Committee's Clerk to every member of the Committee and to prevent Delay such Members as appear at the Hour appointed by the Chairman shall be empowered to return Answers to such Letters—but not to dispose of any Part of the Fund.

5th. The retiring Chairman may eventually continue to Office in that Body, to which he belongs infinitum—The Chairman should be chosen annually by drawing lots except the Committee be unanimous in the Choice of one of their Body.

6th. By the Clause respecting the Continuance of this Grant its Existence may cease whenever a majority of voices in the Committee shall so determine, the Consent of at least of every Member of the Committee seems indispensably necessary on a Decision of such Importance.

'Tis thought necessary that the Committee chosen by the Merchants shall constitute a sufficient Committee and be vested with every Power of a full Committee chosen by the Council and Merchants in Case the Council shall neglect to make their Election on or before the Seventh day of March—and that the Committee chosen by the Council shall have the same Powers of acting if the Merchants shall neglect to choose their number of Committee on or before the same Day.

7th. If £250 shall be found insufficient by the Committee they should have a power to call for any sum not exceeding £500 annually if there be no sufficient aggregate fund at the time of such Demand.

Those gentlemen who have a Right to vote in Council for Committee Men should be excluded from all right of voting in the choice of the Burgess Committee Men or interfering in such Election.

The Place appointed for the Committee Room is quite too small.
John Dobson, Chm.

Council Minute [immediately follows in minutes for same day]

26 February 1774[d]

The foregoing Objections or Proposals being this day brought in by Mr. Sparling as he declared from the Assembly of the Petitioners on the Business therein contained after being deliberately read over by the Town Clerk three several times to the Council and after many debates thereon and the Question put thereon Whether this Council do now agree to accept them or not, carried nem. con. against accepting them.
[signed] Francis Gildart, Town Clerk

Printed Report 28 February 1774[d]

[reprint of 16 February Mayor's statement; published in London newspapers on the day of the presentation of the Liverpool petition in parliament]

Liverpool 16 February 1774

Whereas Several Merchants of this Town propose immediately handing about a Petition to Parliament, to be signed by the Merchants, Freemen, and Inhabitants of this Town, and all Proprietors of Goods to be imported or landed here, for Leave to bring in a Bill this Session to lay a Tax on Goods to be imported here for the Benefit of Trade, as is alleged, and other Purposes which they have not explained, and speedily to bring such Bill contrary to the said Merchants public Declarations at a late Meeting held in this Town; by which hasty Means the Persons whose Goods are proposed to be taxed will not have so good an Opportunity of considering the Plan to be submitted to the Wisdom of Parliament respecting such Tax, nor will there be Time for having such proposed Bill so well digested as a Matter of such national and commercial Importance requires, and as there would have been, was it not to be brought in till next Session, as those Merchants proposed at the late Public Meeting.

I beg Leave therefore to recommend to the Consideration of the Merchants, Freemen, and Inhabitants of this Town, and all Proprietors of Goods to be imported or landed here, whether it would not be better, in order that they may have full Time to deliberate on the Scheme, at present to postpone signing the Petition.
JOHN PARR, Mayor of Liverpool.

Printed Report 1 March 1774[c]

Yesterday [28 February] … A petition was presented from Liverpool [in the House of Commons], setting forth, that they annually sent persons to reside in London during the session of parliament, in order to be informed of any transactions that might affect the trading part of the nation and Liverpool in particular; that the sending of such persons was very expensive, and praying parliament to give them authority to impose a tax upon all goods imported and exported to and from Liverpool, in order to raise a fund to defray such expenses, and others as might accrue.

Mr. Gascoigne was against the petition; he said he thought taxes sufficient were already laid upon trade more than it could well bear, and if Liverpool must send people up to attend parliament, let the Corporation defray their expenses, and not impose a tax upon Merchants of all countries to defray a whim of that corporation. He said, they desired 'leave to raise a fund to defray the expense of sending persons to attend parliaments, and other purposes'. Now those other purposes might be to bribe at elections, oppose the Customs or Excise, or any other such illegal proceedings; he therefore thought it an unprecedented petition, and should be against it. Sir William Meredith spoke a few words in favour of the petition, setting forth that Bristol had the same. [Additional comment in *London Evening Post,* 1–3

March: Meredith requested the petition be sent to a Committee, which was almost unanimously opposed. He demanded a division].

The question was put, whether it should be referred to a Committee: the House divided: Ayes 21, Noes 122.

Printed Report 11 March 1774[a]

To the MAYOR of LIVERPOOL.

SIR,

WHEN you disbursed in hand bills through this Town your Address to the Inhabitants, dated the 16th of February, charging a considerable body of Merchants with duplicity, and a public Breach of Faith, *your abuse passed unnoticed; as it was concluded, that thro' misconception, or misrepresentation, you did not* then *know you subscribed and published a falsehood.— For this reason, and conscious of the uprightness of their own manifest intentions, and of the light in which their conduct appeared to* that Public *you addressed, they thought it unnecessary, as derogatory of their honour, either to confute your slander, or reply to the charge of your groundless and unworthy insinuations. It was also the determination of the Gentlemen you impeached, to avoid every step that even might* eventually *tend to foment any party altercations, which they deemed your letter solely calculated and published to provoke; thereby to render unworthy of public protection, a scheme founded upon the fairest principles of general utility.*

But now, Sir, when even the feeble excuse of ignorance about the facts you have misrepresented, can no longer be pleaded; and you have spread your abuse beyond [orig. behold] that circle, where *a general knowledge of those facts set the Gentlemen above the Reach of your calumny; the honour of that set of men you have so publicly traduced, requires a public defense.—The circumstances you would allude to, were as follow:*

*The Deputy Recorder of this town, who was sent by the council to oppose the intended application from the Merchants to Parliament; said,—"He apprehended it was the intention of those who were anxious for the success of this scheme, to apply for an Act this session of parliament." When one Gentlemen answered, "*No*, not this Session:" —upon which, the Gentleman who first publicly moved this business, rose up, and said, "We do not yet know whether it will be applied for this session or not,"— And these words, I very well remember, were so particularly spoken to the Deputy Recorder, that I must conceive it utterly impossible he could mistake them.— Of these circumstances, however, you were apprised: and yet, adding insolence to injustice, you have republished, even in the London News Papers, the same advertisement subscribed with your name. It would be extremely irksome to the writer of this letter, to reproach in this public manner, even a* private *Man:—but, Sir, it is not his fault, if the*

turpitude of uttering a falsehood recoils upon the Worshipful the Mayor of Liverpool. The writer's intention is only to clear a body of Merchants, of whom He is one, from so foul an aspersion; and to convince You that He scorns the imputation of being an anonymous accuser, whenever the Mayor shall, by a letter to the printer under his own hand, say, he can prove the calumny He has subscribed; He may be assured of knowing the author of this letter.
A Merchant of Liverpool.

Printed notices 19 March 1774[a]

To the FREEMEN of LIVERPOOL
Gentlemen,

THE Honour which you have this Day conferred upon me, not only with unanimity, but with the most genuine Marks of your Regard and Approbation, demands every possible return of my personal Gratitude as well as public Duty,

I Trust, that in whatever Station I may be placed, you will ever find me steadfast to the Cause of Liberty, and assiduous in my Attention to the Interests of Commerce.

I am, Gentlemen, Your most obliged and Faithful humble Servant,
WILLIAM MEREDITH.

THE Half yearly Association *of the Friends of* The Right Honorable Sir WILLIAM MEREDITH, Bart, and RICHARD PENNANT, Esq; *will be held on Wednesday the 6th of April next, at Mr. Banner's, the Sign of the Golden Fleece, in Dale Street.*
Mr. STANIFORTH, in the Chair.[15]
Dinner on the Table at Two o'Clock.

Printed notice 17 & 24 June 1774[a]

Subscribers to the Chamber of Commerce to meet at Pontack's Coffee House at 10.00 on 24th June in order to elect the Committee for the ensuing year. In the meantime those who choose to encourage so laudable an undertaking may see the Deed by applying to John Gore.

[15] Staniforth became the chamber's Vice-President, and was a member of its committee all years 1774–1787.

Council Minute 7 December 1774[b]

Ordered that a Committee of Commerce be appointed out of the body of the Council to consist of Such number, to be subject to such orders and regulations, as should be established at the next Council, &c., and Mr. Peters [Deputy Recorder] is desired to draw up proper rules and orders for that purpose.

Council Minute 5 March 1775[b]

AT A COMMON COUNCIL of the said Town holden in the Council Chamber within the Common Hall of the same on the first Wednesday in April the fifth Day of the same Month 1775 being a General day of meeting of the Common Council there immemorially used.

THE MAYOR Bailiffs and Burgesses in this Common Council assembled taking into their Consideration the great emolument which has arisen and is likely to arise to the Estate and Revenues of this Corporation from the Trade and Commerce of the Town, and being well satisfied that they cannot do any thing, which will more tend to the Furtherance and advancement of the common Profit and Commodity thereof, than by using their reasonable endeavours for the protecting and advancing its Trade and Commerce and they having the prosperity thereof at Hearts DO HEREBY DECLARE IT TO BE THEIR RESOLUTION to extend their Corporate aids for the defence and promotion of all such Trade and Commerce as do or shall concern the Interest of this Town, in such manner and measurers as Exigencies shall from time to time require, and as to the Mayor Bailiffs, and Burgesses in Common Council to be assembled, or the major part of them, shall in their discretion seem meet and expedient for the common Wealth thereof—

AND for the better and more speedy execution of all such matters and things as relate to such Trade and Commerce, It is by and by the Authority of the Mayor, Bailiffs and Burgesses, in this Common Council assembled ORDAINED AND ENACTED,

That from henceforth there shall be every Year Seven Common Councilmen appointed or continued by the Mayor, Bailiffs and Burgesses in Common Council to be assembled for the time being on every first Wednesday in April yearly or at the first or second General Council, which shall be held after that day yearly, to be, and which seven Councilmen shall be and be called, THE COMMITTEE OF TRADE OF THE TOWN OF LIVERPOOL, and shall continue in Office for one whole year next after their Election, and till others shall be chosen in their stead Provided that the Council may continue for any succeeding year or Years, all or any of such Committeemen, and choose others at any Common Council in the room of any Committeeman or Committeemen who may die, to act for the residue of the year after his or their death. And such Committeemen for the time being and the Survivors of them, or any four or three of them to be assembled in the Council Chamber, on three hours Notice in writing to be given or left at the Houses or usual places of abode of all the Committeemen then living for the time being by their Clerk, at the instance of the Chairman or any Committeeman thereof, for the time being, shall have, and are hereby invested with full power and Authority from time to time during their continuance in Office, to do, order, make and execute; or cause to be done, ordered, made and executed, all such ACTS AND ORDERS either for the sending up or employing Deputies, Agents or Witnesses to attend Parliament and else where: and the soliciting for or opposing any Act or Acts of Parliament or any clause or clauses therein: or any other Commercial purpose or purposes: and all such matters and things, as do or shall any way tend to the protection, increase or advantage of such Trade and Commerce, as it is the Interest of this Town to support, acquire or augment, as they in their discretion shall think meet (they or some of them), or their Clerk for the time being, to be chosen as hereinafter mentioned, making Entries from time to time in a Book or Books to be kept and continued for that purpose, and called their COMMITTEE BOOK OR BOOKS of all their Acts Orders and proceedings, which shall as the same are made and entered, be subscribed with the names of the Committeemen making and ordering the same, and shall be by them or some of them, together with their Correspondences touching the premises, reported every year at the Council, when new Committeemen shall be chosen or continued, or when and as often as thereunto required by the Council, by producing such Committee Book or Books, and their Letters and Copies of Letters, and all things required in that behalf, to and for the inspection of the Common Council.

AND for defraying the necessary Expenses of such Committee touching the premises, it is hereby and by the authority aforesaid ORDAINED AND ENACTED That the said Committee for the time being, or such number of them as aforesaid, shall have and they are hereby invested with full power to apply for the purposes of carrying on and executing all such Acts, Orders, matters and things as aforesaid, any Sum or Sums of this Corporate Revenue not exceeding in the whole the Yearly sum of Two hundred and fifty pounds, unless an Act of Common Council shall or any time or times be made, on consideration had of the Committees Report of the insufficiency (if that shall be found) of the Fund hereby established, for augmenting the same, occasionally or otherwise: which Monies the Treasurer of this Corporation is hereby authorized and required to pay, as the same shall be called for to or under the written Order of the Committeemen or the major part of them for the time being, from time to time at any of their Meetings to be assembled: and the Committee for the time being shall cause just Accounts to be from time to time kept in a Book to be provided and continued for that purpose of the application of all such monies.

AND it is hereby ORDAINED AND ENACTED by the authority aforesaid that Aldermen John Blackburn, William Gregson, James Gildart, John Sparling, John Crosbie, Messrs. John Brown and Mr. Thomas Birch (all Common Councilmen of this Town) be and they and the Survivors of them are hereby appointed to be such Committee for one whole Year now next ensuing and until others shall be appointed in their stead pursuant to this Order. And that they and all succeed'g Committees shall meet in the Council Chamber, on the first Monday after their Election respectively, at Twelve o'Clock at noon to choose or Ballot for a Chairman, and shall (if present at each Committee) have the casting Vote, whenever the Committeemen present shall be equal in number, and shall be divided in Opinion. And if such Chairman shall not be present, the Committeemen present shall ballot for the casting Vote at each respective meeting. And such Chairman or any Committeeman shall have power (whenever he shall see occasion) to cause Committees to be Summoned.

AND the Committee shall on the first Monday after their Election annually choose or continue a CLERK who shall keep their Books and papers, and every thing belonging to the Committee in an IRON CHEST to be kept for that purpose, enter all their Acts and Orders, summon Committees and do all their necessary Business, and be therefore paid such Salary as the Committee for the time being or the major part of them, assembled at any Committee Meeting shall (regard being had to such Clerk's trouble in the premises) by any their Order direct. AND as it may sometimes be necessary on very urgent Occasions for the Committee to meet on less Notice than as before mentioned, the Chairman for the time being, when he shall see any such Occasion (but not otherwise) is hereby empowered, to send the Committee's Clerk or some other person to summon every Member of the Committee, to meet in the Council Room, or else where at an hour to be appointed by the Chairman by Personal Notice or leaving a written Summons at his House. And to prevent delay such members who appear at that hour, or the major part of them, are hereby empowered to Act.

AND it is the earnest desire and recommendation of the Mayor, Bailiffs and Burgesses in this Common Council assembled that such Committees for the time being, and the Survivors of them or their Chairman, will from time to time establish and hold such Correspondences as they shall think proper (keeping Copies of their Letters in a Book for that purpose, and filing their Letters received) for the acquiring Intelligence in all matters which relate to such Trade and Commerce, as do or may anyway concern the Town of Liverpool. And that they will (whilst they continue in Office) be attentive to, and use their diligent and utmost endeavours for the protection and augmentation of the Trade and the Furtherance and advancement of the common Profits and advantage of this Town.

AND it is hereby ORDAINED AND ENACTED by the authority aforesaid that this ACT or ORDER OF COUNCIL for establishing the said Committee shall have Continuance only so long as the Acts and Proceedings of the said Committee shall be approved of by the Council.

Committee of Trade, first minutes 5 April 1775[e]

At the first meeting of the Committee of the Board of Trade Established under the act or Order of the Common Council of the Borough and Corporation of Liverpool, held and made on Wednesday the fifth day of April instant [1775] in the Council Chamber within the Exchange of the said Town at 12 o'Clock pursuant to Notice being the General Common Council day according to ancient usage.

Present:

James Gildart Esq.
John Sparling
John Blackburn
William Gregson
John Crosbie
John Brown
Thomas Birch

Merchants

IT IS ORDERED That the Act of Establishment and Constitution of this Committee be Copied in the Committee Book with marginal Notes or References to the same.

ORDERED That John Blackburn Esq. be appointed President of this Committee for the Year ensuing

IT IS ORDERED That Alderman Crosbie the Corporation Treasurer do provide an Iron Chest and Committee Books and Papers and other necessary things as the Committee shall from time to time want for this business.

APPOINTED Then and Elected Alderman John Crosbie to be Clerk of this Committee for this year [he was also Corporation Treasurer].

ORDERED That the first Monday in every Month be appointed the stated Committee day at Eleven o'Clock in the afore noon in the Council Chamber of each day.

4.3 Nottingham chamber of commerce 1795, 1813, 1835–8

The first successful attempt to establish a chamber in Nottingham was initiated in 1860, which falls outside the period covered in this volume. However, there were several previous attempts, only one of which seems to have been briefly successful, over 1835–c.1838 (see Chapter 1). The Nottingham efforts give insight into tensions which differed from almost all other chambers in trying to overcome conflicts with local workers and worker organisations. A first founding of a 'Nottingham chamber of manufacturers' began sometime in 1785, with a first record of it in December when it gave 'an elegant dinner to David Parker Coke MP for … exertions against the Irish propositions'. This report is noteworthy because the local MP Robert Smith had supported the Irish proposals and the divergence of opinion of Smith and a Nottingham local delegate (Mr. Hayne) had been published in the *Nottingham Journal* in March and April 1785 (see documents below; also Chapter 8). Hence, the local chamber's activities were closely interlocked with the General Chamber, to which it gave strong support, using Coke to circumvent the other local MP's opposition. Nottingham's links with the General Chamber thus mirror tensions in other areas.[16] This first chamber was probably no more than a group of delegates who had worked with other localities during the early efforts of the General Chamber,[17] or it could have been a town committee stimulated to use the brand of 'chamber' by the then current General Chamber. It seems to have existed for about two years since another reference to it occurs in 1787 when it offered a reward of 20 guineas for arrest of rioting framework knitters who broke up hosiery frames in October 1787. This type of reward was similar to the way in which the Nottingham Association for Prosecution of Felons operated, which was active in the city at the time. It was buttressed by the MP Coke who introduced a Bill to parliament on 5 May 1788 to make the destruction of weaving frames a capital offence. He was reportedly less interested in actually using capital punishment than promoting this Bill as a deterrent.[18]

However, as the reproduced documents show, the 1780s actions created animosity from the local frame workers, which remarkably was carried forward for 30 years in local memory to the second attempt to found a chamber in 1813. The 1813 attempt was quickly abandoned in the face of opposition from local hosiery workers, and the response to them by business leaders who did not want to inflame an already tense situation during strong local and national Luddite riots which had been ongoing over 1811–13 and focused on the stocking manufacturers. Their business leaders had adopted new manufacturing methods over this period and had lowered prices, which threatened workers and led to frame-breaking in March 1811, with the local magistrates and corporation taking repressive action continuing up to 1813.[19]

The third Nottingham attempt at a chamber in 1835 was more general and seems to have operated as a normal chamber for about two or three years

[16] Bennett, *Local Business Voice* (2011) 404–10.
[17] The two named were Mr. Carpenter Smith and Mr. Northage: see Chapter 8.
[18] Namier and Brooke, *House of Commons* (1954).
[19] Summarized in Walton, *History of the Nottingham Chamber* (1960) 12–14.

(see Chapter 1). However, it may have been diverted into considering industrial controls through developing collaboration with workers. Events are unclear, but an attempt was made to found an 'Artisans Chamber of Commerce' by Gravener Henson in Nottingham in 1838 and it seems likely that this was either a rival employer association that displaced the chamber, or was an evolution of the 1835 chamber into an employer association that failed to take off. Henson was influenced by the French *Conseils de Prud'hommes*, which were used to settle industrial disputes. Henson's concept was a workers' chamber and a manufacturers' chamber. This may reflect a plan for the 1835 chamber and the workers' chamber to collaborate. However, any co-operation broke down after two months and the initiative seems to have come to nothing.[20] There are similarities in concept to the collective silk body in Macclesfield mooted in 1827, which led to various co-operations, eventually resulting in the establishment of a Macclesfield Board of Trade over 1849–52.[21] This produced a list price for silk weaving, which was to be binding on each party (the employees and manufacturers), with activities financed by levies on both parties. Macclesfield copied the *Conseil de Prud'hommes* at Lyons, with which it was closely in touch as another major silk town. The Macclesfield Board broke down after only three years due to undercutting by manufacturers of each other and resistance by some workers, illustrating the problems of voluntary collective regulatory action. This seems to have also occurred in Nottingham and took the chamber down with it.

By the 1860s Nottingham had, however, certainly developed a successful local employer-employee cooperation for the lace and hosiery trades, which was held out as the leading example of local conciliation boards by the Trades Unions Parliamentary Commission of 1867–9. The Commission even recommended local Boards of Conciliation should be more generally developed, using Nottingham as its leading example since it had had a major effect on reducing strikes.[22] This Board was independent of the Nottingham chamber founded in 1860, but the chamber did maintain a closer relationship with the Board than occurred in almost any other area. In general, chambers, Boards of Conciliation, and employer associations kept apart from each other in Britain.[23]

[20] R. A. Church and S. D. Chapman, 'Gravener Henson and the making of the English working class', in E. L. Jones and J. D. Chambers, eds. *Land, labour and population in the Industrial Revolution* (London, 1967) 131–61.

[21] K. Austin 'The Macclesfield Board of Trade', chapter 13 in *Troubled Times: Macclesfield 1790–1870* (Macclesfield, 2003); Bennett, *Local Business Voice* (2011) 583–4.

[22] Trades Unions Commission, *House of Commons Papers*, XXXI (1867–9) xxvii; see also *Local Business Voice* (2011) 569–73.

[23] See Bennett, *Local Business Voice* (2011) 39–40, 465–6, 569–73.

Sources
[a] J. F. Sutton (1879) *The Datebook of Remarkable and Memorable Events connected with Nottingham and its Neighbourhood, 1750–1879,* Printed by H. Field, Nottingham; BL.
[b] *Nottingham Journal.*
[c] *Nottingham Review.*

Published report 13 September 1785[a]

The Nottingham Chamber of Manufacturers gave an elegant dinner to David Parker Coke MP as a complement for his patriotic and manly exertions in Parliament against the Irish propositions for the admission of their manufactures; and for his polite and zealous attention to their remarks on, and objections to, that absurd and pernicious system.

Published report 26 October 1787[a]

A large number of framework knitters assembled in the market place in a riotous manner, marched to the house of a person named Greaves, in Narrow-Marsh, and broke a frame to pieces, the property of Mr. Hooton, hosier, High-Pavement. The mayor immediately swore in a number of special constables, and issued a handbill of a cautionary nature; and the local Chamber of Commerce offered a reward of 20 guineas for the discovery of the offenders. There was consequently no further break of the peace.

Published notice 3 November 1787[b]

CHAMBER OF COMMERCE, NOTTINGAM, 27 October 1787

A great number of framework knitters, with their faces blacked and otherwise disguised, assembled in the market place in a riotous manner and marched to feloniously seize and take a wide standing frame standing in the dwelling house of John Greaves and broke to pieces.

This Chamber, foreseeing and dreading the destructive and fatal consequences which must result from such practices if not timely and effectively checked and prevented, and conceiving it incumbent on them, as Guardians and protectors of the interest, welfare and prosperity of the trade and manufactures of this town; and … that they are bound to secure protect, at all events, the property and every individual concerned in the said trade—

GIVE NOTICE that a reward of 20 guineas to be paid by the treasurer for information leading to the discovery of the offenders.

Samuel Turner (sec.)

Published report 24 December 1813[c]

To John Allen Esq., Mayor.

We, the undersigned, request you convene a meeting of the bankers, manufacturers and others interested in the trade of Nottingham on an early day to take into consideration the eligibility of establishing a Chamber of Commerce in this place.

Dated Nottingham, 21st December, 1813.

[Signed but printed: 14 names: see Appendix, no. 23]

Having received the above requisition, I do hereby in pursuance thereof convene a general meeting of the bankers, manufacturers and others interested in the trade of this town to be held for the purpose of the above mentioned at half past ten o'clock in the forenoon on Wednesday, 29th December instant at the Guildhall.

John Allen, Mayor

Published report 31 December 1813[c]

An unfavourable impression had been made on the minds of many of the working class respecting the Chamber of Commerce. In consequence of an establishment under that name having been attempted in this town some years ago, which they conceived was intended to cramp and control them. Unfortunately that impression had not been removed by a previous display of the intentions of the present projected institution; and the name was sufficient to induce them to oppose it. On the first Resolution being finally put there was a majority of hands against it; in consequence of which the meeting hastily broke up without any further consideration.

4.4 Cork 1814

The chamber in Cork formally began in 1819, but there was an effort five years earlier triggered by dissatisfaction with the Committee of Merchants of Cork, which had been founded in 1769. The committee had become controlled by a small group overlapping with the city aldermen and other officials. It was relatively inactive on a number of the issues of the time. It had refused to collaborate with the Waterford chamber over 1814–16 on a lobby for a tax on foreign butter and cattle imports as the 'subject is more a political than a commercial one'. The committee also appeared inactive over convoying.[24] Perhaps the immediate cause of anger with the Committee was

[24] Waterford chamber letters show the Cork committee of merchants gave either no responses or negative responses to the chamber's efforts. Waterford Archives: chamber minutes, 28 March 1814 over mail coaches; 14 September 1814 over taxation; committee of merchants in-letters

excessive expenditure and inefficiency in the weigh house, which was managed by the Committee, but was in disrepair. A fund had been established for rebuilding it, paid for contributions from the corn and butter merchants and the Committee. Work had begun in March 1814 but became a protracted and delayed by the death of the committee's treasurer. Bills had to be drawn on the Committee's members before funds from the former treasurer were released.[25] Also critical was the committee moving its meetings in 1813 from the Liverpool Arms Hotel, which involved minimal cost, to a committee room at the Commercial Buildings rented at £409 per year.[26] These buildings were a major source of discord since the Commercial Buildings Company, led by a 'junta', was seeking an Act to allow it to tax local citizens for every entry in the Customs House. This led to a petition against it on 19 July 1814.[27] A day later a meeting of merchants (as reproduced here) called for the establishment of a chamber of commerce as an alternative to the Committee, objected that the president of the Committee had agreed that the Customs House could work only one day per week and that the committee was 'self-created' and no longer held authority to represent, not least over any obligation to pay increased fees for butter weighing. The embryo chamber elected a chair, Sir Anthony Perrier, and secretary, Samuel Lane. The Committee was slow to respond, eventually producing a resolution in November (reproduced here). This defended its president and its status, but it was forced to admit that it drew its authority from the merchants and traders who could change its regulations as they saw fit. It stated that having two bodies was 'inconsistent and may prove injurious' and that the public authorities, admirals of the port etc. should for the present send all communications to the mayor.[28] It is unclear whether this early Cork chamber developed. In November 1819 the first minutes of the modern chamber show that only one of its committee (Francis J. Maloney) overlapped with members of the 1814 meeting; but the chamber immediately resumed its attack on the Committee with conflict continuing over the following years until the chamber took over most of the Committee's functions of managing the weigh house, butter market, etc., and relations with the Custom House. The extracts from the minutes for 1819–20 reproduced here show the nature of the conflict of status between a 'self-appointed' body (the Committee of Merchants) and

Cork City Archives, 5 March 1814 (U401/258), 3 August 1814 (U401/ 1330), 28 October 1815 (U401/149), 10 April 1816 (U401/267); convoys in committee minutes, 23 July 1814 ff.

[25] Cork City Archives: Cork committee of merchants minutes, 29 July and 11 August 1813; 5 March 1814.

[26] Ibid., 31 August 1813.

[27] *The Freeholder*, 19 July 1814.

[28] Cork City Archives: Cork committee of merchants, minutes, 17, 21 and 16 November 1814; summarised in document[b].

an elected chamber's committee, and the continued efforts to understand the abuses in the Committee's accounts and wrest control of the market functions from the Committee. Repeated efforts in 1821 and 1822 to obtain detailed accounts from the Committee of Merchants finally yielded information and the chamber took over the butter, hide and skin markets, and crane in 1822, having appointed a committee to administer this in 1821.

Sources
[a] *Cork Mercantile Chronicle,* 20 July 1814
[b] *Cork Mercantile Chronicle,* 29 November 1814; also in minutes of Committee of Merchants 28 November 1814; Cork City Archives U 401/1
[c] Chamber minute book; held by current Cork chamber.

Report 20 July 1814[a]

AT A MEETING OF THE MERCHANTS & TRADERS OF CORK, Convened by Public Advertisement, and held at THE COMMERCIAL BUILDINGS, ON WEDNESDAY, THE 20TH JULY, 1814, Sir ANTHONY PERRIER in the Chair;

The following RESOLUTIONS, proposed by ISAAC MORGAN, Esq. and seconded by ROBERT BURKE, Esq. were put by the Chairman, and unanimously adopted.

RESOLVED,

That we have seen with surprise a Paper signed "GERARD CALLAGHAN, President," dated Committee of Merchants' Room, 5th July, stating, that an arrangement had been made with the Surveyor-General of Customs and Storekeeper of this Port, whereby the Sampling and Inspecting of Warehoused Goods should be confined to one Day in the Week.

RESOLVED,

That such arrangement having been entered into, without our Knowledge or Concurrence, by a self-created Body, improperly styled the Committee of Merchants of Cork, who, however respectable the Individuals may be have no authority to legislate for, or represent us, it is not in the least obligatory, and We hereby Protest against it.

RESOLVED,

That the aforesaid arrangements, if acted on, would be highly injurious to the Commercial Interest of this City, and that we cannot consent to relinquish any Right granted us by the Legislature, at the same time that We shall ever be ready to accommodate the Officers of the Revenue in the performance of their duty.

RESOLVED,

That to protect our own Rights, and to further the general Trade of Cork, it is necessary to form an Association, from the Merchants and Traders at large, which will possess the Public Confidence.

RESOLVED,

That such Body be called "THE CHAMBER OF COMMERCE"; That it consist of 24 Members, one-third of whom to withdraw annually, and the vacancies to be filled by the Merchants and Traders at a General Meeting, and that no two individuals from one House, shall be Members at the same time.

RESOLVED,

That the following Gentlemen be requested to act for the present Year:

James Keene,	Thomas Wise,
Sir Anthony Perrier,	Francis J. Malony,
Nicholas Murphy,	J.K. Cummins,
Thos. S. Reeves,	Robert Burke,
J.B. Foley,	Denis Moylan Sen,
Samuel Lane,	Robert McClure,
Samuel Periott,	John Browne,
Richard N. Nettles,	Barth. Gibbings,
Frederick Honan,	William Large,
Owen Madden,	Pat Purcell,
Thomas Dunscombe,	Henry Hewett,
Joseph King,	James B. Church.

RESOLVED,

That the foregoing Resolutions be published.

ANTHONY PERRIER, Chairman.

Sir A. Perrier having left the Chair, it was Resolved, That the Thanks of this Meeting be given to him for his highly proper conduct therein.

SAMUEL CROOKSHANK.

SAMUEL LANE, Secretary.

Report 29 November 1814[b]

[Emphasis of italics in printed report, not contained in minutes, which were unanimously agreed 28 November 1814]

AT A MEETING of the "COMMITTEE OF MERCHANTS" of the CITY OF CORK, Holden at their Rooms in the Commercial Buildings, the 28th Day of November, 1814, THOMAS HARVEY, Esq, Vice. President, (in the absence of THOMAS MCCALL, Esq. President,) in the Chair,

RESOLVED UNANIMOUSLY,

That the term of our late President GERARD CALLAGHAN, Esq. having, in rotation, expired, we deem the present the proper time to notice a

Publication, dated *20th of July last, containing Resolutions of a Meeting on that day, purporting to be a Meeting of the Merchants and Traders of Cork*; wherein "*The Committee of Merchants*" is styled *"a self-created Body"*, and the Traders at large are called on to form *"an Association which will protect their Rights, possess the Public Confidence, and further the general Trade of Cork."*

That the name of our late President having been introduced into the Publication alluded to, we feel ourselves called upon thus publicly to acknowledge the diligence, zest, and ability with which, as Chairman, he discharged all the duties of that Situation.

That we *deny the allegation of "The Committee of Merchants" being a self-created Body; because the "Committee of Merchants" was originally founded by the Merchants and Traders at large*, in the year 1769, and since continued by an Annual Election of Members, in conformity with the prescribed Rules, as appearing on the Minute Book of the Committee.

That the *"Committee of Merchants" professes to hold no other authority*, but what the acquiescence for nearly half a Century of the Merchants and Traders at large is the utility of the Institution—the characters of the Individuals composing it—their gratuitous labours—the rectitude of its acts, and its acknowledged services in advancing the Trade of Cork, have acquired for it.

That it is at all times competent to the Body of Merchants and Traders from whom the *"Committee of Merchants"* derives its appointment, to make such changes either in its form or its regulations as they shall see fit; and that it is the duty of the *"Committee of Merchants"* in acquiesce in, and give effect to any alteration, that shall appear to conduce to the Advantages and Prosperity of the Trade of Cork.

That, defying all Malignity to point out any act of the *"Committee of Merchants"* which is not grounded on positive good or expediency—we will continue to act, governed by the same principles as ever, for the prosecution of those objects for which we were instituted; persuaded that the *"Committee of Merchants"* continues to possess the full confidence of the Body at large.

That, as the existence of two Associations whose object should be the same, (the promotion of our Trade) is inconsistent, and may prove injurious, we direct that our President do address Vice-Admiral SAWYER ['our Port Admiral' inserted in the minutes], and such other Authorities as usually correspond with this City on subjects connected with its Trade, requesting that their Communications may for the present be addressed to the Mayor of Cork.

That these Resolutions be signed by each Individual of the Committee, in order that the Public may judge whether those who transact such a portion of the Trade of Cork, are qualified by the Interests they have at stake, to guard its Commercial Rights ['interests' in minutes], and watch over its Commercial Concerns. ['Ordered to be printed in the Cork newspapers' in the minutes].

Thomas Cuthbert.	Thomas Harvey.
James Fagan.	William Beamish.
John Cotter Jun.	John Lecky.
David Gallwey.	Simeon Hardy.
William Maxwell.	Joshua Carroll.
Robert Carr.	Robert Barry.
George Waters.	Reuben Harvey.
Henry Bagnell.	Daniel Callaghan.
John N. Wrixon.	John Cotter.
William Crawford.	Archibald Maxwell.
	William Allen.

Minute 31 December 1819[c]

Some proceedings have appeared in the public prints, of meetings held at the Commercial Buildings [where the Committee of Merchants met and which they controlled], at which some persons are represented to have observed upon the absence of a conciliating disposition on the part of those who possessed influence at the Chamber of Commerce.

The Committee cannot avoid this publicly rejecting it, and charging those who uttered with palpable insincerity inasmuch as, no opportunity was afforded them of evincing any disposition—whether conciliatory or otherwise.

Minute 13 January 1820[c]

The Committee considered certain charges in the *Cork Mercantile* [*Chronicle*] but will not proceed on them and agree not to report their proceedings outside the chamber.

Minute 9 February 1820[c]

Report of the delegates of the Committee on their meeting with Mr. Cotter [the Secretary of the Committee of Merchants]. He could not in any way recognise the Committee of the Chamber of Commerce but was ready to grant us individually, as respectable merchants, an inspection of the accounts, and all other information we may require, relative to the Butter, and Hide & Skin Cranes. The delegates replied that it being of no importance to the Chamber of Commerce to be recognised by the Committee of Merchants. … It was unwise of the Committee of Merchants—(whose work of appointment has been objected to; and whose authority, to assure or control over any branch of the trade of Cork, has been abused: even by those now forming a considerable proportion of its actual members) thus to impugn an Institution which has emanated from 400 citizens, amongst who are comprised bankers, merchants, manufacturers and traders of great wealth and respectability—that to contact individually the members of other bodies, would be invidious but if the question be, the constitution of either [the Committee of Merchants or the chamber], it cannot be objected to the Committee of the Chamber of Commerce that it is self appointed! Mr. Cotter then showed the delegates four sheets of paper he had prepared referring to a book and other documents from which the delegates have made a transcript.

Minute 17 February 1820[c]

[The chamber's committee having now been able to access the Committee of Merchants' accounts, the Committee of the Chamber draft a response to the Committee of Merchants]

That your accounts are objected to, because they do not sufficiently enter into details … and have no breakdown of individual payments of income and expenditure. That you have distributed your funds … of large sums for entertainments and wines. … from the documents made available to subscribers to the Commercial Buildings Coffee Room, both purposes wholly unconnected with Butter & Hide & Skins which should only be taxed to defray charges balancing or indigent thereto.

Minute 8 March 1820[c]

After occurrences in their Room on two preceding evenings the Committee have posted the following notice

The Committee do not attempt to restrain the free expression of sentiments and opinion; they are convinced that the Subscribers will distinguish between such free communications and the pubic harangues of any individual. The Committee will promote order and propriety in the Room.

Minute 5 April 1820[c]

The Committee of Merchants is self appointed and included individuals with no interest in Butter, Hide & Skins; it has no righto the control which it has exercised. … The Committee is appointing a Committee of 25 to manage the Butter Hide and Skin Cranes—eleven exporters of Butter, seven Butter burgers, three dealers in Hide and Skins, and four Country Gentlemen being owners and occupiers of Land.

4.5 Bristol 1822

The Bristol Society of Merchant Venturers acted like a chamber over much of the early period, co-operating with other chambers from the 1770s, especially Liverpool over 1774–94, but also with Manchester and Glasgow (as summarised in Chapter 5).[29] The Venturers were strongly interlocked with the local municipal corporation, and the Dock Company, which they had helped to promote. As the Venturers already comprised most of the major merchant interests of the day it is not surprising that Bristol, despite being such a prominent city and port, had a relatively late chamber foundation in 1823. When the first chamber was founded this was mainly because of a breakdown in the effectiveness of the Corporation, Dock Company and Venturers. Especially important was a campaign protesting against the Dock Company's high rate of harbour dues, with the Venturers granted relief from dues.[30] The early Bristol 'floating harbour' to dam the river as a wet dock, promoted by the Venturers from the 1770s, was completed in 1809. The dues had to be set high initially to recover the costs. No dividend was paid to investors until 1823, but from that date the pressure built up to reduce the dues. The Dock Company had been slow to respond to the increasing uproar, and the chamber, eventually with support from the Venturers, was founded mainly to take up this cause. The pressure began with a petition in 1822, reproduced here, to return revenues from the corporation to the freemen (which included most chamber members). Exchanges between the chamber, the Venturers, mayor and common council in 1822–4 led to the council resolution sent to the Dock Company and Venturers, reproduced here, making no concessions: 'this corporation will not yield'.

A poem of c. 1822, written by Corporation sympathisers, demonstrates the council's position. This poem is especially valuable for its recognition of Glasgow as the other leading chamber at the time, and the early Liverpool chamber of 1774–c.1796 now in abeyance. The tone and style of the poem is also reminiscent of the minutes of the Liverpool common council and Committee of Trade, and the responses by John Dobson chair of the Liverpool chamber during that chamber's establishment in 1774–5, which are reproduced in section 4.2. The battle between Bristol Corporation and the chamber was extended over many years. It appears that the corporation tried to subvert the chamber. Reports by 'A. Burgess', reprinted from the *Bristol*

[29] For the activities and history of the Venturers see: J. Latimer, *The History of the Society of Merchant Venturers of the City of Bristol* (Bristol, 1903); P. McGrath, *The Merchant Adventurers of Bristol: A History* (Bristol, 1975); K. Morgan, *Bristol and the Atlantic Trade in the Eighteenth Century* (Cambridge, 1993). None of these sources have observed the relationships with chambers.

[30] Letter from Robert Brush, master of Venturers: BRO, Red Lodge papers 13748/5 (Bundle 4: f. 7).

Mercury of 1836, claimed that a group of leading members of the chamber had become suspect: the 'complainants have now become directors of the chamber' and had failed to press their views:[31] the chamber had been subverted to support the Dock Company and corporation by various personal inducements. The chamber was split between the 'liberal' campaigners supporting the closed corporation, and those who were 'timid with dislike' against the corporation.[32] The Municipal Commission in 1835 recognised 'the chamber in collision with the corporate bodies of the city'.[33] The chamber fell into difficulties after 1848, and was revived when Bruton became chamber secretary in 1853.[34]

Source
Red Lodge Books, Letters 'written to Mr. J. M. Gutch in answer to those who wrote to Felix Farley's Journal under the name of *Cosmo*' and on the chamber of commerce: BRO 13748/5

Printed sheet 'Miller Lines' [loose in Bundle 8] c.1822

'A CHAMBER? Yes, A CHAMBER!
'I hope the days are near at hand when *Chambers will be safe'* MACBETH

A Chamber of Commerce, presided by S—k,
To control the Comptroller, and open the Dock:
The fees of the Corporate Body to stint,
Whose gripe is as close as the closest to flint:
To silence all brawlers, who brawl for their dues,
Quay-wardens and Bailiffs—all water rat crews:
This Chamber has met its Directors to name,
When all are desirous that honour to claim.
A list being demanded, I handed mine in,
Having master'd the difficult point—'To begin,'
For sure none could so properly shew the right way,
Or *smooth a rough road*, as M'–m, they say.
And as merit should never be suffered to rust,
Who next could I name, but the good S—n P–st:
Or if doubt should arise in classing of names,
No loss would be felt, when I recollect J-m-s,

[31] BL: *Strictures on the later reports and proceedings of the Bristol Chamber of Commerce*, A. Burgess, reputedly authored by Leonard Bruton; see also Goldsmiths-Kress: J. M. Gutch, *Letters on the impediments which obstruct the trade and commerce of the city and port of Bristol: from Felix Farley's Bristol Journal*, 'Cosmo' (1823).
[32] John Barnett Kington (1834) *Thirty letters on the trade of Bristol* (Bristol: John Wright); spelling as original.
[33] Municipal Commission, *Parliamentary Papers*, XXIV (1835)1208.
[34] B. D. G. Little, *The City and County of Bristol* (Birmingham, 1954); C. Wells, *A Short History of the Port of Bristol* (Bristol, 1909) 79–101.

So modest, so able, so bland, so polite,
No idler is he, for he'll prate till it's night.
H–y B–n is the next—like a jewel he shines,
When of 'Chambers', and 'Floats', 'Rooms', and 'Bridges', he whines.
The S-nd-rs, a trio—George, Thomas, and John;
The first is a Beau, of the very high ton;
The second a Quaker, or else he's a Quis;
If we judge by his brim, or the cut of his phiz.
The third, like Oberon, king of the Sprights,
Having nothing to do, puts others *to rights*;
For ever annoys you with some scheme or other,
Contriv'd by himself, and approv'd by his brother.

Forty Directors! By twenty too much,
Unless you take F-sh-r, R-yn--ds, and G–h,
With Ly-ns, and R-ng-r, and P-r-y, and M–re,
And *quantum sufficit* to make up a score.
These jumbled together would make a hotch-potch,
Equal to any, so fam'd with the Scotch,
And Bristol may possibly rival Glasgow,
Tho' Liverpool long since has given it --- the go.
Such a chamber as this will all Chambers surpass,
If its roof be of iron—*its Supporters are* BRASS.'
For Tumblewayte and Co.—J. T.

[Presumed names referred to in the poem, in order, are: Thomas Stock, first chair of the chamber (also a William as member from Brice Stock & Fery); Stephen Prust (chair of the committee that drew up the Rules, q.v. Chapter 1); Maurice James & Co.; Henry Browne; George, Thomas and John Sanders of Thomas Sanders & Co.; Francis (?) Fisher; Reynolds of Reynolds Tomlinson & Co.; John Matthew Gutch; James Lyon(s); R-ng-r (not in first membership list; possible R. W. Ring); James Perry; James Moore: see Appendix, no. 3]

Petition: Handwritten draft [Bundle 4: fo. 1 and 2] 1822

To the Honourable the Commons of the United Kingdom of Great Britain and Ireland in Parliament assembled.

The humble Petition of the several Persons whose Names are hereunto subscribed being Burgesses and Resident Merchants or Traders of the City and County of the City of Bristol associated under the Designation of "The Bristol Chamber of Commerce & Trade with Manufactures".

Sheweth

That the Corporation of the City of Bristol is composed of the Mayor Burgesses and Commonality of that City.

That all the Rights Privileges Immunities and Property of the Corporation of the City of Bristol granted by His Majesty's Royal Predecessors have been and now are possessed for the benefit and advantage of the Burgesses of the said City of whom the Mayor and other Officers of the Corporation are Representatives and for whom they are Trustees.

That the privileges and possessions of the Corporation of Bristol granted by his Majesty's Royal Predecessors Kings and Queens of England have been granted either of the Royal Favour with a view to the encouragement of new Trade of the City and the advancement of the Commercial Prosperity of the Freemen at large or in consideration of money paid by the Freemen at large or of Services by the said Freemen performed and none of such privileges or possessions have been granted to any Individual Freemen exclusive of the whole Body of the Freemen of the said City.

[Two pages missing] ... as a Foreign Port and estimate and exact their Toll upon Merchandize to and from that part of the United Kingdom accordingly.

That the Common Council also exact as Mayor's Dues on all Vessels Coasting as well as others of 60-Tons and upwards 40s. and 5s. for the Water Bailiffs fee for every voyage and on Vessels of less tonnage & for each time of their entering the Port.

That the average number of voyages made by a Coasting Vessel annually is from 18 to 24.

That no service whatever is performed or professed to be performed in recompense of the Taxes thus exacted and that these Dues are by the mere Will and Authority of the Common Council imposed in addition to Dock Dues received in Bristol on Shipping and Goods by virtue of recent Acts of Parliament and in addition to anchorage moorage wharfage pilotage plankage and cranage.

That the Members of the Common Council have been and for the most part now are persons extensively engaged in Trade in the Articles of Sugar Wine and Tobacco and that with a most gross partiality the Members of that Body have exempted from the ad valorem tax these Articles of their own Trade exclusively and have substituted on such Articles an easy package rate

That the humble complaint of your Petitioners is that the Common Council have not reduced the Tolls and Dues upon all Articles in similar proportion with the tolls upon these favoured Articles nevertheless your Petitioners also refer to this instance to evince to your Honourable House that the Common Council are fully aware of the ruinous effect produced upon Commerce by the exactions that with manifest partiality and for their [~~the greediness of~~] exclusive Gain they have exempted their own admissions [~~themselves~~] from a burden which if it is at all to exist should be shared [~~by them~~] in common [~~with their fellow Burgesses~~] by the general Trade of Bristol and that as all the Revenue of the Corporation is the property and ought to be applied for the general advantage of the Burgesses of Bristol the Common Council which they wholly disregard the ruin brought by their imposts upon your Petitioners and the Burgesses in general in their Trade have not hesitated for their private and exclusive benefit to relinquish part of the Common Property while they affect to want legal power to equalise and regulate the Burthen which operates upon the general Body

That from the causes stated the Export and Import of Goods from and to Bristol are more expensive than at any other port in the United Kingdom

That on the Export of 13 Bales of Cloth valued at	£1839	19s.	3d.
The Town dues at Bristol are	10	–	0d.
and the total shipping Charges at Bristol are	12	5s.	1d.
While total shipping charges on the same Merchandize at Liverpool are only	3	18s.	–
That on 97 Packages of Manchester Goods valued at	£7436	4s.	5d.
The Town dues at Bristol are	£38	–	–
and the total ~~shipping~~ import Charges at Bristol are	£42	12s.	5d.
While the total ~~shipping~~ import Charges on the same Merchandize at Liverpool are only	3	3s.	2d.
That on 300 Bales of Clover seed the Town dues at Bristol are	6	11s.	0d.
and the total ~~shipping~~ import charges at Bristol are	16	3s.	4d.
While the ~~shipping~~ import charges in London on the same Merchandize are only	7	10s.	0d.
and the total ~~shipping~~ import charges in Hull on the same Merchandize are only	4	18s.	4d.
That on 61 Tons 9 Cwt. of Flax the Town dues at Bristol are	23	17s.	10d.
and the total shipping charges at Bristol are	45	13s.	–
While the total ~~shipping~~ import charges at Hull are only	10	15s.	–
That on 56 Tons of Gallipoli Oil the Town dues at Bristol are	16	16s.	0d.
and the total shipping charges at Bristol are	29	17s.	4d.
While the Total Shipping Charges at Hull are only	5	12s.	0d.

That the Port Charges on an American Vessel of 292 Tons measurement are at Bristol £73 18s. 7d. while at Liverpool those charges are only £47 13s. 6d.

That the Port Charges on a Ship of 350 Tons measurement laden with Timber including the Cargo are at Bristol £111 14s. 6d. and at the neighbouring Port of Chepstow they are only £14 16s. 6d.

That in and before the year 1777 the annual produce of the Town dues was £500 or thereabouts but that after that year the annual amount of these imports increased so greatly that in the year 1810 the same was £4500 and upwards.

That the dues and valorem thus [deleted: levied] claimed of their own authority by the Common Council of Bristol are 60 per Cent higher than the Government Export duly.

That Chiefly in consequence of the excessive Local Charges the Merchants and Manufacturers of the several Counties before named who have heretofore resorted to the Port of Bristol and would naturally continue to resort thither if not discouraged have almost ceased to export and import at Bristol and have carried their Commerce to other Ports and particularly that the Manufacturers of Gloucester, Wilts., Somerset ~~Worcester~~ and Devon now usually transmit their Cloths and other Manufactures through Bristol by Land Carriage to Ports 160 Miles off to avoid these exorbitant local charges.

That the natural Commercial intercourse between Bristol and the South of Ireland which the Common Council rate as a foreign Country is materially restricted and injured in consequence of the oppressive burdens complained of to the great injury of Ireland as well as of Bristol.

That the Town dues being charged both on the import and export of the same Goods operate as a prohibition of a warehousing Trade and rendering the bonding system as regards Strangers in a great measure nugatory except as to the favoured articles above mentioned.

That a Trade which was opened by some of your Petitioners direct with the East Indies has been unavoidably abandoned in consequence of the heavy local charges of the Port.

That the Trade between Bristol and the United States of America was formerly most extensive and is now from this and other causes nearly at an end.

That from the same cause your Petitioners are prevented from engaging in any Commercial transactions with South America upon the Trade with which Country the mode of taxation ad valorem would operate with distinctive severity in as much as almost all the commodities to be imported from South America are of small bulk and of great value.

That the trade in the articles excepted from the ad valorem dues is the only trade which remains to any considerable extent. That the Package rate on these articles in the year 1823 amounts as nearly as your Petitioners can compute to £1400. While if charged at the ad valorem rate imposed on other goods the dues on these articles in that year would have amounted to £8000.

That although the exorbitant charges upon Commerce at Bristol are ruinous to your Petitioners and the Burgesses of Bristol the disastrous effects [of this excessive local taxation] are not confined to the Burgesses inasmuch as those taxes are levied upon the trade of the whole Kingdom so far as that trade does or may pass through the Port of Bristol and that industry and commerce are consequently materially restricted in the South of Ireland and in those Counties of England and Wales of which Bristol has heretofore been the usual port of import and export and which are equal in value and population to one fourth of the whole United Kingdom.

That the Common Council of Bristol although they refuse adequate relief to your petitioners are fully conscious of the existence and the extent of the grievances complained of which is apparent from their having relieved those branches of trade in which they are personally interested and freed those trades ~~themselves~~ from equal participation in the burthen with which they load those of your petitioners Burgesses of Bristol and other their fellow Burgesses and is further apparent inasmuch as the Common Council after many previously unheeded remonstrances from your petitioners, Burgesses of Bristol and other Burgesses of that City did in this present Session of parliament obtain leave of your Honourable House to introduce a Bill by which they admitted the ruinous effects of their exactions but that the sole object of this Bill was to give power to the Common Council to reduce the amount of those exactions when and as they should think proper and again after such reduction to increase them, it being (as your petitioners conceive) strangely considered by the Common Council that the relief they had afforded to their own Commercial Interests without the authority of parliament they could not legally afford to the Commercial Interests of their Fellow Burgesses unless previously sanctioned by such authority.

That your petitioners respectfully expressed a desire to the Common Council that in the Bill that introduced some reduction of the Charges complained of should be censured and that a time should be fixed for such reduction whereupon and in resentment of the desire thus humbly expressed the Common Council wholly abandoned the Bill and declined to submit it to the consideration of your Honourable House and now refuse to give your petitioners any relief.

That your petitioners have no resort for the redress of grievances utterly ruinous to their trade and prospects in life destructive of the prosperity of their ancient City and injurious to the Commercial Interests of the Country except only to the wisdom of parliament.

That your petitioners therefore as Burgesses and inhabitants of Bristol and a part of the Corporation of that City humbly pray

> That your Honourable House will please to institute such Enquiry as to your wisdom shall seem proper into the present state of the Trade and Commerce of the port of Bristol and into the dues and charges imposed upon the trade to and from the port of Bristol and will be pleased to afford such relief to your petitioners and others interested in the trade of Bristol as upon the result of such enquiry shall seem proper.

And your petitioners shall ever pray &c.

Hand-written copy of resolution sent to the chamber [Bundle 4: fo. 1–17]
1 November 1823

At the Common Council at a Special Meeting
A Memorial to [it] being read

'Thereupon it was unanimously Resolved that this Corporation will not yield in inclination to any class of their fellow citizens in an anxious desire to promote the commercial or general prosperity of the city of Bristol; and it having been represented to this Corporation by the Board of Directors of the Chamber of Commerce, that the trade and commerce of this city are in a depressed state and still decreasing from local taxation (of the accuracy of which representation this Corporation is not convinced) They now invite the Public Bodies of the city to take into consideration this most important subject, & at their mutual [?] convenience to transmit to this Corporation their respective opinions thereon, with such documents & papers as they may think best adapted to the elucidation of the subject.

Ordered that Copies of this Resolution transmitted to the Society of Merchants, the Board of Directors of the Bristol Dock Company, & the Board of Directors of the Chamber of Commerce of this City.'

4.6 London 1823–4

London was the last major city in the UK to have a chamber of commerce, founded in 1882. It was then about the 70th chamber established in the UK. It developed within a few years to become the largest in the country. There had been a number of previous efforts to establish a generally based chamber. Weskett in 1782–1800 was seeking to use an opportunity for personal advantage to develop an arbitration service and as a training academy. Initiatives of a more general nature probably predated Weskett, and continued over most of the period up to 1882. They became focused and active during four main periods: 1817–18, 1823–24, 1850–5, and 1867–72.[35] The efforts in 1823–4 have left a valuable record of the issues and tensions involved and these are reproduced here from three newspaper reports to demonstrate the range of opinions existing in the metropolis. The first documents mainly focused on specific proposals to improve the law of merchant and factor relating to how money and credit was held. This was essentially the foundation

[35] The discussion here extends the documentary coverage in the previous assessment of London developments in Bennett, *Local Business Voice* (2011) 193–200, which should be referred to for the wider context; some additional mention of the early developments has also been discovered in F. L. Payne, (1967) *The London Chamber of Commerce: A History of Service to the Business Community* (1967).

of a lobby campaign, which proceeded and had a successful outcome in leading to a reform of the law (see Chapter 5). Its value here is to demonstrate the sort of issues that engaged a group of London merchants and bankers, and from which a proposal for a chamber emerged. On the one hand it is clear from this first document and the following two reports that a specific issue brought people together, and then this was developed into a chamber proposal with a committee to take formal proposals forward and draft rules. On the other hand it is also clear that the view that a chamber was needed in London was running among some of the participants, and they were using the specific occasion of concern about the law of factors and agents as an opportunity to galvanise activity.

The previous effort to establish a chamber in 1817–18 is commented on in the documents here, which make clear that it involved some of the same personalities. The 1817 proposal is remarkable in the level of support the London prime movers sought from government; this was not usually an issue in the provinces. The proposal emanated from H.S.H. Woollaston, who had been in close contact with Frederick Robinson, who was vice president, then president of the Board of Trade in 1812–23. Woollaston claimed that this proposal 'nearly succeeded', that the 'government was amicable to such an institution'. It had received support from Robinson, but the government was not going to initiate a chamber, or 'pledge itself on the subject; … it should stand or fall by its own respectability'.[36] Thomas Wilson MP believed that the proposal foundered 'principally for want of a sufficient number of respectable names to carry it on'. Henry Brougham had also pressed for the chamber in 1817. As far as can be determined, the government was very resistant to this proposal. Robinson supported it, but then reneged. Brougham, and one of his main contacts Alexander Baring, were key to the 1823–4 proposal. This discussion makes clear that the 1817 proposal went further than purely the 'The Equitable Trust Society' which tried to offer arbitration (see Chapter 6). Commenting in 1819, it was stated that 1817 was the *tenth* attempt to establish a chamber in London, but 'The Equitable Trust Society … [was] not … adapted to the temper and disposition of Englishmen—at least not in the metropolis'.[37]

The 1823 proposal seems to have derived from continuation of some of the same individuals as in 1817, but also gained greater encouragement by some success flowing from a petition on 8 May 1820 led by the MP Alexander Baring in the Commons who presented the 'petition of the merchants of

[36] H. S. H. Woollaston, quoted in the second document here.

[37] Goldsmiths-Kress: *The London Tradesman: a familiar treatise on the rationale of trade and commerce* (London, 1819) 322. The nine other attempts, other than Weskett, have not been discovered, although some may relate to Whiston and Davenant.

London in favour of free trade' which had been drafted by Thomas Tooke. This interlinked with activities in Manchester that helped re-establish its chamber in 1820.[38] The 1820 petition has been claimed to be a turning point towards free trade policy.[39] For the 1823 proposal Baring was again in the lead and the documents reproduced illustrate the significance of the Liverpool American chamber, which organised meetings in Liverpool. But this also confirms that it was London in the lead with this lobby, even though some of the initial stimulus had come from merchants in Liverpool. The lobby was successful in changing the law through a new Act, though this did not go as far as many of the lobbyists wished, as is evident in the discussions in these documents. Subsequent correspondence is useful in indicating how Lord Liverpool and William Huskisson (MP for Liverpool) interacted to overcome the opposition by petitions from 'master manufacturers' which was stimulated by Lord Stanhope.[40]

Sources
[a] *Morning Chronicle*
[b] BL Add. MS. 38744, ff. 225–8

Printed Report 2 May 1823[a]

MEETING OF MERCHANTS AND BANKERS

Yesterday a Meeting of the most eminent Merchants and Bankers of the City of London, took place at the London Tavern, for the purpose of adopting measures for the greater security of the money advanced by them, in the course of their commercial transactions, upon the deposit of merchandise and goods, and for a more adequate protection than is at present afforded by the English Law against the fraudulent conduct of Foreign Merchants.

JOHN SMITH, Esq. M.P. was unanimously called to the Chair.

The CHAIRMAN said it was known to them that Merchants, Bankers and other Capitalists, were in the habit of advancing money on the security of merchandize to a considerable extent, as well on the deposit thereof as in payment of bills of exchange, drawn by the consignors from foreign parts, or from one port to another within the United Kingdom. To encourage the employment of capital by means of such advances, by which the amount of capital actually engaged in commercial operations was increased, and the trade of this country was carried to a vast extent, was a sound principle of policy; but it was to be lamented that no adequate protection was afforded by

[38] Redford, *Manchester Merchants* (1934) 69.
[39] W. D. Grampp, 'How Britain turned to Free Trade', *Business History Review*, 61, 1 (1987) 86–112.
[40] See extended correspondence in Add. MS. 38744 ff. 229–39.

our law to such transactions. On the contrary, the English capitalist advanced his money at his peril and to his loss, if the goods proved to be the property of any other person than the individual borrowing or drawing upon the credit of them, although such fact was unknown and undiscoverable by the person making the advance. To provide against such a hardship, it became the great body of the capitalists of the nation to make every effort. It was worthy of remark that our Scottish brethren had exhibited upon this, as well as upon other questions, a much greater degree of prudence than we had exercised, as would be shown in the course of the discussion. In fact, the English law was unfair and absurd in the highest degree; for it went to prevent the circulation of capital beyond any measure that, perhaps, had ever been brought before Parliament.

Mr. FARRAND, M.P. rose to submit certain Resolutions, which had, he said, been drawn up under the legal opinion and advice of Messrs. Kaye, Freshfield, and Kaye. He observed, that the rule that a factor, though clothed with apparent ownership of goods, and the power of sale, could not pledge them, or dispose of them by barter, originated in cases determined a century ago, and turned principally on apparent fraudulent collusions between the factor and the individual with whom the goods were deposited—the Courts of Law had carried the principle to such as extent as to render all advances on goods extremely dangerous, by exposing English Capitalists, who advanced money on merchandise, to frauds on the part of foreign merchants. Any dereliction of duty, as between the principal and his factor, ought to be visited with severe penalties, such as were provided in the case of agents who embezzled securities and other effects deposited for safe custody, but so far as other persons were interested in the transaction, without knowledge of any breach of confidence committed by the factor, the principal ought to be bound by the act of his own agent. He cited cases to shew the great hardship arising from the present state of the law, and observed, that even the freight and duties on goods could not be safely advanced unless the bills of lading shewed that they were the property of the party for whose account such advance might be made. The Scottish law gave to the Scots capitalists the same advantages over the English merchants which foreigners possessed, and it was obvious that it would be for the advantage of commerce that this anomaly should be abolished, and the laws of neighbouring trading communities should be assimilated as much as possible. He concluded by proposing the Resolutions, and moving that a Petition should be presented to Parliament for an inquiry to be instituted into the state of the law, and a remedy provided for the evils complained of.

Mr. SHAW (the Banker) said, it was well known that Bankers were affected by securities of a different description from those alluded to. Bankers were in the habit of receiving Exchequer Bills and East India Warrants as securities for money. Exchequer Bills were often placed in the hands of brokers to sell, but the bankers, instead of making the sale, borrowed money on the bills, and the security became unavailable if the principal made his demand. The same was the case with East India Warrants. Against such losses the Bankers had no sort of protection.

Mr. HANKEY (the Banker) pressed the same objection.

Mr. FRESHFIELD said there was a striking difference between securities representing goods, and securities representing money. With respect to goods they might be traced to their apparent source with ownership, and yet the law gave no protection to the person who advanced money on them, as a third person might come forward to prove his claim. No intelligence would secure the Merchant. It was different with the Bankers. If the Exchequer Bills left with them as securities were made "payable to bearer," they were according to the decision of the Courts negotiable. None, in fact, of the consequences attached to goods would attach to Exchequer Bills.

Mr. THOMAS WILSON, M.P., said he felt much for the Foreign Merchants. Care should be taken to protect them from abuse of trust.

Another Merchant said, that in consequence of the knowledge of the state of the law, foreign capitalists would not advance their money, but if the evil were remedied, there would be no hesitation amongst them. He suggested a Select Committee.

The CHAIRMAN thought that nothing could be more uncertain in general than the conjecture as to the opinion of the Law Officers of the Crown: but he believed they were not hostile to the proposition of remedying the existing evil. Indeed, he understood their disposition is friendly towards a change. If the proceedings of the Meeting were brought to a speedy termination, a Bill might be brought into Parliament this Session.

The Resolutions were agreed to, and the Merchants and Bankers signed a Petition to Parliament.

Hand written report forwarded to Huskisson by Thomas Booth 18 June 1823[b]

At a General Meeting of Merchants, Bankers, Brokers, Corn Factors &c. who signed the petition to the House of Commons for modification of the Law of Principal and Factor convened by circular [from the American Chamber] at the Corn Exchange Committee Room the 18t June 1823, Thomas Booth Esq. in the chair.

The Report of the Committee having been read and Mr. John Ashton Yates having very fully reported the measures adopted by the petitioners in London and the investigations which took place before the Select Committee of the House of Commons.

It was Resolved

1st That this meeting having considered the report of the Committee highly approved of the measures which have been pursued, and requests the committee to accept the thanks of this meeting for their past exertions, which they are requested to continue....

2d. That this meeting having considered the report of Mr. John Ashton Yates as to the transactions which have taken place in London, requests that Gentleman to accept the thanks of this meeting … to which, and the active co-operation of the London Committee this meeting considers the petitioners are indebted for the elaborate investigation which this question has undergone before the Select Committee of the House of Commons.

3rd That this meeting has learned with satisfaction the Select Committee of the House of Commons have in their report which they submitted to the House on Friday last recommended the adoption of the propositions which were expertly formed by Mr. Freshfield[41] the Legal Advisor of the Petitioners in London, which propositions, although not affording all the relief which it appears to this meeting the true interests of commerce require, seem well calculated to produce by very simple and consistent means a remedy for many of the evils complained of. That this meeting cannot refer to that highly respectable Gentleman without expressing its thanks for his indefatigable attention and for his very able and luminous address to Select Committee of the House of Commons calculated to bring back to the standard of justice and common sense, a mercantile question which has been dangerously perverted by legal subtlety.

4th That it appears to this meeting highly expedient that the proposed remedy as recommended by the Select Committee of the House of Commons should receive the sanction of parliament during the present Session, since the publicity given to the present defective state of the Law will necessarily aggravate the evils complained of, and will annihilate confidence among Merchants—cause abstraction of capital from commerce and very much tend to the depression of Merchants and general derangement of Trade.

5th That a copy of the resolutions be forthwith transmitted to the Right Honourable William Huskisson … and the Chairman convey acknowledgements of the meeting for his zealous and active attention …

6th That General Gascoign, Mr. Gladstone, Mr. Birch and Members of the County be respectfully requested to give their support to a measure so essential to the interests of commerce.

7th That Mr. Eason, Mr. Barclay, Mr. A. Maxwell, Mr. William Rathbone, Mr. Joseph Sandars, and Mr. Hutchinson be added to the present committee.

8th That the thanks of the meeting and of the mercantile community are especially due to Mr. George Ashby Pritt for the able manner in which he,

[41] A major figure in the London debates; a prominent London solicitor: see *ODNB*.

first, expressed the injustice and inconsistency in the existing Law and for his laborious and vigilant attention to the interest of the petitioners.

[signed] Tho. Booth

That the thanks of the meeting be given to Thomas Booth Esq. for his able conduct in the chair.

Printed Report 29 August 1823[a]

LAW OF MERCHANT AND FACTOR.—METROPOLITAN CHAMBER OF COMMERCE.

Yesterday a General Meeting of Merchants, Bankers, and others, was held at the City of London Tavern, for the purpose of receiving the Report of the Committee, appointed at a former Meeting to investigate the state of the Law relating to Merchants and Factors, and of adopting such farther measures as might be deemed expedient, with a view to the more complete revision of the laws affecting those interests. Among the Gentlemen present were Mr. J. Smith M.P., Mr. B. Shaw M.P., Mr. Alderman Thompson M.P., Mr. Alderman Bridges M.P., Mr. T. Wilson M.P., Mr. R. Farrand M. P., Mr. Martin M.P., Mr. J. Masterman, Mr. Loughman, Mr. W. Buckle, Mr. Bainbridge, Mr. Soltan,[42] Mr. Mille &c. &c.

Shortly after one o'clock, Mr. T. WILSON moved, that Mr. J. Smith take the Chair, which was unanimously agreed to.

Mr. J. SMITH proceeded to open the business of the Meeting. The Committee, he said, which they had appointed to inquire into the laws relating to Merchant and Factor, and to apply to Parliament for such alterations therein as would render them conformable to just principles, were desirous of stating to them the result of their labours, in a Report which he trusted they would have the goodness to hear read, and in which they would find detailed the history of the late proceedings in Parliament relative to that subject. It was not his intention to occupy any considerable portion of their time; but he hoped he should be permitted to make a few observations, to which it was in some respects necessary to call their attention before reading the Report. A Parliamentary Committee had been appointed for the purpose of considering those grievances, which, much as they oppressed the commercial interests, were not, perhaps, generally known to the public, until the inquiry to which he alluded took place. The publicity which that inquiry gave to the state of the law, which was before scarcely known, was perhaps calculated to produce rather a discouraging effect upon commerce, until more could be achieved than they had yet been able to effect. It was essential, however, that the whole subject should be examined to the bottom, and he believed he

[42] George Soltau of Plymouth and a founding chamber member there; see Appendix.

might say without impropriety, that the Committee exercised great industry, and all the ability they possessed, in the investigation of this subject. A Bill was at length framed in conformity with the almost unanimous sentiments of the Committee. There was but one exception to that unanimity. An Honourable Friend of his, of great eminence, did not concur in the general sentiments of the Committee, but with that single exception they agreed in the measure which was recommended to the adoption of Parliament. That measure was in his (Mr. Smith's) judgment, and in the judgment of the other Members of the Committee, whose opinion was much more valuable than his own, a complete and adequate remedy for all the grievances of which they complained. But, unfortunately for the success of the measure of which they all approved, a strong feeling against it was entertained and expressed with some warmth by some eminent persons in the profession of the law, whose opinion controlled in a great degree the legislative measures of this country. The principle of the law, which allowed no factor to pledge goods, appeared to those eminent persons of great importance to the interests of the Merchants of England, while they overlooked the numerous and distressing instances of fraud and oppression which had been stated before the Committee. Attached to the legal principle to which he had alluded, they shut their ears against all reasoning which might be offered against it. [Summarises the difficulties of the lobby, and how they were overcome] …

There was another point, which he [John Smith] broached with some degree of doubt and difficulty, because he did not know that he had any right to introduce such a topic. He would take the liberty, however, of shortly calling their attention to it. It appeared to him that the commercial inhabitants of the metropolis had on this occasion received very substantial benefit by means of unanimity and co-operation. The Merchants of London formed a most important body of men—he did not like to say *the* most important—whose prosperity and success were intimately connected with the prosperity, success, and happiness of the Empire. The Gentleman now at the head of the Board of Trade, was extremely well disposed to attend to any suggestions of the Merchants of London, and he (Mr. S.) could not help thinking that it might be of great advantage to the commercial interests of the Metropolis, if they had some permanent Board, such as other great public bodies had, to whom commercial difficulties and grievances might be entrusted, and who, by their zeal and talents, might obtain redress. To select such a body of men would no doubt be a matter of some difficulty; but when he looked around him, and considered how many individuals there were connected with the commerce of this metropolis distinguished for their high character and talent, he felt that much of that difficulty might be surmounted. Other Companies [sic; recte 'Cities'] had such Associations, which they found extremely beneficial, and he thought the first commercial community in the world ought not to be without one. He apologised to the Committee for introducing a subject in which perhaps he had no right to interfere; but he confessed that he for one should feel great satisfaction, if such an Association were formed. The Report would now be read, to which he begged the earnest attention of the Meeting. He wished more particularly to direct their attention to that part of the Report which related to the objects they had failed to obtain, and with respect to which he doubted not they would agree with the Committee, in thinking that all their efforts ought to be strenuously directed to the attainment of a complete remedy for their remaining grievances.

Mr. HALL then read the following Report to the Meeting: REPORT.

"The Committee, appointed at a general Meeting of Merchants, Bankers, and Others, held at the City of London Tavern, on the 1st May, 1823, 'To adopt such measures as they might think expedient, for giving effect to the object of the Meeting,' which was declared to be 'an application to Parliament without delay, to investigate the state of the English Law, on the subjects of Goods intrusted to a Factor; and to make such alterations therein as would render the same conformable to just principles; beg leave to Report to the Merchants, Bankers, and others of the City of London, the result of their proceedings, as follows:—

"The Petition, adopted at the General Meeting, was signed within a very few days by 280 persons connected with mercantile establishments of the first respectability within the city… [Long report follows on the exchanges and difficulty of the lobby]

… "In the course of the proceedings in Parliament the views of the Petitioners were most ably supported in the House of Commons by Mr. Huskisson, Mr. Smith, Mr. Wallace, Mr. Baring, Mr. Thomas Wilson, Mr. Ricardo, Mr. John Martin, Mr. William Courtenay, Mr. Serjeant Onslow, Mr. Sykes, Mr. Hume, and Mr. Alderman Bridges, and Petitions were presented in favour of an alteration of the law from the Chamber of Commerce in Dublin, and the Chamber of Commerce in Bristol. …

"The labours of the Select Committee are already before the public, and carry their own recommendation; it is to their unwearied perseverance, as well as to their judgment, that Commerce is indebted for the full investigation of the subject necessary to enable the Legislature to apply a limited measure of relief within the Session; and to show that less exertion would have fallen short of the object, it is only necessary to state, that the Act received the Royal Assent but one day before the prorogation.

"The Committee cannot do adequate justice to the constant and efficient exertions of Mr. John Smith, who presided, with the exception of one day, throughout the sittings of the Select Committee; and the success of the measure, even in its limited form, is greatly to be attributed to those exertions, and to the able support which he, together with the Right Honourable

Thomas Wallace, Mr. Baring, Mr. Thomas Wilson (Member for the City), and Mr. Farrand, gave to it, in the different interviews with the Members of Government; nor ought the Committee to close this part of their Report, without expressing their acknowledgements to Mr. Farrand, their Chairman, for the various and important services rendered them in that capacity, and to Mr. J.W. Freshfield, for the unwearied attention, zeal, and ability displayed in the discharge of those highly important trusts which were confided to him.

"To several Members of this Committee particular acknowledgements are due for information furnished by them, and for having favoured the Select Committee with their evidence, the importance of which appears upon the Report to the House of Commons. Of this number they beg leave to mention James Cook Esq., Lewis Doxat Esq., Robert Farrand Esq., John Henry Freese jun. Esq., Robert Holden Esq., John Hall Esq., Edward Bedwell Kemble Esq., Maximilian Kymer Esq., Joshua Lockwood Esq., Andrew Loughman Esq., John Martin Esq., and Richard Ryland Esq.

"It is not generally known, that, although great dissatisfaction had been felt by many of the Merchants and other Capitalists of London, from the state of the Law, many of whom had suffered from its injurious operation, and a feeling of surprise and corresponding alarm was entertained and rapidly increasing, in consequence of some recent applications of the law, yet no practical measure of relief was suggested, until the arrival in London of John Ashton Yates Esq. of Liverpool, who communicated to Mr. Farrand, and a few leading individuals in the City, the information collected more than two years previously by a Committee of intelligent commercial men at Liverpool [through the Liverpool American chamber: Chapter 5 q.v.], whose suggestions had met with opposition and discouragement at the time, and on that account had not been pursued, but ultimately constituted the nucleus upon which the measures of the General Meeting, held in May last, were formed. The Committee have, therefore, not only to acknowledge this important service on the part of Mr. Yates, but are also indebted to him for constant and invaluable assistance in the course of the investigation, and to him and John Hall, Esq. for their information, attendance, and assistance, during the sitting of the Select Committee. …

"To obtain so important an object, it is indispensably necessary, that the attention of the Merchants and other Capitalists in London, should continue, during the recess, to be applied to the subject, so as to be prepared to renew their application to Parliament at an early period of the ensuing Session, when your Committee are of opinion, they may rely with confidence upon they continued co-operation of the Committee in Liverpool, and may hope to derive additional assistance from the Mercantile Community in various parts of the United Kingdom.

City of London Tavern, July 30, 1823."

[Lengthy discussion then followed, not reprinted here, which contains some divergences of opinion; it then moved to briefly discuss the proposal for a chamber:]

Mr. MILLE felt that there could be no difference of opinion among commercial classes, as to the expediency of a complete revision of the laws respecting the interests of merchant and factor. It was unnecessary for him to point out the zeal and ability with which this important subject had been prosecuted. He should move that the Report of the Committee be received and printed, and that copies be transmitted to the gentlemen who signed the Petition to Parliament, and such other merchants, bankers, and others, as the Committee might direct.

Mr. Alderman THOMPSON seconded the Resolution, which was agreed to unanimously.

Mr. SHAW expressed his cordial concurrence in all the observations which had been addressed to the Meeting by the respectable Gentlemen who preceded him. In moving the second Resolution he should occupy very little of their time, and he was aware how valuable time was to commercial men, and how small a portion of the twelve hours in the day could be devoted to mercantile purposes. It was unnecessary to add any thing to what had been so luminously explained in the Report of the Committee, and he should confine himself to expressing the gratitude which he felt to that Committee for the zeal and ability which they displayed in the prosecution of objects so essentially connected with the commercial prosperity of the country. This subject was brought under the notice of Parliament at so late a period of the Session, that it was matter of surprise to every one that the little which had been done was effected. When he said that little had been done, he meant that little had been done with reference to the attainment of a complete remedy; but much undoubtedly had been effected, when they considered the information which had been conveyed to the leading Members of the State, who had not only been led to entertain the measure, but had arrived at a complete conviction of its necessity. Some observations had been made from the Chair upon the disadvantageous situation in which the commercial community of the Metropolis were placed, from not having a representative body of their own. The Merchants of the City of London might be considered, to use a grammatical illustration, as a disjunctive conjunction. They were united with respect to their general interests, but disunited with reference to their separate interests, when those interests were opposed to each other. This opposition, however, was of the most amicable kind, and would readily give way for the benefit of the whole body. He felt himself standing on tender ground, as the subject was not immediately under the consideration of the Meeting. He trusted, however, that a Meeting would be held, at no distant period, for the purpose of considering in what manner a Chamber of Commerce might be best formed. He felt confident that Government would receive the representations of such as Association with respect. Indeed, Ministers would themselves derive a sort of security from the consideration that every subject had undergone the investigation of such a body before it was propounded to the Government.—He might refer the Meeting to the advantages derived to the shipping interest of the City of London, from the appointment of their Committee. He might refer to the Committee at Lloyd's, the advantages of which he knew from his own personal experience, and to similar associations connected with the West India and East India trade. At Manchester an Association of that sort was formed at the express wish of the Government. If the Merchants of the City of London would apply themselves to the consideration of this subject, he had no doubt that the formation of such an Association would not only be highly beneficial to the commercial interests of the metropolis, but extremely acceptable to the Government. He concluded, by moving the second Resolution (as it will appear in the Advertisements), which was agreed unanimously.

Mr. BUCKLE, in moving the second Resolution, stated his conviction, that every Gentleman connected with the Commercial Interests, would feel himself highly indebted to the zeal, diligence, and ability of the Chairman, and the Members of the Committee, to whom the direction of their interests had, in this instance, been entrusted. In proposing the thanks of the Meeting to those Gentlemen, he would only observe, that although much was done, much remained to be done, and he was confident that the Meeting could not entrust their concerns to better hands than those which had so ably managed them. He then moved the thanks of the Meeting to the Chairman, and the other Members of the Committee.

Mr. BAINBRIDGE seconded the motion.

Mr. WOLLASTON observed, that he could not but agree in the most decided terms with the Resolution just proposed, but there was another object of great importance to Commerce, for the attainment of which the present moment was most favourable, on which he must say a few words, and that was the establishment of a Board to watch over the mercantile interests for the future. He would beg leave to ask, whether it would not be proper to add to the Resolution now proposed, that the Committee nominated be requested to consider of the expediency of establishing a Chamber of Commerce in the City of London? He stated, that the advantages of such an institution to the commercial world were abundantly proved by experience. In the case of the law in question, there were Petitions to Parliament in favour of it from the Chambers of Commerce in Dublin and Liverpool. A similar establishment had been found very beneficial in Manchester. In several parts of the Empire the superintendence of a Select Body over the interests of trade had been found of essential service, and there were two incorporated by royal charter, namely, those of Dublin and Glasgow. The disadvantage of the want of such a body was severely felt in the metropolis of the empire, and he was sure there were few commercial gentlemen, who, under the existing law, were aware of the tenth part of the risk they ran in making advances. He hoped the meeting would not disperse without expressing their sense of the propriety and usefulness of a body permanently constituted for the purposes described. He stated that some time ago he had made exertions with the view of procuring the establishment of a similar institution, and had nearly succeeded. He had now the Resolutions in his pocket which he had at that time proposed. If the meeting demanded it he would submit them to their inspection, but he was aware that they required revision. What he intended to propose was, that the members he now nominates on the Committee would be requested to consider the expediency of the erection of a Chamber of Commerce, and to suggest a basis for its establishment. He was aware, that unless it was constructed on the highest pinnacle of respectability it would be of no use. An Hon. Gentleman had stated that the Government was amicable to such an institution, and he had reason to say such was a fact. He had an interview, on the occasion to which he alluded, with Mr. Robinson, then the President of the Board of Trade, and the right Ho. Gentleman had stated that the formation of such a body was highly desirable, but that Government would not pledge itself on the subject, as it should stand or fall by its own respectability. It was further observed, that when the shoe pinched most, the removal of the inconvenience would be most earnestly attempted. He was perfectly convinced that the inconvenience which he wished to remedy was most severely felt at the present moment. He was sure that every one saw the great risk which was run by merchants in general for want of a proper focus through which to seek and afford information. He would therefore suggest that the Committee appointed be requested to consider the subject as described. …

Mr. FREESE moved the next Resolution. He stated that he felt but one difficulty in moving a Vote of Thanks to their worthy Representative, Mr. Thomas Wilson, and that was the presence of the Honourable Gentleman, who, however meritorious his exertions in the cause of his fellow-citizens, had an extraordinary reluctance to receiving the meed [reward] of public applause to which he was so eminently entitled. His exertions in favour of the general interests were so well known, that to comment on them would indeed be needless, and they were in this instance in perfect unison with his conduct on former occasions. He (Mr. F.) knew that he took a most lively interest in supporting the commerce of the country, and it was the main pillar of our resources—as it was upheld, so the national prosperity would flourish (hear, hear, hear!). He would not trespass on their valuable time with any remarks on the immediate question before them. It was sufficient to say that his opinion was conformable to the luminous exposition of the Report, and therefore any observations from him on the subject would be not only unnecessary, but impertinent. There was one subject, however, connected with this on which he must be allowed to say a word. He alluded to the object which had been long contemplated—that of the establishment of a select body to watch over and protect the rights and interests of commerce, and which would form a focus of communication for the removal of obsolete laws, and the redress of bad regulations, which most injuriously affected the main spring of national welfare. The want of such a body had been long felt and severely lamented; but at length the light had burst upon us, and we were about to follow the useful example which had been set to us by other parts of the empire. It was a singular circumstance, that a similar argument was urged in support of the measure whose final success they contemplated to that which might be used in the advocacy of the object which arose out of its consideration, and which, he hoped, they were no less anxious to promote. With respect to the Bill relative to Principals and Factors, it had been urged, that this was the only country in which the unjust, unreasonable, and anomalous rule affecting the law of pledge existed, and he could say with equal truth, that this was the only part of the empire, of any importance, in which there was no establishment to defend and protect the commercial interests, and certainly commerce had not suffered less from that circumstance than from the others. They were all aware that the trade of London was running away from them. They should have then a point round which commerce might rally, and again be established (hear, hear!). He had been lately in the counties of the North, and there it was tauntingly observed to him, that the trade of London was going, and that what remained of it would soon be gone. It was also said, "You merchants in London are all Lords, you are no longer traders, you have your mansions at the West end of the town (a laugh), and every measure of importance to commerce originates in some provincial place, whether it may be Liverpool, Dublin, or Glasgow." The Gentleman who had adverted so strongly to the necessity of establishing a Chamber of Commerce, had given that subject the attention of his experienced abilities. He had obtained an interview with some of the principal men in Administration, relative to the subject, and it was emphatically remarked to him at the time, that when the shoe pinched most, the evil would be got rid of. The inconvenience arising from the want of a permanent body to watch over the interests of trade was now so manifest, that he trusted it would be very soon obviated (hear, hear!).

The motion was then duly seconded, and carried unanimously. …

The CHAIRMAN now called upon Mr. Woollaston to submit the proposition to which he had previously adverted.

Mr. WOOLLASTON proposed, that the Committee now nominated be requested to consider the expediency of establishing a Chamber of Commerce in London, and to report thereon to a future Meeting.

Mr. HALL suggested a modification of the Resolution, by incorporating with it the opinion of the Meeting, in order to add weight to the question, which was adopted, and a Resolution to that effect proposed by Mr. Woollaston.

Mr. Alderman BRIDGES, in seconding the motion, alluded to the flourishing state of the Funds of the Corporation of London.

Mr. HALL expressed a hope, that as the funds of that body were so flourishing, they would spare them a little from their superfluity (a laugh).

On the motion of Mr. RYLAND, it was ordered that the Resolutions be inserted in such Newspapers as the Committee should think fit, and the Meeting adjourned.

Printed Report 18 March 1824[a]

CHAMBER OF COMMERCE.

Yesterday a very respectable and well attended Meeting of the Bankers, Merchants, Ship Owners, and Traders of the City of London, was held at the City of London Tavern, in pursuance of the following Advertisement:—

> "Chamber of Commerce.—A Meeting of Merchants, Bankers, Ship-owners, and Traders, connected with the commerce of the City of London, will be held at the City of London Tavern, on Thursday, the 18th inst. To receive the Report of the Committee appointed to consider of the expediency of forming a Chamber of Commerce in the City of London. The Chair will be taken by John Smith, Esq. M.P. at two o'clock punctually."

Amongst those present were: Mr. J. Smith M.P., Mr. Pascoe Grenfell M.P., Mr. Thomas Wilson M.P., Mr. Francis Loughnan, and several of the most eminent Merchants of London.—Precisely at two o'clock.

Mr. THOMAS SMITH moved that Mr. J. Smith be requested to take the Chair. The proposition having been acceded to, unanimously,

Mr. JOHN SMITH accordingly took the Chair, and said, as the Meeting had done him the honour to place him in that situation, he should feel it his duty to state the object for which the present Meeting had been assembled. Several months back a large Meeting had been convened, containing some of the most respectable names in the City, at which it was determined, that consequences exceedingly favourable to the Commercial Interest of London would arise from the establishment of a Chamber of Commerce, in imitation of institutions of a similar description in other countries, and in various parts of the United Empire. A Committee was accordingly appointed, to take into their consideration this important subject. And he could himself bear testimony to the incessant labours and constant anxiety of the Gentlemen who composed that Committee, and particularly of one individual (Mr. Hall), whose absence to-day was occasioned, he feared, by indisposition. The Report of that Committee would, he understood, be laid upon the table, and, as he had been informed, the object of the present meeting would be to receive that Report, in order that Gentlemen might take it home and consider the subject at their leisure, and then, at some future day, not very distant, another meeting would be convened of the citizens of London, whose duty it would be, to consider the propriety of either rejecting or adopting the recommendation of the Committee. He had felt it his duty to state these particulars, because it appeared to the Committee as well as to himself that, until after the Report had been well considered (for it was obvious the details of the proposition would require much consideration), any debate in the present state of the question would be superfluous. He could not suppose that Gentlemen were at present prepared to discuss the question; however, he merely stated his opinion as an individual, which it was competent for any Gentleman present either to confirm or disavow (hear, hear!). With the permission of the meeting the Report would now be read.

Mr. WOLLASTON, who officiated as Secretary to the Meeting, was about to read the Report, when

Mr. PASCOE GRENFELL interposed and said, that as it seemed to be understood there would be no decision come to this day, it would perhaps be better not to waste the time of the Meeting by reading the Report, as every Gentleman present could have a copy of it to read at his leisure.

This suggestion was adopted, and it was agreed that the Report, which is as follows, should be considered as read:—

"REPORT.—The Committee appointed at a General Meeting of Merchants, Bankers, Traders, Ship-owners, and others, held at the City of London Tavern, on the 28th August, 1823, to whom (*inter alia*) was referred, to consider of the propriety of the formation of a Chamber of Commerce in the City of London, and to convene a Public Meeting of the Merchants, Bankers, and others interested in the Trade of the Metropolis, whenever they shall have prepared a Report upon the subject, having fully and deliberately considered the same,

"Beg leave to Report—That from certain documents, to which your Committee have had access, the advantages to be derived from the establishment of a Chamber of Commerce in the City of London, appear to have engaged the attention of several of its leading mercantile characters for some time past. In the year 1817, private meetings were held, at which the subject was considered and discussed, the expediency of forming such as Institution was unanimously admitted, and the propriety of convening a General Meeting of Merchants, Bankers, Ship-owners and others, at some convenient period, for the purpose of carrying the object into effect, was determined upon. From a variety of circumstances, none of which, however, have been influenced by any change of opinion as to the expediency of the measure, the convening of a general meeting has been hitherto suspended; the delay has nevertheless operated to give additional force to the sentiments which now so generally prevail in favour of the forming of an association of merchants and others interested in the trade, manufactures, navigation and commerce of the Metropolis, the objects of which shall be to promote the interests of those classes of the community in general, and of the commerce of the Port of London in particular. In the expectation that much useful information might be acquired from the several Chambers of Commerce, and other Mercantile Associations already established in the principal ports and manufacturing districts of the United Empire, your Committee applied for and obtained the rules and regulations by which most of them are governed, accompanied by detailed Reports of their respective proceedings, from these, much highly important and valuable information has been collected; and your Committee take the earliest opportunity of expressing their sense of obligation towards those Gentlemen who have been instrumental in procuring it for them, and also to the respective Officers of the several establishments in the following places, for the readiness with which they have furnished the desired information, viz. Dublin, Glasgow, Greenock, Edinburgh, Leith, Newcastle, Liverpool, Bristol, Manchester, Birmingham, and Plymouth.

"In the consideration of the subject your Committee have derived much assistance from the proceedings detailed in those documents, they furnish conclusive evidence of most important advantages having been derived by the Commercial Interests through the medium of those Institutions, and establish proofs beyond contradiction, in support of an extension of the system to other parts of the United Kingdom. Your Committee, in the course of their investigation, found reason to regret that the Merchants and others connected with the Commerce of the Metropolis, impressed as they appear to have been with the importance of the benefits to be derived from such as association, should not more zealously and effectively have exerted themselves to secure those advantages to the City of London. An Institution comprising in itself an union of every description of Mercantile interest, possessing a practical acquaintance with the Trade and Navigation of the Empire, and an intimate knowledge of all that locally concerns the Port of London, cannot fail to be attended with great and peculiar advantages. Placed near the seat of Government, it would be ready to furnish his Majesty's Ministers accurate and practical information on all points connected with the Commerce of the Empire, and to submit, as occasions arise, such suggestions as may contributed to improve the regulations, and the municipal and fiscal laws affecting the trade, manufactures, and navigation of the United

Kingdom; it may also point out such restraints and burthens appearing to operate injuriously upon any branch of our commerce.—In looking for a period favourable to the establishment of such an institution, it would be difficult to find one in which it promised to contribute more to the public advantage than the present. The attention of the Legislature, and of his Majesty's Government, has lately been particularly drawn to the subjects of commerce, trade, and navigation. The defects under which the system arising out of our code of commercial law has long laboured, have been clearly demonstrated; and the invaluable labours of the Parliamentary Committees on Foreign Trade have led to the enactment of laws distinguished by a more enlarged and enlightened policy, which have thus given a new character and improved principle to the commerce of the country, as well as in its mercantile relations with foreign States. Important advantages have also resulted from the inquiries of the Commissioners into the branches of the revenue of the Customs and Excise, by which great relief and new facilities, in the operations of trade, have been afforded, and remedial measures are in progress in respect of the fiscal regulations by which these branches of the revenue are governed. In the further prosecution of similar objects of national importance, such as institution bust be of value to the Government itself. The Board of Trade & other of the public departments would find it advantageous to possess the means as occurrences might require, of resorting to those, who, from their habits and experience, would be qualified to afford the best information, and which being furnished by an associated public body, embracing in itself so many interests, would not be exposed to the suspicion of interested or partial motives; but entitle their opinions to respect, and aid most powerfully in resisting importunities which have for their object undue protection in favour of particular classes, or the establishing of regulations for partial purposes, in matters of commerce, manufactures, or navigation; a system which has been the source of all those restraints falsely called Protections, that up to a recent period had, by degrees, so interwoven itself with our commercial legislation, as deeply to affect the best interests of the British Empire. The Association would likewise afford an easy mode of conveying to the Councils of the nation the deliberate opinion of the great mercantile body upon any public commercial question which might come under its consideration, and if required, furnish immediate evidence on any particular points to either of the Houses of Parliament. Merchants and others desirous of making representations to his Majesty's Government, or to the Boards of Revenue, touching Commercial matters of importance, might avail themselves of the practical knowledge so respectable and useful a body would be supposed to possess, and resort to it in the first instance for information and advice. The Chamber might, in many cases remove misconceptions, satisfy parties by explanation, and thereby render such representation unnecessary;

whereas, in cases in which it might be expedient to memorialise the Government, the applicants might derive the advantage of such suggestions as the Chamber could afford; and where conflicting pretensions of parties, involving commercial questions of a general character, shall appear dangerous to the public interests, the Chamber might also advantageously lend its assistance to conciliate or reduce those pretensions within just and proper limits. Your Committee, in the progress of their inquiries, have also availed themselves of such information, as they were able at the moment to acquire touching the Chambers of Commerce in Foreign Europe. They find that the establishments in France and Holland are in each country regulated and governed by legislative enactments; they are also invested with a power of hearing and determining matters in dispute between parties relating to Trade and Navigation, and of undertaking, under certain regulations, references, which are confided to Sworn Arbitrators selected by the Directors or Boards of Management of the respective Chambers.

"To the advantages which such a regulation presents in countries in which the parties engaged in any suit, whatever may be its issue, are compelled to pay their own costs, your Committee can, in many cases, bear testimony; at the same time they are sensible that a system which unavoidably exposes parties to have their commercial differences adjusted by Judges, some of whom frequently have an indirect interest in the question propounded, and others who from local connections and prejudices, must find it next to impossible to administer justice impartially or with satisfaction to the litigants; is open to serious objection. It appears, indeed, to have been complained of, and the facilities of appeal which exist in those countries, frequently deprive the successful party of the benefit of the judgment he may have obtained. An attempt has been made in some of the British Commercial Associations to establish a regulation founded upon a similar principle, with a view to the mere speedy and economical settlement of disputes arising out of commercial transactions. Your Committee cannot but approve of that principle, yet consider it in practice surrounded by great difficulties; and they are confirmed in that opinion by the fact, that the measure does not appear to have been actually brought into practical operation by any of the institutions before referred to. Some Insurance Companies, indeed, lately established in the Metropolis, have adopted a regulation of the like description in the adjustment of disputed demands, the claimants being entitled to the option of having them determined by arbitration. The subject, however, is one of considerable importance, and your Committee entertain a confident opinion, that great advantage might be derived from the nomination of referees, under suitable regulations, to whom recourse might be had, particularly in questions involving matters of account and the usages of commerce; the subject may therefore usefully occupy the consideration of the proposed Chamber of

Commerce; but it should rather be entertained as one of the many measures of improvement which will be well deserving of its attention, than as constituting a fundamental rule in its formation.

"The importance and utility of Chambers of Commerce have been so far admitted by the highest authority, as to have led to the incorporation of some of them by Royal Charter, and as that mark of favour has been graciously conferred upon establishments in some of our principal out-ports, your Committee confidently hope that the same high and distinguished patronage will not be withheld from the proposed Chamber of Commerce in the City of London. Your Committee, therefore, after diligent inquiry, and an attentive consideration of all the circumstances before referred to, have no hesitation in recommending the forming of such an Institution, to be designated The London Chamber of Commerce, and that as soon as the details shall have been finally arranged and determined upon the necessary application be made through the proper channel to his Majesty, for a Royal Charter of Incorporation. A draught of rules and regulations, recommended for the government of the Chamber, will be found in an Appendix to this Report.

"Your Committee are sensible that no measures of permanent or of substantial efficacy can be successful, without cordial union and co-operation; that to give full effect to such an Association it is indispensably necessary that it should receive the support of the leading mercantile establishments, and also unite the talents and experience of the most eminent commercial characters of this Metropolis, that it should be conducted upon general and liberal principles, free from every influence of party prejudices, or distinction, and that its Direction be selected from those connected with the several branches of commerce, manufactures, trade, and navigation, as well as acquainted with the local business of the port of London. And in order effectually to secure the permanent connexion of the Chamber with the great commercial interests of the metropolis, it appears desirable, that the Representatives in Parliament for the City of London, and the heads of leading corporations and other institutions connected with its trade, should have seats at the Board of Directors during their continuance in office. Your Committee have particularly in view—

The Governor and Deputy Governor of the Bank of England.

The Chairman & Deputy Chairman of the Hon. E. India Company.

The Governor, Sub, and Deputy Governors of the Royal Exchange Assurance Corporation.

The Governor, Sub, and Deputy Governors of the London Assurance Corporation.

The Governor and Senior Consul of the Russia Company.

The Governor and Deputy Governor of the Levant Company.

The Sub-Governor & Deputy Governor of the South Sea Company.

The Governor and Deputy Governor of the Eastland Company.
The Master and Deputy Master of the Trinity Corporation.
The Governor & Deputy Governor of the Hudson's Bay Compy.
The Chairman and Deputy Chairman of each of the following Companies:—West India Dock Company, London Dock Compy., East India Dock Compy., Commercial Dock Compy., East Country Dock Company, Surrey Canal Dock Company.
The Chairman of the East India Trade Committee.
The Chairman and Deputy Chairman of the West India Merchants.
The Chairman and Deputy Chairman of the Society of Merchants trading to the Continent.
The Chairman of the Wine and Spirit Trade Committee.
The Chairman of the Committee of the Ship Owners' Society.
The Chairman of the Society of British North America Merchants.
The Chairman of the Committee for managing the affairs at Lloyd's.

"Your Committee are equally impressed with a necessity of the immediate management being confided to hands every way qualified for so important a trust. Upon such a selection many of the advantages to be derived from the Association must depend; whether that object may be best accomplished by appointing a Managing Director or a Committee of Management, who shall undertake the active superintendence, or whether the duties may be assigned to the Secretary alone, with equal advantage to the Commercial interests, your Committee will not take upon themselves to determine; the office of Secretary, however, will be one of honourable distinction, from which no Gentleman, whatever be his mercantile station, need to shrink, and who, in accepting and fulfilling his duties of it, will render a most valuable service to his country. In conclusion, your Committee beg to disavow most distinctly, that in the recommendation they have felt it their duty to make, any disrespect has been intended to the Mercantile Associations in which already exist in the City of London; no desire is felt to interfere with their functions on particular objects; nor is there in the opinion of your Committee any reasons which should prevent the respectable individuals who compose those Associations from enrolling their names amongst the members of the proposed Chamber of Commerce; their cordial co-operation and support, will, on the contrary, be anxiously looked for in favour of an Institution which is intended to be an encouragement and support to every description of mercantile interest. The objects of the Chamber will be general, and such as an Institution of a general character alone will be qualified to effect. Its aim will be the improvement and extension of British Commerce in all its branches, and by those means to contribute its aid in strengthening and extending the prosperity of the United Kingdom.—12th January, 1824,"

Mr. WOLLASTON then proposed, that some day should be fixed for the next Meeting; he should say this day week, or perhaps, this day fortnight; he was aware that that would be the 1st of April, but that was no objection, he presumed, as they were not school-boys. It would be most desirable that the Gentlemen at Lloyd's should attend, and he apprehended that two o'clock would be an inconvenient hour for them to attend.

It was then suggested that it would be well to call the Meeting for Thursday next at Twelve o'clock precisely. This was agreed to.

Mr. WOLLASTON said that he thought it had been very properly arranged that there should be no discussion on the present occasion; but he trusted the Meeting would allow him to state one advantage, which he thought was likely to arise from the proposed establishment of a Chamber of Commerce in London. Some Gentlemen might suppose that this institution might become somewhat arbitrary in its proceedings, and would generate a system which might impose restrictions on trade; but he was persuaded, if it were patronised and countenanced by the leading commercial characters in the city, it was impossible it would not be productive of extensive advantages, not only to London, but to the country at large. There were many instances on record of the advantages which had arisen from similar establishments. He happened in the course of the morning to have lighted on a memorandum which he had made some years ago, of a great service which the country had derived from the Chamber of Commerce at Manchester. He alluded to the withholding of the island of Singapore. The Dutch were exceedingly anxious to get possession of that island, and it was in the contemplation of the Government to give it up, as Java had been before; but in consequence of the representation of the Chamber of Commerce at Manchester, in conjunction with those of Liverpool, Birmingham, and Glasgow, the island was retained in our possession. Therefore it was, that seeing the advantages which such institutions were capable of producing, and conceiving that it would be desirable to have, as it were, some focus to which gentlemen might resort, when occasion required, for information on commercial questions, he felt anxious to promote the present undertaking. He merely mentioned this single circumstance as an example of the good that might be done, not wishing in the least degree to provoke any discussion, as the object of the Meeting was simply to receive the Report (hear, hear!).

The Honourable Gentlemen then proposed the following resolution:—

1. "That the Report of the Committee appointed at a public meeting of Merchants, Bankers, Ship-owners, and others, held on the 28th day of August last, to consider the expediency of the formation of a Chamber of Commerce in the City of London, and report their opinion, now read, be printed, and copies be distributed for the information of the merchants, bankers, ship-owners, and others connected with the trade of the metropolis; and that a

general meeting of the Merchants, Bankers, Ship-owners, and Traders connected with the commerce of the Port of London, be convened for Thursday, the 1st of April, at 12 o'clock precisely, to take the Report into consideration, and adopt such measures in respect thereto as may then appear advisable."

Mr. THOMAS WILSON seconded the Resolution.

Mr. GEORGE HIBBERT[43] said, that if the Resolution had not been prefaced by some observation from the Honourable Gentleman who proposed it, he should have abstained from making any remarks on the present occasion. Nothing could be more fair than that the Committee should set forth with ability the object they had in view, and appoint a day for the discussion of the subject. He did not mean to say there was any thing unfair in the observations made by the Honourable Gentleman, because it was very natural, that having been a Member of the Committee, and no doubt deeply impressed with the advantages likely to arise from the proposed measure, his mind should be warmed with the subject. But as those remarks would go forth to the public, he thought it right to state, that he was one of a number of Gentlemen who, at their next meeting, would be prepared to state why they thought the establishment of a Chamber of Commerce was not necessary and might be prejudicial: and he was satisfied, that when the names of those Gentlemen came to be read, it would be found that they must have great influence over all questions of this nature (hear, hear!).

The Resolution was carried.

Mr. WOLLASTON then proposed a Resolution, the object of which was the appointment of a Committee to carry the recommendations of the former Committee into effect.

Mr. TOOKE put it to the Honourable Gentlemen, whether, after what had occurred, and before the Report had been considered, it would not be premature to pass that Resolution.

Mr. PASCOE GRENFELL perfectly concurred in the justice of the observation. No inconvenience could arise from postponing that Resolution, but in the present state of the subject, it would not only be premature, but would have the effect of prejudging the question.

Mr. THOMAS WILSON said, that as a Member of the Committee, although an unworthy one certainly, for he had not attended frequently, he thought it fit to state the motives by which they were guided in proposing this Resolution. An attempt had before been made to establish a Chamber of Commerce, which had fallen to the ground, and, he believed, principally for the want of a sufficient number of respectable names to carry it on. And the

[43] George Hibbert had two direct relatives who had been founding members of the Jamaica chamber 1778–86: Robert Hibbert and Thomas Hibbert junior; see Bennett, 'Collective action when needed' (2015).

gentlemen who had undertaken the subject at present, were anxious to shew that they were prepared with a list of substantial names to carry their plans (if approved) into full execution (hear, hear!).

Mr. TOOKE said, that until the Report had been adopted he should consider all further proceedings premature.

A GENTLEMAN, whose name we could not learn, stated, that some apprehensions were entertained that particular interests might be neglected, if this Institution were founded. But if commercial men of eminence were selected from every department, then no jealousy would be felt by any particular interest. He therefore thought it desirable that the Resolution be carried.

Mr. HIBBERT said, it appeared to him that the reasoning applied the other way. He was satisfied that if they applied to any respectable Gentlemen for their names, they would at once say they could not consent until they were fully acquainted with the nature of the proposition. If they were to apply to him for his name, he should say, "Wait, until I understand what you are about; I am at present hostile to the measure, but perhaps when I have fully canvassed it, I, who now announce my opposition, may then give you my support (hear, hear, hear!)."

Mr. WOLLASTON said the object which he had in view was to promote the trade of London generally, and not any exclusive interests (hear, hear!), and he certainly should not force this Resolution contrary to the sense of any man who considered it premature. When the Report should have been adopted, then would be the time to consider the means of carrying into effect the intentions of the Committee. But Gentlemen must be aware that the entire success of the undertaking must depend upon the respectability of the names which were enlisted in its support (hear, hear!).

The Resolution was then withdrawn.

The CHAIRMAN said, it had just been suggested to him that on Thursday next there would be a Bank Court held, and he submitted to the Meeting whether it would not be expedient to alter the day, in order that they might ensure the attendance of those whose presence would be so desirable (hear, hear!).

Thursday fortnight was accordingly substituted for Thursday week.

Mr. COMBALD proposed that the thanks of the Meeting should be returned to the Committee for their valuable Report.

Mr. BROWNE: Had not you better wait until we see whether it is valuable (hear, hear!)?

The proposition was withdrawn.

Mr. THOMAS WILSON said it would be very desirable that a Chairman should be appointed for the next Meeting, as he understood his Honourable Friend (Mr. Smith) might not be able to attend; and there were other reasons which perhaps would render it advisable that another Chairman should be appointed. He should therefore propose

2. "That William Manning Esq. M.P. be invited to take the Chair appointed at the meeting to be held on Thursday, the 1st of April."

Mr. PASCOE GRENFELL said he really thought it should be distinctly stated that his Honourable Friend (Mr. Smith) had declined taking the Chair. Otherwise it might give rise to strange remarks.

Mr. SMITH: Should any remarks be made, I shall hear them with the most perfect philosophy (hear, hear!). But I think that on a question of such importance it is highly expedient, that at our next meeting, some person should preside of extensive experience and knowledge, such as would entitle him to take a lead; and I think my situation as a Banker would disqualify me from filling the chair, and it must be obvious to every man that no individual could be better qualified to preside over a question of this sort than Mr. Manning, who was a Bank Director, a Gentlemen of great experience, and high character (hear, hear!).

Mr. HIBBERT: I presume that those who propose that Mr. Manning should take the chair, are apprised of his disposition to do so.

The CHAIRMAN: I have no knowledge on the subject.

Mr. HIBBERT said, it would be desirable to ascertain that point, for he had some reason to suspect that Mr. Manning would not feel disposed to take the Chair.

Mr. WOLLASTON: I cannot presume to say what may be the inclination of Mr. Manning on the subject, but I rather think it is not adverse.

Mr. WARRE then said, he had a Resolution to propose, which he was sure would receive the most cordial approbation of the entire Meeting. It was, that the Meeting should return their warmest thanks to Mr. J. Smith, for the manner in which he had conducted himself in the Chair.

Mr. WOLLASTON said, he was just about to submit a Resolution to that effect, which, perhaps the Honourable Gentleman would be kind enough to adopt.

2. "That this meeting is deeply impressed with value of the services rendered by John Smith, M.P., upon this and various other occasions, for the promotion of the commerce of the United Empire, and whilst they hereby testify an imperfect acknowledgement of such services, they also solicit a continuance of the same."

Mr. J. SMITH returned thanks, and said, he should be at all times ready and willing to undertake any task which might be imposed upon him by his Fellow Citizens (hear, hear!).

Chapter 5

Advocacy and Campaigns

The central purpose of the chambers was to represent interests, which is very clear from their rules, charters and founding objectives. Their campaigns were very numerous and it is impossible here to reproduce all documents.[1] The aim instead is to meet five objectives: first, to provide new material that has been previously little known or entirely unknown. Second, to evidence the type of approach adopted and the range of campaigns pursued. For this the Liverpool *Abstract* covering 1774–7 gives a powerful overview. Other documents expand from this forward in time and over other dimensions. Third, it is sought to show how the different chambers were collaborating over advocacy and exchanging with each other, chiefly using the examples of Liverpool-Bristol from 1774, and Glasgow-Liverpool-Bristol-Birmingham and other centres after 1783, which includes the very focused attacks on the Irish propositions, and Arkwright's patent, both in 1785. Collaboration began from the outset of the mainland chambers and continued into the 1800s. The examples re-balance the literature that suggests that the General Chamber of Manufactures of 1785–7 was something new as a national collaboration; rather it was new only in the centralised decision-making it sought. Fourth, the examples produced seek to demonstrate how the lobbies were mounted, with the Liverpool petition on lumber in 1777 giving an example of how central government departments received and processed petitions—in this case turning it down. Fifth, the aim is to give an overview of some of the issues on which lobbies were developed. These ranged from many campaigns against local officials and petty fees (by municipalities, land waiters, the Customs House, and other officials), to efforts to establish local infrastructure projects. In choosing documents the main objective has been to illustrate examples from different places, as well as the emerging core of activity around the major port cities of Liverpool, Dublin, and Glasgow, with Bristol. This volume deliberately stops before the campaign to abolish the Corn Laws, which became one of the greatest achievements of the chambers in 1846, especially for the Manchester chamber, although of course much was also owed to other lobbyists.[2] However, it should be noted that the

[1] For an overview of lobby issues pursued up to the 1840s, see Bennett, *Local Business Voice* (2011) 373–424.

[2] Bennett, *Local Business Voice* (2011) 438–4.

Corn Laws were a long-standing concern of chambers, which is evident in some of the documents reproduced (e.g. Liverpool's *Abstract*). Corn law abolition was also part of the Glasgow chamber's founding objectives (see Chapter 1). A key insight into lobbying is also provided by Glasgow's 'Report of the Delegates' on the various lobbies in which they engaged in early 1785 during the campaign of the General Chamber (reproduced in Chapter 8). It evidences the subtleties, persistence and care required in the lobbying process to avoid 'opposition', radicalism and party, and shows the local chambers operating in an entirely different, more subtle, and more effective way than the General Chamber.

A key element of the documents reproduced is also to demonstrate for some important cases the continuities and evolution from earlier styles of campaign before chambers were established. Significant examples which are reproduced here are the Liverpool Stamp Act Committee of 1765–6, and Liverpool-Bristol-Hull efforts to found 'chambers' to expand the structure of the EIC in 1768. Similarly, some documents are reproduced to evidence the existence of a chamber, or chamber-like committee, at an early date for which little else has yet been discovered: e.g. Guernsey in 1776, Blackburn in 1779, Hull in the 1780s, Lancaster in 1781 and 1785, Exeter in the 1790s, Portsmouth in 1797–8, and Wolverhampton in 1820.

5.1 Liverpool Abstract 1774–7

This document of 16 printed pages is the only systematic material on the activities of the chamber as no minute books survive. It is of enormous significance as a summary of the main activities of the first mainland chamber of commerce in Britain, and as one of the few guides that exists of a self-assessment of effectiveness on each of the main representations it made. The *Abstract* is also valuable in containing information on some member names not otherwise available, on developments of the Rules following its *Deed* of 1774 (q.v. Chapter 1), on its desire for a fixed meeting place and room to store its papers, and aspects of the advocacy process: sometimes using MPs, delegates from the chamber, or others to make its case in London; at other times sending memorials and petitions directly to government officials through MPs (usually the local MP William Meredith). This *Abstract* had been referred to previously for two campaigns only by Checkland,[3] but its full contents and wider significance were not grasped; indeed it may be that Checkland was not actually able to see the full document.[4]

[3] Checkland, 'Economic attitudes in Liverpool' (1952) 58–9.
[4] See Bennett, *Voice of Liverpool Business* (2010).

Source
Liverpool Athenaeum library Misc. Pamphlets Vol. LXV; also Library Company of Philadelphia, Am.1777.Lib/Log.2251.0.11.

Printed pamphlet June 1777

An ABSTRACT of the Proceedings and Resolutions of the Several COMMITTEES of the **Chamber of Commerce** for the Port of *LIVERPOOL*,

From their First Establishment on the 24th June, 1774, To the 24th June, 1777,

Is humbly submitted to the Public, as the truest test of the usefulness of this institution, and the fairest foundation for a judgment, how far it is deserving of further support.

AN ABSTRACT, &c.

1774 The first public application made in the name of this Society was to the Postmaster General, for an indulgence of One hour, in the time of the Posts going out from hence, on Tuesdays and Fridays.

> The *Answer* receiv'd from Anthony Todd, Esq; Secretary to the Postmasters General, was, *That no alteration can possibly be made in the time of the departure of the Posts on Fridays, without often depriving the Inhabitants of Liverpool, and all the Towns north of Warrington, of the benefit of the North Post: and as the indulgence of an hour on Tuesdays, would destroy the regularity of having One constant, and certain hour every day alike, which has always been wished for in the large trading towns thro' out the Kingdom; His Majesty's Postmaster General thought it most advisable, not to make any alteration.*

November 3d. It appeared, that a duty of 4s. per head upon Negro Slaves imported into Jamaica, was likely to prove extremely prejudicial to the trade of this Port. A Memorial was therefore drawn up, and presented to the Earl of Dartmouth, Praying the interposition of his Lordship, towards suppressing an Act of the Assembly of Jamaica, imposing a duty of Forty Shillings per head, payable wholly by the Importer, upon all Negroes imported into that Island.

December 1st. A correspondence was entered into with Governor Pownall, upon the Corn trade, which was productive of much important information upon the subject, and some new regulations, of great moment, were intended to be offered to the consideration of the Legislature: but the unhappy disputes, which soon after broke out in a flame that still continues burning, have hitherto prevented the execution of these salutary schemes.

December 29th. It was resolved, That in the then precarious state of British property in America, some part ought to be taken by the Mercantile interest in Liverpool. A circular Letter was therefore ordered to be transmitted to the principal trading Towns, connected with this Port, requesting to be informed, whether any, and what measures, were intended to be adopted by each Town respectively, upon the alarming state of the Commerce between Great Britain and America.

1775 January 5th. A Memorial was ordered to be drawn up, which was afterwards presented to the Lords of the Treasury, Praying for an additional number of Landwaiters, Scale Porters, and Scales for the use of this Port.

The addition prayed for was soon after granted.

January14th. It was unanimously resolved to petition Parliament upon the unpromising appearance of our Commerce with America.

A Petition was accordingly drawn up against the 18th January, which being approved of, and signed, was presented by Sir William Meredith.

This Petition Set forth the importance of the connection between Great Britain and North America; the losses likely to arise (if the unhappy divisions subsisting were not speedily healed, and mutual confidence and credit restored) from the great debt owing by America to Great Britain; from the baneful effects, which an actual breach with the Continent would produce in the West India Islands; and the ruinous consequences resulting from thence to the African Trade.

January 26th. It was Ordered that a deputation from this Body do attend Parliament during the process of the American business through the House.

> *Mr. Dobson, Mr. Haliday and Mr. Walker accordingly attended several weeks in London; but no security could be obtained for the property of the Merchant.*

The Chamber of Commerce at this time offered their service, to conduct the prosecution, necessary for the recovery of the duty, levied on Negroes, imported into Jamaica; provided a proportionable subscription was entered into by the parties concerned, to defray the expenses of such prosecution.

> The want of unanimity in those Gentlemen who had paid the duty, has hitherto prevented any further proceedings in this business.

February 2d. A memorial was presented to the Committee, complaining of unusual delay in the delivery of Letters at the Post Office in this Town: Application was accordingly made to the Postmasters General, *who immediately afforded all the relief at that time in their power*.

February 11th. Information being given to the Committee, that an attempt was making to continue the former illegal impositions, and lay some new, and still heavier burthens upon the British Merchants, importing Slaves into Jamaica.

February 14th. A Memorial was presented to the Earl of Dartmouth, Setting forth, that the Assembly of Jamaica have by a new Act, continued the duty upon Negroes, of Two Pounds Ten Shillings, payable by the Importer; and imposed a further duty of Five Pounds upon every Negro, which at importation shall be reported to be above 30 Years of Age, by any two of 74

Inspectors, to be appointed by the Magistrates in the Island; which duty of Five Pounds, with the addition of One Shilling a Head for every Slave examined by these Inspectors, is likewise to be paid wholly by the Importer: and Praying to be heard by themselves and Counsel against the said Act.

> *A numerous deputation from hence attended the Board of Trade upon this business, who pursued such measures as obtained a report from that Board to His Majesty, dated Whitehall December 19th 1774, wherein it is given as the opinion of the Lords of Trade, that the Act in question was improper, as will upon its general principle, as from the manner in which it had passed: a disallowance of it is therefore humbly recommended to His Majesty by that Honourable Board; who further give it as their advice, that His Majesty's Governor should be instructed not to give his assent for the future, to any Law for increasing the duties upon Slaves imported, as those duties stood, before the law complained of was passed. His Majesty's disallowance was dispatched by the Mail for Jamaica on Wednesday the 5th July 1775. The Merchants of Liverpool had paid for this duty, in little more than six Months* £15,609. *6s.*

February 14th. A Petition was sent to Parliament, Praying for a continuance of the Bounty of 40s. per Ton, upon Shipping employed in the Greenland Fishery.

> *Nothing further has been since done in this business.*

February 21st. Information being received from Mr. Pennant, that application was intended to be made to Parliament, for an act to render perpetual, a Grant of the Smalls in St. George's Channel, and to impose a perpetual duty upon Shipping for the support of a Lighthouse to be erected thereon;

> *It was Resolved, That in the opinion of this Committee, the Sums already exacted from Shipping, under the pretence of contributions towards the support of Lighthouses, are become so exorbitant, as justly to require public attention.*
>
> *That a very small part of the money, so exacted, is actually expended in the building and supporting of Lighthouses and Lights, for the benefit of navigation; the chief share being applied to the partial emolument of individuals.*
>
> *That every such application to Parliament ought to be opposed, so far as to guard against abuses, and impositions upon the Public.*

March 2d. A Petition to Parliament was resolved on against a Bill then depending in the House, for laying a perpetual Tax upon all ships navigating any part of St. George's Channel, between Cape Clear in Ireland, and the Land's End in England, for the support of a Lighthouse, intended to be erected upon the Rocks called the Smalls: A certain, perpetual, and almost general Tax, for an uncertain, limited, and partial advantage.

Mr. Edward Chaffers, and Mr. Ambrose Lace, attended and gave evidence in the House of Commons in this business. The Bill was thrown out at the third reading.

A Petition to Parliament was presented, against a Bill then depending, for enlarging the Term of Letters Patent, for the sole use of certain materials for making Porcelain. *This restraint, it was apprehended, would prevent such further improvements, as might be productive of most important advantages to trade.*

It was at the same time ordered, That an answer should be given to a letter from Bristol then read; signifying the willingness of this Society to concur in the application to Parliament therein proposed, for providing County redress, to the sufferers by the plundering of shipwrecks; and to correspond with them upon the previous steps necessary to be taken.

N. B. This Business was many months afterwards brought into Parliament, by Petition from Bristol; without their taking any further notice of this application, for concurrence and support from hence. The Bristol Petition was rejected by the House of Commons.

September 6th. The exportation of Arms and Ammunition being prohibited by authority, the Trade to Africa was likely to be greatly prejudiced thereby; it was therefore resolved to present a Petition to His Majesty in Council, Praying permission to ship off Arms and Ammunition, of the Customary quality, for the purchase of Negro Slaves, in Vessels, trading to Africa.

A deputation from hence being found necessary, Mr. Case, and Mr. Thomas Hodgson, Jun. attended in London upon this business; and obtained leave for Vessels going to Africa, to take Arms and Ammunition without the restraint and expense of any Licenses, which are still required for Vessels carrying Gunpowder or Arms to any other parts.

November 20th. It appearing that the West India Islands were deprived of the usual supply of Provision from the Continent of North America, a Petition was prepared, and presented to Parliament, Praying for leave to export Wheat, Wheatmeal, Biscuit-bread, and Pease, to any part of the British Islands in America, during the continuance of the unhappy disputes with the Continent.

This permission was obtained under certain restrictions.

December 7th. Information was given of an intended application to Parliament from the City of Chester, for a power to erect Lighthouses upon the Point of Ayr, and collect duties from Shipping for their support. An immediate correspondence commenced with the Managers of this Application, and such stipulations were agreed upon, as seemed calculated to prevent any inconveniences to the Port of Liverpool, from the operation of said Bill when passed into a law.

An application was at the same time ordered to be made to James Clemens, Esq; Mayor of this Borough, setting forth, that many inconveniences daily arise, from the want of a house for the confinement, and due correction of Vagrants, in this Town, or neighbourhood; recommending the necessity of the undertaking to his confederation, and the speedy execution of it, to his patronage.

1776 February 1st. It was resolved to petition the Lords of the Admiralty, to appoint Convoys to the homeward bound ships from the West India Islands.

> *An answer was received from the Secretary to the Admiralty, dated 27th February, with information, that their Lordships had given orders for Convoys, to see the Trade from Jamaica, 80 to 120 Leagues clear of that Island; and those from the other Islands, the same distance from Anguilla.*

March 7th. Upon considering the foregoing answer from the Admiralty, it was the opinion of the Gentlemen present, that the Convoys there mentioned, would not answer the important purposes, of securing the Trade, and reducing the advanced premium of insurance.

To accomplish these intentions, the Convoy ought to proceed as far as North Lat. 45, so as to see the Fleet fairly clear of the Banks of Newfoundland. A further application to their Lordships was, for these reasons, judged necessary.

> *In answer to this renewed application, information was given, that instructions had been sent to Vice Admiral Montagu, Commander in Chief on the Newfoundland Station, to give orders to the Commanders of the Ships appointed to protect the fishery on the Grand Bank of Newfoundland, to stretch occasionally to the outer edge of that Bank, to look out for, and secure the Trade of His Majesty's subjects passing that way: and in the instructions to the Commander in chief of his Majesty's Ships in North America, the further protection of the Trade of His Majesty's subjects, passing within the limits of his command, would be particularly recommended to his care.*

August 1st. It appeared necessary to make fresh application to the Admiralty, for more effectual protection to the African, and American Trade: particularly that a sufficient number of Ships of War, be properly, and constantly Stationed, for the protection and security of Trade, upon the Coast of Africa.

> *An answer was received from Mr. Stephens, dated August 27th, with an assurance, that frequent Convoys are, and will be appointed for the outward, as well as the homeward bound West India Trade, and that due attention will be given to the African Trade.*

September 5th. A Petition was ordered, which was accordingly presented to His Majesty in Council, for permission to Arm Ships trading to Africa, for their defence against the enemies of the British Empire, without restraint from the Orders of Council.

This application procured some indulgence, but not effectual relief.

September 19th. Information being received from the Secretary to the Admiralty that a Convoy would be speedily appointed for the West Indies to sail from Spithead; a Petition was presented to the Admiralty, praying, that for the general benefit of the Out Ports, the rendezvous of the West India Fleet might not be at Spithead, but at Cork.

The answer to this petition was, that a Convoy would be appointed to sail from Cork for the West Indies about Christmas.

Ordered, A Petition to the Lords of his Majesty's Most Honourable Privy Council, for Permission to take such quantity of Arms and Ammunition on board all Ships from hence, as is absolutely necessary for their defence; the quantity at present allowed being inadequate to that purpose.

This Petition procured immediate, and effectual relief.

October 3d. Resolved, That great inconveniencies are likely to arise, from the want of Staves, Hoops, Heading and other Lumber, in the Sugar Islands; and that some new mode of supply is necessary, during the suspension of the trade with North America.

In consequence of this resolution, sundry Petitions and Memorials were transmitted from hence to different Boards; and our Representatives in Parliament exerted themselves to the utmost; but no effectual remedy has been hitherto obtained.

October 12th. Resolved, That every extension of Lighthouses, under the management, and calculated only for the emolument of individuals, ought to be opposed by the public.

Nov. 7th. Ordered, That by tomorrow's Post be sent up, A Petition to the Lords of His Majesty's Most Honourable Privy Council, setting forth the hardships the Merchants would labour under, by a compliance with the order of Council dated the 25th of October last, relative to Ships carrying Provision from Ireland to the West India Islands.

Such alterations were soon after made in the Order of Council, as effectually removed the grievances complained of.

December 5th. Ordered, That attention be paid to the Trade from Tortola, in the next application to the Admiralty for Convoy from the Windward Islands.

1777 January 2d. Information was received from the African Committee in London, that Captain Johnson, of the Snow Party, of this Port, had forcibly carried off a Number of Canoemen, from Badagry upon the Coast of Africa, which had occasioned the total exclusion of the English from the Trade of that Port, and was likely to be productive of other disagreeable consequences.

The African Committee in London afterwards commenced a prosecution against Capt. Johnson, who was convicted upon the clearest evidence, and fined Twelve Hundred Pounds, but evaded the penalty by escaping out of the Kingdom.

To revenge this insult, and get back the Canoemen, the Natives of Badagry seized upon Ten Whitemen, and closely confined them in chains, where six of the number died in a most deplorable condition. Every possible method has been used by this Society, to obtain the enlargement of the Survivors; and there is the utmost reason to hope that these endeavours will not prove unsuccessful.

February 6th. An application was resolved upon, to the Lords of the Admiralty, for some protection to the homeward-bound Tortola trade.

Mr. Stephens in reply to this application says, Their Lordships will send orders to Vice Admiral Young, Commander in Chief of his Majesty's Ships at the Leeward Islands, to comply with said request.

Application was likewise made, to have Admiralty Protections rendered more effectual, to Sailors attending their duty on shore, within the Port of Liverpool: *but no indulgence has been hitherto obtained.*

March 6th. Resolved, That this Committee apprehend it to be absolutely necessary, for this Nation to keep up some of their Forts upon the Gold Coast of Africa, so long as other European Powers maintain settlements there.

April 3d. Several well authenticated accounts were about this time laid before the Committee, of the protection and encouragement given to the American Privateers, in different West India Islands, but particularly by the Governor of St. Eustatia; That a Privateer had been actually fitted out in that Island; had then taken and carried in thither, Six Prizes, One of them the Brig May, belonging to Liverpool, as she was coming into the road, to seek for a Market: That the subjects of Britain were in a manner shut up in their own Ports, whilst the Dutch, French, and Spaniards, were carrying on a most lucrative trade to the Continent of America: and their Sugar Islands supplied with Lumber and Provision at an easy price; whilst the profit on their produce and traffic was amazing.

The particulars, supported by evidence, upon oath ,where that could be obtained, were transmitted to Ministry; and it is not to be doubted, that proper measures have been already pursued, to prevent a continuance of such pernicious practices.

May 3d. A Petition was presented to the Lords of the Admiralty, Setting forth, That the ships bound from this Port to Africa and the West Indies, not having the benefit of Convoys, are peculiarly exposed to the depredations of the American Privateers, especially off Cape Finister, and when approaching the Sugar Islands. Prays, that their Lordships would be pleased to appoint a sufficient number of Cruizers to those important nations.

No decisive answer has hitherto been given to this Petition.

May 28th. Undoubted information was received by the Committee, of many illegal practises carried on by the French in the West Indies, which were big with danger to the Commerce and Navigation of Britain, and its Colonies. That Privateers were fitted out at Martinique, and Guadeloupe, manned with French, Spaniards and Portuguese; many of them having only one American on board, who was no more than nominal commander. That the Congress Agents in the French Islands had blank Commissions, which they filled up there, and of which they were very liberal. That amongst many others, a vessel belonging to this Port, from Africa, with Slaves, Camwood [African sandal-wood], and Ivory, had been carried into St. Lucia by a French Sloop of Ten Guns, and Fifty Men, said to be the property of Monsieur Bigora, a Merchant in Martinique, That this Sloop had only one Englishman on board, who was honoured with the name of Captain; but the actual Commander and his Officers were French, or other Foreigners. That the *Venus*, Captain Sharp, of and from Whitehaven for Grenada, had been taken, after a gallant engagement of three hours, by a Privateer belonging to Martinico, manned with French, Portuguese, and Spaniards, having only One American as Master.

These accounts have been transmitted to the proper departments of Government, supported by affidavits, memorials, and Petitions; and have met with such attention, as is likely to be productive of the most salutary effects.

June 3d. A Memorial was sent up to the Lords of the Treasury, Setting forth, That from the great failure in the usual demand for the Trade to Africa, and other incidental circumstances unfavourable to commerce, a large quantity of Rum is now in the King's Cellars, not likely to be disposed of before the expiration of the Bonds for the payment of the Excise duty. Prays for an indulgence of Six Months, from and after the expiration of the present Bonds.

No indulgence could be obtained.

June 19th. At the last annual meeting of the Committee, It was Resolved, nemine contradicente,

That the establishment of this Society has been of public advantage.

That a continuation of subscriptions, limited in amount at the option of the subscriber, under such regulations as may hereafter be agreed upon, is essentially necessary.

That it would probably tend to general satisfaction, if a Room was taken in the neighbourhood of the Exchange, where all the Books, and Letters of this Society should be open to the inspection of the Subscribers every day during 'Change hours; and a suitable allowance made to the Secretary for the additional care and attendance.

That it would be a liberal and useful regulation, to admit any Gentleman a Member of this Society, upon payment of such Sum as may be hereafter agreed on to the present fund, and an annual subscription of not less than One Guinea a year.

The COMMITTEE for the present Year, ending JUNE 24, 1778.
GILL SLATER, President,
THOMAS STANIFORTH, Deputy-President,

WILLIAM BOLDEN,	RICHARD KENT,
JOSEPH BROOKS, Jun.	THOMAS LAKE,
THOMAS CASE,	HUGH H. LEIGH,
JOHN CHORLEY,	ALEX. NOTTINGHAM,
EDWARD CHAFFERS,	HENRY RAWLINSON,
JOSEPH DALTERA,	THOMAS SMYTH,
JOHN DOBSON,	GEORGE VENABLES,
THOMAS FOXCROFT,	WILLIAM WALLACE,
JOHN HODGSON,	RICHARD WATT, Jun.
THOMAS HODGSON, Jun.	

SAMUEL GREEN, Secretary.

5.2 Correspondence of Liverpool chamber with other outports, London, and Bristol SMV

This correspondence, mainly preserved at the Bristol SMV, supplemented with newspaper reports, and the minutes of the London West India Committee, provides valuable insight into the activities of the first Liverpool chamber which is otherwise almost entirely lost. It demonstrates how different local organisations could co-operate to help develop national campaigns, the sort of deference they showed to each other's view, and how to manage an 'opposition' to government policies. It also shows how the Bristol SMV operated as a quasi-chamber in this period, and how the provincial bodies co-operated with well-established more specialist interests such as the West India Committee. Both had long histories of campaigns on commercial and trade matters, and may well have suggested to Liverpool the sort of chamber model needed. However, the SMV was a very different and closed body with a charter and closely interlocked with the local corporation. This was the antithesis of the Liverpool chamber in terms of local co-operation, but the closed, formal, and charter type of structure may well have been something that Liverpool corporation was endeavouring to replicate with its committee of trade. The West India Committee may have been more what the Liverpool chamber was seeking, but for a locality not a single field of trade. The documents reproduced begin with the Stamp Act exchanges of 1765–6. These, as well as the rest of the documents reproduced here, seem to have been previously almost entirely overlooked by historians. They change our views about the way in which provincial associations in the outports were operating in the run up to, and during, the American War, and in the period before the General Chamber of Manufactures. The petition with the West India Committee and Bristol also evidences that Liverpool chamber had a London agent in 1782 (also see Chapter 7).

The correspondence here should be compared with the Liverpool *Abstract* of minutes for 1774–7 (see above) and campaigns by other chambers covered in this chapter. The correspondence reproduced is an almost complete record of what exists in the SMV and West India Committee archives, but a few items are omitted that are repetitive, and one letter from Green in Liverpool catalogued in the SMV archives is now missing. Other correspondence of the Liverpool chamber is preserved in TNA, African Company and Treasury papers, in BL Additional MSS, and in some other sources. These are mostly referenced in Liverpool chamber's history,[5] but the West India Committee minutes here are additional to material quoted therein. One of the most intense co-operations between many of these organisations, against slave trade abolition, appears not to have included the Liverpool chamber (section 5.13 below).

An important part of the SMV correspondence also evidences exchanges on a 1768 plan for reconstituting the EIC at the end of its current charter. This set of correspondence appears to have been entirely overlooked in the many previous assessments of the EIC. An opportunity appeared to open in 1768 for the outports to participate in a reconstituted EIC. The government needed revenue and the negotiations for a new charter were used by Shelburne (Lord Lansdowne), under Chatham's influence (then prime minister), to press for greater controls on the company and yield more revenue to government. The Directors of the EIC seem to have conceived an alternative plan to bring in new capital into the EIC from the outports through local 'chambers' like those in the Dutch East India Company (the VOC). The EIC itself made approaches to the outports through Mr. Harris (probably Frederick Harris).[6]

[5] Bennett, Voice *of Liverpool Business* (2010).

[6] Probably an EIC figure; likely to be 'Frek (?) Harris': see L. S. Sutherland, 'Lord Shelburne and East India Company Politics 1766–9', *English Historical Review*, 49 (1934) 476, who states Harris was part of the political campaigning in the Commons in May 1767, along with Samuel

Townshend as minister, and Gascoyne (the MP mostly used by Liverpool corporation and key figure at the BoT), instead favoured using the EIC directors for internal reform,[7] which after prevarications Chatham agreed, though by then he was incapacitated. Hence, the charter was renewed without any involvement from the outports.[8] The ministry of Chatham, Townshend, Shelburne, Rockingham and others, were divided about how to proceed.[9] Preoccupation of the government with the Wilkes affair over 1767–71 and growing difficulties in America encouraged an early settlement of the EIC charter. Rockingham and other opposition groups only belatedly engaged in this initiative, which was indeed mostly negotiated behind closed doors. It is described by Sutherland as 'a tangled skein of politics within the Chatham ministry'.[10] It is notable that the proposals for the first time used the term 'Chamber', to be established in London, Bristol, Liverpool, Hull, and Glasgow. The chamber concept here being mooted resembled the terminology used for the Dutch VOC. But given the involvement of Heywood and Smythe as the Liverpool delegates to negotiate on this, who were leading founding members of the chamber of commerce in 1774, with Arthur Heywood its treasurer, the 1768 proposal appears to have been a critical contribution to the thinking about the development of a committee of trade and chamber in the town. It also resonated with the earlier Stamp Act activities of 1765–6, in which Heywood and Smythe were also involved. Interestingly, Malachy Postlethwayt, whose impact is reviewed in Chapter 3, was quoted against the EIC by the Liverpool newspaper publisher John Phillips during this period.[11] There may also have been some resonance of this EIC chamber concept with Samuel Garbett in Birmingham who was a frequent correspondent with Shelburne, and had close connections with William Burke over this period (see Garbett-Lansdowne letters, Section 5.5 below).[12]

Touchet (the Manchester-linked MP who had relatives connected to the Manchester Committee of Trade, discussed in Chapter 1 and listed in the Appendix).

[7] See D. S. Klinge, 'Edmund Burke, Economical Reform, and the Board of Trade, 1777–1780', *Journal of Modern History*, 51 (1979) D1185-D1200; Gascoyne and several of the Board of Trade members benefited personally from Africa and East India Companies contracts; Shelburne was a major shareholder: *ODNB*.

[8] See *ODNB* entry on William Petty (Lord Shelburne); Sutherland, 'Lord Shelburne' (1934). For other aspects of Shelburne's links to chamber campaigns see the Birmingham Garbett correspondence, section 5.5. below.

[9] See L. S. Sutherland, *The East India Company in Eighteenth century politics* (Oxford, 1952); C. H. Philips, *The East India Company, 1784–1834* (1962); D. H. Watson, *The Duke of Newcastle, the Marquis of Rockingham, and mercantile interest* (Sheffield, 1968) 46 ff., 466–80.

[10] Sutherland, 'Lord Shelburne' (1934) 452.

[11] *Liverpool Chronicle*, 23 and 30 June, 1 December 1768.

[12] Birmingham was never considered as part of the EIC proposals because it was not a port, and there is nothing specific in the Garbett-Lansdowne letters referring to the proposal.

However, Heywood and Smythe were not able to overcome the intense national political machinations and resistance to EIC reform by the Company, Gascoyne and ministers, with the outports finding it difficult to find allies, especially when so many leading politicians themselves had significant EIC interests (including Shelburne). The East India proposal that was being consulted on by Harris, no copy of which has been found, was clearly very similar to the Dutch VOC. This had been founded in 1602 with a decentralised structure based on six cities: Amsterdam, Zeeland (covering Middleburg), Rotterdam, Delft, Hoorn and Enkhuizen. Each formed a 'chamber' of the VOC with varying capital levels defined for ten-year periods. The VOC charter then defined the participation of the six cities in trade: 50 per cent Amsterdam, 25 per cent Zeeland, and one sixteenth each for the other four centres. The 66 VOC directors we divided in proportion: 20 to Amsterdam, 12 to Zeeland and seven each for the others. The committee of 18 had eight from Amsterdam, four from Zeeland and one each from the others, plus one extra. The directors were appointed by the States of Holland and Zeeland and, being chartered, they had no personal liabilities. Each locality had its own Board which acted locally to organise VOC activities, and after 1645 also became an electoral college to appoint new directors.[13] Subsequently various changes were enacted, but the VOC had the same basic structure in 1768 when it was being discussed in England, by which time it had become a very successful operation, and was poised to expand into China in 1786. The VOC structure was a direct parallel to how Liverpool and Bristol conceived their participation in a reformed EIC.

Sources
[a] Bristol SMV, original in-letters: Bristol RO SMV/2/4/2
[b] Bristol SMV, Outletter book: Bristol RO SMV/2/4/1/1
[c] Proceedings of the SMV: Bristol RO SMV/2/1/1/10
[d] Index of Proceedings of SMV: Bristol RO SMV/2/1/2/3
[e] *Prescott's Manchester Journal*; also *Williamson's Liverpool Advertiser* 10 July
[f] *Liverpool Chronicle*
[g] *Williamson's Liverpool Advertiser*
[h] Committee of West India Merchants: London Senate House M915/1; also National Library of Jamaica.

[13] See F. S. Gaastra, *The Dutch East India Company: Expansion and Decline* (Zutphen, 2003) 21–3.

Original letter [SMV/2/4/2/10 (7(a))] Liverpool 31 December 1765[a]

To Mr Wm. Reeve [master of SMV]
To be communicated to the Merchants of Bristol

Sir

We have received repeated Accounts of the troubles the Stamp Act has occasioned in North America, and finding general letters are received from thence, countermanding all their orders for the manufactures of this Kingdom, We think it highly necessary to exert ourselves, by every constitutional Method, to obtain a Redress; for which purpose, the underwritten Gentlemen are appointed a Committee & Mr Mayor their Chairman.

We enclose you the Copy of a Memorial We have drawn up to be transmitted to our Members and presented to the House, or remain with them as Circumstances may require.

We shall hope, if you approve the measures we have taken, for your Concurrence therein; and request that you will be pleased to transmit us a Copy of any Memorial or Petition You mean to present, that We may be as uniform as possible in our Applications. We are, Sir with much respect. Your mo. ob. Servts.[14]

John Crosbie (president) [current mayor]	Charles Goore (vice pres) [next mayor]
Geor[ge] Campbell [immediate past mayor]	[William] Halliday & [Thomas] Dunbar
	Ar[thur] & Benj[amin] Heywood
	John Sparling & Co. [Ald]
	Thos Falkner
	Jhn Brown [Ald]
	[John] Benson & [John] Postlethwaite
	Samuel Kilner [of Lancaster]
	John Crosbie [jun.] [Ald]
	John Walker
	Thos Smythe
	[Geo] Campbell & [Stephen] Hayes

[14] The signatories had the three main corporation members (the immediate past, current and future mayor) and three aldermen [Ald]; all the rest were merchants with no corporation connection who mostly became chamber members.

Memorial touching the American Affairs [SMV/2/4/2/10 (7(b))]

31 December 1765[a]

To the Honourable the Commons of Great Britain in Parliament assembled The Memorial of the Merchants of Liverpool trading to and from America, and the Coast of Africa Humbly Sheweth

That your Memorialists being Merchants, and Owners of Vessels, usually employed in exporting British Manufactures to the Continent of North America, have, at this time, many Vessels detained there, at a great Expense of Wages and provisions as they cannot be cleared out, until the present unhappy Differences, occasioned by the Stamp Act, be adjusted and determined.

That the Colonies are largely indebted to the Merchants of this Port, and to those of Great Britain in general, who are deprived of all methods of recovering the Money due to them from thence, as the regular holding of Law Courts in the Colonies is, at present, interrupted.

That the Resolutions made by the Merchants and Planters in North America, against the Importation and wearing of British Manufactures put a total Stop to the trade between Great Britain and the Colonies, and particularly to those valuable Branches of it, which are carried on by the Merchants of this Town; from whence great Quantities of Woollens of all Sorts, especially of the Manufactury of Yorkshire, British & Irish Linens, Manchester Checks & Fustians, Hats, Stockings, Shoes, Axes, Nails, Hoes, wrought Iron, and various kinds of Hardware, bottled Ale, Salt, Coals, and Lead are exported.

That the Merchants of this Port are under strong Apprehensions, that the African Trade, which is very extensively carried on from here, will also be greatly injured by the present disturbances in America.

These are the distresses We at present experience, and many more are the Circumstances We have reason to dread; not knowing when our Ships, that are now in America, may be permitted to return, nor daring, in the present state of Affairs, either to send out any more Vessels and Manufactures from hence, or to order any of our African Ships to the Northern Colonies.

Wherefore Your Memorialists, under these present Evils, and alarming Apprehensions, humbly presume to lay this interesting Subject before your Honourable House; not doubting but they shall receive, from the Wisdom of a British Parliament such speedy and effectual Redress as the nature of the Case requires.

And Your Memorialists will ever pray

Printed report 4 February 1768[f]

Reports that the Mayor has invited the merchants to lay before them a proposal from the East India Company for establishing a branch of the Company here.

Printed report 5 February 1768[f]

Yesterday at a meeting of Merchants, and others, held at the Exchange, agreeable to notice given by the Mayor, a proposal was read for opening the East India Trade; the further consideration of which was adjourned to this day. By this scheme it is proposed that Chambers shall be established at London, Bristol, Liverpool, Hull, and Glasgow; the first to furnish to Government £3,200,000, the two next £1,600,000 each, and the two last £800,000 each, in the whole Eight millions; this to bear an interest of 2 per cent—in consideration for which the trade shall be free to the five Chambers only—from which, it is said, very great advantages may be drawn both to the public and adventurers.—But this to be more minutely inquired into at this day's meeting.

Printed report 12 February 1768[f]

At an adjournment of the meeting held on Thursday the 4th inst. to take into consideration the proposals relative to laying open the East-India Trade, a Committee was appointed to attend on the Proposer in the Council-Room in the Exchange, and all others admitted who pleased to attend —The result of several of these meetings it [was agreed], that the scheme appears very practicable, and if it can be completed will be of the greatest advantage to the Ports immediately concerned and to the Public in general. Two of the Committee are deputed to attend the Proposer in London, to enquire still further into so very important a scheme.

Printed report 3 March 1768[g]

A letter has been received from Mr. Heywood and Mr. Smythe, by the Committee of the India affair, expressing a great confidence in the utility of the design, and enlarging on the candid and genteel reception they meet with from all they have occasion to treat with.

Printed report 11 March 1768[g]

We hear from Aberdeen that the merchants there propose to invest a sum of money to enable them to engage in the projected scheme to the East Indies, in common with Liverpool, Glasgow, &c.

Printed report 17 March 1768[f]

Messrs Heywood and Smythe, the gentlemen who were deputed to examine into the proposal respecting the trade to India are returned; and do not report so favourably on the matter as the town generally expected.

Printed report 21 April 1768[f]

Report of the meeting on Friday evening to extend freemen … [tenth toast] shame and disappointment to those who, *for private gain*, have obstructed the trade to India from the outports.

Printed report 23 June 1768[f]

[containing a long article against the current arrangements of the India trade, criticising the author of a pamphlet 'The utility and equity of opening the trade to India' for stealing the ideas of the editor of the newspaper]

Printed report 30 June 1768[f]

[quotes Postlethwayt's Dictionary vol. 1 p. 685 on trade and Dutch competition and in favour of the East India Company opening trade and developing local manufactures, noting that] Postlethwayt was a profound and laborious advocate of continuing the trade to Asia under the direction of a company with the outports able to participate.

Original letter [SMV/2/4/2/12 (3)] Liverpool, 12 February 1768[a]

Gentlemen,

Proposals have been made to the Merchants of this place, for a new Establishment and extension of the Trade to Asia by increasing the Capital Stock, and by allowing your City, Hull, Glasgow and this place to participate [in] such Trade in proportion to the respective Capital assigned them.

Our merchants have no doubt that this proposed scheme has been communicated to you which they look upon as a matter deserving the most serious attention, & I have their directions to acquaint you that they have deputed Two of their body viz. Mr. Benjamin Heywood and Mr. Thomas Smyth to go to London to obtain all profitable information relative to this affair, who will be glad to cooperate with such Gentlemen as you are pleased to appoint on this occasion.

Mr Heywood & Mr. Smyth propose setting out from hence on Monday night, and if in the mean time, we should not be so happy as to receive your Answer, those Gentlemen may be heard of at the Somerset Coffee House in the Strand.
I am with great respect, Gentlemen, You most obed. Hbl. Servt
Scrope Colquitt

Copy letter Bristol, 18 February 1768[b]

To: Scope Colquit Esq., Liverpool

Sir,

I have your Favour of the 12th Inst. relative to Proposals for a new Establishment & extension of the Trade to Asia, and have laid the same before the Committee, but as no particular Proposal have been sent to them they cannot at present give any determinate Answer but shall at all times be very ready to acquiesce with any measures that may tend to the benefit and extension of the Commercial Interest of this Country,

I am Sir, Your most obedt. Sevrt.

A. J. Elton, Master

Copy letter Bristol, 6 May 1768[b]

To: Scope Colquit Esq., Liverpool

Sir,

Mr. Harris has waited on this Society, since I wrote you last, & communicated to them his Plan for opening the Trade to Asia, & it is referred to a Committee to be considered—for this purpose we shall be very ready to open a Correspondence with the Committee of Merchants at Liverpool & to go hand in hand with them in such steps as shall be mutually approved of And we should be glad to know what they have hitherto done and the result of the enquiry made by the Deputies who went to London—So far as the Committee has hitherto considered the Plan there seems no very essential objection to the practicality of it, & this Society will always be ready to use their utmost endeavour to lay open & extend the Trade & Commerce of the Kingdom.

I am, Yr. very hble. Servt.

A. J. Elton Mast.

Copy letter Bristol, 30 June 1768[b]

To: The Mst. Worshipful Geo. Thompson Esq., Mayor, Hull

Sir,

Mr Harris laid before the Committee of this Society a Letter which he received from you signifying that the Merchants of Hull were willing to join with this Society and the Merchants of Liverpool &c. in endeavouring to open the Asiatic Trade, & he desired us to acquaint you with the steps were taken here—as yet we have come to no other resolutions that that if the Government should open the Trade, We should be desirous of having a share of it, the Merchants of Liverpool have entered further into the consideration of the matter & as we go on we shall communicate to you our Proceedings &c. Should be glad of your sentiments & proceedings from time to time.

We are (in the absence of the Master), Your very huble. Servts.

Michl. Miller Jn. }
Henry. Garnett } Wardens

A like letter to the Mst. Worshipful Geo Murdock Esq,. Provost ,Glasgow.

Copy letter Bristol, 30 June 1768[b]

To: Scope Colquit Esq., Liverpool

Sir,

Your Letter to our Master of the 16th Ulto. has been this day laid before, and taken into consideration by, our Committee, & also a Letter from you to Mr. Harris by which We observe that you have transmitted to Hull some Remarks on the Plan delivered in by Mr. Harris entitled The advantages to the Public and the Out Ports—from Mr. Harris's Plan. The Former part of the second resolution of your Committee our Committee humbly concur in, but the latter part touching Trading to the Conquered Provinces, if the whole Trade be not laid opened, seems to us impractical—As to the 1st & 3d. of your Resolutions for Petitioning the Lords of the Treasury to concur with & aid us in preventing the Renewal of the present Charter, & for sending Deputies to London to obtain information & form Petitions to Parliament to be procured from the Neighbouring Cities and Counties, the Committee of themselves cannot go so far but must have the sanction of a general Meeting of our Society—At present they think it must rest with the Ministry to judge of the National advantage or disadvantage of such a measure—In the mean time We desire you would send us a copy of the above Remarks.

We are (in the absence of the Master), Yr. &c.

Michl. Miller Jn. }
Henry. Garnett } Wardens

Copy letter Merchts. Hall Bristol, 4 April 1775[b]

To: H[enr]y Cruger & Edmd. Burke, Esqrs.

Sir,

The Committee have taken in cons[ideration] Mr Phillips's Bill which they find is powerfully opposed by the Town of Liverpool who say their people know the Situ[ation] of the Smalls so well as always to avoid it; however this Society do not wish to oppose it generally, but they think the Bill requires such amendments & insofar that it is intended to Subject all Ships & Vessels using this port to this Duty & that the mode of charging it will be productive of much trouble to them: they desire therefore that an exception may be made as to all ships bound to Bristol to the Eastwd., So.ward. or Westwd. or coming from the Eastwd. or So.ward. or Westwd. & not passing thr'o the No[rth] Channel to Bristol, which will have chargeable all ships passing between Bristol & Ireland, or thr'o the No[rth] Channel & such are the only ships that will be in Common course benefitted by the Light.

The words in p.4 [of the Lights proposal, for charges] according to the burthen of such Ships ought to be amended by adding as the same shall be reported at the Custom house or otherwise there will be perpetual quarrels about the burthen & you may assert that the Holmes Light in the Bristol Channel is charged by that rule.

On the 5th of January last was published in a Journal entitled the Bristol Gazette, a Copy of some Letters which was said to pass Between. Mr. Phillips & Mr. Murdock Mackenzie touching the Light House in question, & also a Copy of Mr. Phillip's intended petition to parliament & therein the Duties ascertained at a half penny per Ton from British Ships & 1d. per Ton from Foreign Vessels, the Blanks ought therefore to be so filled up or this Bill opposed totally.

In the proviso for maintaining the Lights instead of the words a Sufficient Light or Lights it ought to be two Sufficient discriminated Lights one above another of different complexions.

And in the next clause touching repairs after the words (as to make it Necessary to alter or Vary the Lights therein) shod. be added which it shall not be lawful for the said John Phillips his & Heirs and Assistants to do but in Case of repairs under a forfeiture of the duty hereby granted— and instead of the words to give Public Notice it should be Three Months Public Notice.

We hope that these alterations may be obtained & then we have no objecn. to the Bill.

A Gent. has engaged to collect an account of the Facts relative to the plundering of Ships & the Same shall be sent you.

I am Yr. very hble. Servt.
Robt. Smith, Master

Proceedings: Minute Bristol, 24 April 1775[c]

A letter of the 16 Instant from Mr. Dobson President of the Chamber of Commerce at Liverpool requesting this Society to join in opposing Mr. Phillip's Bill for erecting a Light House on the Smalls, which Bill has been read twice in the House & is to go before a Committee of the whole House on Wednesday next, and which in its present form all ships passing to or from Bristol will be chargeable; It is the opinion of the Committee that Mr. Fowler and Mr. Vaughan be desired to go to London to oppose the said Bill if they shall find it necessary. And the Committee also desired Mr. Fowler to purchase such sea charts as he shall meet with and which will be useful for this Society

It is the opinion of the Committee that the Chamber of Commerce be acquainted of the above resolution.

Minute London West India Committee, 4 February 1777[h]

A letter from John Dobson, President of the Chamber of Commerce at Liverpool was read:

'I was duly favoured with your opinion that to lay a duty in that case, would be contrary to every principle in which the duty of Customs has been imposed, which they apprehend is meant to be paid by goods landed and not upon a supposed quantity of such as no longer exist, since a duty would operate as a most oppressive fine upon men, who have already lost their whole property by unavoidable misfortune of the voyage, for a duty so levied by sale, or by drawback on exportation, the commodity being destroyed.'

Your letter of the 26 Ult. which I have laid before a general meeting held last night, and they desire me to enclose to you copies of the minutes of their general meetings of 11 December, 7 January and 4th February relative to applications being made to the Lords of the Admiralty for homeward bound convoys, and which they hope you will find a full answer to your several enquiries.

I likewise by desire of the West India Merchants enclose to your several questions of which the answers that of ships will please to examine (as part) the master who sailed with the *Squirrel*, the examination signed by each Master … to be laid before the Lords of the Admiralty.

The Merchants hope that by their examinations to preserve order among their ships and thereby prevent exorbitant rates of insurance as well as preserve a due obedience on the part of the merchant ships and a strict attention in the Commanders of the Convoys.

Agreed the following memorial presented to Lords of the Treasury [supporting Liverpool and requesting a proper convoy to Tortola].

Minute London West India Committee, 14 March 1777[h]

Letters made to Bristol, Liverpool [chamber of commerce] & Glasgow advising that the Lords of the Admiralty had ordered a Court Martial to inquire into the cause of the separation of His Majesty's ship *Squirrel* from the merchant ships that sailed under her convoy [from Jamaica], & to try Captain Douglas for his conduct.

[Further letters to/from Bristol, Liverpool (Dobson and chamber of commerce) and Glasgow 18, 21 and 25 March concerning the Court Martial at Portsmouth; Liverpool delegates could not attend, but Bristol and Glasgow delegates did].

Outletter Bristol, 17 February 1777[b]

To: Dobson Esq.

Sir,

This Society have lately received a letter from the Secretary to the Lords Commissioners for Trade and Plantations

'desiring the Opinion of the African Traders whether the Management and conduct of the Officers & Servants of the African Company have (in their opinion) tended to the increase and Advantage of the Trade upon those parts of the Coasts peculiarly under their care—And whether the Traders have received that Protection and Assistance for the several Forts and Settlements upon that party of the Coast which might be wished & reasonably expected from the application of such large Sums that have been so bountifully given by Parliament to Maintain Forts and Settlements for the better supporting and extending the Trade upon that Coast; and whether the Trade has been carried on in that free and Open manner as to be without cause of complaint & to the satisfaction on Individuals Trading to those parts.'

The Society apprehend that like application has been made to your Port, & as a Correspondency of Opinion would be most likely to obtain such advantages to the Trade as every separate Trader must desire, this Society wish to know the Sentiments of your Chamber of Commerce and when they have considered the Points and furnished themselves with Authentic proofs of what may be Asserted they will communicate to you what appears to the,

I am, Your very Huble Servt.,

Henry Garnett, Masr

Original letter [SMV/2/4/2/20(8)] Chamber of Commerce Liverpool, 4 April 1777[a]

Sir,

I had the honour to write you the 25th Feby last, from which time have waited, not without some degree of impatience, for the Report from the Lords of Trade, of the State of the African Settlements. From the profound silence observed, One can scarce avoid suspecting, that the intention of Administration is to let the remainder of the Session slip over without further attention to this matter. By this conduct they will avoid the customary Grants, which perhaps, was their principal object. We can not however, be contented to give the matter up so tamely. Convinced as we are, of the hardships suffered by the British Merchant, from the malpractices of the Company's Servants;

we are still willing to entertain hopes, that those abuses may be in a great measure, if not totally removed, and a proper number of Forts upon the Gold Coast, rendered as useful as they are necessary. Shall be glad to be favoured with the Sentiments of Your Body upon this Subject; and to cooperate in such measures as shall appear necessary for the preservation of the little Trade that is left us.

I have the Honor to be Sir Your Most Obedient Humb. Servt.
John Dobson, Presd.

Original letter [SMV/2/4/2/20(14)] Chamber of Commerce Liverpool,
28 May 1777[a]

Sir,

Having no frank by me for the Master of your Merchant Hall, I take the liberty, by direction from Mr. Dobson, of troubling you with the delivery of the enclosed.

I am, Sir, Your Obliged Humb. Servant
Samuel Green, Secry.

Enclosed letter [SMV/2/4/2/20(13)] Chamber of Commerce Liverpool,
28 May 1777[a]

Sir,

By various accounts, from different Persons & Places, undoubted intelligence has been received here, of some illegal and dangerous practices, carried on by the French in the West Indies. A Vessel belonging to this place, with Slaves, Camwood, and Ivory, has been carried into St. Lucia by a French Sloop of 10 Guns & 50 Men, said to be owned by a Mr. Bigora, a Merchant in Martinique. The Sloop had only One Englishman onboard, who was honoured with the title of Captain; but the actual Commander and his Officers were French; and the Crew all French, or other Foreigners.

The *Venus*, Captain Sharp, of and from Whitehaven for Grenada, was taken, after a gallant defence of three hours, by a Privateer belonging to Martinique, manned with French, Portuguese, and Spaniards, having only One American for Master. Many others are fitting out upon the same plan both at Martinique, and Guadeloupe. The Congress Agents have blank Commissions which they fill up there, and are very liberal of them. These proceedings appear to us, so ruinous to the trade of Great Britain, that it has been determined to bring the business before Parliament by Petition. Shall esteem ourselves happy and honoured with the concurrence of the Merchants of Bristol in our intended application.

I have the Honour to be Your Most Obed. Humb. Serv.
John Dobson Presd.

Minute London West India Committee, 3 June 1777[h]

Read a letter from Dobson, chamber of commerce, that a petition to parliament is preparing for the merchants of Liverpool concerning the capture of two Guinea ships by privateers fitted out from the French Islands.

Reply that the men of London have already taken up, and a committee attends ministers tomorrow about the business.

Original letter [SMV/2/4/2/20(15)] Chamber of Commerce Liverpool, 6 June 1777[a]

Sir

Conformable to what I had the honour of writing You on the 18th Ult: a Petition to Parliament was actually drawn up, and signed by the West India, & African Merchants here: but upon more mature deliberation, it was not judged expedient to present it when the Session was so near its end. A Memorial to Lord George Germain was therefore substituted in the place of the Petition, as more likely to be of actual service to the mercantile interest.

I have the Honour to be your Obd. Servt.
John Dobson

Copy letter Merchts. Hall Bristol, 26 February 1778[b]

To: Giles [sic] Slater Esq. [President of the Liverpool chamber]
Sir,

Your letter of the 16th inst. would have been earlier answered but that our Secretary has been ill—

This Society have sent a petition to the Members for this City to be presented to the House of Commons touching the Smalls Lights in which they pursue the Sentiments they adopted in the year 1775, not wholly opposing it, but expressing their opinion that a constant Light cannot be maintained there—Whatever may be the agreement between Mr. Phillips & the Corporation of Trinity House, it is apprehended it will be impractical to prove it before the House of Commons, & therefore dangerous to touch upon it, especially as the Management of the Lights on our Coast is by Law put into their hands and It is the opinion here that though Mr. Phillips may have got some Satisfaction for what he has done yet that he will have nothing to do with the future Income.

The state of the African Company is under deliberation & when a resolution is formed it shall be communicated to You, & in the mean time We should be glad to know the Sentiments of the Merchants of Liverpool.

I am respectfully, Yr. very huble. Servt.
Samuel Span, Mar.

Copy letter Merchts. Hall Bristol, 14 March 1778[b]

To: Mr Thomas Staniforth

Depty. Presidt. of the Chamber of Commerce, Liverpool

Sir

Your Letter of the sixth instant relative to the Smalls Lights & the African Trade this day laid before the Committee of this Society—& I am desired to acquaint You that as to the Smalls Lights this Society consider themselves bound by the Sentiments they have expressed in their Petition to the House of Commons which are correspondt. with those they declared in the year 1775 & that therefore they cannot wholly oppose the scheme of establishing a Light there, but that they shall be ready when it becomes Necessary to send up a proper Deputation to Support their petition & obtain such Rules and Regulations as they have prayed for, in doing which the Gentlemen deputed by you and us may Cooperate and prevent the payment of a Duty unless they receive an adequate benefit.

As to the African Trade the Gentlemen to whom the consid[eration] of the improvement of the present plan was committed have not made their report but when they do you shall be informed of it, and your proposed amendments shall be laid before them.

We presume that you as well as the Trade here, are greatly alarmed at the probability there appears of giving Ireland an immediate correspondence with our West India Islands and that if it shall appear more authentic you will join with us in giving it all possible opposition.

I am very respectfully Yr. Most obedt. Servt.

Saml. Span, Master

Copy letter Merchts. Hall Bristol, 16 April 1778[b]

To: Gill Slater Esq., Presidt. of the Chamber of Commerce of Liverpool

Sir

Your letter of the 20th Ult. came to hand & the receipt of it would have been earlier acknowledged but that I have been absent from Bristol. We are Sorry that the Smalls Light Bill is carried, but find that the Trinity House had address enough to persuade the admiralty that it would be of great use to the Royal Navy.—But we have now a more dangerous blow to ward off,—a blow that Threatens no less than destructn. to the prosperity of the Trade of Great Britain—and yet we fear that our utmost endeavours will not avail.—This Society however, will exert themselves as powerfully as they can & for this purpose we have had a meeting & have prepared a petition of which it is to undergo a full consideration. I enclose also a Copy of a circular Letter which we intend to send to all the Cities, Boroughs & principal Manufacturing Towns & places in this part of the Country, & if you did the same to those in your Neighbourhood it would certainly have a good effect.—We think it that the Holiday intervening and to give us time otherwise our opponents would have been too quick for us. We shall send our Deputies to London on this occasion as we Suppose you will do and we shall be Glad to consult & Cooperate with you—Be pleased to inform us of the Steps you take.

I am &c

S Span, Master

Copy letter Merchts. Hall Bristol, 18 April 1778[b]

To: Gill Slater Esq. Presidt. of the Chamber of Liverpool

Sir

In our Letter of the 16th I forgot to acquaint you that it appears to us that the only method of qualifying the Mischief of the Irish Trade Bills is to propose an Union, but it being a Step of such importance it was not thought right even to point at it in the petition as in that Case too could not retract, it appeared to us also that Ireland would not accept a participation of Trade upon such Terms, and as nothing can be more reasonable on our part than such an offer it seems to be the only means of frustrating the whole Scheme, for Surely the Landed Interest would never join any sort of people whatever in an act which would so evidently tend to lay a heavier load on their Estates, & it is so plain a Conseqce. that in our opinion he that runs may read.—It is hoped you will consider with great attention this important point, & favour us with your opinion on it.

I am &c.

S Span, Master

Minute London West India Committee, 4 February 1777[h]

A letter from Gill Slater Esq. President of the Chamber of Commerce at Liverpool read expressing their apprehension of the defenceless state of the Sugar Islands and that the merchants there would adopt & nurture any method that may be proposed by the West India Merchants of London, and to which the Chairman by desire of a meeting of the Committee on the 26 Ult. sent the following answer.

Letter to Gill Slater Esq., Liverpool

Sir, I was only favoured with your letter of the 21st current [June] stating the apprehension of the merchants of Liverpool on account of the dangers to which our Sugar Islands may be exposed in case any foreign power shall attempt to invade them. I can with truth inform you that the Committee of West India Merchants of London have from time to time applied to government to reinforce the squadrons on those stations by sending out ships of the line, and to use all other means for protection of the Islands, and of the West

India commerce, and they have been constantly assured that the utmost attention would be paid to their requests. The Committee are of the opinion that if the Gentlemen of your Chamber of Commerce think proper to make separate application it will come in aid of the representations already made here by the London merchants.

Printed report 11 July 1778[e]

The following is a letter of thanks from the Chamber of Commerce at Liverpool, to Henry Cruger, Esq; one of the representatives in Parliament for the city of Bristol.

Sir, Liverpool, June 29, 1778

The Merchants of Liverpool assembled in their Chamber of Commerce, direct me to entreat your acceptance of their most sincere and grateful thanks, for the *strenuous support* which you honoured them, in opposing the bills lately depending, for extending the trade between Ireland and the British Plantations in America.

The landed-interest, trade and navigation of Britain, will, we are persuaded, remain clear of numberless disadvantages from the alterations obtained by this opposition.

To our expressions of gratitude, for present services, permit us to add our hopes of your future support and encouragement, in guarding against any future INNOVATION upon the wise, and long established laws, under which the commerce of the kingdom hath so extensively flourished.

I have the honour to be, Sir,
Your most obedient, humble Servant,
GILL SLATER, President.

Copy letter Merchts. Hall Bristol, 13 April 1779[b]

To: Henry Cruger & Edmund Burke Esqs.
Sirs,

A Copy has been sent to this Society of an intended report from the Committee of the House of Commons on the African Trade & they are told it will be made the 16th or 17th inst. It is in favour of a Joint Stock Company & the Chairman of the Committee is directed to move the House to address the King to direct the Board of Trade to consider of such plans or proposals as may be laid before them. If this should be effected it would give the Coup de grace to the Trade of the out-ports already greatly injured & that for the sole benefit of a few Monopolists in London—when we mention a monopoly we apprehend we need say no more by way of Argument to convince you it would prove a national Injury or to induce you to oppose it with all your power. We fear that the best exertion of that power will be wanted for we apprehend it has Board of Trade (Mr. Gascoyne) & able friends in the House.—The Grounds on which the report is founded are—

> 1st. That the African Trade is in a very alarming & reduced State & in danger of being annihilated—&
> 2d. That the present mode of conducting the Commercial interest of this Kingdom has proved ineffectual.

To the first we say that it cannot be denied but we may Safely add that it is owing to the unhappy times for that immediately before the troubles the Trade flourished greatly.

To the 2d. That it has been proved to & admitted by the House over & over again that the present plan for conducting the Trade is the best that can be devised.—That the Forts & Settlements are necessary as marks of Sovereignty & possession but as such marks only, & not otherwise essentially useful to the Trade.

It cannot be denied but that great abuses have been committed & they have been loudly complained of & have been for a Season corrected

Copy letter Merchts. Hall Bristol, 14 April 1779[b]

To: Henry Cruger & Edmund Burke Esqs.

Sirs,

To the Arguments we took the liberty to lay before you in Support of the present System of the African Trade we beg leave to add two facts of considerable weight. 1st that it is not peculiar to the present times to have the Trade [limited] for it did so at the beginning of the last War.— & Secondly, & which we consider the most Material, that for 7 years preceding the dispute with America, the Trade was overdone & such quantities of Slaves sent to the Islands that the planters could not pay for them but by Bills at 3, 4, & 5 years date, which payment no merchants could Support business with.

I am very respectfully, yr. most hble Servt.
Michl. Miller Jr. [Master]

Copy letter Merchts. Hall Bristol, 8 April 1779[b]

To: The Presidt. of Chamber of Commerce Liverpool

Sir,

We presume that you have been apprised that the Committee of the Ho. of Commons on the African Trade have made a report in favour of a Joint Stock Co. & intend to move the Ho. to address the King to direct the Board of Trade to consider of such plans or proposals as may be laid before them for establishing such a Company.—We Suppose also that you are not unacquainted that this measure has been long in agitation and that it has received much advantage from the abuses of the present System which have been complained of but never remedied nor opposed with that vigour which they ought to have been. We hope however that as it is now Rea[ched] to a Crisis, it may be productive of good by rousing the attention of the outports.—There could not be a more favourable time for the Friends of a Joint Stock Co. to move in than the present because the Trade is certainly now at a very low ebb & they will no doubt advantage themselves of that Circumstance, but we hope that the Separate Traders will not add to their advantage by a languid opposition but exert themselves as though the Trade actually flourished in the hopes that the day may come when that will be again the Case. We are advised that it will be moved the 17th Inst. & We shall in the mean time write to the Members for this City & our Officers for same on the occasion & shall be ready to cooperate with You in such measure as shall appear necessary

I am your
Michl. Miller, Master.

Original letter [SMV/2/4/2/22(18)] Chamber of Commerce Liverpool,
12 April 1779[a]

Sir

We have been long aware of the intended attack upon the African Trade, and much alarmed at the advantages the Advocates for Monopoly were likely to receive from the abuses of the present establishment. To remedy those abuses in time, has long been our wish; and we have repeatedly attempted to bring on a Parliamentary enquiry, as the only effectual means of accomplishing a reformation. There is now double cause for lamenting, that so much time has elapsed, without, going into this much wanted enquiry; and the very low ebb to which the trade is reduced, will tend still further, to strengthen the hands of our Opponents. However, we are still ready to cooperate with you in whatever measures may appear necessary to preserve the freedom of this Once valuable branch of commerce; which, we do not despair of seeing again flourish.

We were timely apprised of the disposition and proceedings of the Committee of the House of Commons, and have accordingly made what interest we can, towards defeating its intention in the first instance. The different Members in this and the neighbouring Counties have already been applied to, which is all that can be done at present. If a Bill is order'd into the House, we are determined to give it every opposition in our power. Shall be glad to receive any further information which may come to your hands; and to concert with you proper measures for our mutual defence. I am

Sir, Your very Humble Servant
Gill Slater Presdt

Copy letter Merchts. Hall Bristol, 7 December 1779 [b]

To: Gill Slater Esq. Presidt. of the Chamber of Commerce Liverpool.
Sir

Your Letter of the 13th Ult. enclosing Copy of a Memorial from the Committee of Trade and the Manufacturers at Manchester to the Lords of the Treasury praying for various reasons therein set forth that an Act may be obtained for the Importation of Cotton Wool duty free during the present war in neutral bottoms came duly to hand & I communicated it to the West India Merchts. as requested, but their monthly Meeting being past & a difference of opinion arising between them they came to no resolution. Yesterday I laid it before the Committee of this Society & have written at their request to the Members of Parliament for this City to desire them to enquire at the Treasury what reception the Memorial met with there & in what stage the business is in & as soon as we have an Ans[wer] all due attention will be given to it.

I am Yr. &c.
John Powell, Master

*Printed address, in Minutes*London West India Committee, 29 January 1782[h]

[copy also in *London Chronicle*, 3 January 1782]

To the King's most Excellent MAJESTY.

The humble ADDRESS and PETITION of the PLANTERS and MERCHANTS, whose names are hereto subscribed, on behalf of themselves, and others interested in the BRITISH WEST INDIA ISLANDS.

Most Gracious Sovereign,

We your Majesty's most dutiful and loyal subjects, the Planters and Merchants interested in the British West India Islands, beg leave to approach your Royal presence, with hearts full of the warmest attachment to your Majesty's person and family, and to the happy constitution of this kingdom.

The unhappy breach between Great Britain and the colonies of North America, had no sooner taken place, than the West India Planters and Merchants humbly presented to your Majesty, and to both Houses of Parliament, their apprehensions of the distress and danger, that would probably ensue therefrom.

When the colonies of North America formed an alliance with the ancient enemies of this kingdom, those apprehensions of your Majesty's Petitioners were greatly increased; and they should have considered themselves as deficient in duty to your Majesty, as well as regard to the great interests of this kingdom, had they not represented to you Majesty's ministers, the additional danger to which all the British West India Islands were exposed, from so powerful a combination.

Every effort was, therefore, made and invariably continued, by your Petitioners, to urge your Majesty's Ministers to provide effectual reinforcements for their protection, and particularly to induce them to keep a permanent superiority of naval force in the West Indies, as being the natural, and only certain security of those possessions.

The loss of several of those Islands has afforded a melancholy proof of the propriety of those timely and unremitted applications.

… It is with the utmost concern that your Petitioners are compelled to declare, that the remaining Islands are still so unhappily destitute of protection, that at no moment of the war have they been exposed to more imminent danger, than in the present awful conjuncture.

Your Petitioners, therefore alarmed by the inefficacy of their former applications to your Majesty's Ministers, humbly implore you Majesty to enforce and extend the present assurances they have given us, and to direct that, without delay, reinforcements, naval and military, adequate to the permanent defence of your Majesty's West India Islands, may be sent out, so that, by the blessing of Providence, those most valuable possessions may still be preserved to the British empire.

Any your Petitioners shall ever pray, &c. &c.

Nathaniel Bayley, Chairman, Stephen Fuller, Agent for Jamaica, Samuel Estwick, Agent for Barbados.

[signed by 198 at London].

Hen. Rawlinson, Agent for the Chamber of Commerce of Liverpool.

J. Hering for the following Planters and Merchants of Bristol.

[signed by 79 at Bristol].

Original letter [SMV/2/4/2/24(1)] Chamber of Commerce Liverpool,
4 January 1782[a]

Sir

A very respectable Committee of Merchants here, have been employed for some weeks, in collecting an account of innovations, and useless expenses at our Customhouse.

Amongst other matters merely local, the Isle of Man Bonds appear to be of more general import. "By the Act of 5th Geo: 3rd Ch: 39 Sec: 13 it is enacted, that the Commanders of all Vessels from Great Britain or Ireland, bound for Africa, or any of his Majesty's Dominions out of this realm, shall give Bond, with One Surety besides the Master, that such Vessel shall not during the course of the voyage take onboard any Goods whatsoever at the Isle of Man; or out of any Vessel or Boat, any Goods which shall have been brought from thence."—This Law, since the Isle of Man is become the property of the Crown, seems useless, and rather absurd: for you give Bond not to do, what you may legally do notwithstanding such Bond. You are therefore requested to inform me, whether a compliance with this Law is strictly enforced at your Port; and if the grievance is deemed so weighty, that you would join us in endeavouring to procure its repeal.

A petition to the King is now in hand here, praying that such effectual reinforcements may be immediately sent out, and constantly kept up for the protection of the British West India Islands, as many afford a well founded confidence in the future security of those invaluable Possessions.

I have the Honour to be Sir Your Obedient Humb. Servant
Gill Slater Presdt.

Copy letter Merchts. Hall Bristol, 21 January 1782[b]

To: Gill Slater Esq. Presidt. of the Chamber of Commerce Liverpool
Sir

Your Letter of the 4th Instant informing this Society that a Committee of Merchants in your Town had been employed in collecting an Account of Innovations & useless expenses at the Customhouse—and that amongst the matters which were merely Local the Isle of Man Bonds appeared to be of more general Import, & stating that since that Island had been annexed to the Crown those Bonds were entirely useless & proposing that this Society should join you in endeavouring to procure a Repeal of the Act which requires that Bond—was this day laid before the Committee & they are of opinion that this Society should join in procuring a repeal of that Act—& the Members in Parliament for this City will be applied to on that occasion. As to the other part of your Letter the Contents have already been carried into execution.

I am your very hble. Serv.
Henry Cruger, Mas.

Index record Merchts. Hall Bristol, 8 September 1787[d]

Clerk to approach the Chamber of Commerce in Liverpool regarding the House of Lords proposal for abolition of fees at the Custom House.

5.3 Glasgow—Liverpool—Bristol correspondence 1780–3

A group of exchanges in the early 1780s shows the wider circle of liaison between the major ports and the care of negotiations on specific lobbies. They informed each other, sought support, and tried to coordinate timing of use of different local supporters, mainly their MPs at Westminster. Localities did not agree in all cases. Bristol was rather critical and perhaps drew on greater experience. These exchanges evidence an emerging alliance of the major or principal ports which complements the Bristol-Liverpool exchanges above. It is an antidote to suggestions that lobbies were mainly dominated by the 'new manufactures' in this period,[15] though the manufacturing districts were also included. The exchanges also covered Dublin and followed Glasgow chamber's memorial on sugar and tobacco trades, which it was agreed would 'be sent to several merchants in London and the chambers of commerce in Bristol and Liverpool' (minute 18 February 1783). There was a similar initiative over a memorial on iron manufacturer of Scotland, which was to 'be sent to the chambers of commerce in Bristol, Liverpool and manufacturing towns in England' (minute 7 March 1783).

Sources
[a] Glasgow chamber papers; Glasgow Mitchell Library TD 1670/4/15
[b] Bristol SMV Index of Proceedings; BRO SMV/2/1/2/3
[c] Committee of West India Merchants; London Senate House M915/1

Index record Merchts. Hall Bristol, 31 May 1780[b]

Letter from Provost of Glasgow, Society agree that Mr. Colquhoun was deputed from thence to attend parliament respecting Bill for relief of tobacco trade, Bill agreeable to Society.

Minute West India Committee, 25 February 1783[b]

An application to ministers to be made regarding [opposing] restriction of trade to British built ships for West Indies. Ordered that the minute be transmitted to Bristol, Liverpool, Lancaster and Glasgow.

Minute West India Committee, 7 March 1783[c]

Letter from Liverpool chamber of commerce [response to above]

Your favour of 27 Ult. with copy of an abstract from the minutes of the general meeting of the West India Merchants of London 25 February 1783 were taken into consideration at our monthly meeting held yesterday. I am directed to acquaint you with our unanimous resolution:

'That a partial discussion of this question might in our apprehension prove at present rather dangerous as tending to revive those unhappy divisions which have already long subsisted'
Gill Slater, President.

[15] See e.g. Redford, *Manchester Merchants* (1934); Bowden, *Industrial Society in England* (1965); Ashton, *Iron and Steel* (1963).

Minute West India Committee, 11 March 1783[c]

Letter from Glasgow chamber of commerce [response to above]

Your letter directed to the president of the Chamber of Commerce here containing restriction of trade to British built ships for West Indies … was laid before a meeting of the directors who desire me to inform you that they will most willingly cooperate with the merchants of London in endeavouring to procure such regulations as may be for the benefit of trade in general —That, in the present case, not being fully acquainted with the views of the Gentlemen of London, or all the circumstances attending the present application they beg to refer you to Patr. Colquhoun Esq. their chairman, who will confer with you fully upon the subject, and to whom you will be pleased to communicate such intelligence as you can, in order to enable us the judge how far we can be aiding and assisting to you.

Gilbert Hamilton, Secretary.

Original letter Chamber of Commerce, Liverpool, 23 March 1783[a]

Sir

Your favour of the 15th Curr[en]t came to my hands, in the absence of our President upon whose return which is expected in a few days, the Memorial from the Manufacturers of Iron will be submitted to the consideration of a Committee. In the mean time shall be glad to know when you intend bringing this matter before Parliament, that such aid as we can give, may be thrown in at the proper moment.

Amidst the many important Articles relative to commerce, which have for some time engaged the attention of this Society; the utility of restoring Britain some share in the Export of Tobacco, has claimed much of our attention. The high duty, required by the Laws now in force, to be paid down before landing, must confine our Import to the small quantity necessary for Home-consumption only; and effectually exclude us from a chance of the least share, in supplying other European markets. This Object is considered here, as of consequence sufficient, to merit the attention of every considerable Seaport in the Kingdom; and to require their joint efforts towards accomplishing the arrangement wanted. Be pleased to favour us with the sentiments of your Society thereon. I have the Honour to be,

Sir, Your most Obedt. Humb. Servt.

Samuel Green, Secry

Original letter Chamber of Commerce, Liverpool, 1 April 1783[a]

Sir

Your favour of the 15th and 25th Ult. With the Memorial enclosed therein were taken under consideration of our Committee on Thursday last, being their first meeting since these letters came to hand. I am directed to inquire what further steps you intend taking in regard to a drawback upon Foreign Iron, remu'lt [amended word unclear: 'remade'?] up here for exportation, into nails &c that we may be prepared to support you therein. The opinion of your Society is requested, whether Foreign Hemp, Manufactured into Cordage in Britain, and exported, is not deserving of the same encouragement as Iron.

What I wrote to you on the 23d. of March informed you of our sentiments in respect to Tobacco, and we much wish to join the other principal Places of importation in pursuing that Object with spirit. Sugar, being the production of another Country, it may perhaps be better not to include in the same application, particularly at this time, when the Plantation, & Mercantile Interests in London, Bristol &c. have solicited us to join them in an application to Parliament, for a reduction of the Duties on Sugar & Rum. We very readily closed with the proposal, and only wait their appointing a time for throwing in the petition.

I have the Honour to be Sir, Your Obedient Humble Serv.

Gill Slater, Presdt.

Original letter Merchants Hall Bristol [SMV], 12 April 1783[a]

To: Gilbert Hamilton Esq. [Secretary of the Glasgow chamber]

Sir,

Your letter of the 15th & 25th Ulto., the first containing the Memorial of the Manufacturers of Iron in Scotland, & the last containing the Memorial of the Merchants interested in the Tobacco & Sugar Trade have been this day taken into consideration by the Committee of this Society; being the first meeting they have had since the receipt of those letters; And upon due consideration it appears to them that as to the first mentioned Memorial, the drawback proposed would be impracticable in most instances, & impolitic in all; And as to the Second Memorial, it does not appear that the duties deposited lie inappropriated, and if so, the Argument to be built on that fact cannot be supported, but it will be further enquired into.

I am, Your Hble. Servt.

Sam Worrall, Secry

5.4 Manchester–Liverpool–Lancaster, Arkwright petitions 1785

One of the main activities of the Manchester Committee of Trade was to petition against the renewal of Arkwright's patent. This covered a long and expensive campaign which was initiated by Manchester in 1780–1, and was not successful until 1785. The documents presented here show the last stages, where other centres were enlisted to support Manchester.[16] The rather standardised writing of the petitions shows also that they were highly co-ordinated, for which the aim was not to produce new evidence, but to demonstrate broad support from different places, thus attempting to evidence the 'general public interest'.

With in-letters [SMV/2/4/2/25 f.15a] Liverpool, 1785

To the Honourable the Commons of Great Britain in Parliament Assembled

The humble Petition of the Merchants and Traders of Liverpool whose names are Subscribed

Sheweth,

That your Petitioners observe by the Votes of this Honourable House, that a petition hath been presented by Richard Arkwright of Cromford in the County of Derby Cotton Manufacturer praying for leave to bring in a Bill, to extend the Term granted him by Patent, for the exclusive use of certain Machines said to have been by him invented, for making Cotton into Yarn.

That the said Richard Arkwright, hath already obtained every advantage, which the Laws at present in being have provided for the encouragement of new Inventions, and, by the emoluments arising from this exclusive grant, hath, as your Petitioners are informed and believe, realized such a Fortune as every unprejudiced person must allow to be an ample compensation for the most happy efforts of Genius.

That the interposition of the Legislature to grant still greater rewards, and such as are unwarrantable, by any Statute now in being, might as your Petitioners apprehend give Stability to a dangerous Monopoly, and prove highly prejudicial to the Manufactures, Commerce and Navigation of this Land, by leaving to all other Kingdoms the unlimited Use of Machines, which would in England alone, be thereby confined to the Arbitrary disposal of one Man only,

Your Petitioners therefore humbly pray that the said Bill may not pass into a Law

[16] For early stages and a fuller discussion see Redford, *Manchester Merchants* (1934).

Gill Slater*
John Dawson
Thomas Manley*
Thomas Lake*
Frans. Dawson
Wm. Lloyd
Jno. Brown+
Thos. Staniforth*
Henry Linch
John Parker*
James Roberts
William Roe+
Ellis L Hodgson
Geo. Drinkwater
Thomas Toll
Francis Ingram*
Mattw. Nicholson*
Arth. Heywood*
Geo. Case*
Wm. Grierson+
Wm. Earl junr.*
Jno. Gregson*
Richd. Watson
Jos. Brooke junr.*
Willm Crosbie junr.+
Edwd. Pemberton
Thos. Leyland*
John Lightbody
Richd. Heywood*
Jas. France
Geo. Venables*
Geo. Warren Watts
Peter Freeland
Arnold Meyer*
Thos. Rambold
Joseph Birch
James Gregson
Jno. Danl. Ructe
Wm. Collison
Henry Brown
John Copland*
Edgar Corrie*
Charles Caldwell*
Robt. Berry
John Meyers*
Thos. Smyth*
Thos. Birch+
Jno. Menzies
John Johnson
John Greenwood+
Geo. Warbrick
Jno. Fisher*
Thos. Booth
John Hodgson*
Wm. Bolden*
Henry Wilkens*
John Chorley*
John Blackburn junr.+
Richd. Savage
James Grierson
Benjn. Heywood*
Richd. Tate
Richd. Kent*
John Roberts
Richd. Watts junr.*
Geo. Dunbar*
Richd. Wood
Allan Pearson

* Known or probable member of Liverpool chamber of commerce
+ Member of Liverpool committee of trade

With in-letters [SMV/2/4/2/25 fo.15b] Lancaster, 1785

To the Honourable the Commons of Great Britain in Parliament Assembled.
The humble Petition of the Merchants of Lancaster.
Sheweth,

That it appears to your Petitioners, by the Votes of this Honourable House, that Richard Arkwright Esq. of Cromford in the County of Derby Cotton Manufacturer, has prayed this honourable house for an extension of his Patent for the exclusive right of Manufacturing Cotton into Yarn.

That Your Petitioners have every reason to believe the said Richard Arkwright Esq. has enjoyed his present Patent to his own great emolument.

That your Petitioners presume that a Patentee, being amply rewarded, for his genius and invention, the Public are afterwards fully entitled to its utility, and the more extended the more benefit will be derived.

Your Petitioners therefore beg the extension of the said Patent may not take place. And your Petitioners will ever pray &c.

Thos. Dilworth	Thos. Rawlinson	John Bowes
Thos. Hinde	Wm. Lindow	James Barrow
Wm. Carter	Jno. Dilworth	Edwd. Stuart Junr.
Fra. Carter	David Dockery	Joshua Whalley
Thos. Satterthwaite	Richd. Walker	John Coupland
Henry Hargreaves	Robt. Tomlinson	John Barrow
Henry Tisdall	Robt. Whiteside	John Backhouse
Jno. Hargreaves	James Moore	Richd. Edmunson
John Armstrong	Thos. Warsusick	Thos. Wildman
Saml. Bradford	Edwd. Salisbuy	Wm. Feddon
Thos. Wilcock	Richd. Salisbury	John Peacock
Jas. Carter	Saml. Simpson	John Rawlinson
Joshua Robinson	Robt. Addison	Thos. Moore
Wm. Parke	John Addison	William Watson
Thos. Hinde Junr.	Thos. Parke	
Jno. Satterthwaite	John Watson	
Joseph Whalley	Edward Stuart	

With in-letters [SMV/2/4/2/25 fo.15c] Manchester , 1785

To the honourable the Commons of Great Britain in Parliament Assembled.
The humble Petition of the Cotton Manufacturers of the Town and Neighbourhood of Manchester in the County of Lancaster.
Sheweth,

That your Petitioners observe by the Votes, that a Petition hath been presented to this honourable house by Richard Arkwright of Cromford in the County of Derby Cotton Manufacturer, praying for an Act to give him a further Term for the exclusive Use of certain Machines for making Cotton into Yarn, for which he obtained a Patent in the Year 1769.

That the continuing of the Term of the said Patent as prayed by the said Petition would be of most grievous prejudice and oppression to the Manufacturers in the Cotton Trade.

Your Petitioners therefore humbly pray that they may be heard by themselves or Counsel against the said Application, and that a Bill may not pass for the purpose prayed by the said Petition.

5.5 The Garbett-Burke-Lansdown letters 1766 and 1784

Samuel Garbett has been recognised in various studies as a crucial individual representing Birmingham interests. Here the interest in his activity covers four dimensions: first, as having very early some concept of a local collective organisation, from the 1760s, that became a Commercial Society in 1783 (see Chapter 1); second, at times, he was a prolific correspondent with other places to help stimulate collective campaigns; third, this interacted with, and partly stimulated, the General Chamber, with Garbett acting as a sometimes critical go-between for Josiah Wedgwood, Matthew Boulton and James Watt with other localities and parliamentary representatives. Finally, he was able to engineer close links with some critical MPs or members of the House of Lords. It is possible here only to reproduce a few examples of this material, on which Norris and Bowden have written at some length, drawing largely on Wright and Langford, and used by Redford in his history of Manchester chamber.[17] The first letter is to William Burke, then newly elected as MP.[18] The example quoted is a very early reference to the need for a committee to voice the manufacturing interest; at this stage essentially as a national committee, which of course was achieved during the General Chamber period in 1785–7. This perhaps draws from Garbett's reading of the literature quoted in Chapter 3, of some of which he was certainly aware. The rest of the papers reproduced here derive from his exchanges with the Earl of Shelburne. These

[17] Norris, 'Samuel Garbett' (1957); Bowden, *Industrial Society in England* (1965); Wright, *Chronicles of the Birmingham Chamber* (1913); Langford, *Century of Birmingham Life* (1868) 315–25; Redford, *Manchester Merchants* (1934).

[18] MP for Great Bedwyn, June 1766–1774; an appointment through patronage. He became linked to Rockingham through Edmund Burke, but developed to be seen as an unreliable politically, subsequently developing business interests, with Edmund (probably a relative) becoming the major political figure.

began in the 1760s, overlapping with the letters to Burke—for example, Garbett's letters to Shelburne 1766–8 covering trade with America, Portugal, and the obstruction of the canal serving the Carron Iron Co. from the Clyde.[19] From 1784 he kept up a flow of information to Shelburne about the actions of the Birmingham Committee. Shelburne was still a major political figure, though in eclipse.[20] The correspondence is primarily useful here in providing the list of contacts and exchanges Garbett was engineering between different places, people, and representative bodies. His first letter of 1784 (not reproduced), for example, shows him in contact with 'West Midlands towns and Yorkshire, Stroud and Gloucester, Bristol, Manchester, Norwich, Exeter, Kidderminster, Kendal, Leicester, Nottingham and Hinckley, Nuneaton and Coventry, Paisley, Glasgow, Perth, London, Staffordshire potters and Cornwall tin' miners, concerned that negotiations about Treaties were going on 'without any national plans being attempted to investigate the state of the great manufacturing establishments'.[21] His correspondence evidences the existence of some local chambers or other organisations in some places, and their absence in others, relying on individual 'delegates' or representatives who evolved into roles inside and outside the General Chamber.

Sources
[a] Calendar of State Papers, Domestic, 320
[b] Garbett-Lansdowne Letters, Birmingham Central Library ZZ61B
[c] Printed paper, Birmingham Central Library I/7, 359810

Extract of letter Birmingham, 29 October 1766[a]

Samuel Garbett to William Burke, Esq.

Asks whether his letters of the 23rd and 25th inst. have come to hand. The encroachments that are making in various ways by foreigners on our manufacturers, the fraudulent tricks practicing in our own country which bring our articles into disrepute, the little, very little attention given by Administration to support our manufactures, afford a very mortifying

[19] Birmingham Central Library: Garbett to Shelburne, e.g. for 30 October and 5 November 1766, 8 February 1768; ZZ61B.
[20] Shelburne (William Petty) was a disciple of the Elder Pitt and had been Secretary of State for the Southern Department after the post–1766 Stamp Act change of government; he suggested the review of the EIC in 1767 (q.v. Liverpool correspondence above) and was pro concessions to the Americans. He had dissenter sympathy, and his son was tutored by Joseph Priestley. He had been in the Fox-North administration from 1782–3 and in late 1784 was in a political limbo; he was appointed Marquis of Lansdowne in November 1784. He supported open trade, religious toleration, economical reform and parliamentary reform. He was thus a significant ally for Garbett to develop, but he proved to be an unpopular politician with mixed success: *ODNB*; Sutherland, 'Lord Shelburne and EIC' (1934) 450–80.
[21] Birmingham Central Library: Garbett to Shelburne, 21 May 1784; ZZ61B.

prospect to such as himself who see the ground which is being lost daily. Would rejoice to hear of a committee of warmhearted men being formed to take into consideration the state of British manufacturers for exportation. Till that is done there is little chance of anything effectual being done for their support at foreign markets. There would then be an evident place for men of real business, who cannot lose much time in attendance &c., to give intelligence and make application. Surely such a set of gentlemen could be found in Parliament who would give some attention to a point of such importance. If manufacturers should believe our legislators are so far lost to the public, common prudence may soon influence the most judicious to accept (if not seek for) the advantages they may obtain by leaving Britain. It shocks him to view what passes in his mind on this subject.

Handwritten copy[22] Birmingham, 8 October 1784[b]

At a Meeting of the Commercial Committee in Consequence of the following Notice

"A Meeting of the Commercial Committee is desired at the Hotel, this Afternoon, at Five o'Clock, upon Business of great Importance to this Town & Neighbourhood.
I am, respectfully, Your obdt. hble. Servt.
(Signed) Saml. Garbett."

Present

Messrs. Geo. Russell	John Bingham
John Startin	Jas. Bingham
Chas. Startin	John Hurd
Jos. Green	John Lee
Saml. Glover	Saml. Garbett
Jas. Woolley	John Rickards
Wm. Anderton	Saml. Riland
Anthony Frey	Thos. Simcox
Wm. Walker	Jos. Gibbs
Jos. Jukes	

Samuel Garbett Esq. in the Chair.

The Chairman represented to the Meeting several Things relative to a Treaty of Commerce now negotiating with France, & also the Insufficiency of the Laws which were intended to prevent English Workmen being enticed to leave this Kingdom, & particularly in a recent Instance where the Magistrates declared they did not consider themselves authorized to summons

[22] Ibid.: this document was sent to Shelburne on 14 October, and Percival (a leading Manchester Dissenter) on 13 October.

a Person before them who from Circumstances attested upon Oath left no Room to doubt was seducing an Artist to go to Ostend to work at his Trade, & that Tools for that Purpose were put on Board the same Ships in which the Artist was to go, & that Lord Sydney had in Writing requested the Commissioners of the Customs to stop, who had acquainted his Lordship there is no Law at present which prohibits the Exportation of them,—and that there is now reason to believe both Tools & Artist are gone to Ostend.

He likewise laid before the Meeting an authentic Account which had been received by last Post from Vienna, shewing that the Emperor had prohibited (after the 1st November next) the Entry & the public Sale in his Dominions of many English Manufactures and produced Copy of a Letter from thence proposing to an eminent Manufacturer in this Town to bring his People & settle in that Country. And it appeared that several Merchants present had sent & were now packing Goods for Vienna which could not arrive there before the 1st Nov. & that considerable Quantities were also making & in an unfinished state, & that these Goods were contracted for by Commission from the Emperor's Subjects at certain stipulated Prices.

After deliberating upon the several Particulars here recited.

Resolved That it is expedient to correspond with any eminent Merchants or Manufacturers in different Parts of the Kingdom, & particularly with the Committee of Trade at Manchester, & also with any Gentlemen at Sheffield, Leeds, or Norwich, & with the neighbouring Towns of Wolverhampton, Walsall, Dudley, & Stourbridge. That

Mssrs. Welch	Wm. Russell
Startin	Geo. Humphrys
Chas. Startin	Wm. Humphrys
Jos. Green	John Rickards
Saml. Glover	Salt
Anthony Frey	John Bingham
Palmer	Saml. Ford
Perkins	Wm. Walker

together with the Chairman, or any five of them, are requested to take the Charge of that Correspondence—that the Merchants & Manufacturers in different Parts of the Kingdom may write in proper Measures for the common Interest of the whole.

Copy of letter to Doctor [Thomas] Percival, [Manchester]

Birmingham, 13 October 1784[b]

Dear Sir,

I have had a Letter of Thanks from the two young Frenchmen that I took the Liberty of recommending to your Notice, permit me therefore to offer you my Thanks & to hope that I may some Way have an Opportunity of testifying the high Esteem I have of your character & Friendship.—I beg to refer you to the annexed Extract from Minutes of a Commercial Committee Meeting at this Place which I promised to send you.—It appears to us that the proper Trade to obtain Admission of such Goods into the Emperor's Dominions as his Subjects long since directed might be bought for them is by our Ministers representing to his Ambassador in London the Equity if not the Legality of our Claim on his Subjects, & by the English Ambassador at Vienna making similar representations there.

As the Frost will soon render the Conveyance of Goods into the Imperial Dominions impracticable for some Months, it seems necessary not to lose Time in requesting the Merchants at Vienna to acquaint us what in their Opinion will be the best Arguments & best Mode for us to adopt so that we may not counteract their Views for introducing the Goods as soon as the Season will permit; in the mean Time we are ready to consult & to unite with your Committee of Trade, & with Gentlemen at Sheffield, Leeds, Leicester, Norwich, or any other eminent Tradesmen who are interested either in the immediate Object of the Emperor's Prohibition, or in what may relate to the Treaty of Commerce with France & other Countries with which such Treaties are in Contemplation—And in endeavouring to devise more effectual Means to prevent our Artists being enticed beyond sea,—And to prevent the Exportation of Machines & Tools for manufacturing,—Or, to join with Manchester in what Influence we have for the Protection of our Manufactures in general as a common Interest.—I do not consider this an official Letter, I write that to Mssrs. Wm. Barrow & Sons—And which other Gentlemen here also write to Mr. Potter & to Mr. Phillips but I believe they do not send the annexed Extract.

I am Dear Sir, Your affectionate & obedt. Friend

Saml. Garbett

Letter Birmingham, 14 October 1784[b]

The Earl of Shelburne &c. &c. &c.

My Lord,

I had the honour to send your Lordship on Saturday last Copy of a Minute made at a Meeting of our Commercial Committee on Friday—in which I see by a Print taken therefrom that there was two Slips of the Pen which are allowed in the enclosed Extract from it, & I wish they might be so allowed in the Copy I sent you.

The Committee of Correspondence then appointed met on Tuesday when Messrs. Glover, Son & Frey brought of a Letter which they proposed should be wrote to Merchants at Manchester, Leeds, Sheffield &c. &c. which with little Alterations was approved, and several Gentlemen undertook to write the Same to their Friends at different Towns—Viz.—,

Messrs. Glover Son & Frey to Messrs. Horner Turner & Kighley at Leeds.

Messrs. Copper Palmer & Perkins, to Messrs. Greaves Woodhead & Remington.

Messrs. Welch Wilkinson & Startin to:

Messrs. Staniford Parkin & Co., Sheffield
Messrs. Chamberlane Markland & Co., Leicester
Messrs. Unwin & Co., near Leicester
Mr. Potter at Manchester
Mr. Mark Howich [Hewish?], Nottingham

Messrs. Alexander & Wm. Walker, to Mr. Phillips at Manchester

Mr. Garbett to Messrs. Wm. Barrow & Sons at Manchester [&] to
Doctor Percival at Manchester

Enclosed I send your Lordship Copy of the Letter thus approved to which I suppose every Gentleman would make some little addition. I did not write it to Doctor Percival but referred him to that which I wrote to Messrs. Barrow,—enclosed is Copy of my Letter to Doctor Percival, to whom I sent the same Extract from the Minutes of the Meeting as You receive herewith. —

The Tax laid upon Silver last Sessions of Parliament proves a deadly Blow to the Silver Buckle Manufacture in this Town, it will be a Prohibition to Nine Tenths of the Trade,—to obtain Drawbacks upon Such an Article is impracticable in the Mode proposed, or, in any Mode,—it was at Random putting an insurmountable difficulty upon an improvable Article of Export that we had thoughts of applying to Parliament about to render it extremely Extensive, & if the Law is not Repealed a valuable Trade is utterly Ruined

None but Enemies to our Country could Rationally Devise Taxes upon Exportable Manufactures, either directly or indirectly—pray pardon my plain Speaking.

I am always with great Respect, My Lord Your Lordship's
Most obedient Friend
Saml. Garbett

P.S.

Since writing the other side [of this paper] I am disappointed of Sending your Lordship Copy of the Letter I wrote to Doctor Percival by having lent it to Gentlemen who wished to write to the Same Tenor this Evening to Leeds, Sheffield Norwich & Exeter—Viz.,

Messrs. Oatridge & Marinden to

Messrs. Ridsdale & Beaumont, Leeds
Messrs. Rayner & Turner Sheffield

Mr. Timothy Smith to
his Partner who is now at Norwich
to a particular Friend at Exeter

This Moment application is made to me in the Name of the Gunsmiths of Birmingham where more than Nine Tenths of the Guns made in this Kingdom are made. Their Trade suffers very much by the Game Law of last Session. Orders are countermanded from various parts of the Country and many workmen want employ in consequence of it

Copy of letter [sent to Shelburne] 29 October 1784[b]

From Mr. Gilbert Hamilton of Glasgow to Mr. [James] Watt at Birmingham

I have had a good deal of Conversation upon the Subject of your two last Letters, & think their opinions are gaining Ground, but we are rather slow in this Country. —However the present Taxes on our Manufactures here begin to be severely felt, & Remonstrances & Memorials are preparing to be sent up by the Meeting of Parliament, in which I have no Doubt they will hint at a new System, & point out the ruinous Consequences of burdening & oppressing our Manufactures, on which our Existence as a Nation depends; but I am convinced this will be a difficult undertaking, & would require the whole strength of the manufacturing & mercantile Interest to accomplish. Both Bounties & Drawbacks I reckon to be bad, & I am persuaded if such a Scheme could be brought about of freeing our Manufactures from the monstrous Load they are at present oppressed with, we should in a very little Time see Great Britain the most flourishing Country in the World. Should any of your Commercial Committees have any Thing to communicate, I shall be very happy to lay it before our People here, but one solid extensive Plan should be laid to comprehend the whole of the Commercial & Manufacturing Interest to be pursued by the whole, & the Framing of such is a Matter of great Difficulty, & must be very well digested.

Printed notice[23] Commercial Committee, BIRMINGHAM, 3 February 1785[c]

THE Commercial Committee did at two public meetings, on Tuesday the 25th of last Month, and on Tuesday the 1st instant, UNANIMOUSLY order the following entry on their Journal, and desired the same might be inserted in such news-papers as their Committee of Correspondence might think proper; and that copies might be sent to the Knights of the Shire for the

[23] Parts of this notice were widely reproduced in other newspapers; e.g. the numbered paragraphs 5–7 and the resolution were printed in the Liverpool *Williamsons Advertiser*, 3 February 1785.

Counties of Warwick and Stafford, and to other Noblemen and Members of Parliament, viz.

THIS Committee having with anxiety observed the various methods devised to raise a public revenue, in such a manner as materially to impede the improvement and extent of manufactures designed both for home consumption and foreign markets; it is therefore, with great pleasure that they observe, and do entirely concur in the sentiments expressed in the resolutions published by the very respectable quarterly meeting of iron markers and others, concerned in the making of iron in Great Britain, and of the manufacturers of iron in the several counties of Salop, Worcester, Stafford and Warwick held at Stourbridge, in the county of Worcester, on the 7th of this month; viz.

"That it is highly expedient for those who have the good of their country at heart, to express their sentiments freely on those commercial subjects on which its population and riches most essentially depend.

"That the population and riches of this kingdom essentially depend on its manufactures, and taxes laid upon them are impolitic.

"That property acquired by trade and manufactures is a fit object of taxation, but not the manufactures themselves."

In concurrence with these sentiments, this committee are unanimously of opinion.

1. That manufactures and commerce should only be considered as a means of acquiring that real property which is the proper object of taxation.

2. That property, while exposed to the extreme uncertainty which it is necessarily subject to, while engaged in manufactures and commerce, cannot be fully deemed substantial until it is withdrawn from those dangers.

3. That every tax on manufactures, or on the raw materials employed in them (whether imported from abroad or the produce of our own country) is impolitic, as it tends to depress, or crush the ardour of invention,

4. That in general, every excise law is irreconcilable with the freedom and secrecy every manufacturer has a natural right to demand, in his own workshops, and in the exercise of his business, and they subject him to numerous inconveniencies, are an encouragement to smugglers, while they oppress the fair traders and that by the frequency of taking oaths, which it is the deponent's interest to falsify, they lessen the reverence for that sacred ceremony, and tend to sap the foundations of moral honesty.

5. That it is the opinion of this meeting, That a spirit of rivalling and supplanting our manufactures is now operating in various parts of Europe, to a degree truly alarming; and that our present laws are found ineffectual for preventing our ingenious tools being exported, and our most expert and valuable workmen and artificers from being inveigled away to other countries, where raw materials and other necessaries for manufactures are exempted from duty.

6. That it is the opinion of this meeting, That the present times open a new era in the commercial world, and that many circumstances render it necessary not only to remove all taxes upon manufactures, but likewise to hold out every possible encouragement to commercial people, to continue to hazard their property in trade.

7. That the impediments, difficulties, and various prohibitions our commerce meets with in almost every quarter of the globe, requires the early notice of Administration, and that the public interest will very materially suffer if speedy and effectual attention is not granted; and as it is not probable that the gentlemen who devised the taxes were acquainted with these difficulties, or were sensible of the encouragement given to manufacturers in foreign countries, or with the inducements that are continually offered (and with some success) to entice artists to leave this kingdom, it is therefore

Resolved, That in order, as far as in us lies, to counteract the opinion which has long prevailed, that manufactures are proper objects of taxation, it is become necessary to correspond with the Commercial Committees and eminent Merchants and Manufacturers in different parts of the kingdom, in order to represent such particulars to Government, respecting exports to foreign countries, and to the manufacturers which are establishing there, as may be thought most effectual for the protection of British Manufactures in general; and also to represent, that mines of coal, iron, copper, tin, lead, calamine and clay, together with manufactures, very much contribute to the rank this country bears among nations: And that it is essential for persons, who are most intimately acquainted with all the connexions relative thereto, and most immediately interested in the prosperity of mines, manufactures and commerce, to form some mode of corresponding, in order to remonstrate against injudicious taxes upon any article of export, and thereby to afford such information to Ministry, as may be of great importance to our commerce with foreigners.

This resolution is recommended to the Committee of Correspondence, and also that they may take an opportunity of declaring in the most explicit terms, that we would cheerfully pay any taxes upon our expenditures, but let them earnestly pray that we may not be impeded in the means by which we honestly and industriously enrich ourselves and our country, and promote population.

Samuel Garbett, Chairman.

5.6 Embargoes, Liverpool 1776

An example of a Memorial from Liverpool to import lumber direct to the West Indies in December 1776 well illustrates the process of how a petition was framed, dealt with and responded to. This is referred to briefly in the Liverpool *Abstract* (above) for 3rd October. The example here, although unsuccessful, shows (i) the petition itself; (ii) how it was dealt through the government ministerial process, by being sent to the appropriate government officials for comment, and (iii) the response from the Commissioners of Customs, and (iv) how Liverpool sought to engage the Committee of West India Merchants in London.

Sources
[a] TNA T1/523 fo. 66–69
[b] Committee of West India Merchants; London Senate House M915/1; also National Library of Jamaica.

Memorial of the Merchants of Liverpool November 1776[a]

TO THE RIGHT HONORABLE THE LORD NORTH and the other LORDS COMMISSIONERS of HIS MAJESTY'S TREASURY
The MEMORIAL of the Merchants in Liverpool, Traders to the West India Islands, whose names are subscribed
HUMBLY SHEWETH

THAT REPEATED informations have been received from their Correspondents in the Sugar Islands, by many of Your Memorialists; that their Stock of Lumber in those Islands being nearly exhausted, and the Trade with the Continent of North America from whence for a course of years they have been wholly supplied with that Article, under a temporary suspension; they are apprehensive, that without some new mode of supply, their Sugar and Rum can not, for want of Casks, be conveyed to Great Britain.

THAT THE PORTS in the BALTIC appear to your MEMORIALISTS, the only certain fountains for an immediate, equal supply: but the very heavy expense and delay, in landing and reshipping in Great Britain, so great a quantity of Lumber, are almost insurmountable bars to the attempt.

THAT A repeal for a limited time, in the single Article of Lumber, of so much of the Act of the 15th of Charles the 2nd as relates to the Productions of Europe exported to the British Plantations; and liberty granted to export, without previously landing and reshipping in Great Britain, Staves, Hoops, Heading and other Lumber, to the British Sugar Islands only; under such regulations restrictions and appointments as may appear needful; WOULD, as Your MEMORIALISTS apprehend be an important and seasonable assistance to His Majesty's Loyal Subjects.

[Signed]

James Caruthers*	John Chorley*	Will Crosbie, Mayor
Arthur Bayer	Thomas Case*	John Dobson*+
John Hodgson	Thos. Foxcroft*	Thos. Hutton Rawlinson*
Geo. Venables*	Wm. Bolden*	Hen. Rawlinson
Saml Sandys	Thos. Hodgson*	Jos. Brooks Jun.*
Richd. Bamber	Richd. Milford	Francis Ingram*
George Warren Watts	Richard Watt & Nephew*	Gill Slater*
Tho. Wycliffe	Alexr. Nottingham*	Tho. Hodgson Junr.*
Thos. Rumbold	Christ Wetherherd*	

* known or probable member of the chamber of commerce

\+ chamber president at the time

Referral by Treasury 23 November 1776[a]

Whitehall Treasury Chambers

The Right Honourable the Lords Commissioner of His Majesty's Treasury are pleased to refer the aforegoing Memorial to the Commissioners of His Majesty's Customs who are to consider the same to report to their Lordships a true state of the Case together with their Opinion what is fit to be done therein.

John Robinson

Response from Commissioners of Customs 6 December 1776[a]

Custom Hse. London

May it please Your Lordships

In Obedience to Your Lordships Commands signified to Us by Mr. Robinson, on the annexed Memorial of the Merchants in Liverpool Traders to the West India Islands representing the Distress of their Correspondents in the said Islands, for want of Casks to convey their Sugar and Rum to Great Britain; that the Ports in the Baltic are the only certain fountains for an immediate Supply of Lumber for that purpose, and that a repeal for a limited time in that single Article, of so much of the Act of the 15th Chas. 2d as relates to the Productions of Europe, Exported to the British Plantations as may appear needful, would they apprehend, be an important Assistance to his Majesty's Subjects.

We report, that by the 12th Charles 2d. Chap 18th no Goods can be Imported into or Exported from the Plantations, in any other, than Ships built, Owned and Manned by British Subjects, but this Restraint not being thought Sufficient by the Legislature, it was further enforced by the 15th Chas. 2d Chap: 7th which Enacts, "that no Commodity of the Growth, Production, or Manufacture of Europe shall be imported into any British

Colony, or Plantation, but what shall be laden and shipped in Great Britain, and carried directly from thence in British built Ships legally Navigated," with an Exception however, as to Salt for the Fishery, and a very few other Articles.

That the principal reasons for passing this last mentioned Law, as appear by the recital were, "to keep the Plantations in a firmer dependence upon this Kingdom, and to make it a Staple not only of the Commodities of those Plantations, but also of other Countries and places for the supplying of them."

That the Colonies however with great reluctance, submitted to this necessary restraint on their Trade, and continued to carry on a Clandestine Correspondence with the other Countries of Europe, as appears by his Majesty's Orders of Council of the 6th and 22d March 1664, and by a Proclamation dated 24th November 1675, and there is but too much reason to apprehend, that if the British West India Islands, should now be indulged with the liberty prayed for in their Traffic, it may be productive of the same ill Effects, as were intended to be remedied by the 15th Chas. 2d.

That the subsequent relaxations from the beforementioned Acts by other Statutes, allowing the Inhabitants of the Plantations to carry several Articles of their own Produce directly to other parts of Europe, seem greatly to have Contributed to give them a Spirit of Independency and Enterprise in Trade and Navigation, that may with great probability be considered as one of the Sources of the present Rebellion in the British Colonies, and therefore any further deviation, should not as We conceive, be admitted without the greatest Caution and most Urgent Necessity.

That the Word Lumber, as it seems to be described by the 8th Geo: 1st Chap: 12th and 14th Geo: 3d Chap: 11th includes Timber, Deals, Barks, Spars, and a great Variety of other Woods, no way necessary for the fabrication of Casks, and is a very extensive and indefinite Expression, and therefore the opening of a Door to the Introduction of the various Articles, which may be alleged to be comprehended under this Term, may be of the most dangerous Consequence.

That there are a very small Number of Revenue Officers in the West India Islands, scarcely Sufficient for the guard of the Extensive Coast, and Numerous Bays and Harbours Surrounding the same, even under the present Security of no Ships being permitted to Trade thither, but what comes directly from this Country, and were loaden under the Examination of the proper Officers here.

That it will be impossible to take such Caution or Security, from the Ships going to the Baltic, for obtaining Lumber as shall prevent them from procuring, and taking on board at the same time, all manner of Commodities, such as Drillings and other Linens from Russia and Germany, as well as East India

Goods, which are easily obtained there from the Swedish and Danish East India Companies, and from introducing with the Lumber, all those foreign Commodities into the British West India Islands, to the vast prejudice of the British Manufactures and of the Plantation Trade, which the prudence of the Legislature hath so carefully restrained to this Kingdom.

Lastly, that even if the want of Casks (which is all the Distress that is Suggested) to convey the British Plantation Sugar and Rum to Great Britain, was fully proved; yet it does not appear to Us, to require so extensive a Relaxation, as is contained in the Prayer of the Memorialists, unless it was also proved, that they could be in no reasonable degree supplied from hence, or from Canada, the Floridas or the Mississippi. But as Our Collectors and Comptrollers in the several British West India Islands have not suggested to Us, that there is any want of Casks there, nor have made use of that as a pretence, (which a real Occasion would in all probability have given them) for retaining the produce of his Majesty's 4½ per Cent in their hands, We cannot easily believe that any urgent distress exists there; tho' even if that was the case, Yet as the principal Officers in the Long Room have reported to Us, that from the best Information they can obtain, there are sufficient Quantities of the Articles in Question now in England, to answer any Demand that may be made for the same, We can by no means recommend it to Your Lordships to favour the prayer of the Petition.

Js. Jeffreys
Edwd. Hooper
H. Pelham
W. Musgrave
Ch. Morris

Minute West India Committee, 5 November 1776[b]

Read a letter from John Dobson Esq. President of the Chamber of Commerce at Liverpool respecting an application to parliament intended to be made by the merchants of that port for the better supply of lumber from the Baltic to the West India Islands, and desiring the opinion of the men of London, and to know if they are willing to take the lead in the intended application or how they think it deserving of their assistance and support.

Minute West India Committee, 3 December 1776[b]

[Dobson's letter laid before monthly meeting 3 November, but as small attendance was deferred]

Mr. Dobson's letter again read. Reply, that previous to this meeting the house of commons has appointed a day to consider the matter, there is no necessity of West India Merchants to take a lead.

5.7 Shipping in neutral bottoms: Manchester, Liverpool and Lancaster 1779

In 1779 rival petitions from the cotton interests were sent to the Treasury concerning the importation of cotton in neutral shipping during the American War. The first came from the Manchester Committee of Trade seeking this leave, but two others from Liverpool (which overlapped closely with chamber members) and Lancaster opposed it. The Bristol SMV was asked to consider it, but after referring to a committee took no action.

Sources
[a] TNA T1/553/299
[b] TNA T1/553/298
[c] TNA T1/553/300
[d] London Senate House Library: Committee of West India Merchants; M915/1

Memorial Manchester, November 1779[a]

TO THE RIGHT HONOURABLE the Lord North and the other Lords Commissioners of his Majesty's Treasury
THE MEMORIAL of the Committee of Trade and Manufactures at Manchester:

Sheweth,

THAT for some time past the Demand for their Cotton Manufactures has been greatly reduced, particularly at foreign Markets—

THAT the Island of Grenada has for several years last, furnished a very considerable Share of the Cotton used in the British Manufactures—

THAT since the taking of that Island by his Majesty's enemies, the Price of Cotton Wool hath been such, as to induce the Manufacturers, in some Degree, to lessen the extent of their Trade, and of course, in some measure, to lower the former prices paid to the generality of their Artificers; which your Memorialists are sorry to find they have erroneously and unhappily conceived to be the effect of spinning Jennies and other ingenious Machines, by the use of which the Manufactures of this Country, as well as the Artificers themselves, have hitherto been materially benefitted.

THAT from the present high Price of Cotton owing as your Memorialists conceive, to the before mentioned circumstances, and to the high Freight and Insurance on British Bottoms, and the monopolizing of this Article by a few Individuals, and from the declining demand of their Fabrics: your Memorialists apprehend they shall find it necessary still further to reduce their present Stocks of Goods.

YOUR MEMORIALISTS therefore beg leave to represent to your Lordships that the most likely means, as they conceive, by which the present prices of Cotton may be reduced—the Monopolies which have lately

advanced the Article more than thirty per Centum, in future, prevented,—the demand of their Manufactures at Foreign Markets promoted, and the poor Artificer secured in his employ; will be by permitting the Importation of Cotton Wool, Duty free, during the War, on neutral Bottoms.
For the Committee of Trade and self
[signed] Josiah Birch

Memorial Liverpool, November 1779[b]

TO THE RIGHT HONORABLE LORD NORTH &c. AND THE OTHER LORDS COMMISSIONERS OF HIS MAJESTIE'S TREASURY

THE MEMORIAL of the Merchants, Mariners and Tradesmen of Liverpool, whose names are subscribed.
Sheweth

THAT An application having, as your Memorialists are informed, been made to your Lordships in the name of the Committee of Trade and the Manufacturers of Manchester, setting forth some pretended reasons for permitting the Importation of Cotton Wool, duty free, during the War, on Neutral Bottoms; our Memorialists therefore beg leave to represent to Your Lordships,

THAT The price of Cotton Wool, has in former years been higher than it is at this present time, and at the commencement, as well as during the whole continuance of the late unhappy riots in this County, was much lower that at present.

THAT The method proposed of giving so deadly a blow to the Act of Navigation, the Palladium of Britain; is not likely to cause a certain, and lasting reduction in the price of Cotton Wool; nor could, as Your Lordships' Memorialists conceive, in the smallest degree conduce, to prevent monopolies in that Article; to promote the demand of our Cotton Manufactures at Foreign markets; to secure the poor Artificer in his employ; or to prevent riots, and insurrections.

THAT On the contrary, such a measure would assuredly tend greatly to discourage; and in a little time, might put an entire end to the cultivation of Cotton Wool in the British Plantations: prove highly prejudicial to the Merchant, the Mariner, and every branch in Arts, Manufactures, and Commerce, supported by and dependent on our Naval equipments, and protection: deprive the Nation of a principal nursery for seamen: strengthen the hands of our Rivals and Enemies: and may soon reduce our Manufactures to depend entirely upon Foreign Nations for the supply of an Article, upon which the existence of their trade entirely depends.

Your Memorialists therefore beg leave to submit to the consideration of Your Lordships, whether the adoption of such a measure, as permitting the

Importation of Cotton Wool, duty free, during the War, on Foreign Bottoms, would not be certainly productive of such real evil, without affording a single hope of any substantial good.

[signed by 54 names, of which 16 (30 per cent) were known or probable members of the chamber of commerce, though most members signed later in the lists indicating probable leadership from the corporation; the exception to this was Gill Slater, the current president, which signed at the top of the fourth column.]

Memorial Lancaster December 1779[c]

TO THE RIGHT HONORABLE LORD NORTH AND THE OTHER LORDS COMMISSIONERS OF HIS MAJESTIE'S TREASURY
THE MEMORIAL of the Merchants, Mariners and Tradesmen of Lancaster.
Sheweth

THAT your Memorialists are apprised of an Application made to your Lordships from the Committee of Trade and Manufactures of Manchester giving pretended Reasons for allowing the Importation of Cotton Wool (Duty free) during the War in Neutral Bottoms.

THEREFORE your Memorialists humbly beg leave to represent to your Lordships—

THAT in former Years the price of Cotton Wool has been higher than at present and supported the prices for a length of time and the Cotton Manufactury Trade is now good—

THAT the loss for the present of the Island of Grenada and its Dependencies and the brisk demand for Cotton Manufactures your Memorialists apprehend has been the occasion of the advance in Cotton Wool—

THAT there are great Quantities of Cotton now in the Kingdom—

THAT there have always been Dealers in Cotton whose business is to serve the small Manufacturers and that they are as useful and necessary in that Branch as the Woolstapler is to the Woollen Manufactury—

THAT the proposed method of reducing the price of Cotton Wool by striking so immediately at the Act of Navigation your Memorialists are of Opinion would not have the effect of promoting the Sales of Cotton Manufactures and not be a means of answering any good purposes—

THAT on the contrary your Memorialists apprehend it would tend to the ruin of the Cotton Planters in the British West India Islands and that in length of time our dependence would be on foreign Nations for the supply of that Article which has always been paid for in the West Indies by British Manufactures and been a very considerable part of the Imports of your Memorialists and upon which their Trade greatly depends—

THAT your Memorialists apprehend allowing the Importation of Cotton Wool in Neutral Bottoms would prove hurtful to the Merchants Mariners all Arts Manufactures and Commerce deprive the Nation of the Nursery of Seamen and in every degree tend to the hurt of the Kingdom at large—

YOUR MEMORIALISTS beg leave to submit to the Consideration of your Lordships whether the proposed method of permitting the Importation of Cotton Wool in Neutral Bottoms (Duty free) would not be certainly productive of a more general loss to the Kingdom than any real good or the least hopes of a national Advantage.

[Signed by: list of 52 Names]

Minute West India Committee, 23 November 1779[d]

Letter from Gill Slater Esq. of Liverpool [president of the chamber] to chairman enclosing a copy of a memorial from the manufacturers of Manchester [see above], to the Treasury, praying for an importation of cotton in neutral bottoms duty free was read. Referred to a committee of tobacco planters and merchants [no further action taken].

5.8 Customs fees

Challenges to the level of Customs fees, arbitrary 'inventions' of new fees, and the efficiency of local Customs officials were a frequent subject of chamber lobbies. This was part of the local response to the patronage system and sale of offices. Patents and offices given out or sold by government were then manned by others who in turn had to pay for the position and needed to make as much from it as possible to pay their costs and make an income. This became a spiral. Attacks by chambers were often on those at the bottom of the chain who collected the fees and were responsible for the invention of new fees and abuses, such as breaking bills of lading or customs clearances into smaller batches and taking a fee on each element rather than the bulk, and issues of groupage. Attacking the junior functionary was also less challenging than attacking the holders of the senior posts who were more directly linked to powerful government patrons. But sometimes chambers worked their way up the feeding chain, as shown in the documents from Liverpool and Waterford. The first documents derived from a large number of joint meetings held between the chamber and the Liverpool Committee of Trade (the Municipal corporation's rival body; q.v. Chapter 4) and represent a period of rapprochement after earlier conflicts. The minutes from the Liverpool Committee of Trade provide the detail on chamber activity otherwise lacking. The Hull Customs correspondence shows evidence of a Committee of Trade in 1784 which otherwise has left few records.

Sources
[a] Liverpool Committee of Trade Minutes; LRO 352 MIN/COM I 2/1
[b] Dublin Chamber of Commerce Minutes, 17 April 1784: TNAI
[c] Hull Committee of Trade; Hull Archives Centre CWM/9
[d] Londonderry chamber; PRONI D562/15425
[e] Chamber minutes; Waterford Archives WCOC1/01

5.8.1 Liverpool 1782–4

Minute 25 March 1782[a]

At the several meetings of the Committee's of the Board of Trade and the Chamber of Commerce held in the Council Chamber within the Exchange for Establishing the Fees of the Officers and Clerks in the Custom House

William Gregson Esq. }
Gill Slater Esq. } Presidents.

Viz.
On Thursday the thirteenth day of December 1781
On Thursday the Twentieth day of December 1781
On Thursday the Twenty seventh day of December 1781
On Saturday the Twenty third day of February 1782
On Monday the Twenty fifth day of February 1782
On Monday the Fourth day of March 1782
On Monday the Eleventh day of March 1782
On Friday the Fifteenth day of March 1782
On Saturday the Sixteenth day of March 1782
On Wednesday the Twentieth day of March 1782

[Reported that]

At a numerous meeting of the Merchants and others, paying Customhouse Charges at this Port, held agreeable to public Advertisement in the Exchange on Tuesday the 26th of February; and, by adjournment from thence, on Wednesday the 20th of March 1782, the following Rules, Regulations, and List of Fees, to be paid to the Officers and Clerks in the Customs here, were after due deliberation, settled and agree'd on; and it was resolved, that, from and after this Twenty fifth day of March 1782 no more than the Respective fees undermentioned shall, in future, be paid, for Customary Duty and legal attendance.

RULES AND REGULATIONS.

That the Officers of the Customs up Stairs, be required to give attendance in their proper offices during the full time established by Law, agreeable to the Act 12th Cha: 2nd. Ch. 4. viz.

from Nine to Twelve in the forenoon }
from Two to Four in the afternoon }
on Saturdays in the afternoon } Holidays excepted.

That the Officers of the Customs below Stairs, and upon the Quays, be required to attend punctually in their proper places, during the Hours by Law established … viz.

from 10th day of March to the 10th day of September } Between the hours of Six in the morning and Six in the Evening

from the 10th day of Septem: to the 10th day of March } Between Seven in the morning and four in the afternoon

On Saturdays in the afternoon. Holidays excepted.

That All goods inwards be included in one Entry }
All British Goods Outwards in one Entry }
All Foreign Goods Outwards in one Entry } being the property of one Concern.

A LIST OF FEES

		s.	d.
IN THE COLLECTORS OFFICE		[s.	d.]
To the Clerk who takes the Report of Ships inwards			
For every Ships Report	from Foreign parts	1.	0.
	From Ireland or Isle of Man	0.	6.
To the Clerk for filling up each Linen Debenture		0.	6.
To the Collector for taking Affidavit to each Linen Debenture		0.	2.
	For every Stamp'd Bond so long as the Duty shall be 5s. [or more]	6.	6.
	For a Duplicate for Salt to Ireland	1.	0.
	For a Damage Certificate or an over Entry	0.	6.
IN THE CUSTOMERS OFFICE			
To the Customer	For Report of a Ship from the Plantations or E. Country	7.	1.
	For . . . do . . . from other Parts	5.	1.
	For Entry of Goods inwards, every Warrant	2.	0.
	For . . . ditto . . . Outwards, every Cockett	2.	0.
If the Value of the Goods enter'd Inwards or Outwards be less than £5 then the warrant or Cockett shall be only		0.	6.
For a Post Entry, when the Custom duty is under 40s.		0.	6.
For Stamp for Swearing to Goods Outwards so long as the Stamp Duty shall be 1/4d. [or more]		1.	8.
For every Stamp'd Debenture on a large piece of Parchment		3.	1.
For . . . ditto . . . on a Small . . . ditto		3.	0.
For every London Debenture, additional		0.	6.
For every Sail Cloth Debenture		1.	2.
For a Duplicate for Salt to Ireland		1.	2.
For a Damage Certificate or an over Entry		1.	2.

For every Outvoice		3. 1.
For a Plantation Certificate and Bond		9. 2.
For the Clerk, For filling up Bond for Plantation Certificate		1. 0.
For drawing Outvoice of a Ship to Foreign Parts		1. 0.
For . . . ditto . . . to Ireland or the Isle of Man		0. 6.
For Copying Outvoice into the Book		0. 6.
For filling up and Figuring each Debenture		0. 6.
IN THE COMPTROLLERS OFFICE		
For Copying Invoice	from Foreign parts	1. 0.
	from Ireland or the Isle of Man	0. 6.
	For every Debenture for Examining and Writing Receipt	0. 6.
	For a Duplicate for Salt to Ireland	0. 6.
	For a Damage Certificate or an over Entry	0. 6.
SEARCHERS OFFICE		
	For every Foreign Cockett [sic]	10. 6.
	For every Cocket to Ireland or Isle of Man	2. 6.
	For every Salt Cocket to Ireland or Isle of Man	3. 6.
	For Certifying a Debenture	1. 6.
STOREKEEPERS		
For every Bale or Box	if Repacked	1. 0.
	if not Repacked	0. 6.
JERQUER [customs fees for searches ships for smuggled and un-entered goods]		
For a Jerquering Note	from Foreign Parts	1. 0.
	from Ireland or Isle of Man	0. 6.
COAST WAITERS		
For each Permit Excise Goods Included		0. 6.
PASSENGERS BAGGAGE		
To the Clerk for filling up and Passing each Entry		1. 0.

Nothing more to be paid by any Passenger, to any other Person, except upon Holidays, or out of legal hours

5.8.2 Dublin 1784

Minute Dublin, 17 April 1784[b]

Mr Pim for the Committee appointed to prepare Resolutions relative to fees to Custom House Officers reported that they had prepared Resolutions according to which he was ready to report whenever the Council will please to receive the same.

RESOLVED that said Report be now received and read.

RESOLVED that this Council do agree with their Committee in the said report which is as follows:

THAT the exactions of many of the Custom House Officers in the Port of Dublin under the Titles of fees are become of late so enormous and oppressive that they ought to be resisted by every fair trader.

THAT the Council consider it as an especial duty to support and assist any Member of the Chamber of Commerce who shall be put to expense or inconvenience by asserting the legal rights of a Merchant of Trader.

RESOLVED that these Resolutions be thrice Published in Saunders's News Letter.

5.8.3 Hull 1784

The lobby by the Hull Committee of Trade in 1784 may have had some role in convoying in previous years during the American War. The Hull Committee on Convoys minutes finish on 9 July 1782 (see Chapter 6). Links between the convoy committee and the Committee of Trade are possibly indicated from the overlap of membership. Four of the 12 committee were members of the 1780 Committee on Convoys (indicated by *). It is also possible that a new Committee was founded after the American War in order to promote trade, perhaps following the model of the Manchester Committee, re-established in 1782 (see Chapter 1). Some form of committee or group of delegates continued at Hull in 1785–7 as the city is mentioned at various points in the activities of the General Chamber of Manufacturers (see Chapter 8). Hull was again actively in contact with other chambers and local committees over convoys in 1794–9. Hull also had an earlier committee on convoys in 1757.[24]

Minute [CWM/9/1] 20 August 1784[c]

At a Meeting of the Committee of Trade,

Present. Sir Hen. Etherington*, W. Horner*, Mr. Jonas Brown, Mr. Fr. Taylor, Mr. Knowsley, Mr. Harneis, Mr. Bine, Mr. Schonswar, Mr. Terry, Mr. Wilkinson*, Mr. Thompson, Mr. Wm. Williamson*.

That the following Letter this day agreed upon be signed by the Chairman and sent to the Commissioners of Customs.

That the following Letter be also signed by the Chairman and sent to S. Thornton & W. S. Stanhope Esq. Enclosing the above Letters to the Commissioner.

[24] Useful discussion of Hull convoying in the various periods in G. Jackson, *Hull in the Eighteenth Century* (Oxford, 1972); *The Trade and Shipping of Eighteenth Century Hull* (York, 1975).

That the Copy of the above Letters to the Commissioners & the Affidavit be sent to the Collector of Customs of this port.

That the thanks of the American War the meeting be given to Mr. Fran. Taylor for writing the Letter to the Commissioners

That the Secretary Collect the Money Subscriptions and pay it to Sir H. Etherington.

Copy letter [CWM/9/3] Kingston upon Hull, 20 August 1784[c]

To the Honble. the Commissioners of his Majesty's Customs
Gentlemen,

I am desired by the Committee of Trade chosen at a general Meeting of the Merchants and others of this town, to inform your Honble. Board of a practice, which if suffered to be continued, will probably prove injurious to his Majesty's Revenue, and be otherways dangerous to the trading interest of this country.

The Committee have had intelligence of vessels passing this port up to a place called Selby a town of 40 miles up this river, and then taking in various cargoes, which they brought down here, & cleared at this Custom house coastwise for Yarmouth; where they were permitted to clear out for Abroad without delivering & reloading their Cargoes. Concerning one vessel called the ____ [space left, later revealed as *Jane*] which loaded at Selby the End of the last month, and cleared for Bilbao from Yarmouth the ____ July, without delivering her Cargo there the Committee have attested Intelligence (as by the annexed affidavit); and they have strong reasons to think the like illegal practice has been carried on for upwards of 12 months.

The Committee need not intimate to your Honble. Board how detrimental such irregular & lax proceedings of the Officers at Yarmouth may ultimately prove to his Majesty's Revenue: —For, however, watchful faithful in the performance of his duty the Officer at Selby may be, and however just his manifestation to the Collector of the Customs here, of the cargoes taken on board at Selby; yet he cannot guard the shores for above of 40 miles up the river Humber and other rivers communicating therewith; in every stage of which, there are opportunities of taking in goods which ought to pay a Duty outwards, contraband goods, models of manufacturing machines &c. &c.

The Vessels which land at Selby for Yarmouth are cleared at Hull on the supposed Correctness of the Docket signed by the Officer resident at Selby; & on its agreement with the oath of the Captain but if strict examination be not made at Yarmouth & legal delivery demanded there, there must necessarily be a great opening for fraudulent proceedings. I am therefore desired by the Committee to call the Attention of your Honble. Board to this matter, not doubting but you will immediately give such orders and apply such remedies, as its very great importance requires.

I am Gentlemen with perfect respect, Your most obedient and very humble servant
A B Chairman to the Committee of Trade

Letter [CWM/9/4] Custom House Hull, 24 August 1784[c]

The Collector presents his best Compliments to Sir Henry Etherington had the Honour of receiving his Note Yesterday enclosing a Copy of a Letter from the Committee of Trade to the Commissioners of the Customs, relative to the present Practice of Vessels loading at Selby, and afterwards being suffered to depart on Foreign Voyages from Yarmouth (whither they went from this Port under Coast Dispatch) without discharging their original Cargoes before they were permitted to take on board other Goods. The Collector is very happy to say that he thinks the Letter judiciously drawn up, and in other Respects well calculated to have the Grievance complained of removed.

Letter [CMW/9/10] London, 22 December 1784[c]

To: Sir Henry Etherington Bart.
Chairman of the Committee of Trade, Hull
Sir,

I have the pleasure to inform you that the Commissioners of the Customs have come to a determination upon the Petition I presented from the Committee of Trade at Hull, & as in the Case of the *Jane*, Captain Clifton, they are in possession of the Bond given by the Master for the landing his Goods at Yarmouth. They have resolved to proceed against him for it by Law, as soon as the time for the Return of the Certificate is expired & to disallow any Certificate that may have been collusively granted. They have order'd a still further Investigation into the Conduct of the Officers at Yarmouth which will probably issue in the Dismissing of the Deputy Searcher as being the ostensible Offender tho' perhaps not more to blame than his Colleagues.

I think these Proceedings will give every Check to the Matter of Complaint which the Town of Hull can wish, but if notwithstanding the punctuality that will doubtless in future prevail at Yarmouth the Practice should still continue, the Solicitor of the Customs assures me that if any Individual communicates to your Collector a Suspicion that a Vessel has taken improper Goods in, he has a Power & it becomes his Duty to examine them minutely as they pass the Port of Hull.

I beg my respectful Compliments to the Gentlemen of the Committee of that you will believe me.

Sir, Their & Your obed hum. Serv.
Saml Thornton

5.8.4 Londonderry 1790

Printed pamphlet 6 November 1790[d]

Resolutions by Londonderry chamber in favour of the simplification of customs duties

To Rt. Hon. John Foster[25] M.P., Dublin [readdressed] Collon.

Resolved 1 That customs, excise and duties payable upon a great variety of merchandise are (owing to the numerous additions which have been made from time to time to the original duty), so extremely complicated, that the simplification of them in a manner similar to that which has taken place in Great Britain is necessary to help both merchants and the Revenue ....

Resolved 2 That an application should be made to parliament

Resolved 3 That these Resolutions should be transmitted to all merchants of the different principal ports of the Kingdom [of Ireland].

If an appointment is made to represent the commercial interest of this Kingdom ... for the purpose of entering into exploration, or communicating with the Irish Minister, we will depute a member of our body to meet with the representatives of the other trading cities and towns, at the Royal Exchange in Dublin'.

5.8.5 Waterford 1796

The Waterford conflict with local Customs officials led to a proposed boycott, documented here. As an extra-legal action, it may have been very divisive. The half page with the signatories to the boycott was cut out of the minute book, and the chamber suffered divisions that put it into abeyance for a few years soon afterwards.

[25] Secretary of the Irish House of Commons and Chancellor of Exchequer of Ireland. His salary was paid from the Customs of Dublin over 1779–84; 'the most dangerous and virulent Irish opponent of Pitt' in championing of Irish free trade and economic benefits for Ireland: Thorne, *History of Parliament*; *ODNB*.

Minute 10 August 1796[e]

Whereas it appears to us that the Fees at the Custom House have of late increased unreasonably and a Committee having been appointed by a general meeting to digest a list of fees to be produced at a future general Meeting for approbation.

Resolved unanimously

That when said list of Fees shall be so agreed on, We do bind ourselves to each other not to pay or suffer to be paid on our account higher fees than those so settled

Whereas it has been intimated, that, some threats have been thrown out by some of the officers in the long room, whether serious or otherwise doth not fully appear, but in order to counteract said threats if intended to be put into execution we do bind ourselves to each other that we will consider a common cause any attack that may be made on, or any interruption that may be given to any individual in the prosecution of his Business at the Custom house or otherwise, by any officer, in consequence of his adhering to said list of Fees.—And in order that no person may be at a Loss in seeking redress; We do think it expedient to appoint a Committee to whom any person so aggrieved may apply and that said Committee be instructed on receiving information from any subscriber of such grievance, to meet, and on our behalf to apply to such officer demanding redress which if not immediately obtained said Committee is to send a notice in writing to each subscriber acquainting them that such officer has made an attack on said individual in consequence of adhering to said list of fees.—And we do bind ourselves to each other that from the time of receiving such notice we will not pay or suffer to be paid on our account to said officer, for transacting any Business for us, any other fees than that which he is entitled to by Law until full satisfaction shall be obtained by the party aggrieved and notice thereof sent to us by said Committee who is empower'd by us to apply to the Commissioners of the Revenue on our behalf, on any grievance occurring to any of the subscribers in consequence of said List of fees if such a step should appear necessary to said Committee.—And should the urgency of the case require it we do empower said Committee to commence and prosecute a suit at Law for redress, the expense to be paid by us as such committee shall direct.—And whereas some disagreements may at present exist between some Merchants and officers of the Custom house and a stoppage of fees be the Consequence, in order that such differences may be adjusted we agree to submit the same to said Committee and to abide by its decision thereon as also on any difference that may arise between us and any officer in future -- Waterford

[rest of page cut out from this point, which probably contained a list of signatures]

Minute 15 September 1796[e]

At a general Meeting of the Merchants at their Committee Room on Thursday the 15th Sept 1796

Resolved that all vessels coming to this Port with Potatoes & out in Ballast should not pay fees.

Resolved that we are unanimously of opinion that no Person is entitled to Fees in the Long Room or any other department who does not hold an employment therein.

Resolved unanimously that the Dockets of Fees of the several officers in the Long room The Surveyor & Landw[aiters] returned to this meeting by their Committee as now attend do stand in their present form until a conference may be had with the different officers concerned Therein.

Resolved unanimously that having taken into consideration the rise of Times and the increase of Trade in this Port the Fees paid in Dublin Cork and other Ports, and having drawn a comparison it appears to us that the several Fees as stated in our schedules, are fair and equitable Fees to be paid in the Port so long as the several officers continue as heretofore attentive & obliging and as it is our wish if possible to give satisfaction our Secretary is directed to serve the several officers with the schedules attached to their departments in order if they have any just cause of objection they may state the same for our future consideration and determination.

Resolved that our President do write to the Commissioners to know who in the Long Room shall in future hold and see the Bonds executed.

5.9 Notaries' fees

Notaries' fees were an issue taken up repeatedly by the first Dublin chamber. Notaries were not state officials, but were mainly used because laws obliged them to be used, whilst many chambers felt they could offer similar quasi-legal assurances themselves; indeed from the 1880s they developed a system of their own export certification. Dublin lobbied the Commissioners of the Revenue over these fees in 1783 and eventually a mutual agreement was reached. The concerns overlap with the regulation of bills of exchange discussed in Chapter 6, below.

Source
Dublin Chamber of Commerce Minutes; TNAI.

Minute 1 July 1783

RESOLVED that the following Advertisement be published three times in Saunders News Letter.

The Council of the Chamber of Commerce conceiving themselves called on by the duty of their appointment to notice any attempt to enhance the charges upon Trade and having therefore taken into consideration Advertisements of the 10th June signed by the Public Notaries of this City declaratory of their Intentions to exact for the future the sum of one shilling and six pence upon every Bill for which they shall demand and receive payment think it necessary to inform the public:

THAT by an Act in the Kingdom in the eighth year of Queen Anne relative to Inland Bills of Exchange and Promissory Notes, it is directed that for the protesting that there shall be paid for each a sum not exceeding two shillings.

THAT with the laying on of the Stamp Duties the Notaries contented themselves with demanding the said sum of Two shillings of Protesting Inland bills or Notes and two shillings and six pence for foreign bills which latter charge the Council suppose might have been established by ancient custom.

THAT upon the Stamp Act being passed, the Notaries raised their charges for protest of English Money instead of Irish which additional charge the Council apprehend was acquiesced in by the Public merely on account of the trouble incurred by the Notaries in calling with bills which were paid to them.

THE Council conceive that the new regulation for the more punctual payment of Bills and Notes does not lay any reasonable Foundation for an extra charge upon the public and it is the opinion of the Council:

THAT the Public Notaries are not entitled to demand more for the protesting of an Inland Bill or Note than two shillings and a foreign bill (under an established custom as already stated) two shillings and six pence with the legal Stamp Duties, and that persons discharging Bills and Notes when called on to do so cannot be obliged to pay more than the actual contents of such Bills or Notes.

Mr Vice President [Daniel Marston] from the Chair informed the Council that he and Mr. Vice President Dermott had been to wait on the Commissioners of the Revenue but there was no board.

RESOLVED that the Secretary do enclose said Memorial to Mr. Winder Secretary to the Commissioners.

Minute 12 March 1785

A Letter directed to the Council and Signed by Robert Day, Thomas Rainey, John Robinson, William Shannon and Francis McNally on behalf of themselves and other Notaries in Dublin being made.

RESOLVED that the Letter be entered on the Books of the Council.

12 March 1785

Gentn. We take the Liberty to enclose you a Copy of a Petition and Bill which we have in contemplation to lay before Parliament with a view of obtaining some reasonable increase to our present fees on Protesting Bills.

We think it our Duty to consult you in the matter before we take any Step therein and hope on perusing our Petition and considering the hardship of our case, this application will meet with your approbation and concurrence especially as an increase of our fees in that part of the business concerned cannot operate as a Tax upon Trade but on defaulters and will in all probability be productive of beneficial consequences by inducing greater punctuality.

We as Gentn., your very humble and obedient Servants, on behalf of ourselves and the other Notaries in Dublin [signed]

The Copy of the Bill mentioned in said Letter being read.

ORDERED that the same do lie on the Table for the perusal of the Members.

The order of the day being read to take into consideration the propriety of endeavouring to procure a Law for the better regulating the payment of Bills of Exchange and Promissory Notes and establishing with certainty the responsibility of Promisers Acceptors and Endorsers.

The Resolutions of the Chamber of Commerce held the [2]7th of May 1783 relative to the want of punctuality in the payment of Bills of Exchange and Promissory Notes being read:

RESOLVED that it is the opinion of this Council that it is proper to endeavour to procure a Law to declare all Drawers and Endorsers of Bills of Exchange whether Foreign or Inland and Endorsers on Promissory Notes of the amount of five pounds and upwards released from Responsibility unless such Bills and Notes shall have been Protested on the day they fall due if not Sunday and on the day before when due if a Sunday allowing three days of Grace on each Bill or Note.

THAT our worthy President be requested to move for leave to bring in a Bill for enforcing the more punctual payment of Bills of Exchange and Promissory Notes.

Minute 15 March 1785

The Secretary informed the Council that he had according to order furnished the President with a Copy of the Resolutions of the Council of last Saturday [12 March] and in consequence thereof received a Letter from the President which was read and ordered to be entered on the Books of the Council:

> Mr Hartley presents his compliments to Mr. Shannon. He acquainted the Speaker [of the House of Commons] yesterday with the intentions of moving

for leave to bring in the Bill for enforcing the more punctual payment &c. &c. but found him extremely averse to it.

Mr. Hartley used the arguments which occurred to him in favour of the measure but they made no Impression. He afterwards talked to Mr. Latouche who also disapproved of it.—To put forward the Bill under the circumstances he thinks would be very imprudent as the Rejection of such a Bill would do mischief. Mr Hartley thinks that before any step is taken in this business the fuller information with respect both to the Law and usage should be got from London.

Bude St., 15 March 1785

RESOLVED that in consequence of the information communicated in said Letter by our worthy President the Idea of applying for a Bill for enforcing the more punctual payment of Bills of Exchange and Promissory Notes be for the present laid aside.

RESOLVED that the Secretary be desired to communicate the foregoing Resolution to our worthy president.

Abuse of [by] the Public Notaries of the City of Dublin being read.

RESOLVED that the Council be Summoned for Saturday next at two o'Clock to take the said Case into consideration.

Minute 19 March 1785

The Order of the day being read to take the case of the Public Notaries of the City of Dublin into consideration.

The Public Notaries of Dublin having intimated to the Council their intention of applying to Parliament this Session for an Increase to their fees for Acting and Protesting Bills and Notes and requesting our opinion and concurrence therein.

RESOLVED that it is the opinion of the Council that on Account of the Additional Stamp Duty on Protests which will take place the 25th March inst. and for other reasons Stated in their case such their intended application appears to us to be reasonable. And we are also of opinion the following prices exclusive of Stamps should be allowed them viz. for Protesting all Foreign Bills four shillings each and all Inland Bills and Notes exceeding Twenty pounds four shillings, and if under that sum two shillings and six pence and for the Noting Bills and Notes one shilling and six pence each.

5.10 Bankruptcy Laws

Reform of the laws of bankruptcy became a long-running campaign by chambers through to the 20th century. The lobbies by Dublin from the 1770s show how the issue was emerging very early, and was a major part of the objectives of the chamber's predecessor (Committee of Merchants) before being taken up by the chamber. The episode also demonstrates how a law agent was used (also see Chapter 7).

Sources
[a] Dublin Committee of Merchants and Traders, Rough Minute Book; RIA MS.3 C25
[b] Dublin Chamber of Commerce Minutes; TNAI

Minute 22 October 1771[a]

The Law Agent acquainted the Committee that as the Bankruptcy Bill was to be brought into the House of Commons the 20th Instant he therefore though it would be proper that the Speaker and other Members of the House should be waited Upon as soon as possible to request their aid and assistance in forwarding that Bill.

ORDERED that Henry Betagh our Law Agent proceed in soliciting the said Bill in the most Effectual Manner.

Minute 6 February 1772[a]

RESOLVED that the following persons be appointed a Committee to wait upon the Honl. Members of Parliament in respect of the Bankruptcy Bill.

The Speaker	Mr. R. Jaffray
Mr. Ponsonby	Mr. R. Dermot
The Prime Sergeant	Mr. T. Hartley
Sir Lucius O'Brien	Mr. Edwd. Strettell
The Attorney General	Mr. Tho. Thompson
Mr. [Anthony] Malone	Mr. Wm. Colvill
The Solicitor General	Mr. A. Wilkinson
Mr. Flood	Mr. G. Magnay
Mr. Hussey	
The City Members [MPs for Dublin]	

AND that the above Gentlemen be summoned to meet here at 9 o'Clock next Saturday Morning to proceed upon that Business.

Minute 22 February 1772[a]

Mr. Betagh our Law Agent having informed the Committee that an Opposition was intended to be made to the Heads of the Bankruptcy Bill now defending in Parliament it was

RESOLVED that the following Petition in the names of the Merchants & Traders of the City should be drawn up and presented to this Committee on Monday Morning for their Approbation.

Minute 5 March 1772 [mislabelled February in Rough Minutes]

The following matter was agreed to be delivered to the Speaker of the House of Commons by Some Gentlemen of the Committee.

THE COMMITTEE OF MERCHANTS beg leave to recommend it to the Consideration of the Speaker whether in Case the Insolvency Bill is intended to be passed into law, A Clause of the following kind may not be useful and necessary to prevent the Numberless Frauds foreseen by Men of Trade in the operation of the Act from their experience of former Acts of the like nature, and from the number of Knavish attempts on the humanity of this House. They now observe depending, That no person indebted above £100 in the whole, shall have this Benefit of the Act, unless two third in number or value of his Creditors do Sign a Certificate of their Bal[ances] that the Debtor has made a full and fair Discovery and Surrender of his Effects.

Minute 12 March 1772[a]

Mr. Henry Betagh having reported to the Committee that the Heads of the Bankruptcy Bill have passed the House of Commons & are this day to be presented to the Lord Lieutenant by Couns. Hellen.

RESOLVED that Mr. Betagh do attend said Bill in its future progress both here & in England, that it may be passed into a Law, & that he shall be paid by the Committee the Expenses Consequent thereon.

Minute 26 May 1772[a]

RESOLVED Nem. Con. That Mr. Henry Betagh be allowed the sum of Four Hundred Guineas for 'three weeks attendance in Comparing the Draft of the Present Bankruptcy Bill, with the British Statutes, and also the Printed Copy of a Bill which Had been drawn many years ago referring to the different Clauses in said Laws and Acts for [the] Irish petition of said Committee; for attending said Bill three Sessions, & for going to England his expenses there & for a Great Many Attendances on the Several Persons Necessary for Canvasing the said Bill this, & many other expenses that was Necessary to it'.

ORDERED that the Treasurer do Pay Mr. Henry Betagh the above sum of four Hundred Guineas -- taking His Receipts into account.

Resolved that the Treasurer be allowed the Sum of Twenty Five pounds Seven shillings and 8d. being so much paid to Mr. Betagh for Sundry Expenses as for his account.

Minute 19 February 1807[b]

To The Right Honble George Ponsonby Lord High Chancellor of that part of the United Kingdom of Great Britain and Ireland called Ireland
The Memorial of the Merchants and Traders of the City of Dublin
HUMBLY SHEWETH

THAT your Memorialists Solicit permission to Submit to Your Lordship a Statement of the Chief defects and inconveniences that they experience in the present Code of Law and proceedings concerning Bankrupts, as Your Memorialists are encouraged by a Sense of Your Lordship's able and Vigilant administration of Justice to hope that a better System will be adopted, when these defects and inconveniences shall have been more Known to you.

[full memorial not reproduced, but main elements are in the Suggestions below]

Minute 24 February 1807[b]

SUGGESTIONS for the amendment of the Laws in relation to Bankrupts which are referred to by the Memorial of the Merchants and Traders of the City of Dublin humbly submitted to his Lordship.

THAT a Court of Bankruptcy be constituted with power to sit from day to day throughout the Year and to exercise in the first resort a Summary civil jurisdiction and immediate superintendence over the Commissioners individually Assignees Messengers Agents & Bankrupts in Bankrupts affairs and also to exercise the several Authorities herein after mentioned subject to an appeal to your Lordship but the Orders Judgments and Decrees of that Court of Bankruptcy to be executed provisionally on security being given when appeals are lodged that appeals may not be interposed merely for delay.

THAT the number of established Commissioners be reduced to Ten or such other small convenient number as your Lordship shall think proper and that every Commission be directed to all the Commissioners, and enable any one or more of them to transact the business of each and every Commission in order that the number of acting Commissioners in each Commission may be Occasionally and from time to time proportioned and appointed by the Court of Bankruptcy to the magnitude of the affairs or the number of debts to be proved and other particular circumstances of each Estate these Commissioners to be paid as at present out of the Effects, it being conceived that such an increase of emolument would arise to the Commissioners individually by the reduction of their numbers, as would amply remunerate them for relinquishing the business of the Bar and for employing their whole time in acting as Commissioners and yet at far less expense than at present to each particular Estate; providing however that no business shall be commenced or entered upon by the Commissioners at a later hour than one O'Clock P.M.

and that the fees on all adjourned Sittings, shall be only one half of the fees on original Sittings, unless in case of the absence of some necessary party not a Commissioner, or that such adjournment shall be made with permission of the Court of Bankruptcy, and also declaring that the proceedings shall be void, and that a Commissioner shall not be paid for a Sitting during which he shall attempt to transact the business of more than one Commission at the same time or at which another Commr. shall act as an advocate before the Sitting Commissioner. By these means it is humbly conceived, that the office of a Comr. of Bankrupt would be rendered in itself a distinct & sufficiently lucrative profession with benefit and yet Oeconomy to the public.

THAT provisional Assignees should be abolished on account of the expense attending the appointment of them and of vesting in them the Bankrupt's property, as the next following Suggestion would render them unnecessary.

THAT encouragement should be given to qualified persons to undertake the office of an Assignee as a distinct profession Trade or calling, by granting Licenses for that purpose to eligible and responsible persons, who however shall not be Creditors of any of the Bankrupts whose Estate and Effects shall be assigned to them, and the power of appointing one or more assignees as shall be necessary out of such select and licensed persons to be vested either in the Court of Bankruptcy or in the presiding Commissioner or Commissioners instantly after the party shall have been found Bankrupt and not at the election of the Creditors, but removable at the desire of a moderate proportion of the Creditors in number and value or by the Court of Bankruptcy or the Lord Chancellor, those Assignees to give Security by recognizance as in Holland to account for the property vested in them, and for their wilful default in respect of it, and to be allowed either a fixed per Centage on the amount received by them as in Spain, or a quantum merit[ed] in the opinion of the Court of Bankruptcy as in Holland, to remunerate them for their trouble and exertion, in addition to such necessary and reasonable Courts and Expenses as shall be allowed by the Court of Bankruptcy, those Assignees by profession to be obliged to keep public affairs, and to keep distinct and proper Books for each Bankrupts Estate accessible together with the Books and papers of the Bankrupt at seasonable hours to every approved Creditor of any such Bankrupt under a penalty in case of refusal to be enforced in a summary way by the Court of Bankruptcy, and to open distinct Accounts with the Bank of Ireland in the name of the Estate of each Bankrupt and not merely in the name of the Assignee himself, also to pay in to the Credit of such Bank accompt the produce of the effects weekly or oftener when it amounts to £100 or in default thereof to be chargeable by the Court of Bankruptcy periodically as herein after mentioned with penal Interest in the Sums with-held as is at present directed by Law to be done by the Commissioners at their Option or the instance of Creditors but ineffectually, and none of the money so lodged to be issued out of the Bank unless the draft of the assignee shall specify the purpose and shall be countersigned by an Officer of the Court of Bankruptcy.

THAT assignees shall be prohibited from selling debts due to the Estates of Bankrupts and if any such debts shall remain outstanding after a final dividend they should be vested in the Lying In Hospital or some other Charitable institution with power to sell them, such a regulation being necessary to take away from Assignees the means of collecting with the Bankrupts respecting outstanding debts, or of having recoverable debts uncollected until after a final dividend.

THAT quarterly or other periodical days of recall & revision of the conduct and accompts of each assignee should be held by the Court of Bankruptcy until he shall have obtained his quotas by an order for that purpose, and those periodical accompts to be kept on record.

THAT the marriage Settlement of Traders shall be enrolled to obtain at full length, and not merely registered within the same period at which they are required by Law to be registered.

THAT for a Merchant or Trader to convince his Creditors and exhibit at such meeting a wilfully false Settlement of his or her affairs purporting to show his or her inability to pay his or her debts shall be held an act of Bankruptcy.

THAT every Merchant and Trader who shall suffer an execution obtained upon his or her Bill of Exchange or promissory Note to be enforced against his or her person or effects, shall be deemed a Bankrupt from and after the time such execution was executed.

THAT on issuing a joint Commission against Co-partners it shall not be necessary to prove an act of Bankruptcy by each party but that an Act by any one partner at the Compting House or Known place of Business shall be sufficient to support a joint Commission against all the partners.

THAT Commissions of Bankruptcy shall be issuable against the effects of deceased Merchants and Traders who shall have done acts of Bankruptcy and that such Commissions shall bind the Executors and Administrators of the deceased to make a rateable distribution of the effects under the direction of the Court of Bankruptcy and the Lord Chancellor, or in case such Executors and Administrators refuse to act that assignees shall be appointed under such Commissions to stand in the place of such Executors and Administrators until the debts shall have been paid and then to hand over the residue (if any) to the Executors and Administrators of the deceased to be disposed of in the usual course of Administration.

THAT the Bankrupt shall on surrendering sign a Bond or Recognizance not to depart the Kingdom without leave of the Court of Bankruptcy or of the Court of Chancery uncertified.

THAT the Bankrupt shall have a moderate allowance for his or her maintenance until the final examination is closed and afterwards when in attendance on the Court of Bankruptcy Comrs. or assignees excep. when obtained as a public delinquent.

THAT an officer of the Court of Bankruptcy in the nature of a public Accompant selected for his Knowledge of Trade and Mercantile Accompts should be especially charged to examine and report upon the Books of every Bankrupt and to superintend the preparation of each Bankrupts Schedule.

THAT at a Sitting appointed for the final examination of a Bankrupt no other business shall be transacted.

THAT a Bankrupt who shall not surrender, or who shall conceal or embezzle, or convey out of this Country, his Estate or effects or Books of Accompt or who shall have made, and shall conceal, any fraudulent disposition of them in favour of another person or who shall produce false or fabricated or wilfully defaced altered or torn Books of Accompt shall on due Conviction be transported for life.

THAT all other persons who shall wilfully conceal embezzle or fraudulently acquire, or convey out of this Country any of the Estate or effects of a Bankrupt, or who shall wilfully make Oath to a false or excessive demand on a Bankrupts Estate with an intention to defraud the general Estate shall on due conviction be transported for Seven Years.

THAT all persons who shall be accessories or abettors to the last mentioned frauds or in fabricating of false or fraudulent liens and covers of property of a Merchant or Trader by Bond and Execution or otherwise in Contemplation of his or her Bankruptcy and to defraud the general Estate or in fabricating false or fraudulent Books of Account for a Merchant or Trader in Contemplation of his or her Bankruptcy shall on conviction be punished as for a conspiracy to cheat.

THAT the major part in value of the Creditors or the majority in number when equal in value on being convened by public notice shall have power to order a certain proportion of the effects to be applied in prosecuting offenders against the Bankrupt Laws for frauds prejudicial to the particular Estate of which they are Creditors.

THAT every document requisite for supporting prosecutions for offences against the Bankrupt Laws should be of record, and that such legal requisites should be simplified and abridged as far as may be expedient.

THAT the proof of debts should not conclude against the Estate but shall be open to examination and revision at the instance of the Assignee or any one Creditor liable to pay Costs if he fails in supporting his objection to such proof.

THAT it should be Settled whether an affidavit of debt sworn before a Master of the English High Court of Chancery and not attested by a Public Notary is admissible as a regular proof of debt under an Irish Commission, as at present such affidavits are received by some Commissioners and rejected by others.

THAT the Court of Bankruptcy should have a Civil Bill Jurisdiction within the County of the City of Dublin and a convenient surrounding district for the recovery of debts due to Bankrupts Estates and not exceeding £30 on the Trials of which the attested Copy of that Assignment to have the same effect in evidence as at present respecting debts under £20 and that no action at Law or Suit in Equity for debts exceeding the limit of £30 shall be brought by or in the name of an Assignee without leave from the Court of Bankruptcy or of the Commissioners on enquiring into the probability of benefitting the fund by such action or Suit.

THAT the production of the commission and Deed of Assignment should be evidence on Trials of Actions at Law for the recovery of Debts against all third persons of the Assignees right to sue without proving, heading Act of Bankruptcy or the petitioning Creditors debt, but Actions for the Trial of the fact of Bankruptcy to be excepted from such regulation.

THAT one general qualification of a Commission upon undertaking the office in any Case, should be sufficient to support his Authority under every subsequent Commission in which he shall act so as to take away the present needless repetition of Oaths.

THAT the Commissioners shall have power to order the expense of the Bankrupts Certificate to be paid out of the effects in case they are satisfied with the Conduct of the Bankrupt and that such order shall be contained in the Certificate.

THAT the allowances to Bankrupts whose effects pay more than 10s. per pound should be directed to be calculated on the gross produce of the Estate.

THAT the several clauses of the Acts of 11th & 12th Geo. 3rd and 17th & 18th George 3rd which subject all the future property of a person after a Second Bankruptcy for all his or her debts contracted after the time of such second Bankruptcy unless his or her effects shall have paid under such Second Commission 15/- in the pound pursuant to said first act or the full amount of such debts, pursuant to the said last mentioned act should be repealed not only on account of the inconsistency of the said two claims but on account of their manifest injustice it being obvious that a person may become Bankrupt a Second time without being Culpable altho' his Effects may pay under such second Commission but a small or even no dividend.

THAT a Record Room should be appointed for the special purpose of preserving the files of proceedings. Counterparts of the Deed of Assignment and Bargain and Sale periodical accompts of Assignees and Documents for the support of prosecutions open to the public at all times except when in use before the Commissioners or some Court of Judicature.

THAT all Motions proceedings and Orders in Bankrupts Affairs should be free from the duty on advertisements to enable the proprietors of Newspapers to insert them gratis and of their own accord for public information.

THAT the temporary act of Grace which gave the Lord Chancellor power to instigate [an action against] the obduracy of Creditors by generating a Certificate without the Conduct of the Statudable [i.e. that defined by law] proportion of Creditors to Bankrupts who have passed their final Examinations within a limited Time should be permanently revived and extended to every instance of oppression or that a Bankrupt who has passed his final Examination shall have a right to a Trial to be Tried by a Jury in the Court of Bankruptcy for the purpose of determining whether he is entitled to his Certificate.

THAT the several Topics comprised in the last Paragraph of the Memorial to which these Suggestions refer may have the benefit of Your Lordships consideration and of Your influence for the better adjustment of them in such manner in Your Lordships shall deem expedient.

IN presenting these humble Suggestions to Your Lordship the Merchants and Traders of Dublin beg leave to be understood as wishing at the same time that every similar suggestion which may be received from the Merchants and Traders of the rest of Ireland should have their due weight; as local convenience more especially in case of executing Commissions in provincial Towns may render it necessary in some instances to qualify the practice here proposed by other adoptions which the parties interested are best qualified to recommend.

Commercial Buildings Dublin 24th February 1807

By order and on behalf of the Merchants and Traders of Dublin, George F. Carleton—Chairman of the Chamber
R. MacDonnell
Arthr. Guinness

5.11 'Equal trade' with Ireland

One of the most important trade issues to engage chambers was proposals for open trade with Ireland that began under Lord North's government in 1778. These were opposed by the Liverpool corporation and chamber, which marshalled other towns to follow suit.[26] It was also one of the core issues for the General Chamber when Irish propositions were considered for opening trade with Ireland in 1785 (q.v. Chapter 8). The documents reproduced here

[26] Liverpool RO: Corporation minutes; Committee of Trade minutes 28 March, 6, 15 and 18 April, 2 November, 24 December 1778; 22 February and 15 March 1779.

aim to cast a different light on the debates by showing Dublin's view, which evidences the manifest inequality of the status quo. Also reproduced is a memorial from one of the smaller towns not usually reported on, Blackburn. This is the only record we have of an early chamber or committee at Blackburn. This document may reflect an isolated activity or part of a more general body formed to copy or in reaction to the Manchester committee of trade of 1774–86 and the Liverpool chamber of commerce of 1774–c.1796. The actual petition being discussed, against liberalisation of Irish trade, was in line with many positions taken by localities (including Liverpool) against a reform sought by Lord North's government in 1778–9 and thus may be no more than an isolated activation purely on that issue.

Sources
[a] Rough Minute Book of the Dublin Committee of Merchants, RIA MS. 3 C 25.
[b] Dublin Chamber of Commerce Minutes; TNAI.
[c] Bristol SMV; Bristol RO SMV/2/4/2/22(3)

Minute Dublin, 29 January 1780[a]

At a Meeting of the Committee of M[erchan]ts. on the 29th January 1780.
Present
Thos. Thompson in the Chair

Travs. Hartley	Geo. Sutton
Saml. Dick	Alexr. McDonnell
Ab. Wilkinson	G. G. Hoffman
Hugh Crothers	Dens. Thos. O Brien

The Committee having invited several persons concerned in the Linen Trade to Assist them in their deliberations the following Gentlemen were pleased to attend.

Robt. Stephenson	Jno. Cowan
Evelyn Peerpont	Wm. Stewart
Alexr. Stewart	Jno. Russell
James Davis	

And on Mature Consideration the following resolutions were unanimously agreed to.

RESOLVED that it will be of advantage to the Linen Manufacture of Ireland that the like Bounties should be allowed on the Exportation of white & Brown Linen from hence as are granted in England on the Export of British & Irish Linens from thence.

RESOLVED that it will be of advantage to the Linen Manufacture of Ireland that the like Bounties should be allowed on the Exportation of Striped & Chequered Linens the Manufacture of this Kingdom from hence as are given in Great Britain on the Exportation of that Species of goods manufactured in Great Britain from thence.

RESOLVED that it would tend to the Extension of the Linen Trade & Commerce of these Kingdoms if that Bounties granted on the Exportation of plain Linens of British & Irish Manufacture were Extended to Painted Linens.

Minute: Adjourned Meeting 12 February 1780[a]

[Same committee present]:

Ordered that the annexed Petition be engrossed by Mr. Day to be Signed by the Merchts. of Dublin.

TO THE HONBLE THE KNIGHTS CITIZENS & BURGESSES IN PARLIAMT. ASSEMBLED

THE PETITION OF THE MERCHTS. OF THE CITY OF DUBLIN MOST HUMBLY SHEWETH

That your Petition[er]s hold in the highest Veneration the Patriotic Dignity of those Proceedings of the Parliament of this Kingdom which have and long happily awakened the attention of the British Legislature to the Just Rights of Ireland and at the same time produced on the Part of Great Britain a liberality of Sentiment, comprehending the General mutual Interests of both Countries. To that enlarged Idea Your Petitioners consider this Kingdom indebted for the proposed participation in the Trade to the British Colonies in America & Settlements on the Coasts of Africa which they do not View as a Matter of strict Right though all Circumstances Considered not entirely Devoid of Reasonable Pretensions to it. They receive it therefore gratefully as a favour. As such they conceive it to be sincerely intended and it is therefore necessary to point out to this Honourable house such Concomitant Regulations as may make the Grant answer the kind Intentions of the Donor.

The present Principal & professed object is a direct free Intercourse of Trade between this Kingdom & the British Islands in the West Indies, the Capital & most Valuable article of produce in those Islands is Sugar, in that article this Country must look for the greatest part of the returns for her Exports to the West Indies, the Existence of this Trade & all the hoped for benefits arising from it your Petitioners humbly Conceive absolutely to depend on securing a Market here for the Sale of Raw Sugars when Imported from the West Indies. That this can only be done by a Careful Guardianship of the Sugar Refineries of this Kingdom & that therefore the Example of Great Britain should be followed in Subjecting all refined Sugars imported here to the Same duties imposed on them there as it is understood that all raw

Sugars imported here are hereafter to pay the same duty which they pay in Great Britain.
May it therefore please this Honourable house to take this important Matter into Consideration & Your Petitioners will Pray.

Minute 30 October 1783[b]

To the Honble the Knights Citizens and Burgesses in Parliament Assembled.

The humble Petition of the Merchants composing the Council of the Chamber of Commerce of the City of Dublin.

SHEWETH

That your Petitioners, appointed by a numerous and respectable body of the Traders of this Metropolis, to watch over and promote their Commercial Interests, flatter themselves they will not be thought too presuming, if moved by the distresses of Multitudes of their Fellow Citizens, and in compliance with the Duties of their Delegation, they humbly entreat the attention of this Honourable House to the present depressed state of various of the Manufactures of this City and Kingdom.

That your petitioners humbly conceive this unfavourable situation principally to proceed from the very unequal and unjust Terms on which Great Britain and Ireland at present trade—Ireland opening freely her Ports at low Duties to all the Manufactures of Great Britain, Great Britain prohibiting by excessive Duties almost all the Fabrics of Ireland.

That your Petitioners beg leave to assure this Honble House that they feel as well as profess for their Sister Kingdom the most cordial affection and fully acknowledge this Country to be so connected with her that they must stand or fall together, they however consider it incumbent on them, humbly to represent that British Manufactures imported into Ireland should pay the same Duties that are imposed on Irish Manufactures of a similar Species imported into Great Britain.

Your Petitioners humbly beseech this Honble House to take the premises into consideration and to grant such relief as to its great Wisdom shall seem meet and your Petitioners will pray.

Resolved that said Petition be signed by the President and Vice Presidents and presented to the House of Commons as speedily as possible.

Resolved that our worthy President Travers Hartley Esq. be requested to present the said Petition to the House of Commons.

Resolved that 500 Copies of the said Petition be printed.

Minute 13 December 1805[b]

Quarterly Meeting

John Duncan Esq. Chairman
John Todhunter
Alderman Hone
Vale. O'Connor Junr.
Samuel Stephens
Richd. Darling

The Chairman reported that pursuant to the Order of the ____ Ultimo the Deputation of the Council appointed to wait on the Right Honble John Foster the Chancellor of the Exchequer had a conference with that Minister upon the Several Topics comprised in the Letter of the Council dated the ____ Ultimo and that the Chairman had to report the answer of the Chancellor of the Exchequer relative to the Topics to be as follows

No. 1 That care would be taken in the ensuing Parliament to restrain private Bankers from making their Notes or Post Bills payable at any other place than that for which they are Registered as Bankers in order to confine the Circulation of each Bankers Paper to its proper district.

2. That every endeavour in making for the better promulgation of Irish Laws, which is at present prevented by the privileges of the Kings Printers for Great Britain & Ireland having interfered with each other since the Union & that the Council might rely that in the mean time he would take care to transmit to them timely notice of all Bills of Regulation interesting to the Commerce of Ireland.

3. That the Irish provision Trade would continue to have his best support & that he thought the Exporter entitled to a Drawback of the duty on the Salt used in curing Provisions.

4. That the impediments complained of in regard to the Sending of Colonial produce to Ireland had been considered on the application of the Merchants of Cork & had been or should be removed.

5th. That means are taking to render the increased Duties on Wines & Tobaccos mentioned by the Council more productive by adopting a more effectual mode of levying those duties as well as the Duties on Spirits so as to restore in some degree the consumption of Wines.

6. That the Chancellor of the Exchequer is aware of the necessity of introducing some general regulations in the Butter Trade throughout the whole of Ireland & requested to be furnished with certain heads of a Bill for that purpose now in the possession of the Council & which the Deputation promised to present to him accordingly.

7. That the subject of River Laws being a Question of local Police he wished the Council to confer with the Magistracy of the City on the subject.

8. That the subjects of under & overpayments of Duties at the Custom House have been for some time under the consideration of the Board of Enquiry from whom he expected Shortly to receive a Report on that subject as well as upon the possibility of distinguishing as far as possible with Permits & Custom House Fees excepting Fees for attendance during extra hours for the accommodation of the Merchant.

9. That the Prisage duty is at present the subject of a negotiation between Government & the Earl of Ormond for the purchase of it & that he thought any interference of the Mercantile Interest respecting that Duty would be unreasonable at present.

10. That he would take into consideration the propriety of modifying the late prohibition of Grocers from retailing Spirits.

The Chairman reported that agreeably to the Order of the last Meeting he had waited on Mr. Secretary Lees of the Post Office and that Mr. Lees had informed him that it was determined to change the time & mode of dispatching Mails for England agreeably to the wish of the Mercantile Community & that a printed Table, having the hours of dispatch would be sent to the Merchants of Dublin Individually, by Post previous to the 1st of January next.

Resolved on the Motion of Alderman Hone seconded by Richard Darling Esq. that Randal McDonnell Esq. be requested to act as Chairman of the Council for the ensuing three Months.

Resolved on the Motion of Vale. O'Connor Jun Esq. seconded by John Todhunter Esq. that the cordial thanks of the Council be presented to John Duncan Esq. late Chairman of the Council for the zeal & ability with which he filled that Office.

Original letter Blackburn 12 January 1779[c]

To: Committee of trade in Bristol

Information being given in the House of Commons that the Members in the Irish Interest propose bringing in a Bill for a further extension of their exports, and other Advantages to the detriment of this Kingdom, And our Manufacture in particular, I am ordered by the Committee of trade here to Acquaint you, that a powerful, Opposition will be made to endeavour to prevent such proceedings taking place, at same time request you would be kind enough to furnish them with an exact account of the Square Yards of Cottons and British Calicoes exported from Bristol, to America, the West Indies, Coast of Africa and different parts of Europe, Since January 1768 to January 1779 Noting each year respectively, such Account to be Signed by the Collector or some other proper officer in the Customs. We are provided, with a Similar list from our Neighbouring Ports, Liverpool, and Lancaster, As it is not doubted but the City of Bristol will have Gentlemen to attend on this business in London [I] am Warranted to add, [that] those deputed, from hence will be happy to meet them and concur in whatever is thought beneficial to the whole.

Any Expense Occasioned in obtaining particulars from the Custom House will be carefully repaid at any House in London or where you mention.

I am with Suitable respects to the whole of your committee.

Your Obedt. Servant
Bertie Markland
Chairman to the Committee

5.12 The 'State of trade'

The general situation for traders and merchants was a key lobby issue for chambers when trade was depressed. If trade was going well government was not approached. Generally the concerns for trade rose during wars and in economic crises. The examples here show the specific concerns of Guernsey, a major entrepôt affected by the war with America in 1776, Glasgow in 1783 which had a standard letter which it was using to engage other ports in a joint lobby, and Galway in 1822 (which is also the only early record of this chamber). There are no records of advocacy that can be definitely traced to the first Guernsey chamber founded in 1769. The only significant item that has a likely relationship to the chamber is the 'Canary Wine petition' of 1776. The handwritten documentation is reproduced below because it is an important indicator of the likely actions by the first chamber, and it may indicate some of its main members. It is also a valuable example in itself of the lobbying of this period. If it was a chamber-led petition then it is likely that only a proportion of the membership was represented (the wine merchants), and that non-members were also included (other significant wine merchants). For these reasons the full list of signatories is given here rather than in the Appendix.

Sources
[a] TNA T1/520/59–61
[b] Glasgow chamber papers, letters; Glasgow Mitchell Library TD 1670/4/15
[c] TNAI CSO/RP/1822/834/A

Petition Guernsey, 20 March 1776[a]

TO THE RIGHT HONBLE the LORDS COMMISSIONERS of the TREASURY
The Humble Petition of the Merchants Traders and other Inhabitants of the Island of Guernsey.
Sheweth

That by the Act of Parliament the 12th of King Charles the Second Chapter the 18th section the 4th it is enacted 'that no goods or commodities that are of foreign growth production or manufacturer, and which are brought into England Ireland Wales the Islands of Guernsey and Jersey or Town of Berwick upon Tweed in English built shipping, or other shipping belonging to some of the aforesaid palaces, and navigated by English mariners as aforesaid, shall be shipped or brought from any other Place or Places, Country or Countries, but only from those of the said growth production or manufactures, or from those Ports where the said Goods and Commodities can only, or are, or usually have been first shipped for transportation, and from none other Places or Countries under the penalty of the forfeiture of all such of the aforementioned Goods as shall be imported from any other Place or Country contrary to the true intent and meaning hereof, as also of the Ship in which they were imported with all her Guns Furniture Ammunition Tackle and Apparel one moiety to his Majesty his Heirs and Successors, and the other moiety to him or them that shall seize inform or sue for the same in any Court of Record, to be recovered as is before expressed' and THAT notwithstanding which said Act that out of such Goods and Commodities, Wines, and Wines only, which have been imported into this and the Island of Jersey from the Canary Islands had from time immemorial been admitted hence into Great Britain and Ireland on paying the Duties due thereon, as if imported directly from the said Canary Islands into the places aforementioned.

But an objection having been lately made and a stop put to such importation in the Port of London, and as Your Petitioners conceive, not justly being in conformity to the aforesaid Act, Your Petitioners are therefore humbly moved to represent to Your Lordships that great prejudice and detriment must ensue not only to their and the Trade of Jersey, but to that of Great Britain, if that part of the said Act which relates to Canary Wines imported to the said Islands from the said Canary Islands should continue in force, and any Wines be thereby prevented from being imported to Great Britain and Ireland from the said Islands of Guernsey and Jersey.

For that several of the Newfoundland Ships who sell their Fish in the Canary Islands, either bring their Returns in such Wines or get a freight of such Wines for their Ships for account of the British Merchants, which Wines having no other Market than Great Britain & Ireland, the being deprived of such Markets must put a total stop to the advantages accruing from that branch of the Trade. And as of late Years the People of the Canary Islands have taken to making of a dry wine called Vidonia Wine, which tho' it falls short in quality of the best Madeira, yet is now brought to that perfection that a great quantity thence has of late Years been imported into Great Britain; and as the first cost thereof does not exceed for the best quality twelve pounds per Pipe, and that Madeira, Lisbon, and Sherry Wines are purchased at or near 50 per Cent higher, the encouraging of the consumption of the said Vidonia Canary Wine in Great Britain and Ireland must occasion a saving to the Nation equal to the difference of such first Cost.

And as such Vidonia Wine is mostly carried into the Out Ports, none of which Ports can take off a whole Cargo at a time, the landing of such Cargoes into the said Islands of Guernsey and Jersey, and importing them thence into the Ports of Great Britain and Ireland in small Parcels is a great convenience to the Merchants, and must be, as well as to the British navigation, seeing moreover that by the Act of Parliament the 8th of His present Majesty's Reign Chapter 23d. no wines imported from this and the Island of Jersey into Great Britain or Ireland can be entitled to the 12 per Cent allowed for Leakage, unless Certificates on Oath are produced to the Officers of the Customs in Great Britain and Ireland of such Wines having been imported therein for British Account and in British Shipping.

Your Petitioners therefore humbly conceiving the foregoing enumerated Advantages would result by the repeal of that part of the aforesaid Act respecting Canary Wines and be productive of no bad Consequence whatsoever, humbly pray Your Lordships would be pleased to use Your good Offices with the Parliament for the repeal of the part of the said Act as relates to Canary Wines so that after being landed in the said Islands of Guernsey and Jersey in British shipping for British accounts they may be legally admitted into the Ports of Great Britain and Ireland under the Rules and Regulations contained in the aforesaid Act of Parliament the 8th of His present Majesty's Reign Chapter 23d. or suggest to Parliament such other Relief of Your Petitioners in the Premises as Your Lordships in Your great Wisdom and Goodness shall think meet. [Signed]

John Tupper junr.	Thomas Dobrée
Peter Dobree	Elisha Tupper
John Rivoire	John Carey junr.
John Solomon Lauga	John de Havilland
Robt. Porret Le Marchant	Jno. Carey
Paul Grut	Henry Le Mesurier
Thomas Lihou	Richard Le Jersey
Charles Mollet	Danl. Tupper
Peter Mourant	Peter Bonamy
John Cornelius	Dan. De Jersey
Peter Hubert	Peter De Lisle
Peter Le Lievre	Solomon Lauga
Anthony Isemonger	Daniel Watkins

Original letter Glasgow, 10 May 1783[b]

Sir,

By order of the committee of commerce of this Port, I have the honour to transmit you enclosed a copy of a letter which they have addressed to the Lord Mayor of London on two points relating to the Trade of this Kingdom with the United States of America as also to form a Chain of Correspondence between the Principal Ports, so that the best probable means may be adopted for improving and securing the several important Branches of Commerce which have been the Source of the Wealth and Dignity of this Kingdom.

The Committee request the favour of you to lay the same before your Board of Trade, and would be glad to be favoured with the Sentiments on the objects of the enclosed Letter, and will readily concur in the support of any measure which may either be of local or general advantage—

I am with great respect, Sirs

Your most obedient Humble Servt.

John Wilson

Memorial Galway, 6 July 1822[c]

TO THE MOST NOBLE MARQUIS WELLESLEY LORD CHIEF GOVERNOR OF IRELAND

We the Chamber of Commerce for ourselves and the other Inhabitants of the ancient, populous and loyal Town of Galway accompanied by our Collector of Customs beg leave with great respect to call your Excellency's attention to the ruinous state of the docks and quays of this port, which are alike insufficient for the purposes of Commerce and revenue. We beg leave also to submit to your Excellency the many advantages which would arise to both, from a junction by means of a Navigable canal less than a quarter of a British Mile in length, between Lough Corrib and the Bay; an improvement of essential importance and of cheap and easy attainment. The dilapidated state of our Docks and quays has long proved seriously injurious, being found quite insufficient for the proper accommodation and protection of Vessels. Accordingly, amidst the greatest natural advantages, we have had the mortification to see our Trade and Shipping gradually decline, from the eminence at which they once stood, to their present depressed state. Vessels have often been injured in our Dock, or blown out of it on the rocks by rough weather, and Cargoes detained till the market was lost. Foreign Captains have declared they would not return here except at an extravagant freight. The Collector and Custom House officers have had occasion to complain to the Board of Customs of the insufficient accommodation and insecurity to his Majesty's revenue.

We have reasons to believe, that strongly impressed with these Considerations, the Honourable Board of Customs, after a minute enquiry made a representation on the Subject to your Excellency's predecessor, which was favourably entertained immediately before his departure from Ireland, and we anxiously hope it has been reserved for your Excellency to rescue the Commerce of the Chief Town and Seaport of the Province of Connaught, from so fallen a condition, and to give a most beneficial impulse to its internal Trade, with a vast extent of Country, by the navigable communication alluded to. Perhaps in no part of Ireland can improvements of so material importance be effected at so little expense and we confidently refer to the reports of experienced Engineers on their utility necessity and easy accomplishment. We may also refer to an urgent representation very lately made to the Right Honourable H. Goulburn on the same Subject by the Members of Parliament for this Town and County.

At this Crisis of severe and unprecedented distress, we have seen with great satisfaction and gratitude a large Sum of money placed by the Legislature at your Excellency's disposal to alleviate the wants of the poor in Ireland by useful employment. The extreme poverty of our extensive population is notorious and we strongly apprehend the present distress will be continued next Year attended by Typhus fever, as the poor are beginning to consume the New Potatoes unripe, unless, some very extensive public Works are immediately commenced to enable them to buy wholesome food. As therefore the improvements we have mentioned are of great necessity and lasting importance We most earnestly hope your Excellency will give such directions as in your Wisdom may lead to their speedy accomplishment.

5.13 Slave Trade abolition 1788

Slave trade abolition was a difficult issue for the chambers, because many of their members were deeply engaged in the trade especially in Liverpool, whilst others became vehemently opposed. It was therefore deeply divisive. The documents reproduced here show how the issue was handled in different local situations. In Glasgow the chamber adopted the recommendations of a committee that was set up to consider the issue: that it was better for the chamber to stand back and have no view, leaving it to members individually to take whichever position they wished. In Liverpool it is probable that the chamber took the same approach. Explicit records of the chamber's position do not survive, and might in any case be unreliable as many of those supporting abolition in Liverpool were reluctant to give public voice.[27] For example,

[27] F. E. Sanderson, 'The Liverpool Delegates and Sir William Dolben's Bill', *Transactions of the*

Liverpool's chamber member Edgar Corrie wrote *secretly* to the president of the BoT in February 1788 supporting abolition: 'I am a merchant of Liverpool, and it might be attended with irreparable prejudice to some branches of the business in which I am engaged, that I stood forth with any opinion that could favour the abolition of the slave trade'. Therefore he 'begs that this private letter may not be communicated to any person unless to Mr. Pitt' and that 'my name must remain an invisible secret'.[28] However, many other chamber members joined with the corporation in vigorously opposing abolition, led by chamber member John Tarleton, but through the corporation and the corporation's committee of trade, not the chamber.[29] The Liverpool chamber's secretary also played an active role in opposing abolition. However, he did this from the Liverpool Africa Committee Room, never mentioned the chamber, and his salary was paid by the corporation.[30] Hence, the Liverpool chamber itself appears to have made no statement on the slave trade either way. This is in strong contrast to the Bristol SMV. Explicit opposition to abolition was organised on a large scale in conjunction with the Liverpool Corporation's delegates led by Tarleton. The London West India Committee was also an important opponent of abolition.[31]

The situation in Dublin indicates the effect of taking a different line. Although few in Dublin had direct involvement in the slave trade (it is usually claimed that none did), the issue seems to have been very divisive when the Dublin chamber on 29 March 1788 called for abolition. This call was the only item minuted for 29 March and the publicity sought and given in local and London newspapers demonstrates the intent to make a very prominent statement. The eight members present for the meeting had a strong Dissenter presence: Pim was Quaker, Jaffray and Wilkinson were from Quaker families, and Hartley and Crosthwaite Presbyterians. Although the committee of the chamber was adjourned to meet again four days later, there is no further

Historic Society of Lancashire and Cheshire, 124 (1972) 57–84; 'The structure of politics in Liverpool 1780–1807', *Ibid.,* 127 (1977) 65–88.

[28] BL: Edgar Corrie to Hawkesbury 24 Feb 1788; and 'memorandum by M.J.'; Add. MS 38416, f.35–6, 37–44.

[29] Thorne *History of Parliament* (1986); the other members of the delegation were Robert Norris, James Parry, John Matthews and Archibald Dalzell, none of whom are known chamber members; Bennett, *Voice of Liverpool* (2010) 49–53. The role of the committee of trade was mainly to provide financial support through use of its unspent balances; see Bennett, 'Searching for new models' (2014).

[30] BL: Samuel Green to Hawkesbury 21 and 30 May 1788; Add. MS 38416, f. 93, 96; Bennett, *Voice of Liverpool* (2010) 49–53.

[31] There are extensive documents already published on this campaign; see e.g. R. E. Donnan, *Documents Illustrative of the History of the Slave Trade to America* (Washington, 1931); Harlow, *Second British Empire* (1952); Harlow and F. Madden, *British Colonial Developments 1774–1783* (Oxford, 1953).

minute until three years later on 27 May 1791. This is effectively the same chamber with the minutes in the same form and in the same secretary's handwriting. The 1791 meeting had two items of business: to agree a petition on the rum duty, and to authorise payment of the secretary's expenses. The expenses of £86 claimed are more than double any previous year (the last and largest claim was on 12 August 1786 was for £36 2s. 4½d.), which suggests that the secretary was claiming for the previous two or three years which have no minutes. The minutes after 1791 stop again until 27 May 1805, which was an explicit re-launch of the chamber with revised rules, new committee and referral back to the old treasurer for any remaining balances. From this run of minutes, reproduced below, it is clear that the slave trade issue was a crucial element in the break in continuity in 1788–91. This appears to be due to the fracture between the Dissenters who were enthusiasts for abolition and the rest. We do not know the views of the rest of the committee but, given that there was no direct slave trade of significance from Ireland, we may assume that they were neutral and probably did not wish to see the chamber embroiled in a 'political' debate. The meeting of March 1788 also followed quickly on a previous divisive debate about changing the rules of the chamber to increase subscriptions. From this earlier debate it is clear that some members and some committee had not been paying at all (see Chapter 1). Indeed attendance at the committee and general meetings had reduced to small numbers. It appears that in the meeting of 29 March 1788 the 'radicals' took the opportunity of ebbing support to push through a radical position on abolition, which further undermined support from the wider community.[32]

The only other chamber with any comment on the slave trade shows the tension of the issue for the later political discussion in the 1830s. In Dundee the slave trade was discussed in two resolutions at the last director's meeting of December 1830, before the chamber went into abeyance (to be revived in 1835). The first resolution stated: 'That the abolition of slavery in the British colonies, at the earliest period ..., is demanded by every consideration of justice and humanity'. The second resolution stated 'But as this chamber is properly intended for the protection of commercial interests of this town and country, the meeting do not think it expedient to petition Parliament on the subject of slavery.' These two resolutions were clearly contradictory. The first resolution is similar to that in Dublin, but the second shows the same response as in Glasgow, to remove the chamber from involvement. However, this may have been a factor in the demise of the chamber over 1830–35. Edward

[32] See also discussion by Cullen, *Pirates and Princes* (1983) 50–4, and MacMahon, *Most Respectable Meeting* (2014) 72. However, neither attempts to interpret the slave trade resolutions in the context of the chamber's demise 1788–91, and MacMahon claims decline of support was due to failure to obtain a charter, for which there is no evidence.

Baxter, who was a key founding figure of the preceding Forfarshire chamber in 1819, had resigned shortly before 1830 over the payment of a salary to the secretary. There were clearly other tensions between the early and later members at the time. The resolution on slavery seems to have been divisive and the last straw for some members, as the contradiction between the two resolutions indicates. The demise of the chamber in Dundee immediately after debate and resolutions is similar to the evolution in Dublin.

Source
[a] Glasgow chamber papers, Glasgow Mitchell Library; TD 1670/4/52
[b] Dublin chamber of commerce minutes; TNAI
[c] Index of Proceedings of SMV; Bristol RO SMV/2/1/2/3
[d] Bristol SMV Outletter Book; BRO SMV/2/4/1/2

Handwritten report Glasgow 14 October 1788[a]

[Agreed as the chamber's policy: Minutes, 14 October 1788]
Report of the Committee on the Slave Trade

The Committee have attentively considered the papers transmitted from London, and have individually formed opinions on the subject; but finding that there are different opinions, not only in the Committee but among the Directors and in the Corporation [chamber members] at large, they do not think it expedient that the Directors as a chamber should take any decisive resolution on the occasion; leaving it to every member to take such part in the question as to each for himself shall deem ['deem' heavily amended] proper; and trusting that the wisdom of Parliament, before whom it at present depends, will devise means for settling this very interesting business on principles of moderation, humanity and Justice.
Archibald Graham, Convener
John Gordon
James Gordon

Minute Dublin 29 March 1788[b]

[The text of the resolutions is identical to that published except for some additional punctuation, changes in capitalisation, and one trivial word change]

Travers Hartley Esq. President

Joshua Pim	Abraham Wilkinson	William Cope
Leland Crosthwaite	William Rawlins	John Bins
Alexander Jaffray Junr.		

The order of the Day being read to take into consideration the Slave Trade.

The Chamber of Commerce of the City of Dublin having observed with much satisfaction the generous disposition prevalent among their fellow Subjects in Great Britain to effect an abolition of the Slave Trade a disposition so congenial to the character of an humane and enlightened Nation and at the same time having indulged themselves in the reflection that the Traffic in the human Species does not appear to have been ever carried on from this Kingdom, yet wishing to be in any degree assistant to the great and good works ['work' in printed] of relieving Numbers of their fellow Creatures and desirous that any apprehension of this Country engaging in that odious Traffic may be obviated, have deem'd it expedient to come to the following Resolutions.

RESOLVED that if the British Legislature shall think fit to pass a Law for abolishing the Slave Trade it will be desirable for the Legislature of Ireland to cooperate with that humane and wise measure by the enaction of a similar Statue in this Kingdom.

RESOLVED that the Chamber will not fail at the proper time to make humble application to the House of Commons for that purpose in which they cannot question having the support of every rank and description of Irishman.

RESOLVED that a copy of these proceedings be transmitted to Granville Sharpe Esq. Chairman of the Society in London for abolition of the Slave Trade and that our worthy President be requested to Sign the same.

ORDERED that these proceedings be printed in Saunders's News Letter, the Dublin Evening Post and in a London news paper.

Adjourned to Wednesday at 8 o'Clock [2 April 1788]

[Minutes continue in the same hand of the secretary, William Shannon, on the same page with a ruling identical to that between earlier meetings, but no further meetings are minuted until:]

Minute Dublin 25 February 1791[b]

Abraham Wilkinson Esq. in the Chair

Joshua Pim	Edward Forbes	R. McDonnell
William Rawlins	John Lindsay	Danl. Marston Esq.
Leland Crosthwait	Frederick Geale	Alex. Jaffray
William Colvill		

RESOLVED that a Committee be appointed to prepare a Petition to Parliament relative to the proposed additional duty on Rum.

RESOLVED that said Committee consist of Mr. Rawlins, Mr. James Hartley, Mr. P. Wilkinson, Mr. Crosthwait, Mr. McDonnell, Mr. Lindsay, Mr. Lunell, Mr. Forbes, Mr. Pim, Mr. O'Connor, Mr. Hone, Mr. Litton and Mr. E. Hutchinson.

The Secretary presented his account of disbursements amounting to £83. 17. 7½

Ordered that the Treasurer do pay the same.

Adjourned till tomorrow at one o'Clock.

[Next minutes continue in the different hand of Joseph Miller as Secretary, on the same page but with a much heavier triple ruling; next meeting minuted is:]

Minute Dublin 27 May 1805[b]

LIST OF THE COUNCIL OF THE CHAMBER OF COMMERCE ELECTED MONDAY 27th MAY 1805.
Vide Journal of the Chamber.

[a list of 21 names then follows, and minutes continue from 13 June 1805 thereafter in the new hand. The 'Old Chamber' is first referred to on 23 July: see below. The 'Journal of the Chamber' referred to, for which this constitutes the only reference, no longer exists]

Minutes Dublin 23 July 1805[b]

The Secretary presented the following Letter that he had received from Joshua Pim Esq.

Ordered that Mr. Pim's letter be entered on the Journal and that it be referred to the consideration of the Council at large.

12 July 1805[b]

Dear Sir,

The Old Chamber of Commerce stands indebted to me as Treasurer, the sum of £210. 8. 10 without any charge of Interest which would probably make it £50 more—

Of their Property there are, or ought to be in the Brown Case at the Royal Exchange, sundry volumes of the Irish Statutes and any of the Journals which are there I believe belong to Mr. Hartley.

I have in my hands

Ruffhead's British Statutes complete down to 1785, with general Index—ten Volumes.—Manuscript List of Imports & Exports as laid before Parliament from 1782 to 1805. Twenty three large volumes, one wanting, which is to be made good,—these alone would cost nearly £400, and prefixed to the first Volume is a digest or abstract of Imports and Exports of the Principal Articles for twenty years preceding—

These valuable documents I consider as Public Property if redeemed, & on that condition they are at the service of that respectable Association who have had the good fortune to acquire the assistance of your eminent Talents—

I am truly Dear Sir, Your sincere Friend,
Joshua Pim

Index of Proceedings, Bristol SMV 6 March 1788[c]

A Memorial to the Lords of the Council of Trade on the Importance of the African Trade sealed and the business referred to the standing Committee.

13 March 1788[c]

Mr. Anderson and Mr. Bailie requested to attend in London on the African Business.

27 March 1788[c]

An Answer returned requesting attendance of the Gentlemen deputed to support [the] Society's Memorial on the African Business.

7 April 1788[c]

Committee proceeded to collect Information in support of their Memorial on the Slave Trade.

5 July 1788[c]

Petition to the Lords against African Regulation Bill sent to Stephen Fuller Agent for Jamaica.

24 July 1788[c]

A letter from the Deputies from Liverpool respecting the Slave Trade read.—The Society having paid the expenses of the Gentlemen they deputed are of the opinion the Application from the Liverpool Deputies should be made to the African Company.

Outletter Merchants Hall 31 July 1788[d]

To: John Tarleton Esq. Liverpool

Sir,

The Letter of the 11th Inst. from you and the other Gentlemen deputed from Liverpool to oppose the Slave Bill was laid before the Committee of the Society of Merchants here—they were of Opinion that the Society having deputed Gentlemen to attend in London on their part, whose Expenses they have of Course borne, any Application respecting those incurred by the Gentlemen of Liverpool should be made to the Members of the African Company,

I am Sir Sinc.,
William Randolph, Warden.

Outletter 25 April 1789[d]

To: Henry Cruger Esq, Parliament Coffee House, Parliament Street, London

Sir,

The Committee for conducting the Opposition to the intended Abolition of the Slave Trade have just learnt that Mt. Brickdale will be prevented by Illness from attending the House [on] Monday so that the petitions agreed to by the Hall, the planters, Manufacturers &c. cannot be delivered to him at Bath, on his Road as proposed—They directed me to acquaint you that they would be sent to you by the Mail Coach Tomorrow addressed to the Parliament Coffee House, Parliament Street, but lest you might not be in the Way, not being apprised that you were to Exhibit them, I have written by their Orders to Mr. Gordon & Mr. Thos. Daniel to beg they would, should you be absent, put them under the Care of Mr. [Edward] Phillips or Mr. [George] Berkeley. …I am Sir &c.

Jere Osborne

[Similar letters to Wm. Gordon and Thos. Daniel]

5.14 The manufacturing lobbying networks 1825

A letter was sent in 1825 from the Manchester chamber to other committees and chambers around the country with a copy of the chamber's address on allowing the free importation of machinery, subject to only very restricted exceptions. This gives a grasp of how one network of chambers at this time was operating, the extent to which other bodies were involved, and the individuals who were called upon to support chamber opinion where no chamber existed. Thirty-six places were circulated, as well as all of Manchester's chamber members. Of the 36 only six were chambers. Of the others, four were Mayors, one a Boroughreeve, and in Sheffield the Master Cutler, eleven were single individual businessmen, and 13 business partnerships. The list of chambers for 1825 for mainland UK omits Edinburgh, Greenock, the Liverpool American, Newcastle, and Plymouth. The list also misses Jersey and Guernsey, and in Ireland omits Cork, Limerick, Newry, Sligo, and Waterford. It does not, however, list any location which has a chamber using an alternative contact. The Manchester list is therefore useful more to indicate the locations which Manchester sought to network with, rather than to check on the existence of chambers. But it also demonstrates the gaps in chamber systems at this date, and the continued ad hoc involvement of delegates. The locations contacted have a heavy bias towards textile manufacturing in the North West and generally ignored the ports, unless they were also textile manufacturing locations (such as Belfast, Dublin and Glasgow). Bristol is the only exception to this. It can be compared with the network of the General Chamber (see Garbett's correspondence in section 5.5 above), and the much narrower network used for the 'Union 'of chambers in 1794–1805, with which Manchester was also involved (see Chapter 9).

Source
Proceedings of the chamber of commerce; Manchester Central Library GB127. M8/2/1

List added to minute 30 March 1825

Manchester	Every member of the ***Chamber***
Birmingham	***Chamber of Commerce***
Blackburn	Wm. Maude Esq.
Bolton	The Boroughreeve
do.	Messrs E. & W. Bolling
Bristol	***Chamber of Commerce***
Bury	Messrs. Howarth Hartman & Co.
Carlisle	The Mayor
Chorley	Messrs. John Harrison & Co.
Coventry	The Mayor
Derby	Messrs. Strutts
Dudley	W. Hodgett Esq.
Halifax	Rawson & Saltmansheet
Huddersfield	Mr. Haigh Esq.
Keighley	Mr. Clayton Esq.
Kidderminster	Rd. Watson Esq.
Leeds	John Marshall Esq.
do.	Benjamin Gott Esq.
Leicester	Messrs. Pares Heygate & Co.
Macclesfield	Messrs. Charles Wood & Co.
Norwich	Messrs. Oxley & Sons
Nottingham	Francis Hardwick Esq.
Preston	Messrs Horrockses Miller & Co.
Rochdale	Messrs Fenton & Co.
Rotherham	Samuel Walker Esq.
Sheffield	The Master Cutler
Stockport	Thomas Marsland Esq.
Warrington	Messrs. Cockshott & Grun
Wigan	The Mayor
Glasgow	***Chamber of Commerce***
Dundee	***Chamber of Commerce***

Belfast	***Chamber of Commerce***
Dublin	***Chamber of Commerce***
Frome	Messrs. H. G. & W. Sheppard
Gloucester	The Mayor
Taunton	Newbery Son & Co.
Wey	Edward Sheppard Esq.

Chapter 6

Services and Activities

As noted in the Introduction, the chambers for the period from the 1760s to the 1830s developed a bundle of services and activities that was to change significantly in the next period. Although there was variation between localities, the service mix for the early chambers generally covered eight fields:

1. Representation and lobbying (active in all chambers).
2. Commercial arbitration (in about 50–60 per cent of chambers).
3. Market management, e.g. of prices, quality standards, output, etc. (in about 10–15 per cent of chambers, mostly in Ireland).
4. Local promotion and improvement initiatives (varying greatly over time, but followed in almost all chambers for some periods).
5. Coffee houses, reading and newspaper rooms (in about 30 per cent of chambers, with an additional 10–15 per cent with libraries).
6. Information supply, mainly through formal and informal meetings —discourse (all chambers).
7. Services in a crisis: e.g. convoy, naval and impressment arrangements; financial crisis assistance (most chambers at some times).
8. Support to the state: e.g. information provision to the Board of Trade (most chambers)
9. Ad hoc and opportunistic services, such as lotteries (a few chambers).

The mix varied over time, but all the successful and longer-lived early chambers developed two or three services in addition to the services that all supplied: of representation, information supply, and meetings and discourse. A graph of their evolution shows how the mix varied over time from the early chambers up to the present.[1] The documents below seek to highlight some of the features and tensions that arose in the provision. The first set of documents covers the arbitration function, which was developed first as a formal body in the Dublin Ouzel Galley Society, which became part of the Dublin chamber. This was never a high-volume service, but it was high status—demonstrating the quasi-judicial status of chambers—and drew on their expertise and elite position as efficient arbiters to resolve disputes

[1] R. J. Bennett, 'Chambers of Commerce: From Protesters to Government Partners', *British Academy Review*, 20 (2012) Figure 2; for services in Ireland see R. J. Bennett, 'Management adaptation of business association services', *Irish Journal of Management*, 35, 1 (2016) Figure 1.

cheaply and quickly. The second set of documents shows some of the activities of market management for the Irish chambers. The third group of documents covers examples of promotional activities, whilst the fourth and fifth groups cover help in crises: convoying and naval issues, and helping overcome financial crises and specie shortage. The sixth group introduces an initiative whereby the chambers were first explicitly recruited by the state as information sources, by the Board of Trade in the 1830s. Finally two groups of documents cover ad hoc services related to Marine Societies for distressed seamen and their widows, and to fund-raising opportunities provided by lotteries. This set of examples excludes the coffee houses, reading and newspaper rooms, and information supply through formal and informal meetings that were critical features promoting discourse within chamber memberships, which are covered extensively in Bennett, *Local Business Voice* (2011) 501–38.

6.1. Commercial Arbitration

The Ouzel Galley Society in Dublin founded in 1705 was one of the first bodies mainly for the conduct of commercial arbitration, although also as a social organisation. The rules of the society as a whole are reproduced below in their earliest complete form in 1799 when the rules of the Society was regularised. Its relevance is that it cooperated with the chamber and, in effect, provided one of its services. The society's officers are referred to by ranks as on a ship. Before 1799 the first surviving record is for 1748 when the society was re-established under a new committee, which was ordered to prepare a new set of rules. No further records survive until 1751 when its committee positions had been filled, but no rules are recorded. The transaction books of the society are then continuous and record various amendments and developments of the rules but no complete statement.[2] It cooperated with the Dublin Society of merchants, and from 1783 with the chamber of commerce. In 1888 the Ouzel Society was voluntarily wound up and passed all its papers and activities to the chamber. Its origins, activities and history have been covered in more detail elsewhere.[3] The arbitration rules are given below. Griffith argues that there may have been little actual arbitration activity in its early life, and there are only three surviving records of arbitration over the

[2] RIA: Ouzel Galley Transactions Book, 15 February–18 December 1823: MS 12 F 48E.

[3] C. L. Falkiner, 'Some Illustrations of the Commercial History of Dublin in the Eighteenth Century', *Proceedings of the Royal Irish Academy*, 24 (1902–4) 133–153; G. A. Little, 'The Ouzel Galley', *Dublin Historical Record*, 3 (1940) 1–30; *The Ouzel Galley* (Dublin, 1953); Cullen, *Princes and Pirates* (1983); and L. M. Griffith, 'The Ouzel Galley Society in the Eighteenth Century', 165–185 in Michael Brown and Seán Patrick Donlan eds. *The Laws and Other Legalities of Ireland, 1689–1850* (Aldershot, 2011).

early period 1748–99.[4] The first was a minute in 1756 that 'Any Member of this Society, who shall have a difference in point of trade with any person whatever and shall refuse to leave the same to the Arbitration of indifferent Judges to be chosen out of the Galley, shall not be allowed any longer to continue a Member thereof, but shall be expelled from this Society'. Second, the Society declined to arbitrate in a case in 1775, ruling that the case was not a point of trade, but a point of law. The third reference is the rules reproduced below, which were part of the new rules of the society regularised in 1799. The arbitration rules below immediately follow these. Falkiner states that 364 arbitration awards were made 1799–1869.[5] The analysis here shows 412 cases over this period, but some resulted in no conclusion or award. The full arbitration records of the Society reproduced below cover 1799–1879, when cases appear to have ceased being referred to the Society.

Many other chambers provide examples in their minutes of occasional settlement of disputes. These often seem to occur irrespective of whether there was a specific provision in the rules for arbitration. The example reproduced for the first Leeds chamber is the only case in its early history covering 1785–93. Another significant example is John Weskett's *Plan of the Chamber of Commerce* in 1782 (reproduced in Chapter 3). This was both for a chamber and to offer an arbitration function. He may have taken forward the idea from the Ouzel Galley. It operated in London 1782–1800.[6] The chamber offered that business people 'may have a *constant*, or an *occasional* recourse to this office … in like manner as they might have to a confidential friend, agent or correspondent' (Article I); 'immediate, and confirmed appointments are given for *verbal* consultation and conference' (Article II); 'from consultation, opinion, advice and information naturally result' (Article III), which include representation to government and others. The chamber could also act as a legal representative or agent for 'attending or transacting with other people, bodies, courts, MPs, government', thus 'forming and drawing of minutes, memorials, petitions, remonstrances, appeals, proposals, plans'. Weskett charged subscriptions of three guineas annual fee 'for constant resort for advice' (as described by Article II), or five guineas for a two-year service. Although it was limited, this was the first London chamber of commerce, and it operated for 18 years: Weskett is listed in the *Browne's General Law List* for all years 1787–1800 as 'Director of the chamber of commerce, Cornhill'. Weskett's chamber was not a true chamber of commerce, but is a

[4] Griffith 'Ouzel Galley Society' (2011).
[5] Falkiner, 'Illustrations' (1902–4) 146.
[6] See Chapter 3 for Weskett's *Plan* for a London chamber. Sutherland, *London Merchant* (1933) 56–7, 264–5, 518–9, quotes various legal cases he was involved with; some of these must have resulted from actions on behalf of others through his chamber.

valuable early example of an arbitration service developed under the brand of chamber. He may have influenced the development of arbitration in chambers. His activity seems to have been copied by Bignold and Clarke in London in 1817, reproduced here, who explicitly drew on the Ouzel Galley Society. It is not clear that Bignold and Clarke's 'Equitable Trade Society and Chamber of Commerce' actually developed since there are no other reports of it. Unlike Weskett there are no *Law List* or trade directory listings to indicate its existence. The credibility of the proposers also appears somewhat suspect compared to Weskett who was well connected with the African Company and had considerable experience of commercial dealings.[7] The qualifications of Clarke that he prominently quotes (twice) as Member of the Etruscan Academy of Antiquities at Cortona in Tuscany, and Inter Arcades 'Filarco Eldense', at Rome, are unlikely to have been very convincing to a commercial community seeking expertise to sort out complex commercial disputes. Indeed, commenting in 1819, it was stated that an attempt to establish a chamber in London had 'proceeded so far as to enter the names of members under the title of "The Equitable Trust Society" … [but] that it is not the kind of institution that is adapted to the temper and disposition of Englishmen—at least not in the metropolis'.[8] This confirms that that Bignold and Clarke's initiative was still-born. However, some of the supporters quoted, particularly Benjamin Shaw MP and Thomas Smith, were prominent commercial figures in the City, as also were the bankers Smith, Payne, and Smiths quoted as the Treasurers. Hence it is possible that the body had a short life. During London discussions in 1823 (reproduced in Chapter 4), Pascoe Grenfell's Report states that 'In the year 1817, private meetings were held, at which the subject was considered and discussed, the expediency of forming such as Institution [a London chamber] was unanimously admitted, and the propriety of convening a General Meeting of Merchants, Bankers, Ship-owners and others, at some convenient period, for the purpose of carrying the object into effect, was determined upon. From a variety of circumstances … the convening of a general meeting has been hitherto suspended'. Thus although the 1817 initiative was still-born, it may have stimulated later initiatives that sought a more general chamber, and it is notable for including some of the same individuals, such as Thomas Smith, who was still involved in 1823 (see Chapter 4).

[7] See Chapter 3, and Bennett, *Local Business Voice* (2011) 100.

[8] Goldsmiths-Kress/MTMW: *The London Tradesman: a familiar treatise on the rationale of trade and commerce* (London, 1819).

Sources
[a] Ouzel Galley, Transactions Book; RIA MS 12 F 48E; see also Little, G. A. (1953) The Ouzel Galley, pp. 27–9.
[b] Ouzel Galley, Arbitration Books 1799–1884; RIA 12 F 46–8.
[c] Leeds chamber of commerce minute Book; Leeds University Library MS Dep 1951/1
[d] *The Courier*, London.

Minute: Rules of Ouzel Galley Society 1799[a]

Your Committee have blended together the actual Rules, Orders and Customs of the Galley, with such further Rules and Orders as appear to them desirable to be adopted, and report as follows, viz.

The Ouzel Galley consists of a number of Members not exceeding forty.

The officers are the Captain, two Lieutenants, Master, Bursar, Boatswain, Gunner, Carpenter, Master's Mate, Coxswain, Boatswains' Mate, Gunner's Mate, and Carpenter's Mate, of whom the Captain, two Lieutenants, Master, Bursar, Boatswain, Gunner and Carpenter should form the Council.

The Galley has three Annual Meetings, which appear to have been usually held on the 16th of April, the 12th of July or 1st of August, and the 4th November; but these days have been very frequently changed for other days in the same, and even in other months at the discretion of the Captain.

The Captain or, in his absence, the Senior Officer on board, has supreme command at every Meeting of the Galley, and any disobedience to him is mutiny.

The business of the Galley is transacted at the Meeting in November, for which purpose the Council should meet at half-past Three o'Clock, and the Members at Four o'Clock.

No person to be balloted for as a Member, but such as shall be nominated for that purpose by the Captain or Commanding Officer, with the approbation of the Council, and a list of the persons to be balloted for should be exhibited in the room before dinner.

The ballot for *Officers* should take place before dinner, and that for new Members after dinner.

No ballot should take place unless sixteen Members at the least be present.

In the ballot for Officers a majority of the Members present elects.

In the ballot for new Members one black ball out of four excludes.

At each meeting the Captain appoints the junior Member present to be Commissary of Stores; his duty is to take an account of the wine, and examine the bill, which done, the Captain or Commanding Officer certifies it to the Bursar for payment.

The Annual Subscription is one Guinea, which ought to be increased if so required by the Council; such requisition to be first agreed by a majority of the Members present after dinner, at the November Meeting.

All expenses of the Galley are paid by the Subscription Fund.

[Rules of arbitration follow]

Minutes 1799[a]

Your Committee have blended together the actual Rules, Orders and Customs of the Galley, with such further Rules and Orders as appear to them desirable to be adopted, and report as follows, viz.

RULES AS TO ARBITRATIONS

It is the duty of all Members of the Galley to sit as Arbitrators in the settlement of any matter in dispute to them referred, provided all the Arbitrators chosen are Members of the Galley.

Parties are not to make any personal application whatsoever to Members of the Galley, either respecting their appointment as Arbitrators, or the subject of the matter in dispute. Respecting the appointment, the parties, after they have chosen Arbitrators, are to acquaint the Registrar, whose duty it is to inform the Members chosen; and respecting the matter in dispute, it must be spoken of before the Arbitrators, only in presence of the parties or their agents; or where cases or evidence in writing are submitted, they must be transmitted, sealed up, through the hands of the Registrar.

The parties referring matters to arbitration are to deposit with the Registrar a sum of money to insure the payment of the Galley Fees, which are appropriated, after payment of the costs of the award, to a charitable fund.

Parties to have the choice of their Arbitrators; but the Arbitrators, in all cases, to have the appointment of an Umpire, if necessary.

Arbitration Cases 1799–1879[b]

Arbitration cases, count by year

1799[1]	3	1825	3	1851	2
1800	13	1826	4	1852	4
1801	31	1827	3	1853	2
1802	28	1828	1	1854	0
1803	28	1829	5	1855	0
1804	21	1830	7	1856	0
1805	18	1831	1	1857	0
1806	8	1832	3	1858	3
1807	22	1833	2	1859	1

1808	13	1834	3	1860	1
1809[2]	12	1835	3	1861	1
1810	11	1836	0	1862	2
1811	14	1837[3]	2	1863	0
1812	12	1838	6	1864	0
1813	10	1839	1	1865	0
1814	7	1840	2	1866	1
1815	12	1841	3	1867	2
1816	9	1842	2	1868–72	none
1817	5	1843	2	1873	3
1818	9	1844	4	1874	3
1819	6	1845	3	1875	1
1820	2	1846	2	1876	1
1821	11	1847	5	1877	0
1822	4	1848	1	1878	0
1823	7	1849	1	1879[4]	1
1824	7	1850	1	**Total**	**421**

[1] Last two months of year only.

[2] Combines year from end of book MS 12 F 46 and start of book MS 12 F 47.

[3] One page missing (several loose pages at this point): an estimate that it contained one case is included.

[4] No further cases listed after 1879 though there are free pages in book MS 12 F 48.

Leeds chamber Minute Leeds, 21 December 1789[c]

At a meeting held this day specially & at the request of Messrs. Alexr. Turner & Co.

Present Messrs. Bernard Bischoff & Sons, Messrs. Rhodes & Hibblethwaite, Messrs. Thomas Cookson & Sons, Messrs. R. & R Bramley, Messrs. Bros. Oates & Wilson, Messrs. Oates & Kighley, Messrs. Fenton & Wainhouse, Messrs. Dixon & Co., Messrs. Petr. Tolson & Sons, Messrs. Smithson & Rayner, Messrs. Dawson & Smith, Messrs. Ridsdale & Beaumont, & Mr. Robt. Wareing, & Mr. Woolfendale in behalf of Messrs. Brook & Co. of Leghorn—

It was stated by Mr. Alexr. Turner in the name of his House that by order of said Messrs. Brook & Co. of Leghorn they had forwarded & sent 2 Bales of Cloths in the Month of September last year Amo[un]t £210. 3. 3 A. [on account] of Invoice of which Messrs. Brook acknowledged receipt & Credit given for its Import by Letter dated from Legho[rn] the 7th Oct. same Year, but from which Sum the Complainants Messrs. Alexr. Turner & Co. state, that said Messrs. Brook & Co. do keep back a Balance of £119. 3. 9¼. which at this day is still due & owing to them.

At the request therefore of Messrs. Alexander & Co. aforesaid on the one part & as appears by a Letter from Messrs. Brook & Co. on the other part and confirmed by Mr. Woolfendale in person, in their names & at their request, we at this meeting caused to be laid before us the whole of the Correspondence on this Business viz. all the Letters received from & Copies of those wrote to Messrs. Brook & Co. which Letters & Copies of Letters being read & examined & hearing & examining Mr. Turner concerning every circumstance of enquiry which the said Letters & Copies of Letters led to, & this in the presence of said Mr. Woolfendale, we desired the parties to retire into an adjacent Room that deliberation might be enter'd upon more freely & impartially; which deliberation concluded & Mr. Turner & Mr. Woolfendale again present, We signified & made known to them that it was the opinion of this Chamber that the said Messrs. Brook & Co. are justly & truly indebted to the said Messrs. Alexr. Turner & Co. the sum of £119. 3. 9¼. as stated above, which sum or any part thereof said Messrs. Brook & Co. cannot keep back any longer without committing an act of the greatest Injustice.

By order of the Meeting.

Printed Report 26 December 1817[d]

EQUITABLE TRADE SOCIETY and CHAMBER of COMMERCE; Instituted at London, in the Year 1817, No. 38, New Bridge-street, Blackfriars, THOS BIGNOLD Esq. Founder and President.
FRED. ARNAUD CLARKE, Esq. (of Battersea Rise,) F.S. A. Soc. Acad. Etrus. Cortone, et Int. Arcad. Rome &c. Vice President and Secretary:
MEMBERS,

Sir ____ Blakiston, Bart.	Sir John Perring, Bt. Ald. M.P.
Benjamin Shaw, Esq. M.P.	Thomas Smith; Esq. & Ald.
Marc J. Brunel, Esq. F.R.S. &c.	Stephen Nicolson Barber, Esq.
Alexander Lamb, Esq.	Thomas Simpson, Esq.
James Harding, Esq.	John Hanson, Esq.
Solomon Cheek, Esq.	Thomas Wilson, Esq.
Coles Child, Esq.	James Rawlins, Esq.
Christopher Ridout Read, Esq.	Timothy Francis Power, Esq.
John Stachlschmidt, Esq.	John Fry, Esq.
Allen Pering, Esq.	Robert John Bunyon, Esq.
George Le Boutillier, Esq.	James Lewis Kennedy, Esq
Henry Benham, Esq.	Matthew Gilbertson, Esq
John Boden, Esq.	William Bourfield, Esq
Frederick Thornhill, Esq.	John Goldsmith, Esq.

Henry Pybus, Esq.
Samuel Bignold, Esq.
Richard Wilson, Esq.
Thomas Hodgson , Esq.
Joseph Lovell, Esq.
John Pennyman Nodin, Esq.
Mr. Robert Kemp,
Mr. James White,
Mr. William Randall,
Mr. Charles Ball,
Mr. James Douglas,
Mr. Joseph Carter,
Mr. Thomas Baker,
Mr. Benjamin Hughes,
Mr. William Bignell,
Mr. James Adams,
Mr. Thomas Hills,
William Nettleton, Esq.
Goodman Roberts, Esq.
Joseph Rawlins, Esc.
Henry Dobbs, Esq.
Richard Willett, Esq.
Joseph Munn, Esq.
Mr. George Heighington,
Mr. John Warren,
Mr. Robert Ashby,
Mr. John Crowe,
Mr. Joseph Harrison,
Mr. William Joshua Tilley,
Mr. John Sparks,
Mr. Thomas Lay,
Mr. Samuel Rust,
Mr. Garrett Andrews,
Mr. Wm. Atkinson, &c. &c.

TREASURERS

SMITH, PAYNE, and SMITHS, Esqrs. Bankers.

The Chief objects of the Society are, the arbitration and adjustment of disputed Accounts, &c.—the Prevention of Suits at Law—the benefit of the Commercial and Trading Interest of this Kingdom—and for providing a Fund, for the purpose of affording aid to honest but unfortunate Tradesmen, &c. And in pursuance of this plan, the Society have already constituted several respectable Local Committees and Agents in the Country.

The Meetings of the Committee are held every alternate Thursday, at the Society's House, at 11 o'clock, precisely. In order still further to promote the laudable views of the Society, it may be necessary to explain the mode by which the Members are elected, and business conducted. Each Member has the privilege at the Meetings of the Society, or by letter to the Secretary, to propose any person who is desirous to become a Member, provided the proposal contains the name, with the full addition, and place of abode, of the party proposed. The number of Members is unlimited, and the annual contribution Twenty Shillings, in aid of the Funds of the Institution.

All Members are entitled to vote and assist in all the business of the Chamber of Commerce, and the several Committees. Ladies are eligible, as Members of the Society, to all the privileges thereof, and are alone entitled to vote by proxy at elections, through the medium of any Gentleman who is a Member, on his producing a written authority for the same. All communications to the Equitable Trade Society and Chamber of Commerce, are to be made by letter, addressed to the Secretary.

An Annual General Meeting of Members is held on the fourth day of June.

On an application for the adjustment of any matter in dispute, the contending parties are to state the particulars in writing, and direct the same to the Secretary, who will lay, the case before the Commitee, and whose duty it is to inform the Members chosen; or where cases or evidences in writing are submitted, they must be transmitted, sealed up, through the hands of the Secretary.

It is also the office of the Vice President and Secretary to take charge of Papers lodged with him, and lay the same before the Arbitrators;—to issue Notices in writing to the proper persons of all meetings and summonses to the parties and witnesses to attend; to draw up the submissions and awards, and register the same; and to deliver the awards to the parties or their Agents. The parties referring matters to arbitration, are to deposit with the Secretary, a sum of Money, to insure the payment of the Society's Fees, which are duly appropriated, after payment of the Costs of the Award, and incidental charges, to a Charitable Fund, upon the approved plan of the 'OUZEL-GALLEY', of Dublin. Persons have the choice of their Arbitrators; but the Arbitrators in all Cases, have the appointment of an Umpire, if necessary. The Society, anxious to promote the improvement of Trade, further invite the communications of Mercantile and Professional Men, upon all subjects connected with the views of the Society, as such valuable information may afford ground for more extensive exertions, and thus materially contribute to the advantage of the Public. The Law Library of the Society, may receive considerable encouragement from the presents of Members, or other persons who may be inclined to place useful Books, relative to the Laws of Trade, or valuable Manuscripts to form a Digest, in a Repository, at once permanent and conducive to the national benefit. As the endeavours of the Society can be generally successful, only inasmuch as their views are seconded by the Public, the Society request the concurrence of Merchants, &c. to enlarge their Body. The Rules and Regulations may be had (GRATIS), on proper application. All Receipts for Subscription Money, are signed by the Secretary, of whom further information may he obtained.—(By Order of the Society), FREDERICK ARNAUD CLARKE, V. P. and Sec.

Speedily will be Published.

AN EXPLANATION of the PLAN of the EQUITABLE TRADE SOCIETY, and CHAMBER of COMMERCE, instituted at London, in 1817; together with OBSERVATIONS and SUGGESTIONS, connected with the Subject, calculated to promote the IMPROVEMENT of TRADE: —to which are added, the RULES and REGULATIONS of the INSTITUTION.—By FREDERICK ARNAUD CLARKE, Esq, of Battersea-Rise, Member of the Etruscan Academy of Antiquities at Cortona in Tuscany,—INTER ARCADES 'Filarco Eldense', at Rome, &c. &c. &c.

6.2 Management of Markets

Sources
[a] Dublin Chamber of Commerce, Minute Book: TNAI
[b] Limerick Chamber of Commerce, Minute Book 1, entry from page 1ff: Limerick Archives P1/1

Minute: Resolutions on Brokerage 12 July 1783[a]

To the Council of the Chamber of Commerce

The report of the Committee appointed to enquire into the rates of Brokerage and the mode of transacting business by the same Brokers in this City etc. etc.

Your Committee having carefully considered the Subject referred to them are of opinion

That the following fees of Brokerage are proper to be adopted:

SUGARS
per Hhd 1/3 Tierce 1/- Barrel 6d.
Tarpaulins to be found by the Broker
HOPS in Bags & Packets 1/-
TOBACCO
Home Consumption 2/6
Export 1/-
WINE OIL SPIRITS VINEGAR
1/3 per pipe 1/- per Hhd 6d. per Tierce or 3d. per Cask
ASHES
Barrilled in Matts 8/- Pearl in Casks 2/-
Cases per Barrel 4d. American Pearl & Pot 6d. per barrel
FLAXSEED
6d. per Hhd, if sold in parcels of £100—value 1/2 per Cent
other Seeds 1/- per Package
OIL
6d. per Chest. Raisins & other Articles for which one Sample
answers 1/- per lot if sold in Parcells of £100—value 1/2 per Cent
COTTON 1/- per bag
INDIGO, SILK, COCHINEAL, CURRANTS 1/4 per Cent
TEAS 1/2 per Cent
SHIPS
a Guinea or 1/2 per Cent on the value, at the Brokers option, same if by Auction & half Brokerage if bought in for the Seller

Auctions same as by private Sale Goods bought in for the Seller half Brokerage

No goods to be chargeable with Brokerage, unless Sold by the Broker or at his Office except by particular agreement

Your Committee having conferred through the Brokers with the Buyer and Seller frequenting their Offices—are of Opinion:

That it would be highly to the convenience and advantage of Trade were the Offices of the Brokers shut on Saturdays and open the remainder of the Week from 12 o'Clock

Your Committee are of Opinion, that any person professing the business of a Broker should be sworn to act impartially between Buyer and Seller, and not to deal in any article on his own Account in which he is accustomed to act as Broker which Oath signed by the Magistrate should be returned to the Secretary of the Chamber of Commerce and Registered in their Books.

Resolved that the regulations for the rates of Brokerage and the mode of transacting business by the several Brokers of this city be printed and a Copy sent by the Secretary to each of the Brokers a Copy to be also given to each Member of the Chamber who shall call for it.

Resolved that a Committee be appointed to take into consideration the rates of Brokerage on freighting Ships and on collecting freights and to report to this Council their opinion what are the rates at present paid and what rates ought to be paid on Saturday next.

Minute: *Agreement of 21 October 1809* 3 November 1809[b]

ARTICLES OF AGREEMENT made concluded and agreed upon this Twenty first day of October in the year of our Lord one thousand Eight hundred and nine Between the undersigned executing parties hereto of the one part, and John Carroll of the City of Limerick Gentleman Secretary to the Chamber of Commerce of Limerick of the other part WHEREAS the Committee of the Chamber of Commerce aforesaid have taken from the Corporation of the said City of Limerick the Gateage Tolls and Customs of the said City, on Corn, Grain, Flour, Oatmeal and Potatoes from the day of the date of these presents until the full end and Term of one year for the Sum of One thousand Five hundred pounds, with a view to have the power of preventing the Abuses committed by the Collectors of Tolls & Customs in extortion and otherwise and also of exonerating the article of Potatoes from all charge whatsoever.

AND WHEREAS the said Committee have agreed to and with the said executing parties hereto, that no Toll Custom or other charge shall during the said year, be paid on Potatoes—NOW in order to enable the said Committee to carry the aforesaid purposes fully into effect, the said executing parties hereto do hereby respectively each for himself and not the one for the other and for each of their Executors Administrators Partners and Assigns—covenant promise and agree to and with the said John Carroll his Successors and Assigns that they (the said executing Parties) and each of them respectively shall and will from time to time and at all times, from the day of the date hereof, until the Twenty first day of October which will be in the year of our Lord one Thousand eight hundred and ten, pay or cause to be paid to the said John Carroll his Successors, or Assigns on all Corn Flour Oatmeal Pease Beans and Rapeseed which either of them or either of their Partners shall purchase during the said year the Rates following that is to say the Sum of Three pence per Barrel, for each and every Barrel of Wheat of Twenty Stone—the sum of one penny three farthings per Barrel for each and every Barrel of Barley of Sixteen Stone—the Sum of three halfpence per Barrel for each and every Barrell of Oats of Fourteen Stone—the Sum of Three pence per Sack for each and every Sack of Flour of Two hundred weight—the Sum of three halfpence per hundred weight, for each and every hundred weight of oatmeal—the Sum of three halfpence per Barrel, for each and every Barrel of Pease or Beans of Twenty Stone—And the Sum of three halfpence per Barrel, for each and every Barrel of Rapeseed of Sixteen Stone—Which said Rates they the said executing parties hereto do hereby bind themselves (each for himself and not the one for the other) and each of their Executors Administrators Partners and Assigns to Stop and deduct from the Sellers of Corn Grain Flour Oatmeal Pease Beans and Rapeseed and pay over the same unto the said John Carroll his Successors or Assigns some one day in every fourteen days during the said Year—or for every omission or neglect in so doing to pay unto the said John Carroll his Successors or Assigns the sum of Fifty Pounds—AND that each of them their Executors Administrators Partners or Assigns shall within Ten days after the expiration of the said year pay unto the said John Carroll his Successors or Assigns the Rates that shall be due of them and every of them up to and including the said Twenty first day of October, which will be the year one thousand eight hundred and ten under the penalty of paying unto the said John Carroll his Successors or Assigns the sum of one Hundred pounds for the omission or neglect to do so—AND the said John Carroll Doth hereby for himself his Executors Administrators and Assigns covenant promise and declare that the agreement herein before made to him of the Rates aforesaid was so made and accepted of by him in Trust only and to and for the only proper Sole use, Benefit and behalf of the Committee of the Chamber of Commerce of Limerick and for no other use Intent or purpose whatsoever—IN WITNESS whereof the Parties hereto have hereunto put their hands and affixed their Seals the Day and Year first herein before Written—

6.3 Improvements and Infrastructure

Source
Manchester Commercial Society minutes: Manchester Central Library GB127 M8/1/1

Minute 10 May 1796

The Delegates to Halifax then proceeded to report the Proceedings there, which having done, a Letter from Mr John Lees of Halifax of May 7th was read and also the Proceedings of that Meeting:

[Copy of letter] Halifax 7 May 1796

To: James Edge Esq.

Sir Agreeable to your Request I hand you enclosed a Copy of the Resolutions entered into at the Meeting Yesterday in Consequence of a Proposal made by Mr Milnes of Dewsbury for the Conveyance of Goods from Sowerby, Salter Hebble and Huddersfield Wharfs to and from Hull, that you may lay the same before the Merchants of Manchester, and which hope will meet with their Approbation. The Hurry in which they were drawn up; the Gentlemen attending the Meeting being impatient to return Home many residing at a considerable Distance, will I flatter myself be admitted as a sufficient because for any Incorrectness that may be found in them, this Sketch will however serve as a sufficient Groundwork to proceed upon.

If Mr Milne's Proposal should be generally approved of at Manchester, the principal Object will then be to obtain Subscriptions, and as no less than one Hundred Signatures will be required with so many more as can possibly be got in Order to give greater Influence Stability and Security to the Scheme, we rely very much on the Zeal and Exertions of the Gentlemen of Manchester, the Number of Merchants here and at Rochdale being few in Comparison to those of Manchester

It gives me Pleasure to add that Mr Milnes having been introduced by Mr Waterhouse and myself to many of the Merchants attending the Market here today his Proposal has met with their Approbation, and more especially mention a further Conversation with, he has agreed that Wool and many other raw Materials shall be brought up to the Wharfs at the old Rates of Freight, a most material Object and which I think entitles him to the warmest Support of the Country. I have the Honour to be respectfully

Sir, Your Mst. Hble. Servt.
(Signed) John Lees

[Proceedings of meeting] Talbot Inn Halifax May 6th 1796

A Meeting of Merchants of this Town, Rochdale and Manchester … this Day, pursuant to Notice given, for the Purpose of taking into Consideration the present State of Freights and Water Carriage on the Rivers Aire & Calder, in Consequence of certain Resolutions entered into by the Undertakers of the Aire and Calder Navigation, obliging the Shippers of Goods, take the Dangers and Risk of Water Carriage upon themselves

Present

Messrs. James Edge	Manchester
C.F. Brandt	
Lawrence Peel	
Messrs. Thomas Smith	Rochdale
Benj. Smith	
John Walmsley	
Geo. Hamer	
Newall	
Royds	
Messrs. John Waterhouse	Halifax
W. Walker	
Bramley	
Edwards	
Hamer	
Pryme for Mr Stansfield	
R. Swaine	
Rhodes	
James Hoyle	
Knowles	
S. Smith	
Crossley	
John Lees	

Mr John Lees in the Chair

A Proposal having been made by Mr Richard Milnes of Dewsbury to undertake the Carriage of Goods from Sowerby and Salter Hebble and also Huddersfield Wharfs to and from Hull on certain Conditions hereafter specified, viz.

That a Subscription be opened for the Purpose of raising the Sum of Five Thousand Pounds in Subscriptions of and not exceeding Fifty Pounds each, to be furnished and lodged, with the said Mr Miles for the Purpose of enabling him to provide and fit out a sufficient Number of Vessels, so as to furnish one to depart daily from the beforementioned Wharfs, at the undermentioned Rates of Freight, Mr Miles paying the Subscribers 5% commission per, for the said Sum of Five Thousand Pounds, and the Subscribers engaging on their Parts, to bear out of the said Sum, one half of such Losses or Damages, as may accrue to the Goods of the Subscribers to the said Fund, that may not proceed from Mismanagement, Misconduct, or Negligence on the part of Mr Milnes' Servants or Agents in navigating or loading the said Vessels.

Mr Milnes proposing likewise that the Rates of Freight should hereafter be fixed and determined by and under the Control of a Committee of Delegates of the Subscribers of the beforementioned Towns, to meet Annually to determine the Same.

Resolved

That the said Proposal be accepted, and put in Execution, provided the said Sum of Five Thousand Pounds, be subscribed for, and raised in the Manner and Conditions herein beforementioned.

Resolved

That the Rates of Freight shall be for the Present as follows, viz. from Hull to Manchester (including Land Carriage) forty five Shillings per Ton, From Manchester to Hull (including Land Carriage) Fifty Shillings per Ton. From Hull to Sowerby and Salter Hebble Wharfs, Twenty three Shillings per Ton. From Sowerby and Salter Hebble Wharfs to Hull Twenty Eight Shillings per Ton. The Freight of Wool and other Raw Materials from Hull to Sowerby and Slater Hebble Wharfs to be hereafter fixed and determined by a Committee. The said Rules to commence from the Date hereof, provided the Sum of Five Thousand Pounds be raised in the Manner beforementioned and the Plan be put in Execution.

Resolved

That Committees be appointed at Halifax, Rochdale and Manchester to carry the said Resolutions into Effect, and that the following Gentlemen be appointed a Committee at Halifax

Mr James Edwards	Mr Bromley
Mr Rhodes	Mr Rawdon
Mr Rd. Swaine	Mr John Lees

Signed John Lees as Chairman

After the Business had been discussed Mr Milnes attended the Meeting [at Manchester] and was informed that a Committee would be appointed to take the Matter into Consideration and expedite the Business as soon as possible and that the Gentlemen in general approved his Propositions.

It was moved and seconded

That a Committee [at Manchester] be formed to correspond with the Gentlemen at Halifax and Rochdale and conduct the Business; and that the following Gentlemen be the Committee, three of which are sufficient to act, their first Meeting to be on Thursday at Five O'clock in the Evening. Passed unanimously

Messrs James Edge	Messrs. Thomas Richardson
C.F. Brandt	Lawrence Peel
Charles Wood	John Barrow

James Entwisle | Joseph Seddon
Benjn. Potter | Joseph Hardman
Chris. Marriott | James Potter

The Meeting was then adjourned to Thursday at Five O clock in the Evening.

6.4 Convoys, the navy and impressment

Activity to improve the organisation of convoys was a key issue for early chambers in times of war; and indeed was part of the earliest discourse in the 1690s on the need for business leaderships, as discussed in Chapter 3. This activity inevitably spilled over into lobbies where the Admiralty, local naval commanders, or captains were seen as overstepping their powers or ignoring commercial interests. Impressment of seamen was one of the most controversial areas. Generally the chambers sought to take on a role of helping to organise the assembly of ships and cargoes so that it was easier for the navy to provide effective convoys at the right time, or to help man naval ships in a crisis. This was a way of controlling the excesses of some naval commanders. They also sought to give public appreciation of what they considered to be good behaviour by commanders by giving them presents of plate etc. (as in Liverpool, Jamaica and Hull); they hoped this would encourage other naval officers. For some chambers, such as Liverpool (q.v. *Abstract* in Chapter 5) convoy involvement was one element of many other lobbies and activities. However, for other places the documents reproduced here show this activity involved the creation of committees where there was not otherwise an early chamber, such as Hull where a convoy committee had existed in the 1750s and was revived in the 1780s but the first chamber or committee of trade was not established until 1784 and 1801.[9] In other places convoy organisation was a key aspect stimulating a chamber to be established, as in Kingston, Jamaica. In Kingston, naval tensions were also behind an early committee in 1766 for which a document is reproduced here, that had some relation to the local chamber of 1778.[10] Other local committees were used by the Admiralty, or were created by a local commander, in places where there was no chamber.[11] Over the French Wars from the 1790s convoy coordination became a major activity leading to collaboration between chambers, which led to a 'union' to coordinate their lobbies (see Chapter 9), as shown in documents from Manchester and Exeter below.

[9] See Chapter 1.
[10] Bennett, 'Collective action when needed' (2015).
[11] P. Crowhurst, *The Defence of British trade, 1689–1815* (Folkestone, 1977) 62–8, 71–4.

Sources
[a] Hull Committee on Convoys; Hull Archives Centre CWM/3
[b] Bristol RO SMV/2/4/2/23(9)
[c] TNA; CO 137/62, f. 167–76
[d] *Jamaica Royal Gazette.*
[e] Manchester Commercial Society of Merchants; Manchester Central Library GB127 M8/1/2
[f] *The Star*, London

Hull Committee on Convoys 1757 and 1780–82

A committee on convoys was established in Hull on 18 March 1757, which was immediately referred to as a Committee of Trade. The first minute reproduced below gives its basic organisation and membership, including subscription levels, which were graduated, presumably in line with the number of ships or amount of tonnage of ships owned by each member. The minutes, which are reproduced in entirety for the first five meetings, were brief with usually only one item agreed at each meeting, on which action was immediately taken. The attendance from the committee of twelve was variable. For the next war the minutes continue in the same book, re-starting in 1780. On 11 February 1780 the committee was reconstituted with a single one-guinea subscription, but the record is continuous from the immediate previous months as shown by the letter and minutes for 1780–82 reproduced here. The minute book finishes with a last record of a meeting on 9 July 1782, but it may be that it continued as a committee of trade, for which some records survive, reproduced in Chapter 5. At the rear of the minute book are many letters, some detached, which cover 21 March 1757 to 26 July 1757, then 11 February 1758 to 18 October 1758, then 14 February 1759 to 11 August 1759. The war ended in 1760. The records in these letters suggest that the committee was mainly active during the convoy season for the first half or two thirds of each year. Other discussion of the convoy and naval arrangements in Hull is given by Jackson.[12]

Minutes 18 March 1757[a]

At a meeting this Day of the Merchants & Shipmasters, the following Twelve Gentlemen Viz.

Mr. Thomas Broadley	Mr. Leon Collings
Mr. Joseph Sill	Mr. Isaac Broadley
Mr. Richard Bell	Mr. Nicho. Twigg

[12] G. Jackson, *Hull in the Eighteenth Century: A Study in Economic and Social History* (Oxford, 1972) 137, 156–7.

Mr. Samuel Watson	Mr. Henry Maister
Mr. Joseph Sykes	Mr. Robt. Wilberforce
Mr. John Porter	Mr. Jos. Williamson

were chosen (not less than 5 to act) as a Committee of Trade, in order to apply for Convoys & Cruizers & do everything they may judge necessary & beneficial for the general Good of the Trade of this Town.

Towards defraying and Expenses that may arise thereby, the following Subscription is enter'd into, to be collected at the Discretion of the Committee—

[signed]:

Thos. Broadley	2. 2. –	Gase & Eggington		1. 1. –
Joseph Williamson	2. 2. –	Com Popple	pd.	2. 2. –
Sill, Bridges & [?] Blonnt	2. 2. –	Thomas Mow Co.		2. 2. –
Isaac Broadley	2. 2. –	Chris Thompson		2. 2. –
Sam. Watson & Son	2. 2. –	Wm. Beilby		1. 1. –
Richard Bell	2. 2. –	Chris Scott		1. 1. –
L. & M. Collings	2. 2. –	Joseph Peas & Co.		1. 1. –
Nicholas Twigg	2. 2. –	Andrin Perrott & Co.		2. 2. –
Henry Maister	2. 2. –	John Moore		1. 1. –
Thornton & Wilberforce	2. 2. –	John Booth		2. 2. –
Richd. & Joseph Sykes	2. 2. –	Fran. Pryme	pd.	1. 1. –
John Porter	2. 2. –	Hugh Blades		2. 2. –
Messrs Etherington & Son	2. 2. –	Geo. Thompson		1. 1. –
		Joseph Berry		10. 6.
		[?] Jn. Barris & [?] Derefor		10. 6.

Further subscriptions 1757:

[signed]

Jno. Huntingdon	pd.	5. –	John Witty	pd.	10. 6.
Willm. King	pd.	5. –	Will. Cadday		10. 6.
Tho. Chambers		5. –	Mr. Jno. Forton		5. –
Wm. Hammond	pd.	5. –	Cadday & Brown	pd.	10. 6.
Stepn. Rubinson [?]		5. –	Thos. Jackson	pd.	5. –
Lawrence Hill	pd.	5. –	Richard Hill junr.	pd.	10. 6.
Geo Benson	pd.	5. –	Mr. Jno. Barris	pd.	5. –
Jno. Briggs	pd.	5. –	Mt. Aron Anderson	pd.	5. –
Geo. Wellborn	pd.	5. –	Thos. Bromby	pd.	2. 6.
John Baker	pd.	5. –	Willm. Jolliffe	pd.	5. –
Sam. Hall	pd.	5. –			

Minutes 22 April 1757[a]

Present: Mr. Leonard Collings, Sam. Watson junr., Joseph Sill, Richard Bell, Nicho. Twigg & Joseph Williamson

Resolved. That Fifteen pounds, part of the Fund be subscribed towards the Expense of erecting proper Signals on Flamborough Head.

Minutes 24 April 1757[a]

Present: Henry Maister, Jo. Sill, Leo. Collings, Richard Bell, Nicho. Twigg & Joseph Williamson

Resolved, That the letter of this day's date to the Lords Commissioners of the Admiralty be sent by Express.

Minutes 17 May 1757[a]

Present: Leo. Collings, Isc. Broadley, Jo. Sill, Nicho. Twigg, Richd. Bell & Jos. Williamson

Resolved, that a suit of Colours be bought & sent down to Patrick Newmarsh at the Spurn [Head] in order that proper signals may be made to give Notice of any Privateers on the Coast.

Letter in minutes Admiralty Office 29 January 1780[a]

Sir,

Having laid before my Lords Commissioners of the Admiralty your letter of the 25 Ultimo which I had the honour to receive from the Marquis of Carmarthen, requesting that a proper force may be appointed to Cruise for the protection of the Trade, between the Humber & Tynemouth Castle, and to rendezvous in the Humber and Bridlington Bay. I am Commanded by their Lordships to acquaint you that they have Allotted the *Loudoun*, and *Alfred* Armed Ships to supply the place of the *Countess of Scarbro'* and *Bellona*, and that their Commanders will be instructed to Convoy the Trade from the port of Hull from time to time as the Chief Magistrate at the request of the Merchants shall request, and to employ themselves in the intermediate time in Cruising very diligently upon the Coast for the protection of the Trade of His Majesty's Subjects which with the other Cruisers that will be employed on this, as well as on the other side the Humber will, it is hoped, afford a sufficient protection.

I am Sir, Your most humble Servt.

P. Stephens

Minute 11 February 1780[a]

At a Meeting of the Merchants, Ship Owners, and Underwriters to Consider of some regulations to be made for the sailing of Convoys

Present. Mr. Mayor, Ald. Bell, Sir H. Etherington, Ald. Porter, Mr. Ar. Maister, Mr. Rd. Broadley, Mr. Stephenson, Mr. Willm. Williamson, Mr. Wm. Travis, Mr. Staniforth, Mr. Reaston, Mr. Huntington & Mr. Standidge

Resolv'd

That the undermentioned Gentlemen be a Committee for the Regulating of Applications to be made to the Mayor for the sailing of Convoys & agreeable to the Instructions from the Admiralty by their Letter to the Mayor dated 29th Jan. 1780

Ald. Bell, or Son
Sir Hen. Etherington
Ald. Porter, or Son
Ald. Sykes
Mr. Ar. Maister, or Rennard
Mr. Rd. Broadley, or H. Broadley
Mr. Stephenson or Mr. Wilkinson
Mr. Standidge
Mr. Staniforth
Mr. Travis or T. Travis
Mr. Wm. Williamson & Mr. Waller
Mr. Reaston
Mr. Huntington
Mr. W. Horner or Mr T. Horner
Mr. Thorley Senr. or Junr.

That John Chandler be Clerk to the Committee

The above Committee are desired to meet at the Grand Jury Room on Tuesday next to Choose a Chairman

Minute 27 October 1780[a]

At a Meeting of the Committee for regulating Convoys

Present. Sir Hen Etherington, Mr. Jn. Horner, Mr. Rennard, Rb. Broadley, Thos. Reaston & Mr. Huntington

That the following Letter be wrote to the Mayor [Edmund Bramston Esq.]

Sir,

We beg you will be so kind as to acquaint the Honble. the Lords Commissioners of the Admiralty that upon our Application to Capt Kinnier of his Majestys Arm'd Ship the *Lord Amherst* to fetch home our Baltic fleet from Elsingoer [Elsinore] the Capt. informs us she is in want of so many

Repairs and stores as renders her unfit to perform the Service and Cannot proceed. We therefore desire their Lordships will be pleased to direct the Captains of such of his Majesty's Ships as may be coming Convoy from Elsingoer to England to see our Trade into the Humber as we have now at least 50 sails of Ships in the Baltic Loading with very valuable Cargoes for this place

We are Sir &c.

Minute 9 July 1782[a]

At a Meeting of the Committee for Convoys

Present. Sir H Etherington, Ald Porter, Mr Williamson, Mr Staniforth, Mr Reaston, Mr Huntington, Mr Rennards.

Ordered. That the following Letter be wrote to the mayor.

Sir,

As Several Ships will be ready to sail for the Baltic with valuable Manufactures of this Country the last week in this Month. We desire you will apply to the Honourable the Lord Commissioners of the admiralty requesting they will be pleased to appoint a sufficient Convoy to be here against that time to proceed with them to Elsineur and take under their care such Ships as shall be there intended for this Port.

We are Sir, Your most obdt., Humble Servants

That The Mayor be requested to write a Letter of Thanks to Capt Patr. Sinclair of the *Queen* Armed Ship for his great Care of the late Fleet from the Sound to this Port.

Lancaster 1781

The existence of two documents from a Lancaster Committee or chamber, for 1779 (see Chapter 5.4 and 5.7) and for 1781 (below), indicates that a body existed for a few years and, like Blackburn in 1779 (see Chapter 5.11), may have been encouraged by the establishment in 1774 of both the Manchester Committee of Trade and the Liverpool chamber. Its known activities appear to have been lobbying and convoy arrangements.

Original letter Lancaster 1 June 1781[b]

rec'd 4th June

Gentlemen,

The Committee of Trade for this Port having thought it eligible (from the number of depredations committed by the Enemy's Cruizers in St. Georges Channel) to petition the Admiralty for some Ships of Force to cruise in the aforesaid Station for the protection of the homeward Bound W. India Fleet and the Coasting Trade in general request that the Merchants of Bristol will accord the Motion.

I am in behalf of said Committee
Your Obed. hble. Servt.
Henry Tindall

Jamaica 1779 and 1780

Jamaica was often subject to difficulties for shipping during wars, given its proximity to French and Spanish territory, and offered ready scope for American privateers during the war of 1775–83. The documents show how a formal chamber established in 1778 had convoy organisation as one of its prime activities, but one document also shows an earlier pattern of more informal organisation of activities through a local 'Society of Merchants' in 1766 that may have been mainly a social body used as a meeting venue when memorials had to be prepared.[13]

Memorial Kingston 4th March 1766[c]

The Society of Merchants having this Day assembled at Vauxhall to take into Consideration His Excellency's Letter of the 10th Ult. and having formed themselves into a general Committee for that Purpose have agreed to the following Report, Viz.

It appears to the Committee, that the first principal and most fatal Interruption to the Commerce of Foreign Vessels importing Bullion, was given by the seizing and condemning all such Vessels, and their Money, as were found here, when the first Accounts arrived of Hostilities having commenced against Spain, upon the poor pretence that they were the Subjects of a Foreign Prince at War with the Nation; a pretence, that had its foundation in Avarice, and destroy'd all that Confidence and Faith, under which these unhappy People were encouraged to carry on a Trade most lucrative to this Nation at the risk of Incurring the utmost Severity of their own Laws which they were violating.

It also appears to the Committee, that William Murray Esq. acting, Naval Officer, has extorted and received various high and illegal Fees from Spaniards importing Bullion into this Island and that he has made a practice of demanding and extorting such Fees for some time past, which Fees the Committee apprehend, are unwarrantable, and contrary to the Intent and meaning of several Acts of Parliament, and which Fees, it appears to the Committee, are

[13] Bennett, 'Collective Actions when needed' (2015).

not confined to any particular Sum, but are varied agreeable to the Discretion of the said Mr. Murray, that He has claimed and received a Commission of Five per cent upon Goods purchased by Spaniards importing Bullion into this Island, that the said Mr. Murray does also demand and has received from sundry Spaniards importing Bullion, a Fee of a Doubloon for His Excellency's Secretary, which Fee the Committee also think illegal Oppressive and unusual.

But it does not appear to the Committee that any Vessel did at any Time come into any Port of this Island with Eighty Thousand Dollars or other large Sum of Money, on which the said Mr. Murray did demand a Commission of Five per cent and in Consequence of which, such Vessel sailed from hence with such money on board to Hispaniola or some other Foreign Port, where milder Treatment was expected, because, when such Commission has been disputed, the Naval Officer has relinquished it for a certain Sum or the next best Fee he could obtain. The Committee do also find, that the Commanding Officer of the Port does exact and extort from each Spanish Vessel, sailing from Port Royal, the Sum of One Pistole which they are of Opinion is an illegal Fee and a mal practice.

It likewise appears to the Committee, that it has been a practice by the Deputy Naval Officers at Port Royal, to demand illegal Fees from Spaniards, sailing from that Harbour and that Mr. Edward Glasse late Deputy Naval Officer, has extorted from sundry Spaniards, importing Bullion into this Island, the Sum of Six Pounds Ten Shillings under pretence of Pilotage or Anchorage, notwithstanding such Spaniards came into and sailed out of the Harbour of Port Royal without employing any Pilot belonging to this Island.

It has further appeared to the Committee that there has generally been a great Loss of Time to the Persons importing Bullion in such Foreign Vessels, before these several Officers of the Crown have completed the Course or Circulation of their respective Extortions, which in one Instance of a certain Spanish Vessel, computing the Entry and Clearance, has been proved to be a Detention of Twelve Days and the Committee esteem this a Mal Practice and grievous Embarrassment. Finally it appears to the Committee, that upon the whole, the Delays and Obstructions which are given to the Spaniards upon their arrival to and Departure from this Island, together with the abovementioned Extortions, are great Discouragements to the said Spaniards from importing Bullion here and highly detrimental to the Commerce of this Island.

(Signed) Geo. Paplay President

Printed Report Kingston, 27 May 1779[d]

CHAMBER OF COMMERCE.

At a general QUARTERLY MEETING of this Society, held this Day,

PRESENT,

THOMAST HIBBERT, junior, Esq; President,

ALEXANDER ALLARDYCE, Esq; V. President,

MOSES BENSON, Esq; Treasurer,

with the Subscribers at large,

Upon Motion duly made, it was unanimously

RESOLVED—That the thanks of this Society be given to CHARLES INGLIS, Esq; Commander of his Majesty's Ship *Salisbury*, for his great Care of, and Attention to the Fleet under his Charge from Cork, lately arrived.

ORDERED—That a Copy of the above Resolution be transmitted to Captain INGLIS, in a Letter from the Secretary.

This Society having been informed, that WILLIAM LOCKER, Esq; late commander of his Majesty's ship *Lowestofte*, is about to depart for England, for the recovery of his health, it was moved, and unanimously

RESOLVED—That the thanks of this Society be given to that gentleman, for his attention, during his residence amongst us, to the commercial interest in general, and particularly, for having always studiously avoided that practice which, of all others, is the most distressing to trade, the IMPRESSING of Seamen.

ORDERED—That a Copy of the above Resolution be transmitted to Captain LOCKER, in a Letter from the Secretary, and that it be published in the News-Papers of this town.

Extract from the Minutes. J. Hardwar, Secr.

Printed Notice Kingston, 25 November 1779[d]

Chamber of Commerce

The conduct of the CHAMBER, relative to the sailing of the *Thynne* Packet before the usual time, having been misunderstood, and severely animadverted upon, it is thought proper to publish their letter to Vice Admiral Sir *Peter Parker*, and to declare that it was much against their wish that the Packet sailed before the usual time.

Kingston 12 Nov. 1779.

'To Sir Peter Parker, Vice Admiral of the Blue, &c.

Sir

In consideration of the late arrival of the *Thynne* Packet, and that she is not to sail until the 27th instant, and that there has been no great opportunity of giving advice of the large property embarked on the Fleet appointed to sail on the 25th instant,—we beg leave to request, that you will be pleased to order, that the ships intended to sail under the next Convoy do remain at their respective ports five days longer than directed by your former appointment, that the letters of advice may go before the sailing of the Fleet,

—We are, with great respect, Sir, your most obedient servants.'

(signed by the whole meeting of Planters, Merchants, and others)

By Order of the Committee J. Hardwar, Secr.

Printed Report Kingston, 16 November 1780[d]

Chamber of Commerce,

The Admiral having been pleased to signify, that he will appoint a Convoy for the Trade for Great Britain, to sail any day between the middle of *January* and the middle of *February*, that may be most convenient to the concerned.

This is to give Notice,

That a General Meeting of this Society will be held at their room in Kingston, on Friday the first day of *December* next, at eleven o'clock before noon, at which all persons interested are invited to attend, to consider the time that may be most expedient for the sailing of the first fleet, and to make application to the Admiral accordingly. Those who cannot conveniently attend, may give their opinions by letter, addressed to the President, which will be laid before the Meeting.

Alexander Allardyce, V.P.

Printed notice Kingston, 5 October 1782[d]

The Admiral, upon a Representation having been made to him by a Committee of the Chamber of Commerce, has given orders for an immediate stop being put to the Impressing seamen, but has made a requisition of one fourth of the number of seamen employed on board merchant vessels, as being absolutely necessary for his Majesty's service; the remaining part of each crew to be protected; and at a meeting of the Society last Tuesday, it was resolved, "that it should be recommended to all persons concerned in shipping, to adopt a regulation which appears at this time to be necessary, as tending equally to promote the good of individuals and the public."

At a meeting of the Chamber of Commerce, the 26th ult. an addition of Twenty Shillings Currency to the premium or reward already offered by government, was agreed to be given for every straggling seaman or deserter, that should be apprehended and delivered on board any of his Majesty's ships on this station, before the first day of November next.

Manchester and other towns: convoy discussions 1794–9

Minute Manchester 14 April 1794[e]

Proceedings at a Meeting of the Commercial Society of Merchants trading on the Continent of Europe held this Day at Spencer's Tavern.
Present

Mr Chars. Fred Brandt President

Mr T.C. Dawson	Mr Henry Heyer
Thomas Boardman	Nathan Crompton
Christopher Marriott	Thomas Richardson
G.C. Alberti	James Norman
Thomas Harris	James Watkins

Resolved

That this Meeting considers the Periods fixed for the sailing of the different Convoys for the Mediterranean as agreed upon between the Lords of the Admiralty and the Merchants of all the Towns interested ought not to be deviated from.

That the Lords of the Admiralty be requested to give Instructions for the Convoys to sail at the time fixed, notwithstanding any applications that may be made to the contrary.

That Copies of the Periods fixed, may be sent to Leeds, Birmingham, Exeter and Halifax, desiring them to be punctual to the times they engaged for.

Resolved

That the Chairman shall write to Messrs. Thomas & William Earle, requesting them to lay on a Vessel for Salerno & Naples and another for Genoa & Leghorn both to sail from Liverpool with Goods from Manchester the third of June at the latest.

That the Vessels proceed to Falmouth there to avail themselves of the Convoy appointed to sail from Spithead the 15th of June and wait for the same, until the Tenth of July. And in Case the Convoy should not appear by that time, they are then to proceed on their respective Voyages singly.

That Messrs. Thomas & William Earle be requested to provide good and substantial Vessels, and give the Names of them as soon as possible.
Charles Fred Brandt President

Copy of letter Manchester 16 April 1794[e]

To: William Kennaway Esq.
Chairman to the Commercial Society of Exeter

I have received in due Course enclosed to me in a Letter from Mr Samuel Bunfield of your Place dated the 15th of December last, a Copy of the Resolution entered into by the Merchants of Exeter for the Establishment of a Commercial Society similar and for the same purpose, as the one we were then establishing here. We have since more and more experienced the Necessity of such an Establishment, and have extended it on a broader Basis, such as we think may produce the more beneficial Consequences: especially if similar Societies are formed in the principal manufacturing Towns in this Kingdom, and a free and open Communication takes place in all matters of general and mutual Interest, which we have no doubt we shall experience from your Society.

I was directed at our last Meeting to transmit you a Copy of the Rules of our Society together with an English Copy of the Circular Letter we have framed to be transmitted to such of our Correspondents who may stand in need of them. Indeed we consider that those who act upon fair and honourable Principles will see with Pleasure the Steps we take to check the Ill Practices of those who have so long abused a Confidence they did not deserve. We have these Letters in French Italian and German.

We shall be glad to hear that you approve of the general Principles of our Establishment, and I beg leave to renew our Assurances, that we shall on all Occasions be happy to communicate with you on all Commercial Matters, and keep up a friendly Intercourse between your Society and ours.

I am going to write to Mr Stephens to solicit my Lords Commissioners of the Admiralty, that the Convoy which was fixed by the Delegates who met in London in October last to sail from Spithead the 15th of June next, may positively sail at the fixed time without paying any Regard to any application that might be made to alter it, as we are very sensible that prolonging it would endanger the Vessels intended for Salerno of again arriving too late for the Fair. As we are persuaded that you will think as we do we should be glad you would make a similar Application to strengthen ours.

I have the honour to be with great Respect,
Sir, Your Most Obedt. Servant Char. Fred Brandt Presidt.

Minute 9 March 1797[e]

Read the following paper

At a Meeting of Delegates from the Commercial Societies of Manchester, Leeds, Halifax, Birmingham & Exeter held in London.

Resolved unanimously

That, in the present critical Situation of Affairs a general Co-operation of the different Manufacturing Towns of England is highly necessary for the Security of Trade in its present and future Operations.

That during the Course of the present War and more recently since the Progress of the French Armies in Italy and Germany, we have experienced from some of our Correspondents, the greatest Honour and Punctuality in their Dealings, whilst others taking Advantage of the existing Circumstances have abused the Confidence reposed in them by exposing British Property, procrastinating Payments; and raising no just and futile Difficulties to evade Payment.

That in Order to preserve to the Fair and Honourable Dealer the Advantages which such Conduct so justly entitles them to, and at the same time, to expose the Conduct of such as have forfeited the Confidence hitherto reposed in them, we shall from Time to Time communicate to each other such Instances as have or may hereafter occur lending to promote this salutary End.

That each Individual House of our Respective Societies shall be at Liberty to transmit Copies of these Resolutions signed by the Secretary to such of their Correspondents as they shall think proper.

It was moved and seconded

That the President be requested to get the above Resolution translated into French and Italian.

Printed report 21 March 1796[f]

At a Meeting of the EXETER CHAMBER OF COMERCE, held the 16th of February 1796,

The Merchants of Exeter having subscribed a sum for the purpose of expressing to Captain BURGESS of the *Anne*, their sense of his meritorious attention to the Convoy which he conducted to Gibraltar and Leghorn in February 1795, and also [words lost] that which arrived from the Mediterranean in November,

It is resolved unanimously, That the sum so subscribed be remitted to Mr. Clay, and, united with the Subscriptions of the Underwriters in London, for the purchase of a Piece of Plate, with a suitable inscription, and that Mr. Clay be requested to present the same to Captain BURGESS, on the part of the Merchants of Exeter.

By Order of the Committee,
WILLIAM KENDALL, Secretary.

6.5 Financial support, bills of exchange, specie and credit crises

The chambers were pre-eminently concerned with trade and its finance. These became major concerns when disrupted by war, shortage of specie, and financial crises occasioned by bank or other credit failures. The chambers concerned themselves with improving the processes of credit through various lobbies on the acceptance and use of bills of exchange, and were involved in various crisis-management supports. The examples quoted here demonstrate some of these activities, and include self-regulation of bills of exchange, and assurances for transacting bills (which were one of the most important financial instruments of international and inland exchange in the period), and attempts to regulate notaries. Dublin provides one of the best examples of detailed regulations proposed and used, which began under the chamber's predecessor (the Committee of Merchants and Traders) and continued under the chamber. The chief activities of the Jamaica chamber other than convoys were mainly financial assurances. A Portsmouth chamber may have originated in assurances of meeting bills in 1797–9 (see Chapter 1). These efforts all arose in periods of limited specie or other financial difficulties, as in Charleston 1775–80, Jamaica 1778–86, and Waterford 1787 where their meeting room was used 'to transact Bill business'.[14] Attendance was 'by rotation among the committee members, every Tuesday and Friday 1.30–2.30', with a fine of 1s. for non-attendance.[15] The case of the 1793 bank failure of Charles Caldwell's Bank in Liverpool (a chamber member) is not covered by detailed documents, but the basic activity of credit support in Liverpool was engineered through the chamber's members, notably Benjamin and Arthur Heywood, bankers and merchants, and the major merchants Thomas and William Earle. These individuals signed the short-term loan notes issued to provide liquidity needed in 1793. Although previous commentary has credited the Liverpool corporation with this initiative, more recent analysis by the author makes clear that it was the leading individual chamber members and their networks that was crucial to gaining Bank of England support for the loan note initiative.[16] This was a unique local initiative for its time, akin to modern quantitative easing, though similar processes had been used by the Scottish charter banks and the Bank of England.

Source
[a] Dublin Committee of Merchants and Traders, Rough Minute Book; RIA MS.3 C25
[b] Dublin Chamber of Commerce minutes; TNAI
[c] TNA CO 137/62, fo. 167–76.
[d] *Jamaica Mercury*

Minute Dublin, 3 December 1770[a]

Meeting adjourned to the Tholsel[17] where there was a very numerous Meeting of the Merchants and T[raders].

[14] Bennett, *Local Business Voice* (2011) 137–9, 146–8, 514–6.
[15] Chamber minutes, 20 April 1787; Waterford Archives WCOC1/01.
[16] Bennett, *Voice of Liverpool* (2010) 61–2; 'Network interlocks' (2013) 1300.
[17] The Merchants Exchange and Merchants Guildhall, built 1683; this was the main commercial meeting place prior to erection of the new Exchange by the Committee of Merchants in 1789.

Tholsel this day at one o'Clock. On that Occasion. Accordingly at a very numerous Meeting of the Merchants and Traders.

The Rt. Honble. The Lord Mayor in the Chair.

The following Resolution was unanimously agreed to:

RESOLVED that the present low situation of Public Credit & decay of Commerce in this Metropolis & Kingdom make an Association of the Merchts & Traders necessary for the Support of Public Credit. IN Pursuance of which the following Association was entered into.

WHEREAS the Bank of George Colebrooke & Company have advertised themselves under a necessity of deferring the payment of their Notes for a Short Time which may create a Diffidence in the Banks of this City that might prove extremely injurious to the Trade and Manufactures of this Kingdom.

NOW We the Merchants and Traders of the City of Dublin whose names are hereunto Subscribed being thoroughly Sensible of the Secure foundations of the Houses of Messrs. David Latouche & Sons, Messrs Gleadow & Compy., Messrs. Finlay & Compy., and Messrs. John Dawson Coates & Lawless Do hereby declare that we will continue to take Notes of these Banks in all payments whatsoever made To us with the same spirited Confidence we have hitherto Done.

At the same time his Excellency the Lord Lieutenant and Several of the State Officers signed the following declaration.

> WHEREAS the Bank of Sir George Colebrooke & Co. have advertised their being under a necessity of deferring the payment of their Notes for a Short time which may cause a diffidence in the other Banks of this City that may prove extremely injurious to the Trade and manufactures of this Kingdom.
>
> Now we the Lord Lieutenant of Ireland the noble Gentry Merchants and Traders of this City whose names are hereunto Subscribed being thoroughly sensible of the Secure foundations of the Houses of Messrs David Latouche & Sons, Messrs. William Gleadow & Company, Messrs. Thomas Finlay & Co., and Messrs. John Dawson Coates & Patrick Lawless do hereby declare that we will continue to take notes of the said Houses as Cash in all payments whatsoever made to us.

Minute re. Bills of Exchange and Embargoes Dublin, 31 May 1783[a]

[First detailed consideration given to Bills of Exchange; although a later minute refers to a meeting of 7 May, the correct date was 27 May, which called for consideration of the matter. The Resolutions listed below were agreed at a Council meeting on 12 June 1783 and then published in Saunders's News Letter].

THE order of the day being read for taking into consideration the payment of Bills of Exchange and if any and what regulation will be necessary to establish their punctual payment.

RESOLVED that it is the opinion of the Council that the payment of Inland Bills of Exchange and Promissory Notes in the City of Dublin is conducted with great want of punctuality to the injury of Commerce and to the discredit of Traders.

RESOLVED that it is the opinion of the Council that the most effectual mode of Redress will be by a Law expressly pointing out the rule of Responsibility with respect to Drawers and Endorsers.

RESOLVED that it is the opinion of the Council that all Bills and Notes ought to be protested the day they fall due if not then paid and proper notice given to the several parties, in default whereof the said parties ought to be exonerated.

RESOLVED that the President be requested to call a meeting of the Chamber at Large on some early convenient day that these resolutions may then be submitted to their consideration.

[continues without break concerning Embargoes. The lifting of embargoes on the export of provisions to foreign ports after the end of the war with the American Colonies and their allies had been one of the earliest substantive lobby issues taken up by the chamber, on 3 April 1783, initially over trade with Portugal. A memorial had been written on 8 April to the Lt. Governor to ask that he request the government to move quickly to lift embargoes and inform all foreign ports; he replied as reported on 17 April reporting delays, but on 29 April it was reported that the government had agreed the lifting of embargoes, where it was agreed that members should write to their correspondents to inform them]

Mr. Geale reported that in consequence of the Resolution of the Council he had wrote to the following places [confirming the lifting of embargoes]:

Antwerp	Cologne	Konigsberg	Oporto
Berlin	Dantzig	Leghorn	Riga
Brunswick	Drouton	Leuwarden	Stettin
Breslaw	Elbing	Lisbon	Stolpie
Brussels	French fort on the Mayne	Memell	Stralsund
Bremen	Hambro[ough]	Naples	Stockholm
Wolgast			

Mr. Black also reported that he had wrote to Bruges and Rotterdam and Mr. Marston to Stockholm and Petersburg.

Minute Dublin, 19 October 1785[b]

[No further minute on this matter, so presumably was agreed with those concerned]

RESOLVED that it is the opinion of this Council that it will be expedient in future to meet for the Negotiating of Bills at the Exchange on every Monday, Tuesday, Thursday and Friday

THAT a General Meeting of the Passers and Takers of Bills of Exchange be summoned at the Trustees Room in the Royal Exchange on Friday the 21st inst. precisely at half past two o'Clock to take into consideration the expediency of altering the Days for negotiating Bills.

RESOLVED that the said Resolution be published in Saunders's News Letter and Copies sent to each of the Bankers and Posted

Petition: 'Report of Society of Merchants at Kingston'

Kingston, 4 March 1766[c]

The Society of Merchants having this Day assembled at Vauxhall to take into Consideration His Excellency's Letter of the 10th Ult. and having formed themselves into a general Committee for that Purpose have agreed to the following Report, Viz.

It appears to the Committee, that the first principal and most fatal Interruption to the Commerce of Foreign Vessels importing Bullion, was given by the seizing and condemning all such Vessels, and their Money, as were found here, when the first Accounts arrived of Hostilities having commenced against Spain, upon the poor pretence that they were the Subjects of a Foreign Prince at War with the Nation; a pretence, that had its foundation in Avarice, and destroy'd all that Confidence and Faith, under which these unhappy People were encouraged to carry on a Trade most lucrative to this Nation at the risk of Incurring the utmost Severity of their own Laws which they were violating.

It also appears to the Committee, that William Murray Esq. acting, Naval Officer, has extorted and received various high and illegal Fees from Spaniards importing Bullion into this Island and that he has made a practice of demanding and extorting such Fees for some time past, which Fees the Committee apprehend, are unwarrantable, and contrary to the Intent and meaning of several Acts of Parliament, and which Fees, it appears to the Committee, are not confined to any particular Sum, but are varied agreeable to the Discretion of the said Mr. Murray, that He has claimed and received a Commission of Five per cent upon Goods purchased by Spaniards importing Bullion into this Island, that the said Mr. Murray does also demand and has received from sundry Spaniards importing Bullion, a Fee of a Doubloon for His Excellency's Secretary, which Fee the Committee also think illegal Oppressive and unusual.

But it does not appear to the Committee that any Vessel did at any Time come into any Port of this Island with Eighty Thousand Dollars or other large Sum of Money, on which the said Mr. Murray did demand a Commission of Five per cent and in Consequence of which, such Vessel sailed from hence with such money on board to Hispaniola or some other Foreign Port, where milder Treatment was expected, because, when such Commission has been disputed, the Naval Officer has relinquished it for a certain Sum or the next best Fee he could obtain. The Committee do also find, that the Commanding Officer of the Port does exact and extort from each Spanish Vessel, sailing from Port Royal, the Sum of One Pistole which they are of Opinion is an illegal Fee and a mal practice.

It likewise appears to the Committee, that it has been a practice by the Deputy Naval Officers at Port Royal, to demand illegal Fees from Spaniards, sailing from that Harbour and that Mr. Edward Glasse late Deputy Naval Officer, has extorted from sundry Spaniards, importing Bullion into this Island, the Sum of Six Pounds Ten Shillings under pretence of Pilotage or Anchorage, notwithstanding such Spaniards came into and sailed out of the Harbour of Port Royal without employing any Pilot belonging to this Island.

It has further appeared to the Committee that there has generally been a great Loss of Time to the Persons importing Bullion in such Foreign Vessels, before these several Officers of the Crown have completed the Course or Circulation of their respective Extortions, which in one Instance of a certain Spanish Vessel, computing the Entry and Clearance, has been proved to be a Detention of Twelve Days and the Committee esteem this a Mal Practice and grievous Embarrassment. Finally it appears to the Committee, that upon the whole, the Delays and Obstructions which are given to the Spaniards upon their arrival to and Departure from this Island, together with the abovementioned Extortions, are great Discouragements to the said Spaniards from importing Bullion here and highly detrimental to the Commerce of this Island.

[Signed] Geo. Paplay President

Printed notice, 16 October 1779 Kingston, 6 November 1779[d]

In consequence of a Resolution of the CHAMBER of COMMERCE, dated 7 October, directing the Subscribers to forward a sufficient number of BLANK BILLS of EXCHANGE & LOADING, four to the set, instead of three, as usually practiced, to their correspondents in the several parishes, for the accommodation of gentlemen who may have occasion for them;

That they respectfully give Notice, That, in obedience to the above direction, they have printed a proper quantity of the said Blanks, ON THE VERY BEST PAPER, and forwarded them to the Deputy Post-Masters. From whom the gentlemen who want such articles will be pleased to supply themselves.

DOUGLASS & AIKMAN [local printers]

6.6 Information provision to the Board of Trade

The relations of the chambers with the Board of Trade had varied between positive and very negative over the period since their initial foundation in the 1760s. The breakdown of effectiveness of the Board of Trade in the 1760s and 1770s had in part stimulated the foundation of chambers as a substitute for providing information directly to government on the state of manufactures and trade. These exchanges had almost always come from chambers as outsiders seeking the Board to help with various difficulties, or because certain legislation was being considered with which chambers disagreed. A fundamentally different type of exchange took place from the 1830s when the Board established its own Statistics Department. This had very wide-ranging objectives, but one aspect was to use existing business organisations to provide information to help inform government decisions. This might have indicated a coming of age of chambers to become direct sources of information on which government relied, which in turn might have led to contracted or partnership arrangements, and would have stimulated chambers to develop a closer relationship with their members so that a steady information structure was established. Something of this type of interrelationship did develop in the twentieth century, which might have led to registration or other forms of public law status for chambers. The chambers' *Quarterly Economic Survey* initiated in the 1990s plays an important role similar to aspects of the Statistics Department envisaged in 1832.[18]

The 1832 initiative proved far more restricted in practice than originally intended, and it took little time for the Statistics Department to begin to look mainly inward to other government departments rather than using outside organisations. Indeed its objectives were seen as rather limited by the BoT itself: in 1832 its head, George Richardson Porter, was initially envisaged only to 'be temporarily employed in arranging and abstracting the printed Parliamentary Returns in this Office'.[19] It did develop and modestly prosper, increasing its staff from three in 1832, to six people by 1839 (including Porter).[20] It relied heavily in its establishment and subsequent early expansion on Francis Baring, in the Treasury, who was the nephew of Alexander Baring who was a leading figure involved in the initiative to found a chamber in London in 1823–4 (q.v. Chapter 4). Francis Baring had also been a friend since the mid-1820s of Le Marchant, related to the Le Marchants involved in

[18] Bennett *Local Business Voice* (2011) 591–660, 259–73, 351.
[19] TNA: Board of Trade minutes, 17 April 1832; BT 5/40.
[20] TNA: Board of Trade minutes, 1February 1839, accounts and staff of Statistics Department; BT 5/46.

the Guernsey chamber of commerce.[21] The documents reproduced here show how the aims of the Statistics Department were envisaged, and how approaches to chambers were made. It was an important period in which the BoT was becoming a key element in the emerging free trade debate. Indeed its head, Porter, was a great enthusiast for free trade and administrative entrepreneur, in many ways far ahead of his time. He became a critical part of the support on which Cobden and Bright were to draw. Porter's *Progress of the Nation*, released in sections from 1836, was also an influential publication in its own right. Despite the limitations of the Statistics Department, therefore, the initiative of 1832 marks an important turning point for chambers (and subsequently for other industry lobbies) where the BoT became variously a support, partner or the leading intermediary between government and businesses or business groups. The 1832 initiative, though short-lived, thus represents a critical shift towards the modern position of government-business relations, and effectively shifts the terms of debate away from that begun in the 1690s by Whiston and Davenant.

However, whilst Porter's objectives began ambitiously, as summarised in the first document, the objectives were almost incapable of being met. This was an early foray of government into the conceptual arena of assembling economic and social statistics, but Porter's letter can best be likened to a stamp collector trying to assemble pieces of information wherever they might be, without a clear strategy of how they might be used: 'to obtain and systematically arrange Returns upon the Wealth, Commerce, & Industry of the United Kingdom', or more generally to request information on 'the state and progress of manufactures and commerce throughout the United Kingdom' and any other information bearing on 'the subject of statistics'. There was no template of information required or any form of survey design that offered a grid to combine information. In this unfocused trawl Porter mainly saw chambers contributing to reducing the costs of data collection by supplying the information they already possessed or might assemble. The result was a set of first letters to the chambers making a wide trawl, of which the letter to Glasgow letter is an example: to provide 'all information which can be said to belong to the subject of statistics', as well as informing Porter what 'may not be within the province or the purview of the Chamber of Commerce'. Similar letters were sent between August and December 1832 to chambers in Waterford, Limerick, Cork, Newry, Belfast, Dublin, Manchester, Birmingham, and to the Chamberlain of the City of London Corporation,

[21] T. G. George Earl of Northbrook and F. H. Baring eds., *Baring, F. T.: Journals and Correspondence from 1808 to 1852* ... Vol 1. (Winchester, 1905) 43; D. Le Marchant, *Memoir of John Charles Viscount Althorp* (London, 1876) 490; D.R. Fisher *History of Parliament: the House of Commons 1820–1832* (Cambridge, 2009).

Town Clerk of Bristol, and Collector of Customs at Liverpool,[22] as well as consuls in 36 places.[23] The list of chambers reflects the long-term emphasis on the major ports that was apparent from the outset of chambers. The inclusion of Newry offers some substantiation of the existence of an early chamber there. Replies were received from most chambers, which in the case of Limerick led to a series of exchanges where Porter tried to get the chamber to provide ever more detailed information on population characteristics, cattle and animals exported, and other matters.[24]

Source
Statistical Department Board of Trade, minutes: TNA BT 24/1

Minute of letter: Porter to Baring 31 March 1832

Sir,

I am directed by the Lords Commissioners [of Trade of the Privy Council] to request that you will submit to the Consideration of the Lords Commissioners of His Majesty's Treasury the following proposal for Establishing in the Department, a Branch, the Duties of which shall be, to obtain and systematically arrange Returns upon the Wealth, Commerce, & Industry of the United Kingdom for the purpose of preserving Information, and, from time to time, of publishing such reports as have generally been required by Parliament or by His Majesty's Govt.

No System for carefully abstracting in clear and accurate Form, the information which flows through the Board of Trade on these subjects has yet been Established, & it appears to the Lords of this Committee that a distinct Branch for this Purpose, obtaining Returns from the Departments and concentrating the Information already in their possession might be of great public Utility, & although attended with some Expense, yet, that indirectly the saving to the Public upon the costly and desultory Returns which are occasionally called for by the Houses of Parliament would be considerable.

Their Lordships would propose that the most Mass of Statistics Information which is contained in the Returns to Parliament for the last Ten Years should be digested & concentrated under separate Heads, so as to be of Easy reference, & to Establish a Form under which a complete and Extended System may be periodically carried on. Happily a portion of the Labour necessary to this object has been anticipated by private Industry, and the difficulty will not be great Beyond this, it can be only necessary on the present

[22] TNA BT 24/1: Outletters 30 August, 3 September and 21 December 1832; minutes.
[23] TNA BT 24/1: Outletter 10 August 1833.
[24] TNA BT 24/1: e.g. further outletters to Limerick chamber 19 July and 1 November 1833.

occasion very shortly to encapsulate the form the Increase of Information which might be placed within disposal.

The Excise will give a measure of that consumption which marks the general distribution of Wealth & Comfort in the Country with some View by means of the Auction Duty of the Transfer of Duty

The Custom House would afford means of carrying on, with some Improvement and Extension, the Returns upon Trade and Navigation and Receive in the forms which have been most generally approved by Parliament. Inference upon the Wealth of the Country, its Advance or Decline, might be drawn from the Rebate Duty & Legacy Tax and some criterion of the state of commercial Operations found in the Amount of Stamps on Bills of Exchange—The receipts on Policies of Insurance—The House and Window Tax Exhibiting the number of Houses rated at from £10 to £20 and upwards with classified Returns of the Tax upon Horses, Servants and Carriages would mark the distribution of Wealth and of Gains, whilst further Information of Importance would be obtained from the Post Office.

With many subjects of Internal Economy the Public is wholly unacquainted and it will in some cases be difficult to arrive as any accurate Estimate of the Produce of our own Soil; But possibly by the same Machinery under which the Census of Population has been taken, or by Returns from the several markets in the Country, Information might be registered upon the Produce of the Mines and of Agricultural and other Industry, much of which is quite independent of the supervision of any Department. Whether in all the Offices of the Excise and the Departments may be made available for obtaining Information, and to what Extent correspondence for this purpose may be established must be for the present left to consideration. — It is further in the Opinion of their Lordships that Statistic Information upon the state of our Colonies and Foreign Dependencies, though in less Detail, should be collected and registered, Facilities for the purpose may be immediately afforded by the Colonial department, and Board of Control and regular Returns ordered for the Future—It may beyond this be considered how far the Coinage and State of the Circulation the state of Crime and Insolvency—of Mendacity—of Education, The Amount of County Rates, Church Rates and Poor Rates, the distribution of Funded Property—Savings Banks—The Tonnage on Canals and artificial Docks—and other points may eventually be included in the Returns which the Department proposed will classify.

Their Lordships have however not attempted a complete Enumeration of the objects which may be included in a plan capable of Extension. If this Outline should be approved, they would recommend that they should be authorised to make arrangements for the construction of such a Branch of this Department as may appear to them for at least beginning the work they propose.

They cannot as yet presume, with any hope of accuracy to form an Estimate of the Annual Expense of such an Establishment—Once organized the work to be performed would probably grow in Extent & importance but at the same time it should only do so as it may be found useful to the Public; and there can be no doubt that in the Event of success, any additional Expense would be amply compensated by the saving which would accrue in other departments of Government in the preparation of voluminous and irregular Returns for the Houses of Parliament. But Their Lordships believe that they will be quite safe in limiting the Annual Outlay at present to a Sum not exceeding £1500 which they would request the authority of the Treasury to expend if necessary.

I am etc.

Copy of letter 21 December 1832

Board of Trade Office, Whitehall, London

To the Chamber of Commerce, Glasgow

Sir,

It is the wish of the Lords of the Committee of the Privy Council for Trade, to be made acquainted periodically, with the state and progress of manufactures and commerce throughout the United Kingdom, and to combine with a knowledge of these subjects such other matters as will enable the Government and Legislature to form an accurate estimate of the actual and comparative condition of the population.

In enquiries of this kind the Town of Glasgow and the district wherein it is placed must necessarily be considered of much importance; and the existence therein of a Chamber of Commerce, which is presented to them to be managed with much intelligence, seems to offer a great assistance towards the accomplishment of their Lordships wishes.

Before Their Lordships proceed to address an Official letter to the Chamber upon the subject, it has appeared desirable to Lord Auckland to apply to yourself privately and his Lordship has instructed me to request, that you will kindly favour me with a letter at your early convenience, stating upon what points you possess the means of communicating statistical information.

It will be not necessary to enter into further particulars in this private and preliminary communication. Their Lordships object will be sufficiently explained by stating that all information which can be said to belong to the subject of statistics will be acceptable to them.

It will add to the value of your communication if in replying to this letter you will take the further trouble of pointing out other channels which in your

opinion, may be made useful for obtaining such branches of information, as may not be within the province or the purview of the Chamber of Commerce. I am , respectfully, Sir, Your very Obedient Servt.
G. R. Porter

6.7 Ad hoc services and initiatives

The chambers took on all sorts of activities as short-term or one-off initiatives, as and when required (as indeed they still do). The first examples reproduced here develop the idea of a marine society as part of Guernsey chamber's activities. This had been suggested by several of the writers on political economy such as Mortimer in his *Elements of Commerce* (q.v. Chapter 3). It was taken up in several chambers, which encourage it as broader a community initiative; Guernsey's probably had the closest relation directly with a chamber. The second example was developed by the Dublin Committee of Merchants. This body had a range of innovative activities, but its major effort developed soon after its establishment in 1761 was to initiate a lottery. This was primarily for the purpose of building a Commercial Exchange (subsequently the Royal Exchange) as a home for the body; it was subsequently used by the chamber. The Committee's scheme is often referred to as the 'Exchange Lottery'. The construction of the Exchange was begun in 1768 before all funds had been raised, and was completed in 1779. Its lottery continued until 1780. The documents reproduced below give an example of the way in which the lottery was used to fund contributions to local charities as well as create surpluses towards funding the Exchange. This increased the popularity of the scheme. There is no set of complete accounts of income, expenses and prizes for the lottery. Some examples of the charitable disbursements, prizes and potential profits earned are shown here from three separate minutes. It appears the basic structure remained the same throughout so that, on the basis of these figures, each lottery draw would yield a surplus of about £8,000, or £13,000 if all tickets retained were also sold. Each ticket was sold for £1 14s. 1½d. which seems to have included the commission to selling agents. The returns were high, but the potential risks also high, especially if lottery sales were not returned, or if tickets were stolen. The minute for 1782 reproduced here shows the final exchanges to resolve disputes over the payment of accounts to the agent, Christopher Day, which had been running since 1776. This exchange indicates how the agent operated and which of his costs were allowable. As noted by Dudley, lotteries were common in Ireland and England from the 1750s, often used to fund substantial infrastructure or charitable projects; more fun than a simple subscription campaign and generally more successful in raising the money quickly. Dudley quotes that the 1779 Dublin lottery generated £51,756 5s., of which £47,035 went to prizes and costs, with the remainder of £4,721 5s. going towards paying off outstanding debts.[25] In many ways the Committee's initiative was pioneering, with many of its features taken into the Irish state lottery of 1780–1801, which superseded it.[26]

Sources
[a] Printed Notice pasted into minutes; Guernsey Archives AQ/040/01
[b] Rough Minute Book of the Dublin Committee of Merchants; RIA MS. 3 C 25.

Minutes, and printed notice Guernsey, 3 November 1835[a]

CHAMBER OF COMMERCE

THE COMMITEE of the CHAMBER OF COMMERCE request the Merchants, Ship-owners, Masters, Seamen, and others, to meet at the Douzaine-Room, at eleven o'clock, a.m., on Tuesday, the 10th instant, for the purpose of taking into consideration the Acts of Parliament of 4th and 5th year of William IV, abolishing the duty of six-pence per month paid by Merchant Seamen, towards the maintenance of Greenwich Hospital, and levying in lieu thereof in London and the outports a duty of two shillings per month from the Master, and one shillings per month each from the Seamen, "for the relief and the support of maimed and disabled Seamen, and the widows and children of such as shall be drowned in the Merchant service." The Committee being very desirous of providing a fund in this island for the same purpose, and in the hope of its being supported by voluntary donations and subscriptions, will submit the following propositions to the Meeting:—

1—That a Society be established to be entitled "Relief Society for the Merchant Seamen sailing out of the port of Guernsey."

2—That for the purpose of creating a fund for the same, each Master shall pay one shilling per month, each Mate nine-pence per month, and each Seaman six-pence per month; and further, in aid thereof, that there shall be levied one penny per ton annually on every vessel registered in this island. The said contribution to commence from the 1st of January next.

3—That a Committee be named to frame regulations for the management of the Society, and to take such other measures as may be thought necessary.

G.W.H. Davey, Secretary

[25] R. Dudley, *The Irish Lottery, 1780–1801* (Dublin, 2005) quoting *Faulkner's Dublin Journal*, 18–21 September 1779.

[26] Dudley (2005) *The Irish Lottery* (2005) 17–21, 14; also see Falkiner, 'Illustrations' (1902–4).

Minute Dublin, 8 November 1768[b]

[Example of lottery income used for charitable disbursements; it shows that the receipts were held in personal accounts by the Committee members as trustees for the lottery, and charitable donations were paid directly by them]

ORDERED that the Sum of £1000 appropriated for the Purposes of the Blue Coat Hospital out of the Profits of the Exchange [Lottery] Scheme for the present year be paid to Said Hospital by Messrs Rbt. Jaffray, George Sutton & Wm. Thompson.

ORDERED that the Sum of £1500 appropriated in like manner to the United Hospitals be paid by Mr. Wild, Mr. Dermot & Mr. Read.

ORDERED that the Sum of £500 appropriated in like manner to the Lords Hospital & Magdalen Asylum be paid equally between them by Thos. Thompson & Mr. Colvill.

ORDERED that the Sum of £250 be paid to the Hibernian Military School by Mr. Hartley & Mr. Stottell.

ORDERED that the Sum of £250 be paid to the Marine School by Mr. Magnally & Mr. Blake

ORDERED that the Sum of £100 be paid to the Meath Hospital by Mr. George Sutton & Mr. Alexr. Jaffray

ORDERED that £100 be paid to St. Nicholas Hospital by Mr. Cosgrave & Mr. Wm. Thompson.

Minute Dublin, 3 May 1770[b]

[Example of scheme of lottery prize fund and allocation of accounts]

[Prizes]			[Charities and total costs]		
2 of [£]2500	£5000		The United Hospital	1200	
3 of 1000	3000		Lock Hosptl.	200	
5 of 500	2500		Magdalen	200	
10 of 200	2000		Military & Marine	500	
15 of 100	1500		Meath Hospl.	100	
30 of 50	1500		Nich. do	100	
100 of 15	1500				
250 of 5	1250		[total charities]	2300	
1675 of 1. 14. 1½.	27768	13.	[prize costs]	50326	19. 8.
[total prizes]	46818	13.	[total costs]	52626	19. 8.
First Draw 1st 6 Days	600				
Last Draw	200				
Allowances to Subs.	2708	6. 8.			
[total income]	50326	19. 8.			

The above Scheme Unanimously agreed to by the Committee.

Minute Dublin, 20 November 1772[b]

[Example of Lottery tickets distributed]

The Secretary reported that he had delivered to the present night Forty Two thousand Tickets amounting in the whole to ---------------- £47883 6s. 8d.

Amount of Ten thousand sent to England	10833 6s. 8d.
Eight hundred kept by the Secretary	866 13s. 4d.
Amount of those which remain on hand being 5000 Numbers, Viz. 371–430, 471–1000—1541 to 2000 —4001 to5000—5001 to 6000—6001 to 7000, 7801 to 8000—8001 to 8750	5416 13s. 4d.
--	£65000 0s. 0d.

RESOLVED that the above five thousand Tickets be lodged in the Chest to be kept by & at the risk of the Scheme [replaces 'Committee', crossed out] and that in Case any other numbers be returned before the first Act of the drawing be received that they be also locked up in like manner for the same purpose.

Returned from London [ticket nos.]	14001 to 15000
	18001 to 19000
	50001 to 59000

Minute Dublin, 18 September 1782[b]

Report to Committee of Merchants

We the undersigned Arbitrators appointed to adjust and determine a Difference of Account subsisting between the Committee of Merchants and Mr. Christopher Day, having considered the several Matters referred to us as fully as very inaccurate Accounts and unsatisfactory Evidence have admitted of, do declare:

THAT With Respect to the Allowance for managing and conducting the Lotteries We are of opinion and do award that Mr. Day be allowed the Sum of Three Hundred pounds and no more for the Year 1776 and that the several Charges made by him for every other Year be admitted without Diminution.

THAT With Respect to the Sum of One Hundred and thirty pounds, eight shillings and five pence, a Loss incurred by the Transaction with Mr. Weld, We are of Opinion and do award, that the said Loss be charged to the Committee of Merchants, Mr. Day remaining accountable to the said Committee for any Dividend or Retribution which may hereafter be made thereupon.

THAT With Respect to the Sum of One Hundred and fifty seven pounds and five pence, Interest allowed on Payment to Tradesmen, We are of Opinion and do award that the said Sum be reimbursed to Mr. Day.

THAT With Respect to the Sum of Forty pounds, a charge made by Mr. Day for keeping a Bankrupt Calendar, we are of Opinion that the said Sum be not allowed to Mr. Day.

All which We do hereby give and publish as our Award accordingly —Dublin 18 September 1782. [signed]

William Cope Robert Black

Joshua Pim Danl. Marston

Chapter 7

Law/Political Agents and their Costs

An important transition from ad hoc to routine policy exchange for chambers was to develop the use of London agents. They were some of the earliest bodies to do this. Traditionally all successful campaigns used parliamentary solicitor or law agents, otherwise they were operating without specialist knowledge. The 1732–3 Excise crisis and the 1765–6 Stamp Act repeal campaign were probably the most significant campaigns to use agents before chambers were established. Agents were also used by the colonies, particularly the Americans and West Indies as well as UK localities.[1] These were usually solicitor-agents, who provided information on upcoming legislation and administrative changes, drafted Bills, and supported the orchestration of campaigns giving expert advice and contacts.[2] However, chambers began to go beyond using London specialists and appointed their own dedicated agents. Their experience is an important early example of this activity.

Jersey was the first chamber to use its own agent, in 1768. Initially this was through Jersey merchants located in London interrelated with trusted Jersey families: Messrs. James Amicea Lemprière, Gruchy and Le Breton, and Le Gros and Le Gros. These merchants were 'to fix among themselves one of them who may particularly receive instructions and remittances', and to hold a copy of the chamber's rules and list of subscribers 'for them to produce upon any occasion, to show the solidity [i.e. status] of the chamber'.[3] Jersey moved to appointing its own direct agent, termed their 'deputy in London', probably in the 1770s, though the first specific record of John Dumaresq acting is from 1785. At the same time Guernsey chamber appointed Havilland le Mesurier as its deputy, and the two chambers acted jointly on some issues. Jersey's Dumaresq briefed on legislative developments, purchased the Statutes of England, other books and maps, and held meetings

[1] See Bennett, *Local Business Voice* (2011) 291–9; J. M. Sosin, *Agents and merchants* (Lincoln, Nebraska, 1965); M. G. Kammen, *A Rope of Sand* (Ithaca, 1968) 105; A. G. Olson, 'Parliament, the London lobbies, and provincial interests in England and America', *Historical Reflections,* 6 (1979) 367–86; 'The Board of Trade and London-American interest groups in the eighteenth century', *Journal of Imperial and Commonwealth History,* 8 (1980) 33–50; 'The London Mercantile Lobby and the coming of the American Revolution', *Journal of American History,* 69, 1 (1982) 21–41.

[2] See e.g. Rydz, *Parliamentary Agents* (1979); Brewer, *Sinews of Power* (1989).

[3] Jersey Archives: chamber minutes, 14 March 1768 'agents appointed to manage the affairs of the chamber in England'.

to negotiate over petitions.[4] Dumaresq received about £60 per year for his efforts in the 1780s and 1790s, but was also handling an annual account of about £240 for lobbying expenses from 1786.[5] The instructions to him in 1787 and one of his expense reimbursements are reproduced here. Although he acted as the main delegate, he liaised with a London solicitor-agent (Triott).[6] Other Jersey merchants in London were also used as delegates, particularly Paul Le Mesurier during the chamber's charter lobby.[7]

Most other early chambers also used a connected London merchant, or solicitor-agents. In January 1782 Liverpool used a London agent, Henry Rawlinson who was a merchant, to petition the King over defence of the West Indies, in conjunction with the London West India Committee and Bristol (see Chapter 4). Over 1783–95, Glasgow used John Seton, who cost an average of £50–70 per year in agent's fees and expenses.[8] His expenses for his most extensive period of support, for the White Ashes Act and the Thread Act in 1787–8, is reproduced here. Dublin similarly used a London solicitor-agent, Charles Treadgold, costing them £10–15 per year in agent fees in the 1780s for which an invoice is reproduced here. In 1808, London, Liverpool and Manchester merchants used Henry Brougham as their parliamentary agent to lobby against the government's Orders in Council, for embargo of trade to Europe in other than British or neutral ships.[9]

A stage beyond contracting an agent was to establish an agency or office in London. Jersey's agent effectively evolved in this direction; but the most significant early chamber example was Glasgow, which moved away from Seton and established its own agent in 1789–90, following a *Plan* proposed by its chair Patrick Colquhoun in 1788 and reproduced here. Colquhoun was clearly not fully satisfied with John Seton, the *Plan* stating: 'a law solicitor who can have no accurate ideas on such subjects' results in 'enormous fees charged, it is the blind leading the blind' with the result that lobbies 'often fail'. Colquhoun had annotated Seton's bill for 1787–8, reproduced here, and there is a vigorous exchange of letters on costs. Colquhoun recognised that an agent had to carry weight and status to be able to approach ministers. His

[4] Jersey Archives: chamber minutes, e.g. 4 July, 1785, 30 June 1786, 2 March 1787, etc.; see also his negotiations with Pitt in 1790; TNA PRO 30/8/131 ff. 29–32, 35.

[5] Jersey Archives: chamber account books.

[6] Jersey Archives: chamber minutes, 30 June 1786.

[7] Jersey Archives: chamber minutes, 24 January 1788; also see Chapter 2.

[8] Glasgow Mitchell Library: chamber minute books TD 76/1; Seton was a Gray's Inn solicitor, connected to the Touch, Forbes and Coutts banking families, and related to Edinburgh merchants. He was also used for Glasgow's charter: see Chapters 2 and 5.

[9] Bennett, *Local Business Voice* (2011) 293, 389; once appointed, Brougham acted largely under his own initiative with the campaign on the Orders bound up with his own electoral ambitions in Liverpool, though there was some exchange with the Liverpool American chamber; see also *ODNB*.

Plan suggested that this could be achieved by being appointed by a document declaring the support of the Scottish Royal Burghs, the Scottish chambers and committees of trade, and by a 'General Commission' signed by 'a combination of respectable individuals engaged in commerce and manufacturers'. With the *Plan* is inter-bound a letter of support from the local MP, Ilay Campbell (reproduced here), who agreed that the agent needed 'good access ...and constant vigilance and attention ... and in short to act as a solicitor in all commercial matters ... [in] the interest of Scotland'. Campbell was a well-connected heavy-weight politician with whom the chamber had worked closely in 1784–6 over several Bills. Colquhoun himself became Glasgow's first agent for two years, after which the normal parliamentary agents were resumed.[10]

As well as Colquhoun's *Plan*, an account is reproduced here of how Colquhoun saw his role as an advocate for Glasgow commercial interests. This gives important insights into the lobbying process and the role of parliamentary agents. Although self-serving, this account demonstrates many elements of the process of lobby required: status and patronage to get a case heard; continued effort to form, restate, and present a case; and substantial outlay of time and expense. The *Plan* and this account also demonstrate how lobbying had to work from a position of loyalty and claim to be in the public interest: mere protest was a purely radical opposition, and naked self-interest ineffective.[11] Convincing cases had to be built from a position of loyal support for the government, showing how ministers could operate more efficiently for the national good, and to increase their own status and revenues.

Further offices in London were developed by the Liverpool American chamber of commerce, jointly financed with other trade bodies in the town from 1814 until the 1930s (latterly also supported by the corporation),[12] and an Irish chambers' agent in London over 1821–4, which was a co-operation between Limerick, Cork, Waterford, Sligo, Dublin, and Belfast.[13] Another early example was the Salt chamber of commerce (based in Northwich and Liverpool), whose secretary moved to become its London agent over 1853–73. The establishment of the first national chamber association (the ACC) was preceded by setting up a joint 'metropolitan' or 'town agent', which emerged in 1855. When Bristol circulated 23 chambers on 18 April and 6 June 1855 with this proposal, nine already had an agent (Liverpool, Manchester, Glasgow, Edinburgh, Newcastle, Southampton, Plymouth,

[10] Bennett, *Local Business Voice* (2011) 296, 392; also *ODNB*.
[11] See also Brewer, *Sinews of power* (1989); Hoppit, *Parliaments* (2003).
[12] See Henderson, 'The American Chamber of Commerce' (1933); 'The Liverpool Office in London' (1933).
[13] See Bennett, *Local Business Voice* (2011) 297–9.

Dublin and Leeds); seven agreed to go ahead (Belfast, Birmingham, Bradford, Bristol, Hull, Stoke-on-Trent, and Worcester); and four did not reply.[14] The seven going ahead adopted the title of 'united chambers', although the agent himself referred to the 'metropolitan agency' and also the 'association of provincial chambers'. Subsequently six of the initial seven chambers were among the ten first subscribers to the ACC in 1860, but Worcester opted out.[15] The use of London agents was reduced once the ACC was founded, but not all chambers joined, and major chambers maintained their own agent well into the 20th century, whether or not they also used ACC. London agents were thus a stepping stone to the modern successful national association.

Sources
[a] Chamber of Commerce minutes; Jersey Archives L/A/38/A1/2
[b] Dublin chamber of commerce, Minutes: TNAI
[c] 'An account [in his own hand], of the Public Services of Patrick Colquhoun': TNA HO 42/66, fo. 105–29.
[d] Draft in the hand of President Patrick Colquhoun; Glasgow Mitchell Library TD1670/4/52.

Minutes Jersey, 30 January 1787[a]

At a Meeting of the Committee of the Chamber of Commerce held this Day

Mr. Thos Holgrove fined for non-attendance at the Hour appointed.

In Consequence of an Act of the Chamber of the 21st Dec. last the Committee have met and Resolved to recommend to John Dumaresq Esq. that as the Parliament is now Sitting he will take the first possible opportunity of going over to England to prosecute the Several Applications for which he is deputed by the Chamber.

The Committee have further resolved that Mr. Triott of London be desired to Supply Mr. Dumaresq with the Money he may have in hands belonging to the Chamber to be employed for forwarding the different applications they have now depending in England for which purpose the Treasurer will give the Necessary directions to Mr. Triott and that a General Meeting is to be call'd to provide the means of further Supply to carry on the said Matters.

[14] As recorded in Worcester chamber minutes, 20 June, 1855 (held at chamber); see also Bristol chamber, *Annual Report*, 30 July, 1855, p. 8.

[15] For a full discussion of the metropolitan agent over 1855–60, and role of Levi in other chamber initiatives, see *Local Business Voice* (2011) 300–5, 278–87.

Articles of the Memorial which the Committee of the Chamber of Commerce thinks are the most material to be obtained and which they recommend Mr. Dumaresq to lay Stress upon

Art. 1st—Liberty to import from the British West India Island the Article of Rum and to reship the Same from Newfoundland and other parts of the British Dominions where the fishery is carried on.

Art. 2—The whole of this Article should be pressed and if contrary to our Expectations the Oil could not be included it would Still be an advantage to obtain the other produce of the Fisheries.

Art. 3—Idem.

Art. 4th—Olive Oil is the principal Article here, as Tobacco may be exported when Manufactured in the Island.

Art. 5—This is a very material Article & should be pushed as much as any one.

Art. 6th—This would be a very advantageous Article but the Committee are apprehensive that it will be difficult to obtain it, as the Trade with America is not regulated.

Art 9th—Is an Article much wanted & Necessary for the Consumption of the Island.

The Committee also recommend to Mr. Dumaresq to get a Determination as soon as possible of the Application of the Merchants respecting the Harbours.

The Traders from this Island to Southampton have lately been charged with the Portland Lights,—which they had never paid before and which being to the Westwards of both places are entirely out of their Track. Mr. Dumaresq is desired to make Enquiry about this matter at the Trinity House.

Jersey: Bill for John Dumaresq for 1799[a]

Dr[awn on] The Chamber of Commerce of Jersey
To J. Dumaresq

1799 March 23rd	For his attendance in London at the Treasury and Custom House from the 11th Febr. To 23rd March both inclusive on the Memorial of the States respecting the registering of Prize Vessels & for sundry writings & close application to that Business.	Sterling £43.1.–
	For fees and gratuities paid at the Treasury & Custom House & for Coach hire & Porters employed on the Business.	6.5.6

1798 December 14th	For so much paid in Account to Messrs. Le Mesurier, Mr. Cook's Bill for fees & agency in procuring leave to Register Recaptures at Jersey	7.7.–
		£56.13.6

Dublin Minutes Dublin, 20 November 1784[b]

Resolved to make payments

To Mr. Chas. Treadgold of London for English votes last session (English) £2 18s. 9d.

& Ab[raha]m. Bradley King £1 15s. 11d.
for Irish votes.

Account of the Public Services of Patrick Colquhoun Glasgow, 1 September 1802[c]

For upwards of twenty five years Mr. Colquhoun's life has exhibited a series of gratuitous Services. At a very early period of his life, namely in the Year 1777, he contributed a handsome Sum of Money for the purpose of assisting in raising a Regiment for His Majesty's Service at a time when the disasters of the American War and the accumulation of national difficulties rendered necessary Sacrifices and personal exertions obvious to very good effect.

In thus contributing to furnish One thousand men for the Service of the State Mr. Colquhoun was one of very few who subscribed and paid the largest Sum given by any Individual without any personal advantage in obtaining the Appointment of Officers.

From the Year 1779 to 1789 (comprising a period of ten Years) while various pressures occurred which at various times greatly affected the National Commerce and Manufactures, Mr. Colquhoun subjected himself to great personal labour and bestowed unremitting attention year after year upon a number of objects of a public Nature, and by timely applications and various conferences with His Majesty's then Ministers and others in the confidence of Government, he was happily instrumental, not only in averting evils in their nature calculated to check the National Industry but also to promote arrangements calculated to give new opportunities and qualities to the Commercial and Manufacturing Enterprise of the Country which, under the guidance of a wise administration produced that unqualified prosperity which rapidly followed the conclusion of the American War.

As a proof of the confidence placed in Mr. Colquhoun by the respectable Community of which he was a member he was not only placed at the head of the Magistracy by the unanimous voice of the people, at a very early period of his life, but he filled all the other situations of trust and respectability which tended to convey a sense of the Esteem and confidence of the public.

The testimonies he received of public Approbation both from the principal Manufacturers of England and of Scotland were repeated and numerous, and as peculiar Marks of Gratitude these reiterated public services were recorded on various pieces of plate which were presented to Mr. Colquhoun by different respectable public Bodies from the years 1778 to 1786

Vide Appendix A. Nos. 1, 2, 3, 4, 5, 6

In the years 1783 and 1784 when a Committee of the House of Commons was engaged in developing Causes of illicit Trade Mr. Colquhoun at that period and afterwards sacrificed much valuable time in procuring and communicating useful information which while it was entirely gratuitous on his part proved (as he has reason to believe) of no small benefit to the Country.

In the Year 1792 His Majesty was pleased to appoint Mr. Colquhoun one of the Magistrates of the Police under the Act which passed for establishing Seven public Offices in Westminster and those districts of Middlesex and Surrey which joined the Metropolis.

In the Year following and also in 1796 Mr. Colquhoun received the public Thanks of the Silk Manufacturers of Spitalfields for his exertions in detecting and suppressing a System of depredation on the Property of the Master Weavers which had for many years previous to this period been carried on to a very considerable extent and proved highly injurious to this great Branch of National Industry.

Vide Appendix B. Nos. 7 & 8. …

This work has also attracted in a peculiar degree the notice of His Majesty's Subjects in the East Indies and the American and West India Colonies and has produced a Testimony from the Legislative Body of the Virgin Islands who state the following reasons for placing Mr. Colquhoun in the honourable and confidential situation of Agent for the Colony in Great Britain. In the letter announcing this Appointment the Legislative Committee use the following words: 'As the choice which has fallen on you is totally uninfluenced by any private exertions in your behalf and only owing to your elevated Character as a Magistrate and the eminent Services which You have rendered to Society in general and the West India Colonies in particular by your admirable treatise on the Police of the Metropolis We hope much Sir, we expect everything which energy and ability can effect'.

[Summary of contents of the Appendices A and B, each letter giving Colquhoun a gift or some personal tribute; only comment on chambers quoted in full]

A. No. 1 Royal Burghs of Scotland Convention 10 July 1783.

A. No. 2 Chamber of Commerce and Manufactures [Glasgow] 1784: That Fifty pounds be presented in Plate to Patrick Colquhoun Esq. in testimony of the sense which they entertain of his public spirit in establishing this Society and his ability in conducting every part of its Business committed to his Charge. [Chamber minute on this reads (5 August 1783): 'agree to spend 50 guineas on a piece of plate to present to Patrick Colquhoun for his attention in negotiating with London'].[16]

A. No. 3 The Manufacturers of Muslins in the City of Glasgow 1785.

A. No. 4 The Linen Printers of Glasgow 1785

A. No. 5 The Manufacturers of Paisley 1786

A. No. 6 The Linen and Calico Printers of the City of Glasgow 1786.

B. No. 7 Weavers Hall, London, 2 October 1793.

B. No. 8 Committee of the Society for preventing and punishing Embezzlements and other offences in the Silk Manufactures.

Handwritten paper Glasgow, October 1788[d]

[Colquhoun was appointed the 'Commercial Agent for the Chamber in London' soon after this report (minute 12 November 1788). He operated for about 18 months: he was paid £30 for 1789 (part year) and £100 for 1789–90, with no payments in 1790–1].[17]

Plan of a Public Agency in London For Commercial Affairs.

London being the Seat of Government all Public business and all Commercial regulations are settled and adjusted there; either by His Majesty's Executive Government, or by Parliament.

Since Commerce & Manufactures have extended themselves in so great a degree all over Great Britain, regulations of State as well as Legislative protection have become necessary for the encouragement of useful industry; thence it follows that almost every month, nay every week something is occurring at the Seat of Government interesting to one or other of these numerous Bodies of Traders and Manufactures who from their remote distance and from this inability often to act singly, may suffer extreme injury; and in so suffering the Country at large feels the effect of any depression which may come upon the Trade from hasty regulations or Laws not calculated for the general good, as for want of that genuine information which is only to be obtained by the voluntary Communications of Commercial people.

[16] Glasgow Mitchell Library: minutes TD 76/1.

[17] Glasgow Mitchell Library: Annual accounts, in chamber minutes TD 76/1–2.

In London, there are Agents for the Provinces abroad—Law Agents,—Solicitors, and Army & Navy Agents for transacting business at the Public offices: —But hitherto there has been no Commercial Agents Established in London.—No public character appears for the Interest of Commerce & Manufacturers.—No person has yet attempted that particular line: whereby combining a general knowledge of Commerce & Manufactures with a well regulated system—all Precedents with regard to Commercial transactions with the State may be acceptable to mercantile & manufacturing Bodies together with a Public Office where a Collection of all public State papers relative to Commercial affairs are to be found. —Where proper Cases may be drawn in all necessary applications to Government, and where Commercial Bills passing through Parliament often hastily before they can be known to Mercantile Bodies at a distance may be watched and corrected or delayed if found partial or injurious.

No person educated to Commerce & connected by Correspondences with the various Commercial Bodies in Great Britain has yet attempted to stand forth in a line applicable to the general intent of Trade.—And hence it has followed that Government are not seldom deceived by erroneous information and Individuals who are occasionally compelled to go up to London as Delegates find themselves engaged in a business always very tedious and often no less irksome than expensive, principally from the want of these aids which are necessary to men whose time & talents do not permit them (although compelled by interest) to engage in public business without many Disadvantages from a want of System.—from a want of Knowledge of precedents. —from a deficiency of that general Commercial Knowledge which enable men to know and understand how to proceed in a public applications & finally from want of time to pursue the object with steadiness & Propriety.

In many instances Delegates coming from the Country not only subject themselves to an immense labour & expense in a long attendance in London; but being ignorant of the forms of business themselves, application is made to a Law Solicitor who can have no accurate Ideas on such subjects, and who are even unacquainted with the means of obtaining the necessary Knowledge and information, & hence it often happens that while very enormous fees are charged it is the blind leading the blind and in that Case it is not to be wondered that many inaccuracies Creep into Commercial Bills in Parliament and that many just and proper applications for the real Interest of Commerce & the Country often fail because of improper management—want of knowledge, or want of industry in the Conduct of the business.

The Commercial transactions, as well as the various Manufactures of Great Britain have become now so Complicated and extensive, that it requires a regular Education to that particular line as well as years of study &

investigation to be able to explain many points to a Minister, and also to be able to know where the most accurate & proper information is to be found.—To judge at once when a question occurs to what quarter to apply for the best explanation & the most accurate knowledge upon the point of difficulty.

In no one way can these advantages be obtained either to the Country at large as being interested in good and Salutary Commercial regulations, or to the merchants & Manufacturers who may be occasionally aggrieved, but by means of a public commercial agency in London under the management of persons who will turn their whole attention to such objects, and whose general System is such as to give them these immediate aids which are to be derived from a collection of every useful Commercial Record as well as long experience & unremitting Industry.

When it is considered what an immense Sum of money is expended yearly by the Commercial & Manufacturing bodies in transactions with Government in State negotiations, and in Commonplace business with the various public offices.— It is easy to discern the Utility and advantage as well as the great oeconomy of the proposed Institution.—For it may be fairly argued that under the regulations of a Commercial Agency the same aggregate business might be done well & effectively at <u>one third</u>, perhaps at <u>one fourth</u> of the present general expense to the Country, while it might prove a sufficient object to one or more Establishments, where the gratuity should be moderate and in proportion to the labour attending the business.

But that the duty of a Commercial Agent as an Institution now proposed to be Established should be clearly Understood the following outlines are suggested as explanatory of Some part of the general detail.

1st. That the person assuming the Character of a <u>Commercial Agent for public business in London</u> should establish an office with proper and able assistance, in which shall be kept a Collection of all <u>Commercial Memorials</u>, <u>Cases</u>, <u>Informations</u>, <u>and other Manuscripts as well as all publications applicable to the Institution</u>, or <u>calculated to give information in all Cases which may occur</u>.

2. That the business of this Commercial Agent shall be '<u>to attend to all public Commercial Bills in the House of Commons</u>—<u>all investigations at the Board of Trade</u>. <u>To keep open a Constant Correspondence with all Commercial</u> and Manufacturing Bodies who are his Constituents. To inform them of all interesting occurrences by the Earliest opportunity; and all Parliamentary regulations or Bills brought in' where their interests may be affected, and to transmit Copies of Bills in progress through Parliament and other State papers interesting to the different Commercial bodies at a distance.

3. To Transact all public Commercial business—to draw all Cases, Memorials, Commercial Bills, or other public Papers necessary, as the Case may happen.

4. To hold interviews with the King's Ministers, The Board of Trade; and other public Boards according to the nature of the business and the Circumstances of the Case.

5. To find a proper person or persons under the Direction of their Agents to attend the Progress of Commercial Bills through Parliament & to transact all business relative thereto.

6. To [act as] Agent [for] all the claims of Individuals on public offices, or for money due them by the public, and for this purpose to act by a power of attorney when necessary.

7. To assist the Manufacturers in procuring authentic information of the State and progress of Manufactures in foreign parts and in general to Collect for the use of those who may do business through medium of this Commercial office, every species of useful information both at home and abroad which may prove interesting to the Trade at Large.

8. To assist such Manufacturers at all times who are under any difficulty, in London, in giving or procuring the best advice and assistance when the Case may require.

Such are the general Outlines of the plan for Establishing a Commercial Agency office in London.

Upon the Sense of public utility there can be little doubt of the advantage of such an Institution, because it holds out benefits which do not at present exist, and it has an immediate tendency to abridge and lessen the enormous expense which attends all public negotiations at present.—It gives a facility to public business through the medium of a Combination of information & experience upon similar Subjects, from its becoming the business of a certain number of Individuals to turn their sole attention to vast objects and pursuits.—It relieves men closely engaged in Commerce & Manufactures from the hardship and necessity of a long and tedious attendance personally in London to the injury of their affairs at home.—It saves the expense of many and frequent journeys to the Capital.—It enables every person aggrieved to transact many important matters of public business chiefly by Correspondence which at present requires personal attendance.

But in order to obtain these advantages to the Trade it must appear evident at first view that the public Countenance to be given to the Commercial Agent must be such as to render his situation respectable and his authority in all general questions admissible in the Eyes of the King's Ministers and the different public offices of State.

To Effect this purpose so necessary at the Outset & to give vigour and energy to the Undertaking some Document in the form of a general Commission from public Bodies and respectable Individuals will be necessary.

But in order to elucidate this idea it may not be improper at once to Come to particulars—

1st. In order to give weight to the proposed Commercial agency the person who holds it would probably be able to render the office of Considerable benefit to the Trade and Commerce of Scotland by an Appointment from the Royal Boroughs declaring him to be the Commercial Agent of that Body in London.

2nd. Similar Commissions from the Chambers of Commerce and Committees of Trade in Edinburgh, Glasgow, Perth, Dundee, Montrose & Aberdeen &c.

3. A General Commission from a Combination of Respectable Individuals engaged in Commerce & Manufactures approving of the Agent and promising to conduct their public business through the medium of the proposed Institution and to give their Countenance to the general System.

Such respectable authorities would at once stamp a weight and dignity on the office and give to every single body politic or even every single Society of men or Individuals who might have occasions to transact public business, the weight and influence of the whole.

A Commercial Agent thus supported could at all times command a ready Access to every Member of Parliament and even to the great offices of State when Occasion should require.—And hence arises the benefit of a Combination of influences and of a person publically known as authorised to attend to the Commercial Interest of the Country and to assist Members of the Legislature in procuring information by Correspondence with Constituents or otherwise when Bills connected with Commerce or Manufactures are passing through Parliament.

Not that it is meant to Subject any of the public Bodies above mentioned, or any of the Individuals who may Countenance this Institution to the Shadow of expense except for business actually done for them in consequence of a special application.—Neither is it meant to subject such Bodies or Individuals to continue to do their business through the medium of this Commercial Agency unless it shall be conducted to their satisfaction and at an expense more moderate than they have heretofore been accustomed to pay. The Agents own trouble will be all gratuitous.

In short it is proposed that the Commission to be granted shall extend No farther than a testimony of approbation of the Institutions as useful to the Commerce & Manufactures of Scotland and of Confidence in the good Conduct and ability of the agent in rendering it so, by giving His own attention & labour when it Can be spared gratuitously, & only charging for the labour of assistants.—For this purpose the Commission may run the following terms viz.

[letter from Campbell bound into the Plan at here, between pp. 9–10; q.v. below]

'The Annual Committee of the Royal Boroughs of Scotland appointed to transact all business during the recess of the Convention (In Virtue of Conventional powers to us Committed.) Having taken into Consideration the great utility of an Established Commercial Agent in London for the purpose of Collecting information & giving assistance to the Representatives of the Royal Boroughs in Parliament, & in transacting other public business with His Majesty's Executive Government when the interest of the Commerce or Manufactures of Scotland shall require the same,—& having the fullest Confidence in the integrity & abilities of _____ Esquire we do hereby authorise him until the next meeting of the General Convention of the Royal Boroughs to assume the Designation and to act as the Commercial Agent of the Annual Committee of the Royal Boroughs of Scotland in London, and to watch over the general interest of the Trade of the Royal Boroughs and to Correspond with this Committee as occasion shall require, with powers & authority to charge only for such actual business as may be transacted in virtue of specific directions from this Committee

Given under our hands & Sealed with the Seal of the Preceding Borough at the office of the Convention of the Royal Boroughs in the City of Edinburgh this day of _____ In the Twenty Eighth year of His Majesty's Reign.'

The Commission from the different chambers of Commerce and Committees of Trade may run nearly in the same stile as the above. viz.

'We the Directors of the Chamber of Commerce & Manufactures established by Royal charter in the city of _____ that from our remote distance from the Seat of Government and for other reasons equally obvious the Establishment of a public Commercial Agent in the City of London would be of great utility to the Commerce & Manufactures of this District of Great Britain. Do hereby nominate & appoint _____ Esq. to Act in Our behalf and in the behalf of our Constituents as Commercial Agent for transacting public business in the City of London.—And having the fullest Confidence in the integrity, And ability of the said

We do further authorise him until the next General meeting of the Chamber to assume the title & Designation of Commercial Agent in London for the Chamber of Commerce Manufactures in _____ and to act in that Capacity by attending to whatever shall relate to the general interest of the Commerce & Manufactures of Scotland as carried on by this Body politic, with power to Correspond with our chairman & Secretary as occasion shall require, and also to transact such business as shall be specifically Committed to his charge for which a reasonable gratuity shall be allowed.

Given at the Chamber of Commerce & Manufactures in _____on the _____ day of ____and in the Twenty Eighth year of His Majesty's Reign, In Testimony whereof this Commission is Signed by our Chairman & Secretary & the Seal of our Corporation is hereunto affixed.'

The Above form will with a small variation be applicable to all the Commercial Society's in Scotland.—That which relates to Individuals will however in some respects be different.

The following Specimen is humbly suggested namely.—

> 'We the Undersigned merchants & Manufacturers in Great Britain, Considering that much inconvenience has of late years arisen from the want of a Stationary Commercial Agent for public affairs in the Seat of Government where a Register of Precedents may be kept and where Individuals aggrieved in any particular may want for assistance and information in all public negotiations with his Majesty's Executive Government and for other purposes connected with the general System of transacting public Commercial Business: and being Convinced that much benefit will arise to the trade as well as to the public in General by the establishment of a Commercial Agent in London who will be known and acknowledged as such in virtue of proper person & authority to act in that character.
>
> And we having the fullest Confidence in the integrity experience and ability of __________ Esq in such matters of [missing half line of text on torn page] & appoint him as our Commercial Agent in London with full liberty to Correspond with us as Individuals when our Interest may be affected, and to assume the title and designation of Commercial agent for us who Subscribe these presents and whose Designations are annexed to our respective subscriptions.
>
> Hereby declaring our approbation of the institution of a General Agency for Commercial Affairs in London to give our full Countenances to the said _______ by Committing to his charge such public business as we may consider as falling under his particular department where we do not transact the same ourselves: and to allow him a reasonable gratuity for such specific business as shall be transacted through the medium of the said office.
>
> In Witness whereof we have signed & Sealed these Presents and have annexed Hereunto the names of our respective places of residence our proper designations and also the date of our Signatures.'

Letter from Ilay Campbell M.P., bound into the Plan between pages 9 and 10; 11 October 1788

To Patrick Colquhoun Esq. Garscube [House, Glasgow]

Dear Sir

The Establishment of a general Commercial Agent for this Country in London is a Subject which I have often thought of, & I have long been of opinion that such an Institution properly conducted would be extremely useful.—I am happy to think that this Country is advancing in Trade Manufactures & industry of every kind, & from the Experience of five years as Member for the District of Glasgow, I have good access to know that the Commercial part of this Country has frequently very important Business of a public Nature to transact both in Parl[iament] & out of it, which can only be done in London & which besides occasional assistance from Members of Parl[iament] would require the constant vigilance & attention of some person in the Character of an agent to correspond with Societies & Individuals here to convey Information where it may be wanted & in short to act as a Solicitor in all Commercial matters where the Interest of Scotland or of Scotchmen is concerned.

When great Commercial Points are agitated the Traders of Scotland have not the advantage of being at hand, & they may not always have exactly the Same Interest or the Same objects, with those of the same Class elsewhere. Deputations are often necessary to be sent by them to London at a great Expense, which might in a good Measure be saved by employing an active & intelligent agent on the Spot. I am on these accounts, & others which could be suggested a zealous friend to the Plan hinted at in your Letter, & I know no Person more fit than yourself to give it a beginning.

I am Dear Sir your most obedt. humble Servt.

Ilay Campbell

Chapter 8

The General Chamber of Manufactures

The General Chamber of Manufactures was not a local body, nor constituted in the same way as the other chambers discussed in this volume. However, it was a very prominent early body adopting the title 'chamber', and its short life had great influence on local chambers. Its activities have also had disproportionate scholarly attention which has distorted the literature so that presentation of some of the General Chamber's key papers alongside those of local chambers is valuable to demonstrate the key differences. There has also been little effort to investigate how different chambers and committees that existed before the General Chamber viewed it. For example, when the prominent campaign over the Irish Propositions in 1785 has been discussed, almost no attention has been given to the Irish chambers' point of view, or other views from local chambers around Britain.[1]

The documents presented here cover the two sets of rules of the chamber, in 1785 (which combines the rules with a series of resolutions about the Irish Propositions), and in 1787 just before the chamber broke up in acrimony. These can be compared with the rules of local chambers. Whilst the General Chamber was centralised and composed of a few nominated delegates who made decisions, the local chambers were local and referred most major decisions to a general meeting. The local chambers had an equality of member status for members who were all individual business people, whilst the General Chamber had an equality of status for delegates: these varied between representatives of whole local chambers and individuals who sometimes represented no one but themselves. Thus whilst local chambers had checks to ensure a majority voice from a whole community, the General Chamber could be swamped by majorities of voice from very small sectional interests. The confused chairing and representational structure also led to potential for high levels of instability of the General Chamber making it vulnerable to violent swings deriving from the personalities of different chairs and leading figures. Whilst the founding chair (Josiah Wedgwood) was tem-

[1] J. Ehrman, *The British Government and commercial negotiation with Europe 1783–1793* (Cambridge, 1962) 50 , 196–200, 491–2; Bowden 'English manufacturers' (1919–20) 18–35; Bowden, *Industrial Society* (1965) 155–67; Redford, *Manchester Merchants* (1934) 11–13, 51, 205–7; Clapham, *Economic History* (1926); Ashton, *Iron and Steel* (1963); Helm, *Chapters* (1897) 60; Beresford, *Leeds Chamber* (1951) 13, 62, 103; V. E. Deitz, *Before the Age of Capital* (Princeton, 1991); Rose, *Firms* (2000) 135.

perate, experienced, skilled in arguing that he was helping the government, and careful to align interests, others (notably Thomas Walker) were keen to use the chamber to support their individual political or 'radical' agendas which were bound to alarm government. The imbalances of representation and its instability proved to be fatal defects leading to its collapse over conflicts in 1787 concerning the Treaty being negotiated with France. The Treaty of Commerce 'New Irish Song' reproduced here shows one of the many personal attacks that resulted from the tensions between the 'generalists' such as Wedgwood, and the 'political activists' such as Walker.

The documents reproduced also show how delegates from localities struggled to align their views. The case of Nottingham, for example, shows how its three delegates could hold and promote different views, and these could be variously aligned with different political or other agendas. Further discussion and documents on the tensions in Nottingham are reproduced in Chapters 2 and 4 of this volume. Another example from Jersey shows how they took a specific view on the parts of the 1787 French Treaty affecting them. The position in Manchester, where a General Chamber delegate was appointed through the Fustian Committee, shows how Manchester was distancing itself from Walker, and indeed subsequently disavowed him as their delegate.

The position of the Dublin chamber on the Irish Propositions, previously largely ignored by historians, shows how it was attempting to manage opposition in the Irish parliament. It is notable that Dublin's chamber meeting on 10 February 1785, which had begun in the afternoon, continued into the night until 2.00 a.m. on the 11th and was then reconvened at 11.00 a.m. Some dissent is recorded in the minutes, but clearly there was more in play than differences between sector interests. The Dublin members were generally against the propositions as conveying no benefit. This can be compared with earlier petitions of the chamber in 1783–4 which had called for equal treatment of Irish trade (see Chapter 5). There was some disagreement between the Catholic worsted manufacturer Richard McCormick who was unhappy with prohibition of the export of wool but otherwise felt the propositions were acceptable, and William Arnold, who disagreed. The committee of the chamber, however, came out strongly against the propositions as not providing the equality of treatment the chamber had been previously seeking. Cullen, reporting this discussion, argues that the manufacturers were more radical than the merchants, but the minutes suggest they were much of the same view, with the merchants in fact more prepared to take a definite stand.[2] The main battle was in the Westminster parliament, but the chamber kept close watch on the matter, reporting developments, but holding

[2] Cullen, *Princes and Pirates* (1983) 50–51.

its fire awaiting developments in Westminster. The intention was to issue opposition if needed. On 9 June merchants in 'other trading towns in Ireland' were circulated asking them to pressure the Irish parliament seeking equality of treatment. But otherwise, at each meeting until 4 August, it was agreed to postpone action. However, on 4 August it was agreed to petition 'expressing their disapprobation of the Commercial arrangements proposed to Ireland by the British parliament'. The petition that followed (reproduced below) is argued by Cullen to be highly political in tone, calling the propositions 'manifestly unjust in their Commercial Operation and in their political object highly insulting to the dignity of this free Nation ... [and] subversive of the independency of its Legislature'. The address became unnecessary as in August Pitt allowed the propositions to lapse. The chamber then sent an address of thanks to the members of the minority of the House of Commons. Between 9 June and 4 August there were 25 meetings where consideration of the propositions was postponed, four more meetings between 4 and 8 August when the petition was agreed, and eight more meetings before news of the defeat of the propositions was reported on 18 August: 37 meetings in all.[3]

In Birmingham there was considerable opposition to the Irish propositions until the end, with much of the documentary material already published by Wright.[4] Here one petition at a late stage aimed at influencing the House of Lords consideration is given, illustrating the more trenchant opposition from different manufacturing sectors which Walker sought to use. The documents from the Staffordshire Committee of Potters demonstrate the influence of Wedgwood, even more experienced in lobbying, in supporting the General Chamber, but with provisos even at the outset in 1785: the General Chamber was supported 'so long as it continues to be conducted for the Purpose of watching over the Manufacturing interest of this Kingdom' and that it 'Proceed in the same line of conduct which it has hitherto absorbed; regardless either of allurements, or menaces, that may tend to divert it from the main Objects'. The enthusiasm of the potters continued, with Wedgwood's influence clearly evident in the call for the General Chamber to seek a charter on 6 November 1786. But the Potters Committee minutes have a gap after that 6 November meeting for over two years, until February 1789 after the General Chamber had failed. Indeed without the General Chamber as a focus the Potters Committee itself seems to have also withered, with its last meeting recorded on 27 July 1790.

In contrast, the documents from Glasgow show how what was now a mature, experienced and well-developed chamber dealt with the machinations

[3] Cullen, *Princes and Pirates* (1983) 51; reproduced by MacMahon, *Respectable Meeting* (2014) 69, who incorrectly states this as 35 meetings

[4] Wright, *Chronicles* (1913) 13–21.

by Walker, the General Chamber, and the potential for faction. The Report of the Delegates for the City of Glasgow on the various lobbies in which they engaged in early 1785 gives important insights into the General Chamber and also the subtleties and persistence required in the lobbying process. It has been entirely neglected in previous historiography. The two delegates, Patrick Colquhoun the chair of the chamber and Alexander Brown the Provost of Glasgow, were both experienced in dealing with government and the need to organise opposition so as to be reasonable and unchallenging to the existing order and ministers, and to be distant from party. The Report is a valuable commentary on the issues, but also provides a unique insight into how experienced individuals moved from a position of friendly influence, to organised opposition but without raising political alarm bells.

Sources
[a] Manchester Central Library GB 127.m.503 f.19
[b] ECCO
[c] Manchester Central Library M503/26
[d] *Nottingham Journal*
[e] *The Merchants' and Manufacturers' Magazine of Trade and Commerce* (2 vols., 1785, 1786): Goldsmiths Kress Collection, London Senate House Library; also in MTMW.
[f] Jersey L/A/38/A1/2
[g] Manchester Central Library GB127.f.1787 2a
[h] Manchester Central Library GB127.f.1787 2b
[i] Dublin Chamber of Commerce Minutes; TNAI
[j] Glasgow Chamber of Commerce minutes: Glasgow Mitchell Library TD 76/1
[k] Birmingham Commercial Committee: Birmingham Central Library C/19/27082[5]
[l] 'Potters' Committee of Commerce', minutes: Wedgwood Archives, MS. E39–28404 'Josiah Wedgwood's commonplace book'.

London foundation

Printed report London Tavern, 10 March 1785[a]

At a numerous and very respectable adjourned Meeting of Manufacturers, from various Parts of this Kingdom;

Sir Herbert Mackworth, Bart, in the Chair:

The following Resolutions having been proposed and read, were unanimously agreed to, viz.

Resolved,

I. That it is the opinion of this Meeting, that the manufacturing interest of Great-Britain has suffered in many instances, for want of a general bond

[5] See also Langford, *Birmingham* (1868) 324–5.

of union among the Manufacturers, and of a free intercourse between them in the different parts of the kingdom; which is more especially called for at this time, to consider matters of the greatest importance, respecting the Commercial Interests of Great-Britain and Ireland.

II. It is the opinion of this Meeting, That a probable means of producing such an union and free intercourse, would be, *the Establishment of a Chamber of Manufacturers* in London, to watch over their interests at large as one aggregate; to communicate and correspond with the several Committees which are, or may be, established in different parts of Great-Britain; and likewise, to be prepared to furnish Government, if required, with such impartial and true information, as they may, from time to time stand in need of, for the protection of the Commerce and Manufactures of the empire at large: for the want of which (or by relying on the information given by interested individuals) the true interest of the whole has been often unavoidably mistaken.

III. Resolved, That the above Chamber of Manufacturers be composed of a Chairman, a Deputy Chairman, and a number of Assistants, to be elected as Deputies from the different Manufactories within the kingdom of Great-Britain, who shall wish to support the measure; and also, of other persons, being Manufacturers; who shall be duly elected according to regulations hereafter to be formed.

IV. It is the opinion of this meeting, That a Committee be now formed, to prepare proper regulations for such an institution, with a secretary to attend them, to sit from time to time as occasion may require, to receive such communications as may be delivered in for the use of the Chamber of Manufacturers, and to transact such other business and affairs as cannot conveniently be delayed from the time of one meeting of the Chamber to another. But all regulations made by the Committee, which may affect the body at large, shall be laid before the next meeting of the Chamber for confirmation. And a Committee was accordingly appointed to meet on *Monday* next, the 14th Instant, at the *George and Vulture Tavern, Cornhill*, at Eleven o'Clock in the Forenoon.

V. That the British manufacturers are greatly interested in the commercial negotiations with Ireland, now under the consideration of parliament.

VI. That the manufacturers of this kingdom ought not to object, and will not object, to any system of fair, equal, and equitable commercial regulations, being adjusted and finally settled between the two kingdoms.

VII. That *each specific article, the produce or manufacture of either kingdom, being made subject precisely to the same duty in one country as in the other*, as held forth by the third resolution of the House of Commons of Ireland, on the 7th of February last, is by no means calculated to produce that equality.

VIII. That in a commercial treaty between two countries, where it shall so happen that the exports, duty free, from the one, consist chiefly of an article of which the other can send very little in return; in order to produce a real equality, this balance against the latter ought to be made up by the admission of such other articles, duty free, as the latter can send to the former.

IX. That the Irish linens imported into England, duty free, amount yearly to about £1,400,000, whilst the British linens imported into Ireland do not amount to more than about £30,000; and that other articles, the produce or manufacture of Ireland, are imported, duty free, into England to the amount of about £700,000; making together upwards of two millions sterling of goods annually imported from Ireland into Britain, duty free; being four-fifths of the whole exports of Ireland.

X. That the fair equality does not consist in stating the *specific* articles of one kingdom against those of the other, as *linens against linens*, but in the value or amount of goods imported, duty free, into each kingdom respectively, being the same, or nearly so: and that in order to balance the advantage which Ireland has over England in this respect, either Ireland should admit articles the growth, produce, or manufacture of Great-Britain, duty free, to the amount of two millions yearly, or Great-Britain should *lay a duty upon Irish linens* sufficient to indemnify her for the duty which Ireland has laid, and is to continue, upon British goods of other species. But the whole exports of the produce and manufactures of Great-Britain to Ireland, being less than one million yearly, it follows, that if the whole of those exports was admitted duty free, Ireland would still fall more than one million deficient, in compensating Great-Britain for the admission of her linens, &c. free of duty into England.

XI. It is therefore the opinion of this meeting, that Ireland not having wherewithal to balance with, or pay an equivalent to, England, for more than one million of her produce being imported into England duty free; it would be as unreasonable in her to expect, as it would be unwise in Great-Britain to grant, a greater indulgence than she is able, if she was willing, to pay for: more especially if we consider, that when we have once bound ourselves never to lay a tax upon Irish linen, we have lost our best, if not our only security, for any equitable regulations of commerce in future, or for settling any commercial disputes which may arise from many unforeseen causes.

XII. That the partiality shewn here in favour of Irish linens, by admitting that article duty free, besides giving a bounty on its exportation from England, and at the same time laying a heavy duty upon the same article, the produce of other states, has already rendered those states unfriendly to the admission of British manufactures. And that when the provisions in the 9th resolution of the Irish House of Commons stating, "that the importation of articles from foreign states should be regulated in each kingdom on such terms as may afford an effectual preference to the importation of similar articles, the growth, produce, or manufacture of the other" shall pass into a law here, it will be extremely difficult for this country to negotiate a commercial treaty with any other state in Europe.

XIII. That unless Ireland will agree to pay equal duties with Great Britain on all articles imported from foreign states, and some regulations be adopted respecting those articles which are objects of exportation, and *subject to an excise* in either country, no scheme of equalization can be devised which will not in effect prove highly detrimental to Great Britain.

XIV. That the thanks of this meeting be given to Sir HERBERT MACKWORTH, Bart. for the very able and impartial manner in which he conducted the business of this meeting.

Printed minute London Tavern, 12 March 1785[a]

At a SPECIAL COMMITTEE.

Having this day received the most authentic information, that no alteration whatever can be made in any one of the Irish Propositions now before the House of Commons, but that the whole must stand or fall precisely in their present form; and as it is evident, from the debates of yesterday, that should the first proposition be passed on Tuesday next, the house is considered as pledged to consent to the remainder: it follows, that any expectations which may have been entertained by any Manufacturers, that their interests in particular will be taken care of, must prove groundless.

The hope that some alteration would be made in these Propositions so as to render them compatible with the manufacturing interest of this kingdom, seems hitherto to have prevented any petitions being presented, against these destructive measures; and it is now urged, that no such petitions appearing, it must be concluded that the manufacturers are satisfied. But that hope being now entirely cut off, speedy and vigorous measures are necessary, to avert the impending evil.

Signed on behalf of the Committee,

JOSIAH WEDGWOOD.

All Letters, &c. for the Committee, to be directed to *Henry Smeathman*, Secretary, at the *George and Vulture Tavern, Cornhill.*

Printed report London, 27 March 1787[b]

PUBLIC PROCEEDINGS OF THE GENERAL CHAMBER OF Manufacturers of Great Britain, ON THE FRENCH TREATY. From the 9th of February to the 27th of March, 1787. Printed pamphlet London, Circular Letter agreed at a General Meeting held 27 March 1787 [Resolution III].

General Chamber of Manufacturers of Great Britain, at a General Meeting held March 27, 1787.

When the plan of the General Chamber of Manufacturers of Great Britain was, for the first Time, formally submitted to those whose interests this establishment was especially intended to protect and to promote, the great objects of our association were declared to be, that, 'the influence and experience of the whole being collected at one common centre, the manufacturers might be the better enabled to effect any salutary purposes for their general benefit; to procure and circulate useful knowledge among themselves; and to communicate to Government such authentic information respecting their various manufactures, as might occasionally be required, untinctured with the selfish designs of interested individuals.'

On the important occasion which gave rise to our institution, we may now, without vanity, say that all these objects were greatly and happily attained. Our combined influence gave success to the opposition, which our united experience dictated, against a measure at that time cherished as the favourite of its adoptive father: The different papers of the Chamber contained a mass of mercantile knowledge, which, as trust, will not soon be forgotten; and such was the authentic information which we communicated to Government, in the face of our country, at the bar of the British Commons; and so truly did it appear to be untinctured with the selfish designs of interested individuals, that a system, affirmed to be wholly unalterable, was in many particulars completely reversed. Yet, too many of its original defects still remained. We renewed our objections, and, though we were not able directly to prevail, yet on the whole, we extorted such modifications as, fortunately for this country, occasioned the ultimate overthrow of the projected arrangement by the legislature of the sister kingdom.

Another question has now arisen of yet greater moment. We sincerely think, that it would have been both unjust and unwise to have made Ireland the workshop of the British dominions; unjust, to have transferred to her the advantages, without the burthens of this country; and unwise, to have divided the feat of Commerce from the feat of Empire. Nevertheless, there would have been one consolation, that Ireland is still subject to the same Sovereign, whose power must be exercised with the advice of the council of Great Britain. Nor can we suspect her of a wish to break the easy bond of such a connection. Thus circumstanced, had our apprehensions been realized, as we are firmly persuaded they would have been under the Irish Propositions, our wealth at worst would but have changed its situation; it would not have totally emigrated. But this is not the case under the present Treaty with France. If our evidence on the subject of Ireland be true, which we conscientiously believe it to be; and if it applies to the present measure, which we ought seriously to consider; then, all that we lose will be gone for ever; nor will the loss only impoverish us, but it will also enrich our ancient rival; a tried enemy of ages, and at best but the suspicious friend of a day.

Soon after the communication of the Tariff, and yet more, when the whole Treaty was published, certain doubts, which struck forcibly on some of our minds, were entered on the books of the Chamber; while these still remained unsatisfied, (as *some* of them do even at this hour) a Committee met, having been partially called by letter. It happened, however, by some neglect or other, that the Chairman and two other Members were not duly summoned. A diversity of opinion prevailed, both in the arguments urged and the correspondence read. But finally, those Members who remained passed a set of Resolutions, and ordered them to be printed; by which, though they in some degree intimated rather too decisive an approbation of the Treaty, yet further information was properly solicited.

A General Meeting was advertised to be held on the 24th of January, but was postponed to the 5th of February, on which day the Meeting took place. The Committee were then unanimously requested, to investigate certain important points there stated, and to obtain information on the doubts expressed on their Minutes, and to Report thereon. That Report was received, approved and ordered to be printed by the General Meeting, held on the 10th of February, when a new set of resolutions passed unanimously, affirming certain great principles, by which the Committee were directed to examine the Treaty, and a moderate and respectful Petition to Parliament was signed, praying time for discussion and deliberation.

The principal doubt respecting the repeal of the laws which prohibit the emigration of our workmen, and the exportation of our tools, has been in some measure *publicly* answered; but some well-founded alarms which still remain on this subject, are stated in the observations of the Committee on the third resolution of the 10th of February. The other great doubt relative to the irreciprocity of drawbacks, by which Great Britain will supply her own Colonies with the products of France, without any similar advantage to her own Manufactures, still exists in its full force, as it is stated in the Report of the 9th of February. As to the general list of laws to be repealed by the Treaty, no denial has been given to the Report of the Committee.

In the first part of the Report on the Resolutions referred to the Committee by the General Meeting of the 10th of February, some facts, which seem to be of indisputable strength, are stated. The answer to the first Resolution contains a general view of the probable advantages which either party may reasonably expect from the present Treaty; and the remarks on the third Resolution comprehend a more minute examination of the Manufactures of this country; how far they are natural or accidental to our soil and climate, and consequently how far they are likely to be permanent or transitory. Under this head too, will be found such a brief account as we could collect of the comparative state of Great Britain and France. In the continuation of the same Report on the IVth, Vth, and VIth Resolutions referred to the Committee, will be found a statement of French duties, on certain articles of their own, of English and of other foreign Manufactures, more particularly detailed, than we presume to be yet generally known to the Manufacturers of Great Britain.

This latter part of the Report has been much longer suspended, than we could have wished. We have, however, the satisfaction to reflect, that the delay did not originate in any negligence of the Chamber at large; but from some respectable Members, to whom, on former occasions and on other grounds, the manufacturing interests of this country have been eminently indebted; yet who in the present instance, feeling themselves bound and pledged by their own Resolutions of the 9th of December, have unfortunately chosen rather to endeavour at defending their precipitation on that day, than to give way with becoming deference to the enquiries repeatedly sanctioned by General Meetings. But we are happy to add, that the sense of the majority has at length prevailed; and we hope without any material interruption of that union in our exertions, which alone can make us truly useful to those on whose behalf we are associated.

The chief benefit resulting from our establishment *here* to the Manufacturers in the country, must arise from the facility of collecting and concentrating in the metropolis, every kind of information from every distant quarter of these kingdoms; and in the subsequent communication of all, which we may thus draw to ourselves. To this branch of our duty we mean for the present, strictly to confine ourselves; and whether our best judgment may ultimately agree with the opinion of the many, or the few; yet while we proceed no farther than to examine, and to report such facts as we can ascertain, and such reasonings as occur on candid deliberation; surely we ought not to doubt the universal approbation and support of all our numerous brethren. We think it necessary, however, to avail ourselves of the opportunity presented by this circular Address, for the purpose of learning what specific assistance we may in future expect; and we shall esteem ourselves obliged to all persons who will immediately signify their intentions on this head to our Secretary.[6]

If it shall finally appear from our correspondence, that the majority of the Manufacturers of Great Britain think, with the majority of this Chamber, we shall cheerfully, and with confidence, both decide and act; but, if we shall happen to be among the minority on the present important occasion, we shall not oppose, where we cannot hope fair success: we shall declare the motives of our dissent, we shall record and circulate our solemn protest; but

[6] Mr. James Penny, No. 38, Fenchurch-Street.

we shall not come to any decisive resolution, which may be thought to set our opinions above the sentiments of the public. If we did more, we might seem to be deficient in respect to the general body of our Brother-Manufacturers; if we did less, we should certainly be wanting in justice to ourselves.
THOMAS WALKER, Chairman.

[Report continued with summary of proceedings of meetings under chairmanship of either Thomas Walker or Josiah Wedgwood, 10 February—27 March 1787, covering details of the French Treaty and differences of views.] ...

PLAN OF THE GENERAL CHAMBER OF MANUFACTURERS OF GREAT BRITAIN.

The Manufacturers of Great Britain constitute a very large, if not a principal part of the community; and their industry, ingenuity, and wealth, have contributed no small share towards raising this kingdom to the distinguished and envied rank which she bears amongst the European nations. Their manufactures are the basis of our foreign commerce, and it is ultimately upon them that the value of the landed property depends.

Their importance to the state, and their influence upon the rest of the community, seem, however, to be little attended to by the politicians of the present day; who, satisfied with the prosperity which the nation has already acquired, and not aware how instrumental the exertions of our artisans have been in procuring it, have proposed and adopted measures, calculated to accelerate that decline of the national prosperity, which many recent circumstances demonstrate to be rapidly advancing.

That this subject is much better understood by the rulers of other European nations, appears by their active endeavours to avail themselves of the supineness of our governors, and by the vigorous efforts they are making, both openly and surreptitiously, to transplant the British manufactures into their respective dominions, by enticing our workmen, instructed in the manual practices, and acquainted with the inventions of their masters;—by procuring from us the tools, implements, and machines of various kinds, invented and made by the ingenuity of British artisans, for perfecting their several manufactures;—by prohibiting, throughout their dominions, the *sale* of articles produced or manufactured in Britain, or laying immoderate duties upon the importation of them; and by applying those duties, not to the exigencies of the state, but to the encouragement of similar manufactures among themselves;—convinced, (to use the just and emphatic expression of the Emperor of Germany, in his edict for that purpose,) that the '*well being of the state depends essentially upon the prosperity of its manufactures.*'

Nor have the manufacturers themselves sufficiently understood their importance to, and connection with, one another. Intent on the particular objects to which they are attached, they have not extended their views beyond their respective spheres, or considered the relation which they naturally bear to one another, as parts of one great whole, embarked in one common interest. Diffident of their own resources, they have not hitherto thought of uniting their strength, of acting in concert, and thereby obtaining that assistance, reciprocally, from one another, which their respective situations have often stood in need of, and which nothing but united counsels and exertions can afford. From this cause it has happened, that the interests of many distinct bodies of manufacturers have, by a variety of unwise regulations, been injured, oppressed, and themselves driven into the open arms of our rivals.

On the manufacturers, of late years, great part of the national taxes have been imposed; and a mode of taxation has been adopted, peculiarly oppressive to the subject, and destructive to that spirit of emulation and improvement, so essential to the progress of arts, and which, if persisted in, and extended to the degree that there are grounds to believe is intended, must finally prove fatal to the most certain sources of wealth and strength to this nation.

It seems hitherto likewise to have escaped the notice of manufacturers, that whilst the *landed* and the *funded interests*, the *East-India*, and other *commercial bodies*, have their respective advocates in the great council of the nation, *they* alone are destitute of that advantage; and it is probably from this source that many of their grievances have arisen, — that they have so repeatedly and perhaps inadvertently been oppressed by ministers unacquainted with their real interests, and misled by the designs of interested individuals.

Common danger having at length brought together a number of Manufacturers in various branches, and from various places, and these having felt the advantages resulting to each from unreserved conferences, and mutual assistance, they are now persuaded, that the prosperity of the Manufacturers of this kingdom, and of course that of the kingdom itself, will be promoted by the formation of a general bond of union, whereby the influence and experience of the whole being collected at one common centre, they will be the better enabled to effect any useful purposes for their general benefit.

By this means, also, they will procure and circulate useful knowledge among themselves, and will be able to communicate to government such authentic information respecting their various manufactures as may occasionally be required, untinctured with the selfish designs of individuals. For as it is their firm resolution to give a general and determined opposition to every attempt to wound the interests of the kingdom through the sides of its Manufacturers; so are they equally disposed not only to submit to, but on every occasion to strengthen the hands of Government, by promoting the patriotic measures of every administration for the general interests of the Empire.

With these views, and on these principles, is the *General Chamber of the Manufacturers of Great Britain* established, as well as the corresponding Provincial Chambers.

London, as the seat of government, and the grand magazine of the kingdom, must obviously be the place of general union, but the members of the body extend over the whole kingdom. In order that this numerous body may be conducted with prudence, and act with vigour, the following regulations are agreed on, as the commencement and first basis of a plan that may be afterwards improved and enlarged.

REGULATIONS.

1. This institution shall consist of Manufacturers, and such Delegates (being commercial men of the same description) as may be appointed by Provincial Chambers; out of which body shall be annually chosen a President, Vice-President, and Treasurer. Every member, not subscribing to a Provincial Chamber, shall pay annually the sum of *One Guinea*. The Provincial Chambers shall pay to this institution at the rate of 5s. per annum for each of their members. Each subscription shall be understood to continue, till the subscriber gives a written notice to the Secretary of his intention to withdraw.

2. A General Meeting shall be held soon after the meeting of Parliament every year, at a time to be fixed by the Committee, besides such other General Meetings as may, from time to time, be called on particular occasions.

3. A Committee shall be annually chosen by ballot at the aforesaid General Chamber, consisting of twenty-one Manufacturers residing at London, who shall meet on the first Thursday in every month; and of this Committee the President, Vice-President, and all Delegates from Provincial Chambers shall be members, and be intitled to vote; any five of whom shall form a Committee. Every member of the General Chamber shall be at liberty to attend, but not to vote.

4. A Chairman shall be appointed to the Committee when they are chosen by the Chamber, by annexing the word Chairman to one of the twenty-one names in the list to be delivered in for the ballot; and the person who has the majority of votes, so distinguished, shall be declared elected, who shall preside when present at all times, unless the President or Vice-President shall attend, both at the Chamber and at the Committee. Their and the Treasurer's accounts shall be audited at least twice in the year, and reported to the General Chamber. The money belonging to this institution shall be lodged in the Bank, and whenever it amounts to more than the sum of 200 L. shall be invested in Exchequer bills, or some productive fund. No money shall be disbursed on account of this institution, except by order of the Committee.

5. A Secretary and proper office shall be provided to this institution. The business of the Secretary shall be to attend all General Meetings of the Chamber, and of the Committee. He shall attend at the office on such days at such hours as shall be directed by the Committee. He shall fairly transcribe all the minutes into proper books, and keep copies of all letters and papers, in due order, for the inspection of the members. He shall preserve all other books and papers belonging to this institution, and shall, on all occasions, follow the directions of the General Chamber, and its Committees.

6. The Committee shall propose to the General Chamber such Regulations as they may, from time to time, think necessary; which shall be confirmed, amended, or rejected, at a succeeding General Meeting.

7. Any five members of the Chamber shall be at liberty to call a Committee whenever they see occasion, by notice in writing to the Secretary. The Committee, in like manner, shall be at liberty to call a General Chamber; and shall be obliged so to do at the request of twenty-one members of the Chamber at least, when delivered to them in writing, signed by such members, through the hands of the Secretary.

8. Any member of this institution may, on application to the Secretary, in London, either by person or by letter, receive information respecting any matter concerning any branch of manufacture, or matter relative thereto; and if it so happen that the question, shall comprise any matter of law to be decided upon, proper opinion shall, if necessary, be taken at the expense of the Chamber.

Printed Pamphlet c.1787[c]

A NEW IRISH SONG.
Intitled and Called THE TREATY OF COMMERCE.
To the Tune of—"Ballynamoniora."[7]

Troth Mr. *John Bull*, y'are a pretty *Milch Cow*!
Oh! what do you think of us Volunteers now?
Sure I told you, the Work we kick'd up in the State,
Before it was finish'd, wou'd all be complate,
With my Ballynamoniora, Ballynamoniora, Ballynamoniora,
The Treaty of Commerce for me.

Troth I said now last Year, if you'd call it to mind,
What we left you *before* we wou'd not leave behind,
And was'nt I right now, by Hook or by Crook?
For all that *we left you*, is all that *we took*.
Ballynamoniora, &c. &c.

[7] All spelling and italics as in original.

But 'twas deadly good-natur'd in you to lay down,
With the *Wrongs* of our Trade, all the *Rights* of your own,
'Twas a mighty *home* Stroke of magnanimous Pride,
To brake your own *Backs* for the Thorn in our *Side.*
Ballynamoniora, &c. &c.

Oh! like Fools, we despair'd that our terms wou'd go down,
Or such sharp Propositions be sweet to the Crown;
Then how pleasing to see your proud Stomachs to fall,
When we'd *thrown 'em up first* that you *swallowed* them *all.*
Ballynamoniora, &c. &c.

Sure I heard Master Orde now relate in his Place,
All your bountiful Gifts of superfluous Grace;
Jesus! how we all star'd, while he empty'd his Sconce,
To find such a big Bag of Blessings at once.
Ballynamoniora, &c. &c.

Oh the brave British Subject! his Looks were so sweet!
When he lay'd down your Case and your Trade at our Feet;
And the Comments he made too, the wise little Elf!
To shew us that Britain's no Friend to Herself.
Ballynamoniora, &c. &c.

Troth, it plas'd him, he said, cou'd a Briton say more?
That the Trade of *your* Country wou'd shift to *our* Shore,
And that Britain's Disasters had sunk her so low,
The good Tidings he brought us wou'd finish the Blow.
Ballynamoniora, &c. &c.

Then he said, 'twas contriv'd too by Part of the Gift,
That without Irish Linens ye can't make a Shift;
Troth now Ladies and that's a good Measure for you,
When the *Linen* comes over the *Yard*'ll come too.
Ballynamoniora, &c. &c.

Now, we took it most kind, that your Ruler of State,
Who they say has no Parts, but the Parts in his Pate,
Should for *Female Commodities* open a Door
And let freely the *great Irish Staple* come o'er.
Ballynamoniora, &c. &c.

'Twould have bother'd my Head now, the Words he let fall,
When ye gave us *so much*, ye gave *nothing at all*;
But in Dublin I heard his Interpreter swear,
That *nothing in England*, means *every thing there.*
Ballynamoniora, &c. &c.

But your Minister says, now we've got all we can,
The Two States must be join'd on a permanent Plan;
By my Soul he's a Joiner of a notable Cast!
Who *loosens all Ties* now, to join us *more fast*.
Ballynamoniora, &c. &c.

And he says when all Duties and Drawbacks are paid,
That the Navy will want what we make by our Trade;
Troth she will, want it all, now he's right on that Score,
And she'll *want it*, God help her, for *ever and more*.
Ballynamoniora, &c. &c.

If you Wish now to know how Cards we have play'd,
Why we took up *our Clubs*, and we threw down our *Spades*;
So ye dealt us all *Trumps* now for that *very Thing*,
And so Pam became civil as well as the King.
With my Ballynamoniora, Ballynamoniora, Ballynamoniora,
The Treaty of Commerce for me.

Nottingham

Printed report Nottingham, 26 March 1785[d]

Report of a meeting of the General Chamber of Manufactures, London 23 March 1785

Mr. [Matthew] Boulton of Birmingham in the Chair; …A letter from Nottingham being received, appointed Mr. Carpenter Smith of Southwick, W. Northage and W. Hayne, manufacturers of Nottingham, as their delegates, but Mr Hayne stated that he declined accepting as he did not agree with the petition and the rest of those signing, and nor did Mr. [Robert] Smith, the representative [MP for Nottingham].

Mr Carpenter Smith stated that he agreed with the petition and stated that the sentiments of Mr. Smith had no weight whatsoever, when put in competition with the petitioners, who must, undoubtedly, know their own interests better than he could.

Mr. Hayne then attempted to give a long opinion of his own, contradictory to the sentiments of the petition; and had the *modesty* to declare that he knew what was for the interest of the petitioners better than they did themselves; and it came out, that the petition had been sent up to him, but instead of acquainting the two other gentlemen named as delegates, he had taken it himself to Mr. Smith (the Member) and gave him his opinion in direct contradiction to the instructions he had received.

Several Gentlemen were of the opinion, that as Mr. Hayne was inimical to the meeting, it was scarcely decent for him to stay in the room; on which he retired.

[petition text follows from the 'Manufacturers of hosiery & stocking against the Irish Proposals']

Printed letter Nottingham, 2 April 1785[d]

Letter from Mr. W. Hayne, Milk St. [Nottingham]

[responds to the 'false representation' in the *Nottingham Journal* report] …

The facts are that I went to the George and Vulture tavern at the request of Mr. Wedgwood who had called that morning at my house, otherwise I should have attended only as a manufacturer with the delegates of Nottingham Mr. Northage & Mr. R. C. Smith. But on reading a letter addressed to Mr. Wedgwood, it appeared that there were three delegates appointed! So he was appointed but he thought it proper to say, that as my sentiments did not coincide with the petitioners, I declined acting as a delegate, and attended as a private manufacturer.

[there was also confusion over delivery of the letter; he objected because] …

The committee at Nottingham had not stated, either to their members, to me, or to any other persons concerned, the grounds of apprehending that any injury would ensue to their manufacturing. … He did not foresee any evil consequences would arise to the standing of manufacturing for the proposed regulations. …

I had an equal right, with every other Gentleman there, to give my opinions;—and that if it was not well founded I should be glad to receive information.

[he would not engage any further in the business of the chamber] …

There are other modes of adjusting differences, much to be preferred by Gentlemen to that of censuring each other, and obtruding it on the public.

Printed report Nottingham, 4 June 1785[d]

The petition of Nottingham manufacturers signed by 2064 persons against the Irish Proposals was presented in parliament by David Parker Coke MP (who seconded the motion to postpone consideration of the proposals).

[Coke was the other MP for Nottingham, largely an independent]

Printed Proceedings Nottingham, 25 March 1785[e]

Read a letter from Robert Smith MP for Nottingham. He presented the petition [in the House] but with opinion of his own that the Irish propositions … would not in a single instance affect … Nottingham. We think such a declaration was uncandid towards your constituents. …

Mr. Colquhoun pointed out the necessity for the Chamber to steer clear of party … ; he particularly advised no resolutions to be hastily drawn up or agreed to until they had been maturely considered.

[This account accords with other records that Robert Smith presented the Nottingham petition against the Irish propositions but then proclaimed his disagreement as not having any effect on Nottingham industry. Smith was the senior MP in Nottingham, a partner in the prominent Payne & Smith bank, but was not an active MP and this is one of his few recorded speeches: Namier and Brooke, *The House of Commons, 1754–1790*]

Jersey

Minute Jersey, 9 November 1786[f]

At a Meeting of the Committee of the Chamber of Commerce held this day

Took into Consideration the Articles of the Treaty of Commerce between England & France and found nothing therein contained prejudicial to this Island except we are not allowed the same leave of importing all French Manufactures in England as we hitherto have enjoyed with respect to the Articles of Wines etc. It has been resolved that we should beg the Lieutenant Governor to write to Lord Beauchamp to desire his Assistance in Parliament to obtain the Privileges of importing French Goods from this Island as if directly from France. Mr John Dumaresq is to be desired to write to his Lordship to the same purpose. The Committee is also to write to Messrs Le Mesurier & Tr[i]ott on that Subject.

It having been represented to the Committee that it was thought that a Vessel should be sent with provisions to meet the homeward bound Ships that may be in Distress for want of [provisions] owing to the long continuance of contrary Winds, it has been resolved that the Chamber should meet tomorrow morning at 9 o'Clock to decide their opinion on that Subject.
Ph. Hamon, Secretary.

Manchester

Printed leaflet Manchester, 27 February 1787[g]

A Public Meeting being this Day convened to take into Consideration the Proceedings of the Committee on the 19th Instant, and particularly the Letters, which the said Committee then wrote to the Members for the County, I am ordered to lay the same before the Public for their Information.
JAMES RADFORD, Secretary

---

19 February 1787
Copy of a LETTER sent to THOMAS STANLEY, Esq.; and to JOHN BLACKBURN, Esq.;

SIR,

By Order of the Committee of Trade and Manufacturers met this Evening I have the Honour to enclose you a Copy of their Resolution, and also to request your support to render the Treaty with France efficacious.
I am. With the greatest Respect, SIR, Your obedient and Very humble Servant
JOHN KEARSLEY, Chairman.

19 February 1787
"At a special Meeting, held here this Evening, of the Committee of FUSTIAN MANUFACTURERS.

Resolved Unanimously

"That as several Resolutions have been published in the London Papers, by the General Chamber of Manufacturers of Great Britain, expressing Doubts relative to the Expediency of the Treaty of Commerce lately concluded between this Kingdom and France, and a Petition signed by some Members of the Chamber having been presented to House of Commons, praying Parliament to defer the Consideration of the said Treaty, until the said Petitioners shall have Time to satisfy themselves relative to the several Points alluded to in the said Resolutions and Petition.

"We, the Committee appointed at a General Meeting of the Fustian Manufacturers for the Purpose of corresponding with the Lords of the Committee of Council, respecting the Commercial Arrangements between this Country and France, think it incumbent on us to declare, that no Person has been appointed by us as a Delegate to the General Chamber of Manufacturers.

"That after the most mature Deliberation, We are unanimously of Opinion, that the Commercial Treaty between Great Britain and France will be highly beneficial to the Cotton Manufacturers of this Town and Neighbourhood, and we hope and trust, that Parliament will with proper Expedition proceed to render the said Treaty efficacious.
"By Order of the Committee,
JOHN KEARSLEY, Chairman."

Printed leaflet Manchester 27 February 1787[h]

To the MERCHANTS, MANUFACTURERS and all Others, interested in the WELFARE of the Town and Neighbourhood of MANCHESTER.

You are called upon this Day by public Advertisement, to attend a Meeting, convened "to take into Consideration the Proceedings of at

Committee, which met on the 19th instant, and particularly, the Letters which the said Committee then wrote to the Member for the County.

This Committee was appointed at a General Meeting of the Fustian Manufacturers to correspond with the Lords of the Committee of Council for Trade, respecting the Commercial Arrangements between this Country and France; a Copy of the Letter addressed to each of our worthy Members may be seen in the *Manchester Mercury* of this day.

This Letter was written by the Committee, for the purpose of disavowing any Connection with a Body of Men, who, calling themselves The General Chamber of Manufacturers of Great-Britain, (tho' it does not appear that the Members have been severally authorised by the different Manufacturers to act for them) have taken upon themselves to Petition Parliament to delay its sanction of the commercial Treaty between these Kingdoms and France; and had published a Number of Resolutions in the London Papers, expressive of Doubts, relative to the Propriety of several of the Articles contained in that Treaty.

To this Measure they were more especially called, as a Gentleman of respectable Character, who had on a former Occasion been delegated by the Fustian Manufacturers to attend Parliament [Thomas Walker], had, at a Meeting of that Chamber, declared his Disapprobation of the Treaty in the most unreserved and unequivocal Terms, and had strenuously promoted the Forming of the Resolutions and Petition.

The Idea which the Kingdom at large entertains, of the Chamber of Manufacturers, is, that it consists of a Number of Persons delegated from the Manufacturers of Great-Britain, to superintend their Interests.—Yet it appears that their Meetings, though held in London, have rarely consisted of above six or seven Individuals; and these self-appointed.—In their late Proceedings they had taken a Part, so diametrically opposite to those of the Committee, and to the Opinions which they had delivered to the Lords of the Committee of Privy Council for Trade, in Consequence of the Power invested in them, and to the known general Sense of the Manufacturers, that it seemed incumbent on the Fustian Committee to declare, that no Person had been delegated by them to attend the said Chamber; and show that they had steadily and consistently persisted in the Principles by which they had been induced, in their Corresponden[ce] with Administration, to approve of the Treaty. This was[a] Measure necessary to the Vindication of their own Ch[ara]cters, and to the Prevention of Misconceptions, which m[u]st have had an injurious Effect on the Proceedings of [Pa]rliament.

To the Committee the General Meeting confided the Correspondence with the Lords of Council, on the Business of the Commercial Arrangement, as far as the Interests of the Cotton Trade was concerned; and, I believe, they have endeavoured to discharge their Trust, with Zeal and Fidelity.

Look back, I beseech you, on the State, to which the Trade of this Town and Neighbourhood was reduced not many Months ago — Small was the Demand for raw Materials; our Warehouses were full of Manufactured Goods; our Weavers, tho' Wages were greatly reduced, were scarcely employed; our Home Trade was at a low Ebb; and, in many Parts of Europe, where our Manufacture's had usually found a Market, the Ports were shut against their Admission—Every thing was drooping, languid, and desponding.

To what is owing the present Alteration in the Face of our Affairs? The amazing Increase in the Price of raw Materials? The great Demand for manufactured Goods? The full Employment of all the working Part of the Community? And the Advance in the Price of Labour? Will any Man lay his Hand on his Heart, and say, That the Change is not produced by the Prospect of the Commercial Treaty with France, being carried into Execution by the Authority of Parliament.

Shall we then be prevailed on, in order to gratify *a vain Spirit of Resentment*, to undo every Thing that has affected us? After [the] Administration has, with the greatest Attention, complied with every Thing we have asked, and secured the *legal* Admission of our Cotton Goods into France, on such Duties as promise considerable Advantages to our Trade; shall we, I say, *ungratefully* to *them*, and *injuriously* to *ourselves*, endeavour to overturn the Fabric which has, with so much Labour been erected for our Accommodation; and plunge again into Distresses and Difficulties, from which we have so recently, so happily emerged? Should such be the Result of our Meeting, This Day, our Conduct will be stigmatised as absurd and inconsistent; and we can never expect that, on any future Occasion, Government will consult our Inclinations, or hearken to our Requests.

Let me then beseech you to attend the Meeting with a Determination [to j]udge impartially, and a Resolution not to be led astray from the pursuit of your real Interests. If the Committee have [acte]d with Diligence, and with Propriety, they will doubtless meet with that Approbation and Support, which is due to a respectable Body of Men, who could have no other Motives for their Conduct, than a desire to promote the general Interests of the Manufacturers, by whose Authority they had been appointed.
A Friend of the Manufactures and the Extension of Commerce.

Dublin

Minutes Dublin, 10–11 February 1785[i]

[Report presented from various different commercial interests that had been invited to comment; only the manufacturers' response is recorded]
Reported …

THAT the Manufacturers are of Opinion that the Propositions if carried into Effect will not convey any benefit whatsoever to their several Branches.

THAT the Duties proposed while they continue the Importation of British Manufactures into Ireland will not allow Irish Manufactures being imported into Great Britain.

Mr. McCormick being asked his Opinion whether under the Propositions those Manufactures would be in a worse situation than they are now in—answered he thinks they would not.

Mr Arnold declared a contrary opinion.

Mr McCormick stated as the opinion of the Woollen and Worsted Manufacturers that the exception to the export of Wool from Great Britain to Ireland destroys any chance of benefit to those manufacturers from the Propositions but that were they allowed to share the Wool of Great Britain the said manufacturers would be content with the Propositions or would freely consent that all duties on the said Manufactures between the two Countries should be entirely abolished.

RESOLVED that the said information from the Gentlemen Deputed by the Manufacturers of the Woollen Worsted Silk Cotton and mixed Goods be referred to the Committee of the whole Council.

The order of the day being read for the Council to Resolve itself into a Committee of the whole Council to take the Resolutions proposed in Parliament by Mr. Orde[8] into further consideration.

....

Mr. Maquay from the Committee of the whole Council reported that they had come to the following Resolutions which were received and read:

RESOLVED that it is the opinion of the Committee that the Intercourse and Commerce between Great Britain and Ireland should be finally settled and regulated on permanent and equitable Principles of mutual advantage and unequivocal reciprocity.

RESOLVED that it is the opinion of the Committee that the Proposition submitted to the House of Commons relative to the mutual interchange between the two Kingdoms of Articles not the Growth Product or Manufacture of the other is fully consonant to the Principles stated in the above Resolution.

RESOLVED that it is the Opinion of this Committee that the Proposition submitted to the House of Commons for establishing between the two Kingdoms the same Duties on the Admissions into each of Articles of the Growth Product or Manufacture of the other will not in some material instances really accomplish that Reciprocity on which the Propositions are professed to be founded in as much as the Maturity of the one Country

[8] Chief Secretary of the Irish Parliament.

causing her Manufacture to be of a fine Fabric while the infancy of the other only allows the Manufacture to be of a coarse Fabric, the same Duty per yard or price being laid on the Coarse as on the Fine may be Admission to one but exclusion to the other.

RESOLVED that it is the opinion of this Committee that where there now exists any Prohibition in either Kingdom on the Exportation to the other of Articles of its Growth Product of Manufacture the encountering such Prohibition with Prohibition is not calculated to encourage and extend as much as possible the Trade between Great Britain and Ireland or reconcilable to that object of Affection and mutual liberality of Intercourse which should prevail between Countries so closely and we hope inseparably connected.

RESOLVED that it is the opinion of the Committee That if a Measure so unfriendly as that of Prohibition shall be persisted in on the part of Great Britain it will be highly impolitic in Ireland to preclude herself for ever from adopting a similar Conduct in respect to the Exportation of the Material of her staple Manufactures.

RESOLVED that it is the opinion of the Committee That an effectual Preference to Articles of the Growth Product or Manufacture of each Country over those of Foreign States on their Importation into the other Country should be Secured by a mutual Engagement that any present existing preference shall in no sort be ever hereafter lessened.

RESOLVED Unanimously this Council do agree with their Committee in the said Report.

RESOLVED that Mr James Hartley, Mr. Wills and Mr. Geale be appointed a Committee to prepare a Petition to Parliament grounded on the said Resolutions.

RESOLVED that the Council do meet this Morning at Eleven O'Clock to receive said Report it being now near two O'Clock [a.m.].

Minute Dublin, 11 February 1785[i]

[preamble omitted]

The order of the day being read to receive the Report of the Committee appointed to prepare a Petition to Parliament grounded on the Resolutions agreed to this morning.

Mr. Geale from the said Committee reported that they had prepared a Petition which he was ready to present whenever the Council will please to receive the same.

RESOLVED that the said Report be now received and read.

RESOLVED that the said petition do stand the Petition ____ of this Council to the House of Commons which is as follows:

To the Honble the Knights Citizens and Burgesses in Parliament Assembled.

The ____ Petition of the Merchants who have been nominated a Council by a numerous body of Trades associated under the Title of the Chamber of Commerce of the City of Dublin.

HUMBLY SHEWETH

THAT the disposition displayed by the Honourable House for Proceeding to a completion of a System of Commercial intercourse between the Kingdoms of Great Britain and Ireland founded on the Basis of mutual Advantage and unequivocal reciprocity has impressed your Petitioners with the most lively sentiments of gratitude.

THAT your Petitioners are peculiarly anxious for the establishment of such a wise and permanent System since in the relative situation those Countries stand it will prove the most durable bond of connection they can have a connection indispensably necessary to the Interest and importance of the whole Empire.

THAT certain Propositions having been submitted to this Honourable House for a final Adjustment of the Trade between the two Countries, Your Petitioners flatter themselves that on an occasion so momentous, so deeply involving their Interest as well as the Commercial Interests of the Nation at large they will not be thought too presuming if they take leave humbly to submit a few observations, which are the result of the best consideration of the subject that the shortness of the time would permit.

THAT your petitioners are of Opinion that the Proposition submitted to the Honourable House relative to the mutual interchange between the two Kingdoms, of Articles not the Growth Product or Manufacture of either, is fully consonant to the Principles and with respect to such Articles forms an equal and fair system between Great Britain and Ireland a measure of Justice long due to the latter.

THAT your petitioners with all Humility represent to this Honourable House that the Proposition for establishing between the two Kingdoms the same Duties on the Admissions into each, of Articles of the Growth, Product or Manufacture of the other will not in some material Instances really accomplish that Reciprocity on which the Propositions are professed to be founded—in as much as the Maturity of the one Country causing her Manufacture to be of a fine Fabric—while the infancy of the other will only allow her Manufacture to be of a coarse Fabric, the same Duty per yard or price being laid on the coarse as on the fine may be Admission to one but exclusion to the other.

THAT your petitioners take the liberty further to observe that where there now exists any Prohibition in either Kingdom on the Exportation to the other of Articles of its Growth Product of Manufacture the encountering such Prohibition with Prohibition is not calculated to encourage and extend as much as possible the Trade between Great Britain and Ireland or reconcilable to that Spirit of Affection and mutual liberality of Intercourse which should prevail between Countries so closely and your Petitioners hope inseparably connected.

THAT your petitioners humbly represent that if a Measure so unfriendly as that of Prohibition shall be persisted in on the part of Great Britain it will be highly impolitic in Ireland to preclude herself for ever from Adopting a similar conduct in respect of the material of her staple Manufactures.

THAT your petitioners humbly conceive that an effectual preference to Articles of the Growth Product or Manufacture of each Country over similar Articles of Foreign Growth Product of Manufacture on their Importation into the other Country, should be secured by a mutual engagement that any present existing preference shall in no sort be ever hereafter lessened.

YOUR PETITIONERS humbly entreat this Honourable House to take these matters into consideration and adopt such measures as to their Wisdom shall seem meet and your Petitioners — as in duty bound will humbly pray.

Signed on behalf of the said Merchants,

Daniel Marston   Daniel Thos. O'Brien

Minute Dublin, 6 August 1785[i]

To the Honourable the Knights Citizens and Burgesses in Parliament Assembled.

The Petition of the Merchants and Traders of the City of Dublin whose Names are hereunto Subscribed.

HUMBLY SHEWETH

That your Petitioners have seen with Alarm and Indignation certain Resolutions of the Parliament of Great Britain for a permanent commercial Arrangement between the two Kingdoms which Resolutions if carried into effect your Petitioners conceive would be partially restrictive and manifestly unjust in their Commercial Operation and in their political object highly insulting to the dignity of this free Nation in as much as they must be subversive of the independency of its Legislature.

That your Petitioners possess such firm reliance on the Discernment and Integrity of the Representatives of the people that they cannot suppose the said resolutions can possibly meet a favourable reception in this Honourable House.

That your petitioners beg leave with the utmost respect to submit to the Wisdom of this Honourable House that the consideration of any General Commercial Arrangement between the two Kingdoms ought not at present to be proceeded on as the contentment and Happiness of the people of

Ireland to promote which was originally the motive that originated the Idea of the settlement of its Commerce with Great Britain would probably be disturbed by precipitating the Adjustment.

That distinct from a reflection so serious and Important your petitioners beg leave to Represent further with all Humility that the season of the year and the time of the Session already greatly protracted are obviously unfavourable to the Discussion of a Question of such magnitude.

Your Petitioners though fully aware of the evil consequences that must follow precipitation do most earnestly intreat this Honourable House that no System whatever of general Commercial Arrangement with the Sister Kingdom be adopted during the present Session of Parliament.

And your Petitioners as in Duty bound will pray

Resolved that the Secretary be instructed to engross the said Petition fair on Parchment and prepare Parchment for the Signatures of the Merchants and Traders.

Minute Dublin, 22 August 1785[i]

The order of the day being read for the Council to Resolve itself into a Committee of the whole Council to take into further consideration an Address to the Members of the House of Commons thro' whose spirited exertions the late proposed Commercial adjustment has been defeated.

A motion being made and the Question put that the Chairman do now leave the Chair.

It passed in the Affirmative.

The Chairman having resumed the Chair.

Mr. Black from the Committee of the whole Council reported that they had prepared an Address to the Members of the House of Commons thro' whose spirited exertions the late proposed Commercial Adjustment has been defeated which he was ready to present whenever the Council will please to receive the same.

Resolved that said Address be now received and read.

Resolved that said Address do stand the Address of this Council … .

> The Council of the Chamber of Commerce of the City of Dublin whilst they congratulate their Countrymen on the Defeat of the System lately proposed for a permanent Adjustment of the intercourse and Commerce between Great Britain and Ireland feel it incumbent on them in the most respectful manner to return their sincere and grateful Acknowledgements to the one hundred and ten faithful and independent Representatives of the People, through whose virtue and Firmness a Measure has been overthrown, which upon mature Considn. appears to this Council to have been pregnant with the most injurious Consequences as unjustly

restrictive to the Trade of this Kingdom subversive of the independency of its Legislature and by tending to interrupt the Harmony of the two Countries likely to endanger the Prosperity of the Empire.

Signed by order

Wm. Shannon Sect.

Resolved that the above Address be printed three times in Saunders's News Letter and the Dublin Evening Post

Resolved that the above Address be printed on a half Sheet fly leaf and transmitted by the Secretary to each of the Members of the Minority of the House of Commons on Friday the 13th inst.

Birmingham

Printed petition to the House of Lords Birmingham, June 7 1785[k]

It is humbly represented, That if a compact should be made between Great Britain and Ireland upon the Terms proposed by the resolutions of the House of Commons, it would prove highly detrimental to the trade and manufactures of Great Britain in general, and of this town and neighbourhood in particular.

That some of the revenue laws act as a great bounty to cause manufacturers to remove from Britain to Ireland, and have already had that effect in the Glass Trade: and unless material alterations are speedily adopted many people who manufacture other articles for exportation will probably emigrate from this neighbourhood.

That it is apprehended that the duties on all articles used for manufactures when imported from foreign states into Great Britain, and into Ireland, should be precisely the same; and that in particular, as the duty upon bar iron imported into this kingdom cannot be reduced without great injury to the making of it at home, which it is very much the interest of this country to encourage, that the duty on that article when imported into Ireland, should be equal to the duties paid upon it in this kingdom.

That the Birmingham Commercial Committee have long hoped for a favourable opportunity entreat his Majesty's Ministers to take the state of the hardware trade into consideration, as an object of national importance; and, therefore, it is with great concern observed that it is proposed, as an unalterable condition, that the importation of articles from foreign countries should be regulated upon such terms as shall effectually favour the importation of linen from Ireland, although the same may be bought much cheaper from Other countries and may not only be bartered for by the labour of our people, but may also occasion other commercial advantages to this kingdom.

That from observations made by the Merchants and Manufacturers of this place, in the course of their transactions, there is reason to believe it is impossible for human prudence to foresee or obviate the many important and perplexing circumstances which may arise, in consequence of any unalterable regulations that can be settled for commercial contingencies; and it is humbly apprehended that the only expedient which can firmly and lastingly unite the interest of the two kingdoms in commercial matters, is a complete union of the two states.

Staffordshire Potteries

Minutes Staffordshire, 21 December 1785[1]

AT A GENERAL MEETING of the Manufacturers, held pursuant to notice at the Swan Inn in Hanley, on Wednesday the 21st day of December 1785 to consider the Treaty of Commerce with France …

With respect to the Chamber of Manufacturers, it was stated, that the different branches of manufacturers in this Island have a natural and necessary connection with one another and ought to unite their Counsels and endeavours for the Protection and extension of their mutual interests:—That the General Chamber of Manufacturers, instituted at London in March last, consisting of delegates or representatives appointed by the various branches of the different Parts of the Kingdom, appears excellently calculated for that Purpose:—And that by the Wisdom, and will-timed exertions, of the Gentlemen who at Present Compose it, a most alarming danger, which threatened the whole body of our Manufacturers at once, and which no single branch could have withstood, has already been happily averted. The further views of the Chamber were likewise particularly stated, respecting both internal regulations and foreign trade, and the Gentlemen Present, under full conviction of the expediency and necessity of such an institution agreed unanimously to the following

RESOLUTIONS

1. That this meeting approves of the above mentioned institution; and that so long as it continues to be conducted for the Purpose of watching over the Manufacturing interest of this Kingdom, it shall have their hearty concurrence and support.

2. That this Meeting recommend it to the Chamber to Proceed in the same line of conduct which it has hitherto absorbed; regardless either of allurements, or menaces, that may tend to divert it from the main Objects of its pursuit.

3. That this Meeting enter into a subscription for defraying the expenses already incurred by the Chamber, and likewise into an annual Subscription for

its future support—And that the Committee be requested to take the trouble of collecting the donations and subscriptions of such of the manufacturers of this neighbourhood as are not now Present.

4. That it is the Opinion of this Meeting that having had many known spies amongst us for the Purpose of carrying our Manufacture into foreign Parts, And having been lately warned by the Chamber that many such are now travelling in different Parts of the Kingdom, it is the duty we owe to our Country, as well as ourselves, to be upon our guard against the admission of any foreigners into our Manufactories.

5. That the thanks of this Meeting be given to the Chairman.

6. That the Resolutions be printed in some of the London and Country Papers.

n.b. Upward of One Hundred Guineas were subscribed before the Gentlemen left the room.

Minutes Staffordshire, 6 November 1786[l]

Ordered

That a Letter be written by the Secretary to General Chamber of Manufacturers signifying That this Committee being sensible of the Advantages which Manufactures and Commerce have derived from the Establishment of the Chamber think it highly important and expedient that so necessary and useful an institution should be rendered Perpetual, and that they therefore beg leave to Recommend it to the Chamber to use their Endeavour to Procure a Charter in the form in which the Chamber may think proper with such Powers and Capacities as they shall judge most suitable and Proper; and the same time requesting to be favour[ed] with a Copy of the Charter when prepared.

Glasgow

Minutes Glasgow, 3 January 1786[j]

... Reports Plan for a General Chamber (founded in March 1785). Agree to write to them and other provincial chambers and pay 5s. for each member of manufacturers.

Minutes Glasgow, 14 February 1786[j]

... Committee reports that the [Glasgow] chamber, being a body corporate of merchants as well as manufacturers, cannot as a society with propriety form any regular permanent junction with the General Chamber of Manufactures at London but should maintain exchange of information.

Minutes Glasgow, 5 July 1785[j]

REPORT, of the Delegates for the City of Glasgow, Commissioned by the Chamber of Commerce & Manufactures to proceed to London in the Month of March 1785 to attend the progress of various matters of public Concern under the consideration of Parliament

To the Directors of the Chamber of Commerce and Manufactures in the City of Glasgow

Your Commissioners having proceeded on their journey the 13th day of March & having reached London on Thursday the 17th of the Same Month. It was their first care to turn their attention to those objects which were most immediately pressing, and the Proposition for a Commercial Intercourse with Ireland being then under consideration of Parliament, and likely to pass very speedily in their original form, Not a moment was lost in visiting those Gentlemen high in the confidence of Government, who were most likely to listen and to profit by such objections as your Commissioners were instructed to offer upon a subject of such great National importance.

These preparatory steps being taken, and much discussion with various members of Parliament having every day occupied the attention of your Commissioners, they had an opportunity on the 26 day of March last to go over the same ground in a conference of above an hour with the Right Honourable William Pitt first Lord of the Treasury, who after a Very full hearing, candidly declined giving the least hopes that it was possible to make any material alteration in the Irish propositions, or to give any Relief whatever with regard to the primary objects of the negotiations, namely a reduction of the duty on Handkerchiefs and other Scotch Manufactures sent to Ireland.—Upon the subject too of the Repeal of the Cotton Tax, the prime Minister was discouraging in his reply, altho' he had been previously prepared by very full Memorials on the subject of both these grievances.

In this situation your Commissioners having no alternative but to establish a regular and fair System of opposition, they proceeded on the 26 March to the adoption of such measures as they conceived best calculated to strengthen their Interest by associating themselves with the Chamber of Manufacturers of Great Britain, and by joining with other respectable individuals from different parts of England, who had the same objects in view, and were embarked in the same pursuits.—Aided and Seconded in Manner your Commissioners did not fail to suggest such arrangements, and to come forward with such papers, and joint Memorials, and Resolutions as they conceived to be best calculated to obtain the objects in view—but in order to convey to the Chamber of Commerce and Manufacturers a more perfect conception of the matters of Public business under the charge of your Commissioners, They will proceed to consider the various branches of Public

Business under their separate heads, and this arrangement they will begin first by considering the

IRISH PROPOSITIONS

During the dependence of this important business in the House of Commons a laborious and constant attention was given to every part of the detail by appearing every day at the Chamber of Manufacturers—By bringing force and assisting Evidences at the Bar of the House—By framing Resolutions and public papers, and by assisting in the instructing of Council who were to plead.

In the course of this Business above Sixty Petitions from every part of Great Britain, including those from Glasgow, were brought forward in the House of Commons, and in order to remove some impressions that had gone abroad, and had led the Members of Parliament for Scotland to conceive that the Irish Propositions could not affect the Interest of that Country, because of the great increase of the Linen Manufacture, your Commissions thought it their duty to publish certain Queries particularly adapted to Scotland, with observations annexed, shewing the fallacy of the received opinion respecting the prominence of the Linens of Scotland.—These Queries were Circulated among the Representatives, for Scotland, a Copy of which (No. 1) is now produced for the information of the Chamber of Manufactures.—In this general struggle to promote a more thorough investigation of these Propositions, your Commissioners also promoted, (and assisted in framing a General Report of the Chamber of Manufacturers in London (No. 2)) which being calculated more immediately for general circulation was universally made public, And thus by a temperate and decent exertion, much time was gained, so that in place of an Ultimate decision being given in this interesting business early in the month of March, a delay was procured until the 12th day of May, during which interval many imperfections were discovered, and to this must chiefly be attributed the various alterations and amendments that were proposed by the Minister, and afterwards adopted by the House.—The circumstance however, of no alteration being made on the fourth proposition alarmed your Commissions exceedingly, and awakened every profitable exertion to procure an Amendment here also.—But finding it in vain to expect success from appealing to the House at large, and feeling how ineffectual every Argument used by the City Member, and other Zealous friends who combated this business in the House, Recourse was had immediately to private negotiation.—A Case was drawn up and printed (No. 3) It was dispersed among those Members who were likely to take up the matter.—A Conference was obtained with the Minister, and the matter again explained.—Applications were severally made to all who were in his Confidence, and aided by the very powerful and Active exertions of the Lord Advocate, a disposition was shown to depart, in some degree, from his former resolution; and accordingly on the 23d May, an Amendment was obtained by Negotiation with the Chancellor of the Exchequer, by which that part of the Business remains open for future discussion.

Having advanced thus far in the progress, your Commissioners became anxious to establish the most perfect Security that these duties should be reduced, and in order to effect this purpose, They were successful in procuring the assistance of the most opulent whole sale Drapers and printers in London & Lancashire, who in Consequence of a previous explanation of their danger, and Interest in the Question, agreed to ask an interview with the Minister, to whom a Deputation was sent on the 26 May, composed of two London Drapers, and one Lancashire Printer together with one of your Commissioners, when it was fully and clearly stated to Mr. Pitt that the unequal duties in Ireland by no means applied to the Manufactures of Scotland alone, but that England was concerned in a much greater degree.—That the business was truly stated in the printed Case, and that it was a matter of the utmost magnitude to Great Britain, That in framing a Book of Rates, a true, just and fair principle of Equality should pervade every article in the Interchange, and that Handkerchiefs, Muslins, and Calicoes of British Manufacture ought in justice to Enjoy the benefit of a free Access into Ireland in the proposed Commercial Arrangement, otherwise the principle could not be followed out.—These observations were strongly urged by Wm. Withers a very eminent wholesale Draper and Printer of London, who is well known to the Minister and had been much in his Confidence.—Having proceeded thus far in leaving these strong impressions upon the mind of the Chancellor of the Exchequer, your Commissioners established a System for procuring every possible information previous to the arrival of Commissioners to settle the Book of Rates, and having previously prepared an additional Case for the Rt. Honorable Henry Dundas, His promise was obtained by Mr. Colquhoun in a conference held on 15th June that on his part every assistance would be given & every exertion made to remove all future cause of complaint. Learning at this conference that Mr. Beresford the Principal Commissioner of the Revenue in Ireland had just come over and receiving at same time an Authorised copy of the Irish duties as they stand at the present moment, no time was lost in framing a General Memorial for the Printers, Dealers, and Manufacturers of Handkerchiefs, Muslins and Calicoes in London, Lancashire, Carlisle and Glasgow, which memorial was carried down to the City by one of your Commissioners on the 18 June—approved and adopted unanimously by all concerned, and in the course of a few days it will be carried to the Chancellor of the Exchequer by Mr. Withers with such respectable Signatures as cannot fail to give the most perfect Security to a Measure that was already considered as nearly Settled.

Thus have your Commissioners stated their progress and general Management with regard to the Irish duties on Handkerchiefs and Cotton Goods.—It remains only to add what has occurred with regard to the Article of Iron, about which several conferences were held with the Minister by Lord Advocate, Mr. Garbel, and your Commissioners as from the whole complexion of this branch of the detail, scarce any doubt remains that the Iron Manufacture in Great Britain will very soon be entitled to such a Bounty, as will place the coarse articles in all respects on the same footing with Ireland.

The Paper No 4 Exhibits the original State of the Irish Proportions with the amendments proposed by the Chancellor of the Exchequer, and the ultimate improvements made in passing through the House of Commons.—These Propositions are now under the consideration of the House of Lords where several additional amendments will probably be made, and at present it is a matter of great uncertainty whether any conclusive progress will be made during the present Session of Parliament, although it is said to be the Intention of His Majesty's Ministers to Ground a Bill on these Resolutions before the present Session is finished.

COTTON & PRINTING TAX

Your Commissioners had no sooner arrived in London than they took measures to circulate a Pamphlet which had been previously prepared & published for the purpose of showing the Impolicy of Taxing Manufactures. —Copies of this pamphlet were sent to the King's Ministers and to every other person of eminence in the State.

On the 26th of March your Commissioners began their progress in preparing a System of temperate opposition.—Having then no hopes from the Minister, they united their exertions with those of the Cotton & Fustian Manufacturers as well as the Printers of Lancashire who were Delegated upon this business, and who acted in concert by bringing forward Evidences at the Bar of the House of Commons.—Many meetings were therefore held with the Lancashire Delegates, and measures having been adopted to bring forward Evidence in behalf of the Cotton and Printing Manufactures in Scotland, Mr. Alexander McAlpine with a Zeal & public Spirit which deserves the Thanks of his Country, agreed to come forward.—In consequence of this your Commissioners prepared a Petition to the House on the 8th of April, applicable to the peculiar circumstances of the Case.—On the 10th April a Case was drawn, and Council was instructed, and on the 13th of the same Month, Mr. McAlpine as a witness and Mr Dallas as Council came to the Bar of House of Commons, when a Very full and Satisfactory Evidence was given which the Council summed up in a masterly manner.

The Chancellor of the Exchequer having proposed the 20th of April for Ultimately discussing the propriety of Repealing the Cotton Tax, your Commissioners prepared and printed a Case now produced (No. 5) grounded on the circumstances and facts that had been Stated, to which was added a Summary Account of Mr. McAlpine's Evidence.—This Case which separately treated of the Tax on Printed Goods, and Muslins, was previously put into the hands of almost every Member of the House of Commons, and every exertion was used to impress upon their minds the Necessity of a Repeal.—Your Commissioners are therefore happy in being able to congratulate the Chamber of Commerce and Manufactures on the Repeal of the Cotton Tax taking place on the 20th April.

The declared intention however, of the Chancellor of the Exchequer to continue the Tax on printed Goods, and having been supported in this by the two greatest Leaders of opposition in the House of Commons, it was a matter of extreme mortification to your Commissioners to find no Case brought forward in behalf of the English Printers, nor any person instructed to appear for their Interest in the House of Commons.

Under these circumstances, the Case published in behalf of Scotland, was of Singular use in awakening the attention of the Earl of Surrey who Supported the Lord Advocate and Mr. Dempster in a proposition favourable to the low priced printed Goods.—But with so powerful an opposition your Commissioners saw no hopes of Success, but by a great and steady exertion in bringing forward and in Uniting the English Printers.—Not a Moment was therefore lost.—A new Case applicable to circumstances of the Moment was drawn and Submitted to the principal parties in Lancashire who were entrusted.—This case being corrected and approved, was immediately printed and presented to the different Members who interest themselves in the Manufactures of their Country.—Several days were spent in visiting these Members.—On the 25th April an interview was procured with the Chancellor of the Exchequer, Accompanied by Sir Harry Houghton, Mr Pultney, Mr Stanley, Mr Blackburn and Lord Advocate, when one of your Commissioners fully explained the case, and left it with patterns of various Substitutes for low priced printed Goods which were at present in the market, for his Consideration, on the 27th of the same month, another conference was held with the Minister where your Commissioners also attended in the Company of Six Members of Parliament and Eighteen Printers and Manufacturers from the County of Lancaster and Cheshire—when at this interview [the] Minister made a conditional agreement to exempt low priced goods from duty, and a Committee immediately proceeded to the Board of Excise to settle upon the mode—a Copy of the Case in Question is now produced (No. 6) and it will be pleasing to the Chamber of Commerce of Manufactures to perceive from the plan of the Signatures when delivered to the Minister that a most perfect Union of Interests and exertions was established between the English and Scotch Printers and Manufacturers.

Having proceeded to the Board of Excise in order to adjust Several points connected with the official part of this business to which the Minister now stood pledged—a long discussion took place, and various interviews became necessary before any regular System could be established—at length however upon the 2d day of May, certain Resolutions were moved by the Minister, grounded on the compromise which had been made.—Immediately, however on these Resolutions being moved, new difficulties occurred on the part of the London wholesale Drapers and Printers, who brought forward a most powerful opposition.—Delayed the progress in the interim, and created infinite trouble.—Your Commissioners however, holding the Minister as pledged cautiously prevented any measure from being adopted that would disturb the Resolutions moved by the Chancellor of the Exchequer—every thing was done to annul them but in vain—At length the Gentlemen of London, Lancashire, Carlisle and Glasgow met upon the 10 May, explanations developed and given from your Commissioners, and a medium suggested to unite all parties.—In this discussion the suppression of the wearing of Cossair [probably Cossais or Cossaes, an Indian muslin] or foreign Muslins was proposed by your said Commissioner, and the expected opposition was in some measure softened.—By degrees the wholesale Drapers of London acquired more confidence, and at length on the 20th May the System was formed for regulating foreign Calicoes and prohibiting the Consumption of Cossair Muslins printed in Great Britain.—Thus were General conferences with the principal London wholesale Drapers extremely beneficial in many respects, and it was the care of your Commissioners to lose no good opportunity of rendering their information and assistance useful to the Cotton Trade of Great Britain with the view the warehouses of foreign Dealers were visited—Cases were stated, patterns and prices were procured, and many materials collected for the purpose of forming a ground work of a future application to Parliament for further checks upon East Indian Cotton Goods in the Home Market.

But to return to the progress of the printing Bill your Commissioner will only state that from the 10th day of May till the 19th of June Scarce a day passed without meetings.—New propositions of ascertaining the value by the Threads in an Inch Square were proposed by the London Drapers.—These propositions went to the Treasury and from thence to the Excise—many days were wasted in fruitless attendance at both Boards, and at length after the most painful attendance at the Treasury, the Excise, and the House of Commons, these propositions were ultimately Rejected.—Various Clauses in the interim were drawn up and suggested by Mr. Colquhoun one of your Commissioners whose only satisfaction in so tedious an Attendance was this, That in every new Discussion fresh matter calculated to improve the Bill came forward, and has been in many instances Ultimately adopted.

The Proposition for ascertaining a Criterion of Value by the Thread has been rejected, and the London Drapers being Hostile in the Extreme to the original proposition of taking the value by the Running yard, the Secretary to the Treasury at length agreed to take the Square yard at Twenty pence on the Cotton and Calicoes. And thus the matter has been ultimately settled after as much trouble as ever occurred in any Public negotiation of the kind.

Your Commissioners do not enter into any details of Differences which arose between the Parties themselves, and the labour it cost in conciliating them and removing these differences, and bringing the London and Lancashire Gentlemen to hold one opinion and to Act in Concert.—It was however at length Effected.— The prejudices against one another are now wiped away, and by acting in concert on every future occasion, much benefit may be expected to the Trade in future negotiations. The united weight and influence of the whole then collected together will be useful.—After the Bill was framed, near a fortnight intervened before it came into the House on Account of various Forms necessary in handing it from the Solicitor to the Board of Excise—From the Board of Excise to the Solicitor to the Customs—from thence to the Board of Customs as then to the Treasury, and after all some inaccuracies which your said Commissioner discovered in the Bill (& which must still be corrected) prevented it from getting into the House of Commons till the 24th of June.—It is now in the train of passing into a Law, and your Commissioners would hope that the Ease in point of Duty which the Trade will experience will repay all the labour and waste of time which this very tedious business has cost.—And the other Regulations will certainly protect the Cotton & Muslin Manufactures in Scotland.

INTERCHANGE OF MANUFACTURES WITH IRELAND

Your Commissioners having already stated their progress in Establishing a System for preventing any unequal duties being ultimately fixed when a Book of Rates is Settled between Great Britain and Ireland, Have now further to add that conferences have been held with a Gentleman high in the Confidence of the Minister on the Subject to whom Copies of all the Original papers have been delivered, and every possible Explanation given of the whole Rise and Progress of this business.—This Gentleman has promised his utmost assistance, and another equally Zealous has taken the business particularly under his Charge.—On the 22d June Mr. Withers from the City of London waited by previous appointment on the first Lord of the Treasury with the joint Memorial of the Drapers Printers and Manufacturers of London, Lancashire, Carlisle, Glasgow & Paisley, a Copy of which as originally drawn by Mr. Colquhoun, and unanimously adopted by the Trade is now produced (No. 7). Thus the business stands at present.—But in the opinion of your Commissioners it is now a matter of some doubt whether any final conclusion will take place till next Session of Parliament, and as it is still impossible even for Ministers to fix a time when any discussion on this subject can be brought forward, your Commissioners had no other alternative than the Establishment of a Committee in London to correspond and to act as occasion shall require, and as this Committee consists of the respectable names of John Withers, Charles Greaves, James West, and Thomas Brown to whose weight, influence and zeal the parties interested have already been much indebted, your Commissioners hope that the respectability and influence of this Committee aided by the vigilance they promise to exercise; and stimulated by the information they may receive occasionally from your Chamber will ultimately effect a purpose of no little difficulty, and which has already cost much labour and fatigue.

TOBACCO LAW

Your Commissioners proceed now to Report to the Chamber the general outlines of their negotiation regarding the Tobacco Law

So early as the 23d March last year Commissioner Mr. Colquhoun was requested to attend at the House of Henry Beaufoy Esquire to assist in Suggesting information for the improvement of this Law—These meetings were repeated on the 26 March, the 14th, 20th, 24th, & 30th April & 9th May during all which interviews much consideration was given to the business —Many improvements were made and after various alterations and additions the Bill was at length brought into its first shape—It then became necessary to prepare the Clauses applicable to the City of Glasgow which were submitted to the consideration of Mr. Beaufoy on the 21st May and forwarded about the same period to your Secretary for the approbation of the Trade.

Mean time Mr. Commissioner Reid and Mr. Menzies Solicitor to the Customs in Scotland were ordered by the Treasury to attend upon this business in London, and accordingly the Local Clauses proposed for the City of Glasgow were submitted to their consideration by the Lord Advocate—Meetings were held at his Lordships House—The Clauses being submitted to Messrs. Reid & Menzies, They after a full Consideration approved in toto of the principle as well as the justice, necessity and expediency of the measure. But the plan adopted by your Commissioners being supposed to impose heavier burdens than were necessary for the security of the Revenue, A new set of Clauses were prepared by the Solicitor to the Scots Customs, Mr. Menzies which were delivered to Lord Advocate and by him handed to Mr. Beaufoy whose consent was soon after procured, not only to admit but to support within the Clauses proposed by your Commissioner or those proposed by the others of His Majesty's Revenue—But to remove all the difficulty as the tendency of both were precisely the same, he very properly recommended the latter clause to be adopted which was accordingly done, and as Copy of the same as finally proposed is now produced in paper (No. 8).

On the 30th May it came to be generally supposed, and indeed known that no Reduction, of the Duty on Tobacco would take place at this time, and that it was the determined Resolution of Government to make an Experiment by Regulations, Only to make the Revenue Efficient, and to prevent illicit Trade—From that moment almost every spare hour of your Commissioners time was employed in suggesting Arguments against this System, and of enforcing the same with every person who was supposed to have influence with the Minister on this business—and although success in almost every Instance attended these exertions, and although not a few high in confidence of the Administration as well as the Commissioners from Scotland were clearly of opinion, that the Duty ought to be reduced, and although every exertion was made to impress this upon the mind of the Chancellor of the Exchequer, He remained steady to his first purpose.

Under these circumstances your Commissioners not willing to abandon a negotiation of such importance to the City of Glasgow, determined to make a further sacrifice of their time—New Ground was taken up, and a proposition made to divide the Duty between the Importer and Manufacturer—This plan was early hinted to Mr. Beaufoy, but it was not Digested nor brought forward in perfect form until the 3d and 8th of June, when a very full discussion took place and the whole System (No. [9]) was soon after submitted to the First Lord of the Treasury, which produced an interview between one of your Commissioners and Mr. Pitt on the 13th June when a full discussion took place and the propriety of adopting the System of an after period was admitted but various circumstances arising out of the Nature of the Case and the State of the Bill, Rendered it impossible at present—In the paper (No. [9]) now produced to the Chamber is contained the Heads of the plan submitted to the Chancellor of the Exchequer.

Your Commissioners notwithstanding the Evident wish of the Minister to try the Experiment of continuing the high duties, knowing how Ruinous this measure was likely to prove to the Trade of the City of Glasgow, were still willing to make a further exertion—With this view Petitions were suggested as necessary and were accordingly sent up from the out Ports—Various meetings were held with the London Importers of Tobacco—A Conference was obtained between Mr. Beaufoy and the Trade at which your Commissioners were present—Similar meetings were held with the London Tobacconists, all tending to procure the wished for Reduction and with a view still more to Impress the necessity of a new System—Your Commissioner Mr. Colquhoun went to the Excise Office at the period the Bill was under discussion of that Board and fully set forth the distresses of the Trade, and the Necessity of the System he proposed to the Minister, which he then fully explained to the presiding Commissioner,—This coming in aid of what had formerly been done, your Commissioners trust may be useful in maturing the ultimate System which is to come forward in December next, and in modelling the same in a manner calculated to promote in a greater degree the Ease and advantage of the Out Ports as well as London—on the [blank space] of June the Chancellor of the Exchequer opened his intended plan for a new Tobacco Law in the House of Commons, but being previously obliged to abandon that part of the Bill which Extended the Excise Laws on account of the Board of Commissioners having Reported to him the impossibility of maturing the System in time for the present sessions, no very material alteration will take place by this interim Law, Excepting the Extension of Excise to Tobacco Manufactured for Exportation—In addition to this the present Bill will probably introduce Licences and other Regulations under the Customs, calculated to check illicit Trade—But so often has the Bill already been mutilated, altered, and amended, and so various have been the difficulties suggested by the two Boards of Customs and Excise as well as the Solicitors and Law Agents employed in the business of the Revenue—That your Commissioners dare not hazard a Conjecture respecting the precise state of the Bill when it shall be brought forward on the 29th Instant which is the earliest day that is proposed for that purpose—Upon the whole the Bill now in question can only be denominated an Interim Expedient, far short of what was originally intended, and only forming a prelude to that System which must be brought forward Early in the Next Session—The difficulties attending its completion during the present Session were not fully foreseen, nor is it to be expected that a System so Complicated and so new, can be perfected at once, Especially when so many Prejudices are to be combated and when the Mass of business which presses not only upon the Minister but also upon the two Revenue Boards is great beyond example.

Your Commissioners cannot sufficiently lament that these causes outweighed the Arguments they brought forward stating the danger of any delays and the absolute necessity of rendering the System complete at once by a Reduction, at least of the Port Duties—It is perhaps no little satisfaction however to have the Repeated assurances which your Commissioners have had, That the System they proposed in general meets with approbation, and that there is the highest probability that it will be adopted early in December—If this shall be the Case your Commissioners will hope in a few months to congratulate the Chamber of Commerce and Manufactures on the establishment of a System which cannot fail of being productive of all those benefits which Result from protection to the Fair Trader and a free scope to the Industry of the Importer and Manufacturer by such a plan as shall promote their Convenience and extend the Consumption of Tobacco in the hands of the Fair Trader—Your Commissioners cannot close the observations which have occurred to them on that part of Report which relates to Parliamentary negotiation without lamenting that the Introduction and discussion of the Irish Propositions wasted such length of time, and so totally occupied the attention of His Majesty's Ministers as not only rendered it extremely difficult to get forward such business as had been marked out for the Session, but also rendered it impossible to suggest or bring forward any new or extraneous matter however necessary.

On this Account the proposed Bill for Regulating the

THREAD MANUFACTURE

was necessarily postponed, and the long depending negotiation for the purpose of Warehousing Sugars and paying the Duties on being delivered on a Sale and Removal or Cancelling the Bonds by Exportation, was in the same predicament. But your Commissioners have made considerable progress for completing this System next Session when the Tobacco Regulations are finally adjusted—with this View measures have been taken to Interest, some Merchants in the City of London for the purpose of Reconciling the principal Importers, who are at present Hostile to the measure, and if a petition can only be obtained to smooth the way, your Commissioners have procured the promise of a Very able and intelligent English Member of Parliament, that he will bring forward the business early next Session—Matters are therefore thus far advanced in the Progress, and nothing but the opposition of the opulent Merchants of London will prevent the Completion of this business—On the part of Government there will be no obstacle.

AMERICAN DEBTS

Your Commissioners now proceed to Report their progress in the establishment of a System for the purpose of Uniting the Merchants of the Principal Trading Towns of Great Britain in one General Memorial to Government for the purpose of opening a representation for the more Effectual recovering of the property belonging to the Merchants Trading to America previous to the late War—A Subject of so much importance to a very numerous and respectable part of the Chamber of Commerce and Manufacturers, That your Commissioners considered it as incumbent upon them to Exert every endeavour to place this Negotiation on such a respectable footing as might of profit [?] insure Success—With this view, in consequence of a letter from the Chairman of the American Committee at Glasgow the Negotiation opened by an Interview with the First Lord of the Treasury procured by the Lord Advocate who was attended by your Commissioners on the 18th day of May—This interview having produced some Important Information, your Commissioners in consequence of an Invitation from the Chairman, attended a Meeting of the Old American Merchants in London, and having previously collected and digested the information received on this Subject in the form of a Case, after stating to the meeting the various particulars which had been collected on the Subject, one of your Commissioners proposed a plan for writing the Merchants of the principal Trading Towns in Great Britain in one application and in one Memorial to Government to be presented by the

Marquis of Carmarthen in Consequence of the advice and desire of the Chancellor of the Exchequer—This proposition being Acceded to certain Resolutions were proposed by the meeting, and copies of the Same, and of the Case ordered to be transmitted to Bristol, Liverpool Whitehaven & Glasgow for the Information and Concurrence of the American Merchants at these respective Ports, and the meeting was adjourned for 16 days till answers could be received—During this interval your Commissioners having received Authentic information that an American Minister had Actually arrived in London, and having opportunity by the friendship of an American Merchant to procure a ready and favourable interview, your Commissioners considered themselves called upon to avail themselves of it—Their Object being merely information to Act on the United discussions of the Merchants at large—They proceeded with every possible Caution, and previously Resolved to wait on the American Minister merely as individuals in no respect Authorised to represent any Body of Men whatsoever.

Accordingly upon the 2d of June your Commissioners attended Mr. Adams at his Hotel in Piccadilly, and the Substance of the Conversation will be found in the paper (No. 10) now produced—On the 9th of June following your Commissioners attended a Second meeting of the American Merchants to receive the answers and Reports of the Merchants in Bristol, Liverpool Whitehaven & Glasgow, all of which having Committed full powers to the meeting to Act under the System proposed.

A Memorial founded upon the Case addressed to the Marquis of Carmarthen was read and approved of—a Copy of which (No. 11) is now produced—This memorial so approved was ordered to be presented to the Marquis of Carmarthen by a Committee consisting of Mr. Duncan Campbell the Chairman, Messrs. Samuel Gul, Christopher Court & Patrick Colquhoun, and Copies were at the same time ordered to be prepared to be presented to the First Lord of the Treasury and to Lord Sydney as Secretary of State—On the 14th June this Committee waited on the Marquis of Carmarthen by appointment—The Memorial was delivered to his Lordship together with a list of the money, paid into the public Treasuries of Virginia and Maryland, upon which he expressed the greatest desire to procure every possible Relief for so respectable a Body of men whose case certainly deserved and would meet with every possible attention—In the course of the conversation his Lordship stated that a British Minister would probably now go to America as the States of America had placed Mr. Adams at the Court of Britain as a permanent Plenipotentiary and that from the train matters were now in, there was a greater probability of Success than heretofore—The Committee proceeded from the Marquis of Carmarthen to the Office of Lord Sydney where the same professions of attention were repeated, and your Commissioners have since had occasion to hear that the business has been

already under the Consideration of the Cabinet; and that it is likely to be warmly espoused by Government—Mr. Dundas to whom a Copy of the memorial has been delivered, has most obligingly undertaken to give it every weight in his power and to facilitate the completion of such a System as shall put this property in the train of being collected—Thus far have your Commissioners been able to accelerate the progress of a System which from various concurring Circumstances, they are happy to think now promises better Success than at any period since the war—The Representation of the whole Merchants United comes forward with peculiar weight, and by recommending and effecting this point your Commissioners hope these effects will be considered by those more immediately Concerned as at least well meant in so far as they have been able to Connect the Interest of so numerous a Body who were afloat, without plan, and without any regular System Calculated either to give weight to their applications, or Consistency to the General Measures necessary to be adopted—In the course of the present summer it is fully expected that the adjustment will be Completed, and every Impediment Removed that may at present stand in the way of the Recovery of British Debts in America.
CONCLUSION

In the course of a Laborious attendance for upwards of Fifteen weeks in this Metropolis your Commissioners had occasion to assist in various other matters Connected with the Commerce of Scotland—In particular they were called upon to assist & attend the English Manufacturers at the Secretary of State's office to Solicit a removal of sundry obstructions that at present shut out the Printed Goods and other British Manufactures from Spain.—They have likewise assisted in the progress of the measures now adopting for improving the British Fisheries, and in the plan proposed for Commuting the Duty on Salt and Coals in Scotland.—These objects are in the progress of being settled in the Course of the ensuing Sessions.—Your Commissioners cannot close this Report without stating to the Chamber how much they have been on all occasions Indebted to the Lord Advocate for his zealous attention to the Interest of his Constituents nor can they omit mentioning their Singular Obligations to Mr. Dundas, Mr. Beaufoy, Sir Adam Ferguson, Mr. Dempster, Mr. Pultney, Lord Surrey, Mr. Blackburn, Mr. Stanley, Sir Henry Houghton & Mr. McDonald who have on every Occasion manifested the utmost Readiness to promote whatever your Commissioners recommended as beneficial to the Trade of Glasgow.

And to Mr. Dundas, Sir Adam Ferguson, Mr. Dempster, & Mr. Beaufoy this Committee are still to be obliged for the readiness with which they have undertaken to support the Local Clauses in the Tobacco Bill, and to assist in other matters after the departure of your Commissioners which takes place tomorrow. Signed at London the 25th day of June 1785.

[Signed] Patk. Colquhoun
[Signed] Alexn. Brown

Chapter 9

Union of Chambers

After the brief period of the General Chamber of Manufactures, 1785–7, there was continuing liaison between the local chambers in other major national lobbies; collaboration did not break down as claimed by Redford, Bowden and others.[1] But, as far as can be determined, the tensions arising in the General Chamber seem to have discouraged any attempt to revive a national organisation for this purpose. However, from about 1793 a conference of chambers developed, which evolved into a 'union'. The Manchester chamber, which was reactivated in 1794, provides an important record of exchanges between some of the local chambers of this time. Helm and Redford quote many of the exchanges in this record, and these are not further reproduced here, but should be read with the documents below.[2] The documents reproduced here relate to two additional episodes: the tensions over adverse press coverage in 1796; and negotiations with Pitt in 1797–8. The co-ordination began as 'conferences' and evolved into a 'union' of chambers chiefly as a result of negotiations over European Treaties and problems of naval convoying. The Admiralty issued various instructions calling for co-operation from 'the merchants of London and other principal towns', which included those chambers or local committees then in existence:[3] in Manchester, Exeter, Hull, Halifax, Wakefield, Norwich, Birmingham, Liverpool and London. Conferences were called on particular trade routes, with Lloyds emerging as crucial to inducing co-operation by insisting on convoying as a condition of insurance cover. The bottlenecks caused by convoys increased the pressure for a stronger voice from the ports.[4]

A first chamber conference was held in London in 1793 over convoys, and again in 1796–7, stimulated by French occupation of Leghorn. Another

[1] Bowden, *Industrial Society* (1965) 155–67; Redford, *Manchester Merchants* (1934) 11–13, 51, 205–7; also see Chapter 8.

[2] see Helm, *Chapters* (1897); Redford, *Manchester Merchants* (1934) 25–62; also Bennett, *Local Business Voice* (2011) 394–400.

[3] For example, letter from Lords of the Admiralty, received by Manchester chamber, minutes, 9 June 1796.

[4] Crowhurst, *Defence* (1977) 62–8, 71–4; S. P. Ville, *English shipowning during the industrial revolution: Michael Henley and Son, London shipowners, 1770–1830* (Manchester, 1987) 10–13; N. A. M. Rodger, *The Command of the Ocean: A naval history of Britain, 1649–1815* (London, 2004) 559–60; also see R. Davis, *The rise of the English shipping industry in the seventeenth and eighteenth centuries* (London, 1962).

conference focused on the Spanish and Italian trade. John Turnbull, chair of the first conference, became formally the chair of the 'Union' in 1796.[5] Turnbull, although noted by Redford, has not been well understood. He was of considerable status in the merchant community, having been a joint adjudicator with Samuel Bayard, representing the United States, over 1794–5 certifying claims in the Admiralty Court from agents regarding vessels captured or condemned as part of the efforts to resolve disputes with America leading up to the Jay Treaty of 1795.[6] Now the sequestration of British property in Spain led to a campaign by the Union from 1796 until 1805. The Union was primarily a body for manufacturers and their traders dealing with southern European markets. Turnbull was energetic and appears to have been politically adroit. As a merchant he dealt with the local representatives on equal terms, managed the tensions between areas, and had the political connections to allow him ready access, providing Pitt with an important sounding board for policies. A good example of Turnbull's approach to Pitt is provided by exchanges over taxes on convoys in 1798, reproduced below. Turnbull states that 'I am inclined to hope that I may be able, on representing the matter in a favourable, and just point of view, to reconcile them [the delegates] to it, provided that you are pleased to authorise me to say … '. It shows how Turnbull hoped to deliver agreement if Pitt was able to deliver assurances. The Union continued at least until 1805 as shown in the document here. It did not collapse in 1802, and nor did Turnbull give up, as suggested by Redford.[7] Turnbull also chaired a meeting in 1800 to consider Colquhoun's proposals for setting up the first marine police force on the Thames, an interconnection with chambers not previously noticed.[8] The committee formed on that occasion appears to have been part of the London committee of merchants and Union of chambers, with the main members being Thomas Bonar, John Brickwood, John Dumage, Edward Foster, Beeston Long, Albert Roberts, and Robert Thornton.[9]

All the actions were being done very quietly behind the scenes. As Ehrman noted, Pitt was becoming very personally involved and directive in trade negotiation,[10] but very discreetly; the Union made little attempt to use MPs or petition parliament directly. The emphasis on discreetness is illuminated by an incident in November 1796 when information was given to the *Courier*

[5] John Turnbull was a merchant partner in Turnbull and Macaulay in 1793, trading in Quebec; later in Turnbull and Forbes, with trade in Leghorn in 1797–8 with links to naval victualing. Turnbull had debts of about £10,000 in Italy in 1793 for which he sought Pitt's help in recovery; TNA: PRO 30/8/184, f. 174–5. He also sought Pitt's help over advances of £9,256 to estate proprietors in St. Domingo on 6 July 1798; TNA PRO 30/8/222 f. 55–6.
[6] Bennett, *Local Business Voice* (2011) 393.
[7] Redford, *Manchester Merchants* (1934) 61–2.
[8] The founding president of the Glasgow chamber, and then stipendiary magistrate in Shoreditch.
[9] Quoted in Yeats (1818) 29; Bennett, *Local Business Voice* (2011) 398.
[10] Ehrman, *British Government* (1962).

about a proposed memorial from the union of chambers by the Exeter chamber. The Manchester minutes record that in Exeter 'they are acting on different grounds to other manufacturing towns and are more politicians than merchants'. Exeter was censured by Manchester that any publication 'may influence our application' to the government for attention. The actual report of 13 November is reproduced here.[11] The Exeter president replied to James Edge and Thomas Richardson (the past and current presidents of the Manchester chamber) that 'Exeter disavows any publication which occurred without their knowledge and has asked the editor to say who inserted the entry'.[12] The exchange demonstrates the desire to avoid the noisy campaigns of the General Chamber; Thomas Walker's activities had convinced Manchester to eschew party and public attention. Subsequently, Exeter was invited back into Union, but their delegates (Cole, Kennaway and Tremlett) were forced to affirm that 'they have no intention of interfering or appearing in a political light, but merely as commercial men'.[13] Subsequently Kennaway was one of those negotiating with Grenville and 'delegates of the various manufacturing towns' regarding Exeter ships held up at Gibraltar waiting convoys.[14]

It is important to note that the other major chambers of the time, Glasgow, Edinburgh, Dublin, Waterford, the Liverpool American chamber, and Bristol Venturers, were not involved in the national Union. One group of chambers was organising joint working, whilst others acted separately. The main focus of the Union was on manufacturing and European trades, whilst the other chambers were chiefly concerned with America, Africa and the West Indies which had other routes for influence.

Sources
[a] *London Chronicle*, 13 November 1796.
[b] TNA PRO 30/8/184
[c] TNA PRO 30/8/150

Printed report 13 November 1796[a]

STATE OF COMMERCE EXETER

A general meeting of the Merchants and Manufacturers of Exeter was held here on the 10th inst. and the state of trade having been taken into consideration, it was unanimously resolved, 'That from the beginning of the

[11] It is impossible to find this issue of the *Courier*; the *Chronicle* report appears to be the one referred to.
[12] Manchester Central Library: chamber minutes, 22 and 23 November 1796; see also quotes by Redford, *Manchester Merchants* (1934) 18, 57–8, who misses its significance.
[13] Ibid., Manchester chamber minutes, 29 November 1796.
[14] TNA: William Kennaway to Grenville, 10 December 1796; FO 95/5/8 f. 623; Bennett, *Local Business Voice* (2011) 397–8.

present war the trade of this city has laboured under great and unprecedented disadvantages; and that lately, by the shutting of almost every port in Europe to which the manufactures of this country were exported, there appears serious reason to apprehend the most ruinous consequences, the labouring poor in these parts being generally deprived of employment by the total stagnation of commerce.'

The following Memorial to the Privy Council was also drawn up and agreed to, and ordered to be transmitted to all the manufacturing towns of England:

TO THE LORDS OF HIS MAJESTY'S MOST HONOURABLE PRIVY COUNCIL

The Memorial of the Merchants and Manufacturers of Exeter and its vicinity, assembled at a General Meeting of their Chamber of Commerce, for taking into consideration state of their trade.

The measures of relief which your Lordships were pleased to suggest in reply to our Memorial of the 25th July last, having been all defeated by subsequent events, and the state of our trade becoming every day more critical, we presume to solicit your Lordships' attention to our increased distress.

In the North of Italy our property is confiscated; to the South we have no longer access; recent occurrences having rendered the navigation of the Mediterranean so perilous that we cannot be covered by any premium of insurance which our trade will bear. The vessels dispatched from this port for the fair of Salerno, by the July convoy, to the amount of £100,000, appear by the last advices to be still at Gibraltar, waiting farther convoy. (Accounts are since received that they are obliged to return to England with their cargoes) The *Queen of Naples*, another of our vessels, worth above £40,000, is now under embargo at Genoa.

To Spain and Portugal we look with extreme anxiety. The ports of the former country (a chief mart for our manufactures) are not only shut against us, at a moment when our warehouses and vessels are filled with goods prepared for the winter consumption, but reports prevail of an actual sequestration of British property, and a prohibition to discharge Bills of Exchange: measures which, if carried into effect, must be attended with fatal consequences. In these ports also many of our vessels are embargoed with cargos to a very great amount.

In Germany, the operations of War render credit precarious and property insecure. The markets of Flanders and Holland are no longer open. With the other parts of Europe and of the Globe we have little intercourse.

To this consideration of our property, detention of our funds, and annihilation of our trade, is added an extraordinary embarrassment arising from a failure of credit.

Your Lordships need not be informed that the trade or this port consists in the exportation of woollen goods, manufactured in this city and throughout the county of Devon; a suspension, therefore, of our exports, especially under the circumstances we have enumerated, puts an entire stop to the industry of these parts; and the distresses of our labourers, already very great, must soon become extreme.

Under the pressure of these evils, we conceive we are discharging a duty in presenting this Memorial, that your Lordships may be aware of our situation &c.

Exeter Nov. 10th 1796 Edmund Grainger, Chairman

Letter, John Turnbull to William Pitt [f. 180–1] London, 2 March 1798[b]

I will not in any degree, presume to anticipate the Result of the General sentiments, of the different Bodies of Merchants in London, Concerned in the foreign Trade of this Country, & which will be soon Communicated to you, by Mr. Forster, the respectable Chairman of the Gentlemen who had the honour of waiting on you in Downing Street, respecting the increase of Convoys, and the duties on Exports and Imports.

On these important subjects, I beg, however, to be permitted, to Comply with the request of the great Manufacturing Towns, in submitting to you, the Resolutions of their different general meetings, & the Observations that have been made thereon.—It appears to be generally admitted, that under present Circumstances, it is highly expedient, & even incumbent, on Government, to prevent any British Vessel, sailing from a British port, without Convoy—more frequent Convoys will necessarily be required; but from Manchester, Leeds & Exeter, they are decidedly of opinion that the Manufacturing Interest of this country would be materially injured, & the demand for our Manufacturies, would be greatly lessened, by the new Duty which is proposed to be laid on Exports & Imports.—From Birmingham, they also disapprove of it, but appear to be moderate; and that they would be satisfied with certain modifications.—At Halifax, they greatly approve of the Plan, but that the duty on exports to Hamburg should not exceed 1 percent.—These, I believe, are generally the sentiments of the Manufacturing Towns, but in Case you may choose, Sir, to know them more particularly, I take the liberty to transmit herewith, the original letters, which I have received on these subjects [from each town]. At your leisure, you will have the goodness to order that they may be Returned me—Although four of these Towns seem to be adverse to the measure, of imposing any Duties on the Manufactures, that may be exported, I am inclined to hope, that I may be able, on representing the Matter in a favourable, and just, Point of View, to reconcile them to it, provided that you are pleased to authorise me to Say, that it is your Intentions, as I have always understood it to be, That the Duties in Question, are only to Continue, during the Continuance of the War; and

That they shall be laid on the different Branches of foreign Trade, in proportion to the length of Voyage, & the Consequent degree of protection, that they may be afforded. The scale of such Proportions would not be difficult to be made, nor the gradations many.—

These two points, are not explained, nor even noticed, in the drafts of the Bills. The Advantage or saving that would result, on long Voyages, from the Risks being Covered, at the short Commissions, presented with Convoy, would fully Compensate for the Duty, but it would be very hard, and unequal that a short Voyage to Hamburg, or Portugal, on which but a small premium is now paid, should be subject to the same duty as very distant Voyages, on which four or five times the amount of the Same premium may be now demanded.

Sir, Your most obedient & most Humble Servant

John Turnbull

[added at end] The Chamber of Commerce at Exeter appear to be desirous that you will take the trouble to read the letter that has been written to me from that Place.

Letter, John Turnbull to William Pitt [f. 182] London, 15 March 1798[b]

Sir,

I have the honour to transmit herewith the Resolutions of the Merchants & Manufacturers of Birmingham, respecting the proposed duties on Exports & Imports.—

At Halifax they now appear to be likewise much dissatisfied & I am afraid that the Measure will meet with very decided Opposition, from all the Manufacturing Towns, which I am extremely sorry for, as I sincerely think, that its Principle is just, & with proper Modifications, it might have been made Serviceable to Trade, & productive to the Revenue.—

As you have not been pleased to honour me with your Sentiments with regard to the Duration of the Duties, & their being apportioned, According to length of Voyage, I have not been authorised to give any Explanation Respecting these two essential Points, which are left perfectly uncertain from the Expression of the drafts of the bills.—The trading people of Norwich have at last united with the other Manufacturing Towns. Their Chairman has been with me, & I have endeavoured to Reconcile him to the duties in Question, when properly modified.

I have the honour to be very respectfully, Sir, Your most obedient & most Humble Servant

John Turnbull

Letter, John Turnbull to Pitt's secretary [f. 183–4] London, 11 May 1798[b]

Yesterday I Accompanied the Committee Merchants, who again waited on Mr. Pitt, on the subject of the proposed Duties on Exports and Imports—Mr Pitt appeared to have read with attention, & maturely considered the letters and Resolutions that had been sent me, from the different Manufacturing Towns, & which I had transmitted to him.—I am Convinced, that you may be fully persuaded, that Mr. Pitt would not be induced, from any Consideration, to adopt a Measure, that in his opinion, Could be detrimental to the demand for British Manufactures, or to their sale, in foreign countries.—He Seems to be still far from Satisfied, that the duty in question would produce the very prejudicial Effects which is apprehended & Represented in the above mentioned Papers—however, to avoid even the possibility thereof, he appears to have it in Consideration, totally to exempt Spanish Wools from the proposed Duty, & greatly to moderate it on British Manufactures exported to foreign Markets in Europe.—Such exports sent to other Quarters of the World, Certainly Cannot be exposed to, nor suffer from, Competition.—In other Respects I should hope that the Bill, which is merely Occasional & temporary, & at this juncture, from being productive, is necessary, will meet with general satisfaction.—A small universal tax on all Property, Landed & Personal, which has been frequently recommended, would no doubt be more equitable, but it is hardly possible, with any degree of Accuracy, to ascertain the Amount particularly of floating Personal Property.—We all Contribute abundantly to the State, for what <u>we enjoy</u>—but there is a large description of Men, who escape from all Contributions, for the Protection of the immense Wealth, which they possess, but which <u>they do not enjoy</u>—[underlining added in Pitt's copy]

I am always & with sincere Regard, Sir, Your most obed. hble. Servt.
John Turnbull

Letter, John Turnbull to William Pitt [f. 185–7] London, 6 June 1798[b]

Sir,

I have the honour to submit herewith, for Your Consideration, Certain Resolutions that have been today unanimously agreed to by a General Meeting of the Merchants of London, & of Delegates from the principal Manufacturing Towns in England.

I have the honour to be very Respectfully, Sir, Your most obedient & most humble Servant,
John Turnbull

[enclosure with above; also in BL Add. MS. 43770 f. 155] London, 6 June 1798[b]

At a general Meeting of the Merchants of London, who had been, before the present War, largely concerned in the Trade between this Country and Spain, & of Delegates of the principal Manufacturing Towns, the following Resolutions, after having been maturely Considered, were unanimously agreed to.—

That there are many Articles of Merchandise—Wools, Cochineal, Burillar [?], Drugs, &c. which are indispensably necessary for the Manufactures, Agricultures and Commerce of this Kingdom, & that are only produced in Spain and Spanish America; that they cannot be had from any other Country; & that no adequate Substitutes can be found for them.—

That His Majesty's Ministers, it is presumed, from being convinced of the necessity of introducing these Articles into this Kingdom, notwithstanding the present existing War, were pleased, by an Order of Council dated 27 April 1798, to offer to grant of Licenses to Neutral Ships, that were bona fide intended to be loaded from any Enemy's Country to England, except those under the immediate Government of France.—

That it has been found that such Licences could not be safely granted, as no Neutral Vessel would run risk of having such Licence on board from the fear of its being discovered in case of being insisted [compelled by search] by the Enemy [the French].—

That it be therefore, with great deference, Submitted to the Lords of His Majesty's most Honourable Privy Council, that the following mode occurs to the present Meeting as the most eligible to secure & protect at Sea, & in Port, from interception by our Cruisers, the produce of Spain & their Colonies that may be bona fide, meant to be brought to Great Britain & Ireland; & at the same time to prevent fraudulent Consequences and improper Conduct in such transactions—Viz. That such persons, as may have reason to believe, that certain Shipments of any innocent Article, are to be made to their Consignment, from Spain, by Neutral Vessels, Ostensibly bound to a Neutral Port, but really destined to Great Britain, Ireland & the adjacent Islands, should make a declaration thereof, at the Privy Council, & should obtain a Licence for the protection of such Articles; under which Licence, in case of their Stoppage & Detention by any Ship of War, or Privateer, they may be immediately released—The delay attending Adjudication being to many Articles ruinous and destructive.—

That the Merchants of England, concerned with Trade to the Southern parts of Europe, have perused, with much uneasiness & concern the draft of the Act, which has been brought into Parliament by the Attorney General, prohibiting His Majesty's Subjects to reside in an Enemy's country, & any Correspondence whatever to be held, with those who may do so, during the War—There must be many British Subjects in different parts of Spain, Italy, & Switzerland who may be compelled from various motives & Circumstances to remain in those Countries who may be ignorant of the necessity, or may not have the means of applying to His Majesty's Council, for a license in the Country where they may be—The present Meeting, most humbly conceiving that the prohibitions, & Provisions of the Act, are chiefly directed towards France, & that no prejudice could ensue from their being confined to Persons residing in, or corresponding with that Country.—At any rate, it is with Submission presumed that no danger can be apprehended from British Subjects residing in Spain, or Italy; or from Commercial Correspondence being kept up with them.—They therefore fully trust that His Majesty's Ministers will have the goodness to take into their immediate & Serious Consideration the very distressing Consequences that must result from the Act being passed in its present form, & that its farther progress for the present may be suspended.—

That the Chairman be directed to transmit copies of these Resolutions to the Right Honourable Wm. Pitt, the Duke of Portland, Earl Spencer, & the Earl of Liverpool; and to request that the Earl of Liverpool will have the goodness to appoint a time when a Committee of the Merchants may have the honour to attend the Lords of the Committee for Trade of His Majesty's Most Honourable Privy Council, to Receive their Lordships Sentiments & Instructions on these very important matters.

John Turnbull, Chairman

Letter, Henry Lascelles, MP to William Pitt [f. 97] Hanover Sq.
20 February 1805[c]

Sir,

A Deputation from the Manufacturing Towns has requested me to deliver to you the accompanying Memorial relative to the unsatisfied claims of British Subjects upon Spain; and at the same time that I would solicit on their part the honour of an interview on as early a day as may be convenient to you. I am also requested to communicate to them the day you may think proper to appoint.

I have the honour to be, Sir, Your Most Obt. Humb. Servt.
Henry Lascelles

Memorial [f. 98–9] Hoyland's Hotel, Cecil St, Strand 18 February 1805[c]

The Deputies from London and the Manufacturing Towns of Birmingham, Bristol, Exeter, Halifax, Leeds, Manchester, Norwich, Rochdale and Sheffield charged with reclaiming the British Property sequestered in Spain in 1796, and who adjourned their last Meeting in London of November 1804 until the Issue of the Discussions then pending with the Spanish Government was known, have the Honour to request in behalf of the Towns and Districts they represent and in virtue of a special Appointment for the purpose that the Rt. Honourable the Chancellor of the Exchequer will be pleased to grant them an Interview as soon as may be convenient, for the purpose of ascertain His Majesty's gracious Intentions as to the Indemnity intended to be granted from the Frigates and other Spanish Vessels detained, for the Property of which the Claimants have been so long and unjustly deprived.

The Deputies have the Honour to annex, for the Purpose of more easy Reference, a statement of the Facts supporting their Claims and to request the Time of the Interview may be communicated through the Honble. Mr. Lascelles

Jno. Milford for London	Sam. H. Oates for Leeds
John Startin for Birmingham	John Rapp for Manchester
J[ohn] Ebsworth for Bristol	James Hamer for Rochdale
Samuel Banfill for Exeter	Wm. Brittain for Sheffield
John Bramley for Halifax	J. G. Bazeley for Norwich

PART 2

Appendix: Membership of Chambers of Commerce 1767–1839

This chapter provides a complete listing, as far as possible, of the membership of the earliest chambers.[1] These are reproduced in alphabetical order of chamber, with subsequent lists for later dates under the same chamber title, as shown in Table 3. It should be noted that complete lists are not available in several cases as they were not published, not recorded, or have not survived. Where there are no lists an attempt has been made to construct a list as far as possible from notes in minutes or other sources. In most cases this is possible for all committee members, but not for all other members.

The lists include additional information on the 'exogenous' characteristics of each member's business: their sector of activity and their main field of trade, where known; if unknown the entry is left blank. This information is derived from local and national directories, local newspapers and other local sources; where multiple descriptors are given in different sources, all are reproduced here. As far as possible the format is standardised, but differences between places, between the members, and the different levels of information available locally from directories or from survival of documents means that coverage cannot be uniform and consistent. Also the opportunity has been taken of including some additional information on some case where this is significant for interpretation (e.g. on religion). All of this information is subject to the constraints on accuracy in the original sources. Some of the documents were printed, although even these contain errors and misspellings, but many were handwritten, often as signatures or derived from minutes and scribbled listings kept by busy secretaries or treasurers. Therefore the spelling of names cannot be fully relied upon. In any case, many spellings at the time were not standardised, and it is quite frequent to find the same individual's name spelled differently, even on the same document page. There are special problems with spellings of foreign names, especially in Jersey and Guernsey. Brackets [] in names in this Chapter reflect alternative spelling or detail in different lists. In some cases a member is noted by name (or company) but subscribed by someone else on their behalf.

[1] But excludes the early American chambers for which membership lists are given at: http://www.geog.cam.ac.uk/research/projects/chambersofcommerce/

Table 3. Chambers with membership lists reproduced here, with dates covered; incomplete lists shown in italics (almost all have complete committee lists).

1.	Belfast	1783	14.	Leeds	*1785–90*
2.	Birmingham	*1783–4; 1790–5; 1813*	15.	Limerick	1807–15
3.	Bristol	1823	16.	Liverpool	*1774–94*
4.	Cork	*1814; 1819–22*	17.	Liverpool American	1801
5.	Dublin	1783–6; *1805; 1820*	18.	London	1823–4
6.	Dundee	1819; 1836	19.	Londonderry/Derry	1790–3
7.	Edinburgh	1785; 1786–91	20.	Manchester	*1774*; 1781–2
	Fife (*see* Kirkcaldy)		21.	Newcastle	1815–6
	Forfar (*see* Dundee)		22.	North Staffordshire	*1785, 1789*
8.	Glasgow	1783–4	23.	Nottingham	*1813*
9.	Greenock	1813	24.	Plymouth	1813–14
10.	Guernsey	*1769*; 1808–9		Potteries (*see* N. Staffs.)	
11.	Hull	1801; 1837; 1838–40	25.	Waterford	*1787–96*; 1805; 1815
12.	Jersey	1767; 1769–85	26.	Wolverhampton	1819
13.	Kirkcaldy	*1825*	27.	Worcester	*1839*

The details in the list are necessarily brief and only intended as a guide for subsequent research. Standard abbreviations are used throughout this chapter, as follows:

A	Anglican (or Church of Ireland in Ireland)
C	Committee or Board member of chamber
Cath	Roman Catholic
Co.	Company (includes partnerships)
D	Dissenter (P: Presbyterian; U: Unitarian; Q: Quaker. Usually based on information given at birth, otherwise at marriage or death)
d.o.b.	Date of birth
F	Fustian
I	Individual sole proprietor
jun.	Junior, usually the son of someone of the same name
MC	Manchester
Mer.	Merchant
mf.	Manufacturer
MP	Member of Parliament current with time of list
P	Presbyterian
Pres	President of chamber (or chairman)
Q	Quaker
ptnr	Partner
S	Secretary of chamber
sen.	Senior, usually the father of someone of the same name
T	Treasurer of chamber
VP	Vice-president of chamber (or vice-chairman)
w/h	Warehouse
WI	West Indies
w/s	Wholesale

1. Belfast chamber of commerce, 1783 (N=66)

Source: list of first 66 subscribers in minute book and loose papers: PRONI D1857/1/AB/1

Name	Business	Role
Andrews, Thomas	Merchant Taylor; linen draper & flour merchant	
Auchlinleck, William	(& Co.) tobacco merchant	
Batt, Narcissus	(& Co.) wine merchant & shipper	
Black, George	Wine importer & shipper	
Boyle, John	(& Co.) merchant & importer, Discount Office	
Boyle, William	(& Co.) merchant & vitriol mf	
Bradshaw, Robert	(& Co.) linen mf and importer, Discount Office	1st Committee
Brett, Charles	W/s wine merchant	
Brown, John	(J. S. & W.) grain, wine & linen merchants & banker (Belfast Bank), Discount Office	1st Committee
Brown, Samuel	Merchant	
Brown, Thomas	(J. S. & W.) grain, wine & linen merchants	
Brown, William	(J. S. & W.) grain, wine & linen merchants & banker (Cunninghams'), Discount Office	1st Committee
Campbell, John	(& Co.) Rope mf. & banker (Cunninghams'), Discount Office	
Cavan, Thomas	Grocer & merchant	
Crawford, Hugh	Linen merchant & shipper	
Cunningham, John	(& Co.) brewer	
Cunningham, Waddell	(& Co.) Merchant, brewer, mf., banker (Cunninghams'), Discount Office & MP	1st Chair
Dunsmore, David	Merchant	
Edwards, Benjamin	(& Co.) Glass mf.	
Ewing, John	Shipping & banker (Belfast Bank), Discount Office	1st Committee
Ferguson, James	Spirit dealer and tavern, Discount Office	
Getty, Robert	Merchant & insurance	1st Committee
Gordon, David	Lawyer & mf.	
Greg, Cunningham	(& Co.) merchant	
Greg, Thomas	(& Co.) Merchant & vitriol mf.; large landowner & property developer	1st Committee
Griffith, Amyas	Surveyor of Excise	
Hamilton, John	Cork cutter & banker (Belfast Bank)	
Hardin, Thomas	Merchant & shipper	
Haslett, Henry	(& Co.) draper	
Henderson, John	Merchant, shipping & insurance	
Holmes, James	(J. J. & Co.) Russia merchants, Discount Office	
Homes, John	(J. J. & Co.) Russia merchants & banker (Belfast Bank), Discount Office	1st Committee
Hyde, Samuel	Linen merchant & draper	
Hyndman, Hugh	Snuff mf.	
Hyndman, James	(& Co.) wholesale & retail wool merchant & tobacco mf.	

Jones, Valentine	(& Co.) wine & WI merchant	1st Committee
Joy, George	(G., H. & Co.) printing, paper mf., cotton mills	
Joy, Henry sen.	(G., H. & Co.) printing, paper mf., cotton mills	1st Committee
Joyce, Valentine	(& Co.) wine & WI merchant	
Kennedy, James Trail	(& Co.) merchant, glass mf. and brewer	
Knox, Robert	Merchant	
Luke, John	(Bros.) merchant, woollen draper & pottery shop	
Lyons, Thomas	Linen bleacher	
Milliken, Thomas		
Montgomery, Hugh	(& Co.) importer & retailer	1st Committee
Neilson. John	(& Co.) wool warehouse & haberdasher & tobacco mf.	
Orr, Alexander	Merchant	1st Committee
Park, James	Cotton mf.	
Robinson, John	Hatter & linen trader	
Russell, John	Merchant & linen bleacher	
Scott, Archibald	Grocer	
Scott, Robert	Merchant & draper	
Seed, William	(& Co.) merchant	
Simms, Robert	(& Co.) merchant	
Sinclaire, William	Linen bleacher, Discount Office	
Smith, John Galt	Wool draper, mf. and broker	
Smyth, John	(Co.) linen merchant, draper & printer	
Stevenson, James	(& Co.) linen merchant, mf. & retailer	1st Committee
Stewart, Robert	(& Co.) linen bleacher & cotton spinner	
Suffern, James	Linen merchant	
Sutherland, Alexander	Merchant	
Tennant, William	(& Co.) sugar merchant	
Thomson, Robert	(& Co.) sugar refiner, Discount Office	1st Committee
Thomson, Samuel	Linen merchant & grocer	
Tomb, David	(& Co.) merchant	1st Committee
Wilson, Nathaniel	(& Co.) merchant & textile mf.	1st Committee

2. Birmingham chamber of commerce, 1783, 1790 and 1813

Sources: printed notices of meetings, circulated minutes/reports in *Aris's Birmingham Gazette*; Langford's *Birmingham* (1868); Wright, *Chronicles* (1913). No lists are complete; information mainly covers committee.

2.1 Members of first Birmingham Commercial Committee, 1783–4 (N=47)

Name	Business
Alexander & Co.	Ptnr with Walker, Merchant
Anderson, William	Button maker
Barrs, Thomas & Co.	Merchants
Bingham James Bros.	Merchant & buckle maker
Bingham, John Bros.	Merchant
Boulton, Matthew	Merchant & metal mf.
Clay, Henry	Japanner to HM
Conquest, Richard	Wine merchant

Ford, Samuel	Merchant
Francis, John & Co.	Brass founder (with Cotterill)
Freeth, Sampson & Co.	Ptnr with Glover, Merchant (with Bayley)
Frey, Anthony & Co.	Merchant (with Glover)
Galton, Samuel jun. & Sons	Gun merchant; ptnr Gibbins Bank after 1802
Garbett, Samuel	Refiner and sword mf. Pres
Gibbs, Joseph & Co.	Button and cutlery manufacturer
Glover, Samuel & Co.	Ptnr with Frey, Merchant (with Frey)
Green, Joseph	Merchant, chapemaker, & snuff mf.
Hayes, Samuel	Merchant
Humphreys, George	Merchant
Humphreys, William & Sons	Merchant & estate
Humpreys, John & Sons	Merchant
Hurd, John & Sons	Merchant & Steel manufacturer
Ingram, Thomas & Co.	Ptnr with Duncan and Davies, Merchant and manufacturing agents
Jukes, Joseph	Merchant
Lee, John	Gilt button manufacturer
Mar[l]inde, J. P. & Co.	Button maker (Grimqult, Malinde & Paust)
Mason, Wallis & Bros.	Merchant
Oatridge & Marinden	Merchant
Palmer, Edward & Co.	Ptnr with Prentice; merchant & plater
Palmer, Thomas	Steel button maker
Perkins, Edward & Co.	Merchant
Perkins, Henry	Merchant
Richards, John	Merchant & button mf.
Rickards, John	Attorney
Ryland, John	Wire drawer & pin maker
Ryland, Samuel	Pin maker
Russell, George	Merchant & sword hilt & toy mf.
Russell, Thomas & Co.	Merchant (with Smith)
Russell, William & Co.	Merchant & sword hilt & toy mf. (with Smith)
Salt, John	Merchant
Simcox, Thomas & Co.	Tin buckle mf.
Smith, Timothy	Brass founder, toy & Staffordshire ware mf. (with Russells etc.); ptnr Bloxhams Bank in 1790
Startin, Charles	Merchant
Startin, John	Ptnr with Wilkinson & Welch, Merchant; ptnr Wilkinsons Bank after 1808
Turner, William	Gilt toy mf.
Walker, William & Bros.	Ptnr with Alexander, Merchant
Welch, William & Co.	Ptnr with Wilkinson and Startin, Merchant & iron founder
Wilkinson, John	Staffordshire ware mf.; ptnr Wilkinsons Bank after 1802
Woolley James & Co.	Sword & weapons mf. etc.

2.2 Additional members of Birmingham Commercial Committee, 1790–5 (N=31); all the previous members are believed to have continued for this period; Garbett remained the leading figure and chair.

Name	Business
Alston James	Chemist & refiner
Benton, James	Button, buckle & toy makers
Blythe, B.	Merchant & brass founder
Chance, William	Merchant & factor
Coales, Robert	Sword mf., and lead ptnr Coales Bank 1766–90
Daniels, George	Merchant
Garbett, Francis	Sword and metal mf.
Gill, Thomas	Iron, steel & sword mf. to HRH Prince of Wales etc.
Goddington, James	Brass & iron founders; ptnr Bloxhams Bank
Green Thomas	Jeweller & factor
Grundy, Jona	Merchant
Grundy, Thomas	Merchant
Guest, John	Japanner
Harvey	Sword manufacturer
Hawkins, William	Button maker
Homer, Edward	Provisions merchant
Hunt, Harry	Button & thimble maker
Rabone, Joseph	Merchant
Russell George	Merchant & sword hilt & toy manufacturer
Ryland, Samuel	Pin maker
Ryland, William	Plater
Scale, John	
Shorthouse, William	Acid manufacture
Smith, Robert	Factor
Smith, Joseph	Button maker
Stokes, Benjamin	Merchant
Villers, William	Wholesale braziers, pewterer & dealer in metals
Watt, James	Steam engine manufacture
Willmore, Thomas	Silver plate buckle maker
Walker, Alexander	Merchant
Yates, James	Brass founder, coach and harness plater; ptnr Bloxham's Bank

2.3 Birmingham Chamber of Commerce, known members 1813 (N=48)

Name Business	
Anderson & Ashmore	Button makers
Attwood, George	Steel & iron warehouse
Attwood, Jones Henry	Steel & iron warehouse
Attwood, Mathias	Ptnr Attwood & Spooners Bank
Attwood, Thomas	Steel & iron warehouse
Baker, James	Brass founder
Barrs & Hands	Brass founders
Biddle, John	Glass manufacture
Blair, David	Gun maker
Blythe, Robert	Brass founder
Bragg, George	Jewellers & toy manufacture

Chance, William	Merchant
Clark, Thomas	Toy maker
Cooper, W. W.	Wire maker
Crompton, J. W.	Wire maker
Daniel, George	Merchant
Dickenson, John	Ptnr Goodhalls Bank
Francis, William	Clock maker
Frears, Edward	Bank
Frears, William	Bank
Galton, Samuel Tertius	Ptnr Gibbins Bank
Harrold, William	Merchant
Hawkes, Thomas Lakin	
Jones, Paul Mann	Factors; ptnr Gibbins Bank from 1812
Lawrence, John T.	Furrier
Lloyd, Samuel	Ptnr Taylors & Lloyds Bank
Mason, O.	Brass & iron founder
Messenger, Thomas	Brass founder
Neville, William	Estate
Pearson, James	Jeweller
Person, Joseph	
Pemberton, Thomas	Jeweller
Perkins, Henry	Merchant
Payton, Richard	
Phipson, Joseph	Saw manufacturer
Phipson, Thomas	Metals
Potts, Thomas	Merchant
Redfern, William	Gun maker
Ryland, John	Wire manufacturer
Ryland, Thomas	Pin maker
Scholefield, Joshua	Plane maker
Shakespear, William	Manufacturer
Shorthouse, William	Acid manufacture
Small, Thomas	
Smith, Richard	Merchant
Spooner, Isaac jun.	Merchant & ptnr Attwood & Spooners Bank
Spooner, Richard	Probably at Attwood & Spooners Bank
Turner, John	Toy maker
Walker, Simon	Provisions
Webster, Joseph	Bailiff and factors

3. Bristol chamber of commerce, 1823 (N=185)

Source: Minute book, Bristol RO 38605/A/1 Founding members, 1823. There are significant legibility problems from handwriting.

Member	Business
Acraman & Jones	Deal & timber merchants
Acraman, W. D. & W. E.	Shipping agents and materials
Alexander, M. J. F. & A.	Merchants & commission agents
Allies [James] & Son	Paper makers

Ames, J. A.	Shipping and harbour
Ames, J. G. & Co.	Bank
Ariel [William] & Son	WI broker
Arlidge [Joseph] & Co.	? Aldridge, carpenters
Badham, J. B.	Linen draper
Bailie [Evan] Sons & Co.	WI merchants & ptnr Old bank
Bangley & Fyson	Merchant
Barnes, Francis M.	Timber merchant
Betts & Drew	?tailors
Bevan, Edward	Paper manufacture
Brice, Durbin	Sugar refiner
Brice, Stock & Fery	Sugar refiners
Brookman, William	Accountant
Browne, Henry & Co.	Silversmith & Bristol Bullion Bank, & lead ptnr
Browne, Samuel	? Bristol Bullion Bank
Browne, William	Bristol Bullion Bank ptnr
Bush, Henry	Merchant
Bushell [William] & Co.	Merchants & manufacturers
Busvine, John	Ironmonger
Cambridge, L. & A.	Colour merchants
Casey, Edward	? Tailor
Cave, Steven	Ptnr Ames Cave Bank
Chapman, William	Agent, commission agent & accountant
Clark, Gilmore & Clark	? Sugar refiners
Clark, Thomas	Oil & composition manufacture
Clements & Price	Ship brokers
Clift [John] & Sons	Russian, Saxon, German & Irish linen importers
Cole, Thomas	Wholesale linen draper, former Savery Bank ptnr
Cooke & Bengough	attorney; ex banker (ex Under-Sheriff)
Cookson, J. & J.	Glass bottle manufacture
Cossick [Alex J.] & Co.	Merchants ?
Cross, William	Ship broker
Cross [John] & Co.	Wholesale druggists
Cunningham, James	Tin plate maker
Dalton [Edward] & Co.	
Davies, Thomas	Leather factor
Davis [Richard Hart] Son & Co.	Merchants & ptnr Harfords Bank
Evans, J.	Coach maker
Fargus, John	Auctioneer
Ferrell [William] & Son	
Fisher [George] & Son	? Ropemakers
Fisher, Francis	Merchant
Fisher, George	Candle manufacture
Ford, Alexander & James	Hoopers
Frigram & Gooklen	Lawyers
Fripp Daniel	Soap maker; family banking link
Fripp, Edward Brice	Merchant & ptnr Birch Pitt Fripp Bank
Gadd, Thomas	Anchorsmith
George, C., Hills J. B. and P. S. & Co.	Patent shot Co. & former ptnr Castle Bank
George, Philip jun.	Patent shot Co.
Grace, Josiah	Flour factor
Granger [Charles] & Son	Hoopers & warehouse

Gresley, Charles	? Milliner
Griffiths & Lewis	Anchorsmiths
Grimes & Bargeir	Merchants
Gutch?, John Matthew	
Hall [Samuel] & Co.	Spanish wool merchants
Hall, J & Son	Merchant
Hall, Joseph	Grocer
Harding, Robert	Distiller
Harfords Bros & Co.	Bank
Harley & Lany	Ironmongers
Harwood & Blackwell	Merchants & leather factors
Hassell, James	Leather factors
Hellicar, Thomas	Merchant
Hiddell Hood & Co.	Merchant
Hobbs, T. M.	Wholesale ironmonger
Holden & Vining	? Grocers
Howell, John	Deal merchant
Hunt, Richard jun.	Chocolate maker?
Hunter, Robert	Merchant
Husenbeth [Fred. Chas.] & Son	Provision curer
Jackson, David	Drysalter?
Jackson, J. & Son	Watchmaker
James [Maurice] & Co.	? Seed factors
Jeffreys, Humphrey	? Corn factor
Johnson, William & Edward	Wholesale & tinware manufacture
Jones [Lediard] & Mortimer	Dry salters
Kidd, Edward	Saw mill
King & Brettell	? Merchants
King [Thomas] & Son	
King, George	Merchant
Lo[a]rymer, James	Corn factor
Lawrence, Ward & Tanner	Chandlers?
Lane J & Co.	Spanish wool brokers
Leonard, S. & Co.	Wholesalers & tobacco
Lewis, John	Woollen draper
Lewis [William] & Well	Ironmongers & anchorsmiths
Lindsey, George	
Loters & Richardson	? Linen warehouse
Lucas Coathope & Co.	Merchants & Glass bottle manufacture
Lucas [Samuel] & Sons	Confectioner
Lyon, James	
Maggs, Bigg & Maggs	? Tobacco merchants
Manchee/ Matchie, F. J.	? Potter
Marshall, W. H.	
McAdam, John Loudon	Merchant & manufacture
Meaby, Robert	Wharf
Meredith, Abraham	Brick and tile manufacture
Metford, Landsdown & Hooper	Linen merchants
Moens, Adam	Merchant
Montague [Ralph] jun. & Son	
Moore, James	
Morgan & Brown	Tea dealers

Nash & Hill	Drapers
Nash, Jonathan	Brewer
Nash son, Isaac	Hooper
Nassaway, John	Leather dresser
Nicholas [John] & Co.	Coal merchants
Nott, Richard	Ironmongery and cutlery warehouse
Ogden, Benjamin	Corn factor
Oliver, Lionel	? Tea dealer
Palmer, William	Hat manufacture
Park End Co.	
Parsons Charles & Co.	Wholesalers & linen merchants
Payne [Charles] & Son	Merchants & furniture broker
Perry, James	Spirits dealer
Perry, John jun.	Carriage manufacture
Peters, James	Cooper & carpenter
Phillips, J. R. & Co.	Wine & brandy merchants
Phippen, James	Fell monger
Pinney, Ames & Co.	Manufacturers
Poster & Beck	? Grocer
Pountney & Allies	Earthenware manufacture
Price, John & H. C.	Solicitors
Pritchard, William	Ironmonger
Pritchett[ard], G. W.	? Coachmaker
Protheroe & Hunt	Merchants
Protheroe [Thomas] & Son	WI merchants
Protheroe, John jun.	Hat manufacture
Protheroe, William	Ironmongers
Prust, Stephen	Perfumer
Rankin, Robert	Sugar refiner
Rankin, Thomas	Sugar refiner
Reed, Charles	Liquor merchant
Reynolds Thomlinson & Co	Wholesalers
Richard [Henry] & Son	Merchant
Richards & Butcher	Sugar refiners
Ricketts [Henry] & Co.	Glass manufacture
Ricketts, George & Co.	Pattern makers
Ricketts, Leonard, Ricketts & Co.	Tobacco merchants & ptnr Castle Bank
Ring R, W.	Coopers & lime merchants?
Roach, [Thomas] & Son	Warehouse
Robertson & Forthergill	Importers
Roche [William] & Co.	Raisin wine makers and rectifiers
Russell, James Graves	Merchant
Sanders, J. M.	Pin manufacturer
Sanders, Thomas & Co.	Seed, corn & hop merchants
Savery Towgood & Co.	Bank; & agents Prideaux Bank (Kingsbridge)
Savery & Seward	Merchants?
Sheppard, William	Surveyor
Shute Edwards	Chemists
Shute Purnells & Co.	Wholesalers & merchants
Slade, Edward	
Smart, John N.	Barge owner
Smart, Robert	Surgeon

Smith, Son & Co.	Brokers
Stanton, Daniel	Wholesale grocer
Steger, Robert	Linen draper
Stevens, John	Ship owner and broker
Stock, Thomas/William	(President)
Stuckeys, Lean & Co.	Bank
Taylor, George	Maltster & brewer
Thomas [John] & Co	Wholesalers
Tozer & Were	Tea merchants & porter brewers
Vaughan, John & Philip	Spanish wool merchant & banking family
Vining, Charles	Merchant & grocer
Visger, Harman	Merchant
Wait & James	Dry salters
Ward, Thomas	Land surveyor
Waring, Edward	Ironmonger
Wasbrough & Duggan	Brass founders
Waters [William] & Co.	Importers
Watson [William] & Co.	
Whitechurch, James Joseph	Insurance
Wilcox, James	Shipping
Wills Ditchett & Co.	Spirit importers?
Wreford. John	
Wright, Thomas	Merchant & banking family
Wyld [George] & Sons	Rectifiers, distillers and wine merchants
Young [Joseph] & Co.	Land surveyor?

4. Cork chamber of commerce, 1814 and 1819–22.

4.1 Cork chamber, 1814 (N=25)

Sources: *Cork Mercantile Chronicle,* 20 July 1814. The 1814 attempt to begin a chamber failed. * indicates also in chamber after 1819

Member	**Business**
Browne, John	Merchant
Burke, Robert	Esq.,
Church, James B.	(Church, Busteed & Co.) Merchants
Crookshank, Samuel*	
Cummins, J. K.	Grocery warehouse
Dunscombe, Thomas	Merchant
Foley, J. B.	Draper?
Gibbings, Barth.	(Gibbings Thos & Son) brewers
Hewett, Henry	Shipping Capt.
Homan, Frederick*	(Homan & Meade) ironmongers
Keene, James	
King, Joseph	Merchant
Lane, Samuel [S]	
Large, William	
Madden, Owen	Merchant
Malony, Francis J.	Tallow chandler?
McClure, Robert	Merchant

Moylan, Denis sen.		Merchant
Murphy, Nicholas		
Nettles, Richard N.		
Perrier, Sir Anthony	[P]	(& Co.) Merchants
Perrott, Samuel		
Purcell, Patrick		Merchant
Reeves, Thomas S.		
Wise, Thomas		(W & T) distillers

4.2 Cork chamber, 1819–22 (N=54)

Source: Minute books 1819, at modern chamber. The 1819 foundation has no complete list of members, the following comprises attendees at meetings, mostly committee members; chair rotated between meetings.

Member	Business	Role
Baldwin, David	(& Beamish) woollen drapers	
Balshaw, Herbert	M.D.	
Barry, J.	Pottery warehouse	
Blayne, Barth.		
Bullen, William	Attorney (& Sons) Butter merchant	C
Callaghan, P. W.	(& Co.) Merchant	
Cleary, Thomas J.	Grocer	
Cogan, John	Vintner	C
Crawford, William jun.	(& Co.) Brewer	
Crookshank, Samuel*		
Daley, James	(& Co.) Rectifier & distiller	C
Dillon, Thomas		
Fitzgibbon, Thomas	(Perrier, Fitzgibbon & Co.) Merchants	C
Fitzgibbon, William	Butter merchant	
Foley, Dan	Glass warehouse	
Galbuy/Galway, Michael		
Graver, Dan		
Hackett, Barth.	Leather works?	
Hannan, Fred	Vintner?	
Hargreaves, Joshua	Merchant	
Harley, Corns	(& Co.) Merchant	
Harrington, William	Chemist	
Homan, Robert*	(Homan & Meade) ironmongers	
Lugnan, Charles		
Lynch, David	Merchant	
Lyons, Henry		
Lyons, Thomas	Woollen draper	C & S
Mahony, Martin	(& Tim Co.) Woollen & worsted mf.	
Maloney, Fr. J.	Vintner	C
McCarthy, Alexander	Butter merchant	
McSweeney, Paul	Merchant	
Meagher, Dan	Wine merchant	
Mullens, Denis	Grocer	
Murphy, Daniel	Leather merchant	
Murphy Jeremiah	Linen draper	C

Murphy, Jeremiah jun	Linen draper	C & T
Murphy, John	Butter merchant	C
Murphy, Nicholas	Shipper	
O'Connell, Geoffrey	Grocer	
O'Connell, John	Boot & shoe maker?	
O'Connor, Corns	Merchant	
O'Daley, James	Rectifier	
O'Driscoll, Richard		C
O'Keefe, Keefe	Butter merchant	
O'Leary, Arthur		C
Penrose, Edward		
Percival, Sir John		
Regan, William	Merchant	
Roche, James J.	(Stephen & James) Bankers & wine merchants	
Runayne, Richard	Glass manufacturer	C
Scanlon, John	Butter merchant	
Shinkwin, Thomas	Coffee House & hotel	
Sugrue, Charles	(& Co.) Wine merchant	
Waters, George	Wine merchant	

5. Dublin chamber of commerce, 1783, 1805 and 1820

5.1 Dublin chamber of commerce, 1783 (N= 220)

Source: Printed leaflet of initial subscribers photographed in Cullen *Princes and Pirates* (1983) p. 55

Member	Business
George Adamson	(George & Thos) Sugar bakers & merchants
Wm. Alexander	Alderman and magistrate
Wm. Alexander	Merchant
John Allen	(& Sons) Merchant, Director Bank of Ireland
James Anderson	Merchant
Joseph Anderson	(& Co.) Linen printer
Garret Andrews	Ship broker
Alexander Armstrong	(& Co.) Merchant, Director Bank of Ireland
Archibald Armstrong	Linen merchant
James Armstrong	Bookseller
Wm. Arnold	Silk weaver
Joseph Barcroft jun.	(& Co.) Merchant
Patrick Bean	Ironmonger
Edward Beatty	(E. & David) paper and wine merchants
John Binns	Merchant & ironmonger
Robert Black	Tea man
Hans Blackwood	(H. & P.) Merchants
Price Blackwood	(H. & P.) Merchants
Mark Bloxham	Tallow chandler
Richard Bolton	Sheriff's peer
Oliver Bond	Wholesale woollen draper
Thomas Bond	
Charles Bourns	(C. & F.) Haberdashers

Brabazon Noble	(& Co.) Merchants
Patrick Bride	Merchant & Sheriff's peer
Robert Brooke	
Thos Digby Brooke	
Richard Brown	Merchant
Arthur Bryan	Merchant (possibly related to brandy merchants Baker & Bryan of 1750s; Cullen, 1998, p.174)
Patrick Burke	School master (English & Mercantile School)
Thos Burnett	(& Co.) Seedsman
Edward Burroughs	Paper mf.
Edmund Byrne	(Edward Byrne & R. McDonald & Co.) Merchants
Edward Byrne	(Edward Byrne & R. McDonald & Co.) Merchants, including brandy (Cullen, 1998, pp.99–100)
Joseph Byrne	Merchant
Francis Cahill	Merchant
Nathaniel Cairns	Tallow chandler
William E. Calbeck	Gunpowder mf.
George Campbell	Merchant
James Campbell	Merchant & Sheriff's peer
Mathew Cardiff	(& Co.) Whisky & corn factors
John Carleton	(& Co.) Merchant
Joseph Church	Merchant
Benjamin Clarke	Merchant
Charles Clarke	
Hugh Cochran	Merchant
John Collins	Mercer, linen draper & haberdasher
William Colvill	Merchant, Director Bank of Ireland
John Comerford	Merchant
Valentine O'Connor	(Valentine & Malachy) Merchants
William Cope	(Cope, Binns, Hautenville & Downs) Silk merchants
Michael Cosgrave	Merchant
John Coftley	Ribbon weaver
John Cowan	Merchant
John Creathorn	Butcher
James Crosby	Silk weaver
Leland Crosthwait[e]	Merchant, including brandy (Cullen, 1998, p.84) (Deputy Gov. Bank of Ireland 1807–8)
Hugh Crothers	Merchant & Sheriff's peer
West Darby	Merchant
John Darragh	Alderman
Patrick Dease	Merchant
John Deeluzeau	Wine merchant
Robert Deey	
Jeremiah D'Olier	(& Sons) Goldsmiths, jewellers & Sheriff's peer, Director Bank of Ireland
David Dick	(& Co.) Merchant
Samuel Dick	(Bros.) Merchant, Director Bank of Ireland
Daniel Dickinson	(Joseph, Wm. & Daniel) Merchants
Joseph Dickinson	(Joseph, Wm. & Daniel) Merchants
William Dickinson	(Joseph, Wm. & Daniel) Merchants
Richard Dillon	Wholesale linen draper
Wm. Bruce Dunn	(& Co.) Ship brokers & banker (Coates & Lawless)

Richard Eaton	
John English	Wine merchant
Geo Eskildson	Merchant & Danish Consul
Patrick Ewing	Flax dresser
Joseph Fletcher	Merchant
John Folie	Merchant
Edward Forbes	Merchant
Joshua Forbes	(& Co.) Merchant
William Ford	Merchant
Robert Foster	Merchant
George Fox	(& Co.) Merchant
John Galloway	(& Co.) Merchant
Samuel Gamble	Linen draper
Samuel Garner	Pin mf.
Benjamin Gault	Merchant & Sheriff's peer
Daniel Geale	(Ebenezer, Fred & Daniel & Co.) Merchants
Ebenezer Geale	(Ebenezer, Fred & Daniel & Co.) Merchants
Frederick Geale	(Ebenezer, Fred & Daniel & Co.) Merchants
Joseph Goff	Merchant
Joshua Green	Merchant
Thos Green	Alderman
Andrew Grehan	Merchant
Arthur Guinness	(& Co.) Brewer
Hugh Hamill jun.	(Bros.) Merchant
Hugh Hamilton	(& Co.) Sugar baker
Robert Hanna	Grocer
James Hartley	Merchant
Travers Hartley [P]	(& Son) Merchant, Director Bank of Ireland, MP
John Hendrick	Merchant & brewer
Geo. Hamilton Hoffman	Director Bank of Ireland
Joseph Hone jun.	Merchant
Nathaniel Hone	Merchant
Nathaniel Hone jun.	Merchant
James Horan	Alderman
Martin Howard	Wine merchant
Peter Howard	Dry cooper
John Hughes	Cooper
John Hunt	Clothier
Ephraim Hutchinson	Merchant
Alexander Jaffray	(& Hautenville) Merchant, Director Bank of Ireland
Christopher James	Merchant
David Jebb	
Caleb Jenkin	(& Co.) Druggist
Thos Jordan jun.	Hosier
Patrick Kavenagh	Sugar baker
John Fred. Kelly	
Alex. Kirkpatrick jun.	(& Co.) Merchant & Sheriff's peer
Thos Kirwan	Brewer
Henry Lanauze	Grocer
George Lamprey	Cutler
George Lang	(& Hawthorn) Merchant
James Leckey	

Thomas Lee	Merchant
John Lindsey	(& Co.) Sugar baker & merchant
William Lindsey	(& Co.) Sugar baker & merchant
Richard Litton	Merchant
Robert Lloyd	(R. J. & W.) Merchants
John Locker	Merchant
George Lunell	Merchant
Joseph Lynam	Merchant & banker (Finlay's), Alderman
Henry Lyons	Merchant
Robert Magee	(R & W) Merchants
Foliott Magrath	Merchant
Simon Maguire	(& Keighley) Merchants
Alex. Maitland	
George Maquay	(G. & J. L.) Sugar baker and merchant
John Leland Maquay	(G. & J. L.) Sugar baker and merchant
James Marsh	Ironmonger
Daniel Marston [VP]	Merchant & Sheriff's peer
Andrew Maziere jun.	Tea dealer
Francis McAnnally	Linen merchant
Anthony McDermott	Merchant, incl. brandy & wine (Cullen, 1998, pp. 217–8, 222)
Anth. McDermott jun.	Merchant, with father
Farrell McDermott	Gun maker
Owen McDermott	
Patrick McLoughlin	Woollen draper & sheriff's peer
Edward Medlicott	Factor
David Melville	(& Co.) Merchant
Robert Mercer	(R. & R.) Merchants
Stephen Miller	Merchant
Richard Mitchell	
Thomas Mitchell	Merchant
Edward Moore	Wine merchant?
Edward Morgan	Hosier
Ralph Mulhern	Shoe mf.
Denis Murphy	(D. & J.) Merchants
George Murray	
John Nairac	Sugar baker & merchant
Wm. Netterville	Merchant
Richard Neville	Banker (Findlay's); MP for Wexford
John Nevin	Cotton mf.
Richard Nunn	Paper mf.
Charles O'Brien	Woollen draper
Dennis Thos. O'Brien [VP]	(& Co.) Ironmonger & merchants
Oliver O'Hara	Wine merchant
John Orr	Merchant
John James Pache	(J. J. & Co.) Merchants
George Palmer	(& Co.) Hosier, Director Bank of Ireland
Alexander Patrick	Umbrella maker
John Patrick	Merchant
Paul Patrick	(& Co.) Merchants
William Penrose	
John Phelps	Merchant
Joseph Pike	

Joshua Pim [T]	(J. & J.) Merchants
Michael Plunkett	Tea merchant
Richard Plunkett	Sale master
James Potts	Printer
Philip Prossor	
Thomas Rainey	Merchant
Smith Ramadge	Merchant
William Rawlins	Timber merchant
Edward Reynolds	Silk mf.
Robert Shaw	Merchant & banker (Shaw & Sons)
James Sheil	Tanner & Alderman
Abraham Skeys	Merchant
William Smith	Stockbroker
Robert Smith	Merchant
Robert Smith jun.	Merchant
William Speer	Wine & mineral water mf.
Arthur Stanley	Merchant
William Stephens	Merchant
Robert Stephenson	Merchant
James Stewart	(J. & J.) Merchants
Alex. Stillas	Merchant
Amos Strettle	Merchant, Director Bank of Ireland
George Sutton	Alderman
John Sutton	(Beresford St.) Merchant & Alderman
Patrick Sweetman	(P. & J.) Porter brewers
James Napper Tandy	Merchant & Alderman
William Trocke	(& Son) Merchants
Thomas Tweedy	(& Lindsay) Haberdashers
Godfrey Vaughan	(& Litton) Merchant
Jeremiah Vickers	(& Co.) Linen drapers, Director Bank of Ireland
Jeremiah Vickers jun.	(& Co.) Linen drapers
Charles Ward	Merchant
Rt. Hon. Nath. Warren	Mayor & Commissioner of the Peace
Ingratius Weld	Merchant
Luke White	Wholesale bookseller
Robert White	(& Bernard) Hatters
Abraham Wilkinson	(A. & P.) Merchants, Director Bank of Ireland
Peter Wilkinson	(A. & P.) Merchants
Henry Williams	Linen draper & banker (Williams & Sadleir)
James Williams	Coachmaker & banker (Williams & Sadleir) & Sheriff's peer
Benjamin Wills	Goldsmith
William Wilson	Printer & stationer
William Worthington	Merchant & Alderman
Other members 1783–6	
Joseph Sandwith	Merchant
William Shannon [S]	Lawyer & public notary

5.2 Dublin chamber of commerce, 1805 (N= 23)

Source: first chamber minute book, TNAI; printed *Articles of Association*: RIA HP 878/5.
Initial proposers; first committee/council; * also member in 1820; chair rotated frequently; list incomplete.

Member	Relig.	Business
George F. Carleton# Pres# & C	A	(& Co.) merchants
Richard Darling# C T	A	Merchant
John Duncan C		(Wm. & John) merchants
Arthur Guinness C	A	(A, Ben. & W. L.) brewers
Nathaniel Hone# C	A	(& Son) merchants
William Hone C	A	Merchant
William Humphreys C		Merchant
Alexander Jaffray, jun. C		Merchant, banking family
Richard Litton# C	P	Merchant
Randal MacDonnell# * C	Cath	(Edw. Byrne, R. MacDonnell & Co.) Merchant
Bartholomew Maziere# C	P	(& Co.) merchants; C Comm. Building Co.
James M'Call# *	P	Merchant
Hugh O'Connor#	Cath	(V.H. & H & E) merchants
Valentine O'Connor, jun.# C	Cath	Merchant; C Comm. Building Co.
John Orr C		(Wm. & John) muslin mf., merchants
Peter Roe C		(& Sons) merchants
James Ryan# C	Cath	? Merchant; or (Ja. & Ed.) calico printers
Richard Sayers C		(Gordon & Co.) merchants
John Townsend Sinnett C		(& Co.) w/s silk merchants
Samuel Stephens C		(Edw. & Sam.) merchants
John Todhunter# * C	Q	Merchant, and corn merchant
Richard Verschoyle# C	A	(R.J. & Co.) merchants; land agent; C Comm. Building Co.
Joseph Wilson# C 1st Pres	P	Merchant & US consul; C Comm. Building Co.

5.3 Dublin chamber of commerce, 1820 (N= 26)

Source: Officers, in *Laws and Regulations* (1821): RIA HP1220/6. (Full 1820 membership, not reproduced, available in *Annual Report*, 1823: RIA HP1284/12). See also Cullen, *Brandy Trade* (1998); MacMahon *Most Respectable Meeting* (2014).

Member	Role	Business
John Barber	C	Director, Stock Exchange Co.
Samuel Bewley	C	(Bewlay & Fowler) w/s mercers Q
Peter Brophy	C	Merchant
James Chambers	C	(Chambers Todd & Co.) merchant & Linen Hall factor
James Con[n]olly	VP	(& Co.) merchants
Leland Crosthwaite	VP	Merchant; dep governor Bank of Ireland; Comm. Building Co. Cath
Thos. Crosthwaite	C	Merchant Q
George Drevar	C & Sub-T	Merchant

Hen. Higginbotham	C	Merchant
John E. Hyndman	C	? Merchant
James Jackson		(& Son) tallow chandlers
John Lindsay	VP	Merchant
Randal MacDonnell	VP	Merchant (chaired initial meetings estab. chamber) Cath
Thos. MacDonnell	C	Paper mf., printer bookseller
Thomas Maxwell	C	(Connolly Maxwell & Co.) merchants
George McBride	C	? Merchant
James McCall	C	Merchant
John O'Brien	C	(& Co.) merchants
Robert Orr	C	(& Co.) merchants
Joseph R. Pim	C	(J & J) merchants Q
Joshua Pim	Pres	(J & J) merchants; Comm. Building Co. Cath
Richard Robinson	C	Brewer
Robert Roe	C & S	Merchant
John Todhunter	C	Merchant
Robert Turbett	C	Merchant
Thomas Wilson	C	? (Mills & Wilson) merchants

6. Dundee (and Forfarshire) chamber of commerce, 1819 and 1836.

Abbreviations of main shipping companies (many multiple partnerships in ship ownership not noted):
DPS Co.: Dundee & Perth Shipping Co. (launched 1798).
DPUS Co.: Dundee & Perth Union Shipping Co. (launched 1819 by George Wylie, William McGavin, Blinshall Small)
DPLS Co.: Dundee, Perth & London Shipping Co; merger of DPS & DPUS in 1826 (James Gray, James Soot, Robert Sterling ptnrs in 1826).
DHS Co.: Dundee & Hull Shipping Co.

6.1 Forfarshire chamber, 1819 (N=101).

Source: First minute book; Dundee Archives GB251/GD/CC

Member	Business
Alison, John	Merchant & distributor of stamps
Anderson, Patrick	Wine merchant
Anderson, William	Merchant & sail cloth manufacture
Anderson, William jun.	Merchant
Archibald, James	
Balfour, Alexander	Flax spinner, Russia merchant (Provost); also Bell & Balfour major linen & timber exporters to America 1829 (1st Vice chair)
Blair, David, jun.	Stamp master (inspector)
Barclay, George	Agent and banker (London)
Baxter, David	Director Dundee Sugar Refining Co.
Baxter, Edward	Linen, Baltic merchant, sail cloth and bag manufacture
Baxter, Henry	Linen, Baltic merchant, sail cloth and bag manufacture

Baxter, John	Merchant & shipowner; ptnr of Dundee New Bank ; 1st chair DPLS Co. (1st Pres)
Baxter, Thomas jun.	Linen, Baltic merchant, sail cloth and bag manufacture
Baxter, William	Linen, Baltic merchant, sail cloth and bag manufacture
Bell, David	Merchant, Russia; also Bell & Balfour major linen & timber exporters to America 1829; family link to Dundee New Bank
Bell, Thomas	Flax spinner; family link to Dundee New Bank (Provost)
Bissett, William	Merchant & saddler
Blair, David	Merchant & stamp master (inspector) (JP)
Brown, Andrew	Flax spinner
Brown, David	Merchant, and agent for whalers
Brown, James	Flax spinner
Cack James	(possibly James Crockatt, grocer)
Calman, John	Shipbuilder
Cassels, Walter G.	
Chalmers, Charles	Flax spinner
Cloudsley, A. C.	Wine merchant
Collier, John	Yarn, linen & Baltic merchant
Crichton, Archibald	Shipowner & and insurance agent; family link to Paisley Bank
Crichton, Peter	Baker
Crichton, Patrick	Major shipowner (DPLS)
Croom, John	Merchant
Davidson, James	Fish curer
Duff, James	Manager of Dundee New Bank
Duncan, James	Linen & Baltic merchant
Duncan, James jun.	Linen & Baltic merchant
Ellett, William	
Fairweather, James jun.	Flax spinner & linen merchant
Gavin, Robert?	Merchant
Gray, James	Manufacturer & iron merchant (ptnr DPS & DPUS Cos.)
Hackney, William	Merchant and flax spinner
Hawe, William	Shipbuilder?
Hay, James	Merchant &shipowner
Hi[y]nd, William	Shipowner and second largest linen exporter 1829; Atlantic, Baltic & Russian trade
Jobson, David	Merchant, agent for whalers; Director of Dundee Bank (1st S, with Christopher Kerr as clerk)
Jobson, John	Merchant; cashier of Dundee Bank
Jobson, Robert	Merchant & Riga factor
Johnston, Charles	Merchant
Justice, James jun.	Ironmonger & Shipowner
Keay, Alexander	Merchant (Keay & Rattray), port warehouses etc. (Provost)
Keiller, James	Wholesaler
Kinmond, Andrew	Flax spinner; also Kinmond & Hill, major linen & timber exporters 1829
Kinmond, Peter	Engineer, flax spinner; also Kinmond & Hill, major linen & timber exporters 1829
Leighton, David	Linen & Baltic merchants
Lindsay, William	Corn merchant (JP)
Mainz, John	Agent
Martin, David	Flax merchant & agent (senior prtnr DHS Co.)

Martin, James jun.	Merchant
Martin, Patrick	Merchant and agent
Miller, John B.	Baltic & linen merchant
Miller, Robert	Baltic & linen merchant
Miln[e], David	Director Dundee New Bank
Miln[e], George	Director DHS Co.; Major shareholder Dundee & Leith Shipping Co.; whale fishing involvement
Mitchell, James	Coloured thread manufacture
Morton, John	Sewing machine manufacture
Morton, Mungo	Merchant and manufacturer; link to Paisley Bank
Muir, David	(of Arbroath)
Nicoll, George	Grocer & merchant
Nicoll, James	Clothier
Peter, John	Engineer
Powre, Thomas	Linen merchant and manufacturer
Reid, Alexander	Linen and sail cloth manufacturer
Renny, Samuel	Merchant & linen manufacture (of Arbroath); agent for Dundee New Bank with Airth
Renny, William jun.	Merchant
Rob, Alexander	Weaver
Roberts, William	Cashier of Dundee New Bank
Ross, Colin	Manufacturer
Russell, John	Merchant & insurance broker; manager of whale fishing Cos.
Sandeman, William	Bleacher, brown & white linen merchant
Sanderson, John	Newspaper proprietor (*Dundee, Perth & Cupar Advertiser*)
Scott, James	Agents, ship and life insurance and brokers, lottery agent; ptnr Dundee New Bank; ptnr Paisley Bank
Scott, John	Flax spinner
Scott, John jun.	Flax spinner
Scott, Peter	Agent and broker
Smart, David	Shipping (Neish & Smart) and flesher
Souter, James	Sail cloth manufacture
Spaldin, Thomas	
Stirling, Robert	Agent & linen merchant (inventor, engineer); part owner DPLS Co. (with Gray & Soot)
Thain, John	Merchant and shipowner (John & James)
Thanntay, Robert ?	Merchant
Thoms, Patrick H.	Merchant and flax spinner
Thomson, Peter	Merchant, sail cloth and bagging manufacture
Warrack, Alexander	
Watt, Isaac	Russia and linen merchant
Watt, James	Flax spinner, merchant & largest linen exporter 1829
Webster, George	Merchant and agent
Webster, James	Solicitor
Webster, Thomas jun.	Merchant & sail cloth manufacture, Custom House controller
Whitson, Patrick jun.	Major merchant, shipowner, linen manufacturer and banker
Whitten, James	Railway proprietor
Whitehouse, John jun. ?	Carrier
Wyllie, George	Flax spinner, linen & Baltic merchant; DPUS Co.

6.2 Dundee chamber of commerce, 1836 (N=75).

Source: member list from Dundee Chamber, *Chamber of Commerce Centenary Souvenir* (1936).

Member	Business
Balfour, Alexander	Merchant, flax spinner & manufacturer
Balfour, John	Flax spinner and manufacturer; also Bell & Balfour major linen & timber exporters to America 1829
Baxter, David	Merchant and flax spinner
Baxter, Edward	Merchant & Vice Consul for USA
Baxter, Francis	Merchant
Baxter, John G.	Merchant and flax spinner
Baxter, W. Gordon	Merchant and flax spinner
Baxter, William	Merchant and flax spinner
Bell, Thomas jun.	Merchant and manufacturer; also Bell & Balfour major linen & timber exporters to America 1829
Boyack, William	Flax spinner
Brodie, Samuel	Merchant and agent
Brown, Andrew	Merchant and flax spinner
Brown, James	Merchant and flax spinner
Brown, John	Merchant
Browne, Alexander	Agent
Buist, James	Merchant and manufacturer
Collier, William	Merchant
Crichton, Archibald	Manager of Sea Insurance Co.; family link to Paisley Bank
Dick, Alexander	Merchant and flax spinner (Dundee & Blairgowrie)
Duff, David	Merchant
Duff, Robert	Merchant
Duff, William	Merchant
Duncan, P.	Merchant
Edward, Alexander	Merchant and flax spinner
Edward, Allan	Merchant and agent; coastal shipowner
Gavin, Will M.	Merchant & Vice Consul for Brazil
Gilroy, James	Merchant and manufacturer
Graham, John	Merchant and agent
Gray, John	Merchant and flax spinner
Guthrie. Alexander	Merchant
Hackey, William	Merchant and flax spinner
Hadden, John	Merchant
Halley, John	Merchant and flax spinner
Halley, William	Merchant and flax spinner
Hill, I.	Merchant, flax spinner & Prussian Vice Consul; also Kinmond & Hill, major linen & timber exporters1829
Howe, Will	Merchant and manufacturer
Jobson, Robert	Merchant and agent
Johnston, W.	Merchant and flax spinner
Keith, David	Merchant
Kinmond, Alexander	Merchant and flax spinner
Kinmond, Peter	Merchant and flax spinner
Kirkcaldy, W.	Merchant
Learmonth, Robert	Merchant
Lindsay, David	Merchant and flax spinner

Lyall, James	Merchant and agent
Martin, David	Merchant & major long distance shipowner (senior prtnr DHS Co.)
Martin, David jun.	Merchant & major long distance shipowner
Matthew, Robert	Merchant and flax spinner
Millar, Robert	Merchant
Miln, T. W.	Agent
Molison, Francis	Merchant and agent
Moncur, David	Merchant
Neish, Thomas	Shipping, merchant and agent (Neish & Smart)
Newall, G. H.	Merchant
Nicoll, George	Merchant and manufacturer
Paton, John jun.	Merchant and agent
Pennycook, James	Merchant and agent
Peters, David	Merchant
Pitcairn, Alexander	Merchant
Ritchie, William	Merchant
Row, James	Merchant and flax spinner
Rowan, Alexander	Merchant
Sanderson, J[ohn]	Merchant and flax spinner
Symers, George	Merchant; family link to agents of British Linen Bank
Thain, John	Major merchant and shipowner (John & James); shipping from Liverpool
Thoms, James	Merchant
Thomson, James	Merchant and manufacturer
Thornton, W.	Merchant and agent
Turnbull, George	Merchant
Turnbull, Hector	Merchant and bleacher
Walker, James	Merchant and flax spinner
Webster, Andrew	Merchant and manufacturer
Webster, William	Merchant and agent
White, Alexander jun.	Merchant
Wrongham, W.	Merchant and agent

7. Edinburgh chamber of commerce, 1785 and 1786–91

Sources: Edinburgh Chamber, *A brief account of the rise, progress and present position* (1861); Edinburgh Chamber, *Edinburgh Chamber of Commerce* (1945); membership roll subscription books: Edinburgh Archives ED005/8/3. Some uncertainties with handwriting; subscription book starts in 1786 and several 'founding' names are missing. CM is formally named in charter.

7.1 Founding and Charter members, 1785 (N= 118)

Name	Office or role in 1785–6	Business
Aitchison, John	CM	Distiller (St. Clements Wells)
Aitchison, William	Merchant	
Allan, Alexander	Merchant; and banker	
Allan, William	CM	Soap boiler & merchant (Queensferry)

Allan, Robert	CM	Allan & Steuart's Bank ptnr
Anderson, James	Merchant (Leith)	
Anderson, Robert	Merchant (Leith & Edinburgh)	
Anderson, Samuel?	Merchant (Leith); banker, then joined Forbes Bank	
Balfour, Elphingston	Bookseller	
Balfour, John	Bookseller	
Balliny, William	Soap boiler (Leith)	
Bartlett, James	Bank ptnr (Forbes)	
Bell, Hugh	Brewer	
Bell, William	CM	Merchant (Leith)
Blair, James Hunter	CM	Forbes Bank ptnr (MP 1781–4; Provost 1785)
Bonar, Alexander	Mansfield's Bank ptnr	
Bonar, Andrew	Mansfield's Bank ptnr	
Brough, John	Cabinet maker & upholsterer	
Brown, Alexander	Merchant	
Cadell, William	CM	Merchant (Carron Park)
Campbell, James	CM	
Carlier, John	Sugar house	
Carnochan, William	Grocer & merchant	
Cassells, Andrew	Shipmaster (Leith)	
Chalmers, George	CM	Merchant
Chalmers, John	Merchant (later in London)	
Cheape, William	Linen manufacturer	
Cowan, Andrew	Merchant (Kirkcaldy)	
Craig, James	Baker	
Creech, William	CM& joint S	Bookseller
Crichton, Alexander	CM	Coach maker
Davie, John	CM	Merchant
Dewar, Alexander	Distiller (Blackhall)	
Dewar, James	Merchant	
Douglas, William	Merchant (Leith)	
Downie, Patrick	CM	Merchant (Prestonpans)
Edington, Thomas	CM	Merchant (Cramond)
Elder, Thomas	CM	Merchant
Elliot, Charles	Bookseller	
Fettes, William	Merchant	
Forbes, Sir William Bt.	CM& Pres	Forbes Bank ptnr; of Pitsligo
Forrester, Peter	CM	Merchant (Leith)
Gadsell, John	Merchant (Cockenzie)	
Geddes, Archibald	CM	Glasshouse & merchant (Leith)
Gladstones, Thomas	Merchant (Leith)	
Grant, John	Merchant (Charleston – Fife)	
Grindley, George	Merchant	
Haddaway, John	Merchant (Leith)	
Haig, James	Merchant	
Haig, James	CM	Distiller (Canonmills & Lochrin)
Haig, John	Distiller (Lochrin)	
Hamilton, David	Merchant	
Hart, Orlando	CM	Shoemaker

Hay, George	Banker (ex. Musselburgh)	
Hay, John Sir	Banker	
Heggie, George	Merchant (Kirkcaldy)	
Hepburn, Andrew	Merchant (Prestonpans)	
Hill, Alexander	Boatbuilder (Leith)	
Hog, Walter	General manager, British Linen Bank	
Hunter, Andrew	Merchant (Leith)	
Hutton, John	Paper manufacturer	
Hutton, John	Merchant (Leith)	
Hutton, Robert	Manufacturer (Dunfermline)	
Inglis, Sir John Bart.	CM	(of Cramond)
Jackson, William	Merchant (Leith)	
Jamieson, John	Merchant (Leith)	
Jamieson, Thomas	Soap boiler (Leith)	
Jamieson, William	Mason	
Keir, Adam	Banker (and banker for the chamber)	
Kerr, William	Merchant (Leith)	
Kinnear, George	Banker, Kinnear's	
Learmonth, John jun.	Tanner & merchant	
Learmonth, John sen.	CM	Merchant
Lister, George	Merchant	
Mansfield, James	Mansfield's Bank ptnr & merchant	
McDonnell, Angus	Merchant	
MacDowal, Archibald	CM	Merchant
McLaine, Donald	Merchant	
Milne, David	Merchant	
Morrison, James jun.	CM & joint S	Merchant (Leith)
Murray, Robert	Shoemaker	
Paterson, David	Merchant & insurance broker	
Paton, Andrew	CM	Soap boiler (Leith)
Paton, Ninian	Soap boiler (Queensferry)	
Pillans, James	CM	Merchant (Leith)
Ramsay, David	Printer	
Ramsay, William	Mansfield's Bank ptnr; major shareholder RBS	
Ramsey, William jun.	Mansfield's Bank ptnr	
Re[a]nnie, James	Merchant (Leith)	
Richmond, John	Seedsman	
Robertson, Charles	Printer & bank ptnr (Robertson's)	
Robertson, John	CM	Printer & lead bank ptnr (Robertson's)
Rosebery, Earl of	Director RBS	
Scott, Mark	Manufacturer (Dunfermline)	
Scougall, John	CM	Merchant (Leith)
Sherriff, Alexander	CM	Merchant (Leith)
Sherriff, Robert	Merchant (Leith)	
Sibbald, William	CM	Merchant (Leith)
Sime, John	Shipbuilder (Leith)	

Simpson, William	Cashier RBS	
Sligo, John	Merchant (Leith)	
Somervail, Alex	Merchant (Leith)	
Somervail, Patrick	Merchant & flax dresser	
Steuart/Stewart, David	CM & T	Allan & Steuart's Bank ptnr (Provost 1780–2)
Stirling, James	CM	James Stirling's Bank
Taylor, John	Soap boiler (Queensferry)	
Thomson, Alexander	Grocer & banker (Thomson's)	
Thomson, James	Merchant, insurance broker & banker (Thomson's)	
Tod, Richard	Merchant (Leith)	
Trotter, Thomas	Upholsterer	
Walker, John	Merchant	
Watson, John	CM	Cooper (Leith)
White, Adam	Merchant & cooper (Leith)	
Williamson, Thomas	Merchant (Leith)	
Wood, James	Merchant (Ely)	
Wright, Malcolm	Merchant	
Young, John	Wright	
Young, Robert	CM	Upholsterer/carpetmaker

7.2 Additional members, 1786–91 (N= 68).

Sources: as above. Business details from chamber records, supplemented; in Edinburgh unless otherwise stated. Some uncertainties with handwriting.

Name	Business and location
Addison, Charles	Merchant (Bonness)
Addison, James	Merchant (Bonness)
Allan, John	Merchant (Queensferry)
Baird, Thomas	Merchant (Bonness)
Balleny, William	Merchant (Dalkeith)
Bertram, James	Merchant (Bonness)
Biggar, Robert	Linen manufacturer (Sheens)
Biggar, Walter	Linen manufacturer (Sheens)
Brown, George	Merchant (Leith)
Burns, Robert	Architect
Caddell, John	Merchant (Cockenzie)
Cam, Mathew jun.	Brewer (Leith)
Cameron, Robert	Merchant & chamber clerk
Carron Company	Manufacturer
Cochran, James	Printer
Comb, Matthew jun.	? brewer
Crichton, Patrick	Coach maker
Dickson, James	Bookseller
Donaldson, James	Bookseller
Dover, Rt. Hon Lord	
Fall, Robert	Merchant (Dunbar)
Gardner, Ebenezer	Bank ptnr Bertram Gardner

Gilchrist, Ebenezer	Manufacturer
Grieve, William	Merchant (Queensferry)
Haddaway, Peter	Merchant (Leith)
Hay, Charles	Merchant (Dunbar)
Henderson, Alexander	Bank prtnr (Wardrop's)
Henderson, Sir John Bt.	
Horner, John	Merchant
Kerr, Charles	Kings stationer
Kinnear, Thomas	Bank ptnr Kinnear's
Laing, William	Baker (Leith)
Leslie, George	Merchant
Martin, Ellis	Merchant (Leith)
McAlpine, William	Manufacturer & Banker (Stormontfield & London)[ex. Clerk at Paisley Union Bank, Glasgow]
McDougal, Alexander	Merchant (Fingask, Perth)
McVicar, Neil	Merchant
Melliss, George	Merchant (Perth)
Mitchell, James	Merchant (Leith)
Murdoch, Thomas	Pistol maker (Leith Walk)
Pinkerton, James	Merchant (Otterston)
Primrose, James	Custom House (Leith)
Renton, James	Merchant (Berwick)
Ritchie, Charles	Banker
Ritchie, George	Shipmaster (Leith)
Sanderson, Patrick	Banker
Scott, Thomas	Farmer
Scott, William	Bank ptnr Scott, Smith & Stein
Scougall, Richard	Merchant (Leith)
Sharp, Francis	
Sharp, Francis	Merchant
Simpson, William	Paper maker (Polton)
Sinclair, George	Linen draper and manufacturer
Sinclair, George	Merchant (Leith)
Slerant [?], William	Merchant (Leith)
Smith, Donald	Bank ptnr Scott, Smith & Stein
Staig, David	Merchant (Dumfries)
Stark, Mark	Manufacturer (Dunfermline)
Stein, James	Distiller (Kelbugie)
Stein, John	Bank ptnr Scott, Smith & Stein
Strong, Robert jun.	Merchant (Leith)
Thomson, John	Insurance broker
Trotter, William	Merchant
Walker, Robert	Chaplain (& chaplain to chamber)
Wardrop, Alexander	Bank prtnr Wardrop's
Wardrop, John	Bank prtnr Wardrop's
Watt, John	Merchant (Leith)
Whyte, James	Merchant (Leith)
Young, John	Wright

8. Glasgow chamber of commerce, 1783–4 (N=191)

Source: Initial subscription lists: Glasgow Mitchell Library TD 1670/1/8. Canvasser recruiting the member (if known): * John Campbell and Archibald Ingram; # David Dale. The lists are hand-written and difficult to read.

Name	Business	Location or where recruited
Allan, Alex*	Merchant	Glasgow
Allan, Arthur		Anderston, Glasgow
Allan, Richard*	Merchant, Esq.	Glasgow
Allan, Richard*	Merchant	Glasgow
Anderson, Andrew	Boot & shoe mf.	Glasgow
Anderson, George*	British Linen Bank agent & WI merchant	Glasgow
Alston, John jun.*	Merchant	Glasgow
Auchincloss, John#	(& Co.) Merchant	Glasgow
Austin, John	(& Co.) Lawn & cambric mf.	Port Glasgow
Bannatine, Dugald*	Merchant	Glasgow
Barbour, Humphry	Sugar mf.	Kilbarchan
Bell, Thomas*	Merchant	Glasgow
Bell, James*		Glasgow
Black, David*	Tobacconist	Glasgow
Bloch [?], John	(& Co.) Calico printers	Paisley
Bowman, John*	Esq., Merchant & banker (Arms Bank)	Glasgow
Bogle, George*	(& Co.) Coach makers	Glasgow
Bogle, George*	Merchant	Glasgow
Bogle, Robert*	WI Merchant, Esq.	Glasgow
Brauford, George*		Glasgow
Brown, Alex*	Merchant	Glasgow
Brown, Andrew*	Auctioneer	Glasgow
Brown, James*	Merchant	Glasgow
Brown, John jun.	Merchant, muslin mf. & banker (Ship Bank)	Glasgow
Brown, George*	(& Co.) Merchant	Glasgow
Buchanan, Andrew jun.*	Merchant	Glasgow
Buchanan, George jun.*	Merchant	Glasgow
Buchanan, John*	Merchant (chair)	Glasgow
Buchanan, Robert*		Glasgow
Buchanan, Thomas*	Merchant & banker (Ship Bank)	Glasgow
Buchanan, Bernard	Dry salter	Paisley
Burnie, Alex*	Merchant	Glasgow
Carr [?], John*		Glasgow
Campbell, John*	Merchant	Glasgow
Campbell, John* jun	Merchant & banker (Thistle Bank)	Glasgow
Carmichael, William#	Merchant	Glasgow
Carrick, Robert	Merchant & managing banker (Ship Bank)	Port Glasgow
Carlisle, William		Paisley
Christie, John*	Banker at Paisley (Paisley Union Bank)	Paisley
Coats, William*	WI Merchant	Glasgow

Collins, Richard	(& Co.) soap mf.	Dalmuir
Colquhoun, Patrick	Attorney & WI merchant; 1st Pres	Glasgow
Colquhoun, Walter*	Merchant	Glasgow
Corbett, Cunningham*	Merchant	Glasgow
Connell, Thomas*	Merchant	Glasgow
Corse, Robert	Banker (Paisley Bank)	Paisley
Cowan, Robert	Wholesale merchant	Glasgow
Craig, John*	(& Co.) Ironmongers	Glasgow
Craig, William	Timber merchant & banker (Ship Bank)	Glasgow
Craig, John	Victualler	Paisley
Crauford, Thomas*	Merchant	Glasgow
Cross, Hugh*	Insurance broker	Glasgow
Cunningham, A.*	Merchant	Glasgow
Cunningham, G.*	Merchant	Glasgow
Dale, David#	Banker (RBS co-agent) and mf.	Glasgow
Dun, James*	Grocer	Glasgow
Dennistoun, James jun.*	Merchant	Glasgow
Dinwiddie, Robert*	Merchant, Esq.	Glasgow
Donald, Thomas*	Merchant	Glasgow
Dunlop, John*	Merchant	Glasgow
Dunlop, Robert	(& Co.) Merchant	Port Glasgow
Dunlop, Robert*	Insurance (& Ship Bank)	Glasgow
Dunmore, Robert*	(& Co.) WI Merchant	Glasgow
Ewing, Walter*	(& Co.) Merchant	Glasgow
Findlay, Robert*	Merchant (chair)	Glasgow
Finlay, James	Merchant	Port Glasgow
Finlay, William#	Merchant	Glasgow
Fleming, William	Merchant	Port Glasgow
Fleming, William jun.	Merchant	Port Glasgow
Freeland, John	(& Co.) yarn merchant	Port Glasgow
French, William	Merchant, Esq.	Glasgow
Fulton, Robert	Banker (Paisley Bank)	Paisley
Gammel, James	Banker (Greenock Bank)	Glasgow
Gardener, William	Innkeeper	Port Glasgow
Gillespie, William	(& Co.) linen & calico printer	Glasgow
Glassford, John*	Merchant & banker (Thistle Bank); Stamp Act protester	Glasgow
Gordon, Alex*	Merchant	Glasgow
Gordon, James*	Merchant	Glasgow
Gordon, John*	WI Merchant	Glasgow
Govan, Archibald*	Merchant	Glasgow
Graham, Archibald*	Bank cashier Merchant Bank, 1783 Thistle Bank	Glasgow
Graham, Walter	(& Co.) Merchant	Port Glasgow
Gray, William*	Silk mercers & drapers	Glasgow
Hagg, John*	Manufacturer	Glasgow
Hamilton, George*	Merchant	Glasgow
Hamilton, Gilbert*	Merchant, mf., agent, banker (Gilbert Hamilton & Sons), S	Glasgow
Hamilton, John jun.*	Esq. and banker	Glasgow
Hardie, Henry	Wholesale linen drapers	Port Glasgow

Harling, John*		Glasgow
Hay, John*	Merchant	Glasgow
Henderson, Archibald*	Merchant	Glasgow
Henry, Alex#	Manufacture and wholesale	Glasgow
Hirling, Walter		Port Glasgow
Hopkirk, James*	WI Merchant, Esq.	Glasgow
Houston, Andrew*	Banker (Greenock Bank)	Glasgow
Houston, Robert*	WI Merchant	Glasgow
Howan, Robert*		Glasgow
Howe, John		Kilbarchan
Hunter, Robert	Banker at Paisley (Paisley Union Bank)	Paisley
Ingram, Archibald	Merchant (& Arms Bank)	Glasgow
Ingram, Warren*	Merchant & insurance broker	Glasgow
Kippen, John	Merchant	Greenock
Kippen, George*	Merchant	Greenock
Lang, William#	(& Co.) Merchant	Glasgow
Lawrie, John*	Merchant	Glasgow
Leitch, John*	Merchant	Glasgow
Leckie, W.	Merchant	Anderston, Glasgow
Lightbody, Adam*	(J. & A. Co.) WI Merchant	Glasgow
Lindsay, John*	Merchant	Glasgow
Loudon, James*	Canal collector	Glasgow
Low, Alex*	Merchant	Glasgow
Lowdes, James	Merchant & banker (Paisley Bank)	Paisley
Lowdown, M.*	(& Co.) Merchant	Glasgow
MacAlpine, A.*	(& Co.) wholesale linen printers	Glasgow
MacApline, Alex	Cambric & linen printer	Port Glasgow
Macbrayne, Donald	(& Co.) cambric & linen printer	Port Glasgow
Macintosh, Robt.	Merchant	Glasgow
MacKay, Bob*	WI Merchant	Glasgow
Macmorly, George*	Merchant	Glasgow
McCall, James*	Merchant and Stamp Act protester	Glasgow
McCaul, Alex*	Merchant	Glasgow
McDonald, John*	Salt & barley office	Glasgow
McDowall, James*	Banker (Greenock Bank, Glasgow agent) & WI Merchant	Glasgow
McGrigor, James	Wholesale linen draper	Port Glasgow
McNair, Robert*	Salt merchant	Glasgow
Marshall, Richard*	Tar works manager	Glasgow
Maxwell, James*	Banker (Thistle Bank)	Glasgow
Miller, Andrew	Yarn merchant	Port Glasgow
Miller, George jun.*	(& Co.) Merchant	Glasgow
Miller, James	Merchant	Paisley
Mitchell, James#	Merchant & banker (Thistle Bank)	Glasgow
Moncreieff, Robert Scott	Banker (RBS co-agent) & merchant	Glasgow
Monteath, Walter*	Merchant	Glasgow
Monteith, James	Major cotton manufacturer & twist dealer	Port Glasgow
Moodie, Hugh	Barber & perfumer	Glasgow
Morrice, Robert	(& Co.) Merchant & hosier	Port Glasgow
Murdoch, Peter*	Merchant & banker (Arms Bank)	Glasgow

Muir, David	Grocer	Glasgow
Neilson, Claude	Merchant & banker (Paisley Bank)	Paisley
Neilson, Walter*	Merchant	Glasgow
Orr, John	Advocate and City Clerk	Glasgow
Park, James*	Merchant	Glasgow
Pearston, Mathew#	(& Co.) Lawn & cambric mf.	Glasgow
Provan, George	(& Co.) Dry salters	Port Glasgow
Reddell, John*	Provost	Glasgow
Reid, John	Vintner	Port Glasgow
Reid, William	Vintner	Glasgow
Riddell, John	Merchant, Provost	Glasgow
Riddell, Henry*	Merchant	Glasgow
Ritchie, James	Merchant & banker (Thistle Bank)	Glasgow
Robertson, James	Bank treasurer	Port Glasgow
Robertson, John*	Cashier (Arms Bank) & WI Merchant	Glasgow
Robertson, William*	Merchant	Glasgow
Rodger, John	Lawn & cambric mf.	Port Glasgow
Rugull, Daniel*	Merchant	Glasgow
Scott, James	Linen wholesaler	Paisley
Scott, Joseph*	Merchant	Glasgow
Shedden, John*	Merchant	Glasgow
Sheddon, Thomas#	(& Co.) lawn & cambric mf.	Glasgow
Sheils, John		Port Glasgow
Shibble, James		Paisley
Shortridge, William	Merchant	Port Glasgow
Sibbald, Andrew	Yarn merchant	Port Glasgow
Smith, Archibald	Merchant	Glasgow
Smith, William*	Printer & bookseller	Glasgow
Sommerville, James#	(& Co.) Wholesale linen drapers & WI Merchant	Glasgow
Speirs, Messrs*	(& Co.) Merchant	Glasgow
Stewart, Thomas	Manufacturer & wholesaler	Port Glasgow
Stirling, John	Merchant	Glasgow
Stirling, Andrew	Esq.	Port Glasgow
Stirling, Walter	Merchant	Glasgow
Tait, William*	Gauze & muslin mf. & wholesaler	Glasgow
Temple, John		Finniston, Glasgow
Thennibough, George		Port Glasgow
Thompson, Andrew*	Merchant & banker (Thompson's Bank)	Glasgow
Thompson, George	Merchant & banker (Thompson's Bank)	Port Glasgow
Thompson, John jun*	Tobacconist	Glasgow
Thompson, Robert#	Banker (Thompson's Bank)	Glasgow
Todd, David	(& Co.) wholesale linen printers	Port Glasgow
Tomorwell, James*		Glasgow
Ure, Alex#	(& Co.) woollen linen drapers	Glasgow
Wardlaw, William	Merchant	Glasgow
Watson, David*	Calico & linen printers	Glasgow
Whitlow, William#	Grocer	Glasgow
Will [?], James*		Glasgow
Wilson, ____*		Glasgow

Wilson, John*	Writer, City Clerk	Glasgow
Wilson, John*		Paisley
Wilson, John*	Manufacturer	Anderston, Glasgow
Young [?], Robert*	Cooper?	Glasgow
Young, John#	Merchant	Glasgow

9. Greenock chamber of commerce, 1813

Source: Watt Library, Greenock, first minute book TD 508/1; charter, BG1/3/1, R34593, 647.9625. Full list of 63 members at end of charter, plus 19 further Directors appearing in minutes, listed in pencil at the end of the charter, and joining within the first few months. Some businesses were also members of the Glasgow chamber q.v.

9.1 Founding members on original charter (N=63)

Name	Business
Baine, Robert	(Lang, Baine & Co.) merchants and shipowners (one Baine, probably Robert, was agent to Leith by canal)
Baine, Walter	(Lang, Baine & Co.) merchants and shipowners, Port Glasgow
Baine, Walter jun.	(Lang, Baine & Co.) merchants and shipowners, Port Glasgow
Beatson, Henry Dundas	? Merchant, Glasgow
Byrne, Charles H.	? Merchant, Glasgow
Campbell, Duncan	Silk & cloth merchant
Campbell, Robert	Warehouse
Dempster, George	Wood merchant & joiner
Duncan, James	Merchant
Fairrie, James	(Esq. & Co.) sugar refiner & Bailie of Town Council
Ferguson, Dugald	(with John) merchant; Harbour Commissioner
Ferguson, Duncan	General agent, & agent for Liverpool packets and to Leith by canal
Forsyth, William	(Robertson, Forsyth & Co.) Merchant & Counting house
Gairdner, James	? Merchant, Glasgow
Galbraith, William	(& Co.) counting house and merchant
Holmes, John	Merchant
Hunter, James	(& Co.) Insurance broker, merchant & shipowner; Harbour Commissioner
Hunter, John	(& Co.) merchant
Hunter, Patrick jun.	(Patrick Hunter, James Tasker & Co.) Counting house
Hyde, David	Merchant and Harbour Commissioner
Kerr, Alan [Pres 1817]	(& Co.) Merchant & agents, ship agents Co.
Kerr, George	Grain merchant
Laird, Alexander	(Muir & Laird) shop
Lang, Thomas	(Lang, Baine & Co.) merchants and shipowners
Leitch, Quintin	(& Co.) Merchant, Harbour Commissioner
Leitch, William	Merchant
Lindsay, William A.	(Kippen & Lindsay) general and ship agents & insurance brokers
McCunn, Thomas	Merchant & Harbour Commissioner
McDougall, Donald	? Merchant, Glasgow
McFie/Macfie, William	(McFie & Lindsay) Merchant and grocer

McGoun, Archibald	Merchant
McGoun, Archibald jun.	Merchant
McGoun, Duncan	Merchant
McGoun, John	Merchant
McGoun, Robert	(McGoun, Watson & Co.) counting House
McGregor, Dugald	Feuer & shipmaster
McGregor, Gregor	Merchant
MacLellan, John	(Wilson, MacLellan & Co.) Merchant & ship agents
Macnaught, Duncan	(Esq. & Sons) Merchant & packet agents to Dublin & Belfast
Millar, Alexander	(Stevenson, Millar & Sons) ship agents
Oughtenson, Arthur	Merchant & Harbour Commissioner
Oughtenson, James	Merchant
Pringle, John	(& Co.) Manager, Dumbarton Glassworks Co.
Ramsay, James jun.	Merchant & counting house, Treasurer of Town Council
Rankin, John	(Rankin & James) Merchant, counting house, Harbour Commissioner; also (Denny & Rankin) shipbuilders, Dumbarton
Robertson, George	(Robertson, Forsyth & Co.) Esq., Counting house
Robertson, George jun. [Pres 1815]	(Robertson, Forsyth & Co.) Esq., Counting house
Robertson, James	Merchant
Robertson, John	(Oughtenson, Robertson & Co.) wine & spirit dealer
Robertson, John jun.	(Oughtenson, Robertson & Co.) wine & spirit dealer
Scott, James	Wine & spirit dealer
Scott, John	(& Son) Merchant
Scott, John jun.	(& Son) Merchant
Shannan, Alexander	Merchant
Smith, Duncan	Accountant & ptnr Renfrewshire Bank Co.
Stewart, James	(James & William) Merchants
Stewart, John	Ship master
Stewart, Sir Michael Shaw (life)	(? Stewart, Rennie & Co.) counting house, Baronet, MP
Stewart, Roger	Merchant
Tasker, James	(Hunter, Tasker & Co.) Counting House
Thomson, John	(Thompson & Buchanan) Merchant & ship agents
Watson, John	(McGoun, Watson & Co.) merchant & counting house
Wilson, Archibald jun.	(Wilson, MacLellan & Co.) Merchant & ship agents, Town Treasurer 1815, packet agent to Charleston

6.2 Members added immediately after foundation, 1813 (N=19)

Name	Business
Baine, Archibald	(Lang, Baine & Co.) merchant
Balderston	Hemp warehouse Port Glasgow
Buchanan, John jun.	(Thompson & Buchanan) Merchant & ship agents;
(Bunchanan jun.) coopers	
Denniston, John jun.	Merchant etc.
Dunlop, Alexander [Pres 1814]	Esq., Manager & ptnr, Renfrewshire Bank Co.
Ewing, Robert	Merchant; ?(Ewing, Miller & Co.) shipowners
Hall, James	(McFarlane & Hall) boot & shoe merchants

Hamilton, Hugh	(Wm & Hugh) merchants and shipowners Port Glasgow [probably connected to John Hamilton, ex ptnr Hamilton, Gardner Bank of Glasgow]
Kippen, James	(Kippen & Lindsay) general and ship agents & insurance brokers
Leitch, James	(& Co.) Grocer & merchant
McKenzie, John	Ship master
Miller, John	(Stevenson, Millar & Sons) ship agents; ?(Ewing, Miller & Co.) shipowners
[Mc]Naught, John	(& Sons) merchants
[Mc]Neill, John	(Neil & Gray) cloth merchant & ship agents [Andrew was teller of Greenock Bank]
Nellson, John	Town cashier
Ritchie, James	Merchant & Harbour Commissioner
Ross [? Walter]	Ship chandler Port Glasgow
Stevenson, Tho.	(& Co.) packet agent to Charleston
Stewart, Graham	(Stewart & Rennie's) Counting house
Others attending early meetings	
Dunlop, John [S]	(Dunlop & Liddell) writers
Andrew Houston	(Greenock Bank Co.) bank partner, Glasgow
Watt, James	(& Co.) Ship master & brewer

10. Guernsey chamber of commerce, 1769 and 1808–9 (N=68)

Sources: No list of members for the chamber of 1769; only known member was its London agent Havilland Le Mesurier (1758–1806: *ODNB*), merchant with Le Havre and London. However, the signatories to the Canary Wine petition of 1772 may have constituted a partial list of members (see Chapter 5). 1808 list from chamber minutes: Guernsey Archives AQ/040/01. Uncertainty about spelling of names, as well as many alternative spellings used, sometimes in French and sometimes not.[2]

Member	Role	Business
Allaire, John jun.		(1763–1846) Highly successful privateer in French wars (Marr, pp. 2–3, 208) Ptnr Macculloch's Bank
Angel, John		
Arnold, John	C	Merchant
Arrivé, Peter		Left Guernsey shortly after 1808
Bardel, Peter		
Bishop, Charles	C	Linen draper, merchant & ptnr De Jersey's bank
Bonamy, James/John		Merchant & shipping; family links with Dobrée's bank and Macculloch's bank
Brehaut, John		Shipping & imports wine/fish; family connected to Newfoundland & Quebec (Cox, p.78)
Brock, Matthew	C	Merchant & large land owning family; Bailiff 1820s; family links de Lisle; and to Perchard's bank

[2] Further information from Marr, *Guernsey People* (1994); G. S. Cox, *Guernsey Merchants and their World* (2009). See also Cox, *Guernsey Chamber of Commerce* (2009).

Carré/Cané, Hilary		
Carey, Thomas		Wine merchant & large land owning family
Carr/nel, Amos		? Connected to Canel wine traders, Nantes (Cox, p. 137)
Collings, John, jun.		(1745–1821: Marr, p. 208) Merchant, shipping & large land owner
Collings, Joseph		Merchant, shipping & large land owner
Collings, William	C	(prob. 1781–1854: Marr, p. 183) Merchant, shipping & large land owner; jurat; founded fund for poor relief; Knt.
Corbin, William		Shipping, family were prtnrs with de Jersey 1770s
Cowan, Robert		
D' Auvergne, Charles		Rope maker
Davy, Joseph		
De Carteret, John		Major shipping and merchant
De Jersey, Joseph		Gent., banking family
De Jersey, Peter		Gent., banking family
De Lisle Brock, Daniel	Pres	(1762–) Gent, major merchant, banker; jurat, Bailiff 1829–
De Lisle, Daniel	C	Gent., major merchant, ptnr in States of Guernsey Bank 1827–
Dobrée, Bonamy	VP	([Peter] Bonamy Dobrée, 1755–1825: Cox, pp. 64, 186–8) Major merchant, banker; agent for Dobrée London bank; fish and wine trade; later in Barcelona
Duniere, Lewis		Merchant, privateering during American War; from Quebec (Canadian DNB: Cox, p. 189)
Gellings/Sellings, Thomas Jun.		
Giffan/Giffard, Nicholas		Shipping capt.? in Spanish trade
Goodwin, Samuel		
Gue[v]rin, Elias		Corn merchant, leading trader (Cox, p.190)
Ham, John		Weymouth brewer (Cox, personal comm.)
Harvey, John		(1771–1820) Shipping and merchant in wine & brandy (Cox, p. 192)
Haynes/Hayter, John		Coal & ship agent?
Isemonger, Ay.		Shipping to Newfoundland (Cox, pp. 164, 192)
Jeremie, H. Durrell		Family of shipping and privateers American War (Cox, p. 192)
Jeremie, James		Family of shipping and privateers American War
Jolley/Sallas/Tallas, Thomas		
Jones, William		Agent, shipping
La Serre, John		Merchant
Lauga, Nicholas		Shipping, corn merchant, later with Priaulx
Le Li[e]vre Nicholas		Merchant & shipping
Le Li[e]vre, Peter, son of Wm.		Merchant & shipping, privateer Am. War (Cox, p. 194)
Le Marchant, William		(1721–1809) Major merchant family & shipping, Bailiff 1770–1800 & large land owner (Marr, pp. 99–101; Cox, p. 195); family links to States of Guernsey Bank 1827–

Lukis, Frederick C.		Merchant & family links to States of Guernsey Bank 1827–; close links to Collins family (Cox, p.199)
Macculloch, David	C	Merchant & French trade
Macculloch, Thomas		Merchant & French trade, banker in Macculloch's
Maing(u)y, Peter, 'for Nicholas'		Large land owning family, Nicholas ptnr in States of Guernsey Bank 1827–
Maing(a)y, Thomas sen.		Leading merchants and traders, Am. War privateers (Cox, p. 199) Large land owning family, family links to States of Guernsey Bank 1827–
Maire, John		
Mallebay, John M.		
Manley, John		Shipping
Mansell, Frederick		Brewer, family connected to EIC (Cox, p. 199)
Mansell, John		Ditto and ptnr of States of Guernsey Bank 1827–
Mauger, Joshua/Joseph		Miller & shipping & wine trade (Cox, p. 200)
Mellish, John	C	Corn merchant & shipping
Mollity, Peter		
Murie, T/J[?]		
Naftel/Nafflet, Daniel		(Naftel: Cox, p. 190) Merchant and shipping
Pint [?], Peter		
Priaulx, Anthony		Merchant, shipping & large land owner; major privateers Am. War, traders in WI & S. America; closely linked with Janvrins of Jersey in Newfoundland cod trade, (Cox, p. 201–2)
Priaulx, Carteret		Merchant, shipping & large land owner; as Anthony
Priaulx, Thomas	C	Merchant, shipping & large land owner, ptnr of Guernsey Banking Co 1827–; as Anthony, and influential in founding of chamber (Cox, p. 202)
Price, Frederick sen.		Merchant from major merchant family European & WI trade (Cox, pp. 203–4)
Price, Frederick jun.		Merchant, ptnr Guernsey Banking Co 1827–
Ring, David		
Rougier[uer], John jun.	C	Wine merchant; family links to States of Guernsey Bank 1827–
Tupper, John sen.		(prob. 1743–1810: Marr, pp. 201, 212; Cox, pp. 208–9) major privateer making fortune in Am. War; Wine merchant, shipping & large land owning family; jurat; family links to De Lisle, De Havilland, and Brock; Huguenot family
Tupper, John		Son of John sen. Wine merchant & shipping
Watson, David		Tobacco merchant

11. Hull chamber of commerce, 1801 and 1837

11.1 Hull Chamber, 17 November 1801 (N=27)

Source: *Hull Advertiser*, 14 November 1801.[3]

Name	Business name and trade	Other links
Bolton, Wm. Watson	(William & Christopher) Merchants & oil millers; shipbuilders, shipping to New York, ship sales, major whaling, underwriter.	Sheriff 1792, Alderman 1810
Bowden, James S.	(Wright, Bowden & Wright) Merchants; shipping to Elsinore & St. Petersburg	
Brown, Jonas	(& Co.) Merchants; shipping to Quebec	
Burstall, John jun.	(Samuel & John) Merchants & shipowners; major shippers to Oporto, Genoa, Leghorn, Naples, Messina, etc., underwriter	father was Trinity House asstnt
Clarkson, John	(Clarkson & Parker) Gent., merchants	
Coates, Henry	(& Co. with Jarratt) Merchants & oil millers, insurance broker; large Co.	
Coulson, Edward Foster	(Edward & George) Merchants & insurance brokers, Esq.; shippers to Rotterdam, Hamburg and Italy e.g. raisins; underwriter	Mayor 1781, Alderman 1801
Egginton, Joseph	(G. & J.) Esq., Oil merchant & insurance broker, major whale shipowner, underwriter; shipping to Koningsberg & Elbing (Prussia)	Sheriff 1793, mayor 1798, JP, Alderman 1801
Fea, Thomas	Merchant & oil crusher, underwriter	
Finlay, Edward	(Finlays, Uppleby & Co.) Merchants; flax from Riga & St. Petersburg, shipping to Madeira and Jamaica (some ptnr with Haworth 1802)	
Fowler, William	(Robert & Co.) Esq., Merchants	
Hall, Francis	(with Hall & Robinson) Merchant to Russia & Scandinavia (iron), major ship broker and owner	Trinity House warden 1790, Sheriff 1795
Hall, Francis jun.	(with Hall & Robinson) Merchant to Russia & Scandinavia (iron), major ship broker and owner	Trinity House warden 1799
Haworth, Jos. jun	(sometimes ptnr with Finlays and Uppleby 1802) Merchant & broker, major shipper to Rotterdam, Amsterdam, Madeira & Jamaica; selling pork from US, wine, brandy, rum and casks	

[3] Useful information on Hull merchants in G. Jackson, *Hull in the Eighteenth Century* (1972); *Trade and Shipping of Eighteenth Century Hull* (1975).

Hentig, John William	(& Co.) Merchants	
Hollingsworth, Andrew	(with Wray) Major merchant, shipping & insurance broker & underwriter, iron and timber	Sheriff 1797, Alderman 1810
Knox, George	Merchant	
Ogle, John Ogle	Baltic merchant & shipper	
Osbo[u]rne, William	(William & Sons) Tar & timber merchants to Russia; leading shipbuilder in fir; saw mill, early steam power 1790s; contractor to HM dockyards; activist against Dock Co.	P 1801 chamber meeting, Mayor 1796, Alderman 1810
Rennard, Richard	(Richard & Thomas) Merchants; shipping to Hamburg	
Sykes, John	(Joseph Sons & Co.) Major merchants; shipping to Elsinore & St. Petersburg; investors in others	Sheriff 1789, Mayor 1792, Alderman 1810
Sykes, Nicholas	(Joseph Sons & Co.) Major merchants; shipping to Elsinore & St. Petersburg; investors in others	Sheriff 1803, Alderman 1810
Terry, A. [Avisor]	(Richard & Sons; broker with Wright) Merchants & major shipowners; shipping to Riga, Elsinore & St. Petersburg; Italian trade with Wright in 1790s	
Thompson, Thomas	(Smith & Thompsons) Merchant & banker (largest bank in1780s; bankers for Dock Co.); chief bank clerk, prev. at Wilberforce & Smiths Bank	Sheriff 1805, son at Queens College Camb., MP 1807
Todd, John	(member of Levant Co. with Popple) Brass & iron founder, merchant	
Tottie, Richard	Merchant & oil miller; shipping to New York, importing cotton, oil, tallow, turpentine	
Uppleby, George	(Finlays, Uppleby & Co.) Merchants; flax from Riga & St. Petersburg, shipping to Madeira and Jamaica (some ptnr with Haworth 1802)	

11.2 Hull Chamber 1837 (N=110)

Source: Initial subscription list, 1 March 1837 in Chamber minute book, at modern Hull and Humberside Chamber. PC = member of provisional committee of 21 elected 14 April 1837; [?alternates] indicates that there is more than one possible business with the same name.

Name	Business	Officers
Allen, John	[?alternates] probably agent to Hull & Selby Tug Co.	
Artrop, John sen. (by Artrop, John junr)	(& Son) General merchant & paper merchant	
Atkinson, John	[?alternates] merchant & seed crusher	
Bamford, Charles jun.	Merchant (senior: wine & sprit merchant)	
Barnby, Wm.	(Barnby, Faukner & Co.) merchants, commission agent & water carriers to Manchester	
Beadle, Willm.	Commission agent	
Bell, Thos F.	Wharfingers, commission agent & shipping broker	
Bell, W. H.	(& Co.) merchants, seed crushers & oil miller	PC
Bell, William	[?alternates] Commission agent & ship broker or pot mf.	
Blundell, Henry (by the brother, Jas. Blundell)	(Blundell, Spence & Co.) Paint & colour mf. & importers of leeches, wharfinger	
Bogdan, F(red)	Corn & commission merchant	
Bowden, James	Victualler & beer house keeper, wine & spirits merchant	PC
Bowden, Saml., W.	Russian broker	
Boyes, Faulkner	Merchant	
Brady, Edward	[?alternates] wharfinger	
Broadbent, William	Merchant, insurance broker, shipping agent & accountant	
Brodrick, John	Merchant, shipowner & broker	PC
Brownlow, W[illiam] B.	(Brownlow & Pearson) steam packet agents & wharfingers, merchants	PC
Bruce, T.	[?alternates] (probably & Co.) merchants	
Buckton, Geo.	Merchant, wharfinger & shipping agent	PC
Carlill, Briggs	Tallow & insurance brokers & general agents; agent for Phoenix Fire & Eagle Life	
Clarke, Peter	Merchant, wharfinger & warehouse; agent for Economic Life Assurance	
Collinson, John	(John & William) merchant, general commission agents & share brokers	
Cramp, Robt.	(& Co.) wine & spirit merchants	
Cunnington, Thos.	Wine & porter merchant	
Day, George & Sons	[? Illeg.] (& Sons) tea dealer	
Depledge, W. N.	(& Bros.) merchants & shipowners	
Dikes, W[m.] H[ey].	(Co.) Manager, Yorks. District Bank	PC
Earle, Thos.	(Geo & Thos) mf. of Roman cement & Paris white	
English, Thos.	Warehouse	
Farthing, Wm.	(& Co.) mercantile agent & broker	PC
Foster, John [S @ £20 p.a., remaining as a director]	[?alternates] probably attorney (Foster & Miller)	PC
Garbutt, Robt.	Merchant, shipowner & insurance broker	

Garton, Geo.	(G. G. & H. Garton & Co.)merchants, tar and turpentine distillers, cork manufacture	
Gee, Joseph	(& Co.) merchants, shipowners & shipping agents	PC
Gibson, Edwd.	Shipowner & ship builder	PC
Good, W. C.	Danish consul & merchant	
Greenwood, Geo.	Merchant, shipping agent, ship & insurance broker; agent for British Commercial Life	
Hadley, George	Ship & insurance broker, agents for Leeds & Yorks Insurance	
Hall, Henry William	[?alternates] Seed crusher or Gent.	
Hall, John	[?alternates] probably merchant & shipowner	
Hall, John	[?alternates] (& Co.) patent rope makers, sail cloth mf. etc.	
Hansell, Thos., T.	(William & John) corn factors	
Hassell, S. T.	(& Co.) merchants	PC
Henwood, James	banker	PC
Hertig , Rob.	(& Co.) merchants and shipowners	
Hewitt, Thos.	(Hewitt & Co.) seed crushers, oil refiners, merchants & commission agents	
Holderness Thos.	(Holderness & Chilton) shipowner, commission agents & Atlas Insurance agent	PC
Hudson, [T/F/J]	(probably Hudson & Cobly) shippers & commission agents, & agents to Harbour Union Steam Co.	
Jackson, Robt	[?alternates] commission agent	
Jackson, Wm.	(& Sons) wine & spirit merchants	
Jameson, Willm.	(& Co.) sail cloth & sacking mf.	
Keddey, Rob	Foreign, colonial & general commission agent & insurance broker	
Keighley, M. J.	(M. & R. Keighley) merchants	
Kemp, Geo. G.	Merchant	
Krushe, C. B.	Commission agent	
Laverack, W[illiam]	Wharfinger, general commission agent & insurance broker	PC
Levett, Henry (by Norrison Levett)	(J. & H. Levett & Co.) oil merchants & seed crushers	PC, VP
Liddell, Geo.	[?alternates] (Pearse & Liddell) bank or (Liddell & Genthorne) wine merchants	PC
Locking, George	(Hull & Selby Rly Co.) secretary	
Lofthouse, D[yas]	(Dyas Lofthouse & Co.) wharfingers & coal fitters	
Lumsdson, Jno.	Mercantile agent	
Malcolm, Jesse	(& Co.) merchant	
McIntosh, Wm.	Wharfinger, general agent & warehouse	

Mitchell, N.	(Mitchell & Field) insurance brokers & commission agents	
Morehouse, Charles (dead, Mr. Brown inher.)	(Morehouse & Brown) General merchants & commission agents [membership passed to partner]	
Morley, Thos. B.	(& Co.) lead & glass merchants, shipping agents	
Newmarch, Tho.	Joiner & timber merchant	
Norman, W. V.	Merchant & commission agent	
Ostler, John	(& Co.) bark & hide merchants	PC
Petchell, John	Merchant & seed crusher	
Petchell, Thomas	Merchant & corn miller	
Piercy, Wm.	Brush mf. & Gent.	
Pimm, Thomas S.	Merchant & shipping agent; manager St. Georges Steam Co. packets	
Popple, Robt. (by Popple, G. W.)	(& Sons) general merchants, seed crushers, paint & colour mf.	
Priest, Wm.	(& Lambert) merchants	
Radford, J. S. (made by Dalton, John)	Accountant, translator & general agent, editor *Hull Month. Comm. Report of Importers & Exporters & Price Current*	
Raikes, Robert junr	(Raikes Thos & Robert Co.) bank	
Reimer, A[ndrew]	Commission agent	
Roberts, Henry	Commission merchant	
Rutherford, A[ndrew] R[iddel]	(Mr.) draper	
Sanderson, Joseph	(Joseph & John) merchants & general shipping agents	
Smith, H. J.	(H. & J. Smith Bros. Co.) bankers	
Smith, John	[?alternates] agent for Aberdeen & Hull Shipping Co.	
Spence, Edwd.	Iron merchant	PC
Spratt, James	General agent	
Stephenson, J.	(? J. H.) Draper	
Stocks, Benj. junr	Ship & insurance broker & general commission agent	
Storry, J. M.	(Storry, Smithson & Newham) general merchants & Turpentine distillers	
Strother, Edwd.	Merchant	
Tapp, Benje. [Ashley[	Wine & spirit dealer	
Taylor, Jno.	[?alternates] (probably Taylor & Clifford) corn factors	
Tealby, R[obert] C[hapman]	(& Co.) timber merchant	
Terry, John	Shipowner & merchant	PC Pres
Thompson, Thomas	[?alternates] solicitor & town clerk or merchant & shipowner	PC
Thompson, W. J.	[?alternates] (probably & Co.) commission merchants & ship insurance brokers	
Tootal, Fredrk.	Corn merchant	
Torr, Jno.	(& Co.) merchants & shipowners	
Torr, Thos. Wm.	Merchant & ship owner (office in Old Counting Ho.)	

Tudor, Wm.	(& Co.) White lead mf.	
Veltmann, N.	Shipping agent	
Wade, John	(& Co.) timber merchant	
Wake, Robt. for	(Wake & Officer & Co.) glue mf. & general merchants	
Ward, Wm.	[?alternates] Merchant & shipowner	PC
Watson, J[ames] K.	(Harrison, Watson & Locke Co.) bank (office in Excise Office)	
Wells, Peter	[?alternates] (Peter & Robert) solicitors or merchants	
West, Wm. junr	Corn factor, biscuit mf. & flour dealer	
Westerdale, Saml.	Merchant	
Wilson, Thos.	[?alternates] merchant	
Wood, Thos	General commission agent and wine merchant	
Later members 1838–40		
Bannister, Mr.	[?alternates] (probably John) clerk to Dock Co.	
Bright, H. S.	?	
Gill, Robt.	(Rob. & John) shipowners, ship & insurance brokers	
Grut, T.C.	?	
Pennock Tigar, Mr.	?	
Staniland, Joseph [S 1845–]	Merchant, broker, agent & spirit dealer	
Tall, John	(& Co.) tar & turpentine distillers & general merchants	

12. Jersey chamber of commerce 1767–9 (N=49) and 1770–85 (N=21).

Source: Chamber minutes and accounts: Jersey Archives L/A/38/A1/1. The first membership list follows the Articles of the chamber reproduced Chapter 1, numbered 1–49 as in the Articles. The later members are listed in the minutes. The subscriptions were calculated from the burthen of the ships owned by each member or partnership. Note spellings of names vary, some barely legible; many members are the whole partnership as named, not a single person.

	Member	Business	Shipping owned (tons)
1	Messrs Cabot, Thos and Jas Amicea Lempriere, Charles Le Maitre and John Hue	Brig *Endeavor*	130
2	James Lempriere and John Hue	Ship *Magdelaine*, Brig *Princessa*	120+70
3	Messrs De Gruchy & Le Breton, James Hilgrove, Charles Payne, John Gissrard, Thomas Durrell	Brig *Neptune*, *Snow Success*, Schooner *Elizabeth*	80+85+ 69
4	Messrs Richard Carteret family, John Carteret, Edward Millais, William Dumaresq, Thos Hilgrove, Nicholas Trott, Matthew Gosset sen.	Ship *Jenny*, Brig *Betty*, Brig *Penguin*	131+91+35

5	Messrs Abraham Gosset, Matthew Gosset sen., De Gruchy & Le Breton, Nicholas Mallett, Peter Mallet	Ship *Mary*	120
6	James Lempriere, Peter Dorey, Peter Mallet	Schooner *Defiance*	67
7	Peter Mallet	Brig *Fortune*	37
8	Messrs Daniel Messervy, Nicholas Le Gros, Peter Mallet, Peter Patriarche, Peter Dutleaume, William Patriarche	Brig *Elizabeth*	115
9	Messrs James Lempriere, Thomas Durrell, Helier Messervy, William Patriarche	Schooners *Jake* and *Molly*, Brig *Good Intent*	45+80+148
10	Messrs Peter Patriarche, Philip Vanmorel, Michael Du Pre, James Hemery	Ship *Tryal*	210
11	Messrs De Gruchy & Le Breton, Thos & James Pipon, Thos Pipon, Philip Marrell, Philip Robin	Snow *Recovery*, Brigs *Hope* and *Seaflower*	118+101+40
12	Philip Laurens and other owners	Ships *Tartar*, *Willing Maid*, Postillion, and *Endeavour*	160+157+ 46+122
13	John Brunet and other owners	Brig *Triton*	160
14	Messrs John Le Geyl, Philip Pelque, Edward Dolbel	Schooner *King's Fisher*	53
15	Philip Winter	Brig *Success*	130
16	Daniel and Philip Le Couteur	Schooner *Jenny*	54
17	Peter Le Cronier		30
18	John Lys and London packet	Sloop *London Packet*	80
19	John Perrochon		30
20	Philip Lerrier sen.		60
21	John Allez		30
22	Peter Amiraux		30
23	Abraham Gosset, Philip Winter sen., John Villeneufoe, Philip Winter jun., Thos & James Pipon	Ship *Charm[ing] Nancy*, Brig Mary	225+ 60
24	John Thoreau and other owners	Sloop *Jersey Packet*	36
25	Philip Lys	Brig *Susan*	50
26	John Dolbel		30
27	Abraham Chevalier and other owners	Sloop *Lucky*	40
28	John Luce and other owners	Sloop *Mary*	15
29	James Lempriere Esq, Messrs Amicea Lempriere, Messrs Le Maitre, Edward Combes, John Hue	Ship *Sally*	160
30	Jean de la Taste sen.		30
31	John de la Taste jun.		30
32	John Kerby		30
33	James Guillet		30
34	Clement Messervy	Sloop *Neptune*	67
35	David Patriarche		60
36	Aaron de St. Croix		30
37	Philip Lyse and other owners	Sloop *Elizabeth*	25
38	Peter Simonet		30

39	Philip de Janvrin	Brig *Mayflower*	60
40	Philip Ingonville		30
41	Louis Gareau		30
42	John Cosnard	Brig *Esther*	80
43	Pierre Avrice	Sloop *Speedwell*	
44	Clement Hilgrove of Southampton and James Hilgrove		50
45	John Boudier	Sloop *Union*	
46	Messrs Corbet Combes and John Hue, from 1 Feb in place of Messrs Corbet, Thomas and James Amicea Lempriere, Charles Le Maistre		
47	John Thoreau		30
48	Guill Patriarche from 1 March 1769	Schooner *Molly*	80
49	Philip Laurens, Nicholas Trott jun. from 13 March 1769	Brig *Nancy and Mary*	60
50	George Rawcliffe by 1770	Ropewalk mf.	
51	Edward Comtees by 1770		

Additional subscribers 1770–85; no tonnage listed

Francis Aubin	Clement Hemery
Francis Anguetet	Thomas Hammond
James Baleinne	Edward Du Heaume
John Benest	Francis Janvrin
Charles Bertram	Philip Lerrier jun.
John B. Le Capelain	Thomas Mallet
Benjamin Le Capelain	John Matthews
Elias Colling	Edward Millais
Charles Coutanche	George Maager
Matthew La Cloche	Edward Nicolle
Elias Durrell	Philip Du Pang
John Dumaresq	Charles Poingestre
Daniel Dolbel	Edward Remon
Edward [Trott/Tiott/Fiott]	James Remon
Matthew Gosset jun.	Elias Robinson
Thomas de la Garde	Charles Renous
Francis Gautier	Philip Renous
Philip le Gallais	Thomas Sivret
Daniel Le Guyt	James Simonet
Philip Hamon	Philip Thoreau
Philip Hamon St Aub	Henry Voy

13. Kirkcaldy chamber of commerce (founded 1825); members 1825 (N=18)

Source : Members present at initial meeting, and founding directors 18 July 1825: Minute book, at modern Kirkcaldy chamber.[4] * first directors.

[4] Name list transcribed from minutes by current chief executive of chamber, Bill Main.

Member	Business	Location
Adamson, Thomas	Merchant	Auchtermuchty
Arthur, Charles	Merchant	Kirkcaldy
Aytoun, James*	Flax spinner	Kirkcaldy
Barber, Michael*	Merchant etc.	Kirkcaldy
Bogie, Heyunter	Merchant	Kirkcaldy
Bogie, James	Merchant	Kirkcaldy
Elder, George	Merchant	Kirkcaldy
Graham, George	Merchant	Kirkcaldy
Hendry, William	Merchant	Kirkcaldy
Landale, David* [Pres]	(Landale & Selkirk, merchants) Flax spinner, bleacher and linen mf.	Kirkcaldy
Millar, George junior*	Merchant & shipowner	Kirkcaldy
Millie, Thomas*	Merchant (family business; David a mf. of ticks and checks)	Pathhead
Millie, William* [VP]	Merchant	Pathhead
Norman[d], James [sen.]	Merchant & shipowner	Dysart
Oliphant, William	Merchant & ship owner; large family concern	Kirkcaldy
Rutherford, Ebenezer	Merchant	Kirkcaldy
Swan, William* [d. 1859]	(Swan Bros.) Shippers & merchants; Wm. the leading shipping partner	Kirkcaldy
Stocks, Robert*	Merchant	Kirkcaldy

14. Leeds chamber of commerce, 1785–90 (N=75 + 8)

Source: Minute books of chamber: Leeds University Library MS Dep 1951/1. No complete listing of members, names drawn from attendance at meetings 1785–90, including 8 representatives from other areas (shown bold). Legibility problems of handwriting.

Member	Role	Business
Beacroft, G.		
Beaumont, George		(& Ridsdale*) Merchant
Beckett, John*		(& Co.) senior director Becketts Bank [mayor]
Beckett, Jonathan*		(& Co.) Becketts Bank
Bernard, Bishoff & Sons		(& Co.) Merchants
Bischoff, G.*		(& Sons) Merchants
Bischoff, N.*		(& Sons) Merchants
Bischoff, Thomas*		(& Sons) Merchants & banker (New Bank)
Blagbrough		
Blaydes, John		Merchant
Bramley, R. & R.		Mercers [separately represented from Robert]
Bramley, Robert		(& Sturdy) Mercers
Brooke, John		Merchant
Mr. Burrell		[representative of Messrs. Milnes of ***Wakefield*** —Stamp Act protesters] Woollen mf. & banking
Cataneo		(& Lloyd*) Merchants
Clapham, – C.,		(& Hall) Snuff mf.
Close, John		Dyer

Cookson, Thomas		(& Sons) Merchants
Cookson, William	Pres 1786–7	(& Son) Merchants
Dawson & Smith		(& Co.) Merchants
Dawson, Obadiah		
		(& Rayner*) Merchants [sole dissenter from support for Eden Treaty] [Stamp Act protester]
Dixon & Co.		(& Lee*) Merchants
Dixon, Jere	Pres 1785–6	(& Lee*) Merchants [mayor 1785]
Dunn		(& Thursby*) Merchants
Elam, Emmanuel		(& Sons) Merchants [Stamp Act protester]
Elam, John jun		(& Sons) Merchants [later bankers]
Fenton & Wainhouse*		(& Co.) Glass & coal mf. [Fenton later in Commercial Bank]
Fildes, Mr.		[representative of ***Rochdale***] (& Co.) Hat mf.
Fisher, William		Merchant & mf.
Forrett, Benjamin		
Fountaine. Jo		(& Wormald) Merchants
Godman, George		(& Sons) Worsted mf. & merchant
Godman, John		(Bros) Merchants & worsted mf.
Hainsworth, Jas		(& Thursby*) Merchants
Hainsworth, Thomas		(& Thursby*) Merchants
Hanner, Samuel Oates		(& Sons) Merchants
Harrop, Mr.		[representative of ***Saddleworth***] Woollen cloth mf.
Hebblethwaite, John		(& Rhodes*) Merchants
Hill, Thomas		Merchant [key representative on Eden Treaty 1787]
Hollins		(& Harrison) Merchants
Holdsworth, Mr.		[representative of ***Wakefield***] (& Co.) Spinners & mf.
Holroyd & Co.		(& Co.) Cotton spinners
Jawitt & Co.		(& Co.) Woolstaplers
Johnson, Nat		(Bros) Merchants
Kighley, George	S & T	(& Oates*) Merchants
Lee, Richard		(R. & Thomas & Dixon*) Merchants
Lloyd		(& Cataneo*) Merchants
Markland, Edward		Merchant [mayor in 1790]
Metcalfe, John		Dry salter & clothier
Nevile, J. P.		(& Co.) Millers
Norris, Pym		
Oates, George*		(& Sons) Merchants & staplers
Oates, Josiah*		(& Sons) Merchants
Oates, S. H.*		(& Sons) Merchant
Oates Bros & Wilson		(& Co.) Merchants & wholesale linen drapers; Wilson* also in Becketts Bank
Oates & Kighley*		(& Co.) Merchants
Rayder, William		[representative of ***Rochdale***] Merchant
Rayner, Milnes		(& Dawson*) Merchants
Read, John		(& Walker) Merchants & dry salters
Rhodes, Tim		(& Hebblethwaite*) Merchants & tanners
Ridsdale & Beaumont*		(& Co.) Merchants
Rodbard, Samuel		Merchant
Routh jun		(& Wainhouse*, Sons) Merchants
Sanderson, Edward		Linen draper

Smith, B[eckwith]	[representative of ***Rochdale***] Merchant
Smithson & Rayner*	(& Co.) Merchants
Smithson, William	(& Co.) Merchants
Soubley	(& Co.) Merchant [of ***Leeds & Wakefield***]
Stansfield & Co.	(& Wolrich) Merchants, ***Quebec***
Storey & Co.	Provisions dealer
Strother	(& Clayton) Merchants
Thompson, William	(& Haltly) Merchant & banker (Thompson & Elam)
Thursby	(& Hainsworth*) Merchants
Tolson, Peter	(& Sons) Brewers
Tolson, Richard	(& Sons) Brewers
Turner, Alex	(& Co.) Merchants [key representative at Committee of Trade 1785–6]
Turner, Joshua	(Bros) Merchants
Wainhouse	(& Routh*) Merchants
Walmesley	[representative of ***Rochdale***] (& Co.) Merchants
Waterhouse Samuel & John	[representatives of ***Halifax***] (& Co.) Merchants
Wareing, Robert	
Wilkinson, Matt	(& Coupland) Distillers
Wrigglesworth, Jas?	(& Eyre) [of ***Leeds & Wakefield***] Ironfounder; tanner, merchant & snuff mf.

15. Limerick chamber of commerce, 1807–15 (N=110)

Sources: Minutes: Limerick Archives Limerick Archives P1/1. Members qualified to vote, with fees based on imports and exports at the port; not certain if this includes all members, or only voters; first complete list for 1813, and in 1815 for charter. Some handwriting legibility problems, with some alternate spellings. First column is all members over 1807–15 (about 60 in any one year, of which about 43–45 voting); third column identifies charter members in 1815 (N=63) of which * were the first directors.

Member	Role	Charter member	Business
Allan, David			Merchant
Alpin, John N.			
Anglim [Auglin] James	Founding C, and 1808, 1809, 1810, 1811	√	Merchant, corn etc.
Arthur, Martin hardwaremen		√	(? Arthur & O'Hara)
Baker, Robert			(& Son) Merchant, corn etc.
Bindon, Francis H		√	
Black, George	C1810, 1811	√	Merchant, corn etc
Bourke, John & Co.			(& Co.) Merchant, corn etc.
Brown, John merchant		√	Woollen draper & cloth
Carroll, John	S 1808–15	√	Attorney
Chaytor, Thomas			Merchant
Clanchy, Bartholomew		√	Merchant

Connell, John		√	Brewer & Merchant, corn etc.
Crawford, Robert & Co.			(& Co.) Merchants
Creagh, Arthur			Merchant
Creagh, Edmund		√	(Edmund, J & P Creagh) Merchants
Creagh, John Michael		√	Merchant, corn etc
Creagh, Martin	C 1813, 1814	√*	Merchant, corn etc.
Creagh, Paul		√	(Paul & Philip) Merchants
Creagh, Philip		√	(Paul & Philip) Merchants
Crilly & Bindon			Merchant, corn etc.
Cronin, William & Co.			(& Co.) Merchant, corn etc
Dickson, Arthur			Merchant, corn etc. & flour factor
Egan, Michael & Co.	C 1810	√	(& Co.) Merchant, corn etc.
Ferguson, Robert jun.			Merchant
Fisher, James sen.	C 1808, 1809; retired 1814		(Fisher, Mark & Fisher) Merchant
Fisher, James jun. Merchant	C 1813, 1814	√*	(Fisher, Mark & Fisher)
Fisher, Joseph	C 1813, 1814	√*	Merchant
Fosbery, George Wm.		√	(Fosbery & Chaytor) Esq., Merchant, corn
Furnell, Edward			(Furnells) Banker
Gabbett, Daniel	C 1811		Attorney
Gabbett, John		√	(John & Poole) Merchant, corn etc.
Gabbett, Poole	Retired 1814	√	(John & Poole) Merchant, corn etc.
Gabbett, Thomas		√	(? Suddert & Gabbett) Merchant
Gabbett, William		√	(? Suddert & Gabbett) Merchant
Gavin, Cornelius			Merchant
Gavin, Michael	C 1811		Grocer, merchant, corn etc
Gavin, Michael, jun.		√	Merchant, corn etc.
Geary, Daniel			(Geary & White) Merchant
Gray, Daniel			Merchant, corn etc
Hart, Thomas		√	Merchant, corn etc
Harvey, Joseph Massy	Founding C, and 1808, 1810, 1811; Pres 1809	√	(Harvey, Fisher & Harvey) Merchant, corn etc.
Harvey, Reuben		√	(Harvey, Fisher & Harvey) Merchant, corn etc.
Hill, John	C 1810 (vice Lyons)	√	(John & William) Merchant, corn etc.
Hill, William	C1813, 1814	√*	(John & William) Merchant, corn etc.
Hill, Joshua			Merchant, corn etc
Hogan, Michael			(& Co.) Woollen draper & cloth merchant

Kelly & Gavin			(Hagen, Michael, Kelly & Gavin) Merchants, corn etc.
Kelly, John	Founding C and 1808, 1809, 1810, 1811, 1814	√	(& Co.) Merchant, corn etc.
Kelly, Thomas	C1813	√*	Merchant
Kennedy, John	C 1811		(Maunsell & Kennedy) Banker
Long, Stephen			Merchant, corn etc.
Lyons, Denis jun.	Founding C and 1808, 1809, 1810 (resigned), 1811		Merchant corn etc
Lyons, James	C 1810		Merchant
Mark, John	Founding C	√	(Fisher, Mark & Fisher) Merchant, corn
Mark, Thomas		√	Merchant, corn etc.
Maunsell, Edward		√	(?Willington & Maunsell) Merchants
Maunsell, Robert	C 1811, T 1807–		(Maunsells & Kennedy) Bankers
McNamara, Charles		√	Merchant, corn etc.
McNamara, James	Pres 1811		(James & John) Merchant, corn etc.
McNamara, John N. Esq.	Founding C and 1808, 1809, 1811, 1814, Pres 1813	√* P	(James & John) Merchant, corn etc.
Meade, Charles	C 1811	√	(Meades) Banker & corn merchant
Meade, John Thomas			(Meades) Banker & merchant
Murray, Richard Thos.		√	(Richard & Terence) Grocers
Nugent, Richard		√	Bank?
O'Brian, Charles	C 1811		Merchant
O'Neill, Alan Francis	C 1813, 1814	√	(& Sons) Merchant
O'Neill, Francis & Sons		√*	(& Sons) Merchant
O'Neill, James		√	(& Sons) Merchant
O'Shea, William	Founding C		Merchant
O'Sullivan, James			Merchant, corn etc.
Pennott, John			
Pennott, Thomas			
Perry [Peny], Thomas			Merchant
Phelps, James		√	(James & Samuel) Merchant, corn etc
Phelps, Samuel		√	(James & Samuel) Merchant, corn etc
Poe, Herman J.		√	(Poe & Carpenter) Merchants, corn etc.
Roche, William	C 1811		(Thos & Wm Roche) Bankers [became 1st Catholic MP]
Rochford, Michael			Miller, merchant, corn etc
Rochford, Michael P.		√	Merchant, corn etc.

Roddan, John		√	Merchant
Rodger[s], Robert	Founding C and 1808, 1809	√	Merchant, corn etc.
Russell, John Norris	Founding C and 1809	√	Merchant, corn etc
Russell, George William		√	(William & George) Merchants
Russell, William		√	(William & George) Merchants
Ryan, Edmund & Sons	C 1808, 1809, 1813, Pres 1810	√	(& Sons) Merchants, corn etc.
Ryan, Lant. & Kennedy Merchants, corn etc			(Lant. & Kennedy)
Ryan, Michael		√	Merchant
Ryan, William		√	Merchant
Ryan, Timothy	C 1810	√	Merchant, corn etc.
Sargent, Joseph		√	Merchant, corn etc.
Seymour, Thomas	Founding C & S 1807, C 1808		(Seymour & Mark) Merchant, corn etc.
Shannon, William			Hardware and ironmonger
Stein, John		√	(Stein, Brown & Co.) Distillers
Stevenson, David		√	Merchant, corn etc
Studdert, Thomas		√	(Studdert & Gabbett) Merchants
Stretch & O'Shea			(Stretch & O'Shea) Merchants
Waller, Henry			(& Co.) Woollen draper & cloth merchant
Waller, Thomas			(& Co.) Woollen draper & cloth merchant
Wallplate, Fitzgibbon			Merchant, corn etc.
Wallplate, Jacob			Merchant, corn etc
Westropp, Ralph	Pres 1812	√	(Ralph & Thomas) Merchants, corn etc. [Capt. Loyal Limerick Volunteers]
Westropp, Thomas	Pres 1813, C 1814; Retired 1816	√* VP	(Ralph & Thomas) Merchants, corn etc.
White, Jasper	Founding C, Pres 1811, retired 1814		Merchant, corn etc.
White, Walter N.			(? Whites & McSwiney) Brewers & merchants, corn etc
White, William	C 1811, 1813, 1814	√	Merchant, corn etc.
Whites & McSwiney			(& Co.) Brewers & corn merchants etc.
Wilkinson, Thomas Francis	C1811	√	(Thomas & Francis) Brewer & merchant, corn etc.
Willington, James		√	(Willington & Maunsell)
Worrell, John		√	Merchant, corn etc

16. Liverpool chamber of commerce 1774–96 (N= 87)

Source: Updated from Bennett, *The Voice of Liverpool* Business (2010), Tables A.1, A.2, A.3. Probable members marked *; incomplete, mainly chamber committee.

Member	Business	birth-death	Markets
Samuel Appleton*	Provisions merchant	?1740–	Ireland and UK
John Armstrong	Merchant	1738–	
Nicholas Ashton	Major salt merchant exporting to America and ship-owner; St. Helens and Dungeon salt works mf.; coal mining and salt at St. Helens (with George Case)	1742–1833	America and UK
Daniel Backhouse*	Merchant and major ship-owner (with Tarleton and others), slaving	1741–1811	America and WI
Robert Bent	Merchant and shipping, slaving (with Ellis Bent)	1744–1831	Africa and WI
Patrick Black*	Shipping capt. for Whalley & Co., and merchant; sugar baker (with Blundell, Hodgson, Sparling et al.), slaving	1728–1816	Africa and America
Jonathan Blundell*	Major merchant, sugar baker (with Black, Hodgson, Sparling et al.), (later canal proprietor with Wm. Earle, Chaffers etc), slaving	c.1723–1800	Africa, WI and UK
William Bolden	Merchant and ship-owner; some slaving	1730–1800	America (Virginia)
John Bolton	Major merchant, Esq., slaving, ship-owner (with Staniforth, Brooks, Slater, Ryan)	1756–1837	WI
William Bootle*	Merchant	?1738–	
Joseph Brooks jun	Merchant and major ship-owner (with Ingram, Staniforth, Carruthers, Slater, Ryan), slaving, turpentine merchant, rope mf., brewing	1746–1823	America
Charles Caldwell	Sugar baker mf, merchant (with Matthews and Wallace) (major banker and also ship-owner with Smythe)	1739–1814	UK and America
James Carruthers	Merchant, major corn trader, ship-owner (with Brooks, Ingram, Staniforth, Heywood), slaving, copper smelting	c.1718	Mainly Africa also Europe

Thomas Case	Merchant, shipping, slaving (with Dobson), colliery, coal agent (with Gregson and Clayton), glass mf, real estate, plantation owner (later prtnr in Gregsons bank)	1731–	São Tomé, Africa, America
Edward Chaffers	Merchant, glass and pottery mf (mugs), some slaving	1734–1810 c.1735–c1810	UK and America America, UK
John Chorley	Merchant and ship-owner of Lancaster (with Rawlinson and Wallace), sugar store, also tanning		
John Copland	Merchant	1727–	
Edgar Corrie [poss. Pres 1791–3]	Beer brewer, corn factor (with Robert Greenham, Roscoe and Gladstone)	–1819	UK, Europe, America
John Cragg	Merchant, iron founder and soap manufacture	1767–1854	UK
Joseph Dalterra	Merchant (with Dobson; Ryan; Walker), slaving, banking (1791—with Ingram, Goore, Staniforth and Bold); bankrupt with Dobson 1778, soon refloated	c.1732–1793	Africa and WI
John Dobson[5] [Pres 1774–77]	Major merchant (with Dalterra; Walker; Rob. Nicholson; Thos Hodgson; Henry Hulton), corn dealer and provisions to Europe, whaling, slaving (with Case); also joint investor with Josiah Wedgwood in Reid & Co china warehouse; bankrupt with Dalterra 1778	1722–96	WI and Africa, Europe
George Dunbar	Major shipping (with Halliday) and major insurance broker and cotton merchant (with George Hall, linen and raffia merchant)	c.1749–1811	Europe, America
William Earle	Major merchant, packet service to Leghorn, major ship-owner (with Thos Hodgson, Ingram and Leyland) (and slaving with brother Thos) also ironmonger	1721–88	WI, Africa, Leghorn and Mediterranean, Amsterdam

[5] John Dobson, the first chamber chair, was probably baptised in St Mary's church Holbeck, near Leeds, 7 December 1722, the son of Rev. Joshua Dobson a dissenting minister and brother of Matthew. First mention of John Dobson in Liverpool in 1749, consigning 33 cheeses to Gibraltar on the account of Henry Hulton & Co, whose partners were Dobson, Robert Nicholson, Thomas Hodgson and Henry Hulton. He was declared bankrupt in 1778, and by 1781 had moved to Hull as a partner in a brewing company with John Richardson, as Dobson and Richardson. He was buried at Holy Trinity church, Hull, 17 September 1796: information provided by a descendant, Mark Dobson, which is to be written up more fully elsewhere.

	and anchorsmith; later coal mining		
Edward Falkner	Merchant and slaving	1750–1825	Africa, America
Thomas Falkner	Merchant (with A. Heywood), major slaving	1719–85	N. Carolina
John Fisher	Major ship-owner, ship builder and merchant, some slaving	1740–91	Africa
Joseph Fowden	Merchant, ship-owner and slaving, Gent.	c.1740–	Africa, America
Thomas Foxcroft	Merchant and slaving, from Lancaster	1733–1809	America, WI, Africa
Anthony Grayson*	Timber merchant, shipping capt. and ship builder (with Foster Cunliffe)	1719–85	America and WI
Samuel Green [S 1774–92]	Merchant, mainly linen	1728–92	America and Ireland
John Gregson*	Boatman in Customs; merchant; later receiver of taxes for Lancashire	1755–1802	UK
Richard Grime*	Merchant	?1702–	
Robert Grimshaw*	Provisions, slaving, capt., from Lancaster	1720–81	America, Gold Coast, WI
Samuel Halliday	Merchant, major ship-owner	1748–	Africa, America
Stephen Hayes	Merchant and coastal shipping (possibly part of Campbell and George Hayes & Co., major ship-owners and merchants; or Hayes Wm & Co., pot warehouse)	1732–	America and Ireland
William Hesketh*	Major ship-owner (with brother Robt), merchant, pottery mf.	?1717–	Africa
Arthur Heywood	Major ship-owner, slaving (with Thos. Falkner), merchant, major banking (with Benjamin)	1717–95	America, WI, Africa, UK
Benjamin Heywood	Major ship-owner, slaving (with Thos. Falkner), merchant, major banking (with Arthur); also glassworks (with Staniforth)	1723–95	America, WI, Africa, UK
Richard Heywood	Banking (with Arthur), insurance; 1783—hotel proprietor (with Slater, Gregson and Ryan)	1751–1800	America, WI, Africa
John Hodgson	Ship-owner (with other Hodgsons), merchant, major slaving	1736–1813	Africa, America
Thomas Hodgson	Merchant, shipping (with other Hodgsons), and insurance broker (with son), also sugar refining (with Black, Blundell, Sparling et al.)	1729–1823	America, Bahamas, Senegal, Leghorn

Thomas Hodgson jun	Merchant, shipping (with other Hodgsons), and insurance broker (with father), major slaving, (probable supporter of slave trade abolition)	1739–1817	America
Nehemiah Holland*	Merchant and pottery mf., capt.	1713–86	America
Francis Ingram	Merchant in tar and pitch, ship-owner (with Earle, Leyland, Staniforth), slaving, banker (1791—with Earle, Dalterra, Goore and Bold, later with Staniforth), rope mf., copperas mf. (ferrous sulphate)	1739–1815	Africa, America
William James	Major cattle merchant, broker, major ship-owner, slaving	1734–98	Africa, Guinea, America
John Chambres Jones*	Merchant, slaving	1715–1833	Africa
Samuel Kelly*	Merchant (with brother Thomas)	c.1730–	
John Kennion jun	Merchant and major ship-owner; grain merchant	1725–81	Africa, America
Richard Kent	Timber and general merchant and ship-owner and builder, salt mf. at Northwich, white lead mf., Winsford flats agent 1767–74	1745–	America
Philip Kewley*	Merchant (with John and Patrick Kewley)	c.1740–c.1800	Grenada and WI
Thomas Lake	Merchant and Irish shipping packet service (with William); potter (with William and Richard); later slaving	c.1745–	UK, Ireland
William Charles Lake	Merchant and Irish shipping packet service (with Thomas); potter (with Thomas and Richard); later slaving	1753–1836	UK, Ireland
Joseph Leay	Merchant, earthenware warehouse	c.1746–	UK, America
Hugh Hindley Leigh	Merchant and ship-owner	?1738–79	Africa
Ambrose Lace	Merchant and shipping captain, wine, slaving (with Roscoe and Aspinall)	1727–94	Africa, America, Iberia
Thomas Leyland	Major merchant, ship-owner (with Earle and Ingram; later with Tuoy), Irish meat and provisions; olive oil, wine, major slaving, later banking (with Clarke and Roscoe)	1752–1827	Africa, America, Ireland, Europe, Spain
Thomas Manley	Wine merchant	c.1760–	Europe
Edward Mason	Grain merchant and ship-owner, slaving	1735–1814	Africa, America

William Mason*	Tobacco merchant, shipping and sales	1740–	America
William M. Mears*	Merchant, wine trade	1740–	Mediterranean
Arnold Meyer	Linen merchant and shipping (some with Wilckens)		Africa, America
John Myers	Corn merchant (with Trotter)	?1727–	America, UK and Europe
Jacob Nelson	Merchant, shipping; Merchants Counting House (with Pearson)	c.1735–	UK, America
Matthew Nicholson	Linen and textiles merchant and shipping (with various other Nicholsons); copperas works (Paisley and Wigan) (1788 banker with Heywoods in Manchester)	1759–1849	WI and America
Alexander Nottingham	Merchant and major ship-owner (with son), slaving	1737–81	Africa, America
William Ormandy*	Bookseller	1751–	UK
Thomas Parke*	Linen merchant, shipping (with Ingram, Carruthers, Dennison, Heywoods etc.), later bank with Tuoy, Gregson, Morland etc.); fire insurance with Heywoods etc.; slaving	1729–1819	America
John Parker*	Merchant (with Tarletons and others), slaving	1740–95	America
Joseph Rathbone	Timber merchant; also brewing, earthenware, glass, soap, salt and coal	1746–c.93	America
Thos Henry Rawlinson	Merchant and ship-owner (with Chorley), in Lancaster and Liverpool, sugar store	1743–86	America and West Indies
Thomas Rawson	Merchant	?1734–c.1815	
Thomas Ryan	Wine merchant, major broker (also slaving with Dalterrra), ship-owner (with Brooks, Slater, Bolton, Staniforth); of Montserrat in 1776 (payments from John Tarleton); 1783—hotel proprietor (with Slater, Gregson and Heywood)	1738–1802	Africa, America, WI, Europe
John Shaw*	Merchant, insurance broker with father Samuel, slaving	1743–1807	Africa and UK
Gill [Gilbert] Slater [Pres 1777–83; poss. also 1789–90]	Major provision merchant and ship-owner, insurance, slaving; 1783—hotel proprietor (with Gregson, Heywood and Ryan)	1737–1802	America, Grenada, St. Vincent, Africa
Thomas Smythe [VP 1774]	Major merchant, also banker and ship-owner (with Caldwell)	1737–1824	UK

Wm. Spe(y)ers*	Capt. and ship-owner (with Tuoy), slaving (with Thomas Speers, Tuoy, et al.)	1755–	Africa, America
Thomas Staniforth [VP 1777, 1781]	Major ship-owner, Greenland fisheries (with Charles Goore), merchant, banker (1791—with Dalterra, Ingram, Bold), major slaving, real estate; rope mf., glassworks (with B. Heywood)	1735–1803	Africa, America; also Europe, Greenland and Canada
John Tarleton [poss. Pres 1793–6]	Sugar baker & merchant (with Thomas), major ship-owner (with Brooks, Backhouse etc.), whaling, major slaving; MP for Seaford	1755–1841	Curacao and Grenada, Greenland
Thomas Tarleton	Merchant and ship-owner (with John Backhouse and others), sugar refining, major slaving, insurance	1753–1820	WI estates
Tyzack Trotter	Corn merchant (with Myers)	?1750–	America
David Tuohy*	Capt. and ship-owner, slaving (with Heywoods, Speers; later with Leyland), Irish provisions, later bank (with Ingram, Dennison and Parke etc.)	1734–88	America, Africa
George Venables	Linen and general merchant	1720–	Jamaica, America
Benedict Paul Wagner	Merchant, shipping, shipping agent (and merchant with Armstrong and Taylor): later Venetian consul at Liverpool	c.1730–	America, Europe
John Walker	Major merchant (with Dobson & Dalterra; some with Richard Watt's uncle) and shipping captain, slaving	?1747–	Africa, America
William Wallace	Grain merchant, merchant (with Carruthers); shipping (with Chorley and Rawlinson)	c.1745–	Africa
Richard Watt jun	Merchant, shipping and WI estates (with uncle), rope mf. (with George Green)	c.1740–1801	WI
Christopher Weatherherd*	Merchant, broker	1726–c.1795	America
Henry Wilckens	Shipping (with Meyer); Cheshire salt mf. and general merchant/dealer	1751–1821	America and UK

17. Liverpool American chamber of Commerce 1801 (N= c.165)

Source: Minute book: Liverpool RO 380 AME/4. First subscribers to chamber; extreme legibility problems with many names also crossed out as they lapsed or died. To enable easier use and checks by others the list is kept in its original order and placement on pages noted; this results in some repetition, and where later possible duplicates are found these are noted; number of members about 165. All were by definition merchants, traders, agents or factors, to or from America.

Page 1, Col 1.

James Maury; merchant and American consul [later Maury & Latham & Co.] Pres
W. M Duncan [later W. M. Duncan & Rathbone Hughes; then W. M. Duncan for Hughes & Duncan]
Coppin & Benson [Benson T for early years]
William Barber & Co. [first P]
Humble & Holland & Co.
Lees & Rundles
Quentin Hamilton for Hamilton Maher & Co.
Adam Lodge (for) Lodges & Tooth
Nicholas Harry & Co.
John Richardson & Co. [later also Michael Richardson] [VP then P]
H. Mc Corquodale for Mc. Ivor, Mc Viccar & Mc Corquodale [VP then P]
Thompson & Nelson
David Shaw
Hannory & Loqcase
Abraham Binns & Sons
L ….. Cumber & Co.
Francis J. Walker
Taylor [?] & Park
Greatham & Greer
Swirent Cook
D. A. Caruthers [David]
Hannay & McCall

Page 1, Col. 2

Campbell & Frears
Charles Tayleur & Co.
W. W. Thompson & Sons
Rolf [?] …. & Co.
James Chapman
Worrall & Williamson [later Worrall &] Borland
Ed. H. Wilson
V. [?] Lawrence for Robinson & Lawrence
Coway [?] & Carmill…
Clough Wilkes & Clough
A. Coates & Co.
Hamnat Roscoe & Wilson

Page 2, Col 2 (continued)

Duff Findlay & Co.
Thoms. & Willm. Earle & Co.
Maury & Latham
Dan. & S. A. Willin & Co.
James Browne
T. & G. [?] Hawker & Maker &Co.
Richardson & Bolton
N. Worthington
King & Gracie
John McCarmick [?]
N. & E. Lawrence & Co.
Edw. George & Sons
Shipley, N. Caleb & Co.
George G. Brown
Brown Wanson Danson & Co.
Peck & Phelps
Edw. Martineau
Blundell Hollinshead & Slavell
Salisbury Turner Hall
Anthony Molyneaux
Withington & Meyles
George Son & Charles
John Johnson
Wm. Oxley

Page 3, Col. 1

Cearns & Cravy
Latham & Gair
Ewart, Myers & Co.
Thos. F. Dysin
Collman Lambert & Co.
Henry Dixon & Co.
John Jackson & Co.
Fitz Hugh & C. Grimshaw
Maury Latham & Co.
Bolton Ogden & Co.
Tho. & john D. Thornely
Cropper [James], Benson & Co. [later James Cropper & Co.]

Page 1, col 3.
George Exciss
Geo. Garder junior for G. Garder [?] & Sons
Leigh & Sherlocks
John Hunter
Wm. Gibson & Co.
Francis Boult
Alexander Mein for Wm. & Alexr. Mein [later Davison & Mein]
John Houghton for P. [?] Wainewright & Co. [later Green & Wainewright]
Tho. Bolton for Hobson & Bolton
Ewart Rutson & Co.
William T. Cape jun. for Martin, T. Cape & Thornely [Thorneley]
Cyrus W[M]orrall & Jack Borland
Greaves Yates & Co.
B. Gray [later & partners]
Thomas T Wookleave [?]
Henry Gardiner for Thomas Epsquire & Co.
Wm. Dixon & co.
Joseph Bailey
Alexander MacGregor & Co.
William Little & Co.
Page 2, Col. 1
Ryland Child
Will. Smith & Son
C. Humbarton
Thomas McCall
R. & A. Harrison & Latham [later Richard Harrison]
John Eason
Abraham Garnett [entered twice]
Willm. & Richd. Rathbone
Mason, Hodgson & Co.
Anthony Mann [later Mann, Barnard & Co.]
Hugh Mathie & Son
Buchanan & Benn [?]
Carter & .....
W. & A. Maxwell
Wm. & Edgar Corrie
James F. Leitch
Wm. Brown & Co.
Marmaduke [?] & Mar
Robert & Turple Garathmey
Hayes & Storr
Wm. Hempe for Lyne Brothers Hempe
Pearson Hodgson & Gardiner
George Bunley & Co.
McOwen & Johnson
Wm. & James Brewes & Co.
Sands Hodgson & Co.
Richd. Bateson & Co.
Buchanan Laird & Co.
Peter Serjeantson
Aleton Finlay & Co.
Jos. Robinson
Drummond Heyworth & Co.
Wm. Shaw & Co.
Rathbone Bros. & Co.
Jas. Brown & Son
Wm. H Gilliat
Martineau Huith [?] & Co.
John Orred
Wm. Robinson & Co.
Edwr. Hamnet & Co.
Thos. Wright & Watson
Hunter & Alexander
Waddington Holt & Co.
Page 3, Col. 2
J. Hobson & Sons
Bateson & Horsfall
Bayard [?] & Reasoning
Hollinshead & Tesley
Melly Stewart & Co.
Booth Dixon & Co. [also P. J. Dixon]
M. Smith & Co.
Thos. Wilson & Co.
Todd Brothers & Co. [later Thomas Todd; then Todd Jackson & Co]
Humphreys Brindle [?]
Purton Parker & Co.
Fletcher Alexander & Co.
Roskill Ogden & Co.
Wainwright Sheils & Higgin
Molyneaux Witherley & Co.
Elland & Trott[e]r [?]
McCalmont Broths.
Reid Iring & Co.
A. Dennistoun & Co.
Blandin Brown & Co.
J. & D. Malcolmson & Co.
Chapman Bowman & Co.
Curm & Telo
J. H. Schöden & Co.
Fredk. Huth & Co.
A. St. Nylie [?]
Wm. Burton [?] Co.
Boyd Edwards & Beddy

Page 2, Col. 2
Ogden Nixtiances ? & Gibson ?
Natl. [?] Hazard & Co.

18. London chamber of commerce, Members 1823–4 (N=68)

Sources: Reports of chamber meetings in the *Morning Chronicle*, 19 and 29 March 1823 and 5 April 1824; Bennett, *Local Business Voice* (2011), pp. 100–101, 193–200. Initial meetings had 280 subscribers; only 55 names of standing committees of the chamber in 1823 and 1824 recorded, plus 13 whose comments are reported.

Other sources: *ODNB*; History of Parliament, (Thorne and Fisher); City of London inhabitants; London Metropolitan Archives catalogues; London Lives; Bunhill Fields burials.

Abbreviations used here:

BoE Bank of England
BoT Board of Trade
EIC East India Company

Name	Birth/death	Political role	Business
1823 Standing Committee			
Baring, Alexander	1773–1848	MP, modest reformer; Bullion Cttee 1810 with Manning; significant parl advocate for trade	Merchant, banker (dominant ptnr 1810–) retired 1830; BoE director 1805–17, Pres BoT 1834–5
Bernal, Ralph	1783–1852	MP, pro-reform	Lawyer, son of WI merchant
Brougham, Henry	1778–1868	MP, Attorney Gen 1820–1, Chancellor 1830, pro-reform	Lawyer; ex-Liverpool and Manchester chamber agent, etc.; later Social Science Assoc.
Courtenay, William	1777–1859	MP, Master of Chancery 1817–26, independent and modest reformer, mainly followed Canning	Lawyer, specialist in bankruptcy; family from Atwells bank (failed 1770); South Sea Co.
Davis, Richard Hart	1766–1842	MP for Bristol, pro-reform, opposed EIC and Corn Laws	WI merchant, ptnr in Harford Bank, Bristol [SMV & Bristol chamber member]
Farrand, Robert	1792–1855	MP, pro-reform; assisted Smith with Bill on Factors	Corn factor and agricultural interests
Gladstone, John	1764–1851	MP, pro-reform, opposed EIC, linked to Canning	Corn merchant, shipping & WI estates, ptnr of Edgar Corrie in Liverpool and others
Grant, John	1778–1866	MP, Vice Pres BoT, pro-reform of Corn Laws	Lawyer, supporter of Canning

Haldimand, William	1784–1862	MP, supported resumption of cash payments	Director of BoE
Huskisson, William	1770–1830	MP, President of BoT, pro-reform, Bullion Cttee 1810	
Irving, John	1765–1845	MP, opposed BoE resumption of cash payments, conservative	Merchant & financier, Alliance Insurance; Cork agents and property in WI
Marryat, Joseph	1757–1824	MP, modest reformer, independent	WI merchant, colonial agent for Grenada, formerly for Trinidad; chair of Lloyds; bank ptnr
Martin, John	1774–1832	MP, pro-reform	Ptnr Grasshopper Bank (Martins)
Newport, Sir John (Simon)	1756–1843	MP for Waterford, pro-reform, opposed EIC	Ptnr Newport Bank, Waterford [Waterford chamber member]
Onslow, (Sergeant) Arthur	1759–1833	MP, opposed Corn Laws, pro reform	Lawyer, bankruptcy specialist
Phillimore, Dr. Joseph	1775–1855	MP, generally conservative, sought offices	Lawyer, merchant family
Plummer, John	1780–1839	MP	Rum & WI merchant & plantation owner; insurance broker
Ricardo, David	1772–1823	MP, pro-reform, supported resumption of cash payments, leading Bullion Cttee member	Author, broker & loan contractor for govt. stock; free market supporter
Scarlett, James	1769–1844	MP, conservative, opposed Bill on principal and merchant	Lawyer and judge
Scott, Samuel	1772–1849	MP, conservative, pro-govt.	Corn merchant, director Royal Exchange Assurance; son of principal of Scott, Dent & Co. bank
Smith, John	1767–1842	MP, opposed BoE resumption of cash payments; introduced Bill on Factors	Ptnr Abel Smith bank of Notts.
Smith, William	1756–1835	MP, modest reformer, opposed EIC	Merchant, grocer & dissenter; director London Assurance, Albion Assurance, British Herring Co.
Sykes, Daniel	1766–1832	MP, Whig (& family supported Rockingham)	Merchant, lawyer, iron ore interests, Hull trade etc.

Wallace, Thomas	1768–1844	MP, Vice Pres BoT, pro-free trade	Master of Mint, lawyer
Wells, John	1761–1848	MP, conservative, Sheriff of Kent	Shipping, local land development, EIC & navy contracts
Wetherell, Charles??	1790–1846	MP, Solicitor General, generally conservative	Lawyer
Williams, William	1774–1839	MP; pro-reform	Bank ptnr in Dorchester
Wilson, Thomas	1767–1852	MP for City, Alderman; modest reformer, supported resumption BoE payments shipping	Grenada merchant and (Co.), director Phoenix Assurance; banking connections
1824 Standing Committee (additional members)			
Bainbridge, John			Merchants (Co.); later bank ptnr
Birkett, Richard			Corn with Thos Fothergill; ptnr Birkett's bank
Bridges, George	? 1762–1869	MP, Alderman, mayor 1819–20	Wine merchant
Buckle, John William	–1846		Wine and brandy merchants & insurance brokers (Co.), manager & ptnr in ship *Batavia*
Cook, James			Stockbroker (Co.)
Dorrien, George		(Brother, Magens, was an MP)	Merchants at Old South Sea House; ptnr Dorriens Mello bank; director BoE
Doxatt, Lewis	1778–1871		Editor, *Morning Chronicle*
Freese, John Henry jun.			Merchants, brokers (Co.)
Glynn, George Carr	1797–1873	MP later	Ptnr Glynn's bank, railways, dir St. Katherine's Dock, & Globe Insurance
Hall, John			Insurance broker (Co.), colonial broker; ptnr Hankey's and Child's banks
Hankey, W. A.			Ptnr Hankey's bank
Hodgson, John	–1831		Merchant with Chas Stokes; tea broker (Co.), son of WI planter
Holdon, Robert			Merchant, bank (Co.)
Kemble, Edward Bedwall			Tea brokers (Co.)
Kymer, John			Merchants, coffee w/h, brokers; ptnr of Max
Kymer, Maximilian R.			Merchants, coffee w/h, brokers; ptnr of John
Loughnan, Andrew			Merchants (Co.)
Masterman, J.			Peters, Walker, Milched bank
Morton, Robert H.			Brewers (Co.)

Richardson, C.			Wine merchants, brokers (Co.)
Ryland, Richard	–1832		Stockbroker & banker with Stonard; corn factor (Co.)
Shaw, R[obert]	1774–1849	MP for Dublin, modest reformer	Merchant & Ptnr Leighton & Shaw's bank [Dublin chamber member]
Smith, H. W.			Stockbroker / barrister ?
Thompson, William	1792–1854	(MP for City 1826–37), Alderman, moderate reformer, opposed Corn Laws, then turned Tory	Shipping, insurance, iron merchant & Welsh iron mine owner; Chair of Master Ironmongers Co.; (BoE director 1829); connected to Attwoods Bank
Ward, H.			Agents and brokers (Co.)
Wilkinson, T.			Brokers (Co.); ex ptnr Mackworth Dorsetts & Bloxham bank
Wollaston, H. S. H. (Henry Septimus Hyde)			Merchant; director London Assurance; mf. of Roman cement with Astides F. Mornay
Other members 1823–4			
Browne, (J. K.)			Corn factor (Co.)
Combauld, (Honorius)			Merchants (Co.)
Freshfield, James Joseph Wm.	1775–1864		Solicitor for BoE, Royal Exchange Assurance, & Smiths bank
Grenfell, Pascoe	1761–1838	MP, pro-reform & critic of BoE	Cornish copper smelters; governor of Royal Exchange Assurance
Hibbert, George	1757–1837	MP (1806–12), Alderman	WI merchant, director of WI Dock, agent for Jamaica 1812–30 [family of Jamaica chamber members 1778–85]
Lockwood, Joshua			Grocer & hop merchant
Lyon, David	? 1794–1872	(MP later, 1831–2)	Scotch factors & merchants (Co.), WI merchant
Manning, William	1763–1835	MP, Bullion Cttee 1810 with Baring, defended BoE	Stockbroker, BoE director & governor, president London Life Assurance; WI planter family, agent for Grenada
Mille, ______ [? Thomas]			? Silk manufacture (Co.)
Shaw, B(enjamin)	1770–1843	(MP 1812–18) defended BoE	Merchant, EIC shareholder, Ptnr Perring, Shaw bank

Soltau, William			Geo & Wm. merchants; [Geo a bank ptnr in Plymouth and a leading Plymouth chamber member d. 1819]
Tooke, Thomas	1774–1858		Author, merchant (Co.); director Royal Exchange Assurance
Warre, Sir William??	1784–1853		BoE director; ex-governor of Cape Colony etc.

19. Londonderry (Derry) chamber of commerce, 1793 (N=55)

Source: Londonderry chamber, *Translation of the charter* (1793). The committee and officers are as in 1790; Committee of 13 in 1790.

Member	Role	Business
Adams [Adems] Jas.		Soap manufacture, Coleraine
Alexander Andrew		Merchant, agent, Newtown; later bank
Anderson James		Merchant, Belfast
Armstrong Wm.	C 1790	Major local linen mf., and merchant in Belfast
Atcheson James		Brewery
Beaty Wm.		
Buchanan John		Attorney
Burnside Jas.		
Chambers Thos.	S	Lawyer and merchant
Charleton Geo.		
Clark John sen.		Shipping agent
Conningham Dickson	C 1790–3	Merchant
Crompton Adam		Insurance and shipping agent; later shipping chandler and director of Crompton, McKye & Alexander
Curry Samuel	VP 1790–3	Wine/rum merchant and agent
Davison Samuel		
Ewing John		Merchant, shipping
Gilmour James		
Gregg Tho.		Shipping agent
Gwyn John		Rope maker and shipowner to N. America
Hamilton John		Ship captain
Harvey John		Merchant for sherry, bottles, glass and manufacturer
Haslett Geo.		Timber and cider merchant
Horn[m]er Leonard	C 1790–3	Wine, oats and oil merchant; also flour mill
Joy Henry		
Kerr Wm.		Shipping
King Samuel		Grocer
Kyle Tho.		
McClintock John		Paper mill at Clady
McClintock Wm.		Paper mill
McConnell George	C 1793	Merchant
McCrea James		Cider merchant and ship owner; also insurance agent

McKeige Clot.		
Moore John		Tobacco merchant
Moore Robert	C 1790–3	Tobacco merchant and shipping
Murray James	C 1790–3	Timber and cider merchant
Nicholson John	C 1790–3	merchant
O'Donnell Con.		
Orr, Jo.		Shipping
Patterson Daniel	Pres 1793	Oak and bark merchant
Porter David		Merchant
Preston James		
Ramsay Jas.		Ship captain
Ross Samuel		Shipping
Schoales Adam jun.	C 1793	Spanish wine importer
Schoales James		Wine and oat meal merchant
Scott David		) probably Belfast merchants
Scott Henry		) ditto
Scott Henry		) ditto
Scott Richard N.		) ditto
Scott Tho. P.		) ditto
Scott Wm.		) ditto
Thompson James	C 1793	Merchant, importer of kelp, oats, fruit and wine
Thorp Geo.		
Watt David	C 1790–3	Cider merchant
Whitaker Jo.		
Wilson Tho.		Ship captain

20. Manchester Committee of Trade, 1774 and 1781–2

In addition to the *Manchester Mercury* lists, a very wide range of sources discuss Manchester and all have been used to input information here. [6]

20.1 Manchester Committee 1774 (N=28)

Source: Published list in *Manchester Mercury*, 8 March 1774. Committee of 1774; business as at 1778

Name, office and place if outside	birth-death	Religious affiliation	Co/I	Business
Barrow Thomas	1732–	A	Co.	Check & F mf, woollen draper and mercer (ptnr with Bussey, d.1782) (& Sons)(ptnr with Ryan Liverpool 1775)
Bayley Thomas B. Pres	1744–02	A/D	I	Yarn mf. & Gent. (Hope Hall, Pendleton)
Birch Josiah	1723–86	D-P	Co.	Leading yarn mer; F. mf. (& Sons) (ptnr John Rigby), also cotton &

[6] One of the most useful specific sources is C. Saggus, 'Social Identification, Attitudes, and Relationships in the 1780's of those Cotton Manufacturers of Manchester Listed in the Trades Directories of the Period' (Emory University, 1974). Full references to secondary sources in Bennett 'Alignments, Interests and Tensions' (2014).

				linen mill at Backbarrow [broth Thos at London & Barbados]
Chadwick jun. Thomas	1738–	A	Co.	(& Sons) Yarn mf., w/h, mer
Chippindall Joseph	1738–87	A	I & Co.	Attorney, coroner (scrivener with Nath. Milnes, dissolved 13.7.1779)
Crompton Peter	1735–89	D/?A	Co.	F. mf.
Derbyshire James (Bolton)	1742–	D-P	I	F. mf.; w/h MC
Drinkwater Peter (Bolton)	1742–01	A	Co.	Cotton mf., & foreign mer; also mill at Northwich; 1st major mule investor [mill in MC 1st to apply steam to cotton mf.1790]
Hamilton Robert	1725–81	D-U	Co.	(& Co.) Check mf.
Harrison James		A	Co.	Dyer (ptnr with Houghton)
Hibbert Robert	1717–84	D-U	Co.	Check mf. and WI mer (ptnr with Samuel)
Hodson James	d. by 1797	A	Co.	Check & F. mf. (& Sons)
Hyde Robert		A	Co.	Check & F. mf. (closed bus Feb 1783, passed to ptnr Nathaniel Hyde) WI trade
Markland John	1740–99	D	Co.	Leading check mf. (ptnr with Robert & Sons)
Philips John	1734–24	D-U	Co.	Small-wares weaving mf. tape & handkerchiefs (ptnr with Nathaniel) 'one of largest tape mf in world'; 'the major silk hat mf.'
Potter James	1741–95	D-U	Co.	F. mf. & mer (ptnr with Thos & Benj)
Radcliffe Edmund	1737–78	A	Co.	Major cotton mf. & mer (largest in England 1776), extensive foreign & WI contacts; development of dressing (ptnr with Ross)
Ridgway John (Bolton & Oldenshaw)	1732–	A	Co.	F. & woollen mf.
Ridings John (Pendleton)	1742–	A	Co. & I	F. mf. (ptnr with George)
Ryder Joseph Pendleton; w/h MC	1747–79	A	Co.	Check & F. Mf. (ptnr Thackeray)
Starkie Thomas	1745–	A	I	Silk and check mf.
Stott Thomas	1735–c90	A	I	Yarn mer and F. mf.
Tipping Thomas	1718–83	D	Co.	Yarn and cotton mf., major exporter & linen draper and Irish yarn mer; counting house (with Walker); shipping to America
Touchet James	1743–27	D-U	Co.	Major cotton, linen & check mf. and export mer to WI; Irish trade; family early users of spinning machine; WI estates [uncle was Sam, MP]
Walmsley William		A	Co.	Chapel works; Check and F. mf.; also mill at Backbarrow (with James)

Whitaker Daniel	1738–	A	I	Check, silk, cotton, linen and F. mf.
Withington John	1739–96	A	Co.	Check and F. mf.(ptnr with Birch & Birch, dissolved 1788)
Withington Thomas (Pendleton)	1747–	D	Co.	Check and F. mf., yarn w/h (ptnr with James, bankrupt 1788)

20.2 Manchester members 1781–2 (N=133)

Source: Published list in *Manchester Mercury*, 3 July 1781. Full subscribers for 1781–2: business as at 1778.

Name, office and place if outside	birth-death	Religious affiliation	Co/I	Business
Ackers Holland	1742–01	D	Co.	Silk and cotton mf. (with James & with George)
Ackers James	1753–24	D	Co.	Silk and cotton mf. (with Holland)
Ainsworth Peter (Bolton)		D	Co.	Crafter, cotton mf. (MC and Bolton) (& Sons)
Ainsworth Thomas (Bolton)	1751–31	D	Co.	Cotton & muslin mf. (MC and Bolton) later ptnr with Peel
Atkinson Joseph		Q	Co.	Hatmaker & F. mf.
Barlow James	c1734–	D	I	F. mf. and mercer
Barrow Henry (Prestwich/ Radcliffe)	1745	A	Co.	F. mf., dealer, chapman & printer (ptnr with John), bankrupt 1782
Barrow John (Prestwich/Radcliffe)	c1746–	A	Co.	F. & smallware mf. (ptnr with Henry) bankrupt 1782
Barton George	c1730–	A	Co.	Major F. mf., spinners, chapman & printer (H. J. & Co., then G.H. & J & Co.)
Barton Henry	1728–	A	Co.	Major F. mf., spinners, chapman & printer (H. J. & Co., then G.H. & J & Co.)
Bayley George	1729–	A/?D	Co. & I	F. mf., dealers, chapman and velvet draper (ptnr with John Jones & Jos Scholes, bankrupt 1783)
Beever John	1731–	A	Co.	Check mf. (with Jonathan)
Beever Jonathan	1743–	A	Co.	Check mf. (with John)
Bell Robert (Rochdale)		D	Co. & I	F. mf.
Bentley John	c1740–	A	I	F. cutter & dyer
Bickerdike Gideon Scotland; WI trade		A	I	Cotton mf, cotton mer; also in
Birch John (Bolton)	c1734–	A	I	F. mf., warehouse MC
Blomley Robert			Co.	F. mf. & w/h (with Samuel)
Boardman Thomas	1734–	D?	Co.	F. mf. (with Wm.; later ptnr with Graumann 1784); prob related to Sam of Swinton, m. to Nicholson of L'Pool and ptnr of Bentley (Josiah Wedgwood ptnr)

Boardman William	1722–	D?	Co.	F. mf. (with Thos. cf.)
Bolton Robert (Bolton)		D	I	F. mf.; warehouse MC
Bo[a]rron James			I & Co.	F. mf., printer and spinner (some with Edw & Wm)
Bourne Joseph			I	Quilt mf.
Bowen Joseph		A	I	Cotton mf.
Bradshaw James (Stretford)	1720–		I	F. mf.
Bray Champion		A	I	Check & F. mf.
Brown John (Bolton)			I	F. mf.
Carli(s)le William (Bolton)	1722–	D	Co.	Cotton & F. mf. (2nd largest in 1795) (with Thomas); warehouse MC
Chadwick Adam (Salford)	c1730–		I	Canvas maker & warehouse
Cocker James	1716–	A	I	F. mf.
Cocker William		A	I	Dyer
Cooke Bold		A	I	F. & Cotton mf.
Crane William	1737–	A	I	Yarn mf.
Crompton Ellis (Farnworth)		D	Co.	F. mf. & w/h MC (with John; & with Edge & Bradock)
Crompton John (Farnworth)	1730–	D	Co.	F. mf. & w/h MC (with Ellis; & with Edge & Bradock)
Dearnely William (Prestwich/Eccles)	1751–	A	I	Crafter
Dinwiddie James	1744–	A	Co.	F. mf. (with Wm. & later with G. Kennedy)
Dinwiddie William	1753–	D	Co.	F. mf. (with James & later with G. Kennedy)
Douglas Thomas	1747–	A	Co.	F. mf., spinner and mills (with Wm.)
Douglas William (Pendleton)		A	Co.	F. mf., spinner and mills (with Thos.)
Edge Richard	c1753–	A?	Co.	F. mf. (ptnr with James & John, then Thos., & Bradock)
Edge Thomas	1723–87	A	Co.	F. mf. (ptnr with Rich., & Bradock)
Entwisle James	1734–	A	Co.	Cotton, linen, F & check mf. & dyer, W/h (John & Jas Entwisle Co.)
Fogg Thomas (Bolton)	1738–	A?	Co.	F. mf., warehouse MC
Fowden William (Stockport)	1742–	D?	I	Silk and check mf.
Foxlow Thomas Peter	1722–	A	Co. & I	Silk, cotton, linen, F., check, calico and wire mf (also ptnr with Milne in Stockport)
Gardner James	1731–	D/?A	Co.	F. mf. (with Lawrence)
Gardner Lawrence	1744?–	D/A?	Co.	F. mf. (with James)
Gibson John (Hyde)	1725–	D?	I	W/h
Gorton Thomas	1745–	A	Co.	Smallware weaver & mf. (& Sons)
Grant Ed. B. Thos.	1732–	A	I	F. mf.
Graumann Herman			Co.	F. mf. (with Boardman)
Green William			I	Land surveyor & cotton goods mf. (linked to Thos Parke, L'pool)
Greenhalgh Robert (Horwich)	1719–	D	I	F. mf.; W/h in MC

Griffiths James	1748–		I	Calico printer
Hanson William	1728–	A	I	Check mf.
Hardman John	1719–	A	Co.	Silk & F. mf. & dyer (with Samuel) [family m. Tipping]
Hardman Samuel	1739–95	D-U	Co.	Silk & F. mf. & dyer (with John; & with Mather)
Hardy William	1743–	D	I	Check mf.
Harmer John	1731–	D	Co.	Silk mf. (with John jun.)
Harrison Richard	c1742–	A	Co.	Cotton mf. (with Wm.)
Henshaw Henry (Oldham)	c1748–		Co.	Hatmaker (ptnr with Thomas)
Hilton John (R&O; London)	1715–	D?	I	Major cotton spinner, cloth mf. and linen mer. espec in Europe (? of Blakelay)
Holden[ing] Giles	1735–	A	I	F. mf.
Hope Thomas (Watt engine 1797)	1723–	A	Co.	Hat & smallware mf. (Stockport)
Horridge John	1733–	A	I	Weaver, draper & dyer
Hyde Nathaniel	1752–	D	Co.	Cotton, linen and check mf. (succeeded ptnr Daniel with Robt. 1783) WI trade
Janny Thomas	1741–	A	I	Fustian dyer and cotton mf. (bankrupt 1782)
Johnson Thos	1745–23	A	Co.	Silk, cotton printer & mf.
Kay Daniel (Bolton)	1741–	D	I	F. mf.
Kearsley James		A	Co.	F. mf. (with Joshua 1783)
Kennedy Gilbert		D?	I/Co.	Major F. mf. and mills (later with Dinwiddie)
Lawrence John		A/?Q	Co.	F. and check mf. (with Joseph)
Leigh John		D?	Co.	Irish linen mer. (Richard Leigh & Sons)
Leigh (Rich. & Darwell)	1736	A	Co.	Major F. mf. (also in Warrington)
Lever James Lomas		A	I	Calico printer
Lever John	1719–	A	I	F. mf.
Lomas [& Thwaite]			Co.	F. mf.
Lomas [?Thomas] (& Boardman)			Co.	Cotton mf. & W/h
Lowe Joseph jun	c1742–	A	Co.	F. & smallware mf. & w/h (with Joseph sen. & Peter Marsh); solely Jos. from 1779
Makin William	1734–	A	I	Wool draper?
Markland Robert	c1744–28		Co.	Check mf. (with John)
Mars(c)h Josiah	1717–	A	Co.	F. mf.(with Wilson & Reeve)
Marsh Peter	1724–	A	Co.	F., linen & muslin mf. (with Reeve & Co.)
Mather Samuel Hardman)	1739–90	D-U	Co.	Silk & cotton mf. & mer (with
Metcalf Cornelius	1750–	A	I	F. mf.
Morris James			I	Hatter & F. dyer
Morris Peter	1739–		I	Hatter

Mort John (Chowbent)	1702–88	A	Co.	Cotton mf.; w/h MC (ptnr with Valentine) (salt mf. family at Nantwich)
Nayler James (Bolton)		A ?D	Co.	F. mf.; w/h MC (J & T)
Nayler Thos (Bolton)		A ?D	Co.	F. mf.; w/h MC (J & T)
N[H]eelis Edward		A		F. mf.
Nicholson Thos	?1753–25	D	Co.	Probably T. N. & Co. cotton mer. (ex L'pool family)
Norris Henry	1745–15	A	I	Cotton mf. & mer.
Norris Samuel	1724–	A	I	Check mf. & mer
Norton **Mrs.**		A	Co.	F. dyers & cotton printers (& Co.; Michael & Rachel) [**or** less likely, distributor of medicine drops]
Orme John	1732–	A	Co.	F. & smallware mf. (with Aaron O. & Son)
Philips Thomas Falkner	1744–	A	Co.	F. & smallware weavers & hatters (ptnr with Nath.)
Phillips Nathaniel	1726–08	D?	Co.	Smallware weavers & hatters (with Thos., Phil & John; with Falkner 1783)[m. Eliz Hibbert d. of Robt]
Pilkington John (Bolton)	1753–28	D	Co.	Cotton, linen & F. mf. (ptnr Sam. Oldknow)
Potter Richard	1745–10	D-P	I	Check mf.
Potter Thomas	1746–88	D-P	Co.	Cotton mer., linen & F. mf. & w/h (ptnr with James; James & Benj 1783)
Reynolds Robert	1717–	A	I	Small-ware mf.
Rider John	–1788	A	Co.	F. Mf., dyer & printer (with Thackeray)
Ridgeway John	c1730–		I	Woollen mf. (different from other John Ridgeway)
Ridgeway Thomas (Bolton)	1731–88	A	Co.	(& Sons) Dyer & chapman of Chowbent
Rigby William	1740–93	D-U	I	Yarn mer. (mar. Mary Touchet)
Robinson Robert	c1744–	D?	Co.	(& Co.) F. mf.
Rothwell Edward (Bolton)	1726–	D-P	Co.	F. mf. & dyer (ptnr with Barrow)
Smith [?Thos] (& Briscoe) (Worsley)			Co.	Cotton & F. mf. & smallware weaver; w/h MC (ptnr with Jos. Birch) (later in Gen. Chamber)
Taylor John (Oldham)	1724–	A	I	F. mf.; yarn & cotton mer. & w/h MC; prob shipowner 1786–90
Taylor Lawrence	1724–	D	Co.	F. mf. (? of Jane Taylor & Son) woollen drapers & mantua mf.
Taylor Samuel (Moston)	c1748–		Co.	Major cotton & check mf. & factor & exporter (ptnr with Israel & with Thos)[m. Birch family] w/h MC, WI trade
Tetlow Edmund	1718–	A	I	Cotton weaver & check mf.
Thackeray Joseph	1740–25	A?	Co.	F. mf., cotton spinner, mill built 1785 (ptnr with Ryder); father was steward to Sir Oswald Mosley

Thorp Issachar	1733or 48–	D?	I	Silk dyer & calico printer; w/h MC
Thwaite John (Bolton)	1721–	A	I	F. mf.; w/h MC
Tipping Joseph	1714–	A	Co.	Calico mf. (with Walker)
Varley John			Co.	Dryslater (ptnr Nicholson)
Walker George (Gorton)		A	Co.	Check mf. & cotton mer.; w/h MC; counting house (with Tipping)
Walmsley William			I	F. & check mf. (different from other Wm. Walmsley)
Whitehead John (Bolton)			I	F. mf.
Whitehead Robert (Roch & Oldham)		D	Co.	F. mf.; w/h MC
Whittaker Daniel jun	c1752–	A	Co.	Silk & check mf.
Winter Benj. L.	1731–	A	I	Cotton, linen & F. mf.
Wolstenhome John (Failsworth)	1728–	A	Co.	Check & F. mf.
Wood Charles		A	Co.	(& Co.) Check mf.
Worral Henry	1732–	A	I	F. & hat mf. (jun. d. 1787)

21. Newcastle-upon-Tyne chamber of commerce, 1815–6 (N=60)

Source: Published list of members and officers 1816, in chamber minutes: Tyne and Wear Archives 2401/1/1.

Member	Role	Business
Akenhead, J. & Sons		Booksellers, stationers, printers
Anderson, J. & Sons		Flax importer and dresser
Anderson, John	VP	Russia merchant (ptnr in Lambtons Bank 1822–58)
Armstrong & Thompson	C	Raff [used maritime goods] merchants
Atkinson, L. & M.		Shipping & insurance brokers
Ayton, Parker & Co.		Colour manufacture
Barras, J. & Co.		Merchants and brewers
Bigge, Thomas Hanway	C	Banker (Ridleys 1802–24)
Blackbird, R.		
Bradshaw & Anderson		Merchants & insurance brokers
Browell & Brewster		Coach and harness manufacture
Burnett, G.	C	Surgeon ?
Chapman, W. (N. Shields)		Merchant
Clapman & Foster		Oil merchants
Clarke, John Graham	Pres	Merchant
Clarke, Thomas		Spirit dealer
Clayton, Robert & Co.	VP	Merchants & raff yard (used maritime materials)
Clementson, G.		Wine & brandy merchant, ship insurance & commission broker
Cookson, Isaac & T.		Iron & brass founders; coal mines
Cookson, Isaac jun.	C	Glass manufacture
Coultherd, Thomas		Brewer

Doubleday & Easterby		Soap manufacture
Dunn, G. T. & Sons	C	Major coal mines
Easterby, Anthony & Co.	VP	Lead and soap manufacture
Greenwell, Robinson Robt.	C	Merchants & shipowners
Greenwell, W.		Merchants & shipowners
Hall, A.		(Easterby, Hall & Co.) Lead manufacture
Hawks, W. Sons & Co.		Iron founders & anchorsmiths
Joplin, W. & T. & Co.		Raff merchants (using maritime materials); later banking
Lamb, Joseph	C	Glass manufacture
Locke, Blackett & Co.		White & red lead and patent shot manufacture
Loggan, T.	C	
Losh, Wilson & Bell		Commission merchants & agents
Marshall, R. & Co.		Linseed oil manufacture
Naters, N.		
Newcastle Bottle Glass-house Co.		(Cookson, Isaac & Son) Glass manufacture
Northumberland Glass Co. (Joseph Lamb, manager)		Glass manufacture
Plummer, Matthew	C	Brewer
Pollard, Joseph & Son		Corn factors
Potter, A. L.		(Potter Wm. & Co.)Brewers & spirit merchants
Potts, J.	T	Corn factor
Reay, W., Walker		Flint mills and fire brick manufacture; coal mines
Redhead, W. & Co.		Merchants and insurance broker
Renwick, John & Co.		Esq.
Richmond, W. (N Shields)		
Robertson & Fox (S. Shields)		
Robson, C. L.		Linen draper
Scaife, R.		Merchants & paper manufacture
Sewell & Donkin		Potters
Smith Charles & Co.		Ship & insurance brokers
Smith, Thomas	C	Staffordshire ware merchant
Smith, Thomas		Ropemaker
Sorsbie & Co.		Merchants & founders
Sorsbie, Benjamin	C	Merchant and founder
Straker & Boyd		Shipping agents & insurance brokers
Surtees & Crosser		Wine & spirit merchants; coal mines
Thompson, T. & Co.		Corn merchants
Walkers, Parker & Co.		Lead merchants & manufacture
Winch, Mr.	S	Iron merchant
Winship, Harle & Co.		Ship owner & brokers

22. North Staffordshire Potters chamber of commerce, 1785 and 1789 (N=53)

Source: Josiah Wedgwood Commonplace Book, Minutes of North Staffordshire Potters chamber of commerce: Wedgwood Archives E39–2804. List of those attending initial meeting, or other meetings in 1785 and thus active; with committee for 1785 and 1789 (incomplete: 5 members missing). Those attending the initial meeting may be claimed to be initiators of the chamber, marked ✓. The six marked 'dec' were elected to the first committee but declined to serve and were replaced by others. All are by definition potters. A list of master potters for 1785 in the Wedgwood paper lists 77 firms (commonplace book E39–28408). This may be a list of all members, or a list of all potters. The 53 named here come from about 49 of these firms and thus constitute about 64 per cent of all.

Member (place if specified)	**Initial meeting**	**1785 committee**	**1789 committee**
Adams, William (Burslem & Cowbridge)			C
Baddelely, John			
Baddeley, Ralph		C	C
Bagnall, Charles	✓	C	
Barker, Richard	✓	C	C
Barker, William (Lane End)			
Bold, Jas. Spencer (Burslem)			
Boon, Edwd.			
Booth, Hugh	✓	C	
Bourne, James		dec	
Brindley, Taylor		dec	
Bucknall, Robert			
Cartlich, Samuel			
Chatterley, Charles	✓	C	
Chatterley, Ephraim			C
Clowes, William	✓	C	
Cole, ____			
Daniel, John			
Daniel, Walter	✓	C	
Glass, John			C
Goodwin, Benjamin		C	C
Graham, John		C	
Hales, John	✓	C	
Harrison, John			
Heath, Joshua			
Hollins, Samuel			C
Keeling, Anthony		C	C
Keeling, Edward			
Mare, John		C	C
Mare, Richard			
Mare/Mayer, Elijah		C	C
Mellor, Daniel		dec	
Prince, John		dec	
Robison, James	✓		
Rogers, John		C	
Rogers, John			C
Shelley, Thomas	✓		
Smith, Ambrose	✓		
Smith, Joseph	✓		C
Spode, Josiah			
Taylor, George			C
Turner, John (Lane End)		C	
Turner, William			
Twemlow, George	✓		
Twemlow, Thomas		C	C

Warburton, Jacob	✓	C	C
Wedgwood, Josiah*	✓Pres	Pres	Pres
Wedgwood, Thomas (Burslem)*	✓C	dec	
Whithead, Charles*	✓C	C	
Wilson, Robert	✓	C	
Wood, Enoch*	✓C	dec	
Woolfe, Thomas	✓		
Yates, John*	✓C	C	

23. Nottingham chamber of commerce, 1813 (N=14)

Source: Report of initial committee to found a chamber, *Nottingham Review*, 24 December 1813, referred to as 'bankers, manufacturers and others interested in the trade of Nottingham'. The most complete list of any of the early Nottingham chamber attempts before the successful foundation in 1860; see also Walton, *Nottingham Chamber of Commerce* (1960), p. 11.

Member	Business
Joseph Beardmore	Hosiery mf.
William Burnside	Esq. (Wilson, Burnside & Co.) British lace mf.
Edward Charteris[t]	(& Co.) hosiery mf.
Joseph Churchill	(Churchill & Price) Hosiery mf.; (Churchill & Dickenson) linen & woollen drapers
Francis Hardwick	(Hall, Northage & Hardwick) hosiery mf.
Francis Hart, Jnr.	(Hart, Fellows & Co.) bankers
Kewney & Richardson	(Co.) Hosiery & lace mf.
W. Melville	(Melville Ellen & Sons) India cotton mf. & hosiers
Needham & Nixons	(Co.) Merchants & hosiery mf.
Thomas C. Smith	(Smith & Co.) bankers
John Stone[s]	Coachmaker
W. Trentham, Jun.	(Trentham, Turney & Morton) Hosiery mf.
Francis Wakefield	(Hancocks & Wakefield) Hosiery mf.; (Hancock, Wakefield & Wildsmith) British lace mf.
William Wilson	(Wilson, Burnside & Co.) British lace mf.

24. Plymouth chamber of commerce, 1813–14 (N=40)

Sources: Founding papers, Monkes of Saltram MS, Plymouth and West Devon RO; *Report* reprinted in W. Burt, *Review of the Mercantile, Trading, and Manufacturing State … of the Port of Plymouth* (Plymouth, 1816), Plymouth Central Library P371.1, Accession No. L3730.[7]

[7] Burt was the first secretary of the chamber; see also Worth, *History of Plymouth* (1871) 235–9.

Member	Role	Business etc.
Arthur, John	C	Brewer
Bayly, Richard	C	Chandler and ironmonger
Billing, Thomas	C	Linen draper
Blackburne, Isaac	C	Shipbuilder
Boringdon, Rt. Hon.Lord	Pres	Estates
Bullocke, Benjamin	C	Appraiser and auctioneer, Plym Dock
Burt, William	S	Solicitor
Canning, Henry	C	Merchant
Cleverton, John	C	Lawyer
Collier, John	C	Wine merchant
Elford, Jonathan	T	(Elford, Tingcombe & Clark) Banker, and solicitor
Elford, Sir William	member	1749–1837, Banker (had been MP 1796–1808 Plymouth; generally pro-government)
Forrest, Digory	C	Marines officer
Forsyth, George	C	Merchant
Fox, Thomas Were	C	Agent for family bank in Falmouth
Fuge, Robert	C	Merchant, distiller
Fuge, Robert jun.	C	Merchant, distiller
Glanville, Francis	member	Tea warehouse
Harris, John jun.	C	Banker
Harris, John	member	Banker and attorney
Hawker, John	C	Merchant and ship owner; also Dutch Consul and Vice-Consul for America, Sweden, Oldenburg and Kniphausen
Hawker, Wm. H.	C	Tanner
Hodge, William	C	Timber merchant and banker
Langmead, W	C	Brewer, distiller
Lockyer, Edmund H.	C	Merchant
Lockyer, Wm.	C	Merchant and ship agent
Moore, Joseph	C	Shipbuilder
Nichols, Ambrose	C	Cordage manufacturer
Prance, William	C	Linen draper
Slade, James	C	Agent
Soltau, George [d. 1819]	C	Banker and merchant (with Wm. Soltau)
widow of Symons & Sons	proposer	Husband was bank partner with Soltau
Welsford, Peter	C	Sail cloth manufacturer
Woollcombe, Henry	VP, mayor	Attorney, commissioner of taxes
Additional members listed who were probably honorary		
Bastard, John P.	proposer, MP Truro and Devon	1756–1816, independent, reformist, leading supporter of militia
Bloomfield, Sir Benjamin	proposer, MP Plymouth	1768–1846, solid government supporter, in Prince of Wales household
Lopes, Sir Masseh	proposer, MP Barnstaple	1775–81, Jamaica Jewish planting family; major Plym landowner; huge wealth; pro-government and important patron of elections; Grampound bribery link.
Pering, Sir John	proposer, MP Romney, Hythe	1765–1831, Devon family; woollen manufacture at Exeter; London banker and insurance; pro-government

Pole, Sir Charles	proposer, MP Plymouth	1757–1830, RN Admiral, Admiralty Board; personal enemy of Elford who he dislodged 1808; pro-government, toward opposition from 1812
Pole Carew, Reginald	proposer, MP various Cornish	1753–1835, linked to Lord Edgcumbe, pro-government, held various high offices

25. Waterford chamber of commerce, 1787–96; 1805; 1815.

Some individual business details ambiguous in other sources as some initials or first names not stated; handwritten.[8]

25.1 Members 1787–1796 (N=66)

Source: Minute books, Waterford Archives; WCOC 1/01; committee attendees and others 1787–96; some double counting between individuals and partnerships; full list from 1805.

Member	Business	Also member in 1805
Atkins, J. & A.	(& Co.) Merchants & bankers	
Alcock, Thomas	Alderman	
Allen, John	(Wallace & Allen) merchants	X
Bancroft, A.	(Ramsay, Gatchell & Bancroft) merchants & glass mf.	
Barker, Arthur	Merchant	
Binnie & Bell	(& Co.) Merchant	
Blain, William	(Strongman, Davis & Blain) Merchants	X
Blake, W.	(J. Blake & Son) Merchant	X
Browne, John	Whitesmith	X
Brunskill, Michael		
Cherry, Francis	Woollen draper	
Cherry, Robert	Merchant	
Clancy, Man.	Merchant	
Connell, John	Snuff mf.	
Courtney, John	(& Sons) Butter mf. and merchant	X
Davis, Richard	(Penrose, Davis & Co.) Merchants	X
Delandre, B. & J.	(& Co.) Merchants	
Dwyer, Joseph	Merchant	
Firth, J.	Grocer	
Follett & Co.	(& Co.) Merchant	
Futh, John		
Grant	(Grant & Banon) Merchants	
Grubb	Q	
Hayden, Henry	(& Co.) Merchant (& banker, Hayden & Rivers 1804–20)	
Hayden, P.	Merchant	
Hedgway		

[8] See also Cowman, *Perceptions and Promotions* (1987); *Irish Shipbuilding in Waterford* (2001); Bennett, *Local Business Voice*, 156, 165, 214, 514–6.

Hutchinson, Max.	Merchant	X
Hunt, Henry H.	(Hunt, O'Brien & Hunt) Merchant & banker	X
Hunt, John	(Hunt, O'Brien & Hunt) Merchant & banker	
Hunt, Robert	(Hunt, O'Brien & Hunt) Merchant & banker	
Hurley, John	Tanner	
Jacob, R. J. T.	Ironmonger Q	
Jacob, Richard	(R. Jacob & Son) Major merchants and ironmonger Q	
Jacob, Thomas	Ironmonger Q	
Jones, David	(Kings & Jones) timber merchant, Gent.	X
Keating, Fred	Merchant	
Keating, Wm. Augustus	(Co.) Merchant, & City Club	
Kenna, R. M.	Merchant	
King, Samuel	(King & Jones) timber merchants, Gent.	X
Lecky, J. & J.	(& Co.) Merchants	
Lonergan, John	Merchant	
Lyons & Revell	(& Co.) Merchant	
Max, Simon	Merchant, Gent.	
Murphy, Phineas	Wine merchant	
Murphy, William		
Nevins, Thomas	Merchant	
Newport, Simon	(Newports) attorney and banker, Alderman	
O'Brien & Hunt	(Hunt, O'Brien Hunt) bank	
O'Neill, John	Merchant & banker (1799–1801)	
O'Neill, William	Merchant	
Peck, Edward	Corn merchant	X
Peet, Edward	Merchant	
Pennell, William	(& Co.) Major merchant and ship owner Q	X
Penrose, William jun	(& Co.) Major merchant and ship owner Q	
Penrose, William sen	(Simon P. & Wm. Sons & Co.) Timber merchants; tanning, bacon & coal yards; glass mf. & exporters from 1782 Q d. 1799	X
Pope		X
Power, Robert	Haberdasher & wine merchant	
Quan, James	(Wyse, Cartin & Quan) Merchant	
Quan, Thomas	(Wyse, Cartin & Quan) Merchant	
Rogers		
Russell & Ardagh	(& Co.) Merchant	
Ryan, John		
Sheaman, W.	Merchant	
Sikes, Thomas	Merchant, Gent.	X
Strangman, Joshua	(& Sons) butter merchant Q	
Strangman, Thomas	(& Co.) Major merchant Q	
Strangman, William	(& Co.) Major merchant Q	
Sykes, Thomas	(Cherry & Sykes) Merchants	
Syms, A.	Merchant, Esq.	
Wallace, Alexander	Merchant	
Wallace, Alexander jun	Merchant	
Wallace, Cornelius L.	(& Co.) Merchant, Customs collector?	
Wilson, George	Merchant	
Wyse, Cartin & Quan	(Co.) merchants	

Additional members by 1805

Allen, John & Son	(& Co.)Merchants	X
Archbold, John	Merchant	X
Aylward, William	Merchant	X
Belcher, William	Flour & spirit merchant	X
Cherry, Richard	(Rich & Wm.) Brewers	X
Cherry, Thomas	Salt & lime works, John's town	X
Cherry, William	(Rich & Wm.) Brewers	X
Collins, Joseph		X
Courtney, Edward	(& Son) Merchant	X
Davis, Samuel	(& Co.) timber merchants	X
Devereaux	Salt & lime works	X
Farrell, Matthew	(M., P. & M) Merchants & ship brokers	X
Farrell, Patrick	(M., P. & M) Merchants & ship brokers	X
Fogarty, Richard	Merchant	X
Fayle, S. W.	Merchant	X
Galway, Patrick	Merchant	X
Harris, James	Merchant	X
Harris, John	(W. & J.) Merchants	X
Harris, Wm.	(W. & J.) Merchants	X
Henderson, Abraham		X
Hill, James	(J. & J.) Merchant and tanners	X
Jackson, Anthony	Merchant	X
Jacob, Joshua	Ironmonger & merchant	X
Jacob, Thomas	Timber merchant	X
Kennedy, R. Michael	Merchant	X
Leonard, Joseph A.	Merchant	X
Markefield, Joshua	Merchant	X
Mason, Joshua	Merchant	X
Mason, Simon	Merchant	X
McCheane, Thomas	(McCheane and Hutchinson) merchants	X
Milward, William		X
Moore, Benjamin	(B & F. Moore) merchants	X
Murphy, Phineas	Wine merchant	X
Nevin, John	(Nevins, Pim & Penrose) merchants	X
Newport, John	Merchants	X
Newport, Marmaduke	(Newport & Scott) merchants and bank	X
Newport, William	(Newport & Scott) bankers	X
Owen, Thomas	Sailmaker	X
Peet, Joshua	Merchant	X
Penrose, Samuel	(& Co.) Merchant	X
Pope, Alexander	Merchant & notary public	X
Prosser, Robert J. K.	Merchant	X
Ridgway, George	(H. Ridgway & Son) Butter merchants	X
Robinson, William	Spirit & corn factor	X
Ryan, Jeremiah	Wine merchant	X
Skottowe, Edmund	Merchant	X
Sparrow, Joseph		X
Strangman, Joshua jun	(& Co.) Merchant	X
Wakefield, Joseph	(Procter & Wakefield) merchants & ironmongers	X
Watson, William	(R. & W. Watson) Major merchant Q	X
White, Thomas & Son	(& Co.) Merchant ; sugar & grocery trader Q	X

25.2 Waterford members 1815 (N=87)

Source: full lists for 1815; charter list WCOC 18/01; subscribers to House of Concerns WCOC 2/01; some individual business details ambiguous in other sources as some initials or first names not stated; named as charter members in printed list. Also initial subscribers to 'House of Concerns' (the chamber's premises), listed 10 February 1812 (n.b. John Harris is listed twice); 44 became debenture holders; debenture holders subsequently changed in many cases.

Member	Business	Subscription (£) to House of Concerns 1812	Also member by 1805
Ardagh, William A.	Brewer		
Aylward, William	Merchant		X
Bayly, Henry A.	(& Co.) Merchants	50	
Belcher, William	Flour & spirit merchant		X
Birnie, Arthur	(& Co.) Bookseller		
Blain, Andrew	Merchant		
Blain, William	Merchant, Gent.	100	X
Blake, James	Merchant & shipowner	50	
Boland, Thomas	Merchant		
Cherry, Richard	(R. & W.) Brewers & insurance	50	X
Cherry, William	(R. & W.) Brewers & insurance		X
Courtenay, Edward	Merchant		X
Davis, Francis		100	
Davis, Richard	(& Son) Brewers	100	X
Davis, Richard jun	(& Son) Brewers		
Davis, Samuel S.	(& Co.) Timber merchants		X
Downes, Henry			
Farrell, Maurice	(M., P. & M.) Merchants & shipbrokers		
Fayle, Joseph	(Scott, Fayle) merchants & boot mf.	100	
Fayle, Samuel W.	(Scott, Fayle) merchants & boot mf.		X
Fogarty, Richard	Merchant		X
Gatchell, Jonathan	Merchant & glass mf.		
Gibbons, Peter		50	
Harris, James	(Messrs) Bank	100	X
Harris, John	(Wm & John) merchants, MP	100 + 50	X
Harris, William	(Wm & John) merchants, Gent., insurance agent	50	X
Hill, James	Flour merchant	50	X
Hughes, William	Excise Collector		
Hunt, Henry H.	(Hunt, O'Brien & Hunt) Merchant & banker	50	X
Hunt, Robert	(Hunt, O'Brien & Hunt) Merchant & banker		X
Hunt, William	(Hunt, O'Brien & Hunt) Merchant & banker		
Hutchinson, Thomas	(McCheane and Hutchinson) merchants, Gent.	50	
Jackson, Anthony	Merchant	100	X
Jacob, Isaac			

Jacob, Joseph	(Thomas, R. & J. Jacob)	See Thomas	
Jacob, Joshua	Merchant & ironmonger	50	X
Jacob, Joshua R.	Merchant		
Jacob, Robert	(Thomas, R. & J. Jacob) timber merchants	See Thomas	
Jacob, Thomas	(Thomas, R. & J. Jacob) timber merchants	50	X
Jones, David	(King & Jones) timber merchants	100	X
King, S.	(King & Jones) timber merchants, Alderman, Gent.	50	X
Leonard, Joseph A.	Merchant		X
Leonard, John	Merchant		
Leonard, William	Merchant		
Mason, Joshua	Merchant, tallow chandler & insurance Co.	50	X
Max, Simon	Merchant, Gent	100	X
McCheane, Thomas	(McCheane and Hutchinson) merchants, Harbour Commissioner	50	X
Milward, George			
Milward, William			X
Murphy, Phineas	Wine merchant		X
Nevins, Penrose	(Nevins T., Pim & Penrose) merchants		
Nevins, Thomas	(Nevins T., Pim & Penrose) merchants	50	
Nevins, Pim	(Nevins T., Pim & Penrose) merchants		
Newport, Sir, J. Bart.	Merchant		X
Newport, William	(Newport & Scott) bankers, Alderman	50	
Newsom, Joshua			X
Peet, Joshua	(Edward Peet & Son) merchants	(Edw) 50	
Peet, William	(Edward Peet & Son) merchants	See Joshua	X
Penrose, Francis	(& Co.) Timber merchant and shipping		
Penrose, John		50	
Penrose, William			
Pope, Alexander	Lawyer & notary public		X
Pope, Richard	Merchant & ship broker	50	
Prosser, Thomas	Merchant		X
Ridgway, Henry	(& Sons) Butter merchants	200	
Ridgway, George P.	(& Sons) Butter merchants		X
Ridgway, Henry jun	(& Sons) Butter merchants	50	
Robinson, William	Spirit & corn factor		
Ryan, Jeremiah	Wine merchant	50	X
Scott, Thomas	(Newport & Scott) Esq. bankers		
Scroder, Jacob	Commission agent	50	X
Skottowe, Edmund	Merchant		
Skottowe, Nicholas	(Atkins, Skottowe & Roberts) bankers		
Smith, Francis		150	
Strangman, John		150	
Strangman, Joseph	Merchant	50	
Strangman, Joshua	Merchant Esq.	50	
Strangman, Joshua jun			X
Strangman, William	Brewer & merchant	50	X
Trouton, Charles			
Turner, Mathew J.		50	

Wakefield, Joseph	(Procter & Wakefield) merchants & ironmongers, Gent.	50	X
Watson, Robert	Gent.	50	
Watson, William Penrose		50	
White, Samuel	Boot & shoe mf.	50	
White, Thomas	Russia merchant & wholesale grocer	50	X
White, William	Merchant & rope and ship mf.	50	
		Total £3000	

26. Wolverhampton chamber of commerce 1819 (N=27)

Source: Report of 12 November 1819 'subscribers to the Wolverhampton chamber' reproduced in V. B. Beamont, *The Wolverhampton Chamber of Commerce*, (1956) p. 3. F&B = freeman and burgess of borough; Const. = constable.

Member	Business	Other appointments
Brady, William	? Lock manufacturer	
Briscoe, William & Son	Merchants & factors	C of Sub. for Poor
Dixon, John [Ready Wm. & Dixon]	Cock & brass founder, iron tube & gas apparatus manufacturer	Ready: F&B
Duffield, William	Japanner & enameller	Const. 1818
Duncombe, Samuel	Factor and locksmith	
Earp & Wynn [& Bagnall]	Factors and lock makers	
Elwell, H. B. [Henry Barker]	Japanner and tin plate manufacturer	Bible Soc.
Fletcher, William	Lock manufacture	Sub. for Poor
Halten, Cooper & Himen	Factors	
Jones, Robert	Factors and wholesale ironmongers, japanners	C of Sub. for Poor; F&B
Lang[s]ton & Baker	Merchants and factors	
Mander, Weaver & Mander	Wholesale and manufacturing chemists	C of Sub. for Poor; Bible Soc.; F&B
Pearson, Jos[eph] & Co. [C, T & S]	Brass founders, wholesale ironmongers & factors	C of Sub. for Poor; Bible Soc.; F&B
Rogers, Henry & Co.	Wholesale merchants, factors and ironmongers	Const. 1823; Sub. of Poor
Ryton & Walton	Japanners and tinplate	Sub. for Poor
Savage, Thomas [& Sons]	Factors and ironmongers	Bible Soc.; F&B
Shaw [John] & Crane	Merchants and factors	
Shaw, Benjamin	Ironmonger and brazier	Const. 1815; Sub. for Poor
Sparrow, William & Sons	Factors and iron masters	
Stanley, Benjamin? & Sons	Japanner and tin plate manufacture	
Tarratt, Joshua & Co.	Wholesale ironmongers	C of Sub. for Poor; Bible Soc.
Turner, Edward	Lock manufacturer	Const. 1821

Underhill, Jos[eph]	Wholesale ironmonger & cutler	Const. 1817&20; Sub. for Poor; Bible Soc.; F&B
Walker, John [prob. Joseph]	Japanner	
Ward, William	File and rasp manufacturer	
Wenman & Walker Co.	Factors and wholesale ironmongers	F&B
Wright, Jos[eph]	Japanner and tin plate manufacture	Bible Soc.; F&B

27. Worcester chamber of commerce, 1839 (N=18)

Source: *Report with Rules and Regulations agreed upon for the Formation of the Worcester Chamber of Commerce together with Bye-Laws, 1839*; printed; held at the modern Hereford and Worcester Chamber of Commerce: p. 15, list of initial office holders only.

Name	Role	Business
George Allies	C	(Geo. & Robt.) currier etc.; ? also malster
Thomas Burlingham	C	(& Sons) Glove mf.
John Dent	Pres	(John & Wm. Co.) merchant and glove mf.
Henry Deighton	C	? bookseller & printer
Edward Evans	VP	(Herefordshire Banking Co.) Bank manager
Richard Evans	C	Esq., ? victualler
Thomas Grainger	C	(Grainger, Wood & Co.) china & porcelain mf.
J. M. Gutch	C	
Robert Hardy	C	(Hardy & Padmore) ironfounder
J. Whitmore Isaac	C	(Worcester Old Bank: Berwick, Lechmere, Wall, Isaac & Lechmere) bank ptnr.
J. W. Lea	C	(Lea, Perrins & Smith) chemists etc.
Matthew Pierpoint	C	Surgeon MD
William Stallard	C	(& Sons) Wine and spirit dealer
H[arvey] B[errow] Tymbs	C	(& John) solicitor
John Tymbs	S	(& H. B.) solicitor; member & sec, not a director
James Wall	Auditor	Pipe mf.
T[homas] H[enry] Wheeler	Auditor	Auctioneer
Richard Yapp	C	(Yapp, Williams & Co.) grocers & tea dealers

References

Akins, B., *History of Halifax City* (Halifax, 1895)

Aldrich, H. E., *Organizations and Environments* (Englewood Cliffs, NJ, 1979)

Andrews, C. McL., 'The Boston merchants and the non-importation movement', *Transactions of the Colonial Society of Massachusetts*, XIX (1916) 159–259

Ashton, T. S., *Iron and Steel in the Industrial Revolution* (1963)

Barrow, J. H. ed., *The Mirror of Parliament* (1838)

Barker, T. C. and Harris, J. R., *A Merseyside Town in the Industrial Revolution: St. Helens 1750–1900* (1959)

Basye, A. H., *The Lords Commissioners of Trade and Plantations, Commonly Known as the Board of Trade, 1748–1782* (New Haven, Conn., 1925)

Beaumont, V. B., *The Wolverhampton Chamber of Commerce 1856–1956: Centenary publication* (Wolverhampton, 1956)

Bellamy, J. M., *The Trade and Shipping of Nineteenth Century Hull* (East Yorkshire Local History Society Series, No. 27, York, 1971)

Bennett, R. J., 'The logic of local business associations: an analysis of voluntary chambers of commerce', *Journal of Public Policy,* 15 (1996) 251–79

Bennett, R. J., 'Can transaction cost economics explain voluntary Chambers of Commerce?', *Journal of Institutional and Theoretical Economics,* 152 (1996) 654–80

Bennett, R. J., 'The Relation between government and business associations in Britain: An evaluation of recent developments', *Journal of Policy Studies,* 18, 1 (1997) 5–33

Bennett, R. J., 'Business associations and their potential to contribute to economic development: re-exploring an interface between the state and market', *Environment and Planning A,* 30 (1998) 1367–87

Bennett, R. J., *The Voice of Liverpool Business: The First Chamber of Commerce and the Atlantic Economy, 1774–c.1796* (Liverpool, 2010)

Bennett, R. J., *Local Business Voice: The History of Chambers of Commerce in Britain, Ireland and Revolutionary America, 1760–2011* (Oxford, 2011).

Bennett, R. J., 'Malachy Postlethwayt: Genealogy and influence of an early economist and spin doctor', *Genealogists' Magazine*, 31 (June 2011) 1–7

Bennett, R. J., 'Chambers of Commerce: From Protesters to Government Partners', *British Academy Review*, 20 (2012) 37–40

Bennett, R. J., 'Network interlocks: The connected emergence of chambers of commerce and provincial banks in the British Isles, 1767–1823', *Business History*, 55, 8 (2013) 1288–1317

Bennett, R. J., 'Alignments, interests and tensions over 'Reform' in 18th Century Britain: The Manchester Committee of Trade 1774–86', *Northern History*, 51, 1 (2014) 61–90

Bennett, R. J., 'Searching for new models of business representation: the Liverpool Committee or Board of Trade, 1775–1794', *Northern History,* 51, 2 (2014) 263–89

Bennett, R. J., 'Collective action when needed: The Kingston chamber of commerce in Jamaica, 1778–85', *The Journal of Imperial and Commonwealth History,* 43 (2015) 165–88

Bennett, R. J., 'Management adaptation of business association services: Long-term stability 1783–2012 and "change points" for Irish Chambers of Commerce', *Irish Journal of Management*, 35, 1 (2016) 58–73

Bennett, R. J. and Ramsden, M., 'The contribution of business associations to SMEs: Strategy, bundling or reassurance?', *International Small Business Journal*, 25, 1 (2007) 49–76

Bennett, R. J. and Robson, P. J. A., 'Intensity of interaction in supply of business advice: A comparison of consultancy, business associations and government support initiatives for SMEs', *British Journal of Management*, 10 (1999) 351–69

Bennett, R. J. and Robson, P. J. A., 'Exploring the market potential and bundling of business association services', *Journal of Services Marketing,* 15, 3 (2001) 222–39

Bennett, R.J. and Robson, P.J.A., 'The role of trust and contract in the supply of business advice', *Cambridge Journal of Economics*, 28 (2004) 471–88

Beresford, M. W., *The Leeds Chamber of Commerce* (Leeds, 1951)

Bhattacharya, C. B., 'When customers are members: Customer retention in paid membership contexts', *Journal of the Academy of Sciences*, 26, 1 (1998) 31–44

Bishop, J. B., *A chronicle of one hundred and fifty years: the chamber of commerce of the State of New York* (New York, 1918)

Bladen, V. W., 'The Association of the Manufacturers of Earthenware (1784–86)', *Economic History, Supplement to Economic Journal*, 1 (1928) 356–67

Borsay, P., 'The Culture of Improvement', in P. Langford ed. *The Eighteenth Century: 1688–1815* (Oxford, 2002) 183–212

Bowden, W., 'The English manufacturers and the commercial Treaty of 1786 with France', *American Historical Review,* 25 (1919–20) 18–35

Bowden, W., *Industrial Society in England towards the end of the Eighteenth Century* (1965)

Bradley, J. E., *Religion, Revolution, and English Radicalism: Nonconformity in Eighteenth Century Politics and Society* (Cambridge, 1990)

Brewer, J., *Sinews of Power: War and the English state, 1688–1783* (1989)

Bridenbaugh, C., *Cities in Revolt: Urban Life in America 1743–1766* (New York, 1955)

Bulletin Societé Jersiaise, 'The Jersey chamber of commerce—the early years', 19 (1968) 299–306

Burt, W., *Review of the Mercantile, Trading, and Manufacturing State, Interests, and Capabilities of the Port of Plymouth; With miscellaneous additions by other persons, and notes* (Plymouth, 1816)

Butler, G. F., 'The early organisation and influence of Halifax merchants', *Collections of the Nova Scotia Historical Society*, 25 (1942) 1–16

Cameron, K. J., 'Anti-Corn-Law Agitations in Scotland, with particular reference to the Anti-Corn-Law League', PhD thesis (Edinburgh, 1971)

Castles, F. G., 'Business and Government: a typology of pressure group activity', *Political Studies,* 17, 2 (1969) 160–76

Chambers, G., *Faces of Change: The Belfast and Northern Ireland Chambers of Commerce and Industry, 1783–1983* (Belfast, 1983)

Checkland, S. G, 'Economic attitudes in Liverpool 1793–1807', *Economic History Review,* 5 (1952) 58–75

Cheffins, B. R., *Corporate Ownership and Control: British Business Transformed* (Oxford, 2008)

Christie, I. R, *Wilkes, Wyvill and Reform: The parliamentary reform movement in British politics 1760–1785* (1962)

Christie, I. R., *War and Revolutions: Britain 1760–1815* (Cambridge Mass, 1982)

Church, R. A. and Chapman, S. D., 'Gravener Henson and the making of the English working class', in E. L. Jones and Chambers, J. D. (eds.) *Land, labour and population in the Industrial Revolution* (1967) 131–61

Clapham, J. H., *An Economic History of Modern Britain, Vol. 1: The Early Railway Age 1820–1850* (Cambridge, 1926)

Clark, J. C. D., *The Language of Liberty, 1660–1832: Political Discourse and Social Dynamics in the Anglo-American World* (Cambridge, 1994)

Clark, P., *British Clubs and Societies 1580–1800* (Oxford, 2000)

Cooke, C. A., *Corporation, Trust and Company: An Essay in Legal History* (Manchester, 1950)

Cowman, D., *Perceptions and Promotions: The Role of the Waterford Chamber of Commerce, 1787–1987* (Waterford, 1987)

Cowman, D., *Irish Shipbuilding in Waterford* (Waterford, 2001)

Cox, G. S., *The Guernsey Chamber of Commerce 1808–1983: A celebration of 175 years of activity* (Guernsey, 1983)

Cox, G. S., *The Guernsey Chamber of Commerce, 1808–2008* (Guernsey, 2008)

Cox, G. S., *Guernsey Merchants and their World* (Guernsey, 2009)

Creighton, D., *The Empire of the St. Lawrence: A study in commerce and politics* (Toronto, 1937)

Crowhurst, P., *The Defence of British trade, 1689–1815* (Folkestone, 1977)

Cullen, L. M., *Princes and Pirates: The Dublin Chamber of Commerce 1783–1983* (Dublin, 1983)

Cullen, L. M., *The Brandy Trade under the Ancien Régime: Regional Specialisation in the Charente* (Cambridge, 1998)

Cullen, L. M., *Economy, Trade and Irish Merchants at Home and Abroad, 1600–1988,* (Dublin, 2012)

Cullen, M. J., *The Statistical Movement in Early Victorian Britain: The Foundations of Empirical Social Research* (New York, 1975)

Curl, J. S., *The Honourable The Irish Society and the plantation of Ulster, 1608–2000* (Chichester, 2000)

Cuthbertson, B., *Voices of business: A history of commerce in Halifax, 1750–2000,* (Halifax, Nova Scotia, 2000)

Davidoff, L. and Hall, C., *Family Fortunes: Men and Women of the English Middle Class 1780–1850*, Revised Edition (1997)

Davis, R., *The rise of the English shipping industry in the seventeenth and eighteenth centuries* (1962)

Dawley, D. D, Stephens, R. D. and Stephens, D. B., 'Dimensionality of Organizational Commitment in Volunteer Workers: Chamber of Commerce Board Members and Role Fulfilment', *Journal of Vocational Behavior*, 67 (2004) 511–25

Deitz, V. E., *Before the age of capital: manufacturing interests and the British State 1780–1800,* PhD thesis (Princeton, 1991)

Dixon, M and Verma, R., 'Sequence Effects in Service Bundles: Implications for Service Design and Scheduling', *Journal of Operations Management*, 31 (2013) 138–152

Donnan, R. E., *Documents Illustrative of the History of the Slave Trade to America, Carnegie Institution* (Washington, D. C., 1931)

Donner, R. F. and Schneider, B. R., 'Business Associations and Economic Development: Why Some Associations Contribute More than Others', *Business and Politics*, 2 (2000) 261–88

Dudley, R., *The Irish Lottery, 1780–1801* (Dublin, 2005)

Duffy, M., 'Contested Empires, 1756–1815', in P. Langford ed. *The Eighteenth Century: 1688–1815* (Oxford, 2002) 213–44

Edinburgh Chamber of Commerce, *A brief account of the rise, progress and present position of the Chamber of Commerce and Manufacturers in the City of Edinburgh* (Edinburgh, 1861)

Edinburgh Chamber of Commerce, *Edinburgh Chamber of Commerce and Manufacturers 160th Anniversary 1785–1945* (Edinburgh, 1945)

Ehrman, J., *The British Government and commercial negotiation with Europe 1783–1793* (Cambridge, 1962)

Elwell, Charles J. L., (1988) *Black Country Essays and Reviews* (Black Country Society, Wolverhampton, 1988)

Falkiner, C. L., Some Illustrations of the Commercial History of Dublin in the Eighteenth Century, *Proceedings of the Royal Irish Academy*, 24, C (1902–4) 133–53

Finer, S. E., 'The political power of private capital, Parts 1 and 2', *Sociological Review*, NS 3, 279–94; NS 4 (1955) 5–29

Fisher, D. R., *History of Parliament: the House of Commons 1820–1832* (Cambridge, 2009)

Freeman, M. Pearson, R. and Taylor, J., *Shareholder Democracies? Corporate Governance in Britain and Ireland before 1850* (Chicago, 2012)

Gaastra, F. S., *The Dutch East India Company: Expansion and Decline* (Zutphen, 2003)

George, T. G. Earl of Northbrook and Baring, F. H., eds., *Baring, F. T.: Journals and Correspondence from 1808 to 1852* (Winchester, 1905)

Grampp, W. D., 'How Britain turned to Free Trade', *Business History Review*, 61, 1 (1987) 86–112

Grant, W., *Business and Politics in Britain,* second edition (1993)

Grant, W., *Pressure Groups and British Politics* (2000)

Griffith, L. M., 'The Ouzel Galley Society in the Eighteenth Century: Arbitration Body or Drinking Club?' in M. Brown and Donlan S. P., eds. *The Laws and Other Legalities of Ireland, 1689–1850* (Aldershot, 2011) 165–85

Gross, C., *Gild Merchant: A contribution to municipal history* (Oxford, 1890)

Hansen, J. M., 'The political economy of group membership', *American Political Science Review,* 79 (1985) 79–96

Hansmann, H. and Kraakman, R., 'The essential role of organizational law', *Yale Law Review*, 110, 3 (2000) 387–440

Harling, P., *The Waning of 'Old Corruption': The Politics of Economical reform in Britain, 1779–1846* (Oxford, 1996)

Harlow, V. T., *The Founding of the Second British Empire 1763–1793* (1952).

Harlow, V. and Madden, F., *British Colonial Developments 1774–1783: Select Documents* (Oxford, 1953)

Harris, R., *Industrialising English Law: Entrepreneurship and Business Organisation, 1720–1844* (Cambridge, 2000)

Helm, E., *Chapters in the History of the Manchester Chamber of Commerce* (1897)

Henderson, W. O., 'The American Chamber of Commerce for the Port of Liverpool, 1801–1908', *Transactions of the Historic Society of Lancashire and Cheshire,* 85 (1933) 1–61

Henderson, W. O., 'The Liverpool Office in London', *Economica,* 18 (1933) 473–79

Hirschman, A. O., *Exit, voice and loyalty* (Cambridge, Mass., 1970)

Hirschman, A. O., *Shifting involvements* (Oxford, 1982)

Holdsworth, W. S., *History of English Law, vol. 8* (1925)

Hope W. J., *In the beginning was an orchard: A commentary on the origins of the Hull Incorporated Chamber of Commerce and Shipping* (Hull, c.1987)

Hoppit, J., 'Political arithmetic in eighteenth century England', *Economic History Review*, *49*, 3 (1996) 516–40

Hoppit, J., ed., *Parliaments, nations and identities in Britain and Ireland, 1660–1850* (Manchester, 2003)

Ilersic, A. R. and Liddle, P. F. B., *Parliament of Commerce: The story of the Association of British Chambers of Commerce 1860–1960* (1960)

Innes, J., 'The local Acts of a national parliament: Parliament's role in sanctioning local action in Eighteenth-century Britain', *Parliamentary History*, XVII (1998) 23–47

Innes, J., 'Governing Diverse Societies', in P. Langford ed. *The Eighteenth Century: 1688–1815* (Oxford, 2002) 103–40

Innes, J., '"Reform" in English public life: the fortunes of a word', in Burns, A. and Innes, J., eds., *Rethinking the Age of Reform: Britain 1780–1850* (Cambridge, 2003) 71–97

Jackson, G., *Hull in the Eighteenth Century: A Study in Economic and Social History* (Oxford, 1972)

Jackson, G., *The Trade and Shipping of Eighteenth Century Hull,* East Yorkshire Local History Society Series, No. 31 (York, 1975)

Jamieson, A. G., ed., *A people of the sea: The maritime history of the Channel Islands* (1986)

Jordan, G. and Maloney, W., *The Protest Business* (Manchester, 1997)

Jordan, G. and Richardson. J., *Government and Pressure Groups in Britain* (Oxford, 1987)

Kammen, M. G., *A Rope of Sand: The colonial agents, British politics, and the American Revolution* (Ithaca, 1968)

Keith A., 'The Macclesfield Board of Trade', in *Troubled Times: Macclesfield 1790–1870* (Macclesfield, 2003) Chapter 13

Kington, J. B., *Thirty letters on the trade of Bristol* (Bristol, 1834)

Klinge, D. S., 'Edmund Burke, Economical Reform, and the Board of Trade, 1777–1780', *Journal of Modern History*, 51 (1979) D1185–D1200

Lamoreaux, N.R., 'Partnerships, Corporations, and the Theory of the Firm', *American Economic Review, Papers and Proceedings*, 88 (1998) 66–71

Landale, D., *Report of the trial of David Landale Esq., before the Circuit Court of Justiciary at Perth on Friday 22nd September, 1826* (Perth, 1826)

Landale, J., *Duel: A True Story of Death and Honour* (Edinburgh, 2005)

Langford, J. A., *A Century of Birmingham Life: or, A Chronicle of Local Events, from 1741–1841* (Birmingham, 1868)

Langford, P., *A Polite and Commercial People: England 1727–1783* (Oxford, 1989)

Langford, P., *Public life and the propertied Englishman 1689–1798* (Oxford, 1991)

Langford, P., ed. *Writings and speeches of Edmund Burke, Vol.3, Party, Parliament, and the American War, 1774–1780* (Oxford, 1996)

Langford, P., 'Introduction: Time and Space', in P. Langford ed., *The Eighteenth Century: 1688–1815* (Oxford, 2002) 1–34

Latimer, J., *The history of the Society of Merchant Venturers of the City of Bristol* (Bristol, 1903)

Le Marchant, D., *Memoir of John Charles Viscount Althorp, Third Earl Spencer* (1876).

Lees, R. M., 'Parliament and the proposal for a Council of Trade, 1695–6', *English Historical Review*, 54 (1939) 38–66

Leighton, J. M., *History of Fife from the earliest period to the present time*, vol. 3 (Glasgow, 1840)

Levi, L., *Chambers and Tribunals of Commerce and proposed General Chamber of Commerce in Liverpool* (1849)

Levi, L., *The story of my life: The first ten years of my residence in England, 1845–1855* (private, 1888)

Lindley, N. L., *A Treatise on the Law of Partnership*, 4th edition (1878)

Lindsay, W. S., *History of merchant shipping and ancient commerce*, 4 vols. (1874–76)

Little, B. D. G., *The City and County of Bristol: A Study of Atlantic Civilisation* (Birmingham, 1954)

Little, G. A., 'The Ouzel Galley', *Dublin Historical Record*, 3 (1940) 1–30

Little, G. A., *The Ouzel Galley* (Dublin, 1953)

Londonderry Chamber, *Translation of the charter granted by King Charles II to the mayor and citizens of the citizens of London-Derry* (London-Derry chamber of commerce, 1793)

MacMahon, E., *A Most Respectable Meeting of Merchants: Dublin Chamber of Commerce: A History* (Dublin, 2014)

Mahoney, J. and Thelen, K., eds., *Explaining Institutional Change: Ambiguity, Agency, and Power* (Cambridge, 2010)

Mander Bros. Ltd., *The History of Mander Brothers* (Wolverhampton, 1955)

Mander, Gerald P., *A History of Wolverhampton to the Early Nineteenth Century* (Wolverhampton, 1960)

Marr, L. J., *Guernsey People* (Chichester, 1994)

Marshall, Peter J., *The Making and Unmaking of Empires: Britain, India, and America c.1750–1783* (Oxford, 2005)

McAdam, D., Tarrow, S. and Tilly, C., *Dynamics of Contention* (Cambridge, 2001)

McGrath, P., *The Merchant Adventurers of Bristol: A history* (Bristol, 1975)

Mead, C., *The Magicians of Main Street: America and its Chambers of Commerce, 1768–1945* (Association of Chamber of Commerce Executives, Washington D.C., 2014)

Meister, A., *Participation, associations, development, and change* (New Brunswick, 1984)

Mokyr, J. and Nye, J., 'Distributional Coalitions, the Industrial Revolution, and the Origins of Economic Growth in Britain', *Southern Economic Journal*, 74, 1 (2007) 50–70

Money, J., *Experience and Identity: Birmingham and the West Midlands, 1760–1800* (Manchester, 1977)

Morgan, J., 'The chamber history', 10–17 in *The Bicentennial Handbook, 1779–1979* (Kingston, 1979) reprinted in www.jamaicachamber.org.jm/history

Morgan, K., *Bristol and the Atlantic Trade in the Eighteenth Century* (Cambridge, 1993)

Morris, R. J., *Class, power and social structure of British nineteenth century towns* (Leicester, 1986)

Morris, R. J., 'A Year in the public life of the British Bourgeoisie', in Robert Colls and Richard Rodger eds., *Cities of Ideas: Civil Society and Urban Governance in Britain, 1800–2000* (Aldershot, 2004) 121–143

Morris, R.J., 'Urban Associations in England and Scotland, 1750–1914: The Formation of the Middle Class or the Formation of Civil Society?' in Morton, G., de Vries, B. and Morris, R. J. eds., *Civil Society, Associations and Urban Places: Class, Nation and Culture in Nineteenth-Century Europe* (Aldershot, 2006) 139–57

Mortimer, T., *The elements of commerce, politics and finances, in three treatises* (1772)

Murphy, D., *Derry, Donegal and Modern Ulster, 1790–1921* (Londonderry, 1981)

Namier, L. B., and Brooke, J., eds., *The House of Commons 1754–1790,* 3 vols. (1964)

Norris, J. M., 'Samuel Garbett and the Early Development of Industrial Lobbying in Britain', *Economic History Review,* 10 (1957) 450–60

O'Connor, D. P., *The history and functions of the Limerick chamber of commerce 1807–1902,* MSc. Thesis (University College Dublin, 1938)

O'Connor, T. M., 'The Embargo on the Export of Irish Provisions, 1776–9', *Irish Historical Studies*, 2, 5 (1940), 3–11

O'Gorman, F., *The Emergence of the British Two-party System 1760–1832* (1982).

O'Shaughnessy, A. J., *An Empire Divided: The American Revolution and the British Caribbean* (Philadelphia, 2000).

Olson, A. G., 'The Board of Trade and London-American interest groups in the eighteenth century', *Journal of Imperial and Commonwealth History,* 8 (1980) 33–50

Olson, A. G., 'The London Mercantile Lobby and the coming of the American Revolution', *Journal of American History,* 69, 1 (1982) 21–41

Olson, A. G., *Making the Empire Work: London and American interest groups 1690–1790* (Harvard, 1992)

Olson, M., *The Logic of Collective Action: Public Goods and the Theory of Groups,* second edition (Cambridge, Mass., 1971)

Ostrom, E., 'Collective Action and the Evolution of Social Norms', *Journal of Economic Perspectives*, 14 (2000) 137–58

Payne, F. L., *The London Chamber of Commerce: A History of Service to the Business Community* (1967)

Pearson, R. and Richardson, D., 'Social capital, Institutional Innovation and Atlantic Trade before 1800', *Business History,* 50 (2008) 765–80

Philips, C. H., *The East India Company, 1784–1834*, Second edition (1961)
Picton, J. A., *City of Liverpool: Municipal Archives and Record* (Liverpool, 1886)
Pierson, P., *Politics in Time: History, Institutions, and Social Analysis* (Princeton, 2004)
Porritt, E., and Porritt, A. G., *The Unreformed House of Commons: Parliamentary Representation before 1832* (Cambridge, 1903)
Prendeville, P. L., *History of the Dublin Chamber of Commerce 1760–1860, with an introduction on the chamber of commerce movement,* M.Comm. Thesis (University College Dublin, 1930)
Prentice, A., *Historical Sketches and Personal Recollections of Manchester Intended to Illustrate the Progress of Public Opinion from 1792 to 1832* (1851)
Ramsden, M. and Bennett, R. J., 'The benefits of external support to SMEs: 'Hard' versus 'soft' outcomes and satisfaction levels', *Journal of Small Business and Enterprise Development*, 12, 2 (2005) 227–43
Redford, A., *Manchester Merchants and Foreign Trade 1794–1858* (Manchester, 1934)
Richmond, L. and Stockford, B., *Company archives: The Survey of the records of 1000 of the first registered companies in England and Wales* (Aldershot, 1986)
Rodger, N. A. M., *The Command of the Ocean: A naval history of Britain, 1649–1815* (2004).
Rogers, G. C., 'The Charleston tea party: the significance of December 3, 1773', *South Carolina Historical Magazine*, 75 (1974) 153–68
Rogers, N., *Whigs and Cities; Popular politics in the age of Walpole and Pitt* (Oxford, 1989).
Rose, M. B., *Firms, networks and business values: The British and American cotton industries since 1750* (Cambridge, 2000)
Rowlands, M. B., *Masters and Men: in the West Midlands Metalware Trades before the Industrial Revolution* (Manchester, 1975)
Royal Commission on Labour (1892) *House of Commons Papers*, XXXIV
Rydz, D.L., *The Parliamentary Agents: A History* (1979)
Sadowski, D. and Jacobi, O., eds., *Employers' associations in Europe: policy and organisation* (Baden-Baden, 1991)
Saggus, D., 'Social Identification, Attitudes, and Relationships in the 1780's of those Cotton Manufacturers of Manchester Listed in the Trades Directories of the Period', Ph.D. thesis (Emory University, 1974)
Salmon, P., *Electoral reform at Work: Local Politics and National Parties, 1832–1841* (2002)
Sanderson, F. E., 'The structure of politics in Liverpool 1780–1807', *Transactions of the Historic Society of Lancashire and Cheshire,* 127 (1977) 65–88
Schneiberg, M. and Hollingsworth, J. R., 'Can Transaction Cost Economics Explain Trade Associations?' in Czada R., and Windhoff-Héritier A., eds., *Political Choice: institutions, rules, and the limits of rationality* (Frankfurt,1991) 199–256
Seed, J., '"A Set of Men Powerful Enough in Many Things": Rational Dissent and Political Opposition in England, 1770–1790', In Haakonssen, K., ed., *Enlightenment and Religion: Rational Dissent in Eighteenth-Century Britain* (Cambridge, 1996), 140–68
Sellers, L., *Charleston Business on the eve of the American Revolution* (Chapel Hill, North Carolina, 1934)

Sosin, J. M., *Agents and merchants: British colonial policy and the origins of the American Revolution, 1763–1775* (Lincoln, Nebraska, 1965)

Stevens, J. A., *Colonial records of the New York chamber of commerce 1768–1784*, 2 vols. (New York, 1867)

Streeck, W. and Schmitter, P. C., 'From national corporatism to transnational pluralism: organised interests in the single European market', *Politics and Society,* 19, 2 (1991) 133–64

Sutherland, L. S., *A London Merchant 1695–1774,*(Oxford, 1933)

Sutherland, L. S., 'Lord Shelburne and East India Company Politics 1766–9', *The English Historical Review*, 49, 195 (1934) 450–86

Sutherland, L. S., *The East India Company in Eighteenth century politics* (Oxford, 1952)

Sweet, R. H., 'Topographies of politeness', *Transactions Royal Historical Society,* 12 (2002) 355–74

Taylor, R., *A History of chambers of commerce in the United Kingdom: 1768–2007* (BCC, 2007)

Taylor, M. and Singleton S., 'The Communal Resource: Transaction Costs and the Solution of Collective Action Problems', *Politics and Society,* 21 (1993) 195–214

Thomas J., *The development of the North Staffordshire potteries since 1730, with special reference to the industrial revolution*, PhD thesis (London School of Economics, 1934).

Thomas J., The potters of Staffordshire and their relations with the Manchester Committee of Commerce, 1784 to 1790, *Manchester Statistical Society, Papers* (1934–5) 1–46.

Thorne, R. G., *The House of Commons 1790–1820* (1986)

Touzeau, J., *The Rise and Progress of Liverpool from 1551 to 1835* (Liverpool, 1910)

Tyler, J. W., *Smugglers and patriots: Boston merchants and the advent of the American Revolution* (Boston, 1986)

Van Waarden, F., '"Two logics of collective action?" Business associations as distinct from trade unions: The problems of associations of organisations', in Sadowski, D. and Jacobi, O., eds., *Employers' Associations in Europe: Policy and organisation* (Baden-Baden, 1991) 51–84

Ville, S.P. *English shipowning during the industrial revolution: Michael Henley and Son, London shipowners, 1770–1830* (Manchester, 1987)

Wadsworth, A. P and Mann, J. de L., *The Cotton Trade and Industrial Lancashire, 1600–1780* (Manchester, 1931)

Walton, R., *The History of the Nottingham Chamber of Commerce 1860–1960* (Nottingham, 1960)

Watson, D. H., *The Duke of Newcastle, the Marquis of Rockingham, and mercantile interest in London and the provinces, 1761–1768*, PhD thesis (Sheffield University, 1968)

Wells, C., *A Short History of the Port of Bristol* (Bristol, 1909)

Weskett, J., *Plan of the Chamber of Commerce* (London, 1782)

Williams, O. C., *The Historical Development of Private Bill Procedure and Standing Orders in the House of Commons*, Vol. 1 (1948)

Wolverhampton PL., (1976) *Wolverhampton: The Town Commissioners 1777–1848: Their Story in their Minutes and the files of 'The Wolverhampton Chronicle'* (Wolverhampton Public Libraries, 1976)

Worth, R. N., *History of Plymouth from the Earliest Period to the Present Time* (Plymouth, 1871)
Wootton, G., *Pressure Groups in Britain 1720–1970: An Essay in Interpretation with Original Documents* (1975)
Wright, G. H., *Chronicles of the Birmingham Chamber of Commerce 1813–1913* (Birmingham, 1913)
Young, A., *Annals of Agriculture and other useful arts* (1786)

Index: General and Place

Index: People

This indexes the main text where a name arises, excluding attendance list at meetings. The members of each chamber are listed under that chamber in the Appendix; the General Index indicates the membership lists under each chamber location.